MYSTICS
and
MISSIONARIES

❖

MYSTICS
and
MISSIONARIES

The Jews in Palestine
1799–1840

Sherman Lieber

UNIVERSITY OF UTAH PRESS
Salt Lake City

∞The paper in this book meets the standards for permanence and durability
established by the Committee on Production Guidelines for Book Longevity of
the Council on Library Resources

LIBRARY OF CONGRESS CATALOGING-IN-PUBLICATION DATA

Lieber, Sherman, 1930–
Mystics and missionaries : the Jews in Palestine, 1799–1840 /
Sherman Lieber.
p.   cm.
Includes bibliographical references and index.
ISBN 0-87480-391-8 (alk. paper)
1. Jews—Palestine—History—19th Century.   2. Palestine—
History—1799–1917.   3. Hasidim—Palestine—History.   4. Judaism—
Palestine—History—19th century.   I. Title.
DS125.L53   1992
956.94′03—dc20   92-53605

TO

Peggy Street Lieber

AND

Meshulam Zeeysha Lieber

Pages 9, 22, F. B. Spilsbury, *Picturesque Scenery in the Holy Land and Syria Delineated during the Campaignes of 1799 and 1800*, London: 1908.

Page 14, *Kardum*, Jan. 1983. Permission granted by editor.

Page 90, E. Finden, *Landscape Illustrations of the Bible*, London: 1835.

Pages 92, 96, L. N. P. A. de Forbin, *Voyage dans le Levant en 1817–1818 par le Comte de Forbin*, Paris: 1819.

Pages 94, 287, 355, 350, D. Roberts, *The Holy Land from Drawings Made on the Spot*, London: 1842–49, 3 vols.

Page 97, A. Dumas and A. Dauzats, *Quinze jours au Sinai*, Paris: 1839, 2 vols.

Page 99, E. Schiller, *Jerusalem in Old Engravings and Illustrations*, Jerusalem: 1977.

Page 167 top, J. Wolff, *Travels and Adventures*, London: 1860; bottom, D. H. Finne, *Pioneers East: The Early American Experience in the Middle East*, Cambridge: 1976.

Page 188 top, J. S. Buckingham, *Travels in Palestine, through the Countries of Bashan and Gilead*, London: 1822, 2 vols.; bottom, A. Morgenstern, *The History of the Pach Rosenthal Family*, Jerusalem: 1987.

Page 207, J. Carne, *Syria, the Holy Land, Asia Minor, etc.*, London: 1835, 3 vols.

Page 231, J. Schwartz, *A Descriptive Georgraphy and Brief sketch of Palestine*, Philadelphia: 1850.

Page 248, W. H. Bartlett, *Jerusalem Revisited*, London: 1855.

Page 258, A. W. C. Lindsay, *Letters on Egypt, Edom and the Holy Land*, London: 1838, 2 vols.

Page 261, T. H. Horne, *Landscape Illustrations of the Bible . . .*, London: 1835–1837, 3 vols.

Page 277, J. L. Burckhardt, *Travels in Syria and the Holy Land*, London: 1822.

Page 290, C. R. Conder, *Palestine*, London: 1889.

Page 298, C. Geikie, *The Holy Land and the Bible . . .*, London: 1877.

Page 299, *Jewish Intelligence*, March 1840.

CONTENTS

Introduction   1

1   Napoleon's Invasion of Palestine, 1799   5
2   Nineteenth-Century Palestine: The Land and Its People   16
3   Hasidic Immigration of Eretz Israel, 1777–1807   36
4   Perushim Settle in Safed, 1808–1812   56
5   The Plague Years and the Jewish Community of Jerusalem 1812–1815   87
6   Friction and Factionalism, 1815–1825   120
7   English and American Missionaries in Palestine, 1820–1829   157
8   Jewish Activities in the Four Holy Cities, 1825–1830   184
9   The Egyptian Occupation of Palestine, 1831–1840   202
10   Jewish Immigrants and Their Initiatives in the 1830s   224
11   Organizing the Jewish Community and Building the Hurva Synagogue, 1834–1838   246
12   Pilgrims, Travelers, and Explorers   275
13   Missionary Activities in the 1830s   292
14   The British Consulate in Jerusalem, 1839–1840   318
15   Montefiore's Second Trip to Eretz Israel, 1839   333
16   The End of Egypt's Occupation of Palestine, 1840   367
Epilogue   388
Notes   397
Bibliography   459
Index   475

ACKNOWLEDGMENTS

It is a pleasure to acknowledge the help I have received from many people while researching and writing this book. My sincere thanks to the anonymous librarians at the Tel Aviv and Bar Ilan Universities, the Jewish National and University Library in Jerusalem, the Library of Congress, Oxford's Bodleian library and New York City's 42nd Street library. I am deeply indebted to Menahem Levin, manager of the municipality of Jerusalem archives, and the courteous staff at the Anglican Trust Fund in Jerusalem for making available to me the invaluable journals of John Nicolayson and other missionary documents.

For advice and guidance in a wide and valuable variety of ways, I am most grateful to Steve Arbel, Yohai Goell, Deborah Harris, Shlomo Kadmon, Harvey Lieber, Haviva Meshulam, Mibi Mozer, Rafi Rosenbaum and Orit Wartheim. My thanks to the staff at the University of Utah Press for supporting the book and expertly guiding it through to publication. I was fortunate that Priscilla Fishman, my fellow Yeshiva of Flatbush graduate, skillfully edited the manuscript and shaped it into a more readable text. Credit for suggesting the title of the book goes to Bonnie Fetterman of Schocken Press.

I would like to express my great appreciation to Professor Israel Bartal of the Hebrew University for reading the rough draft, offering incisive and constructive comments and saving me from some egregious blunders.

Last and far from least, I was sustained by the three D's in my immediate family—Donna, Daniella and David—without whose understanding and encouragement this book could never have been written.

OH! WEEP FOR THOSE

I.

Oh! weep for those that wept by Babel's stream,
Whose shrines are desolate, whose land a dream;
Weep for the harp of Judah's broken shell;
Mourn—where their God hath dwelt the godless dwell!

II.

And where shall Israel lave her bleeding feet?
And when shall Zion's songs again seem sweet?
And Judah's melody once more rejoice
The hearts that leap'd before its heavenly voice?

III.

Tribes of the wandering foot and weary breast,
How shall ye flee away and be at rest!
The wind-dove hath her nest, the fox his cave,
Mankind their country—Israel but the grave!

From Lord Byron's "Hebrew Melodies," 1858

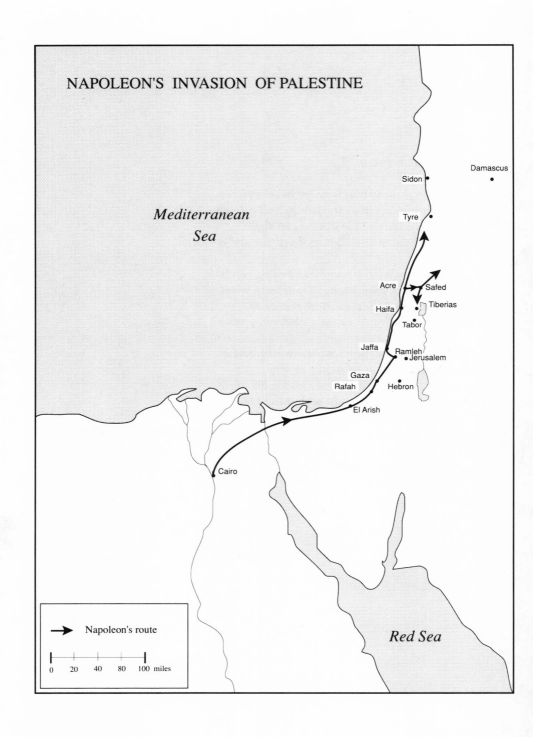

NAPOLEON'S INVASION OF PALESTINE

Mediterranean
Sea

Red Sea

Damascus

Sidon

Tyre

Acre
Safed
Haifa
Tiberias
Tabor
Jaffa
Ramleh
Jerusalem
Gaza
Rafah
Hebron
El Arish

Cairo

Napoleon's route

0   20   40   80   100 miles

INTRODUCTION

Mystics and Missionaries is the story of the Jews who lived in Palestine from 1799 through 1840. This period marks the start of "modern" Jewish history in the land of Israel and delineates a significant era in the history of the Jews in the Holy Land. During this time the direction in which the Jewish community was moving was altered and imperceptible underlying changes started to transform it. For the first time in more than one thousand years, the history of the Jewish people converged with the history of their land.

This narrative begins with Napoleon's invasion of Palestine, the first meeting of East and West in the Holy Land since the Crusades. Napoleon abruptly pushed the country into the glaring spotlight of the nineteenth century, where it came to the attention of the acquisitive European powers. But claims that Napoleon jolted Palestine out of its medieval stupor and plunged it into the swirl of progress were premature. The "stagnation of centuries" proceeded during the following decades. Hardly a trace of Napoleon's short-lived expedition in Palestine was visible after his departure. Instead of achieving concrete results, Napoleon's invasion symbolized the dynamics of change, latent modernization, and impending reform.

At the start of the nineteenth century, Palestine, with less than 5,000 Jews, was a backwater province of the Turkish Empire. The death of Ahmad al-Jazzar in 1804 marked the end of a long era of dictatorial rule. Pashas Suleiman and Abdullah governed the country in a manner less cruel and absolute than that of their predecessors. Yet Palestine remained a desolate province in the Ottoman Empire where corrupt local authorities greedily extorted money from the farmers and townspeople. This stultifying "sameness" ended only in 1831 with Egypt's conquest of Palestine.

Modern Jewish settlement in Eretz Israel is sometimes viewed as beginning in 1777 when 300 members of the Hasidic group came to Safed. Most scholars, however, believe that 1777 was not a juncture point that initiated substantial innovation and sustained changes in the small Jewish community. The Hasidim lived the same life of religious exuberance in Safed and Tiberias that they had in Poland. They had no ambition to transform Eretz Israel; that God would do in good time. After an initial period of misunderstandings, disagreements, and clashes with the established Sephardi community, the Hasidim conformed to their new Ottoman environment, adjusted to the long-established ways of the Sephardim, and tranquilly coexisted with them. The community in the Galilee became a holding operation that kept watch over Eretz Israel for the Hasidic movement then revolutionizing the religious life of East European Jewry.

In 1808, when the first convoy of Perushim Jews from Eastern Europe came to Safed, a process of slow, incremental change began to stir within the Jewish community in Eretz Israel. Perushim spoke in a different idiom and acted at a faster pace than the old-time Sephardi settlers and the Hasidic immigrants. Displaying a vitality lacking among the Hasidim, the Perushim played a catalytic role in the growth and development of the Jewish community in Eretz Israel from the time they settled in Safed. The ability of the Perushim to observe events and people, evaluate new conditions, weigh risks, and then act with ruthless realism was unique in the Jewish community. However, the Perushim, like the Hasidim, did not want to recast life in Eretz Israel. They did not come as pioneers eager to introduce new modes of thought or practice a new way of life. They viewed themselves as a religious vanguard dedicated to serving God in study and prayer and to maintaining Jewish historical continuity in the Holy Land. Like the Hasidim and Sephardim, the Perushim were motivated to live in Eretz Israel by the traditional Jewish yearning to leave Exile, return to Zion, and be redeemed in the Holy Land.

From 1815 onward Perushim initiatives sparked disquieting changes that altered the long-standing status quo and shook the institutions of the Jewish community. Diversity of interests and disagreements about objectives inevitably led to irreconcilable differences that spawned interminable conflict among the Perushim, the Sephardim, and the Hasidim, as well as within each of the three groups. Perushim innovations, especially the founding of a community in Jerusalem, established a new rhythm for the development of the Jewish community in Eretz Israel. Between 1815 and 1825 the Perushim stirred up a small, stagnant community, achieved a separate communal identity, secured independent financial means, and obtained approval to build their central religious institution.

Aggressive Perushim actions crippled the economic position of the Sephardim and damaged their standing as the representatives of all Jews in Eretz Israel. The hegemony of the Sephardim drew to an end as their numerical strength in the Jewish community dropped from 95 percent in 1800 to just under 70 percent in 1840. A more surprising demographic fact was the tremendously high mortality rate—80 out of 1,000 Jews annually— especially among newborn babies. The family heartbreak and psychological suffering of mothers unable to conceive at an early age can be imagined. This tribulation of women was compounded by a high divorce rate; Jewish law permits a husband to divorce his wife if she fails to give birth after a number of years. Such a divorce rate reflected a highly charged emotional situation and greatly disrupted the social fabric of the Jewish community.

During the period of Egyptian rule from 1831 through 1840, Palestine broke loose from its old ways and was pushed in new directions that presented opportunities for change. Travelers, pilgrims, and explorers flocked into the country. The English and Americans openly conducted missionary activities. Foreign governments and their consuls intervened in local affairs and spread modernizing influences. For the first time, protecting Jews was declared to be a political goal of some great powers. Restoration proposals were bandied about by Christians, who were the only "Zionists" in sight. Historians view the Egyptian interlude as the dawn of a new era which transformed nearly all aspects of life.

At the time of the Egyptian occupation of Palestine, foreign consuls, missionaries, and Moses Montefiore effectively and frequently protected the Jews. Without the active presence of the consuls it is impossible to imagine the growth of the Jewish community and the development of Palestine. As the weakest minority group, the Jews benefited most from consular protection. Jews wrote that "had it not been [for] the consul's supervision we would have all been destroyed and lost since the Gentiles wish to eat the Jews and accuse them falsely." The Anglican mission led by John Nicolayson was most concerned about the spiritual and physical welfare of the Jews who were recruited for the Christian life so that Christ could return and redeem all mankind. John Nicolayson consecrated his life to the service of God by helping and protecting the Jews of Jerusalem for thirty years.

Thanks to Montefiore's efforts, a spirit of change slowly began creeping through the Jewish community. Montefiore strove to turn Jews into a "productive" group able to earn its own livelihood. He was a symbol that bridged geographic and ideological differences and provided another link between the Jews of Eretz Israel and the Diaspora. Montefiore was the first world Jewish figure to intercede on behalf of less fortunate Jews. For the Jews in Eretz Israel, Sir Moses represented their hoped-for financial salvation and served as a symbol of their economic redemption.

Although Jews in Eretz Israel were greatly helped by consuls, missionaries, and Moses Montefiore, most of all they were sustained by the fundraising efforts of Jews in Europe and the Ottoman Empire that were indispensable to the existence of the Jewish communities in Eretz Israel. World Jewry consistently came to their rescue in times of critical need, and Diaspora Jews derived personal satisfaction and a deepened sense of Jewish identity from their charitable contributions to Jews in the Holy Land.

Lacking an economic and political base, the Jewish community in Eretz Israel could not develop as an organic community but only progressed, like a puppet, in fits and starts that were controlled by outside forces such as Mehemet Ali, the sultan, and overseas Jewish communities. Completely dependent on external elements, the Jews found it hardly possible to develop strong local leadership in Eretz Israel. Heroes of towering stature appear only in the legends and lore of the period.

After nine turbulent years of enlightened Egyptian rule, the great European powers expelled Mehemet Ali from Palestine, closing the door that offered an opportunity for change. When the eagerly awaited Messianic vision turned into an apparition, also in 1840, the Perushim's inner force collapsed—the Jews were spiritually crushed and fell into an apathy from which they recovered only after four decades. Under the influence of this monumental disappointment, all suggestions to institute changes in the material and spiritual life of the kehilla were derisively dismissed as debased ideas of the Enlightenment and Reform Judaism. Nonetheless, Jews in Eretz Israel continued to cherish their Messianic dreams and maintained their centuries-old traditional way of life.

ONE

Napoleon's Invasion of Palestine

1799

When Napoleon Bonaparte invaded Palestine in 1799, he catapulted that backwash Turkish territory and its Jewish population into the international arena, where it has remained ever since. In 1798, at the age of 29, General Bonaparte ambitiously searched for new worlds to conquer after leading French armies to victory over Austria in Italy. Since the Hapsburgs, Prussians, Russians, and English were too formidable opponents for the French forces, Napoleon, like others before and after him, was spurred on by the mystic prize of the Orient—"all great glory has always been acquired there," he is reputed to have said. Napoleon boasted that "Europe is but a molehill—all the great reputations have come from Asia—I shall overturn the Turkish empire and found in the East a new grand empire which will fix my name in the records of posterity."[1]

The strategic importance of the Near East, linking Africa and Asia with Europe, was obvious to Napoleon's keen military mind. Here was the high road commanding the British route to India that would permit Napoleon to deprive England of the rich Asian trade and "turn the British Empire upside down."[2] Bonaparte wrote in 1797 that "really to destroy England we must make ourselves masters of Egypt."[3] As commander of the French "Army of England," he had just aborted a planned invasion of the British Isles because the French lacked naval supremacy and adequate financial resources. At the same time, the revolutionary national aspirations of the French could be fulfilled by dismembering the Turkish Empire, long the "sick man of the Bosphorus" whose death was imminent in the opinion of Napoleon and many others. "We shall see its fall in our time," he prophesied.[4]

The Directory of Five then governing France needed military victory and money to stay in power, so it easily rationalized a lust for land by convincing itself that, if France did not invade the Turkish province of Egypt to protect its own commercial and national interests, other European powers would seize these potential riches. French foreign minister Charles Talleyrand persuaded the Directory that, by invading Egypt, France could fish in the troubled Turkish waters and strike a menacing blow to the British overland route to India as well as "guarantee the peace of Europe" and establish a flourishing colony that would help develop French commercial markets in the Orient.[5] In one stroke, the Directory would establish a base for penetrating the Levant while sending overseas an ambitious inactive general "whose popularity excited envy".[6]

The Egyptian expedition also appealed to many Frenchmen as a way of scientifically exploring the treasures of ancient Egypt and removing the magic veil from the mysterious secrets of the East. After the French revolutionary period, an ecstasy for historic destiny and a martial enthusiasm for civilizing the downtrodden Egyptian fellahin seized reasonable Frenchmen who were drunk with the mixed cocktail of power, glory, and science. "It was the epidemic of madness which seized our ancestors at the time of the Crusades," a French scholar wrote many years later.[7]

On May 19, 1798, Napoleon and his Army of the Orient set sail from Toulon to their secret destination—Egypt. Not since the thirteenth-century Crusaders had a powerful Christian army from Europe invaded the heartland of Islam. After capturing Malta from the piratical Knights of St. John, and luckily evading Lord Nelson's searching fleet in the dense haze of the Mediterranean, Napoleon surprised both the Turks and the British, not to mention the Egyptians, when he landed an army of 38,000 men near Alexandria on July 1. Wielding modern French weaponry and a trained fighting force, Napoleon overwhelmed a brave but outmoded army of Mamluke warriors, the aristocratic, military clique of converted slaves who had ruled Egypt since the fourteenth century. With the capture of Cairo on July 25, Bonaparte set about consolidating his conquest of upper Egypt. Meanwhile Nelson's English fleet finally caught up with the French armada in Aboukir Bay, near Alexandria, and destroyed it, severing Napoleon's sea lanes to

France, cutting off his source of vital military supplies, and stranding the French army in Egypt among a hostile population.

Napoleon immediately initiated a number of diplomatic moves to bolster support for his Egyptian expedition. He sought to convince Sultan Selim III (1789–1807) that the French invasion of Egypt was a friendly act meant to rid the Ottoman Empire of the usurping Mamlukes. Napoleon also tried to secure the support of the strongest ruler in Palestine, Ahmad al-Jazzar, pasha of Sidon (1775–1804), claiming that vanquishing the Mamlukes was in his interest because they were his enemies as well. Jazzar was less impressed by Napoleon's words that "the Muslims have no better friend than the French" than by Sultan Selim appointing him governor of nearly all of Palestine, greater Syria (Damascus, Tripoli, Sidon), and Egypt.[8]

Neither the pasha of Sidon nor the sultan was convinced by the declarations of a military leader of a Christian power intent on grabbing Muslim territory in the Near East. Turkey, in alliance with England and Russia, finally declared war on France during the winter of 1798 and prepared a military campaign against Egypt. Jazzar then announced his aggressive intentions against French-occupied Egypt.

Napoleon's decision to invade the Holy Land was designed to forestall Turkish land and sea attacks on French forces in Egypt, deny British and Turkish vessels sources of supply in Palestine ports, and threaten Britain's route to India. This also was a way to start negotiations with the sultan, who offended Napoleon by taking little notice of his Egyptian expedition. In his history of the campaign in Palestine, written years later, Napoleon stated that his primary objectives were to destroy Jazzar's army, capture Gaza, Jaffa, and Acre, stir up a rebellion among the minority factions of Druze and Christians, "and then let circumstances determine the rest," a most uncharacteristic pose for Napoleon. Such murkiness of purpose has prompted some historians rashly to conjecture that Napoleon planned to march on Istanbul and topple the tottering Turkish sultan,[9] or capture Europe from the rear, or move to conquer India, the Persian Gulf, or Vienna and Petersburg.

On February 6, 1799, Bonaparte marched into the Sinai peninsula with an army of 12,000–14,000 soldiers. Faulty intelligence and disdain for his enemy made Napoleon delay before subduing the El Arish fortification. Then, in the best tradition of the French Enlightenment, he promised to protect the innocent inhabitants of Palestine, to respect all religious practices, and to liberate the people from Jazzar's persecutions.

Pushing past El Arish, French troops quickly overran Rafah and Gaza.[10] They looted Gaza despite Napoleon's order to maintain correct military conduct, and thousands of residents temporarily retreated to the nearby villages of their kin. The few Jews of Gaza also fled and settled permanently in Hebron and Jerusalem.[11]

From Gaza, the French army veered slightly inland and captured Ramleh before surrounding the walls of Jaffa, a large town of 6,000–7,000 Muslims and Christians and no Jews.[12] Jaffa's primitive port enjoyed considerable commercial success and served as the Holy Land's point of entry for thousands of pilgrims traveling to Jerusalem, thirty miles inland.

Before bombarding Jaffa, Napoleon sent an attaché to the Turkish commander, ordering him to surrender. To the horror of the French, the attaché was decapitated and his head was displayed on the town wall. Infuriated, Bonaparte blasted Jaffa with cannon fire before his troops stormed through gaps in the walls. "Anybody with a human face fell victim to their fury," according to the grisly account of a French army doctor who witnessed this scene of horrendous carnage.[13]

The well-armed Jaffa garrison of 3,000 troops surrendered to Napoleon's aides-de-camp on condition that the lives of the soldiers would be spared. However, lacking the will and resources to guard and feed 3,000 soldiers, not wishing to provide safe passage for an army that once again might do battle against him, under pressure from his troops and officers and wanting to impress on Ahmad al-Jazzar that resistance was futile and would be dealt with mercilessly, Napoleon was left with only one alternative. The surrendering soldiers were shot and bayoneted on the Jaffa seashore. While this expedient and bloody massacre was being executed, the bubonic plague struck the French army, as if in divine retribution.

Napoleon ordered his plague-stricken army out of Jaffa and marched northward toward Acre, capital city of the province of Sidon. By March 18 French forces had occupied the undefended town of Haifa with its 1,200 Greek Catholics, Maronites, and Druze, and 50 Jews who lived on a gently rising slope at the foot of Mt. Carmel, eight miles south of Acre. Continuing north, the following day Napoleon set siege to Acre, the largest town in Palestine.

In Napoleon's opinion Acre was an easy target for conquest,[14] a consoling thought when he learned that a British naval squadron had captured ships transporting French heavy artillery intended to smash the walls of the city. Napoleon set up camp on the hills overlooking Acre, blockaded the town, and placed his few artillery batteries on the height, one mile east of the walls, where Crusader Richard the Lion-Hearted had camped in 1191.

The defense of Acre was led by the 65-year-old ferocious fighter Ahmad al-Jazzar, pasha of the Sidon province for nearly twenty-five years. One

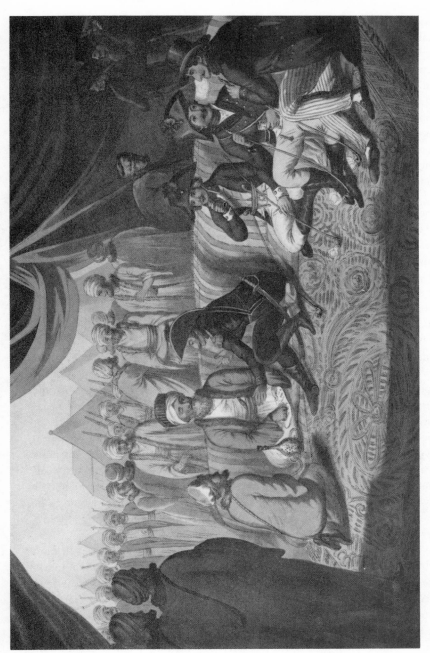

British naval officers in the tent of the grand vizier.

reason for his long rule was his recognition of the Turkish tradition of "habitual duplicity" that led Jazzar to suspect allies as well as enemies.[15] Jazzar Pasha was ably helped in the defense of Acre by the flamboyant English admiral Sir Sidney Smith, the French colonel Louis-Edmond de Phelipeaux, and his Jewish financial advisor, Haim Farhi. While Jazzar, Smith, and de Phelipeaux concentrated on fighting the French, Farhi organized Acre's civilian population of about 9,500. (Some Jewish historians claim that Napoleon so valued the services of Farhi that he tried to win him over to the French side.[16] If Farhi had gone over to Napoleon, it is contended that the outcome of the siege would have been completely different, but there is no evidence backing this opinion.)

Lacking both heavy cannon fire and respect for his opponent, Napoleon repeatedly attacked the walls of Acre using the old tactics of the Crusaders. He made numerous unsuccessful frontal assaults trying to storm the trenches and breach the fortifications. When this failed, French sappers dug tunnels under the walls and exploded mines to topple the masonry, but only minor damage resulted. Unable to achieve a quick victory, Napoleon set siege to the town.

In order to protect his flanks against the invading army of the pasha of Damascus, sent to help Jazzar, Napoleon penetrated deep into the Galilee. French troops conquered Nazareth, a small farm town of 1,250 (750 Christians and 500 Muslims) with no economic, geographic, or political importance. As the site where Christ preached and spent his youthful years, it occupies a venerated place in Christian history, right after Jerusalem and Bethlehem. Then Safed and Tiberias fell to Napoleon and he achieved a dazzling victory near Mt. Tabor by crushing the numerically superior but divided forces of the pasha of Damascus and local soldiers. Napoleon might have followed up his greatest military success in Palestine by invading greater Syria while continuing his siege of Acre. However, he correctly calculated that his depleted 13,000 troops were too few to undertake such a large military operation and that such an invasion might lead him to be swallowed up in Syria and drown in the Orient. Before proceeding any further Napoleon resolved to conquer Acre.

While conducting the siege of Acre and only four days after his brillant victory near Mt. Tabor, Napoleon ostensibly found time to issue a remarkable proclamation to "the Rightful heirs of Palestine" and "to all the Jews of Asia and Africa." Napoleon supposedly implored the Jews "to claim the restoration of civil rights . . . and your political existence as a nation among the nations. . . . Now is the moment which may not return for thousands of years . . . reestablish the ancient Jerusalem."[17] Curiously, this proclamation, which may never have been issued,[18] was recorded as coming from "Grand

Headquarters, Jerusalem," although Napoleon was then tied down by the siege of Acre and never attempted to enter Jerusalem. Perhaps he logically assumed that after capturing Acre all of Palestine would surrender to him.

Despite the lack of hard evidence regarding this publicized clarion call to the Jews, its contents were consistent with Napoleon's expedient practice of spreading the concepts of equality and liberty in the territories he conquered. Throughout his Egyptian expedition, Bonaparte professed a love of Islam and practiced tolerance toward Muslims. This was part of Napoleon's stratagem to foment unrest and rebellion among the disparate population of Christians, Jews, Maronites, Druze, and Muslims. Nevertheless, only the small Roman Catholic minority welcomed the new Latin "Crusader" and scouted the Galilee for their French co-religionists.[19] Greek Catholics, the largest minority group in Palestine, showed a negative attitude toward Napoleon, reflecting their deep-rooted hatred of the Roman Catholics and their traditional French protector. The chief of the Druze rejected Napoleon's overtures and struck a neutral watch-and-wait position. Similarly, Muslims "waited only to see how it ends to join the victor," according to Sidney Smith, who observed a "multitude of spectators on the surrounding hills" watching the siege of Acre.[20]

If Napoleon's proclamation to the Jews was ever issued, it had no effect on its target population. Jews feared the Muslims, expressed skepticism about Napoleon's motives, and were revolted by the barbaric behavior of some French troops in the Galilee. During the short period that 600 to 800 French soldiers occupied Tiberias and Safed, they looted and pillaged the Jewish quarters, and Jews were "greatly maltreated by the French."[21]

Soon after Jazzar Pasha's troops returned to Safed and Tiberias, he charged the Jews with treason and stole what few Jewish possessions the French had left behind. In Safed, "the Jewish quarter was completely sacked by the Turks" and the Jews reported a number of deaths. In greatly exaggerated language, Jews described their plight, which was nevertheless quite terrible:

> They came with axes and began to break in the doors and windows, robbed and pillaged everything, money, outer garments, clothing, not leaving even shirts or trousers, and the women were naked in the streets of the city . . . without bread or raiments. . . . Never has such a thing befallen Israel anywhere. . . . May God repay the doers of evil with the measure of their evil![22]

As a result of Napoleon's invasion, the Jewish community plunged deeply into debt for many years. Safed Jews were fined 50,000 piastres on a "villainous charge" of treachery by Jazzar Pasha and the community debt jumped to 125,000 piastres. Unable to pay this large sum, Jewish leaders were beaten and punished.[23] Heaping insult upon financial injury, Muslims warned that a French victory would have resulted in a massacre of all Jews in Safed, Tiberias, and Jerusalem.

Jerusalem's minorities (2,750 Christians and 2,250 Jews) were in a state of terror as a result of Napoleon's invasion of Palestine. When Napoleon conquered Gaza, Ramleh, and Jaffa, refugees fled in panic to Jerusalem. During the siege of Acre, Jerusalem's Greek and Roman Catholics were held hostage in the Church of the Holy Sepulchre by the belligerent Muslims.[24]

Muslims also accused the Jews of conspiring with no less than 12,000 "brothers, the children of Israel" in the alleged advance guard of Napoleon's army and of wanting to deliver Jerusalem into the hands of Napoleon. Jews lived in great danger:

> Each day there were new tribulations and they punish us for disobedience. . . . Each day they [the Muslims] stand over us to kill and destroy us . . . and every hour we anticipate death. . . . A book would not be sufficient to write about such a record of lamentation . . . [25]

Muslim creditors pressed the Jewish community to pay its debt, and Jews ransomed their lives by paying a "large huge sum" in order that "righteous Israeli daughters should not be defiled, God forbid," and so that "Torah scrolls are not desecrated and profaned." Jews were forced to sell all the silver ornaments adorning the Torah scrolls.

> In addition we levied taxes and fees on all the Jewish residents, from the oldest to the youngest; even scholars, who are normally exempt from taxes, paid. We were forced to sell our clothing to ransom our lives, leaving us naked.

Despite these drastic measures, the debt of the Jerusalem Jewish community swelled from 50,000 piastres in 1797 to the huge sum of 200,000 piastres.[26]

To prove their loyalty, Chief Rabbi Yom Tov Algazi and Rabbi Mordecai Joseph Meyuhas directed Jerusalem's Jews to make a new rampart and bastion around the citadel. The respected 61-year-old Rabbi Meyuhas "stood and dug with spade in hand and he labored with the people."[27] In front of the Wailing Wall the rabbis led the Jews in prayer "for protection and aid for the city against their French army."[28] Prices escalated during these times of war and Jews complained that there is "no exile like the exile of Israel. . . . And from the day that Jerusalem was founded we have never dwelt here in such affliction."

Back at Acre, Napoleon the besieger found himself in a besieged position. The French forces were cut off from their distant Egyptian supply base and were reduced to scrounging for food in a hostile countryside. Lacking the heavy artillery needed to pierce the fortified walls, Napoleon launched fourteen full-scale infantry assaults and innumerable sorties. Jazzar answered the French attacks with aggressive temerity by breaking out of Acre no less than twenty-six times. He spurred his embattled troops forward by awarding cash prizes to soldiers presenting him with the gory head of a Frenchman, which he placed on full view at the top of the wall.

As the siege dragged on into its second month, the discouraged Napoleon saw French casualties mount while receiving news about crises in France and defeats dealt the French by European powers. He ordered a last massive frontal breakthrough on Acre's fortifications. When his last assault was repelled with heavy losses, Napoleon ordered his decimated army back to Egypt. He rationalized that "the capture of Acre was not worth the loss it would entail,"[29] and that now "is the season of the year when hostile landings may be expected," referring to the anticipated joint Turkish-British attack on Egypt.[30]

Exactly two months after the start of the Acre siege and one year after sailing from Toulon, Napoleon started his withdrawal. He who was destined to overthrow thrones and reshape the map of Europe was thwarted before the impregnable walls of Acre. Napoleon later lamented that "the fate of the East" depended "on that petty town." On their way out of Palestine, French forces were stung by hit-and-run attacks of the scavenging Beduins and Jazzar's troops and shelled from the sea by Sidney Smith's flotilla. In defeat and anger, Napoleon blew up fortifications and set the torch to crops and villages from Acre to Gaza. One French officer described the scene: "Our march was illuminated by torches, lighted for the purpose of setting fire to the towns, the villages, the hamlets, and the rich crops of corn which everywhere covered the earth. The whole countryside was one blaze of fire . . ."[31] After a 25-day retreat that covered more than 500 kilometers, Napoleon marched his troops in a stage-managed "triumphal procession" through the Gate of Victory in Cairo. Of the 13,000 French soldiers participating in the Palestine campaign, about 1,200 died of the plague, and another 2,300 were sick or severely wounded.[32]

On August 22, 1799, after decisively defeating an invading Turkish force

Pasha Ahmad Jazzar, the "Butcher," defending the walls of Acre against Napoleon's repeated attacks in 1799.

of 18,000 at Aboukir, Napoleon transferred command of his stranded Egyptian army to General Jean Baptiste Kleber and sailed for France. The Egyptian interlude in Napoleon's career had come to an end. Years later he grandly deluded himself that "the time I spent in Egypt was the most beautiful of my life. . . . In Egypt, I found myself freed from the obstacles of an irksome civilization. I was full of dreams. I saw myself founding a religion . . ."[33] By December 1799 Napoleon had proclaimed himself sole ruler of France. But not until September 1800 did the French expeditionary force of 24,000 survivors—one-third of the original army was buried in Egypt and Palestine—leave Egypt after an agreement was reached with Great Britain.

The scientific achievements of the 150 French savants accompanying the Egyptian expedition in search of a new world of knowledge far outshone the conspicuously nonexistent military and political achievements of Napoleon. No French colony was established in the Orient and no British interests in the Levant were dislodged. France's traditional friendship with the Ottoman Empire was damaged, and its preeminent position in Palestine was lost. Napoleon's only positive contribution in the Holy Land was the Jacotin maps, which marked the beginning of modern cartography of Palestine.[34]

Napoleon's abortive expedition in Palestine caused great suffering and carnage. Villages were laid waste and residents along the devastated coastal strip had their lives seriously dislocated. Foreign commerce and the trading of cotton were disrupted. Bitter antagonisms among the Christian minorities and between Muslims and Christians were exacerbated by Napoleon's proposals. Jews and other minorities were terrorized and heavily taxed by Jazzar Pasha on suspicion that they assisted or sympathized with Napoleon, and their debts soared to unprecedented heights. Only Admiral Sidney Smith's threat to bombard Acre averted a threatened slaughter of Christians in Nazareth and Jerusalem. To intimidate the Muslims further, in 1801 the indomitable Admiral Smith marched his marines, with flags unfurled and drums banging, from the coastal plain to Jerusalem and Bethlehem.

These events were transitory episodes in the history of Palestine. The iron rule of Ahmad al-Jazzar continued. The population was enfeebled and the land languished. Turkish sovereignty over Palestine and Egypt was again recognized by the great European powers. Napoleon's invasion, however, did expose the country to the dynamics of change and Western modernization. Arabs were confronted with Western military superiority that jolted Islamic society.[35] Muslims reluctantly concluded that "Napolis and the French have opened our eyes."[36] Napoleon demonstrated to the continent how easily a trained and equipped army could dismember the Turkish Empire that once aspired to rule Christian Europe and now could not defend Palestine without the assistance of a great European power. More than ever, the English realized the significance of sea power and how easily their overland and sea routes to India could be cut.

Napoleon's grandiloquently proclaimed campaign ended as a poor melodrama. Palestine was paraded in the world arena, where its enticements were exhibited before the covetous European powers. Bonaparte had initiated a new stage in the power struggle for empire, territory, and commercial benefits by drawing Palestine into the international political vortex.

TWO

Nineteenth-Century Palestine

The Land and Its People

Palestine was ushered into the nineteenth century with Napoleon's legacy of a burnt-out Mediterranean coastal strip and thousands dead from warfare and the plague. Bonaparte had unceremoniously pushed Palestine and the Middle East into the explosive tumult of a brand new century[1]—the age of progress and ideology; the day of science and scholarship; the period of Romanticism; the era of nationalism and increased foreign intervention; the time of liberalism, reform, and revolutions in the social, industrial, and political arenas.

In 1800 Palestine was a tiny, remote, neglected area that lacked recognition as a separate administrative entity in the Ottoman Empire. The Turks followed the Persian, Roman, and Arab empires and provided a new imperial force that successfully united heterogeneous peoples of diverse foreign languages, religious practices, tribal customs, and cultural patterns. The unifying life force of this multiracial, multiethnic, multireligious civilization was the spoils reaped by repeated conquests in Europe and Asia. "The Ottoman state was not built to cultivate its own garden";[2] it was primarily built for war against the infidel.

At the end of the eighteenth century this huge empire encompassed vast principalities in Europe, Asia, North Africa, and the Middle East. It

16

stretched from the borders of Morocco to Persia, and from Mecca to Moldavia, penetrating through the Balkans deep into Central Europe.

This massive territory with a motley mixture of people was ruled by a supreme sovereign, the sultan, descendant of Sultan Osman I (1289–1326), founder of the Ottoman dynasty and the first of thirty-six sultans to rule the empire before its demise in 1922.

The sultan, a near absolute monarch, governed his Islamic empire in conformity with the principles of the Sacred Muslim Law, the Shari's, as interpreted by the ulema, the elite class of theologian-scholar-jurists headed by the muftis and kadis. This Sacred Law of Islam gave the empire meaning and purpose and developed a social force of common brotherhood that helped transcend differences among ethnic groups, nations, and classes. As Protector of Islam and Defender of the Muslim faith, the sultan fought sacred battles against the infidels. He conquered immense territories with the military might of the men of the sword—the select Janissary infantry corps and the Sipahi cavalry.

The government machinery controlling this gigantic empire was managed by its chief minister, the grand vizier. Serving at the pleasure and in the name of the sultan, the grand vizier directed and supervised the multitude of government activities from the palatial building called the Sublime Porte. From the end of the sixteenth century he also served as commander-in-chief of the armed forces.

In order that the unwieldy, polyethnic, polyglot empire might be effectively governed and controlled from its capital in Istanbul, it was divided into twenty-five to thirty provinces. Each province, ruled by a sultan-appointed pasha, was in turn subdivided into a hierarchy of smaller, more manageable administrative units. A province was mandated to defray its administrative and military expenses as well as contribute a fixed annual sum to the imperial treasury.

Since economic activities failed to interest the Turks—who considered trade an "inferior activity,"[3] demeaning "to their honor"[4]—commerce was largely conceded to minority groups: Greeks, Armenians, and Jews. To develop trade throughout the empire and thereby swell government revenues, sultans since 1535 signed capitulation agreements granting foreign powers special extraterritorial privileges that exempted them from local laws and taxes.

The Ottoman Empire reached its zenith during the reign of the tenth and greatest sultan, Suleiman the Magnificent (1520–1566). At the end of the sixteenth century, when this warrior state ceased conquering new lands, it started a slow, prolonged slide toward oblivion. During the next 350 years the empire went into an irreversible decline, interrupted by occasional brief periods of restored splendor; its deterioration was marked by government disintegration, social upheaval, financial insolvency, and territorial dismemberment. Most sultans lacked the aptitude and determination to rule, preferring the pleasures of the harem and the blandishments of bribery. Law, as in late Roman times, was "bent by influence, or broken by power or spoiled by money."[5] Government organization atrophied, currency was devalued, coinage was debased, and prices escalated. A matchless public service fell into disorder and disrepute. Nepotism, incompetence, and corruption were rife. Unbridled avarice encouraged violent widespread rebellions. The once great fighting force of the Janissaries failed to maintain order, let alone conquer new lands.

From the end of the seventeenth century the Ottoman Turks suffered a succession of crushing military defeats that diminished the empire.[6] Outmoded Turkish political, social, and industrial structures were powerless to cope with advanced military techniques and incapable of adjusting to emerging world forces accelerated by the French Revolution. The fatal disease that prevented the Turks from solving basic problems was their arrogant belief in the inferiority of the infidel, the superiority of Islam, and the infallibility of the Ottoman. The Muslim frame of mind that mere mortals could never presume to alter the course of events established by the will of God condemned to oblivion an empire in vital need of fundamental changes. The Ottoman Empire was "a medieval state, with a medieval mentality and a medieval economy. . . . In a world of rapidly modernizing states it had little chance for survival."[7]

The process of disintegration was closely watched by England, France, Russia, and Austria, all eager to bite off pieces of the collapsing empire and infiltrate their influence into the Sublime Porte and the imperial provinces. That the Turkish regime was not totally dismembered before the twentieth century was due only to the fact that the carnivorous European powers could not agree who would get what territorial limb. Turkey earned the indignities heaped upon it by contemptuous Europeans such as François Chateaubriand, who remarked in 1807 that "to make an alliance with Turkey is the same as putting your arms around a corpse to make it stand up."[8]

When the reform-minded Selim III attempted to revamp the military forces and reorganize social and economic institutions, the Janissaries and the ulema foiled his efforts at modernization, easily unseated him, and later assassinated him. After Selim was deposed, Mustafa IV was proclaimed sultan in 1807, only to be summarily dropped in favor of Mahmud II (1808–1839).

In such conditions of anarchy, the central government was not able to manage the enormous empire and control its subjects. With a power vacuum in Istanbul, few pashas were willing to "rub [themselves] in the dust before the sultan."[9] Governors heading provinces in Anatolia, Egypt, Arabia, and North Africa defied the inept central authority and threatened to revolt. Some regions were convulsed by insurrections.

Palestine had been part of the Turkish Empire since 1516, when it was captured by Sultan Selim I. A geographically undefined area, Palestine lay between the Mediterranean Sea and the Jordan River, and extended from the Lebanon Mountains to the Sinai desert. The derisive name "Palestine" applied by the Romans was derived from the word "Philistines" and showed antipathy toward the Jews and Eretz Israel. Although Palestine was the gateway to Africa, Asia, and Europe, it had little commercial importance. Whatever position of consequence it occupied was due to the Muslim, Christian, and Jewish holy places in Judea and the Galilee, and to its strategic position straddling the route of the hajj, the Muslim religious pilgrimage, which stretched from Damascus, past Palestine, and down to Mecca and Medina.

At the end of the eighteenth and the beginning of the nineteenth century the Sublime Porte hardly noticed Palestine because it contributed little revenue and only a miniscule military force to the empire. Palestine had a meager population of about 275,000,[10] which had hardly grown since the sixteenth century, indicating the stagnant nature of the country. The languishing territory lacked political unity and had no identity of its own as a specific administrative unit within the Ottoman Empire. Palestine was split between the two administrative provinces of Damascus and Sidon. The province of Damascus consisted of a small part of the eastern-upper Galilee, the mountain range in central Palestine from Jenin south through Nablus and Jerusalem to just beyond Hebron. The Sidon province included the Galilee and the swampy maritime plain, from its capital Acre south past Jaffa to Khan Yunis, bordering on the Sinai desert.

The provinces of Damascus and Sidon were divided into a number of districts (sanjaks) and further broken down into smaller administrative units that included a number of towns and villages. As in other areas of the empire, the two provinces had flexible, ever-changing borderlines determined by the military strength of the mutually hostile pashas. At the start of the nineteenth century, for instance, ten villages between Ramleh and Hebron deserted the province of Damascus and formed an enclave under the protection of the pasha of Sidon.[11]

Pashas used personal armies to battle each other for control over larger areas of territory in order to extend their lands for tax collection purposes. With new revenues a pasha could build larger, stronger armed forces, expand his influence and power, and conquer additional areas. Such was the cycle of events that enriched the pasha and his officials, desolated the countryside, and impoverished the population.

The sultan's major concern was to ensure that monies flowed from the provinces into the imperial treasury. The pasha ruled his province with little imperial intervention as long as he remitted revenues fixed by the Sublime Porte, maintained a semblance of order, and did not visibly challenge the sultan's authority and prerogatives. Occasionally when a pasha became too independent, the Sublime Porte waited patiently until it could regain control, acting according to the Turkish proverb "The hand you cannot cut off—kiss."[12] During critical times, the sultan appointed a strong pasha for his own purposes, as when he selected Ahmad al-Jazzar on four different occasions to serve as pasha of Damascus as well as pasha of Sidon.

Government laws and regulations were issued by the Sublime Porte in the form of imperial decrees. These firmans covered subjects that most interested the sultan: tax collection, currency and coinage, weights and measurements, and the recruitment of soldiers.

The pasha was the vassal of his sovereign, the sultan, and was granted circumscribed authority to promulgate regulations of a strictly limited, provincial nature. Like all officeholders in the empire, the pasha paid the sultan a proper "consideration" to hold office for a set period. If the pasha was strong and rich enough, like Jazzar, he had a good chance of repeated reappointments beyond the normal one- to three-year term of office.

With his autocratic powers, the pasha acted quickly to earn back the money he paid to the Sublime Porte as well as to reap a hefty profit. In the words of one eighteenth-century official, "What happens in the future does not concern me. Yesterday I was posted in Marash, and tomorrow, maybe in Jedda; so why should I deprive myself of a secure present in place of a future without hope?"[13]

The system of selecting the pasha and provincial officials for a price determined that the major job of all functionaries was to collect taxes. By authority of their appointment, officials were granted monopolies to collect a bewildering array of taxes, customs, rentals, a poll tax on minority members, special levies, and other fees. One way for the pasha to earn a quick return on his appointment "investment" was to sell to the highest bidder the subordinate positions in the province. In turn, these officials sold tax and commodity concessions to powerful families, clans, and strong-armed professional tax collectors. Every functionary intensively farmed his tax concession. Exercising the minimum functions of government held no interest for rapacious, incompetent officials. As a result, law and order were replaced by arbitrary rule and anarchy.

From 1775 to 1804 the staunch defender of Acre against Napoleon, Ahmad al-Jazzar, entrenched himself as pasha of Sidon, dominated Palestine, and ruled most of the northern part of the country. Born in Bosnia about 1730, Ahmad ran away from home at the age of 15 to escape punishment on charges of raping his sister-in-law. He served bravely as an officer in Egypt, where he earned his nickname Jazzar, the butcher, for his cruel treatment of enemy soldiers. After serving as the sultan's governor of Beirut, Jazzar soldiered for Dahir al-'Amr, the ruler of the Galilee (c. 1840–1875), and then defected to the Turkish side and was appointed governor of the Sidon province.

Jazzar found it "convenient and profitable" to acknowledge loyalty to the sultan.[14] Cunning and crafty, he realized how affairs were settled at the Sublime Porte when he said that "the Sultan is like a coquettish maiden who will grant her favour to none but the highest bidder." He distributed gold to the sultan's influential functionaries and sent to Istanbul the annual tax allocation fixed for the Sidon province even if he frequently delayed payment and remitted it in debased coinage. In 1784, before paying the sultan's annual tribute estimated at 1,875,000 piastres, Jazzar collected for his own use about 9–10 million piastres.[15]

The gigantic revenues he amassed from his comprehensive tax system and his agricultural lands and commercial enterprises enabled Jazzar to construct the most splendid city in Palestine. Acre was the most populous town in Palestine because it was the administrative capital of Sidon province, the commercial center of the country, and its main port of commerce.

Jazzar Pasha ruled the province of Sidon with a private army of 4,000 to 15,000 soldiers. His navy of ten gunboats guarded the coastline against smugglers, cutthroat Barbary corsairs, and Malta-based pirates.

Playing the role of a satrap, Jazzar sat as judge of his people. After rendering sentence, he frequently beheaded a prisoner or "ripped up a Mason with an axe."[16] Whipping, hanging, and drawing and quartering were frequent forms of justice. When Jazzar suspected the fidelity of the women in his harem he had them all killed except his most beloved, whom he personally disemboweled. Cropped noses and lopped-off ears were the trademark of Acre residents and "plainly indicated whence they came."[17]

Jazzar conducted the civil administration of the province with the

Pasha of Acre, Ahmad Jazzar, holding the rod of punishment while sentencing his subject. Note the axe to his left. On his right stands his chief financial office, Haim Farhi, holding the charge sheet. While Farhi was in temporary disfavor, Jazzar had gouged out one of his eyes, cropped his nose and cut off his ear.

assistance of Christian secretaries and Jewish accountants. For his chief financial officer, he selected Haim Farhi, a Jew, who served in a similar position under pashas Suleiman and Abdullah.

As a member of the wealthy, well-connected Farhi family of Damascus, Haim, a talented diplomat and financier, developed a strong network of connections in centers of Turkish power. At a time when finance and commerce were inextricably bound together, a "banker-trader" in the employ of the pasha could achieve spectacular economic results. European travelers believed that Farhi was "the actual source of all influence in Acre" and that the government and private persons owed him large sums of money.[18] The Farhi family fortune was estimated in 1812 at the magnificent sum of 300,000 pounds sterling.[19] Not surprisingly, Farhi was envied and hated by the Muslims and Christians who competed for office, power, and money. A contemporary Christian historian wrote, "Hayim the Jew has been holding all reins of government and has been doing whatever he wishes. It is said that a Jewish person dominates the Muslims and the Christians, the great and the small, the near and the far—without any restriction."[20]

The rewards garnered by Farhi were great, but the risks were quite high. When he temporarily fell out of favor, Jazzar gouged out one of his eyes, cut off an ear, and slit the tip of his nose. A discerning traveler wrote prophetically that "there is hardly a case . . . of a Christian or a Jew enjoying power or property for a long time. These people are always cut off at the height of their success."[21] In order to survive in their rewarding yet dangerous positions Farhi and other Jewish accountants in the Turkish Empire (and in Eastern Europe) kept their accounting records in Hebrew, tantamount to a secret code. Thanks to the protection of Farhi, Jews in the Galilee enjoyed "perfect religious freedom."[22] In Acre, Farhi helped merchants, artisans, and laborers in the Jewish community of a few hundred persons.[23]

Even after Jazzar reached age 70 and defeated Napoleon, the pasha of Sidon did not mellow. He fought against the grand vizier, the pasha of Damascus, and the ruler of the Druze, while continuing to tax and terrorize his people.

Under the strong-armed rule of Jazzar Pasha, Palestine experienced "the violent tenor of life" that characterized the waning years of the Middle Ages. Rural, town, and nomadic populations were divided and violently antagonistic. Prolonged tribal enmities and blood feuds led to frequent fights between the pashas, the Beduin, and the feudal chiefs. Brutality was taken for granted and insecurity was the normal way of life. This era was "rough, coarse, brutal; a world for the muscular and the aggressive and the cunning."[24]

Tribal marauders and Beduin vandalized the sparsely settled maritime plain from Acre south to Gaza, a wasteland of malaria swamps and wild brush. Beduin and brigands spread destruction in the country's most densely populated area, the mountain range from Nablus through Hebron. With the exception of garrisoned towns such as Jerusalem, Jaffa, and Gaza, the urban and agricultural populations were in perpetual disorder. Property was looted, fruit trees cut down, crops set afire, wells blocked, and villages devastated. No government existed to protect the people.

Only the few administrative towns were guarded, by a small number of Janissaries and other Turkish troops paid by the sultan. Pashas recruited their own private armies from local villages and tribal clans. These ruffians, accurately called "empty heads," were distinguished by a spirit of rapine and a duty to pillage villages they were paid to protect. A French traveler described this scourge of the peasants: "He is a real robber under the name of a soldier; he enters as a conqueror and commands as a master."[25]

Some powerful tribal chiefs could recruit large numbers of infantry combatants who fought so effectively in their natural mountain habitat that they occasionally challenged the authority of the pasha. Rival tribal clans of punitive passions and predatory ways frequently fought each other. Robbery and plunder were the rewards of the warrior who believed, as did many nineteenth-century Mediterraneans, that "he who does not steal is not a man."[26]

The Beduin, estimated at 40,000 at the start of the nineteenth century,[27] were no longer "faithful children of the desert" (Chateaubriand) but "sedentary nomads" camped in tents. Beduin preyed on the people in the Judean desert just outside Jerusalem, in the Galilee, and near the swampy coastal plain of Samaria and controlled lands around Ramleh, Jaffa, and Jerusalem. In order to graze their herds without hindrance, Nazareth sheep-owners paid a protection fee in 1806 to the prowling Beduin, who regarded banditry as legitimate work no less honorable than cultivating the land. In some coastal areas Beduin performed the goverment functions of collecting taxes and protecting the population, for a price. What the Beduin once coveted they were now invited to defend.

The Palestinian population, in self-protection against the combined forces of the marauding Beduin, undisciplined "empty heads," the conflicted tribes, and the not-so-protective soldiers of the pasha, organized their own military forces into two rival factions: the Kays (Qaysi) and the Yamani, divided on the basis of geography and logic-defying historical tribal affiliations and groupings of common interest.

Most villages joined one alliance or another so as not to be attacked, but their allegiances were constantly in flux. The Yamani camp around Jerusalem was led by the powerful Abu-Ghosh family living in a village about ten miles west of Jerusalem called "robbers' village" as late as 1841.[28] Acting as the warlord of Jerusalem, Abu-Ghosh controlled the road between Jerusalem and Ramleh and "found the pilgrims a profitable prey."[29]

In the endemic spirit of hostility long-simmering rivalries were amplified by the tradition of retaliation—the blood of the injured must be avenged by his family as a point of honor. Vengeance was mandated by a government that failed to provide elementary justice. Blood feuds were passed from father to son, leaving the populace in a "perpetual civil war."[30] Violated honor was vindicated in the reigning spirit of revenge and retribution. "Ottoman society approved if the offended person smiled and then waited until his enemy was weak and vulnerable, to avenge past humiliations."[31] Pity and forgiveness were nowhere in evidence.

This was the Palestine jungle that Jazzar Pasha ruled. After a lengthy reign of twenty-eight years of strong, central rule that oppressed the population, Ahmad al-Jazzar died in 1804. There was a "universal shout of joy. God gave men rest from the tyranny of Djezzar and cast him to eternal punishment" in his grave in the magnificent mosque he had built in Acre.[32]

After numerous intrigues and fights, and with the support of Haim Farhi, the Sublime Porte appointed Suleiman as pasha of Sidon (1805–1819). Pasha Suleiman was called "the just" because he was such a stark contrast to his cruel predecessor. He proved loyal to the sultan; after he put down an 1807 insurrection by the governors of Jaffa, Lod, Ramleh, and Gaza, Palestine was relatively quiet.

Nineteenth-century Palestine was predominantly a rural society. About 220,000 village fellahin or peasant farmers constituted 80 percent of the population. For security reasons 600 of the 700 remote villages were sited in the easily defensible central mountain range and in the Galilee mountains with nearby sources of water and roughly accessible roads. Most villages were of no economic or political consequence and were inhabited by a small number of families. Three and four generations of families dominated by a patriarch dwelled close together in primitive living conditions.

A village was an independent, insular, self-contained agricultural community supplying its own essential food, clothing, and shelter. In a barter economy fellahin brought fruits and vegetables to town and traded for goods such as dyed cloth and soap. Village raw materials of cotton and olive oil supplied the weaving looms and oil presses of Gaza and Nablus.

Village dwellings were surrounded by agricultural land whose fertility was critically determined by the long winter rainy season that stretched from late October through March. Fellahin tended their land using methods and tools dating back to biblical times—a plough was "frequently no more than the branch of a tree."[33] Unable to change their methods of cultivating orchards, vineyards, and field crops, the fellahin were confined to perpetual drudgery. Few villages found it worth while to raise flocks of sheep and goats, for such movable stock was tempting to the eyes of robbers, and poor people ate little red meat except at times of weddings, holidays, and festivals.

By far the largest areas were cultivated by the villagers on government-owned land. In return for the privilege of working this miri land,[34] villagers paid the government a land tax. Very few villages were sited on mulk or private land, which could be owned only by Turkish citizens. A third type of landholding was the waqf property that belonged to religious groups and was consecrated for the upkeep of religious organizations.

Villagers paid their miri tax, usually 10 percent of their produce, or an equivalent sum fixed for the whole village. Tax collection for state-owned property was sold by the pasha to rulers of the districts and subdistricts, who contracted their territorial concessions to powerful tax farmers. These tax collectors squeezed out of the fellahin ever-growing taxes, which, even more than the weather, determined the villagers' level of subsistence.

The rapacity of the tax collector determined the level of tax extortion—anywhere between one-sixth and two-thirds of the crop's value.[35] A reliable traveler reported that fellahin were forced to pay

five or six miris in the year... last year (1811) many peasants were obliged to sell a part of their furniture to defray taxes. It may be easily conceived therefore in what misery they live: they eat scarcely anything but the worst bread and oil or soups made of the wild herbs of which tyranny cannot deprive them.[36]

These authorized abuses fleeced the peasants, divested them of their property, and destroyed any possibility of their repaying long overdue taxes.

What could the defenseless, despairing peasants do against grinding taxation, constant plunder, and continuous oppression that robbed them even of the hope of recovering their crops and possessions? In order to survive in a static society with a distinct hierarchy, most peasants apathetically submitted to their destined fate. Obedient Muslim fellahin believed that "if you try a thousand times you can in no way change what is determined." Nevertheless, they tried to hide produce from the tax collectors, and many produced only what they could quickly consume.

TABLE 1 Population of Towns in Palestine in 1800

Acre	9,500
Jerusalem	9,000
Gaza	8,000
Nablus	7,500
Hebron	6,000
Safed	2,500–3,000
Ramleh	2,000
Tiberias	2,000
Bethlehem	1,600
Nazareth	1,250
Jaffa	1,250
Haifa	1,250
Lod	1,000

Numerous fellahin surrendered their tenuous independence and became tenant-vassals in servitude to the arbitrary tax collector. Another large group of peasants left the land they had previously cultivated; in northern Palestine 25 percent of the land was abandoned at the end of the eighteenth century.[37] Some landless peasants settled in town; others fled the province or withdrew to new lands; a few turned to robbing the remaining fellahin.

One out of five persons (about 55,000) lived in the thirteen towns of Palestine in 1800.[38] In order of size, the populations in these towns ranged from 9,500 to 1,000 (see table 1).

These population figures showing that not one town was inhabited by 10,000 people accurately reflect Palestine's unimportance. By comparison, in 1800, about 260,000 people lived in Cairo,[39] 150,000 in Aleppo, and 100,000 in Damascus.

Palestine was a land bridge for commercial traffic between the trade centers of Cairo and Damascus. Towns were located on or near the two major overland transportation routes—the hilly route and the Via Maris. Otherwise they were of negligible commercial, military, and administrative significance. Towns served as minor trade centers for nearby villages. The five towns of Jerusalem, Nazareth, Bethlehem, Hebron, and Nablus were religious centers for Muslim, Christian, and Jewish populations. Members of minority groups and people with common connections lived together in separate town quarters whose physical layout and buildings hardly differed from village houses. Due to abominable sanitation and health conditions, epidemics decimated the town population, but it was constantly replenished by villagers and Jewish and Christian immigrants from Europe. Minimal educational facilities and the municipal offices of the provinces and districts were located only in the towns. Another distinguishing characteristic of most towns was the presence of Jews, except in Lod, Ramleh, Gaza, and the Christian centers of Bethlehem and Nazareth.

Town life was permeated by the spirit of the countryside. For many town dwellers, life was an extension of agrarian life in the village. In fact, the smaller towns of Lod, Haifa, Nazareth, Bethlehem, and Ramleh were over-grown, sprawling villages. Some townfolk were employed as farmers on land located just outside the town gates and on vacant plots inside the town walls. Outside the walls and borders of towns was desolation and the ever-present danger of attack. Towns were protected by their topographic positions, citadel fortresses, garrisoned troops, and fortified walls. Jerusalem, Acre, Haifa, Jaffa, and Tiberias were walled towns; towns without walls were located in the mountains, with the exception of Gaza, Lod, and Ramleh.

Darkness extinguished activity in town. With the setting of the sun town gates were locked, not to be opened until sunrise. A traveler entered the town gates before sunset or remained prey to the robbers roaming the countryside. At night townfolk were forbidden to walk the unlighted streets without a torch; transgressors of the curfew were arrested as thieves.

Towns in Palestine were constructed in Oriental style dating back to Crusader and Byzantine times and were adapted to the mode of living in a warm climate. Houses in the homogeneous town quarters were built of clay, sometimes mixed with large rocks. Only in the mountain towns were homes constructed of hewn stones to insulate against winter's cold and summer's heat.[40] Houses stood close together because of the need for security, the lack of available space, and the desire of the people to huddle close to each other.

The basic housing unit in town was a one- or two-story building of separate rooms, built around an open courtyard, where all members of the tightly organized family lived. Rooms grouped around a courtyard were most suitable for the warm climate and helped strengthen the already strong sense of family. For the men, the courtyard provided a refuge from work and the pressures of the outside world; for the women, the courtyard was the center of social life. Into this constricted housing compound the whole family of grandparents, parents, and their numerous brood crowded together. Adding to the congestion was the family livestock of chickens and goats. Privacy was an unknown notion; no one felt the need to be alone.

Streets were dirty, narrow alleys winding from the town gates through the various quarters and around clusters of housing units. Down the middle of the street ran a drainage canal that served as a sewage system and overflowing cesspool. During the rainy winter season streets became stagnant pools of mucky water that were quickly turned into quagmires by the sloshing feet of humans and animals. Slanting streets of mountain towns were transformed into oozing streams moving fetid garbage from one place to another. During seven months of the year townfolk walked in pebble-littered streets and choking clouds of dust. As a "receptacle for whatever is useless,"[41] streets were littered with piles of refuse, dung, and putrefied animal carcasses. A town was no less smelled than seen, causing Europeans to wonder if "the organs of sense have in the East the same susceptibility as in the West."[42]

Because of the ever-present filth, the absence of garbage disposal and toilets, befouled water, and poor diet, endemic diseases ravaged the population. The most dreaded illness was the undefined and fatal plague that periodically thinned out the towns' populations. In all of Palestine there was not one certified doctor or hospital to care for the sick. When quarantines were imposed on plague-struck towns many Muslims fled town and returned to their family villages until the danger had passed, usually with the approach of the winter cold.

Towns also served as markets, but commercial activities in Palestine were conducted on a small, inconsequential scale. There was not much need for buying and selling in a country where 80 percent of the population lived in poor, self-sufficient villages and the remaining town dwellers barely eked out a subsistence living. After the harsh economic measures of Jazzar Pasha and Napoleon's destructive invasion, it was impossible to activate the feudal agricultural economy and the barter-based market system.

Other factors that depressed trading were the absence of a postal service and the deplorable means of transportation. Business could be transacted by mail only with the greatest difficulty because a postal service was introduced in the Turkish Empire only in 1834. Mailmen in Palestine were travelers bound for Istanbul and European cities. Unpaved roads between towns and villages were pitted dirt paths littered with rocks and stones. During the rainy winter season it was impossible to travel through flooded wadis or to transport produce over soggy roads where pack animals sank in the mud.

Port facilities were as antiquated as the roads were poor. The two major port towns of Jaffa and Acre lacked breakwaters, quays, and lighthouses, and Gaza and Haifa were dangerous ports exposed to winter storms. Once ashore, people and cargoes were frequently consigned to fifteen to forty days of quarantine to prevent the spread of infectious diseases.

Trading opportunities that surmounted the obstacles of primitive ports, quarantine delays, rutted roads, and no mail service were threatened by robbers stalking the countryside. During a three-day trip from Tiberias to Jaffa in 1827, a British tourist "was five times in the hands of robbers" and was forced to pay the robbers a small "toll tax"—a genteel term for protection money.[43] Since a lone traveler was an exposed target, transportation between towns was organized in caravans that traveled with guards. Lacking wagons or carts, travelers were carried on the backs of docile mules, horses, or donkeys except in the Sinai desert, where the camel was used. There was no wheeled transportation in Palestine until the 1860s.

Traders and tourists traveling in escorted caravans could not stay at hotels and inns because they did not exist in the Palestine of 1800. Caravansaries (khans) and monasteries provided shelter and protection in towns and on trade routes. Most of the khans, however, were so primitive that Christians preferred to lodge in the more comfortable monasteries of their personal denomination. Jews and Protestant missionaries were refused accommodation in many monasteries.[44] During Napoleon's 1799 expedition, the general stayed at Armenian and Franciscan monasteries in Ramleh, Jaffa, and Nazareth. Under such trying traveling conditions we may wonder "what motive has a man to bestir himself in a country . . . where everything, in short, invites [him] to stay at home."[45]

Despite the trifling trade potential, there was a small merchant group in the towns. Muslims as well as Armenians and Greek Catholics but hardly any Jews played key roles in the commercial life of the country. Merchants paid for transactions in cash or in barter, because only in large cities such as Beirut (not in Jerusalem) could merchants transfer money by bills of exchange. Bills of exchange were cashed in Beirut and then coins were transported to Palestine in guarded caravans. The merchant was both banker and moneylender, as in medieval times, and provided financial services not supplied by the government or private banks. Loaning money at high interest rates was one of the banking services provided by the merchants, who disregarded the Muslim ban on usury. More sophisticated merchants found that dealing in the silver-based Turkish currencies was even more profitable than granting high-interest loans. Juggling the coinage was the art of the merchants, just as tinkering with the currency was the profitable delight of the sultan. The Turkish system of minting debased coins, declaring arbitrary discounts, and paying with short-weighted, clipped coins led to strong inflationary pressures and successive devaluations of the Turkish piastre. From 1814 to 1840 the piastre was devalued in relation to the English pound sterling by more than 450 percent, dropping from 23 to 107 piastres per pound sterling.[46]

Local merchants could not compete in the conduct of foreign trade because the capitulation agreements issued by the sultan provided foreign traders with special privileges and exempted them from local laws. In order to expand commercial enterprise and stimulate trade throughout the Turkish Empire, foreign traders were granted the benefits of immunity from local and Turkish laws, guaranteed religious freedom, and exempted from payment of some or all taxes and custom tariffs. Capitulation agreements required the presence of a consul representing a foreign power, who had exclusive, sweeping, and binding judicial powers over European nationals. Of greater importance were the dual diplomatic and commercial functions of the consul: to strengthen the influence of the foreign power he represented and to develop its commercial interests. That is why consuls, vice-consuls, and consular agents were stationed in or near the coastal towns of Jaffa, Haifa, and Acre.

Foreign powers with capitulation rights were represented by local dignitaries, not natives of the foreign country they represented. For example, the prominent Jewish Picciotto family represented a number of foreign powers in consular posts in Aleppo and other towns in Syria.[47] Consuls received no salary for their services, but benefited by receiving protection and prestige from the governments they represented while trading on their own. A consul was a trading agent with almost no diplomatic functions to perform.

The capitulation agreements empowered the consuls in Palestine to protect not only the commercial rights of foreign nations but also the members of Jewish and Christian minorities, who enjoyed some tenuous connection with a European power. France was the guardian of Roman Catholics and Russia protected the Greek Catholics in the Turkish Empire. The Russians had inseparable religious ties with the Greek Orthodox Church and actively supported its 20,000 members, who were by far the largest minority group in Palestine.[48]

Russia's diplomatic position and presence in Palestine were further strengthened by the thousands of Russian peasant pilgrims who streamed into the Holy Land each year, in comparison to the few Roman Catholic pilgrims. The Russian-backed Greek Orthodox Church was able to gain the upper hand in control of the Christian holy places in Palestine after Napoleon's expedition seriously damaged French influence by turning Muslims against Roman Catholics.

Russia's strong interest in Palestine was evidenced by the appointments of George Mostras as Russian consul in Jaffa in 1812 and Anthony Katafago as Russian consul in Acre about 1815.[49] In contrast to Russia, Britain played a passive role and was only interested in safeguarding its gateway to India at the start of the nineteenth century.

Because of the capitulations and the long-standing Islamic tradition of tolerance for members of the minorities, Christians and Jews were granted special status in the pluralistic, ideologically permissive Ottoman society. Muslims tolerated minority groups, but never doubted the inferiority of the Jews and Christians and never let them forget it.

Minority groups coexisted as separate ethnic, social, and religious communities with freedom to conduct their own internal affairs. No attempt was made to Ottomanize the Christian and Jewish minorities; minorities were a "medley of peoples . . . they mix but do not combine."[50]

Religious communities of minorities, millets, were separate islands of distinct cultures within the Turkish Empire. A millet was a self-governing community organization of minority members who were legally granted independence to select their leaders and to manage their own religious, economic, cultural, judicial, and educational life without interference from the Turkish authorities. In return for such extensive autonomy, minority groups were responsible to the ruling power for the proper behavior of their members and for carrying out administrative functions, such as collecting revenues and promptly remitting taxes to the government.

A wide variety of taxes and fees were imposed on minority groups. As a token of their subservience to the Muslims, and as payment for religious tolerance and protection of life and property, dhimmis—the people of protection—paid a progressively rated poll tax for each male 15 years of age and above. Instead of serving in the Turkish army, members of minorities paid a bedel tax exempting them from military conscription. For a license to bury their dead, the minorities paid a fee to the kadi (religious judge) and his functionaries. There were also "insurance" fees and obligatory gifts that were "donated" by the millet on special occasions. Revenues from minorities were so large that they reportedly provided the principal source of income for Jerusalem's governor.

In exchange for tax payments and a host of extortionist rebates, the authorities protected the dhimmis yet proscribed their activities by imposing upon them stringent legal restrictions and social disabilities. Minority members were forbidden to worship in public and could not build new places of worship or repair existing ones except by the long and costly procedure of securing a firman from Istanbul. Dhimmis were prohibited from entering Muslim holy places. Christians were prevented from ringing church bells or carrying the cross in public. Jews and Christians were not allowed to carry arms; they could not ride a horse in town so as not to be higher than a Muslim; they could not serve in the Turkish army or be appointed to important imperial administrative positions; they were banned from buying property and could purchase land only with the greatest difficulty, because Muslims were forbidden to sell land to non-Muslims; they were not permitted to give evidence against a Muslim in a kadi court; and they could not own Muslim slaves for fear of proselytizing among true believers.[51] Jews and Christians were ordered to wear distinctive clothes of specific colors to distinguish them from true believers. Many Jews reacted to their designated dress not as a mark of discrimination but as a clear identification of the religion they proudly practiced.

Minorities were frequently prone to economic discrimination and physical persecutions whose severity depended on local levels of Muslim tolerance and the ability of the minority to pay bribes. Generally the "position of dhimmis was . . . tolerable but insecure. Humiliation was part of the pattern."[52] Only in isolated instances did officials resort to physical violence and threaten the existence of the Jewish community, although some nineteenth-century language and actions appear intimidating from the perspective of the twentieth century. When the Jewish community could not pay its debts, Muslims greedily confronted Jews, callously heaping scorn and contempt on them. In certain cases minority members were forced to sweep the streets and carry heavy bundles for Muslims. Other dhimmis were publicly reviled, attacked, and even robbed. When minority members were maltreated it was normally for the purpose of extorting money. Minorities were usually able to achieve the level of tolerance they could afford.

The major minority groups in Palestine in 1800 were the Greek Orthodox, the Roman Catholics, the Jews, and the Armenians.[53] The few Protestants living in Palestine secured protection from a consul representing their country of origin and were not organized in a millet until 1850.

Most of the 25,000 Christians of Palestine lived in Jerusalem, Bethlehem, Nazareth, and villages surrounding these towns. The almost 5,000 Jews in Palestine at the turn of the nineteenth century grouped together mainly in Jerusalem, Hebron, Safed, and Tiberias. The 30,000 Christians and Jews together constituted only 11 percent of the total population of 275,000 but made up more than half of the 55,000 town dwellers.

The Greek Orthodox Church, which had split off from the Roman Catholic Church in the eleventh century, comprised about three-quarters of the Christian population. Greek Catholics were the most influential minority group in Palestine because of their numbers, wealth, and the strong backing they received from their Russian benefactor. The Greek patriarch of Jerusalem resided in Istanbul and showed his disinterest in Palestine by hardly ever visiting his diocese.[54]

Nearly 3,000 Latins belonging to the Roman Catholic Church were staunchly supported by France and were represented by the Franciscan order, which guarded the Catholic holy places.[55] Not until 1847, in response to the lead taken by the Greek Catholics, did a Roman Catholic bishop take up residence in Jerusalem.

Most of the fewer than 1,000 Armenians in Palestine lived in Jerusalem's Armenian quarter, near the Armenian convent, "more splendid than anything else in Jerusalem."[56] Armenians belonged to the most homogeneous, the most united, and the most prosperous millet. The leader of the Armenian millet was their patriarch, who resided in Jerusalem.

Jews constituted the second largest minority community but numbered less than 2 percent of Palestine's residents. In a world population of 2.5 million Jews,[57] only 1 out of 500 Jews lived in Palestine. About 60 percent of world Jewry lived in European countries, mainly in the Kingdom of Poland, which was the population center and the scholastic core of the Jewish world. The remaining 40 percent, or 1 million Jews, resided in the Turkish Empire. At the beginning of the nineteenth century only 3,000–3,500 Jews lived in the United States.[58]

Jews settled in their four holy towns in Palestine: 2,250 Jews resided in Jerusalem, 800–900 in Tiberias, 600 in Safed, and 300 in Hebron in 1800. Another 300 Jews worked as farmers in the northern villages of Peki'in, Kfar Yasif, and Shfar-Am; 100 Jews lived in Nablus and 50 in Haifa; another 300 settled in Acre, under the protection of Haim Farhi.

About 95 percent of the nearly 5,000 Jews in Eretz Israel were of Sephardi origin—Jews from Oriental countries who had settled mainly around the Mediterranean basin after their expulsion from Spain and Portugal at the end of the fifteenth century—and long-time residents of Palestine called Musta'rabs.[59] Arabic-speaking Sephardim came to Eretz Israel from the North African countries of Morocco, Algiers, and Tunis and from Egypt, Turkey, Asia Minor, and the Balkan states.

Sephardim were non-Muslim Ottoman subjects, or rayahs, with the privileges and responsibilities of other minority groups. Only about 200 Jews in Eretz Israel were Ashkenazim who had immigrated from Germany, Holland, the Austro-Hungarian Empire, and the East European regions of Poland and Russia.

The economic situation of the Jewish communities in each of the four holy cities was far more depressed than that of the Greek Orthodox, Roman Catholic, and Armenian millets. The Jewish millet lacked the protection provided the Greeks and Roman Catholics by Russia and France and the financial assets of the Greek and Catholic churches, which received generous financing from rich overseas benefactors. Only the contributions of Diaspora Jewry enabled the poverty-stricken Jewish community to cling precariously but stubbornly to the Holy Land.

THREE

Hasidic Immigration to Eretz Israel

1777–1807

In 1777 a group of 300 Polish Jews arrived in Palestine and settled in Safed. This was the first large organized group of Jewish immigrants to the Holy Land since Rabbi Judah HeHasid led a retinue of 400 Jews to Jerusalem in 1700.[1] During the intervening decades, a small but constant trickle of individuals, families, and small groups composed mainly of elderly people settled in Eretz Israel. Most immigrants or olim (a Hebrew word meaning "ascending" to the Land of Israel from the Diaspora) came from Sephardi communities in the Turkish Empire. However, some new settlers, such as R. Abraham Gershon of Kuty, were Ashkenazim from the Kingdom of Poland. Rabbi Gershon's family were the first Ashkenazi settlers in Hebron, but they later moved to Jerusalem,[2] unable to adjust to Hebron's Sephardi environment. Other elderly Polish Jews settled in the Galilee holy cities of Tiberias and Safed.[3]

Some of the 300 settlers in Safed in 1777 were members of the newly founded Hasidic movement, which first appeared in the Polish provinces of Podolia and Volhynia during the middle of the eighteenth century.[4] The founder of Hasidism was Israel Ba'al Shem-Tov, "the Master of the Good Name," whose religious folk and revivalist movement based on the love of a merciful God and expressed in a clamor of joy and ecstasy made religion

36

accessible and meaningful to the mass of East European Jews. Hasidism was an emotional, mystical convergence of religious faith, Messianic hope, divine salvation, cathartic exuberance, scholastic ignorance, and an exorcism of evil spirits, all affirmed in unpredictable, inexplicable ways of the most personal kind. "God-intoxicated" Hasidim elevated themselves and their mundane existence to heavenly heights by remaining in a constant state of exultation, expressing spontaneous feelings during their fervent communions with God and while engaged in their daily activities. Life ceased being an onerous burden as Hasidim ornamented the grim realities of East European life with a splendor fancifully woven by their religious imagination.

In reaction to a religion that constantly exhibited the agony of the spirit and "set the largest, most edifying standards of despair,"[5] Hasidism chased sorrow from the Jewish heart by exploding in tumultuous prayer and partaking in the pleasures of dancing, singing, and making merry. Rabbi Abraham of Kolisk, like other devout Hasidim, turned somersaults, performed pranks and practical jokes in public,[6] and was accused of standing on his head during the prayer service. For such frivolities R. Abraham was harshly chastised by the successor of the Ba'al Shem-Tov, Rabbi Dov Baer of Mezhirech. (In the eighteenth century most Jews had no family name; they were known by the towns they lived in and by their father's first name.)

A crucial figure in Hasidism was the zaddik, "the righteous one." A new type of Jewish leader, the zaddik attained his venerated position by force of personality and charismatic leadership, rather than by scholarship and erudition. He guided his flock in religious and personal matters and advised them on business and personal affairs. Hasidim gained self-esteem from the sacred stamp of their zaddik, were elevated by his spiritual fervor, recognized his absolute authority, and contributed to his upkeep. The zaddik and his Hasidim were inextricably bound together in a reciprocal relationship.

The 300 Jews in the Hasidic group who reached Safed in 1777 migrated to Eretz Israel for a variety of spiritual and practical reasons. One menacing factor motivating them to leave Eastern Europe was the wave of blood libels and persecutions that swept through the Kingdom of Poland nearly every year. The worst atrocities occurred in 1768 when Haidamak cossacks and rebellious peasants rampaged through the Ukraine and parts of Poland where most European Jews lived, destroying synagogues and homes and slaughtering the population. These massacres uprooted entire Jewish communities, and their members scattered in search of new homes.

These assaults were followed by the first partition of Poland in 1772. Russia, Prussia, and Austria, the three absolute monarchies sharing common borders with Poland, started to dismember the Kingdom of Poland,

and many Polish Hasidim found themselves placed under Russian rule. New borders divided some Hasidic communities between rival countries and forced Jews to move out of territories in which they had long lived.

Another reason for Hasidic migration to Eretz Israel in 1777 was competition and conflict with other Jews. During the Passover holiday in 1772, the Vilna gaon, a preeminent rabbinical authority and the leader of the opponents of Hasidism (called Mitnaggedim), "ostracized, cast out and isolated" the Hasidim from the entire Congregation of Israel.[7] Hasidic prayer services were banned and Mitnaggedim were prohibited from maintaining religious and social contact with the rival group. This 1772 excommunication launched organized persecution against the Hasidim and initiated a state of strife between the two groups that lasted well into the nineteenth century.

Why did the Mitnaggedim so fiercely oppose the Hasidim, who were not preaching a new religious doctrine or trangressing the Jewish law, but were trying to infuse a new spirit of joy into the stolid religious practices of Judaism? The Vilna gaon and his followers declared war because they believed that the Hasidim scorned scholars and scholarship, replaced study with communal celebrations, presumed a special intimacy with the Lord, elevated the inspirational personality of the zaddik above rabbinical authority, and contemptuously disparaged the conventional values and courtesies in Jewish life. The Mitnaggedim were battling a new type of leadership that threatened the existing establishment within the Jewish community. They charged the Hasidim with introducing innovations into the liturgy, reciting prayers after the designated hours, and ritually slaughtering animals with specially honed knives rather than with ordinary sharpened knives.[8]

In an effort to placate the Vilna gaon, two Hasidic leaders traveled to Vilna in 1775 seeking reconciliation. But the gaon refused to meet with people he considered to be organizers of apostasy, who were continuing the corrupt and divisive work of the false Messianism of Shabbetai Zevi and Jacob Frank that was destroying the unity of the Jewish people. The disparity between the innovative Hasidim and the truly pagan, heretical Frankists was ignored. In times of stress it is difficult to differentiate between reform and rebellion.

In December 1772 the Hasidic movement was struck a cruel blow when its leader, Rabbi Dov Baer of Mezhirech, died. Lacking this dominant personality, the movement started to split into separate sects. While the Hasidim were still mourning the death of their leader, two political events, one in Europe and one in Palestine, influenced their actions. In 1774 the bitter six-year Russo-Turkish War was drawing to an end. Russian subjects, such as the Hasidim, could now travel and transfer funds to Turkish-controlled territory like Palestine.

Between 1770 and 1775 most of Palestine had been in a state of chaos. A Russian flotilla sailed off the Syrian coast fighting the Turkish Empire in a side skirmish of the Russo-Turkish War of 1768–1774. The Egyptian Mamlukes revolted against the sultan and captured large parts of Palestine with the aid of the ruler of the Galilee, Dahir al-'Amr. Dahir and the Mamlukes conquered Nablus, Jaffa, and the coastal area south to Gaza; they laid siege to Jerusalem in an effort to gain control over virtually all of Palestine.[9] In the ensuing battles Palestine suffered widespread destruction. Frequently the Galilee was cut off from the southern part of the country. Jews in Tiberias, Safed, Jerusalem, and Hebron were incarcerated in their towns and suffered from heavy taxes, large debts, high interest rates, and escalating prices.[10]

In 1775 the Egyptian rebellion was quelled, Dahir al-'Amr was killed, the sultan regained control over Palestine, and Pasha Ahmad al-Jazzar began to impose order in northern Palestine.

In Poland, the situation of the Hasidim in 1776 was an unenviable one. They lacked a dominant leader, were excommunicated and tormented by the Mitnaggedim, and were persecuted by the Russians. Some Hasidim, inspired by the ideal of praying and studying in the Holy Land, decided that it was a propitious time to start anew by settling a small, elite group in a newly peaceful Palestine. By going to Eretz Israel, the Hasidim would be delivered from Exile and from the hands of the Poles and the Mitnaggedim. Moreover, trumpeting the message of Hasidism from Zion for all Jews to hear would strengthen the movement, increase its prestige in the Jewish world, and achieve "a valuable gain in the odor of sanctity" in their struggle against the Mitnaggedim.[11] They would also hasten the coming Redemption, although it was obvious to all Jews that deliverance would be accomplished by divine intervention, not by the efforts of mortals.

The group's desire to establish a center of Hasidism in the Holy Land reflected its religious beliefs and revealed its spiritual needs. The Hasidim, like other Jewish settlers, came to pray, study, and fulfill the commandment (mitzva) of living in Eretz Isreal. From the time God promised Abraham, "To your descendants will I give this Land," an indissoluble connection and mutual obligation had been established between the Jewish people and Eretz Israel. Jews wanted to be buried among the tombs of their forefathers in order to be assured of quickly entering the next world,[12] after the Messianic Redemption. Living in Eretz Israel, Jews would be spared the ordeals of transmigration—the rolling of the dead underground from the corners of the scattered Diaspora to Jerusalem's Valley of Jehoshafat where they would be redeemed and resurrected.

A strong incentive drawing Hasidim and other Jews to Eretz Israel was the yearning to obey commandments that could only be performed in the Holy Land, particularly those tied to agriculture, such as the sanctification of the first fruits collected from the fields of the Land of Israel. Rabbis sermonized on the duty of every Jew to settle in Eretz Israel. Had not God ordered the patriarchs to possess Eretz Israel by "working the land and guarding it" (Genesis 2:15)? How could the Jews "sing the Lord's song in a strange land"? Rabbis decreed: "Every Jew must abidingly and firmly resolve in his heart to ascend to the Land of Israel to live in it." But they tempered their words with the cautionary advice that a Jew should migrate only after having "acquired the expenses and some position to afford him a living"—and they remained in Europe.

Nonetheless, Eretz Israel exerted a powerful attraction for religious Jews who yearned for the coming of the Messiah, their deliverance from Exile, and their ingathering in the land of their forefathers. Without the Land of Israel there could be no salvation. This central concept of Redemption in Zion was woven into the beliefs, prayers, and customs of the Jewish people wherever they lived. Jews considered Redemption by the Messiah part of God's working out of His purposes in history, with events like the Exodus from Egypt placed on an uninterrupted continuum of time that would conclude with the ingathering of the exiles in the Holy Land.

The sanctity of the Holy Land and the concept of Messianic deliverance were inherent in Hasidic thought, but settling in Eretz Israel was not a cornerstone of the movement. Moving to Zion did not inspire Hasidim, motivate them, or explain the success of their movement. Nevertheless, some early Hasidic leaders were seized by an intense Messianic tension that moved them to Eretz Israel in 1777. They wrote that they had left their "permanent homes" in the Diaspora and settled "near the Lord's devastated mountain . . . because of the love of the holy, to work and to maintain a sanctified watch" over the Holy Land.[13] "We are standing in the courtyards of the Lord's house and on His holy mountain as emissaries of His holy people . . . to perform the commandments . . . written in the Torah . . ." For these Hasidim, the dictum of the Jewish sages that "the merit of living in Eretz Israel is balanced against all the precepts of the Torah" had a real and imminent meaning. Select Hasidim yearned to open the heavens over Eretz Israel so that the prayers of Diaspora Jews would be accepted by God. By maintaining a vigil in Eretz Israel for all Jews, they would awaken love for Eretz Israel and strengthen the bonds of all Jews with the Holy Land.[14]

In March 1777 dozens of Hasidim left their homes in White Russia and started a five- to six-month trek to Eretz Israel.[15] They were led by 47-year-old Rabbi Menahem Mendel of Vitebsk, who was assisted by R. Israel of Polotsk and R. Abraham Hacohen of Kolisk, the somersaulting Hasid. During the spring the convoy wended its way southward through Volhynia and Podolia, where Jewish communities collected funds for their voyage. As was their custom, the Hasidim celebrated by eating, drinking, and dancing to stimulate "joyous worship."[16] The holy pilgrimage to Eretz Israel was indeed a festive occasion worthy of a Hasidic celebration.

The attention heaped on R. Menahem Mendel and his followers attracted many impoverished and homeless Jews who had been uprooted by the 1772 partition of Poland and the subsequent anti-Semitic persecutions.[17] Swept along by the enthusiasm of the Hasidim and their vision of security in Eretz Israel, these destitute people joined the group. In fact most of those who continued on the voyage were strangers and not Hasidim,[18] according to R. Israel of Polotsk. However, the righteous impulses of the Hasidic heart could not deny the desire of these Jews to fulfill the commandment of settling in the Holy Land, to arouse God's benevolence, and to pray for all Jews.[19] Since this was the "will of God,"[20] the Lord would help the Hasidim find a way to support them.

After passing through the Ukrainian province of Podolia, the Hasidim continued overland through Moldavia to the Black Sea ports, from which they set sail on small barges to Istanbul.[21] One barge carrying 80 Hasidim sank in a storm and only 30 were saved. In desperation, some of the survivors asked to return to Poland. Others who reached the Turkish capital could not endure the hardships of the trip and also decided to return, for it was "not the will of the Creator" that they should reach Eretz Israel.[22] R. Menahem Mendel openly admitted that he was not unhappy about these departures, for "were they all to come [to Eretz Israel] they would cover the entire land."[23]

In Istanbul the Hasidic group was helped by the Jewish community and the major fundraising organization for Eretz Israel, the Istanbul Officials for Palestinian Jewry, which twice a year chartered ships for Jews traveling there. The Istanbul Officials rented a ship to transport the Hasidim, along with 130 "rich, poor, and scholarly" Sephardim from North Africa.[24] After an uneventful seven days on the Mediterranean, the Hasidic group of more than 300 persons landed in Acre in September 1777.[25]

On arriving in the Holy Land, the joy of the Hasidim knew no bounds. R. Menahem Mendel blessed the Lord, "who has sustained and maintained and enabled us to reach this place which has been glorified by our fore-fathers. . . . Who can tell about its brilliant splendor. . . . " They prayed rhapsodically that "God has heard our lament and started gathering us to-gether from all corners of the world. May He soon send us the sainted Mes-siah in our lifetime. . . . This is the day we hoped for. Let us rejoice and make merry in the land of our love . . ."[26] From Acre the group traveled all day by donkey to reach Safed, spending about 2,400 piastres for transport, plus daily living expenses, and tariffs imposed by the authorities.[27]

Some Hasidim might have preferred to live in the holy city of Jerusalem. In fact the Jerusalem Jewish community (kehilla) of about 3,000 asked the Hasidim to join them,[28] but this was more a gesture of friendship than a practical invitation, for Jerusalem had been closed to Ashkenazi settlers since 1720, when Polish followers of Judah HeHasid were run out of town after defaulting on their debt payments. The Hasidim feared that if they entered Jerusalem the Muslims would immediately demand payment of that debt. Even the 50 or so Ashkenazim who lived in Jerusalem felt obliged to dress like Sephardim to mask their identity.[29] It is difficult to conceive that the 300 members of the Hasidic group would blend inconspicuously into the Sephardi community. Moreover, since the mid-eighteenth cen-tury, Jerusalem had been out of bounds to poor settlers, whether Ashkenazi or Sephardi, by decision of the Istanbul Officials, who were unable or un-willing to pay the poll tax and other expenses of a debt-ridden and plague-stricken community.[30]

The Tiberias Jewish community also invited the Hasidim to settle in its midst,[31] alongside 40–50 Ashkenazim and 450–550 Sephardim. The Hasidim were tempted to live near the tombs of famous sages such as Maimonides and join a tranquil and more prosperous community than those in Jerusa-lem, Hebron, or Safed. However, the Tiberias invitation was not re-alistic—the small, walled Jewish quarter of 10 dunams (2½ acres) was short on housing after having just taken in 130 North African Jews who had traveled to Eretz Israel on the same boat with the Hasidim.[32] To house and absorb another 300 immigrants would have overburdened the Tiberias community physically and drastically upset the balance between Sephardim and Ashkenazim.

Nor was the holy city of Hebron a viable settlement alternative for the Hasidim. Hebron's 300 Sephardim and handful of Ashkenazim,[33] crowded into a small Jewish compound, were the most poverty-stricken and perse-cuted of the communities in the four holy cities. It was socially impractical, economically unfeasible, and physically impossible to double the size of Hebron's Sephardi kehilla by adding 300 Polish Jews.

The Hasidim were quite willing to settle in Safed. They were attracted to the town's mystical religious past: the kabbalistic belief that the Messiah would come from Safed conjured up alluring visions. From Safed the Hasidim could fulfill the religious custom of visiting the graves of rabbinical authorities buried in nearby Meron, such as the shrine of Rabbi Simeon Bar Yohai, the reputed author of the classic kabbalistic *Book of the Splendor*, the *Zohar*. The Hasidim would also benefit from the peace imposed on the Galilee by Jazzar Pasha and from his tolerant attitude toward the Jews.[34] About 1777 Jazzar levied an annual poll tax of only 2,000 piastres on the Jewish community in Safed, wiped out their old debt of 20,000 piastres, and allowed the Jews to rebuild synagogues and study halls damaged by the earthquake seventeen years earlier.

Furthermore, the cold mountain climate of Safed, with its elevation of 2,750 feet, was somewhat similar to the even colder Polish climate. On a more prosaic level the new arrivals discovered that living expenses in Safed were low and food was plentiful.[35] Most important were the welcoming attitude shown by the 200 Sephardim, the presence of a few Ashkenazim in Safed who could help the Hasidim adjust more quickly, and the availability of many houses,[36] which had been vacated after the 1759–1760 earthquakes, which had leveled many buildings, killed about 150–200 Jewish residents,[37] and caused most of the Jews to flee town.[38]

The newly arrived Hasidic group tripled the number of Ashkenazim living in Eretz Israel, raising it from about 150 to 450, and more than doubled the Safed Jewish population, increasing it from 200–250 to 500–550. The group quickly settled into roomy houses in the Jewish quarter of Safed.[39]

The 100 bona fide Hasidim belonged to about 20 to 25 families.[40] The other 200 settlers probably included children and households.[41] Thus, most of the 300 individuals in the Hasidic group were young and middle-aged people looking forward to a new life, rather than old people interested in spending their last years in the Holy Land. The Hasidim were scholars possessed by a feeling of "religious elitism" who viewed their move to Eretz Israel as a mission on behalf of all Jews. In contrast, most of those who joined the convoy en route were the first group of eighteenth-century Ashkenazi immigrants who were not scholars.

The Hasidim transplanted to Safed their religious values and practices and their East European way of life. They dressed, spoke, prayed, and studied as if they were still living in Poland, speaking to each other in Yiddish. In summer as well as winter the bearded Hasidim dressed in the heavy black gabardines and fur hats they had worn in Poland. They tried to converse with the Sephardim in their one common language, Hebrew, but this was difficult because the Hasidim pronounced Hebrew words with a sing-song Yiddish inflection and accented the syllables differently from the Sephardim. Eventually, the musically oriented Hasidic ear adjusted to the lilting Sephardi pronunciation of stressing the last syllable in Hebrew words.

R. Menahem Mendel of Vitebsk and the other scholars spent their days and nights as they had in Europe, "following the path of Torah," unraveling the intricacies of the Talmud, and trying to solve the kabbalistic mysteries of the *Zohar*. They labeled the 200 non-Hasidim, far from the world of study, a "mixed multitude,"[42] a clear allusion to a motley crowd.

Life started each day for the Hasidim when they recited their first prayer upon awakening. Three times every day—in the morning, the late afternoon, and early evening—the Hasidim prayed in one of Safed's three synagogues according to the liturgy of the kabbalistic sage Isaac Luria, which gave the Hasidic prayers a "Sephardi coloring."[43] The inspiration of praying in the Holy Land, in the kabbalistic town of Safed, according to the ritual of Rabbi Isaac Luria, must have driven the Hasidim to pray with an extra measure of devotion, ecstasy, and noisy turbulence.

The Hasidim arrived late at the synagogue, made long preparations to enter into concentrated devotions, and then shouted out their heartfelt prayers in a terrible tumult. "The din and confusion of their prayer can split a city asunder,"[44] complained a European. Violently shaking back and forth, bowing down and leaping up, gesticulating, swaying, and dancing, "the whole congregation was in motion."[45] A convulsive frenzy of communal rapture would seize the congregants. Out of joy in performing the mitzva of praying in Eretz Israel they would roll on the floor. Hasidim clapped their hands, stamped their jumping feet on the floor, and uttered ear-splitting cries. "Everyone tries to shout louder than his neighbor, with the result that it is completely impossible to respond 'Amen.'"[46] While they skipped and whirled, Hasidic voices were lifted in rhythmic, resonant song, and strident laments were transformed into melodic harmony, in an attempt to bridge the distance between the joy of heaven and the gloomy despair on earth. One Christian observed that the Hasidim "appeared as if determined at once to take heaven by storm, springing upon their toes, beating their breasts, and groaning and crying simultaneously at the highest pitch of their voices."[47] A Hasidic prayer service in Tiberias was described by a startled Swiss traveler (1812):

The congregation frequently imitate by the voices or gestures the meaning of some remarkable passages; for example, when the Rabbi pronounces the words "praise the Lord with the sound of the trumpet" they imitate the sound of the trumpet through their closed fists. When "a horrible tempest" occurs, they puff and blow to represent a storm; or should he mention "the cries of the righteous in distress" they all set up a loud screaming; and it not infrequently happens that while some are still blowing the storm others have already begun the cries of the righteous, this forming a concert which it is difficult for any but a zealous Hebrew to hear with gravity. [48]

No member of the Hasidic group earned a living. Even had they wanted to work this would have been impossible because, according to R. Israel of Polotsk, "We do not know the language and the customs of the country."[49] In fact, the Hasidim did not intend to work; this would have diverted them from their true occupation of prayer and study. Lacking employment ambitions and work skills that could be used in their new environment, most Hasidim subsisted on funds contributed by Diaspora Jewry. Some Hasidim of means lived off the income from overseas assets.[50] No effort was made to study Arabic, the language in daily use in the country, and negligible interest was shown in the Muslims, whom they derisively called *ara'ber* in Yiddish—with the same negative connotation as the word *goyim* applied to Gentiles. In 1778 the Hasidim did not even know how many people lived in Safed and masked their indifference with the argument that this town of about 2,000 persons was too large to be counted.[51] As they had kept their distance from Gentiles in Poland, so the Hasidim stayed far away from the Muslims of Safed, meeting them only in the market while buying food.

While the Hasidim studied, it is not clear what filled the days of the many nonscholars who had come with them. Since letter writers habitually ignored ordinary, commonplace daily events, no written record remains. We may conjecture that this large group of people who were unsuited to study and unable to work idled away many hours socializing and gossiping. The relaxed rhythms of their day permitted them the leisure of emulating the Hasidim not only in joyous devotions, but in their merrymaking and in the retelling of popular Hasidic folktales.

In sharp contrast to the Hasidim, the Sephardim dressed like Muslims, spoke Arabic, knew the local customs, and earned their living working at a wide variety of jobs—as porters, construction workers, silversmiths, silk-weavers, storekeepers, and peddlers in the nearby Arab villages.[52] No Jews followed the Muslim practice of working as farmers in the fields, groves, and vineyards surrounding Safed. Despite the labor of the able-bodied men, the Sephardim were poor and some required financial help. The Istanbul Officials contributed to the upkeep of elderly and indigent Jews unable to work.

One may presume that the 200–250 Sephardim of Safed, suddenly reduced to a minority within the Jewish community, felt somewhat overwhelmed and slightly put off by the 300 Polish Jews and their incongruous appearance, rough manners, unfamiliar prayer habits, and clamorous celebrations. Nonetheless, the two groups developed feelings of mutual respect based on common kinship, heritage, and history. R. Abraham reported that "all of us find favor in the eyes of the Sephardim."[53] Indeed, upon the arrival of the Hasidim in Safed, the Sephardim provided them with the use of the House of Joseph synagogue and graciously undertook to refurbish for them one of the synagogues that had been damaged in the 1759 earthquake. "They are building for us a new synagogue,"[54] R. Israel wrote six months after their arrival.

Hasidim and Sephardim worshipped in separate synagogues because of different prayer customs developed in widely separated countries during hundreds of years. Although the Hasidim adopted the Lurianic-Sephardic rite, their prayer liturgy, benedictions, and customs were different. Even the synagogue behavior of each group was at variance. The Sephardim arrived at their synagogue at sunrise, decorously chanted their prayers, and then quickly left for work. The Hasidim arrived at the House of Joseph synagogue long after sunrise, loafed about socializing, and prayed in a bedlam of fierce energy before slowly dispersing.

The mystically oriented Hasidim did not reveal what they regarded as the "true Torah" to others. As late as 1801 R. Abraham wrote that they were careful not to expose their hidden beliefs and practices before the Sephardim.[55] This indicates that the Hasidim in Safed, unlike the few Ashkenazim in Jerusalem, did not study with Sephardi scholars or seek to learn the distinctive Sephardi system of talmudic interpretation. Such reticence to share Jewish thought and concepts did not antagonize the Sephardim but kept them at a distance and prevented the development of close, convivial relations between the two groups.

Daily contact between the groups was courteous and cordial. Before the arrival of the Hasidim, the few Ashkenazim in Safed had cooperated with the Sephardim in raising money from Diaspora Jewish communities.[56] One of them wrote that the Sephardim "love us dearly . . . and please us by sharing with us their money, despite poverty and privation."[57] Some letters written by Hasidim evince a certain admiration for the Sephardim, who spoke as equals with Muslims, were knowledgeable about Muslim customs and behavior, and earned their own living. Such esteem was tempered by faint Hasidic disapproval of a people stagnating in what they regarded as a primitive, albeit holy, environment.

There was some intermarriage between the two groups, with greater social prestige being granted to the Sephardi pedigree. The leader of the Hasidim, R. Menahem Mendel, married his son Moshe to the daughter of a distinguished, wealthy Sephardi family in Jerusalem. The dowry of 800 piastres was so large that the young couple was able to live off the annual interest payments. R. Menahem Mendel advised his son to act tolerantly and "not to pay strict attention to details when dealing with the Sephardim and their leaders, whatever their behavior may be."[58] This "mixed" marriage reflected the need for mutual accommodation; the young bridegroom did adjust to his marriage, after complaining that his Sephardi wife was unable to prepare good Polish borsht.

One source of contention between the Sephardim and Hasidim was the ritual slaughter of animals. The Sephardi ritual slaughterer used whetted, normally sharpened knives (like the Mitnaggedim in Europe), instead of the specially honed knives mandated by Hasidic ritual. Consequently R. Menahem Mendel declared that meat slaughtered by the Sephardim was not kosher for the Hasidim. The Sephardi rabbis were dumbfounded. How could meat that was kosher for them and the followers of the rigorously orthodox Vilna gaon be declared unclean by the Hasidim? This incident stirred up bad feelings. Not only had the Hasidim rejected an established Sephardi ritual practice, but they had deprived the Sephardi treasury of a significant source of income from the profitable meat tax.

Soon after the Hasidim settled in Safed, they found their treasury running dry. They could not have foreseen that the authorities in White Russia would prohibit the emigration of Jews and ban the transfer of money to Palestine.[59] Nor had the Hasidim anticipated that the original group of 100 would have to support all those who joined them. R. Israel contended that it was impossible that "the few support the many in Eretz Israel," but when the many "asked for bread they did not have," the Hasidim could not resist their pleas, although their budget and their patience were sorely tried by the constant complaints of those whom even kind-hearted R. Israel called "paupers" and the "affliction" of the Hasidim. At one point he was reduced to exclaiming, "We did not want them."[60]

Sephardi leaders expressed misgivings about the perilous financial situation of the Hasidim. As Turkish subjects (rayahs) and members of the Safed millet, the Sephardim were responsible for paying to the government taxes and fees levied on all Jews, both Sephardi and Ashkenazi. Since the Hasidim could not earn a living and were dependent on overseas contributions, the Sephardim feared that they would be forced to bear the tax burden for all Jews. The Sephardim asked the Hasidim to pay a share of the Jewish community's financial obligation—a reasonable request considering that members of the Hasidic group constituted the majority of Safed's Jews. However, the Hasidic community, already in great financial distress, regarded this request as completely unfair. It had to pay for the daily upkeep of 300 people while the Sephardim were in the favorable position of not having to support most members of their community, who were able to earn their own living. The Hasidim felt that the least the Sephardim could do was pay the community taxes for all the Jews while they struggled to raise money overseas to feed their group.

To aggravate money matters, in 1778 Safed was hit by a plague of locusts and a drought.[61] Was this God's way of testing the faithful, the Hasidim wondered? Prices for wheat and food shot up tenfold, according to R. Abraham; twenty-five-fold according to the Sephardim. In order to feed their group the Hasidim borrowed money at a high rate of interest, in anticipation of receiving contributions from overseas. This initiated a cycle of escalating interest payments that was to plague the Hasidim over the years. The Sephardim also took loans, incurred high interest charges, and paid taxes in arrears.

When the Hasidic "well was not refilled,"[62] R. Menahem Mendel sent R. Israel back to Poland, to collect donations so that "all Israel will be strengthened by settling the Holy Land." R. Israel managed to send the Hasidim 3,000 piastres "to keep them alive." Of this amount, 2,000 piastres were allocated for payment of the poll tax, 250 piastres covered R. Israel's travel expenses, and 750 piastres were earmarked for the maintenance of the Safed Hasidic community, a paltry sum hardly sufficient to support the group for two weeks. During the following decades a Hasidic emissary, or shaliah, was sent overseas almost every year to raise funds.

Despite the efforts of R. Israel's far-roving fundraising missions (he traveled as far as Holland and died abroad in 1783), the Hasidim were unable to provide for the needs of the 300 members in their group. R. Menahem Mendel complained that "expenses in Eretz Israel are four and five times the expenses overseas." One hard-pressed Hasid, R. Isaac, who arrived in Safed with a small group eighteen months after the 1777 convoy, asked his father for money "to save an endangered life" because "there is no poor person in your country more poverty stricken than we sitting here in the Holy Land." R. Isaac reminded his father that it is "proper" to send financial support because "there is no more important commandment than maintaining a settler in the Holy Land. And this way they will be considered as if they had performed the commandment themselves."[63] He described hunger in the land and the escalating prices for wheat and olive oil, but noted that the 1780 prices of these items had dropped by 400–450 percent compared to the previous year.

In a similar vein, R. Menahem Mendel related that "all the privations which we suffered during the last three years are the sufferings of Eretz Israel. . . . We suffered so much that all other Jews were free of affliction because of our torment . . ."[64]

While the Hasidim were trying to solve their financial problems, they were attacked by their old nemesis, the Mitnaggedim. Warnings and recriminations against the Hasidim had been sent from Europe to the Sephardim and to the few Mitnaggedim living in Safed, and the conflict was transferred to the more sacred battlefield of Eretz Israel. An attitude of contempt and a "mutual lack of tolerance" prevailed among the Ashkenazim of Safed.[65] R. Menahem Mendel vilified the Safed Mitnaggedim: "They are ignorant and oppress and bully the true worshippers of God." At the same time he sent placating letters to Polish Jewry, seeking a reconciliation between the two groups. Paraphrasing Malachi (2:10), he pleaded: "Have we not one father? Hath not one God created us? Why should a man betray his brothers and desecrate the covenant of our Father? . . . All we ask for is peace . . ."[66] But these pleas went unheeded; the European Mitnaggedim continued to malign the Hasidim, and the Mitnaggedim in Safed joined in the fray.

The vitriolic attacks of the Safed Mitnaggedim against the Hasidim triggered negative feelings on the part of the Sephardim, who suspected that letters sent to Poland and Germany contained criticism of their actions.[67] The Sephardim also continued to be offended by the challenge to their ritual slaughtering practices. When the 2,000 piastres sent by R. Israel to pay the poll tax were received, the relieved Sephardim firmly insisted that the Hasidim continue to pay taxes and community charges. The Hasidim refused to accept this permanent financial obligation, not having money to pay for both food and taxes. When the Sephardim adamantly pressed their demands, R. Menahem Mendel called them "completely wicked believers of Shabbetai Zevi, may his name be blotted out" and heatedly charged the head of the Sephardim community with "defaming" and endangering the lives of the Hasidim.[68] The financial situation of the Hasidim continued to deteriorate. Funds from Eastern Europe were usually late and always

inadequate. Lacking sufficient money, R. Menahem Mendel favored the
100 true Hasidim in his group and, reluctantly, stopped paying for the daily
upkeep of the 200 non-Hasidim. "And when they no longer received help
from us," he wrote, "they joined the others to cause us suffering and to
curse us."

Now the Hasidim were at loggerheads with all the Jews of Safed—the
Sephardim ordered them to share in the millet community taxes, the Mitnaggedim bitterly antagonized their traditional opponents, and the 200
non-Hasidim turned against their old benefactors.

After struggling for more than three years to establish the Hasidim in
Safed, in 1781 R. Menahem Mendel moved an estimated 75 followers to
Tiberias, ten miles southwest of Safed. Only about 25 Hasidim stayed in
Safed with R. Abraham, who "took upon himself the burden of exile" during the next two years.[69] Out of the 200 non-Hasidim in the 1777 convoy,
about 50–75 remained in Safed and an estimated 100–125 "were forced to
return to their native land."[70] A few families headed by physically able,
farm-experienced non-Hasidim settled in the village of Peki'in, a three-
hour donkey ride from Safed.

The decision of R. Menahem Mendel to move the Hasidim from Safed to
Tiberias was influenced by the positive impression made by the Tiberias
Sephardim. During a visit there in 1778, R. Menahem Mendel and R. Abraham had been received with great honor and respect. R. Abraham wrote,
"In Tiberias they asked us many times to live amongst them . . . and we
stayed there two weeks and it seemed like only a few days because of the
great love and desire that we all have to live in one place . . . " After moving
to Tiberias, populated by about 2,000 Muslims, 50 Ashkenazim, 650–750
Sephardim, and a few Greek Catholics, R. Menahem Mendel found the Sephardic community to be "completely righteous."[71]

The Hasidim lived in the Jewish quarter of Tiberias, which extended two
hundred meters along the shores of Lake Galilee and fifty meters inland.
Surrounded by high walls on three sides, the constricted neighborhood was
entered through a single gate that was locked every night. Housing the
members of R. Menahem Mendel's group and preparing shelter for additional Hasidic settlers was a major problem.

Soon after the group's arrival, an Ashkenazi merchant from Russia who
lived in Acre rented from Jazzar Pasha courtyards just outside the Tiberias
Jewish quarter. He planned to rent the large compound with its many
apartments to the Hasidim for 1,000 piastres a year. This rental scheme was
attacked and declared illegal by the chief Sephardi official, who feared that
rentals outside the Jewish quarter would decrease the income of the
Sephardi house-owners. In heated exchanges with the Sephardim, R.

Menahem Mendel denied involvement in any illegal rental scheme, and despite Sephardi opposition he appeared before Jazzar Pasha, who did not punish the Hasidim for irregularities, but prevented them from moving into the housing compound outside the Jewish quarter.[72]

Hasidim and Sephardim now clashed over the establishment of a separate Hasidic synagogue.[73] Since the newly arrived group did not have a firman to establish a new place of worship, the Sephardim had generously agreed to partition their own synagogue into two sections, with a thin wall dividing the two congregations. To their surprise and horror the Sephardi prayers were drowned out by the cacophonous outpourings of Hasidic devotional passion. The Hasidim "roared aloud as if they wished to be heard at Jerusalem," driving the Sephardim to distraction.[74] In an attempt to placate the Sephardim, the Hasidim transferred their prayer service to R. Mendel's spacious house, "the best and prettiest of all houses" in the Jewish quarter.[75] But this arrangement was opposed by the next-door neighbor, the chief Sephardi official, who was prevented from quietly enjoying his Sabbath lunch while the Hasidim worked up to a cascading crescendo of raucous prayers. The Sephardi official threatened the Hasidim that the Muslims would fine them and destroy R. Menahem Mendel's house if they conducted prayers in a building not officially approved as a place of worship. The dispute was resolved when R. Menahem Mendel refurbished his three-story house and relocated the Hasidic synagogue on the far side of the Sephardi official's home.

After these initial controversies, the Hasidim and Sephardim learned to live in peace with each other. What first appeared to the Hasidim as an oppressive, discriminatory millet tax was later understood to be the Ottoman tax system. And what the Sephardim once considered to be ridiculous rituals and a bedlam of prayers were later understood to be true expressions of profound religious feelings. Differences were now resolved in a spirit of accommodation based on considerations of mutual interest. Hasidim and Sephardim even cooperated in joint overseas fundraising campaigns.[76]

Although the financial condition of the Tiberias Jewish community was not good,[77] its per capita debt of 55–85 piastres (1805) was the smallest of any of the four holy cities. The Safed community debt (1804) totaled 125,000 piastres or about 200 piastres for each of its 600 Jews.[78] Hebron's 300 Jews were the most debt-ridden (1800), owing 200,000 piastres or 670 piastres per person. The Jerusalem community of 2,250 Jews owed 300,000 piastres (1806) or 135 piastres for each Jew.[79] Another indication that the Tiberias Jewish community was in viable financial shape was its ability in 1805 to pay Pasha Suleiman 12,500 piastres for five dunams (1¼ acres) of land, enabling it to enlarge the Jewish quarter by 50 percent.[80]

During the last two decades of the eighteenth century a small number of Jews—young and old, Ashkenazi and Sephardi—trickled into the Galilee. Families and small groups from Algiers, Morocco, Poland, and the Ukraine filled out the thinning ranks of the Tiberias Jews, who suffered from a high mortality rate,[81] like other town residents in Eretz Israel. By the beginning of the nineteenth century the Tiberias Jewish community had increased only to about 900, due to the successive series of blows it received— droughts, cholera, heavy rains, escalating prices, debts, taxes, and persecutions by Jazzar Pasha and Napoleon's troops.[82]

The Hasidic center in Eretz Israel did not succeed in growing. In contrast, the movement was at its pinnacle of success in Eastern Europe, where its leaders were making concerted efforts to restrain their adherents from settling in the Holy Land. Thus, few Hasidim came to Eretz Israel, because of the irrevocable binding between the zaddik and his followers. The zaddik could not desert his followers, who depended upon him to set them on the path of righteousness; and the Hasidim could not possibly leave their beloved zaddik, on whose indispensable advice they depended. The only way Hasidim could move to Eretz Israel was to have the zaddik shepherd his entire flock to the Holy Land, a move that would cost large sums of money and socially dislocate the Hasidim. Uprooting a Hasidic group from its natural East European habitat and planting it in a strange Muslim environment was contrary to the wishes of all but a few Hasidim.

Neither could the Hasidim in Eretz Israel afford the luxury of persuading their European cohorts to join them in performing the mitzva of settling in Zion. They wrote letters dissuading all but the old and affluent, and the most dedicated scholars, from joining them in Eretz Israel. R. Menahem Mendel beseeched his European followers to contribute to the upkeep of the Hasidic community in the Galilee, but he appealed only to those with financial means to settle in Eretz Israel. In 1781 he wrote:

> Truly they who wish to come to Eretz Israel want to put out fire with straw because the problem of making a living is most troublesome. . . . They should put aside a good few hundred adumim in some very safe investment in order that the profit on the investment be sent to them in Eretz Israel every year. That would be very good. And if they cannot support themselves in such a way, I advise them for their own good to set aside the idea of coming to Eretz Israel.[83]

A few months earlier R. Menahem Mendel had similarly advised European Hasidim wishing to immigrate to write to him first. Then, shocked by his lack of encouragement for new settlers, he added, "I had a thought which should not pass my mouth." R. Menahem Mendel was not only influenced by the practical problems of feeding new settlers, but also by the ideology of his teacher, the maggid of Mezhirech, who had deterred Jews from moving to Eretz Israel, stating that "to serve God in Exile was easier and therefore more within the grasp of the devout than to serve Him in Palestine."[84]

R. Israel of Polotsk declared more bluntly, "I never believed a person without means should come to Eretz Israel . . ." In a clear reference to the 200 poor non-Hasidim, he wrote, "He should not move here if he has little money, as had been mistakenly done by poor and destitute brothers who were much more numerous than we." R. Israel ended his letter with a prayer that "soon Jews will gather and flock together to Zion in the light of the Lord," but this was only a religious slogan devoid of concrete commitment and action.[85]

The Hasidic rabbis were following in the footsteps of other settlers who had advised that only rich, elderly Jews should come to Eretz Israel.[86] In 1760 Yakir, the nephew of the Ba'al Shem Tov, wrote from Jerusalem: "The truth is that living in Eretz Israel is very good for the elderly but not for the young . . . when you reach seventy and have enough money then you may joyously come here . . ."[87] Similar sentiments were expressed by another Ashkenazi settler: "Whoever comes here should bring money with him and not come empty-handed, or he should be a good artisan able to support himself. In this manner Eretz Israel will resemble the rest of the world where no person receives anything for nothing."[88]

The Hasidic sentiments against poor Jews coming to Eretz Israel were in consonance with the views of the Istanbul Officials, who, from the middle of the eighteenth century, tried with mixed success to stop the entry of poor Jews into Jerusalem and Eretz Israel. They believed that immigrants should be self-sufficient and rich enough to contribute toward the support of scholars, instead of draining money away from the poor people already residing in the Holy Land. Residents of Jerusalem and the other holy cities tacitly agreed to this policy of limited immigration, based on the simple calculation that, if the population continued to grow, each Jew would receive a smaller and smaller portion of the fixed financial assistance sent from overseas. Polish Jews also opposed emigration; since their community taxes in Poland were unchanged, the remaining Jews would have to remit larger tax sums.[89]

This negative attitude toward poor immigrants was carried over into the nineteenth century and influenced the thinking of the Sephardim. The

Sephardi chief rabbi of Jerusalem from 1802 to 1806, Rabbi Meyuhas, reflected this view when he wrote, "We have in our community some artisans, too few for our nation . . . because they should be more numerous here . . . and too many for the charities to support them when they are unemployed; more wealthy people should come here."[90]

When R. Abraham succeeded to the Hasidic leadership upon the death of R. Menahem Mendel of Vitebsk in 1788, he continued to discourage the immigration of poor settlers. At the same time he stressed the need for spiritual adjustment in Eretz Israel rather than the requirement of financial resources. In a sonorous letter filled with Hasidic fervor, R. Abraham advised only the strongest to attempt a transformation of body and soul in Eretz Israel.

> How many changes and transformations and events lasting an infinity will pass over every one who comes to this Land until it grows upon him and he finds pleasure in her stones and cherishes her dust and loves the ruins of the Land of Israel and prefers its dry crust of bread. This is not a race of the swift; not for one day or two, not for one month or a year. . . . He who comes to this sacred place must be reborn, suckled anew and again raised from infancy until face to face he beholds the countenance of the Land and his soul is bound to the soul of the Land. . . . Each person must decide of himself how and when and with how much, according to his own personal affairs and behavior and based on the depths of his soul. Therefore he who enters the Holy Land has to prepare himself for all eventualities and must test his soul to see if he has the strength to stand up to all this without endangering himself . . . [91]

The sublime truths about adjusting to life in Eretz Israel have never been better expressed, but they could hardly have inspired any but the most dedicated to settle in the Holy Land.

The message of the Hasidic leaders was loud and clear. Poor people should not come to the "wild and desolate" land of Eretz Israel, where they could not earn a living.[92] If they came they would become an economic burden on the poor Hasidic community, which would sink deeper into debt. Only an elite group of scholars and wealthy, resolute people should consider settling in the Holy Land. The economic exigencies of feeding the Hasidic flock took overwhelming precedence over the religious ideology of ingathering the Jews from Exile. This line of argument lends support to the view that Hasidim were not motivated by a singular, dominating Messianic yearning for Zion, but came to Eretz Israel for the same religious reasons shared by other Ashkenazim and Sephardim.

Because the Hasidic group in Eretz Israel did not grow, it remained a stable but inert operation. The vigor and vitality that characterized Hasidic activities in Eastern Europe were lacking in Tiberias and Safed. Dynamism and innovation would have to come from another source outside of Eretz Israel. Ironically, the catalytic agent for modifying Jewish community life in Eretz Israel came from the indomitable opponents of the Hasidim—the Mitnaggedim.

FOUR

Perushim Settle in Safed

1808–1812

The first large, organized group of European Jews to settle in Eretz Israel during the nineteenth century were disciples of the Vilna gaon, the ideological opponents of the Hasidim. This group, called Perushim (scholars who separated themselves from other Jews), dwelled in the twin worlds of contemplation and action. Not prone to the heartfelt instincts so common to the Hasidim, the systematic Perushim achieved success in worldly pursuits while being sustained by an unshakable conviction in the inspired Word of the Lord as expressed in the Torah given by God to His Chosen People at Mount Sinai.

Pious faith and practical reason led the Perushim to formulate both revelations about the next world and rational rules regulating the present life. Logic and faith were twin anchors that enabled them to frame rational premises in an attempt to reveal the ineffable essence of the Lord. Biblical revelation and talmudic elucidations provided the Perushim with the framework of an orderly society that bound them in the faith of their fathers in partnership with God and instructed them how to live, think, and feel in a world filled with people of free will.

For the Perushim, living in the Diaspora was a temporary event tainted with sin that required correction by carrying out the mitzva or religious commandment of settling in their homeland, Eretz Israel. The Vilna gaon explained the meaning of "You shall take possession of the land and settle in it."[1] "By virtue of possessing it, shall you dwell therein. And how will you possess it? Through occupation. From this you are to learn that dwelling therein means obtaining through occupying." He preached the necessity of gathering the Jewish exiles in Eretz Israel and then redeeming them spiritually. Populating and building up the Land was a preparation for spiritual Redemption.

At the core of Jewish tradition was the concept of Messianic Redemption in the Holy Land; Jews of various ideological schools fervently prayed for deliverance from Exile and the coming of the Messiah. The Redemption message gained greater immediacy for the Perushim when coupled with the clear instructions of the Vilna gaon to "ascend" to Eretz Israel and settle there.[2] Perushim found a "harmonic integration" between religious fulfillment of the return to Zion and the Redemption of the Jewish people, which would be accelerated by Jewish settlement in the Holy Land.[3]

The Perushim believed they were living in a period that marked the end of Jewish life in Exile and that they should take advantage of the imminent Redemption. In contrast to other groups of Jews, they were convinced that it was no transgression to "press for the End" rather than passively wait in the Diaspora for the Messiah's arrival. The Vilna gaon declared that it was within human power to accelerate Redemption and bring deliverance nearer by settling groups in Eretz Israel to study, pray, perform the commandments of the Torah, "and . . . endure tribulations for the rest of their brethren in the Diaspora."[4]

It is related that a "Vision of Zion" conference was held in 1806 in Shklov, a center of foreign trade in White Russia and a predominantly Jewish city with a large concentration of Perushim.[5] Although this assembly apparently was never convened, the story reflects the fact that there were reawakened feelings for Redemption among the Perushim. They determined to finance settlers willing to live in the Holy Land and made careful plans, remembering the warning of the Vilna gaon that a major obstacle to settling in Eretz Israel was its "poor and scanty means of livelihood."[6] It was clear to the Perushim that it would be best periodically to send people of means and groups of selected settlers to Eretz Israel. A large caravan of nondescript immigrants traveling in a carnival atmosphere had not served the Hasidim well in 1777.

Perushim were also motivated to settle in Eretz Israel by the upheavals within Russian Jewry. Czar Alexander I issued the Statute of 1804, which defined where Jews could and could not live.[7] Three years later Jews were expelled from some villages in White Russia, and many were economically ruined and left destitute and homeless. The 1806–1807 war of Russia and Prussia against Napoleon, which threatened an imminent French invasion of White Russia, added to the uncertainty of Jewish life in that region.

It is significant that the Perushim mentioned only the love of Zion and the hope for Messianic Redemption as reasons for their settling in the Holy Land.[8] Perhaps a prevailing opinion intimating that 1810 would be the year of Messianic Redemption played a role in their decision. Without doubt the powerful legacy of the Vilna gaon inspired his followers to settle in Eretz Israel. Nonetheless it is not at all clear why, in 1808, Perushim started to dispatch groups of their members to Eretz Israel.

The elite Perushim settlers in this vanguard were not pioneers intent on creating a new social order in Zion, but a select task force imbued with great enthusiasm and obsessed by the religious destiny of the Jewish people living in Eretz Israel, who would "elevate the status of the Torah."[9] To further Redemption a limited number of Perushim made a total commitment to the Jewish dream of ascending to Eretz Israel.

In 1808 an advance group of Perushim led by R. Menahem Mendel of Shklov (no kin to the Hasidic Menahem Mendel of Vitebsk) explored the Promised Land and made preparations for the settlement of organized groups that would soon follow. Upon their arrival, the Perushim lived briefly in Tiberias, where they met the venerable Hasidic leader R. Abraham of Kolisk. At that time the Jewish population in Tiberias numbered 900–1,000; 200–250 were Hasidim, a few Perushim, and the remainder Sephardim.[10] Despite the available housing and relative prosperity of the Tiberias community, R. Menahem Mendel realized that it was not feasible to settle Perushim near the Hasidim, for such proximity would create conflict due to differences in customs and behavior.[11] Since neither group was able to dispense with the contentious baggage carried from Eastern Europe, it was sensibly decided that the two groups should live apart in different towns.

R. Menahem Mendel of Shklov undoubtedly would have preferred settling in Jerusalem near the holy remnants of the Second Temple and its hallowed Wailing Wall, for the Vilna gaon viewed the settlement of Jerusalem as the cornerstone of building Eretz Israel. But the Perushim in 1808, like the Hasidim in 1777, found that Jerusalem with its 2,250 Jews was closed to groups of Ashkenazi settlers after followers of Yehuda HeHasid had fled in 1720. Reports of opposition by both Sephardim and Ashkenazim to Perushim settling in Jerusalem may have reached R. Menahem Mendel.[12] The few Ashkenazim in Jerusalem undoubtedly feared that the Perushim would seek to share the funds they received from the Sephardi Jerusalem community, and the few Hasidim of Jerusalem may have worried that the destroyed courtyard of R. Yehuda HeHasid would be claimed by the activist newcomers.[13] The Sephardim viewed with apprehension the crowding of Perushim settlers into the overpopulated Jewish quarter and the dangerous possibility that the Jerusalem authorities would claim more tax money from the larger Jewish community.

R. Menahem Mendel did not seriously consider settling his group in Hebron because that town's 300 Sephardim and handful of Ashkenazim still remained the smallest, poorest, and most persecuted Jewish community of the four holy cities.[14] The economic and social infrastructure of Hebron made it impossible to absorb a large number of Ashkenazim.

By this process of elimination, but with high hopes, R. Menahem Mendel chose Safed as the home of the new Perushim settlers. Safed was "peaceful" in 1808–1810 due to the lenient regime of the ruler of the Galilee,[15] Pasha Suleiman of Acre-Sidon, who was described by Safed Jews as an "honest upright ruler, undesirous of false accusations."[16] In contrast to the situation in Jerusalem and Hebron, Jews in Safed and Tiberias were hardly persecuted, and they were lightly taxed, thanks to the protection provided by their patron, Haim Farhi. Like the Hasidim before them, the Perushim were also enticed by Safed's kabbalistic history, the nearby graves of venerated rabbinical sages, the climate and landscape,[17] the good, plentiful, and inexpensive food, and the homes available in the Jewish quarter. The small number of Mitnaggedim already living in Safed helped R. Menahem Mendel's group to settle in.

In 1808 Safed had a population of 2,500–3,000.[18] It was the highest populated spot in the Galilee, situated on a craggy summit surrounded by barren hills, terraced slopes, and precipitous valleys that supported extensive olive groves, vineyards, and fruit orchards. Although on the road between Acre and Damascus, Safed had no khan and was of little commercial consequence. The town was subordinate to the pasha of Acre-Sidon, and was ruled by a governor.

About 300 Jews lived in three agricultural villages in the Safed area: Peki'in, noted for its tradition of uninterrupted Jewish settlement; Kfar Yasif, six miles from Acre; and Shfar-Am, a three-hour donkey-ride from Haifa. Each village contained about 100 Jews, nearly all Sephardim who had gained farming experience locally or in North Africa.[19] These villages provided the Jews of Safed and Tiberias with places of refuge in turbulent times.

After R. Menahem Mendel settled his small group in Safed, he proposed that other Perushim join him "to establish a new, independent settlement."[20] In response to this invitation, a second convoy of 70 Perushim left Shklov in February 1809. This group was composed of families with children as well as men traveling alone. The voyage to Eretz Israel was considered so dangerous that some men temporarily left their families behind in Poland, and a few granted their wives conditional divorces, allowing them to remarry without legal complications if their husbands were never again heard from.[21]

On the long, arduous overland journey in wagons from Shklov to the Black Sea port of Odessa, the 70 Perushim were feted by local Jewish communities. Foresight and financial means had enabled them to book passage in advance on four seaworthy Greek barges sailing from Odessa to Istanbul. When the Perushim arrived safely in Istanbul in the summer of 1809, they thanked the Lord, made contact with the Istanbul Officials for Palestinian Jewry, and planned the next stage of their journey on the Mediterranean, then infested with pirates making forays from hideouts in the Aegean islands.

In the late summer of 1809 the Perushim traveled from Istanbul to Izmir, where they set sail for Beirut, spending an uneventful seven to ten days on a boat chartered by the Istanbul Officials. Seven months after departing from Shklov the 70 Perushim reached Haifa. Upon stepping onto the sacred soil of Eretz Israel, they fell on their knees and blessed the Lord for leading them out of the oppression of Exile and into their Promised Land.

In humble gratitude and quiet reverence, the Perushim wrote about this "eventful day, a day of joy and praise for all upright men." They extolled the "ingathering of Israel from the four corners of the earth" and wrote a hymn of praise about the virtues of Eretz Israel:

> Truly how wonderful it is to settle in this good land! Truly how marvelous is this love of our land! Truly how lovely is the sacred land where it is splendidly glorious to settle, to dwell, to walk about and to live in peace and quiet. Even in its ruins nothing like it can be imagined and even in its desolation nothing can compare with it. There is nothing like its peacefulness; good are its dust and its rocks; plenty are its wheat, fruits, and vegetables; beautiful is its clear air, marvelous are its Torah achievements; blessed are its multitude of mitzvot, blessed is its pure holiness. . . . the Torah has exalted us to its pinnacle and who can glorify the many facets of this magnificent Queen![22]

A third convoy of Perushim arrived in October 1809 to reinforce the 150 "precious souls" in the Safed community. This group was led by Rabbi Israel of Shklov, another outstanding student of the Vilna gaon, who wrote: "I found here some 40 householders. . . . They were learned students of the Law, and elderly worshippers of the Lord, and completely in fear of Him . . ."[23]

The Perushim found it unnecessary to mention anything about the selection process that designated which of their members would settle in Eretz Israel. Most likely it was a self-selection process by those able to secure personal or community financial support. The place of residence in White Russia apparently influenced the choice of immigrants. Many Perushim settlers knew each other in Poland, shared the aspirations, purposes, and principles of the Vilna gaon, and probably prayed together in Shklov.

The new Perushim settlers, like the Hasidim in 1777, were warmly welcomed by the predominantly Sephardi population as well as by Haim Farhi, who told them, "Whatever [you] need I will take care of it."[24]

In contrast to the cordial reception they received from the Sephardim, Perushim reported adjustment difficulties with the Safed Hasidim, who were beginning to increase in numbers at the start of the nineteenth century. Perushim "could not be together with the Hasidim of Volhynia because of the differences in customs."[25] Money matters exacerbated the historic rivalry between the two communities when the Perushim staked an exclusive claim on money donated by their overseas compatriots. Until then, funds contributed for Eretz Israel by East European Perushim and Hasidim were distributed to members of both groups living in the Holy Land. Now the Perushim logically demanded that all donations coming from Perushim in Europe be distributed only to members of their group in Eretz Israel.

This first of innumerable arguments about financial matters between the Perushim and Hasidim was resolved amicably. During the first year of the Perushim settlement in Safed, the Hasidim shared with them the funds donated by the Perushim of Lithuania.[26] Financial support was of critical importance because funds promised by Perushim overseas supporters were late in arriving. R. Menahem Mendel maintained the Perushim "by obtaining loans, solely to sustain life that they might study the Torah."[27] Realizing the need to secure economic independence for his group, R. Menahem Mendel sent two shlihim (emissaries) to Eastern Europe to raise funds and seek new recruits.

By 1810 it was clear that the Perushim had significantly underestimated the financial resources needed to support their growing community. Therefore "all the great men and elders" of the Perushim community sent R. Israel of Shklov to Europe to organize fundraising efforts and collect money for a house of study, a library, and the purchase of agricultural land.[28] R. Israel, a rare combination of scholar and activist, was most reluctant to leave Eretz Israel even temporarily. He did not relish traveling alone overseas after having lived with his family in Safed for less than six months:

Although this heavy burden of leaving the Holy Land, to which I have become attached through great suffering and yearning like a thirsty man to water, is as the weight of a rock and the burden of a load of sand; although the Holy Land is dear and sweet to me above all, the plea of the scholars to leave my home and family and my studies in the yeshiva presses down upon me, and I see that their necessity is dire: for there is an increase in the number of scholars of our community who have come to the Land of Israel and are without food and sustenance.[29]

In March 1810 R. Israel left Safed on a three-year mission to Europe. He traveled overland from Acre to Istanbul because another Turkish-Russian conflict that did not end until 1812 made the sea route extremely dangerous.

R. Israel carried with him a letter explaining to the Jews of the Diaspora the reasons for his fundraising mission. Drafted in a heartrending style, the letter transmits information and ideas about Eretz Israel in Hebrew, the one common language understood by world Jewry. The letter is the manifesto of a young, vital community not begging but demanding rights properly due to settlers in the Holy Land.

Writing on behalf of Eretz Israel, the land that "proclaims," "arouses," "exalts," and "liberates,"[30] the letter asks, "Why am I bereft of honor and desolate, without settlers, bereaved and lonely? Am I not a beloved country?... Why am I disgraced... last among the laggards rather than first among the leaders?" After eulogizing the holiness of Eretz Israel, the letter admonishes Diaspora Jews for not remembering their pledge "if I forget thee Jerusalem." It then warns: "To forget the Holy Land, Heaven forbid, prolongs the Exile, and leads to forgetting the end of days." In conclusion the letter exhorts the faithful to contribute monies to maintain Jews in Eretz Israel so that they can perform the mitzvot commanded by the Lord.

R. Israel was instrumental in getting the Vilna Rabbis, the Perushim parent organization, to ask the Berlin Jewish community to send half of its contributions to the Perushim, with the other half going to the Sephardim. Before then all donations from Western and Central Europe were channeled to the Sephardim alone. The reply of the Berlin community is not known.[31]

In Warsaw, R. Israel came to an arrangement with emissaries sent by the Volhynian Hasidim of Safed. In order to eliminate competition for contributions, it was decided that Volhynian Hasidim and Perushim in Eretz Israel would share on a per capita basis all monies collected in Poland. R. Israel confidently signed this agreement in the belief that the Perushim would receive by far the largest share of the funds now that their community was growing faster than the Hasidic group. But this arrangement was never implemented and in 1818 it was replaced by another compromise that funneled monies from certain geographic areas of Poland to one group or the other.[32]

While visiting Vienna, R. Israel learned that one Simon Winer had bequeathed a large endowment of 22,000 florin paying 4,000 florin or at least 40,000 piastres annually to the Jews of Eretz Israel, which meant to the Sephardi community. Due to R. Israel's strenuous efforts, it was agreed that 50 percent of the Winer bequest would go to the Sephardim, and the remaining half would be allocated to the Ashkenazim—33 percent to the Hasidim and 17 percent to the Perushim.[33] Why did R. Israel settle for a smaller share of the endowment than the more passive Hasidim? Possibly this was the price he had to pay to secure the cooperation of the jealous Hasidim, who previously had failed where he succeeded. Income from the Winer inheritance was less important to the farsighted R. Israel than establishing the precedent that the Ashkenazim in Eretz Israel should get a good share of European bequests.

The two agreements he signed in Warsaw and Vienna and the Vilna Rabbis' letter to Berlin were intended to break the long-standing fundraising monopolies enjoyed by the Sephardim and the Hasidim. They constituted initial successful efforts to change the rules about how money collected in Europe, heretofore sent only to the Sephardim, should be apportioned among the Sephardim, Hasidim, and Perushim in Eretz Israel.

During his productive fourteen-day stopover in Vienna, R. Israel realized how the Lord had blessed the Perushim in Eretz Israel, for he must have heard about the fate of Jews from Bohemia and Galicia. After about 50 families from Galicia left for Eretz Israel in 1811 and 1812, Emperor Francis I forbade other Jews to leave the Hapsburg Empire, fearing the loss of Jewish capital. Less fortunate than the Galician Jews were the 70 to 80 families who set out from Bohemia for Eretz Israel in March 1811. While traveling through the plains of Hungary the Bohemians had to fight bandits and were struck by the plague. Survivors reaching the Croatian border were refused passage and sent back to Bohemia. Out of the original group of some 300, only 5 bachelors reached Eretz Israel.[34]

After establishing the foundations for Perushim fundraising efforts in White Russia, R. Israel returned overland to Eretz Israel in 1813, braving Napoleon's pillaging of Shklov during his bloody conquest of Poland and Russia. Soon after R. Israel's return, the Perushim sent another emissary to collect funds in Eastern Europe, a pattern they would follow throughout the nineteenth century.[35]

While R. Menahem Mendel was sending emissaries to Europe to build a stable financial base for his group, he was observing the separate community organization of the Sephardim, the kollel, and set up a similar framework for the Perushim.

In Safed, as in the other holy cities, the millet representing all Jews was the Sephardi kollel. Like other millets, it was granted complete freedom to conduct Jewish activities and to select its leaders. R. Isaac Abulafia headed the Sephardi kollel of Safed and Tiberias, assisted by a treasurer and an accountant.[36] This executive committee, composed of rabbinical authorities and laymen, was responsible to the Turkish authorities for the self-governing Jewish community. The committee was selected by the influential members of the kollel, although the Istanbul Officials might dictate appointments.

The Sephardi kollel paid the salaries of its functionaries and maintained Jewish community institutions such as the synagogue, study center (yeshiva), cemetery, and ritual-baths. It legislated rules governing the behavior of its members and possessed strong legal, economic, and social sanctions to enforce such regulations. Rabbinical courts of the Sephardi kollel dispensed justice by adjudicating disputes among Jews; it issued binding judgments and meted out punishment. Jews who broke religious or civil laws were not turned over to the Muslim authorities, but were fined, disciplined, and even publicly whipped, imprisoned, and excommunicated by the kollel.[37] The more severe measures were infrequently resorted to, because it was not difficult to impose discipline in a closed community where members shared common beliefs, and where position and status were based on millet membership.

The kollel also was a powerful financial organization that managed the Jewish community's expenditures and revenues. It provided welfare services and distributed money to poor, sick, and old people unable to earn a living, as well as to scholars, whose work was studying. The kollel protected the economic situation of its members by controlling rents and setting maximum prices for essential food products. It organized the collection of funds from Diaspora Jews and was held accountable by the Turkish authorities for remitting a variety of taxes and arbitrary payments, including the annual poll tax of 2,000 piastres, which had remained unchanged since about 1777.[38]

During the second half of 1810 the Sephardi kollel paid the authorities a large ransom for 31 scholars who had been jailed. The reason for the imprisonment and ransom payment remains unclear because "the mouth cannot talk" about it,[39] in the words of Jewish letter-writers in Safed. It appears that the incident was initiated by new revenue demands of Mahmud II, who was proclaimed sultan in 1808. The kollel was fined 75,000 piastres;[40] in 1815 it still owed 50,000, forcing it to borrow large sums, which would indicate that it had a good credit rating. There is no mention of the Perushim paying part of the 1810 ransom tribute; nevertheless, R. Israel claimed that at least on one occasion the Perushim helped defray arbitrary government exactions imposed upon the Sephardi kollel.

Since the Sephardi kollel, like the Jewish millet, represented the total Jewish community and was legally responsible to the authorities for the actions of all Jews, the kollelim of the Perushim and the Hasidim were under its jurisdiction. But this was a loose, undefined relationship that fluctuated according to the will and power of the three groups. Moreover, the Perushim and Hasidim, unlike the Sephardim, were not Ottoman citizens, having chosen to retain their European nationalities. Therefore Ashkenazim were exempt from paying certain taxes, such as the poll tax, that were levied on Turkish subjects. However, as foreign nationals, they could not purchase land or property and have it recorded in their own name.

Borrowing elements from the Sephardi kollel and their East European community experience, the Safed Perushim set up an autonomous kollel framework in order to conduct their religious, educational, welfare, legislative, judicial, and financial affairs. The kollel of the Perushim was directed by a three- or four-man executive committee chosen by the Vilna Rabbis, not by the members in Eretz Israel. In an attempt to guarantee impeccable honesty, the Perushim in Poland appointed a trustee charged with keeping the records in a prescribed maner. Two accountants were appointed to audit the records and certify that they were maintained according to accepted practices.

The two leading figures on the Perushim executive committee were

R. Menahem Mendel and R. Israel. Both rabbis enjoyed public esteem because of their piety, scholarly erudition, sterling character, good deeds, and
judicial abilities. Perushim regulations provided no special status to the
rabbi just because he was clergy. R. Israel omitted his rabbinical title when
signing letters, but he did record that he was an official of the Perushim
kollel and proudly noted the titles of two talmudic books he had authored.
Although the executive committee was not democratically elected by their
constituents, its leaders reflected the views of the Perushim community and
governed by its general consensus.

A crucial function of the executive committee was the allocation of
money to kollel members, based on lists prepared in Safed and approved by
the central Perushim organization in Poland. The executive committee in
Safed wielded great power when it prepared the list of names and the
amount recommended for each person to receive. Procedures for preparing
lists and paying monies were prescribed in meticulous fashion and scrupulously supervised according to detailed regulations governing the distribution of haluka (apportionment of charity).

Jews in Eretz Israel were heavily, but never sufficiently, supported by
benefactors in the Diaspora. Perushim and Hasidim were specifically maintained by their fellow members in Poland. Other funds collected overseas
were distributed to the Sephardi kollelim in the four holy cities. Since about
90 percent of the Jewish population in Eretz Israel was Sephardi, and the
Sephardi millets represented all Jews before the authorities and bore the financial responsibility for the total Jewish community, it was logical that the
Sephardi kollel should receive monies donated to maintain the Jewish community in Eretz Israel. Moreover, the Istanbul Officials collected most of its
monies from the Sephardi communities throughout the Turkish Empire.

The Istanbul Officials, established in 1726 in response to the pleas for
protection and financial assistance of the Jerusalem Jewish community,
used connections with key officials at the Sublime Porte to secure financial
benefits—reducing oppressive taxes,[41] deferring interest payments, and re-
scheduling debt payments—for the Jews in the four holy cities. In return
for collecting large sums of money for Eretz Israel, the Istanbul Officials assumed general supervision over the Jewish communities, established rules
regulating life in the community, and determined how donations would be
distributed.

The Istanbul Officials channeled money to the Sephardi kollelim in the
four holy cities based on the number of scholars and Jews in each (see table
2) and their financial condition.[42]

Since Jews used numbers to paint an impressionistic picture rather than

TABLE 2 Haluka Allocation and Estimated Jewish Population in 1810

Town	HALUKA ALLOCATION		ESTIMATED JEWISH POP. 1810	
	Shares	%	Number	%
Safed	7	25	900*	20
Jerusalem	11	40	2250	51
Tiberias	4	14	1000	22
Hebron	6	21	300	7
TOTAL	28	100	4450**	100

* Includes 200 newly arrived Perushim, 600 Sephardim, and 100 Hasidim.
** The total Jewish population in Eretz Israel in 1810 was just over 5,000, including 300 Jews in Acre, 50 in Haifa, 50–100 in Nablus, and 300 in the Galilee villages of Peki'in, Kfar Yasif, and Shfar-Am.

to define precisely their financial and demographic situation, we can only conjecture, with no small degree of risk, about the financial situation of each town.

Jerusalem received 40 percent of the money distributed, rather than its proportionate population share of 51 percent. This underdistribution could be due to Jerusalem's receiving a large share of special donations from Morocco and of funds earmarked for specific purposes,[43] such as setting up yeshivot and endowments for scholars.

Hebron's 300 Jews, or 7 percent of the total Jewish population, were granted 21 percent of the funds.[44] This is a clear recognition of Hebron as the most destitute, persecuted, and debt-ridden Jewish community in Eretz Israel.

Tiberias with 22 percent of the population received only 14 percent of the monies because it was the most solvent of the holy cities. Its 200–250 Hasidim received money directly from their East European supporters, while its Sephardim enjoyed exclusive fundraising in North Africa and Gibraltar and collected money in Sephardi communities for the Fund of Meir the Miracle Worker.[45]

Safed received 25 percent of the Istanbul Officials' funds, compared to its 20 percent of the population, because it was a poorer town than Tiberias and received less direct funding from the overseas Sephardi communities. Obviously, the 200 newly settled Perushim and their independent financial resources were not included in the Istanbul Officials' allocations.

The allocation formula of the Istanbul Officials was adopted in 1810 by a newly founded fundraising organization called the Officials and Wardens of

Amsterdam, or PEKAM,[46] an acronym of its Hebrew name. PEKAM had been established one year earlier after the Dutch government restricted the authority of the Amsterdam Jewish community to collect money for the Jews of Eretz Israel. Two Sephardi emissaries who were in Amsterdam in 1810 certified PEKAM as the official collection agency in Western Europe for the Jerusalem kollel. A few years later PEKAM was also authorized to collect money for the Sephardi kollelim of Safed, Tiberias, and Hebron.

PEKAM sought to increase the amount of contributions for Eretz Israel by systematizing and centralizing donations; its activities eventually were extended to Germany, Holland, France, England, the Scandinavian countries, and the United States. The PEKAM charter provided an all-embracing, near absolute frame of operation: "to manage all matters of charity for Eretz Israel according to their own best opinion and agreement, without any person being able to appeal or protest against them."[47] The Istanbul Officials heartily endorsed the founding of PEKAM, writing in 1814 that "whatever PEKAM agrees to and decides, as they best see fit, will be implemented, as if it were the decision of the High Court in Jerusalem . . ." Initially PEKAM operated under the general aegis of the Istanbul Officials and transferred its funds to Istanbul, but this situation gradually changed with the increasing penetration of the Great Powers into the affairs of the weakening Ottoman Empire, the incessant Turkish-Russian wars, and the growing financial power of West European Jewry.[48]

Monies collected overseas by the emissaries, the Istanbul Officials, PEKAM, and the organizations of Hasidim and Perushim in Poland were distributed in Eretz Israel by the Sephardim and Ashkenazim in completely different ways. The care each group extended to its poor and elderly reflected its unique circumstances and specific view toward life.

Sephardim allocated haluka to full-time scholars and to needy persons unable to work. The poor obviously had to be cared for, and the scholars, whose sole work was studying, earned their right to be supported. They "ought naturally to have some additional share in the offerings of their wealthier brethren abroad, offerings intended not only for the relief of individual distress but also for the preservation of a religious community."[49] Except for scholars and the old and feeble, Sephardi Jews earned their living and did not burden the community treasury.

In contrast to the Sephardim, the Perushim and the Hasidim distributed haluka to all their members without regard to age, ability to work, or economic status. Every head of household—rich and poor, young and old, scholar and artisan—received a deserved subvention for performing the mitzva of settling in Eretz Israel. Nobody felt shame or embarrassment in accepting haluka funds. Besides, neither Hasidim nor Perushim could work; they did not speak Arabic, know the local customs, or understand Muslim behavior and commercial practices, and they lacked practical work skills.

Ashkenazim also discovered that they could not continue the traditional East European practice of the scholar-husband studying all day while his wife cared for the children and ran a small store to support the family. Wives were forbidden to work outside the home and to have contact with Muslim men.[50] Most crucial, Perushim men were not interested in doing anything that would deflect them from their true work of Torah study and prayer.

The amount of the haluka apportioned to an individual varied in relation to his scholastic and community standing. Perushim regulations rewarded the academic achievements of scholars with a share of the haluka plus a bonus that might reach an additional 50 percent.[51] Privileged persons of importance and lineage were also granted this bonus by the kollel leadership. Haluka rules penalized the few Perushim who worked. Although performing the mitzva of settling in Eretz Israel, workers were granted only half a share of the haluka because they did not study Torah "day and night"; however, over the years, this restriction was relaxed. Working Perushim, categorized as second-class members,[52] were obligated to study "at least" three hour each day in order to deserve their haluka allocation.

The economic power of the haluka gave the kollel great influence over its members, enabling it to resolve large and small problems. For example, the haluka regulations helped solve the shortage of domestic help.[53] Perushim widows and divorcees received only a half share of the haluka and were encouraged to work as domestic servants helping "the young, weak, and sick women"—but only in Perushim homes.

Although we do not know the specific amount of haluka allocated to Safed Perushim, it was higher than the payments to Hasidim and Sephardim. This aroused the envy of the Sephardim, who saw Ashkenazim enjoying at least the same standard of living, without working. The Sephardim exaggerated the debilitating effect of the haluka, which sapped the economic initiative of the Jewish community: "Every man and woman who owes money and is tired of working says to himself or herself, I will go to Safed . . . in order to live off the public treasury and its charity fund. And this town [Safed] was filled with the poor and needy."[54]

The Perushim viewed the situation from a completely different vantage point. They complained about their penurious plight: "Each resident has difficulty finding food and securing an income, and in their homes there is no bread or clothing . . ."[55] This letter, like others written to Diaspora Jews for fundraising purposes, magnified and overdramatized the harsh conditions in Palestine. Although poverty was a fact and an accepted companion, the Perushim were not starving. Jews frequently fed their discontent by "crying out for bread and water and there is none" and groaned about their "naked and destitute" state.[56]

The economic state of the Perushim deteriorated when their emissary, Shlomo Zalman Shapira, who was detained in Istanbul by a cholera epidemic, made a bad investment in wheat and lost monies collected for the community. The Perushim were also forced to pay 6,000 piastres in extortion money to the local authorities because, according to the vague accusations of R. Israel, the Safed Sephardim "informed" on them. To aggravate their financial plight, the transfer of funds from European supporters was delayed in the wake of the Napoleonic wars that devastated Perushim strongholds in Poland and Russia. When funds finally arrived, it was the task of R. Menahem Mendel to distribute them. While contributions from the Diaspora prevented starvation, they could not raise the vast majority of the Jews above the bare subsistence level. When Perushim were unable to cover daily expenses, they were forced to borrow money from Muslims at high interest rates. By 1816, seven years after first settling in Safed, the Perushim had amassed a debt of 42,000 piastres, or 90 piastres for each member of the community.[57]

The financial situation of the Sephardim of Safed was no better. In order to borrow the small sum of 100 piastres from the Sephardi kollel in 1817, a Tunisian rabbi had to sign a promissory note, immediately pay in cash the interest rate of 30 percent, and make periodic payments of 14 piastres.[58]

The debt burden of the Jewish community of Tiberias was less severe despite escalating prices and a shortage of food. Their impoverished life was made more miserable in 1813 when they had to pay the authorities an extortionist tribute of 50,000 piastres in order to be saved from "death." By 1816 the Tiberias community had mortgaged its synagogue for 75,000 piastres and its debt totaled 50,000 piastres, slightly higher than the 40,000 piastres reported for 1802, equal to the reported debt in 1806, and significantly lower than the 78,000 piastres it ostensibly owed in 1805. These elastic figures of indebtedness show that, although the financial condition of the Jewish community was poor, it may not have been as bad as was described in letters sent to East European Jews for the purpose of raising funds. In any event, Tiberias had the lowest per capita debt of the Jewish communities in the four holy cities. The Jews there increased slowly in numbers from 800–900 in 1800 to about 1,000 in 1815, remaining at that level until 1830. There was an influx of a few Perushim settlers (1810), Jewish refugees from Kurdistan (1812), and groups of Hasidim from Poland and Russia (1815).[59]

The 200 Perushim who had settled in Safed by 1810 increased to 462 in 1815.[60] The great majority of the settlers were members of an elite group, promising prodigies and scholars of recognized academic achievements, including five of the six outstanding disciples of the Vilna gaon. A number of Perushim were also affluent persons, who had been encouraged to live in Eretz Israel. "Whoever can support himself on the income from his overseas investments can settle here in peace and quiet and secure for himself the best of both worlds,"[61] advised the wealthy Haim Katz. Then he added a little quoted but revealing phrase, "and he should bring with him a female domestic servant because it is impossible to find a maid here." A small number of Perushim were artisans, such as tailors and silversmiths, who supplied the needs of their community and other Safed Jews.

Some Perushim settlers were learned old men whose pilgrimage to Eretz Israel was the capstone of their life. Yet a good number came with wives and children, indicating that young and middle-aged Perushim migrated to Eretz Israel to live, rather than to die. Despite financial problems and initial adjustment difficulties, the Perushim were satisfied settlers who found Safed "quiet and tranquil . . . let God maintain this until the Coming of the Messiah." Studying and praying in Eretz Israel provided them with a sense of elation. Life in Safed was described by Haim Katz in panegyric terms. "How wonderful it is to settle in this good land," with its fine weather and beautiful scenery. In Safed "adults and children walked without any fear," and even in the countryside Jews could stroll without fear of being molested or beaten. Finally, food is "plentiful all the time and much cheaper than overseas."[62]

R. Menahem Mendel rented houses for the new settlers in the Jewish quarter of Safed. As late as 1819 a letter from Safed, "may it be rebuilt and reestablished," informs us that "there are many houses here for sale, with fine cisterns and good water . . ."[63] The Safed Jewish quarter consisted of about 150 houses built in three tiers, one row on top of another, on the steep, terraced western side of the mountain. The highest level was occupied by the Hasidim; the Sephardim were located in the middle, symbolically separating their "upstairs neighbors" from the Perushim below them. On the sloping mountainside, the roof of each house served as a public pathway for the higher level. A market and a large open area set the Jewish quarter apart from the relatively flat Muslim neighborhood. The Muslim quarters were "so far off that the Jews appear to be in a town which they may call their own."[64] There was no Christian quarter in Safed; Christians lived in nearby villages and visited the town to sell their produce in the market.

The Perushim rented homes, although the purchase price of a house was conspicuously low. After Jews had rented houses and stores from Muslims for a period of three years, they established a long-term legal claim on the property, called a hazaka or holding; they even passed on this right of possession from father to son. The hazaka right of tenured occupancy was a negotiable commodity allowing one Jew to rent an apartment to another Jew or even to mortgage it. Rentals were negotiated not with the Muslim owner but with the Jew holding the right of hazaka. Affluent Jews purchased a hazaka on one or more apartments, or even on a whole courtyard, and then sublet rooms and apartments and received rentals considerably higher than the amount paid to the Muslim owner. This rental practice proved lucrative to the tenant financially able to purchase a hazaka and advantageous to the new immigrant unable to afford the purchase price of an apartment.

Property rights were legally sanctioned by the Sephardi kollel and rabbinical court,[65] which forbade Jews from infringing on the right of occupancy by proposing a higher rental. In this way the Jewish community prevented poor Jews from being evicted from their apartments when a higher rental was offered. To protect the Jewish tenant and his lessor, kollel regulations controlled rentals and prohibited arbitrary increases in prices by establishing a reasonable profit margin of about 20 percent. This regulation of "interminable leases" also stopped "the money of Israel" from passing into Muslim hands.[66] The Gentile landlord was forced to come to equitable terms with the Jewish tenant, knowing that a Muslim would never rent property in the Jewish quarter, and that Jews were legally prevented from bidding against each other.

R. Menahem Mendel purchased agricultural land outside Safed and planned to buy more land "according to the circumstances, the place, and the time."[67] Farm land was purchased "with wheat rooted in the ground," disproving the legendary claim that here the first Jewish farmers established "an agricultural settlement" in Eretz Israel.[68] By purchasing land the Perushim were able to fulfill the biblical injunctions that could only be discharged in Eretz Israel, such as "When you reap the harvest of your land you shall not reap the corners of your field" (Leviticus 19:9). They could now allow poor Jews to glean the sheaves forgotten in the field. Performing agricultural mitzvot denied Jews in the Diaspora was a consecration of the immutable laws of nature ordained by the Lord and manifested in the orderly universe He created. The esthetic beauties of this harmonious world were of no interest to the Perushim; they were only concerned with glorifying the Lord by obeying His commandments. Fruits of the earth were not beautiful to behold; they were holy objects to be sanctified by a benediction and then, most practically, consumed.

Since foreign nationals like the Perushim could not buy property and were legally barred from registering it in their name, it is not clear how the purchase of agricultural land was transacted. Possibly the land was registered in the name of the Sephardi kollel or a trustworthy Sephardi who, as an Ottoman national (rayah), could own land and record it in his name. Or the property may have been "registered in the name of females who by a legal fiction were regarded as rayahs."[69] Such legal subterfuges did not stop the Perushim from encouraging their overseas donors to possess a "share and property" in the Holy Land.[70] One wealthy Jew bought a vineyard in the vicinity of Safed and bequeathed the proceeds of its produce to the yeshiva and study hall named after the Vilna gaon. Other rich Polish Jews bought land in Eretz Israel so that they could import and bless fruits grown in the Holy Land, thereby performing in the Diaspora commandments that could only be performed in the Holy Land.

What was a tolerable income in Safed,[71] and how much did basic food items cost? The wealthy Haim Katz rented a "fairly good-sized" courtyard for about 500 piastres a year.[72] He complained that rentals were "greatly increasing," probably reflecting the growing housing demands of newly arrived Perushim. Katz's annual rent of 500 piastres was an exceedingly large sum relative to the average standard of subsistence. He wrote in 1810 that a couple could live comfortably on approximately 75 piastres a year; 50 piastres was enough for average subsistence, but 33 piastres provided for rock-bottom sustenance "and less than that can lead, God forbid, to depressing poverty." Katz's figures appear on the low side and may reflect low prices in Safed, fluctuating exchange rates for foreign currency, or the insulated view of an affluent person unfamiliar with bare subsistence living. Based on the report of this affluent Jew and other less relevant figures, it is possible to conclude that at the start of the nineteenth century 100 piastres was sufficient for the basic needs of a Safed Jew, while 150 piastres supported a couple.

Food prices tell little about the Perushim standard of living but much about what they ate.[73] Haim Katz wrote that "fruits and vegetables, olive oil and good wine, are always plentiful and much cheaper than overseas. Wheat products are very good and cheaper than abroad." Prices flunctuated wildly in Safed's volatile market due to the catastrophes of nature; for example, after an invasion of locusts in 1817, one rotl of olive oil cost 4½ piastres compared to one-quarter of a piastre in 1819.

As in Poland, Perushim consumed wheat products such as cereals and black bread baked in the public oven. A limited diet of dairy products—milk, butter, and cheese—was eaten. Perushim enjoyed abundant varieties of seasonal fruits and vegetables, some of which they saw for the first time and were unable to name.

On Sabbath and holidays the Perushim celebrated by transforming the physical satisfaction of eating into the spiritual art of serving God. They drank wine and ate poultry, lamb, or beef. Such expensive items were served infrequently during weekdays, when meals were simple and little time was spent on eating. Fish from the Sea of Galilee were also on the menu. The cooking and types of dishes served by the women of the community were strictly Polish in taste and style.

To seek God and study His Torah, the Perushim established a number of batei midrash, combination synagogues and study halls full of books. These were not new buildings, because the authorities prohibited minorities from constructing new places of worship. The practical Perushim, always short of money, preferred setting up rooms for study and prayer in private courtyards of wealthy congregants,[74] at little cost to the community. Not until 1816 did the Perushim repair a synagogue for their use. In the beit midrash, Perushim spent day and night immersed in the dual acts of worship: prayer and study. The house-of-God was the religious and social center of the community. From the compact, confining beit midrash, Perushim viewed the panorama of all that was significant in life; it opened windows on all of life's great possibilities and opportunities.

The daily rhythm of life was set by the hours prayers were recited. Perushim prayed in joyous daily communion with a God they were familiar with, not to a Jehovah they feared. Perushim males above the age of 13 were mandated to assemble in the beit midrash each morning and late afternoon just before the sun set. Obligatory daily attendance was enforced by the inner compulsion of free men acting within a climate of belief accepting the supremacy of the Torah in all facets of human existence.

Jewish observances and ceremonies based on the ritual of the Vilna gaon were steeped in profound values that dictated the behavior of the Perushim, conditioned their conduct, and gave meaning to their lives. As in all religious systems where right and wrong are absolutes, there was no "nearly right" or "almost wrong" in the world of the Perushim. So implacably strong was their conviction in religious values that alien thoughts and emotions could not be tolerated. Tolerance was an abomination.

Religion pervaded the daily practices of the Perushim and all observant Jews. Within the insular confines of the kehilla, religion provided a stable core around which all activities of life revolved. The minutiae of everyday activities were hallowed by religious law, which provided an inexhaustible store of advice about how to live the proper life: what clothing to wear, what food to eat and how to prepare it, and even when to have intercourse with one's wife. Where the spiritual and secular were fused into one totality, religion was the very substance of life and gave shape and content to its events. Birth, bar mitzva, marriage, and death as well as holidays, festivals, and the Sabbath were sanctified by rituals, ceremonies, and benedictions all voicing thanks to the Lord in "an enormous unfolding of religion in daily life."[75]

During the Perushim prayer service on the Sabbath and the Jewish holidays, a sermon was delivered explaining the biblical chapter of the week and other classical texts. The sermonizer was not a shouting preacher exhorting the frenzied faithful, but a public educator expounding the mysteries of the divine Scripture. By aiming at the brain rather than addressing the heart, the sermonizer, frequently R. Menahem Mendel, conducted an open study session before the congregation. Only on solemn, sad occasions, and during holidays prescribing repentance, were impassioned oratorical perorations delivered loudly, to arouse responsive feelings from the lamenting congregation.

In order to conduct a decorous prayer service, Perushim regulations forbade conversing. Those wishing to talk were told to step outside the synagogue, so that some worshippers were constantly wandering in and out of the place of worship. Perushim disturbing the solemnity of the service could be fined.[76] Their sanctity of silence was in stark contrast to the noisy disorder of the Hasidic prayer service.

Daily prayer sessions in the beit midrash also served an important social function in the Perushim community. They drew people together in friendship, bridged the social gap, encouraged shared participation, and established the social standing of congregants. The closeness of the congregant's seat to the Holy Ark holding the Torah scrolls indicated his social status. Sons sat next to their fathers, closing the distance between father and son that might arise in a society that demanded deference, commanded obedience, and imposed discipline. In an environment of physical proximity and accessibility where everything was known and nothing could be hidden, the rich and the poor, the scholar and the unlearned, mingled, scrutinized each other, and freely passed information about who was doing what. This proved an effective method of supervising the conduct of kollel members.

After the Perushim finished reciting their morning and afternoon prayers, R. Menahem Mendel conducted an advanced study session for scholars, while at another beit midrash R. Saadia led a study group on a lower academic level. In an atmosphere of free give-and-take, erudite arguments were heatedly presented and pugnaciously defended in an animated show of frenetic hand-waving and withering verbal battle. "Questions of law and ritual were everywhere assiduously investigated and elaborated, with that subtle analysis peculiar to the Jewish mind, which pursues every idea to its remotest consequences and its most trifling details."[77] In their intellectual endeavors the Perushim achieved exaltation and ecstasy no less than that of the Hasidim, although by temperament and training they expressed their intense devotions differently from the uncontrolled outpourings of the Hasidim, which they scorned.

At the conclusion of the group sessions, most Perushim returned to long vigils of solitary study. A day in the life of the scholar was irretrievably lost if his attention was not riveted on sacred texts for 15 to 18 hours, with short interruptions for food, prayers, sleep, and family contact. All else was idle frivolity and a waste of the limited time the Lord awarded each person in this world.

The pinnacle of scholastic achievement was attained by mastering the Talmud, an encyclopedic compendium of legal discussions that served as the basis of Jewish law (halacha). Since the unalterable, eternal constitution of the Bible did not fully explain itself, it was the task of the Talmud to unearth the hidden logic of the divinely sanctioned legislation delivered from Sinai and elucidate its subtle interpolations so that the Jewish people would understand what was expected of them.

Despite the counsel of the Vilna gaon to study the "concealed treasure" of the Old Testament,[78] learning the five books of the Pentateuch was relegated to a secondary position on the assumption that it obviously was familiar material to all scholars. On the highest, most esoteric level, the Perushim tried to resolve their intellectual dilemmas by wrestling with the kabbalistic "science of the invisible" that tried to unravel the mysteries of Deliverance and Redemption, calculate the time of the coming of the Messiah, and plumb the depths of the unfathomable.[79]

Nothing significant could be discovered by the Perushim outside of Scripture, the sole source of immutable truth about human existence; secular studies of the physical and social sciences were irrelevant. Where all knowledge was contained in one unified compendium, there was no need for arts and literature. Only in the "manuscripts of God" could the Perushim "read what is still unread."[80]

Learning was not the monopoly of the elite few. Everyone was commanded to study the Torah for its own sake and for his own spiritual health. A Jew was measured by the yardstick of how well he expanded the dimensions of the mind. In Eretz Israel the scholar was at the top of the social hierarchy, where he enjoyed social status, prestige, and financial rewards. Perushim haluka regulations convincingly encouraged scholars to make Torah their full-time occupation. Education enabled the scholar to engage in religious pursuits as a teacher, ritual slaughterer, scribe, or rabbinical judge. Another tangible benefit was the large dowry a coveted scholar could secure by felicitously marrying the daughter of a wealthy man.

In addition to studying six days a week, every Sabbath eve (Friday night) the Perushim were divided into two shifts. One shift studied "until after midnight, and the second until sunrise. . . . On the Sabbath and holidays all men were required to assemble in the beit midrash and study according to their ability, during summer and winter."[81] Since books were the real life of the Perushim, one of their first requests from their overseas supporters was to send books of talmudic commentaries. Haim Katz wrote: "And we should make it known that he who comes [to Eretz Israel] should bring with him books that are not found here."[82] A more prosaic yet essential request from a town located at a height of 2,750 feet in the mountains of Galilee was to send wood-burning stoves for the study halls.

In the enveloping society of the Perushim, children were strongly subordinate to the authoritarian wishes and loving pressures of their fathers. Children were inculcated with parental values and community practices from a very young age.

In consonance with the talmudic saying that "the world rests on the breath of the children in the schoolhouses,"[83] Jewish boys began their studies in one-room schools at the age of three or four. Parents were responsible for the education of their children and paid tuition fees directly to the instructor. Sitting on the floor in the crowded home of the teacher, the youngest students learned to read and write Hebrew and to recite the daily prayers and blessings. They next progressed to the weekly portion of the Bible, studying the Prophets, biblical commentaries, and the oral law in the Mishna. Entire passages were committed to memory, since much of the teaching was based on relentless, repetitive recitation.

Zealous teachers maintained discipline by frequently rapping the fingers and boxing the ears of their pupils. Physical abuse was normally not practiced, but there were cases of severe punishment such as a seven- or eight-year-old boy receiving "the bastinado on the sole of the feet."[84] It was common belief that, although scholars could not be produced by beating the student, to spare the rod was to spoil the child. The teacher was responsible for supervising the behavior of his students not only from morning to evening during the weekday study sessions, but also on the Sabbath and festivals when studies were conducted after the morning prayers. Boys played games only on Friday afternoon until one hour before the Sabbath sundown. The Perushim community had no tolerance for frivolous play unconnected with worship and study. A boy was treated as a miniature man.

Finally, boys progressed to the study of the Talmud and its commentaries. Coercive teaching was now replaced by understanding, analysis, and individual learning. The curriculum was a replica of the Perushim study program in Poland. Secular studies such as Arabic, European languages, or arithmetic were considered unworthy of a high-level academic discipline.

Between the ages of 10 and 13 the lives of most boys changed dramatically. While many boys were apprenticed to learn trades passed on from father to son, students with a talent for learning continued their studies, either in the Perushim beit midrash or in the Sephardi yeshiva. This system of education accounted for a high literacy rate among the Jewish men at a time when fewer than 5 percent of the Palestine population could read and write.[85]

Only boys attended school. Although girls were taught at home to recite the prayers by rote, they received no formal education. Like Muslim women, they were confined to the home, where they helped with household chores and learned domestic skills from mother and grandmother. Many girls from very poor families worked as domestics for rich families.

There was only one option for a girl—marriage. Many girls were matched and mated at the age of 12 to 14; unmarried girls of 16 were labeled spinsters. In the Jewish community, marriage was not the culmination of an emotional binding but the performance of a religious duty and the forging of a calculated social and economic alliance between families.

Girls lacked freedom to choose a husband from the limited pool of available men. Only the most strong-minded girls were able to exercise veto power over a prospective mate—for example, when their parents selected an elderly widower as the prospective groom.

Although the world of the Perushim was very much a man's world, women achieved equal standing in the home. After marriage the wife did not assume the role of a meek, silent servant of her master. It was understood that since men and women were physically different each had a distinct, unique role to play in life. The wife became an active family partner. When guests visited Jewish homes, women and girls appeared in the sitting room and freely conversed with the visitors. An English physician was startled to discern that:

the Jewesses in Jerusalem speak in a decided and firm tone, unlike the hesitating and timid voice of the Arab and Turkish females; and claim the European privilege of differing from their husbands, and maintaining their own opinions. [86]

Women produced and reared the children, kept the house, fostered the enveloping atmosphere of domestic piety, and cared for all mundane family matters. Yet, surprisingly, Perushim wives had an easier life in Eretz Israel than in Poland, for they did not assume the burden of earning the family living by running a small shop, as was the practice in Eastern Europe.

How well did the Perushim get along with the Hasidim, the Sephardim, and the Muslims? What language did the Perushim speak with these groups? Perushim conversed with each other and with the Hasidim in Yiddish, as they had in Eastern Europe. Based on a ritualistic language they had developed in Polish study halls, they expressed themselves in a traditional phraseology that reflected their way of thinking. According to a Sephardi saying, "Nobody can understand [Ashkenaziml except one who is well acquainted with them through having studied at the yeshivot for many years." [87] As in all tongues, gesticulations of the hands, shrugging of the shoulders, motions of the body, and the volume of the voice were also integral parts of the Perushim speech patterns.

Extremely few Perushim (and Hasidim) spoke Arabic; this was also true of most Ashkenazim who had settled in Eretz Israel in previous centuries. [88] From an economic standpoint the Perushim felt like "strangers in the country" because "of the hindrance of language." [89] Later R. Israel confirmed this situation:

> The majority of the Sephardim provide for themselves through grocery stores, dealing with the fellahin . . . and from interest arising from lending money. As for us Ashkenazim, the biblical saying, "He hath made me dwell in dark places" [Lament. 3:6] was fulfilled. For we do not know the language, and we are all broken paupers. [90]

Such economic estrangement did not impel the Perushim to study Arabic, if we may judge from the example set by R. Menahem Mendel, who, during twenty years of living in Safed and Jerusalem, never learned Arabic. [91]

Although the Perushim could freely converse with the Hasidim in Yiddish, the two wary contenders kept contact to a minimum after their initial adjustment difficulties over money matters. Such coolness did not prevent a small number of Perushim in 1810 from establishing a beachhead in Tiberias alongside the Hasidim. This settlement opportunity was seized at the behest of the Perushim leadership of Safed right after the death of R. Abraham and the weakening of the Hasidic movement in the Galilee.

Perushim communicated with the Sephardim in their one common tongue, Hebrew, "the holy language" of ritual and response, Jewish legal contracts, and correspondence between Jews in Eretz Israel and the Diaspora.[92] Even Jewish farmers in the villages of Peki'in, Kfar Yasif, and Shfar-Am had a basic knowledge of the Hebrew vernacular. Initially, conversation was difficult because the Perushim, like the Hasidim, pronounced Hebrew words quite differently than the Sephardim, accenting different syllables in a quavering Yiddish inflection. A European rabbi concluded in 1820 that "it is quite impossible for an Ashkenazi to use the Sephardi pronunciation correctly; the adoption of the Sephardi pronunciation by the Ashkenazim would produce a pronunciation which would be neither Ashkenazi nor Sephardi."[93] Eventually the Perushim's tongue and ear became attuned to the soft-singing Sephardi pronunciation.

Sephardim conversed in varying dialects of Arabic, the vernacular of the Muslims. Depending on their country of origin, Sephardim spoke Ladino or Judesmo,[94] a Judeo-Spanish dialect of Castilian mixed with many Hebrew, Arabic, and Turkish idioms, a veritable "Spanish Yiddish." Only a few Turkish-born or secularly educated Sephardim who maintained contact with the authorities spoke and wrote Turkish, the official government language, which was not known by most Muslims in Palestine.

Sephardim regarded Perushim and Hasidim as different and slightly strange because they lived, dressed, and spoke as they had in Poland and made no effort to learn the local language and customs. Bemused Sephardim found it curious that so few Perushim showed any interest in wanting to work but willingly depended upon donations from their Polish supporters.

As old-time settlers, some Sephardim looked down on the Ashkenazim and felt superior, "Jews of the highest caste."[95] Nevertheless, Sephardim acted graciously toward the Perushim, providing them with that most precious possession, a place of prayer, as they had done with the Hasidim in 1777. "The Sephardim are very close to us,"[96] one of the Perushim wrote in 1810, adding that the scholars of the two groups studied together. R. Israel of Shklov reported that the Sephardim and their leader R. Isaac Abulafia acted as hospitable hosts and helped the Perushim during their first years of adjustment.

But close contacts never developed between the Perushim and the

Sephardim due to different religious concepts, customs, prayer patterns, and modes of behavior. It was impossible to bridge the wide differences that had developed between the two groups during the past centuries, and no such effort was attempted. Perushim and Sephardim separately conducted their independent religious, financial, and social lives. Only when the Sephardi millet represented all Jews before the authorities was joint action and common payment required—though not always forthcoming.

The Perushim, like the Hasidim, displayed a haughty disinterest in the Muslims. In Poland they had developed tough inner defenses and outward defiance of the Gentile world. In Eretz Israel the swaggering walk, lustful speech, and violent actions of many Muslims reminded the Perushim of European Cossacks. Both Muslims and Polish Gentiles lived spiritually empty lives, in the opinion of the Perushim. Jews should have as little contact as possible with the *ara'ber*, who had nothing to teach them. So why talk with them?

Sanguine in their belief of superiority, Perushim showed dismissive disdain toward the Arabs by an ominous nod of the head and whispered words of repugnance. Their attitude toward the Muslims ranged from indifference to contempt and during the following hundred years it was "a mixture of scorn and fear—scorn for their low moral, cultural, and material standards, and fear of their physical prowess, greater numbers, and lack of restraint."[97] Unlike the Jews of Jerusalem, who lived in proximity to the Muslims and suffered their constant hostility, taunts, and ridicule, Safed Jews chose to keep their distance and were only infrequently abused or assaulted.

In an effort to maintain tolerable relations and prevent provocative behavior from offending their Muslim neighbors, the Sephardi kollelim in Safed and the other holy cities enacted rules governing the conduct of business with Gentiles. Purchases by Jews from Gentiles of products such as milk and water were regulated in Jerusalem, and there were also regulations about employing Gentiles for construction work and rules controlling lending and borrowing money from Muslims and Christians.

The Jewish community also legislated rules of behavior in order to maintain order and social harmony within the kehilla. Regulations enacted by the Sephardi millet were the authorized law of the land for all Jews. The Perushim willingly adopted Sephardi regulations and drafted their own precise, detailed rules in order to establish close control over the growing congregation to merge individuals into one community and to curtail the bickering that inevitably crops up in a small, closed, inbred group. A review of the Perushim regulations and selected Sephardi codes of behavior that were applicable in Safed informs us about the structure and social patterns of the community and illuminates their mind-set. A description of these ordinances enables us to feel the texture of the Perushim lives and hear the tone of their voices.

Paradoxically, the Perushim were governed by a strong rule of law, while living in the state of anarchy prevailing in Palestine. They systematically drafted exacting strictures that established study hours and prayer habits, mandated standards of dress, behavior, and frugality, and controlled the freedom to move to another town in Eretz Israel, travel overseas, and correspond with overseas friends.

In 1823 the Perushim wrote out their regulations in concise talmudic legalese.[98] Rules were based on the initial guidelines laid down by the kollel and practiced by all Perushim since their arrival in Safed in 1808. By command of their culture rather than by order of a ruling hegemony, the pyramid of values gained the compelling force of law. Perushim unanimously vowed obedience to their regulations, which strengthened group solidarity. In a well-ordered community surrounded by an unfriendly and occasionally hostile population, submission to community law was easily achieved since the kollel controlled the physical existence and the spiritual sustenance of its members by a wide variety of financial and religious sanctions.

The clothing worn by Ashkenazi men required no regulation, since nobody thought of deviating from the traditional Polish dress that made no concession to the subtropical climate of Palestine. Throughout the year Perushim wore long, black gabardine robes (kaftans) and broad-brimmed fur-trimmed hats (shtreimels). Pallid faces were set off by curled side-locks that bobbed up and down like springs on each side of bearded faces and nearly touched the rounded shoulders. In contrast, white-bearded Sephardi men with "grey hair flowing on their shoulders" dressed in loose kaftans that hardly distinguished them from Muslims.[99]

Women's dress and appearance in the market, streets, and other public places were dictated by the kollel to prevent the carnal coveting of Jewish women. Jewish women were instructed that "not even the aged may go to the market without a covering over her garments..."[100] Unlike Muslim women, Jews appeared in public without a veil, but they were well covered: their hair by a kerchief, their arms by long sleeves, and their shoulders by a shawl. They were told not to dress ostentatiously and not to wear ornaments and jewelry in public. Women under 60 were banned from entering Gentile homes.

Both men and women were forbidden "to sell wine and intoxicating beverages to...any Gentile and uncircumcised person," because Muslim law prohibited the drinking of alcoholic beverages. Entry and employment in the public bakeries were regulated,[101] to prevent meetings between members of the opposite sex in the morning darkness. Bakers were ordered "not to hire as workers bearded young men, neither Jews nor Gentiles, unless married." Women under 50 years of age were forbidden "to approach the oven, to insert or withdraw a loaf of bread." For fear of walking the unlighted streets after sundown, women younger than 40 attended synagogue evening prayers only on the holiest holidays of Yom Kippur and Rosh Hashanah, but not on the Sabbath or during the week. Unmarried teenage boys were forbidden to participate in midnight vigils or studies unless they went hand-in-hand with their father or older brother.

Behavior of Jewish men was also circumscribed, but such rules had little applicability among Perushim, who studied around the clock and were not tempted to idle away time on material pleasures. Men were forbidden "to patronize a purveyor of wine and drink." Gambling was a cardinal sin. Playing cards and dice was so repugnant that Sephardi officials in Jerusalem were told to turn the offender over to the "governor of the town who will punish him on his person and in his pocket. No mercy and pity should be shown toward a person who has transgressed the religious law. There is no forgiveness forever for such a person." The tone toward women who infringe the law was no less stern. One Jerusalem regulation stated most categorically: ". . . and if any woman transgresses these regulations we certainly will learn about it, and we will harass her in order that she be made an example and a lesson. We will proclaim it in the markets and streets, in addition to fining her according to the law."

Unmarried men "from the age of twenty and above and sixty and below" were forbidden to settle in Eretz Israel, and single men were ordered to marry promptly or leave the country. Apparently the many widows in the four holy cities were too tempting a target. Perushim agreed with the Sephardi injunction against single men settling in Eretz Israel and warned against the "bitter protest of the Sephardi scholars" if Perushim bachelors came to Safed.[102]

The austere character of the Perushim is visible in their stern admonishment against inviting to a wedding or circumcision party more than ten males outside the family circle. Uninvited guests were sharply warned to stay away from such celebrations.[103] It was not that the Perushim believed in the denial of physical pleasures or that celebrating at a party marking the continuity of the Jewish people was sinful. Rather, they hedged celebrations with rules in order not to distract men from the daily urgency of prayer and study. Life was a serious matter that allowed Perushim little time for levity;

laughter was at a premium and frivolity was absent. Moreover, the frugal Perushim wished to avoid social competition between families and to channel all available financial resources toward the sacred, solemn purpose of settling in Eretz Israel.

The comings and goings of Perushim in Eretz Israel and abroad were closely restricted by kollel regulations. Safed Perushim wanting to travel overseas or even move to Jerusalem, Tiberias, or Hebron required written approval from the kollel. A member of the community traveling overseas by permission of the kollel did not receive his share of the haluka, but members of his family remaining in Eretz Israel were granted their proportionate share. If a man went to Europe without securing the prior approval of the kollel, he and his family forever forfeited their share of the haluka, and the family could be banished from Eretz Israel to prevent it from becoming a financial burden on the kollel.

Sometime in the 1810s it was decreed that haluka support would not be granted newly arrived Perushim during their first three years in Eretz Israel. This regulation encouraged Perushim to arrive in Eretz Israel with substantial financial means and discouraged trips back to Eastern Europe during the first few years after arrival for the purpose of collecting money for their personal needs. Certain scholars were exempt from this travel prohibition, possibly because their overseas trip might financially benefit the Perushim community.

Writing letters to Diaspora Jews was closely monitored by both Sephardim and Perushim. At the risk of losing their haluka allocation, Perushim were prohibited from writing "accusing and indicting letters about individuals in the Holy Land, or the community or its officials." It was forbidden to make derogatory comments about Eretz Israel to a visitor, because such negative opinions might tarnish the holy image of Eretz Israel and cause a loss of revenue. Letters containing charges against members of the executive committee had to be filed with the treasurer "and definitely with no other party," in order that the claim be substantiated or disproved by two distinguished persons of the kollel. Perushim corresponding with overseas relatives and friends were encouraged to write short letters and omit mentioning the subject of haluka. Yet the vast majority of letters sent by Jews were written for the express purpose of soliciting overseas funds.

To enforce this censorship regulation, letters were given to the rabbi or kollel leader before being posted. It was common knowledge that "rabbis and community leaders open and read all incoming and outgoing letters."[104] Kollel leaders sent packets of letters once or twice a year with one of their emissaries, who also might read the letters. Only if no emissary was sent abroad for two years—"God forbid"—could Perushim resort to the postal services of traveling merchants and pilgrims.

When Hillel Rivlin wrote glowing letters to the Diaspora, he was asked skeptically: "Is this really the truth about Eretz Israel?" He answered that "the truth from Eretz Israel is the purpose—the purpose of Redemption because the privations are temporary; Eretz Israel is earned by suffering..."[105] Such a purposeful truth was defined as telling Diaspora Jews what the leadership thought was appropriate and preventing overseas Jews "from knowing what is happening in Eretz Israel."[106] Because of the "greater good" of the community we have two basic types of letters: those describing the fabulous, wonderful Holy Land and those expressing a passion for suffering in Eretz Israel.

The Perushim created their own Jewish community and religious environment in Safed by transplanting from Poland to Eretz Israel their prayer services, customs, rituals, dress, language, and educational system. Little was indigenous to their way of life in Eretz Israel. While dwelling in Poland, the Perushim lived spiritually in the historic past and the Messianic future of the Holy Land. Now, while residing in Eretz Israel, the Perushim behaved as if they still lived in Poland! Another huge difference in living in Safed was the inner contentment and spiritual serenity of living in Zion, which washed over the Perushim despite their lower standard of living and higher mortality rate, as compared to their Polish friends.

The life of the Perushim in Eretz Israel was more spiritually exalted and less physically difficult than that of the Jews in Eastern Europe. Within the millet framework of self-rule, Safed Perushim enjoyed greater freedom of expression and tolerance than their co-religionists in Poland. The community was subjected to extortionary taxes, but these were often ameliorated by the intervention of Haim Farhi and the financial responsibilities assumed by the Sephardi kollel. Any financial burden that fell on the Safed Perushim was borne by East European Jews who by religious fiat supported their brethren in Eretz Israel, albeit in modest style. Since the Perushim, both men and women, were liberated from the constraint of earning a living in Eretz Israel, they stubbornly kept the outside Muslim world at arm's length, not as in Europe, where they were forced to enter the hostile Gentile environment in order to work. Moreover, in Eretz Israel no legal restrictions were imposed on the occupations of minority members, and Jews were not barred from working in trades and professions, as in Poland.

Since the Palestine Perushim were foreign nationals and not Ottoman citizens, they enjoyed protection under the capitulation agreements and were not persecuted by malevolent Christians and the rabidly anti-Semitic Catholic Church. The Perushim did not have to contend, like their East European brethren, with the cruelties of a government that condoned assault, plunder, mob-instigated massacres, blood libels, and mass expulsions. Of course, the Perushim in Eretz Israel were attacked and robbed, like their Muslim neighbors. However, such terrorizing was not sanctioned by government edicts, but reflected ineffectual government, incompetent officials, and bribery-prone functionaries unwilling or unable to enforce the law.

In order to feel free and productive within the narrow confines of the Jewish quarter, the Perushim clung to their tradition rather than fleeing their past, like most Jewish immigrants who settled in the Western world. In contrast to Polish Jews who later migrated to Western Europe and the United States, the Perushim survived and prospered in Eretz Israel by preserving their enclosing religious framework, which enabled them to adjust more easily and rapidly to their strange and harsh new environment. The Perushim traveled to Eretz Israel in groups, continued their accepted behavioral patterns and social norms in Safed, and established their own kollel. The newly arrived Perushim were not alienated individuals in a foreign land; they were not alone and did not feel lonely. They did not have to cope with the problems of practicing traditional rituals in a Gentile world and did not have to search to find God in their own personal way or adjust to changing Jewish values fashioned in the profane Diaspora.

Perushim experienced no "reshuffling of the self."[107] In a world where religion was a comforting reality rather than a disruptive intrusion, the Perushim had no doubts to clarify and no dilemmas to resolve. Uncertainties about Jewish existence and personal identity were unknown to a people who had fulfilled their yearning to return Home.

The Plague Years and the Jewish Community of Jerusalem

1812–1815

From the end of 1812 until 1815, while the Perushim were settling into Safed, adjusting to a new country, and learning to live with the Sephardim and Hasidim, the Galilee was struck by the plague—"a frightful pestilence, a fearful epidemic."[1] Ignorant about the rules of hygiene and the causes of contagion, the Jewish community took no preventive measures. "We knew nothing about quarantine and taking precautions,"[2] in the words of Israel of Shklov, indicating that the Perushim had not learned of the quarantine practices instituted by the Hasidim during the plague of 1786 in Tiberias.[3] In Safed, which was hit hardest by the plague, hundreds of Jews died.[4]

Jews fled Safed and settled temporarily in the nearby Jewish villages and in Jerusalem. The Perushim kollel incurred extraordinary expenses for the upkeep of the refugees and the care of orphans and widows. It undertook "to tend and support the living, that they might live and not die of hunger . . . to raise the orphans and to provide wet nurses for sucklings whose mothers had died." R. Israel of Shklov recorded the travail and agony experienced by Jews during the plague. He reported that "many people fled in convoys to the wildernesses and forests. I and my family also traveled to the Holy City of Jerusalem."[5] On the journey, R. Israel's wife died and was buried in the village of Shfar-Am. After R. Israel arrived in Jerusalem, other members of his family succumbed in quick succession: first his son-in-law Joel, 27; then his two daughters, Esther and 18-year-old Leah; the following day his son Nahman; two days later his 14-year-old son Wolf. R. Israel then received news that both his father and mother in Safed had perished from the plague. He was left with only his small, sick daughter Sheindel. "And I lay on the roof crying, prostrating myself and imploring the compassion of our Father-in-Heaven . . . tears flowed out of my eyes for all that had happened to me, and my heartbreak was as large as the sea." As he wallowed in dark despair, the depths of R. Israel's anguish knew no end. He implored the divine for help and forgiveness: "Please Lord, full of compassion, spare me and take pity upon me and the remaining refugees of the House of Israel."[6]

For R. Israel, a scholar and organizer of prodigious energy and relentless drive, absolute belief provided a refuge from torment in times of desperation. The unshakable convictions of R. Israel and his co-religionists in Eretz Israel enabled them to endure tragic afflictions and sustained them through Job-like crises.

Jews understood that forces rampant in the universe frustrated their puny human efforts. Try as they did, they could not fathom these forces, governed by the indecipherable will of God. But during catastrophes the power of punishment by a wrathful God became shatteringly clear to them. They were convinced that God, who had visited upon them successive calamities in retribution for their sins, must certainly have destined them for a special mission in this world. As people of free will, Jews could not accept the idea that their lives were vulnerable to the arbitrary, unpredictable whims of an inscrutable power and were not part of a divine plan and that God was a lawless tyrant assailing them with random, capricious manifestations of nature. If life was a game of chance, they would have been condemned to the purgatory of a purposeless world.

Instead, Jews perceived a benevolent Providence who condoned suffering while guiding the world toward an intelligible purpose. They believed that God refrained from meddling in the swirl of human events. However, from time to time He intervened when nature was diverted from its ordained direction. Satisfied in this faith, they were not wracked by doubts and learned to endure the divinely foreordained yet inexplicable events that God had willed and to consider the plagues as an instrument of the Lord. In resigned acceptance Jews intoned: "The Lord hath given and the Lord hath taken away; blessed be the name of the Lord." This was the inexorable human fate. "Blessed be the name of the Lord forever and ever."

For Jews, death was a release from the suffering and tribulations of this life. The next world was a triumphal reward for having lived the life of a true believer. So the Perushim gained solace from life's misery by consecrating themselves to living in the sight of God and doing their best in an unpredictable world. Only in their vision of God in heaven could they find the consoling values that made life on earth worth living.

A group of 71 Perushim headed by R. Menahem Mendel of Shklov came to Jerusalem from Safed in July 1814. Before entering town the Perushim were quarantined for eight days, forcing them to find shelter outside the city walls. Sephardi leaders graciously assisted the displaced Perushim during their three-month stay in Jerusalem. "When I saw their sorrow and plight," a Sephardi kollel official wrote, "I was forced to save their lives. I rented for them two courtyards near the wall and I set them up in apartments. . . . I provided for them and spent money to feed, clothe, and house them."[7] The Perushim were favorably impressed by the Sephardim, and it also appeared to them that the hatred of the Muslims toward Ashkenazim had subsided.[8]

The Perushim who had fled the plague-stricken Galilee initially planned to remain in Jerusalem only until they could return home. However, exhilarated and comforted by the timeless historical attachment of the Jews to that holy city, they pondered how to convert the tragedy of the plague into an advantageous opportunity for settling in Jerusalem. They were spurred by the teachings of the Vilna gaon, who considered Jerusalem the life-source of the Jewish people and the final destination of all Jews.

Although Palestine was an unknown territory, the Jerusalem viewed for the first time by the Perushim was intimately known to them from their Bible studies and daily prayers. In their lives Zion was a constant presence of veneration and a place to "rejoice greatly" (Zechariah 9:9). Perushim had returned to "the faithful city . . . full of justice" (Isaiah 1:21), not to build it but to witness the fullfillment of the Lord's promise to "rebuild it soon in our days for evermore." They were encased in an ever-present two-millennial past of memories and images that linked harmoniously with the present.

Jerusalem was a small administrative town of little strategic or commercial importance within the Ottoman Empire and was ruled by a governor subordinate to the pasha of Damascus.[9] Unlike Hebron and Nablus, Jerusalem was not an urban center for its surrounding villages. It was an unruly place of general lawlessness and anarchy that at times was controlled by Beduin, rival pashas, and contending tribal chiefs. In 1808, for example, the governor was so weak that he was run out of town.

A street in Jerusalem.

Muslims, Christians, and Jews recognized Jerusalem as the symbol of hope and redemption. For Muslims, Jerusalem was the third most sacred city, after Mecca and Medina. For Christians, Jerusalem was the city of the Crucifixion and the Resurrection. For Jews, Jerusalem was Zion and the spiritual center of their universe. The walled city of slightly more than 200 acres loomed monumental in their lives.

The towers, turrets, battlements, and four kilometers of hewn stone walls surrounding Jerusalem had been rebuilt in 1537–1540 by order of Sultan Suleiman the Magnificent. Along the top of the creviced wall, and interrupted by the city gates, ran ramparts to facilitate the movement of troops. Entrance to Jerusalem through one of its four gates was impeded for reasons of defense; access was not direct but required entering and then turning ninety degrees before penetrating into the city. From dusk to dawn the gates were locked to shut out robbers and marauding Beduin.

Before entering the "everlasting doors" (Psalms 24:7) of Jerusalem, the Perushim made the traditional tear in their clothing as a sign of mourning for ravaged Jerusalem and the destroyed Temple, and recited, "Zion is turned into a desert, it lies in ruins."

Outside its walls, Jerusalem was bounded by the Judean hills, slashed with deep ravines that protected the town in times of siege. To Jerusalem's east, south, and west, the steep valleys of Hinnom and Kidron were filled with the ruins of centuries and the rubbish of residents. No one dared to live outside the walls of Jerusalem, and few ventured into the dangerous countryside without an armed escort.

Jerusalem was sited "between the Desert and the Sea." To the west lay Jaffa and the Mediterranean Sea, and immediately to the east was the Judean desert dropping down to the lowest point on earth, the Dead Sea. Arid Judean wasteland and bleak desert wilderness were all around Jerusalem, which stood, fortresslike, dominating the surrounding desolate land. The brooding, oppressive silence enveloped the countryside and reached right up to the town walls.[10]

"Before Jerusalem on the east" (Zechariah 14:4) was the Mount of Olives, an effective barrier against the hostile winds and sand of the Judean desert and attacks by desert Beduin. Viewing Jerusalem from its summit made an indelible impression on the Perushim. Before them lay the magnificent city of David; but their attention was riveted on the invisible—the destroyed Temple where Jews once offered sacrifices and prayers. Accustomed to delving into books, the Perushim were blind to the esthetics of nature. Looking at the city so dramatically exposed before them, they remembered their afflictions in Zion and their historical ties to Jerusalem. They

The Jaffa Gate with the Citadel in the background.

didn't know and couldn't care that the Mount of Olives was sacred to the Christians as the site where Jesus prophesied the destruction of Jerusalem, and where he was crucified.[11]

Below the Mount of Olives were thousands of gravestones in the Jewish cemetery in the Valley of Jehoshafat (Hebrew: the Lord will judge). Tradition held that Jews buried in this sacred cemetery would be the first to rise on the day of the Messiah's arrival. For this reason, Jews sent earth from the holy cemetery overseas, to sanctify the graves of beloved ones buried in the Diaspora.

Jerusalem's gray-tinged stone, the congealed mass of dome-roofed buildings, and the dull desolation surrounding the town provided a low-toned background for the exquisite beauty of the golden-capped, blue-ornamented octagonal Dome of the Rock. Situated on a raised platform in the center of a 35-acre foliaged esplanade on Mt. Moriah, where the First and Second Jewish Temples once stood, the graceful structure was built in A.D. 691 over the sacred rock from which Muslims believe the Prophet Muhammad ascended to heaven. Entry into this most holy Muslim site was barred to both Jewish and Christian infidels.

Within its protective walls, Jerusalem was no more than a crumbling village of 9,000 people, divided into four quarters, each housing a specific religious group: Jewish, Muslim, Christian, and Armenian. Full of "signs and sounds of religion,"[12] neighborhood activity focused on the dominant religious institutions—synagogue, mosque, church, and monastery. The exteriors of the quarters were plain, uninviting "blank walls and dull portals."[13] Before the avaricious eyes of the Turkish authorities, Jerusalemites, like modest women, made conscious efforts to reveal as little of themselves as possible.

The Christian quarter in the northwest section of Jerusalem had no Jewish inhabitants and few Muslims. Its 2,250 Christians belonged to the Greek Orthodox (1,400) and Roman Catholic (800) churches and to a bewildering welter of small sects:[14] Copts, Abyssinians, Syrian Jacobites, Nestorians, and Georgians. Characteristic of the Christian quarter were its many open fields, some of which were sown with wheat and barley in the winter. Vacant lots served as a dumping ground for foul-smelling carcasses and rubbish piled up to great heights.[15]

The dominant spiritual and geographic center of the Christian quarter was the Church of the Holy Sepulchre, the traditional site of the Calvary and the mother-shrine for the Greek and Roman Catholics. "Not remarkable for elegance or beauty,"[16] even in the believing eyes of Scottish ministers, the church was deprecated by Muslims as "a heap of rubbish." Church

The courtyard of the Church of the Holy Sepulchre.

esthetics were not helped by the nearby tannery, whose noxious smells assaulted the senses. Leading to the Holy Sepulchre was the most famous street in Christendom, the Via Dolorosa. Before the entrance to the Holy Sepulchre was an open court that served as a bustling bazaar where pilgrims bartered foreign goods for food and souvenirs, and peddlers from Jerusalem and Bethlehem sold rosaries, crucifixes, and Christian icons carved in olive wood and mother-of-pearl. In 1806 about 2,000 Christian pilgrims spent at least 200 piastres each for souvenirs, food, and shelter, leaving a substantial 400,000 piastres in Jerusalem.[17]

The Perushim did not know the Christian quarter, where no Jews lived because of the "visceral hostility" displayed by Christians toward Jews.[18] The first British vice-consul in Jerusalem wrote (in 1839) that "the prejudice of the Christian against the Jew in Jerusalem amounts to a fanaticism..."[19] The Sephardim living in Jerusalem warned the Perushim to stay far from the Church of the Holy Sepulchre or risk loss of limb or life. This was not an easy task because it was difficult to navigate the narrow, winding streets of Jerusalem without losing one's sense of direction.[20] Not only did the Christians express animosity toward the Jews, but they were "all hating each other sincerely."[21] Informing on Christian rivals in the "spirit of intrigue and cabal" aroused most "painful and revolting" feelings on the part of Christian pilgrims.[22] Long-festering antagonisms, "deep hatred,"[23] and "constant intrigues" between the Western and Eastern churches, and internal conflicts among the Eastern sects, led to verbal and physical assaults by religious groups upon one another. Although these conflicts had little effect on the local population, active intervention by European powers involved in the struggle for Christian holy places magnified minor local issues to major international incidents.

The sparsely populated Muslim quarter was by far the largest section of Jerusalem and contained nearly 50 percent of the town's population—4,000 Muslims,[24] and some Jews and Christians who were tolerated by the majority group.

The Armenian quarter, in the southwest section of town next to Mt. Zion and bordering on the Jewish quarter, was populated by about 500 Armenians. This quarter covered 15 percent of Jerusalem's area, but contained only about 6 percent of its population. Armenians lived in the most spacious and clean area of town, surrounded by a high wall—"a little fortress town"[25]—that signaled their insularity and independence. The "opulent" centerpiece of the Armenians,[26] jutting above the town wall, was the tall white monastery, which was "the largest and most comfortable building of its class in Jerusalem, able to house more than one thousand pilgrims."[27]

The Jewish Quarter of Jerusalem in 1818.

The Citadel, commonly called the Tower of David, is opposite the compound of Christ Church.

Next to the Armenian monastery were lovely, extensive gardens and the Church of St. James, first in affluence and second in size to the Church of the Holy Sepulchre.

Best known to the Perushim was the Jewish quarter, about 27 acres located in the southern part of Jerusalem wedged between the Armenian quarter and the Moroccan section of the Muslim quarter. The Jews who lived there, nearly all of Sephardi origin, constituted 25 percent of the Jerusalem population but lived on only 13 percent of its land, meaning that the Jewish quarter was four to five times more densely packed than the Armenian quarter. Of the four quarters of Jerusalem, the Jewish area was the smallest, most crowded, and most filthy. Obvious to all was the abject squalor of the quarter, the streets strewn with refuse, and the pungent stench of the nearby slaughterhouse.

The center of Jewish spiritual life was the large complex of four interconnecting Sephardi houses of worship named after its most prominent synagogue, Yohanan Ben Zakai, where about one thousand Jews prayed. Nearby was the Beth El synagogue, which served as the place of worship, study hall, and meeting place for mystically inclined Sephardim and Ashkenazim.

Lacking a firman for the establishment of an Ashkenazi synagogue, the Perushim prayed unobtrusively on weekdays in the narrow corridor entrance to the four Sephardi synagogues, not wishing to attract the attention of the authorities. When they lacked the prayer quorum of ten males over 13 years of age required for community prayer, they invited one or two Sephardi males to join their decorous service. On the Sabbath Perushim participated in the Sephardi prayer service in the four unornamented, unimposing, neglected synagogues.

Tourists wrote about the ramshackle synagogues with holes in their leaky roofs, whose dismal appearance was accentuated by their being "built almost underground," as in a basement, about three yards below ground level.[28] Inside the plain synagogues a few places on the walls were not whitewashed, in memory of the destruction of the Temple.

Bordering the Temple Mount was the Wailing Wall. This holiest of Jewish religious sites was an impressive wall of huge stones nearly 60 feet high and 160 feet in length, the only surviving remnant of the retaining wall of the Second Temple destroyed by the Romans in 70 C.E. Before the sun set on Friday afternoon Jewish males, dressed in their finest Sabbath attire, flocked to the Wailing Wall through narrow streets and crooked lanes in the Moroccan section of the Muslim quarter. Standing before the Wailing Wall in a small alleyway less than four yards wide, the Jews, in a "vortex of raging sorrow and lamentation," sobbed, "How long yet, O Lord?"

The Wailing Wall.

Christian tourists noted that "bowed in the dust they may at least weep un-
disturbed over the fallen glory of their race. . . . It was a sad and touching
spectacle. Eighteen centuries of exile and woe have not dulled their hearts'
affections, or deadened their feelings of national devotion."[29]

While in Jerusalem the Perushim learned about the activities of the
Sephardi community and the Istanbul Officials, the functions of the
Sephardi chief rabbi, the relations of Sephardim and Ashkenazim during
the last century, how Jews were employed, what amounts of money were
collected by the kollel from what sources, and how these revenues were
spent.[30]

When the Perushim first came to Jerusalem they found a Sephardi community in great debt and distress. Sephardim bitterly lamented their

> life of sorrow and their years of anguish [caused by officials who] drink
> our blood . . . and we are like a flock without a shepherd . . . one lamb
> amongst many wolves who frighten us from all sides . . . and beat us
> with a stick . . . [in order] to save our lives we are forced to bribe the
> wicked men [for] violence and robbery multiply . . . [31]

The Jewish community borrowed money at usurious rates, and "the debt
weighed us down."[32] In the course of thirteen years (1793–1806) the community's debt of 60,000 piastres had swelled to 300,000 piastres, more than
130 piastres per person. This debt was probably the result of the large ran-
soms extorted by the Muslims during Napoleon's invasion.

The Sephardi community was headed by the grand rabbi, who, at the
start of the nineteenth century, was designated chief rabbi or "the First in
Zion" (the title of the present Sephardi chief rabbi in Israel).[33] During the
last quarter of the eighteenth century the Jerusalem chief rabbi was R. Yom
Tov Algazi, who was succeeded from 1802 to 1806 by R. Mordecai Joseph
Meyuhas, both last seen in this narrative reinforcing the Jerusalem ramparts during Napoleon's invasion of Palestine. From 1806 to 1817 R. Jacob
Moshe Ayish served as chief rabbi, and it was he whom the Perushim met
on their first visits to Jerusalem.

The chief rabbi, titular leader of the Jewish community, was recognized
by the authorities as the representative of all Jews. He might be a member
of the kollel executive committee, but this was not mandatory. Selection of
the chief rabbi, for a life term, was ostensibly determined by local scholars

and the distinguished, wealthy members of the kollel, but in fact the Istanbul Officials chose the candidate, set his plentiful salary, and appointed him head of a study academy (yeshiva).

The functions of the chief rabbi were vaguely defined and were determined by traditional customs, past community practices, and the leadership traits of the incumbent. His authority did not stem from an imperial Turkish decree (that was not issued until 1841) or from a structured, obedient organization; a disciplined hierarchy and an incontrovertible authority were inimical to Jewish tradition. The Jerusalem Jewish community was an open society with many pressure groups lobbying for their own interests, making it impossible to issue orders that were not backed by a community consensus. The supremacy of the chief rabbi was determined by the force of his personality, intellectual powers, spiritual standing, competence of scholarship, and gift of articulating oral and written opinions. Powers vested in the chief rabbi were reinforced by the halo of holiness that hovered above Jerusalem; however, he held no sway over the Sephardi chief rabbis of Tiberias and Safed.

A source of considerable power was the chief rabbi's authority to appoint rabbinical judges and convene court sessions. The chief rabbi appointed nine to twelve judges to sit on three or four rotating rabbinical courts that dealt with a great variety of cases, including marriage and divorce, inheritance, legal contracts, and business matters.[34] A High Court of seven judges was assembled by its chief justice, the chief rabbi, to adjudicate the most precedent-setting questions of Jewish law, to legislate special regulations for the community, and to impose discipline on contentious groups. Court decisions were recognized by the authorities as legally binding on all Jerusalem Jews. Ashkenazim were not empowered to establish their own judiciary during the first half of the nineteenth century.

The most distinctive feature of the eighteenth- and early-nineteenth-century Jerusalem community was the dominating influence of the Istanbul Officials.[35] They had saved the community from extinction but had also stifled local initiative and thwarted the emergence of an indigenous leadership. Istanbul Officials intervened in Jerusalem kehilla affairs, dictated the appointments of community officials and the chief rabbi, invoked rules regulating Jewish life, and controlled the collection and distribution of funds.

The unstable, shifting Sephardi population and the interminable squabbles between competing Jerusalem factions also contributed to the weakness and dependency of the Jerusalem kehilla,[36] which lacked a commanding spiritual presence and an outstanding community leader at the beginning of the nineteenth century. The kehilla hardly governed its own affairs and exerted no influence over Jewish communities in the Diaspora, or even in Eretz Israel, with the exception of nearby Hebron.

Another distinctive characteristic of the Jerusalem Jewish community, in contrast to those of Safed and Tiberias, was the sporadic sharp clashes between the Sephardim and the 50 to 100 Ashkenazim. From the early eighteenth century until well past the start of the nineteenth, Ashkenazim vehemently disagreed with Sephardim about the collection and distribution of funds and demanded to receive all donations contributed by Ashkenazim in Europe.

> If an Ashkenazi approaches his Sephardi brother and pleads with him for sustenance, asking for a contribution from one of the Sephardi yeshivot or from the kollel, the Sephardi answers: Turn to the rich European Jews, for what do we have in common with you Ashkenazim? And he is told: You send shlihim to Europe and collect large amounts of money. And you also send fund collection letters to all European cities. . . . All this we [Ashkenazim] deny: from time immemorial there never was such a thing and the poor Ashkenazi leaves the Sephardi in despair and in tears.[37]

Sephardim, on their part, disapproved of Ashkenazi collection campaigns in Europe, claiming that their community responsibilities entitled them to collect money from all Diaspora Jews because

> if, God forbid, Sephardim were not present in the city, the Ashkenazim would not be able to exist. . . . The Sephardi scholars [in Jerusalem] give their share of the donations collected for the Sephardi Talmudical academies to the Ashkenazi scholars . . . and the destitute among the Ashkenazim are cared for by the communal chest together with the poor among the Sephardim, as known to everyone visiting our city. . . . [The Ashkenazim] study in the talmudical academies of the Sephardim; they pray in the synagogues of the Sephardim; and their children study in the Talmud Torahs of the Sephardim. . . .[38]

Peace was temporarily established based on an authoritative Ashkenazi rabbinical opinion that had been written in 1771. According to this accord Sephardim could collect money in Europe on condition that they supported the small Ashkenazi community in Eretz Israel.[39] Despite this agreement

Europeans were periodically pressed to organize separate collection campaigns for the Ashkenazim in Eretz Israel, who complained well into the nineteenth century that the Sephardim financially discriminated against them.

The Sephardim whom the Perushim encountered in Jerusalem in 1812–1815 may be divided into five major groups: scholars; artisans and craftsmen; traders, shopkeepers, and professionals; affluent individuals; and the indigent.

The following general profile of the community's occupational and economic structure includes a gross estimate of the number of Jews in each group.[40] In the absence of substantiating statistics a broad overview, allowing for a large margin of error, must suffice.

Scholars in the Sephardi society of Jerusalem carried on the Jewish tradition of erudition by meditating on "His law...day and night" (Psalms 1:2). They belonged to an elite, academic aristocracy of professions that today we would call professors, judges and lawyers, writers and researchers, theologians and philosophers. Although the scholar subjected himself to the rigorous discipline of a caste, he was not isolated from the activities of the Jewish community and sometimes served as a member of the kollel's executive committee.

Scholars studied in yeshivot, institutions of higher learning intended for adult scholars, not for children. In one typical yeshiva, nine out of ten tenured scholars ranged in age from 30 to 60, with a few fledgling scholars in their teens and twenties. Large yeshivot supplied teachers for Talmud-Torah schools of intermediate learning levels, which they maintained in order to identify young scholars and recruit the most promising talent.

As in all academic institutions, titles of rank distinguished among scholars. At one yeshiva each of the ten scholars "held a different scholastic rank." The "head" of the yeshiva was followed by the "sage" and then by "masters" of the Torah. About half the scholars strove to attain the title of master. Scholars were selected and promoted by the head of the yeshiva and the sages, based upon erudition and purity of behavior, but there were instances of scholarly positions passing in inheritance from father to son.

At the start of the nineteenth century about 180 scholars studied in some dozen yeshivot in Jerusalem,[41] ranging from academies with about twenty-five scholars to others with ten or fewer scholars. There also were three yeshivot for propertied and working men who studied on a part-time basis.

Members of scholar families constituted about 32 percent of the Jerusalem population and numbered 720, based on the substantiated assumption of 4 persons in each of the 180 scholar families.

Jerusalem yeshivot were well endowed by wealthy overseas benefactors and affluent Jerusalem residents. In return for a permanent monthly allowance, rich Jerusalemites made "living bequests"—investing large sums of money in yeshivot and willing this capital to the yeshivot upon their death. Thus, by virtue of their considerable endowments, many Jerusalem yeshivot were powerful financial institutions and supported their scholars in a handsome fashion. This was one reason for the great concentration of yeshivot in Jerusalem, verily "the largest theological seminary in the world."[42] A more spiritual reason was that the greater the number of yeshivot and scholars in Jerusalem, the more intensive would be the study of Torah, which would accelerate the Redemption of the Jewish people.

Not only did the achievements of the scholar secure personal honor and prestige, but his preeminent status was recognized in the form of substantial financial rewards: haluka payments, a yeshiva fellowship, and a special Scholars Fund that was replenished each year by 10 percent of the money collected overseas.[43] This special fund totaled about 6,000 piastres a year. Each of the 180 scholars received an average of 30–35 piastres, a tidy sum in the days when 100 piastres sustained one person and 150 piastres supported a couple on a tolerable level for one year. Exceptionally prestigious scholars received additional stipends from an individual benefactor of a Jewish community in the Diaspora. The fellowship of one head of a yeshiva was 200 piastres a year;[44] other stipends were 100 piastres for the sage, and from 80 to 50 piastres for the next eight scholars; three students received 34, 30, and 28 piastres. The beadle of the yeshiva earned 40 piastres. In 1839 the annual fellowship granted to a scholar was estimated at 100–150 piastres.

Renowned scholars enrolled in more than one yeshiva, lending it their academic reputation in exchange for an additional income, so "that they might support themselves appropriately."[45] A distinguished scholar was frequently offered the lucrative post of shaliah (emissary), which permitted him to travel and achieve fame by publishing scholarly tracts. The job of shaliah also enabled the scholar to raise money for his yeshiva and collect money for his own personal use. Not infrequently the scholar-shaliah was offered a position as rabbi in a Diaspora Jewish community. Therefore, one purpose of the munificent benefits granted prized scholars was to prevent their leaving Eretz Israel for the generous financial blandishments proffered in the Diaspora. Another economic reward enjoyed by scholars was a tax-exempt status, indicating both the community's respect for the scholar

TABLE 3 Jewish Artisans and Manual Workers in Jerusalem in 1806

Coppersmiths and solderers (probably goldsmiths and silversmiths)	5
Tinsmiths	2 or 3
Coffee processors (probably grinders and millers)	2
Butchers	10
Painters	2
Tailors	10
Flax and cotton cordmakers (weavers?)	2
Ritual slaughterers	10
TOTAL	43–44

and his powerful position in the kollel organization.

It has been estimated that the Jerusalem scholar in the eighteenth century earned, from his varied sources of income, at least double the income of a person in the propertied category.[46] Although the 1839 comment that "the yeshivot are not seats of learning; they are rather situations of emolument" may be somewhat exaggerated,[47] there is little doubt that the work of studying provided the scholar with an ample income compared to other Jerusalemites.

The second group in the Jewish community was composed of artisans, craftsmen, butchers, and ritual slaughterers who earned their living by working with their hands. Because most Jews were poor and could afford only the bare necessities, there were limited employment opportunities in Jerusalem for artisans and craftsmen. As late as the 1850s a British traveler observed that "a trade is useless where there is no employment. The Jews are too poor to employ each other."[48]

A reliable German explorer, Ulrich Seetzen, reported in 1806 on 43–44 Jerusalem artisans and manual workers (see table 3).[49]

The large number of butchers (10) and ritual slaughterers (10) is quite unusual in a community that ate some chicken but little meat. From this list of artisans and craftsmen we learn that no Jews worked in the building trades; that there were no Jewish glaziers, upholsterers, tanners, or candlemakers; and that there still was no Hebrew press employing printers, typesetters, or bookbinders. We also have no record of Jewish farmers.[50] To Seetzen's list we must add about 20 artisans performing essential services such as cobblers, morticians and tombstone engravers, bakers, watchmen, and porters. Based on Seetzen's figures and omissions, we may conclude that

TABLE 4 Commercial Pursuits of Jerusalem Jews in 1806

Storekeepers (spices)	10
Storekeepers (sugar, tobacco, etc.)	10
Dealers in sweets, vegetables, etc.	20
Cloth merchants	10
Secondhand dealers	5
Sulphur, thread, and needle dealers	3
Thread and silk dealers	2
TOTAL	60

there were about 60 to 65 artisans and craftsmen whose families totaled 240–260 persons or 11 percent of the Jews living in Jerusalem.

The next occupational group included shopkeepers, tradesmen, and professionals. A Trappist monk wrote in 1832 that "there are Jews of all trades; of all professions." Seetzen recorded that 60 men engaged in a variety of commercial pursuits (see table 4).[51]

Some of the 20 Sephardi storekeepers may have continued the eighteenth-century practice of maintaining partnerships with Muslims, to prevent being looted. Numerous references by Ashkenazi Jews attest to the lack of commercial possibilities in Eretz Israel, particularly for Ashkenazim who spoke no Arabic.

Professionals listed by Seetzen were 3 "doctors" and 5 teachers—5 teachers appears far too few for a population of 2,250 that must have included at least several hundred boys up to the bar mitzva age of 13.

Sick Jews were treated by 3 paramedical doctors practicing a "mystic craft" that combined prescribing herbs, mixing ointments, applying leeches, pulling teeth, expelling evil spirits, counseling patients, and predicting their future.[52] Such folk medicine was engaged in by no less a personage than Chief Rabbi Meyuhas, who "practiced medicine" by enveloping folk wisdom and magic remedies in the garment of religious sanctity.[53] Since sickness was willed by nonhuman power, it could only be spirited away by prayers and magic that depended on the divine will. Doctors prescribed purges, bleedings, and enemas that may have killed more patients than they cured, in a time when it was statistically safer to stay away from a doctor. Other physicians were healers who cured illnesses by conjuring up protective incantations, supplying talismans and magic amulets, praying for miracles, and chasing away the "evil eye."

Missing from Seetzen's list are tradesmen such as vendors, peddlers, and the "professions" of scribes or Torah scroll-writers, cantors, and beadles. Based on Seetzen's figure of 68 professionals, tradesmen, doctors, and teachers—and his omissions—we may estimate that there were 90 to 95 Jewish tradesmen and professionals and 360–380 members in their families.

The fourth group in the Jerusalem Jewish community was composed of well-to-do merchants, men of property, moneylenders,[54] and Jews who lived off an income from their investments in Eretz Israel and overseas. A few well-to-do Jews traded locally, but hardly any Jews engaged in foreign trade, which was controlled by Armenians and Greek Catholics. Some Jews of substance were "bankers," lending money to Jews and Christians.

Numerous affluent Jews loaned their capital to the kollel and in return were guaranteed a fixed income for the rest of their lives. But many Jews with capital preferred to invest it with Gentiles, who paid a higher rate of interest. Most important, loans to Gentiles were usually more secure than loans to Jews because the kollel could unilaterally suspend debt payments to Jewish creditors until interest and loans had been paid to Gentile money-lenders, "those villains" who threatened harsh penalties and physical punishment.

About 10 percent of the Jerusalem Jewish population—225 persons— were in the "rich" category. This figure is based on the difference between 45 percent of the Jews who "did not require [financial] support,"[55] and 35 percent of the Jews who were "totally self-supporting" artisans, tradesmen, and professionals. The somewhat high number of affluent Jewish families living in the poor Jewish kehilla is not surprising considering that wealthy Jews were encouraged to settle in Eretz Israel by the Sephardim, the Istanbul Officials, the Hasidim, and the Perushim. Another indication that there were a certain number of wealthy people in Jerusalem is provided by the community regulation warning Jews not to wear jewelry and ostentatious clothes in public. One tourist reported that an old Jew built a home costing "upwards of 600 sterling" or 60,000 piastres.[56] Other tourists told that "many of the Jews are rich and in comfortable circumstances; and possess a good deal of property in Jerusalem; but they are careful to conceal their wealth and even their comfort from the jealous eye of their rulers . . ."[57]

The fifth group of Jerusalem Jews were the poor—people unable to earn a subsistence living because of their age, infirmity, and lack of work skills and also because of the country's primitive economic condition. Many of the destitute were paupers completely dependent on the modest haluka allocations distributed by the community. Other poor people received small sums of money from overseas relatives.[58] Nearly 700, or 30 percent, of Jeru-

TABLE 5 Population of the Jerusalem Jewish Community, 1812–1815

	NO. OF HEADS OF FAMILIES*	NO. OF PERSONS	% OF TOTAL POPULATION
Scholars	180	720	32
Artisans and craftsmen	60–65	240–260	11–12
Tradesmen, shopkeepers, and professionals	90–95	360–380	16–17
Affluent	55	225	10
Poor, old, sick, and unable to work	330–350	665–705	29–31

*Based on four persons per family with the exception of the "elderly-poor," calculated on two persons per family.

salem's Jews were impoverished and completely or partially dependent on the community for haluka. This figure is obtained simply by subtracting the number of persons in the first four categories already described from the total number of 2,250 Jews living in Jerusalem.

These 700 poor people received from the kollel about the same amount of haluka as the 720 members in the families of scholars. What appears to be an equitable distribution of money on a per capita basis may in fact have been quite unfair, because of possible differences in the size of families. It was the family that was the basic economic unit for determining haluka, so the number of members in the family had a marginal rather than a determining effect on the subsistence level of the family.

The 720 members in the scholar group belonged to 180 families, on the assumption that a family had an average of 4 members. In contrast, many of the poor people belonged to family units of 2 persons—husband and wife—because they were elderly, and their children had grown up and left home. If 2-member families prevailed among the poor, and 4-member families among the scholars, the 180 scholar families were receiving about the same total amount of haluka funds as the 330–350 poor families. This probably unequal distribution of haluka money was one more sign that the Jewish community intended to support an oligarchy of scholars in the Holy Land, rather than establish an egalitarian society.

The population of the Jerusalem Jewish community in 1812–1815 is shown in table 5.

From this table it is obvious that the majority of the 2,250 Sephardi

Jews—scholars, old, and indigent—lived off contributions donated by Diaspora Jews. Three out of ten Jews belonged to the scholars group, and another three out of ten could not support themselves. One out of ten Jews was rich, while the remaining three out of ten belonged to the families of gainfully employed artisans and craftsmen, tradesmen, and professionals. Out of the slightly more than 200 heads of families earning their living from work and investments, more than 25 were employed in "religious" jobs as teachers, ritual slaughterers, and beadles.

Where did the Jerusalem kollel obtain funds and how much did it collect? How much money did it spend, and on what? Figures for estimated income and expenditures of the kollel, like those for occupational and economic groups, are order-of-magnitude numbers that paint a rough picture portraying the composition, activities, and internal operations of the Jewish community of Jerusalem in 1812–1815.

The Jerusalem kollel levied a great variety of taxes and fees on its members. Its major sources of income were overseas donations, inheritance and income taxes, excise tariffs on consumption commodities such as meat, one-time lump-sum tax payments, burial and other fees, the poll tax, and investment of Jewish capital in the kollel. Many tariffs and fees were legally sanctioned in detailed community regulations. These multiple taxes led to the accusation that the kollel burdened Jews with crippling taxes and payments that impoverished the whole Jewish kehilla.[59]

The total estimated income of the Jerusalem kollel was about 170,000 piastres, from the revenue sources shown in table 6.

The major source of income for the Sephardi community was money collected overseas by shlihim traveling to the farthest corners of the world where Ashkenazi and Sephardi Jews lived. These emissaries were sent by the Jerusalem kollel under the auspices and supervision of the Istanbul Officials.[60] A good emissary annually collected about 25,000 piastres;[61] half this money went to the kollel, and the other half covered his expenses and salary. Four Jerusalem shlihim were simultaneously collecting money in the four areas of the world where Diaspora Jews lived—Europe, North Africa, Asia, and other countries in the Turkish Empire. Their gross income totaled 100,000 piastres, which netted the Jerusalem kollel 50,000 piastres. In addition, the Jerusalem kollel received 40 percent of the money collected in Western Europe by PEKAM, a small, unknown sum that we may estimate at 5,000 piastres.

(Revenues and expenses are usually extrapolated from 1855–1856

TABLE 6 Revenue Sources of the Jerusalem Kollel, 1812–1815

Overseas donations collected by emissaries and PEKAM	55,000
Inheritance tax	25,000
Income tax	10,000
Burial plots and tombstones	10,000
Burial fees	12,500
Meat and luxury taxes	15,000
Miscellaneous taxes	10,000
Capital invested in kollel by Jews	30,000
Poll tax	2,500
TOTAL	170,000 piastres

figures by assuming that 1812–1815 financial figures are 50 percent of those for 1855–56.[62] Although the rate of inflation from 1812 to 1856 far exceeded 50 percent, the Jews may not have been financially affected by inflation and the increased cost of living because a significant part of their income came from overseas in the form of foreign currency that was cashed into frequently devalued local currency. Moreover, by 1856 some payments extorted from the Jewish community in 1812 had been abolished. For these two reasons figures may be somewhat biased in the direction of underestimating revenues and overestimating expenses.)

The second largest source of income for the Jerusalem kollel was the inheritance tax,[63] which produced an estimated 25,000 piastres (half the reported income in 1855), because of the advanced age of many residents, the high mortality rate, and the fact that many Jews had no legal inheritors living in Eretz Israel. One Jew quipped that "income from the dead exceeds income from the living." Inheritance regulations stipulated that when a Jew living in Eretz Israel died without a legal heir residing in the country, he automatically bequeathed his money and property to the Sephardi kollel. If the kollel did not collect the inheritance, the Turkish authorities could confiscate such funds, thereby depriving the Jewish community of vitally needed financial resources. The overriding purpose of supporting the Jews in Eretz Israel took precedence over legal inheritors living in the Diaspora. In order to prevent tax evasion, a will was binding only if it was drafted and signed in the presence of authorized rabbis and leaders of the kollel.

So strict was the inheritance regulation that only in 1810 was the surviving husband in Eretz Israel recognized as the legal ineritor of his wife, and he was entitled to only half of the legacy, with the other 50 percent going to the kollel. Even when the wife and other heirs living in Jerusalem inherited the deceased's property, the kollel derived a considerable income from the inheritance tax of about 10 percent. A legal inheritor was taxed on "all his assets—whether in the country or abroad—in silver, gold, gems, pearls, and all manner of merchandise and landholdings."[64] Only books were tax-exempt. An additional 3.33 percent inheritance tax was sometimes levied "to help cover the debts of the kollel." To facilitate tax collection among widows, an 1800 regulation provided that "a widow must show the 'kolelut' of the Holy City of Jerusalem everything in her possession, from thread to shoelace." A widow about to remarry was taxed 20 percent of her dowry, "the reason in principle being that since she had no heir here . . . her legacy would have passed to the kollel of the Holy City." If the widow married a third time, she again paid to the kollel a percentage of her dowry.[65]

Inheritance regulations caused friction between longtime settlers and new arrivals. Old-timers had no alternative but to follow the inheritance regulations and pay up, while some wealthy new settlers left their money abroad, out of reach of the community. It was even claimed that the inheritance regulation dissuaded some rich Jews from settling in Eretz Israel.[66]

An income tax of 5 to 10 percent was levied by the kollel on Jews with an income above the subsistence level of 100 piastres per year.[67] Widows coming from overseas paid 5 percent on their income of 100–200 piastres and 8 percent on annual income above 200 piastres. But "if her income is less than 100 piastres, not even one small piastre should be taken from her."[68] The tax on income received from abroad or "from within the city" produced minimal revenues because the majority of the Jews lived on the edge of subsistence and scholars were exempt from paying the income tax. Widows also were "granted income tax deductions in view of the fact that the kollel was the beneficiary on their decease."[69] Affluent merchants, landlords, and property owners believed that the income tax discriminated against them and sought ways to avoid payment of this tax. Their opposition led to the abolishment of the income tax before 1855. Lacking documentation, we may arbitrarily estimate that the income tax raised about 10,000 piastres for the kollel.

Sale of burial plots and tombstones in the Mount of Olives cemetery netted the community about 10,000 piastres (half the income for the years 1855 and 1856).[70] Burial fees, which brought in about 12,500 piastres (50 percent of the 1855 revenues), were fixed after a "compromise" was negotiated with the inheritors about payment of the deceased's debts to the kollel. If the deceased left no capital from which the kollel could collect the 10 percent inheritance tax, his heirs paid a burial fee equivalent to the amount that had sustained the deceased for one year. Scholars paid a burial fee of only 3 to 5 percent of their annual income plus the burial tax remitted to the authorities.

A miscellany of kollel regulations legislated burial fees for widows, childless women, orphans, and children.[71] Poor people paid a burial fee of 30 piastres to the kollel plus the burial tax due to Turkish authorities. Some immigrants paid the burial fee to the Istanbul Officials before they settled in Jerusalem. Although the wealthy paid a high, progressive burial tax, the total income generated probably just covered the funeral costs of the Burial Society and the burial tax of the authorities.

Members of the Burial Society were called in immediately upon the death of a Jew. As representatives of the kollel, they expeditiously sealed off the assets of the deceased to prevent the loss of inheritance payments. Disagreements between the family of the deceased and the kollel over unpaid debts, the payment of the inheritance tax, and the burial fee could delay the funeral. Since Jewish custom dictated the burial of the body within 24 hours after death, the bereaved family could be pressured into complying with the financial demands of the kollel. Such incidents, showing the strength and style of the kollel, may have been few, but they magnified the potential power wielded by the kollel over the lives of the Jews.

The Jerusalem kehilla, like Jewish communities in Eastern Europe and Turkey, levied a gabella tax on the purchase of luxury items such as tombstones, meat, wine, certain foods, and merchandise.[72] Scholars were sometimes exempted from paying this nonprogressive tax, which netted the kollel about 15,000 piastres a year. The most conspicuous and remunerative gabella tax was that levied on meat. Based on an old firman the Sephardi chief rabbi licensed the ten Jerusalem ritual slaughterers, who thereby secured a monopoly over the kosher meat eaten by Jews. In return for their licenses, the ritual slaughterers paid into the kollel treasury annual fees of about 10,000 piastres.

By common agreement with the Muslims, after the authorized ritual slaughterer killed a lamb, cow, or goat, the animal was examined in the presence of Muslims. Then Jews bought the kosher parts of the animal and Muslims purchased the nonkosher pieces that Jews were forbidden to eat. Muslims consented to this arrangement only if the ritual slaughterer was certified by the chief rabbi as a true Jewish descendant "from the seed of Abraham, Isaac, and Jacob" and a believer in one God. This concord between Jews and Muslims served the common interests of both groups by preventing wastage and keeping the price of meat low. Nevertheless, the gabella tax raised the price of kosher meat about 25 percent, placing meat in the luxury category and out of reach of poor Jews, who could hardly afford to buy poultry once a week for the Sabbath meals.

In addition to the two major sources of income of the Sephardi kollel—the emissaries and the inheritance tax—and the income tax, burial fee, and gabella tax, there were large numbers of miscellaneous taxes that produced an annual income arbitrarily estimated at 10,000 piastres.

A well-to-do Jerusalem settler who came to live off his overseas capital was taxed a one-time payment equivalent to his annual income and then was exempt all his life, or for ten years, from paying other annual taxes, except the poll tax.[73] This was an effective tax collection method, for many new settlers were well advanced in age and would not live many more years. Such large, lump-sum tax payments helped improve the normally distressful situation of the kollel treasury. Often the Istanbul Officials collected the one-time payment from prospective settlers, guaranteed their tax exemptions, invested the money, and periodically sent interest payments to Eretz Israel.

When Jews left Eretz Israel they were taxed 6 percent of their assets, as indemnity for the loss of future revenues. In the words of an 1801 regulation, "the person is obliged to show clearly, how much property and money he has . . . in Eretz Israel and abroad . . . or he must swear a solemn oath about all the assets he has in the world . . ."[74]

Other taxes included:

—Upon betrothal the prospective bride paid half a percent of her dowry.[75] When the couple married, the bridegroom paid another 1 percent of the dowry.

—A Jew selling property paid the kollel half a percent of the purchase price, while the buyer was taxed 1 percent. If the Jew sold his property to a Muslim or Christian he was penalized by paying a 2 percent tax.

—A 3 percent tax on imports and exports paid by Jewish merchants in the eighteenth century may still have been in force in the early nineteenth century.

The sale of the privilege to perform religious functions in the synagogue ceremony and the fines levied by the rabbinical courts were a small source of income.

Affluent settlers provided the kollel with a large source of income. Some rich Jews loaned money to the kollel treasury in return for an annual stipend based on the prevalent 7 to 10 percent interest rate,[76] which could reach

TABLE 7 Major Types of Disbursements of the Sephardi Kollel, 1812–1815

Poll tax, protection money, and "gifts"	35,000
Maintaining the poor and scholars	50,000
Operating expenses of the kollel	at least 10,000
Interest and debt payments to Muslims (60,000) and to Jews (27,000)	87,000
TOTAL	182,000 piastres

15 percent. It is estimated that at the beginning of the nineteenth century Jews invested in the kollel 300,000 piastres (half the sum invested in 1855).

The kollel of Jerusalem was responsible for remitting to the Turkish authorities the poll tax levied on each adult male over 15 years of age. At the beginning of the nineteenth century the poll tax is estimated at 6 piastres per adult male (50 percent of the 1853 poll tax). If all adult male Jews paid 6 piastres in 1812–1815, the kollel would have collected 5,400 piastres, based on 900 adult males in the Jewish Jerusalem population of 2,250. However, it is estimated that only half the adult men paid the poll tax; the destitute could not afford to pay the tax, while scholars claimed exemption, basing their case on a "Torah Judgment." This led the Istanbul Officials to remark cryptically that "if we go according to the Torah Judgment we will not be able to maintain Jerusalem . . . because the Muslims and the Pasha do not know what a Torah Judgment is."[77]

Due to the large number of poor and tax-exempt people, the kollel had to pay a good part of the poll tax out of its own treasury, transforming it from a levy on individuals to a community-assumed tax burden. The kollel negotiated with the authorities on the amount to be paid, doing its utmost to keep the number of Jews in the community a secret.

The estimated 170,000 piastres that flowed into the coffers of the Sephardi kollel in Jerusalem were channeled into the general fund, which supported four major types of disbursements (see table 7).

Jerusalem Jews realized that "basically, our settling in town depends on them,"[78] meaning the Muslims. In order to buy the goodwill of government authorities, Muslim notables, and neighboring villagers, Jews disgorged large sums of money for general protection and for specific services. In effect there was no boundary separating tax payments from compulsory gifts, government fees, and bribery. Like other minority groups in the Ottoman Empire, the Jewish community paid tributes on special occasions such as the appointment of a new town governor. In 1824 an American missionary described how this tax was paid by one minority group in Jerusalem.

> This is the fifth Governor who has had command of the city since my first visit there a year ago. Every new Governor receives a visit from the chiefs of the principal convents with a present of money, I believe 500 piastres, for each convent. Then he returns the visit and receives a similar sum. This is one out of many occasions on which the convents are obliged to make presents, besides paying fixed sums monthly and annually to the Governor, to the Judge, and to a great number of chiefs and principal men.[79]

Other exactions paid to the governor and his retinue were gifts of honey, sugar, velvet, and money to commemorate religious holidays, family festivities, and birthdays, wood, wool, and burial taxes.

In 1821 the Sephardim and the Perushim were forced to pay 156,000 piastres to the visiting pasha,[80] and in 1827 the Jerusalem community was forced to "reward" the new pasha of Damascus with 100,000 piastres. Where the kehilla collected such massive amounts of money is not known (and not included in the list of revenues and expenditures). One may speculate that major sources of funds were emergency contributions from the Istanbul Officials and local Jews, as well as loans borrowed at high interest rates.

Other "gifts" were recurring items. Villagers of Silwan were paid about 10,000 piastres "for guarding, or rather for not injuring," the Jewish tombstones in the cemetery,[81] and for permitting Jewish funerals to pass unmolested to the cemetery on the Mount of Olives. The kollel also had to bribe the Jerusalem governor and other functionaries to permit the burying of Jewish dead in that cemetery. Muslims living in the Moroccan section received money to allow Jews access to the Wailing Wall and to prevent disturbances during the Jewish prayer service. The Abu-Ghosh clan collected passage rights from Jews traveling on the Jaffa to Jerusalem road: 7 piastres per person plus 2 piastres for baggage. Residents of Bethlehem were paid to permit Jews to enter Rachel's Tomb. Jews also paid a poll tax of about 5,000 piastres and protection "presents" amounting to about 30,000 piastres (half the sum paid in 1855).

Fulfilling its function as "one large charity organization,"[82] the Sephardi

The Damascus Gate.

community maintained the scholars and prevented poor Jews from starving. Scholars and the indigent received from the kollel an estimated 50,000 piastres (slightly more than half of the 93,000 piastres distributed to them in 1855).

Supplementing the general community fund were numerous special-purpose funds to help scholars, the sick, orphans, and Jews badly in need of loans.[83] When a special fund ran dry, its deficits were covered by the general fund. The special funds provided the poor, aged, infirm, orphans, and widows with clothing and food for the Sabbath and Jewish festivals; gave a small dowry to poor or orphaned girls; and defrayed the burial costs of the indigent.[84] A Food and Coals Fund that provided the most needy with money for food at Passover time and coal to heat their homes was maintained by taxing 2.5 percent of the income of Jerusalemites living off overseas capital. The income of a Sick Fund that paid for medical care and drugs came from a death tax (not to be confused with the burial tax) that in 1843 was levied on inheritors, at the rate of 40 piastres for a rich man, 25 piastres for a person of average income, and no less than 12 piastres for a poor person.

An Orphans Fund provided food, clothing, and a dowry to female orphans from income received by selling the clothing of deceased persons.[85] A special Scholars Fund distributed monies before the Passover and Shavuot (Pentecost) festivals, and helped scholars pay the dowry needed to marry off their daughters. The Scholars Fund was replenished each year by donations from the affluent and by earmarking 10 percent of the 50,000 piastres collected overseas by shlihim and 10 percent of the funds contributed by overseas benefactors as endowments in memory of deceased members of their family.

Providing for the poor was practiced according to the Jewish tradition that conceived of charity as justice and welfare payments as a community obligation. The philanthropic ideals of the Torah set the social tone of the Jewish community, despite occasional deviations.

The third category of expenditures was the operating expenses of the kollel:[86] the salaries of the chief rabbi, tax collectors, ritual slaughterers, and other community functionaries, and the cost of maintaining public institutions such as the synagogue. Operating expenses are estimated at 10,000 (half the 20,000 piastres spent in 1855). Certain operating expenses, such as the repair of synagogues, may have been financed directly by overseas donors rather than being routed through the kollel treasury, yet this hardly explains such a low expenditure. One authoritative source claims that community and "municipal" expenses consumed one-third of the operational funds,[87] which is at least 35,000 piastres, a far cry from our figure of 10,000 piastres. We can only conclude that operating expenses exceeded 10,000 piastres, but by how much we do not know.

By far the largest expense item in the kollel budget was annual interest payments to both Muslim and Jewish creditors; they amounted to about 87,000 piastres. Debt repayment was the major financial burden on the Jerusalem Jewish community from the 1770s or earlier until well past the middle of the nineteenth century.[88] Estimates are that in 1812–1815 the kollel must have paid Muslim creditors about 60,000 piastres a year, based on a 20 percent interest rate on the debt of 300,000 piastres.[89] The kollel also paid interest of 9 percent on another 300,000 piastres invested by rich Jews (27,000 piastres calculated on a 9 percent interest rate). Efforts to earmark certain taxes such as the burial tax for paying off part of the 600,000-piastre community debt proved unsuccessful.

When the community could not service its annual debt payments, let alone repay part of the loan, additional funds were borrowed, the total debt increased, and the following years' interest payments spiraled ever higher. This explains why the kollel debt to the Muslims rose to 480,000 piastres in 1830–1835,[90] and rocketed to 1.1 million piastres in 1855, at which time the community also owed Jews 600,000 piastres.

The annual income of the Sephardi kollel in Jerusalem is estimated at 170,000 piastres, compared to expenditures of more than 182,000 piastres. The deficit of at least 12,000 piastres appears relatively small and may have been higher, because we may have underestimated the 10,000 piastres for operating expenses. This deficit may have been partially offset by donations from Jewish pilgrims and by income from rental of kollel property in and outside of Jerusalem; we know about such income in 1855. Yet a deficit of 12,000 piastres out of expenditures of 182,000 piastres begs credibility and appears extremely small when compared to kollel deficits of 10,000, 17,800, and 12,000 as early as 1755, 1756, and 1760, out of budgets of 40,000 in 1755 and of 26,500 in 1760.[91]

Other limitations of our gross figures are that they exclude one-time huge extortionist payments and special-purpose funds not channeled into the kollel treasury. Also, the kollel was not the sole collection and disbursement organization for Jerusalem Jews. To further complicate this unclear financial picture, the Sephardi kollel lost an unknown amount of revenues when the Istanbul Officials collected monies from some immigrants and then exempted them from paying certain community taxes in Jerusalem. Despite such serious qualifications about approximations that cannot be verified by nonexistent records, these rough numbers most generally sketch the economic situation of Jerusalem's Jews in 1812–1815.

Income and expenditure figures show the Jerusalem kollel to have been a large philanthropic and welfare organization as well as a powerful financial institution that actively raised substantial sums of money in Jerusalem and overseas.

It has been assumed that the Jews of Jerusalem (and Eretz Israel) were predominantly supported by the largess of overseas Jewry. Figures for estimated income do not support this assumption: Diaspora Jewry annually contributed only about one-third of the total kollel income of 170,000 piastres. Even considering the substantial but unknown sums donated by Diaspora Jews for yeshiva endowments, specially earmarked projects, and one-time extortionist payments, Jerusalem Jews still contributed about half of the kollel revenues. These revenues were generated by imposing on the local population a severe and heavy tax burden "rarely encountered in Diaspora kehillot."[92]

More than six out of ten Jews in Jerusalem received complete or partial economic support. A community that financially supports over 60 percent of its population and heavily taxes the self-supporting minority must come under constant, fierce pressure when deciding who should pay how much tax money and to whom to distribute these and other community funds. By lightening the tax burden of one group or by distributing more money to scholars or poor people, the delicate balance of daily sustenance is disturbed. Under such circumstances each group found it absolutely imperative to battle for financial decisions that would be to its advantage. Such a stressful situation understandably unleashed prejudices, passions, and unseemly contentiousness among the partisan groups in Jerusalem. It also united the scholars, the poor, the propertied, and the rich in their effort to deter poor Jews from settling in Eretz Israel. Inevitably, the introduction of a forceful new interest group, like the Perushim, would upset the community's status quo by changing time-honored practices and subverting traditional agreements.

SIX

Friction and Factionalism

1815–1825

At the end of October 1814, when the plague appeared to have subsided in Galilee, the 71 Perushim who had fled Safed returned to that town. On leaving Jerusalem, R. Menahem Mendel signed a note promising that the Perushim would repay the money the Sephardim had spent on them. He and his group did not wish to be economically obligated and dependent on the patronage of the debt-ridden Sephardi community.

The Perushim heatedly discussed the possibility of relocating to Jerusalem, or at least permanently settling some members of the group there. R. Menahem Mendel advocated putting down Perushim roots in Jerusalem, as their venerable ideological sage, the Vilna gaon, had preached, and interpreted the plague in Galilee as divine retribution for the Perushim's neglect of Jerusalem. He was opposed by R. Israel, who presented ideological, Messianic, and financial reasons for remaining in Safed.[1] As the Perushim fundraiser, R. Israel feared that a Jerusalem settlement would drain the group's already strained treasury and might lead to a financial fate similar to that of the followers of R. Judah HeHasid. Unable to resolve this basic difference of opinion, the Perushim sought a decision from the Vilna Rabbis, who ruled that "the main part of the kollel should be based in the holy mountains of Safed,"[2] but that a limited number of Perushim could move to

Jerusalem after receiving the approval of the Safed leaders.

Twenty Safed Perushim led by R. Menahem Mendel settled permanently in Jerusalem in October 1815,[3] joining a few Perushim such as Shlomo Zalman Zoref and Hillel Rivlin who had made Jerusalem their home a year or two before. R. Menahem Mendel remained the leader of the united kollel for all Perushim in Eretz Israel, while the Safed community was placed in the dynamic charge of R. Israel.

The story of the first Perushim settlement in Jerusalem is "enveloped in fog,"[4] despite the tidy tendency of the Perushim to document their activities. They maintained silence about their intention of settling in Jerusalem in order to prevent negative reactions from the town authorities, the Muslims and Sephardim of Jerusalem, and Haim Farhi. Both Farhi and the Sephardim believed that Ashkenazim should remain in the Galilee rather than upset the Jerusalem status quo by increasing the Jewish population and altering its composition. Sephardim in Jerusalem feared that Muslims would clamor for repayment of the 1720 debt of R. Judah HeHasid's group, that the poll tax would be raised, and that new taxes and tributes would be demanded. Moreover, Sephardim were apprehensive about Perushim scholars asking for money and again stirring up the Ashkenazi-Sephardi conflicts that disrupted the Jerusalem community throughout the eighteenth century.

The Perushim entered Jerusalem separately, dressed in Sephardi garb, and temporarily lived in the Jewish quarter. Until R. Menahem Mendel's family joined him, he lived in a tiny room provided by Sephardi leaders, who once again helped the Perushim. Soon after their arrival, the Perushim moved into the Light of Life courtyard in the Bab-el-Huta section of the Muslim quarter, north of the Temple Mount. Rentals were cheaper in the Muslim quarter than in the more crowded Jewish quarter, and the nearby Wailing Wall was easily accessible. The move was eased by Perushim living together in the same courtyard, where they felt at ease with their ideological kin, spoke Yiddish, and practiced their East European customs.[5]

Perushim strongly desired to communicate with God according to the prayer ritual of the Vilna gaon, so that they "will be worthy of the advent of our righteous Messianic Redemption."[6] But a firman for an Ashkenazi synagogue was not requested because this would have revealed their intention to settle permanently in Jerusalem. During the weekdays, when the vigilant eyes of the authorities were less watchful than on the Sabbath, they dared to conduct a prayer service in an improvised synagogue in their courtyard. When short a quorum of ten adult males, the Perushim "hired" one or two Sephardim to join their prayer service, paying them from the haluka funds in their treasury. By February 1817 the Perushim had settled enough of their followers in Jerusalem to constitute a prayer quorum.

On occasion the Torah scroll had to be spirited out of the Light of Life synagogue in order to escape detection by the authorities. At prayer time four boys were posted as lookouts. When they spotted approaching Muslim officials, the Torah scroll was thrust through a hole in the wall designed for such an escape. Seventy years later this story was embellished with a touch of self-pity:

> When the Muslims heard that the Ashkenazim had established a place of worship they became very angry, attacked the congregants, and tried to take away the only Torah scroll they had. Only by weeping, entreaties, and a gift of money did the worshippers save the scroll. They had to promise the Muslims that they would never again pray in that place. From then onward the scroll was kept at the house of one of the members of the community. A hole was made in the wall of the house and whenever Torah readings were in progress four children functioned as lookouts, and as soon as they reported that the Muslims were approaching, the scroll was removed through the hole to the roof of the house. In this way the Ashkenazim went through a long period of trouble and vexation. More than once they were in mortal danger when the Muslims took them by surprise and found them praying fervently . . . [7]

On the Sabbath and holidays the Perushim joined the Sephardi prayer service. Perushim met and mingled with Sephardim. R. Menahem Mendel was befriended by the future Sephardi chief rabbi, Shlomo Moshe Suzin, who "recognized R. Menahem Mendel's elevated status. He became a true friend, like a brother, and he blessed and honored R. Menahem Mendel."[8] The head of the Beit El yeshiva so esteemed R. Menahem Mendel that he invited him to study at his academy. Perushim in Jerusalem and Safed (unlike the Galilee Hasidim of the eighteenth century) were intellectually curious about the customs and traditions of the Sephardim. Scholars of the two groups discussed the differences in styles of prayer, liturgy, and the reading of the weekly portion of the Torah. They conferred on complicated talmudic problems in an attempt to discover new legal approaches and precedents. Some Perushim even adopted certain Sephardi customs, but in the area of religious doctrine and practices they remained separate.

The small number of Perushim in Jerusalem organized their own kollel branch. But it was an integral part of the larger, unified Perushim kollel centered in Safed, which in 1817 borrowed 10,000 piastres from Haim Farhi and gave some of it to the smaller, poorer group in Jerusalem.[9] Only by establishing their kollel separate from the Sephardim could the Perushim freely develop their own community institutions and consecrate a synagogue in Jerusalem.

From 1815 to 1821 the Perushim population in Jerusalem grew slowly from 20 to about 100 persons. R. Israel reported that "only about twenty heads of families" lived in Jerusalem in 1821,[10] but this figure may be on the low side because it was recorded for a specific purpose—to prove that Abdullah Pasha's huge tariff of 75,000 piastres imposed on so few Jerusalem Perushim was exorbitant and unjust, especially when compared to the tax of 81,000 piastres levied on about 2,500 Sephardim.

Few Perushim settled in Jerusalem because of the staunch opposition of the kollel in Safed, where R. Israel held adamantly to the ruling of the Vilna Rabbis that no Perushim could so much as travel to Jerusalem without securing the prior consent of the kollel branch in Safed. In 1817 R. Israel warned against a shaliah, Shlomo Pach, enticing East European Perushim to settle in Jerusalem because "this is most dangerous as is clearly known to us."[11] This was an oblique reference to the fact that it was illegal for Ashkenazim to live permanently in Jerusalem, as well as to the strong opposition of the Sephardim and Haim Farhi to such settlement.

While vowing love for Jerusalem, R. Israel harbored a partisan interest in the development of the Safed community of Perushim and tried to enforce the injunction that "peace is better than all material matters, such as building. One argument should defer all else," including the settlement of Perushim in Jerusalem. Because "it is not good to cause disagreements in Eretz Israel for nothing,"[12] he observed that it was not worth while to agitate the Sephardim. It is indeed strange that R. Israel would characterize the settlement of Perushim in Jerusalem as "nothing"! He dogmatically declared that "it has been firmly established in practical terms, in Vilna and throughout the land," that most of the Perushim would live in Safed and only a minority would settle in Jerusalem. R. Israel based his case on the theory that Jerusalem should be settled by a few exceptional individuals and great Torah scholars. As a spiritual center, Jerusalem should be free of secular matters and intercommunity politics. This concept of the role of Jerusalem was to remain a frequent point of contention between the Perushim of Safed and Jerusalem.

Praying and studying together helped the Perushim and Sephardim develop mutual tolerance and respect. When the vital subject of financial support from the Sephardim was mentioned, the Perushim treaded softly in a conscious effort not to antagonize their neighbors. Six months after settling quietly but permanently in Jerusalem they expressed self-effacing financial demands: "God forbid, we are not here to deprive [the Sephardim of monies

collected overseas] but only ask that they also take pity on us, the Ashkenazim, because we are of their own flesh and blood."[13] This humble tone of
asking for modest haluka allocations could not be sustained for long. As the
number of Perushim grew, their needs burgeoned, their expectations increased, and their confidence was bolstered.

In order to achieve their goal of an independent self-sustaining community, the Perushim soon clashed with the Sephardim over religious issues
that had strong economic implications. Since the rabbis of each group actively participated in the leadership of their communities, rabbinical opinions went in tandem with kollel policy. Rabbinical endorsements that could
affect revenues created discord between the groups, as happened in cases involving Jerusalem regulations about inheritances, burying the dead, and the
slaughtering of kosher meat.

One of the first efforts of the Perushim toward economic independence
was their demand for a change in the long-standing inheritance regulations,[14] which mandated that a Jew who died without a legal heir living in
Eretz Israel automatically bequeathed all assets to the Sephardi kollel. It
made no sense to the Perushim to funnel the money their members inherited into the Sephardi kollel treasury. R. Israel, in his overpowering fashion, undertook to fight the Sephardim in this battle of the Torah.

The chief rabbi of Jerusalem from 1818 to 1821, R. Joseph Hazzan, vehemently argued that the Sephardim had a legal right, based on Jewish and
Muslim law, to enact inheritance regulations for all Jerusalemites. Without
this income, which provided the Sephardi treasury with its second largest
source of revenue, Rabbi Hazzan insisted, there probably would be no Jewish community in Eretz Israel. Although the inheritance regulations were
not cited in the Torah, they were firmly imbedded in traditional customs
dating back to the fifteenth century, backed by the commanding authority
of rabbinical courts, and unanimously accepted by both Sephardim and
Ashkenazim. Moreover, it is the obligation of every resident to comply
with town regulations and customs, especially in the case of the inheritance
tax, where most of the revenue is spent for the needs of the total community. Since Muslim law provided that when a person dies without an heir in
town he is "inherited" by the government treasury, the Perushim must adhere to the inheritance laws of the Sephardim or suffer the consequences of
breaking the law of the land and allow Jewish money to fall into the hands
of Muslims.

In order to rebut the Sephardi case, R. Israel galvanized heated answers
in the best talmudic tradition.[15] He wrote that he had convinced all the Torah scholars in Europe about the illegality of establishing regulations con-
flicting with the inheritance law of the Torah that permits every Jew to will

property to whomever he wants. Although the Perushim had accepted the inheritance regulation when they first settled in Jerusalem, they were not asked their opinion and so they did not specifically authorize their approval. Not only was the inheritance regulation a badly conceived law, in R. Israel's opinion, but it did not apply to the Perushim, non-Turkish citizens not subject to Turkish laws. R. Israel hinted that he might turn to foreign consuls to invoke the Perushim's tax-exempt status as foreign nationals. On the practical level, R. Israel stated that the Sephardim are inestimably better off than the Perushim, who "do not know the language, have no work, and are all poor"; therefore the "poor" Perushim should not be forced to put money into the hands of the "comfortable" Sephardim.

R. Israel appealed for the positive intervention of European rabbis and the leaders of PEKAM in Amsterdam by declaring that the inheritance tax dissuaded rich Perushim from settling in Eretz Israel. To cap his contentions R. Israel "demanded" the return of all inheritance monies "taken" by the Sephardim throughout the years because:

> Since our very first day in the Holy Land we have never been given our share in the donations, and they do not even pay the taxes for us. They have taken away from the Ashkenazim all legacies as well as commissions from buying houses and the income from the dowries of widowed women, which amounts to more than double all the annual taxes put together, as is clear from our open records.[16]

This high-pitched argument expired out of sheer irrelevance in face of the legal ingenuity of the Perushim.[17] They resorted to the cunning expedient of resolving that all haluka monies paid to members be given in the form of a loan that had to be repaid to the Perushim kollel if the member died without an inheritor living in Jerusalem. Other Perushim wrote wills before they entered the legal jurisdiction of Eretz Israel setting up endowment funds benefiting Perushim scholars. The inheritance tax was also evaded by designating a trustee in Eretz Israel as the legal inheritor of the assets of Perushim. By May 1822 the Perushim of Safed (and, presumably, Tiberias and Jerusalem) had ceased paying the inheritance tax to the Sephardim.

The Sephardim continued to press their right for the inheritance money of the Perushim and R. Israel continued to blast the Sephardim, who

> have stolen more than 300,000 piastres from us, from inheritances and stores [property tax] . . . they took from us more than 20 years of our lives by their grabbing and really we are all in danger due to their re-

newed claim for burial fees and inheritances. They only want to take for themselves and not give us one piastre.[18]

This argument raged until the end of the 1830s, when the Sephardim reluctantly surrendered their claim to the inheritance taxes of the Perushim after having lost the actual money long before.

In another attempt to reduce expenditures the Perushim tried to stop paying burial fees into the Sephardi treasury of Jerusalem.[19] Perushim wanted to establish their own Burial Society in order to break the Sephardi monopoly over burial fees and the sale of burial plots and tombstones, which generated substantial income and strong control over Jews requiring burial services. But the Muslim authorities, probably at the behest of the Sephardim, rebuffed the Perushim. Only in 1856 did the Perushim finally succeed in establishing their own Burial Society, as a result of the Sephardi refusal to bury Shlomo Zalman Zoref until his heirs paid monies he ostensibly owed to the Sephardi kollel.

Trying to stop payment to the Sephardim for the gabella tax on meat was another effort to reduce Perushim expenditures. The Sephardi rabbis insisted that the Perushim must adhere to the Sephardi ritual of slaughtering meat that ensures it is kosher. One important motive behind this rabbinical decision was that this income helped defray Sephardi community expenses; another no less crucial reason was the need to uphold the standing of the Sephardi community and the prestige of its chief rabbi, who had sole authority to select the Jewish ritual slaughterer, according to millet rules.[20]

Perushim found Sephardi claims for their monopoly of the meat tax ridiculous. In Poland the Perushim were authorized to slaughter meat and declare it kosher, but in the Holy Land they were declared incompetent to do so. Uncharacteristically, the Perushim kept their insult to themselves, paid the meat tax, and assumed so formidable a silence on the matter that we do not know when they initiated practical efforts to break the Sephardi monopoly. The realistic Perushim must have known that they lacked sufficient political clout with the Muslim authorities to change the existing arrangement. Not until 1867, thanks to the intervention of foreign consuls, did they win the right to slaughter kosher meat separate from the Sephardim.

While trying to stop payments to the Sephardim, the Perushim acted to secure legal sanction from the authorities in order to settle permanently in Jerusalem. In the first half of 1817, about eighteen months after their arrival in that city, the Perushim of Jerusalem sent Shlomo Pach to Istanbul, charging him to obtain a firman wiping out debts on R. Judah HeHasid's courtyard and synagogue, called the Hurva (Hebrew for ruins). Ashkenazim in Jerusalem—the few Perushim and the fewer Hasidim—were still held responsible by Muslims for the large debt and astronomical interest that had accumulated since the followers of R. Judah HeHasid fled Jerusalem in 1720 after defaulting on their debt payments. Since it was impossible for the Perushim to pay off this huge sum of money, the only alternative was to secure a firman revoking the 1720 debt and "when a firman is issued, with God's help, we will establish a settlement" in Jerusalem.[21]

As novices in the Levantine negotiations for a firman, the Perushim might have been expected to solicit the assistance of the Sephardim and to deploy the influential contacts of the Istanbul Officials at the Sublime Porte. However, the Perushim did not ask ask for outside help, fearing the opposition of the already suspicious Sephardim to yet another move to change the status quo in Jerusalem.[22] The Perushim of Safed were also kept in the dark about the objectives of Pach's mission because of R. Israel's continued opposition to settling all but a few select Jews in Jerusalem. Apparently Pach was not adverse to encouraging immigrants to settle in Jerusalem, for R. Israel accused him of "sitting on the crossroads of Istanbul and pointing important people in the direction of Jerusalem."[23]

Shlomo Pach's mission not only riled his community but also produced friction between Jerusalem's Sephardim and Perushim that was not easily assuaged even after it was learned that Pach had failed to obtain the firman.[24] In 1820, however, the Sublime Porte issued a firman canceling all debts incurred forty or more years before. When the Jerusalem Perushim heard that "from now on Muslims have no legal claim on old debts against Ashkenazi Jews,"[25] they were beside themselves with joy. "This was salvation for the Ashkenazim and a source was opened providing an opportunity to settle in the Holy City." The Perushim promptly dispatched two emissaries to Istanbul to obtain the firman and forward it posthaste to Jerusalem before proceeding on fundraising missions to Eastern and Western Europe.

Having attained the status of debtless legal residents of Jerusalem, the Perushim decided to send Shlomo Pach on a second mission to obtain a firman to repair and rebuild the Hurva synagogue and the buildings in the compound that had been gutted by the Muslims in 1720.[26] They wished to "glorify and uplift the place of our Temple" and hoped that God's Dwelling Place would speedily be rebuilt. Was not the purpose of the Perushim settlement in Jerusalem to pray before the Gates of Heaven for their brothers left in the Diaspora? Now that they had settled so near the Wailing Wall, they wanted to sanctify all Jews in prayers emanating from Jerusalem and establish close contact with the Spirit of the Lord, two essential conditions for hastening the coming of the Messianic Redemption.

It was not surprising that R. Israel and the Perushim of Safed "passively opposed" the rebuilding of the Hurva.[27] R. Israel believed that the building costs would bankrupt the community and that developing the Hurva would enable Jerusalem to supplant Safed as the center of Perushim settlement in Eretz Israel. Buttressing his practical reasons were his ideological beliefs that predicated the rebuilding of Jerusalem at the end rather than the start of the process of Redemption.

In 1821 Shlomo Pach left Jerusalem for Istanbul, despite the Greek revolt which flared up that year and endangered travelers in the eastern Mediterranean. He sought to secure a firman allowing the rebuilding of the Hurva. Pach's mission was not successful. Either he failed to reach Istanbul or, after a short stay in the Ottoman capital, he admitted defeat and returned to Jerusalem,[28] not heeding the pleas of R. Menahem Mendel and Shlomo Zalman Shapira, who urged Pach to intensify his efforts to obtain the invaluable Hurva firman.

In 1823 Shlomo Pach again was sent on a mission to Istanbul and Eastern Europe in order to achieve three major objectives.[29] First, he was authorized by both the Jerusalem and Safed Perushim to collect funds in Eastern Europe for the unified kollel. When appearing before the Polish Perushim, Pach was instructed not to divulge differences of opinion between the Perushim of Safed and Jerusalem. He took "a stern vow" forbidding him to defend or criticize any individual "in the two kehillot,"[30] indicating that personal conflicts were rampant. Second, Pach was once more charged "to secure for the Ashkenazim a firman from the Sultan for the well-known building, the Hurva." Third, he was told to obtain Ottoman recognition of the Perushim in Eretz Israel as an autonomous religious group. The Perushim wanted to split off from the Sephardim and obtain rights granted to foreign nationals, based on the capitulation agreements.

Pach was instructed to secure a firman

> so that we the Ashkenazim living in the four holy cities and any other place in the Holy Land will have all the freedom of foreign nationals so that the pasha and governor should not take from us even one piastre and that the town governor and the kadi will not have the right to judge us for anything; only the vakil [leader of the community of foreign citizens] of the Ashkenazim or the consul normally stationed in a seaport

will have the right over all the Ashkenazim, who will have a place of prayer and study, like a synagogue, so they can recite the Torah among themselves according to their own Ashkenazi traditions and customs. And no person shall prevent them from burying their dead anyplace they wish without having to give a piastre to anyone in the world. And they will be able to build houses in the courtyards they bought from residents of the land . . .

This was a clarion call to establish a second Jewish millet in Eretz Israel, providing the Perushim with all rights of foreign citizens, independence from local Muslim officials, and separate status from the Sephardim.

The aim of establishing the Perushim in Eretz Israel as an autonomous religious group was so crucial that R. Israel wrote "with tears flowing from my eyes" that Pach could "earn his place in the next world and in this world in one hour, because the settlement in the Holy Land" depends upon his mission.[31] Shlomo Zalman Shapira also exhorted Pach: "My friend, my friend, if we were only born just to set right this settlement in Eretz Israel, it is enough and it is the equivalent of performing all the mitzvot . . . " R. Israel told Pach that if necessary he could neglect his fundraising mission to Vilna and concentrate efforts in Istanbul in order to prevent the Perushim from "being chased out of Safed" and losing their homes "because now the Holy Land is in danger . . . and we are all truly in danger . . . " The Perushim viewed the danger as coming not only from the Muslims but also from the Sephardim. R. Israel, no spendthrift, wrote Pach that "if you must spend another one thousand piastres to secure a firman, take the money from us and like a lion conquer and like a deer run . . . " Rather than patiently waiting for a firman to be issued while differences continued to fester between Perushim and Sephardim, R. Israel was willing to settle for a Torah judgment rendered by a seven-man court composed of three Perushim, three Sephardim, and one Hasid.

In a separate letter, R. Menahem Mendel told Shlomo Pach to take upon himself the additional task of encouraging new immigrants to settle in Jerusalem:

And it will be very, very good for a person who wants to go up to the Holy mountain to travel with you . . . and ask him to listen to your words and not pay attention to the fanatics who by nature insult those speaking well of Jerusalem, the Holy City, and the people living there . . . and if he comes and travels with you all will be fine with him.

This letter is most exceptional in unabashedly telling Jews to live in Jerusalem, contrary to the strong opinions of R. Israel, who is obliquely called a "fanatic" insulting Jerusalem. No less remarkable is R. Menahem Mendel's encouraging Jews to settle in Jerusalem without noting any preference for old and rich immigrants.

When the Sephardim of Jerusalem discovered the purpose of Pach's mission, they were livid with rage. In their best bombastic style the Sephardim warned that, if the Perushim persisted in their separatist actions aimed at autonomy, the Sephardim would drive them out of Jerusalem.

The Sephardim appealed to their influential supporters in Istanbul to fight the granting of a firman for an independent Ashkenazi community. Little convincing was necessary because it was obvious to Sephardi leaders in Istanbul that no less than the legal status of the millet in Eretz Israel was at stake. Judging from the Perushim records, opposition mounted by the Istanbul Officials against the granting of an autonomy firman must have been most effective. According to R. Israel, the Sephardim of Jerusalem, Tiberias, and Safed slandered and lied about the Perushim, leading the Istanbul Officials "to give the blood of our souls to the Gentiles."[32] Shlomo Zalman Shapira urged Pach, "for God's sake do not hesitate to go and announce in the markets and streets of Istanbul what the Sephardim are doing to us." R. Israel in Safed appended a note to Shapira's letter, explaining that at least some of the differences of opinion between Ashkenazim and Sephardim arose because of taxes of 15,000 plus another 13,000 piastres that the Perushim were forced to pay Mustafa, pasha of Damascus.

Shlomo Pach was unable to obtain a firman defining the Ashkenazim as an autonomous group, due to uncompromising opposition by the Sephardim in Eretz Israel and Istanbul. However, as a result of Pach's request for a firman, the chief justice of Istanbul instructed the Jerusalem kadi to search the town archives for a previously approved firman allowing Jews to reconstruct the Hurva. After additional efforts by the Perushim and baksheesh payments of about 7,000 piastres,[33] a Muslim court in Jerusalem ruled in March 1824 that Jews had the right to repair their property in the Jewish quarter, including the Hurva. Later the kadi issued a firman granting Jews rights to the Hurva.

Upon receiving the firman, R. Menahem Mendel expressed the elation of the Jerusalem Perushim community:

And now the Lord has helped us take possession of the Hurva in Jerusalem that belonged to the Ashkenazim in bygone days. More than one hundred years ago there was a synagogue in the Hurva compound that was taken by strangers and Gentiles and transformed into desolate ruins. But now God in His eternal mercy and justice has taken it out of their hands.[34]

At last the Perushim had received the right to rebuild this synagogue, the focal point around which they could rally and establish their status as a separate worshipping community.

At great expense the Perushim bought out Muslims who had set up shops in the Hurva ruins. Lacking the financial resources to rebuild the synagogue, R. Menahem Mendel intended to dedicate the royalties from one of his books for the purpose, but this plan never materialized. He wrote fundraising letters to rabbinical leaders such as R. Hirschel, Ashkenazi chief rabbi of London, and to Polish Perushim. One letter dispatched with a Polish Jew visiting Jerusalem in 1819 was confiscated by the Russian authorities. As the mail carrier of a subversive letter,[35] the elderly Shlomo Plonski was imprisoned and died in jail.

PEKAM opposition to emissaries collecting money for the Hurva also blocked the project and aroused the ire of the Perushim, who labeled PEKAM "great delayers preventing the performing of a mitzva."[36] Amid such dissension, the Hurva compound remained desolate in its ruins until the 1830s.

It was a sign of the times that, while the Sephardim were at loggerheads with the Perushim, and there was friction between the Safed and Jerusalem Perushim, the Hasidim in the Galilee were also splitting apart. Fifty-six Habad Hasidim belonging to fifteen families settled in Hebron in 1819 because they could no longer "sit together with the other Hasidim" of Safed.[37] They were obeying the command of the head of the Habad Hasidim in Poland (Habad is the Hebrew acronym for Wisdom, Understanding, and Knowledge) that they establish an independent community base, in order to pray and study according to their own unique customs and traditions. To understand the fractious interests of the Hasidic groups we must recall the ideological chasm and the rancorous personal clashes that had developed since 1797 between the Habad Hasidim and R. Abraham and his Hasidic followers.

After the death of R. Abraham in 1810 the antipathies prevailing between the few Habad Hasidim and the majority of the Hasidim were patched over. But with the arrival in the Galilee of new settlers of Habad persuasion old irritations and new antagonisms surfaced. In 1816–1817 the head of the Habad Hasidim in Poland sent a representative to Eretz Israel to find a suitable place for the independent Habad settlement. Since Jerusalem had been preempted by the rival Perushim and was still closed to the settlement of Ashkenazi Jews, the Habad chose to live in Hebron, twenty miles south of Jerusalem on the edge of the Judean desert. Hebron, with a population of 6,000, was an open city that served as a flourishing commercial and manufacturing town and a market and municipal center for hinterland villages with warlike tribal tendencies that frequently erupted into violence and rebellion.[38]

Hebron was such a center of Islamic religious fundamentalism that no Christians lived in town.[39] Jews settled there because it was one of the four holy cities of Eretz Israel. About 300 Jews, nearly all Sephardim, lived in a large courtyard surrounded by shabby single and multilevel houses. Hebron Jews were scholars or performed religious and other services for the Jewish community; they did not engage in manual labor, possibly because they were quite elderly.

Like the Sephardim in Hebron, the newly arrived Habad Hasidim had a hard life, with periodic uprisings of the Hebron fellahin causing them problems. Very little had changed in Hebron since the second half of the eighteenth century,[40] and Jews continued to live there in unrelieved misery. The small Hebron community was by far the most debt-ridden and persecuted of the four holy cities. In 1813 some rabbis were chained, imprisoned, and tortured after the Jewish community again defaulted on its debt or was accused of transacting an illegal real estate deal.[41]

Initially the Habad group in Hebron partook of the haluka monies distributed by the Hasidic kollel of Tiberias and Safed, but, since these allocations were so modest, the Habad kollel sent its own emissaries overseas. This decision was strongly opposed by the Hasidic kollel in the Galilee, which objected to the 56 Hasidim in Hebron collecting their own funds, thereby reducing the haluka livelihood of the hundreds of Hasidim in Safed and Tiberias. Using inflated rhetoric, an Ashkenazi shaliah from the Galilee wrote in 1821 about the "few thousand" poverty-stricken Ashkenazim of Tiberias and Safed.[42]

There was a great proliferation of shlihim from the four holy cities: emissaries of the Sephardim, of the Perushim, of the Hasidim of Galilee, and of the Hebron Hasidim contended in wildly uncoordinated efforts for the limited resources of European Jewry. In 1821 an emissary from Galilee bemoaned the fact that "this shaliah leaves and that one comes right after. For this reason contributions to the last shaliah are reduced."

The Hasidim of Hebron Habad sent shlihim to areas of Eastern Europe where members of their group lived. But contributions dwindled after the ascension of Czar Nicholas I (1825–1855), who forbade transferring money out of Russia to Eretz Israel. This situation forced the Habad to collect money in Western Europe despite strong oposition from PEKAM. Aggressive as they were in collecting money overseas, in Eretz Israel they showed little interest in issues such as inheritance monies, burial fees, and the meat tax over which the Perushim fought the Sephardim. Not until 1830 did the Habad Hasidim and Sephardim amicably agree to share income from inheritances,[43] reflecting the friendly relations that prevailed in Hebron between the two groups.

As the Habad Hasidim settled into Hebron, and the Perushim maneuvered to stop paying taxes and fees into the Sephardi treasury, the Jewish communities of Eretz Israel were struck a devastating blow. On August 19, 1820, by order of the recently appointed Pasha Abdullah of Acre (1819–1831), Haim Farhi was strangled and his body was thrown into the Mediterranean Sea. The reasons for this monstrous murder are not clear, for "in this country . . . it is very difficult to know the truth"[44] according to an English missionary. Most likely, Farhi fell victim to intrigues,[45] in a power struggle that surrounded the recently appointed, 19-year-old, vain, hot-tempered Pasha Abdullah.[46] Born with the proverbial silver spoon in his mouth, he was given everything he ever wanted and had a highly inflated idea of his own importance.

When the three surviving Farhi brothers living in Damascus "learned [about] the deplorable death of their beloved brother they resolved to be revenged on his murderer . . . "[47] The Farhi thirst for revenge and influence in Istanbul meshed with Sultan Mahmud's directive to the pashas of Aleppo and Adana to help Darwish, pasha of Damascus, unseat the upstart pasha of Acre. It served the purpose of the sultan to get rid of the brash Abdullah, who refused to return the treasure he had inherited in 1819 from his predecessor, Pasha Suleiman, coveted the pashalik of Damascus, and declined to relinquish control over part of Palestine in favor of the Damascus pasha. At that time Abdullah controlled nearly all of Palestine, with the exception of the mountain ridge from Nablus to Hebron, and he saw no reason to surrender such a powerful territorial position simply because it was the will of a distant, weak sultan.

Thus, in 1821, the pasha of Damascus mounted an invasion of Abdullah's pashalik with the blessings of the sultan, the backing of the immense Farhi wealth, and the support of armies from the provinces of Damascus,

Aleppo, and Adana. The combined armed forces of 40,000 soldiers defeated Abdullah's army and forced his retreat to Acre, where he was besieged for about nine months. "In dire distress,"[48] Abdullah begged help from the powerful ruler of Egypt, Mehemet Ali, who was interested in extending his sphere of influence beyond the Nile. He sent provisions to the pasha of Acre, and in gratitude Abdullah declared that his provinces also belonged to Egypt, for he was "Mehemet Ali's creature."

Pasha Abdullah saved his pashalik in 1822 by cunning. The siege of Acre was lifted after the oldest Farhi brother, Shlomo, was poisoned and the besiegers were bribed. By 1824 Sultan Mahmud had pardoned Abdullah for his acts of rebellion and officially reinstated him as pasha of Acre at the intercession of Mehemet Ali, after Abdullah promised the sultan a huge gift of 1,250,000 piastres.

This incident reveals the true state of government in Palestine—the shifting loyalties of the sultan and the pashas and their predilection to change sides in accordance with their needs, ambitions, and whims; the mutual quarrels and periodic hostilities among the pashas; the crucial importance of extortion and bribery; and the ability of powerful clans to ally themselves with rival pashas and agitate local wars.

Two days after Haim Farhi's death Safed's Jews were locked up in the citadel throughout the Sabbath. The reason given for their internment was to count them. It was alleged that Farhi did not report on "thousands of Jews" in an effort to lighten the tax burden on the community.[49] After completing his census, Pasha Abdullah charged the Jews with tax evasion, aided and abetted by Haim Farhi, who had shielded the Jewish community by decreasing the number of registered Jews. Despite R. Israel's protestations, Pasha Abdullah demanded retroactive poll tax payments for the last ten years, which totaled 50,000 piastres.

In an effort to avoid payment, R. Israel sought a new protector for the Perushim and found him in the person of Anthony Katafago, who was the Russian—and also the Austrian, Swedish, and Danish—consul in Acre. Katafago, like most consular agents in the area, was of Mediterranean origin and represented European countries while actively engaged in trade and commerce. He also loaned money to Jews at high interest rates and exchanged foreign currency for them.[50]

R. Israel asked Katafago to enforce the capitulation agreements,[51] which provided protection for non-Turkish subjects and entitled Perushim to exemptions from local imposts such as the poll tax.[52] Protect the Perushim as foreign nationals against "savages trying to sever us from the Holy Land" was R. Israel's request to Katafago, who agreed in return for an annual retainer of 8,000 piastres.[53]

And as soon as the people of Safed—may it be rebuilt and reestablished speedily in our own days, Amen!—heard about it, they went to the [Russian] consul and registered the names of all the Ashkenazim in his book of records and they were exempted from all the taxes which they owed to His Excellency the pasha, which included inheritances and burial taxes that were traditionally levied by our Sephardi brothers . . .[54]

Paradoxically, the protector of Russian Jews in Palestine represented the great persecutor of the Jews in Eastern Europe.

When Katafago protested to the pasha about taxes levied on the Perushim, Abdullah ingenuously said that he had ordered collecting back taxes "only from the Sephardim, subjects of his country,"[55] and not from the Russian foreigners. Based on the pasha's decision, Katafago arranged a compromise agreement with Safed officials that provided for annual Perushim payments of 1,050 piastres in lieu of building and property taxes; payment of the more onerous poll tax was waived. It was stipulated that "with the payment of this amount all due privileges will be accorded" the Ashkenazim as foreign nationals. The use of the capitulations for tax evasion purposes escalated the deteriorating relations between the Sephardim and Ashkenazim of Safed. The Sephardim would now have to shoulder the major tax burden imposed on the Galilee Jewish communities within the jurisdiction of Pasha Abdullah.

Sephardi Jews were frustrated at this new turn of events, and R. Israel accused them of betraying him to the town officials. R. Israel and the leaders of Safed's Hasidic community were imprisoned and ordered to pay their debts within one week. This time R. Israel petitioned the Russian consul in Aleppo, Elijah Picciotto,[56] because Katafago was confined to besieged Acre. Picciotto succeeded in having the Ashkenazi leaders released, but only after R. Israel paid more than 2,500 piastres to the local authorities. The Perushim expressed their gratitude when they wrote (in May 1823) that "if not for the help of Elijah and Moses [Picciotto], all of us would have been dead and lost."[57]

Due to R. Israel's invocation of the capitulations,[58] by May 1822 the Perushim of Safed no longer paid the poll tax, were not held responsible for paying off the debt of the Jewish millet, and had stopped remitting inheritance monies to the Sephardim. These reductions in revenues fell upon the

Sephardim at a time when Pasha Abdullah increased the annual poll tax of the Safed community by 250 percent—from 2,000 to 5,000 piastres.

While the Safed Perushim escaped the poll tax and responsibility for the debts of the Jewish community, the Tiberias Sephardim clashed with the Ashkenazim—Perushim and Hasidim—over payment of enormous taxes levied on the Tiberias kehilla. Apparently the appearance of "a certain number" of Perushim between 1810 and 1820 upset the amicable status quo of the Tiberias community.[59] Nevertheless, Ashkenazim in Tiberias did not ask consul Katafago to invoke the capitulation agreements on their behalf, as the Safed Perushim had done in 1820, for fear of jostling the strong arm of the local authorities, arousing the wrath of the Sephardim, to whom they owed money, and "for several secret reasons that can be divulged only by whispering from ear to ear."[60]

Sephardim and Ashkenazim had signed an agreement that all impositions levied by the pasha would be paid half by the Ashkenazim and half by the Sephardim;[61] thus, when the Tiberias governor arbitrarily levied on the Jewish community taxes totaling 50,000 piastres in December 1821, Sephardim paid 25,000 piastres and Ashkenazim paid the other half. The Tiberias officials then quickly imposed another crushing tax of 150,000 piastres and locked the town gates to prevent an exodus. "Immediately we were driven together in the fortress," an Ashkenazi wrote, "and some us were terribly beaten on the soles of the feet until we agreed to pay the half of it, namely the sum of 75,000 taler."[62] With great difficulty Tiberias Ashkenazim got word to Safed Ashkenazim pleading for their intervention in revoking this huge tax. "Travel to Acre and plead before the pasha and ask that if God forbid he does not revoke his edict that has left us naked and stripped of everything, then let him take our homes and our possessions and all that we have and just put us on ships returning to our country" (Poland). Safed Ashkenazim declared two consecutive days of fasting and then traveled to Acre for a meeting with their protector, consul Katafago. After consulting Pasha Abdullah about invoking the capitulations, Katafago ruled that as foreign nationals the Ashkenazim should pay no taxes even if they had lived in Tiberias for forty years or had been born there. Ashkenazim, however, were instructed by Katafago to pay the Tiberias Sephardim 50,000 piastres as their fair share of the community debt. Since the Ashkenazim were cash-poor they borrowed the money from Katafago and paid the Sephardim 50,000 piastres—one-third, not one-half, of the 150,000-piastre tax levy.

Upon learning that Tiberias Ashkenazim were now protected by the capitulations, the Sephardim realized that they would be stuck with paying all future tribute imposed on the Jewish community. They were outraged by the Ashkenazim unilaterally abrogating their recent agreement to share on a fifty-fifty basis the payment of town taxes. So vile were the actions of the Ashkenazim in the eyes of the Sephardim that they protested to the Tiberias governor, claiming that the Ashkenazim "are no longer under the authority of the Austrian kaiser or the Russian czar,"[63] that they constituted two-thirds of the Tiberias Jewish community and had lived in Tiberias for fifty years, and that many were born in Tiberias, just like the Sephardim. In fact about one-third of the 1,000 Tiberias Jews were Ashkenazim,[64] mainly descendants of Hasidim who initially settled in Tiberias in 1781, forty-two years before. The Tiberias governor, uninterested in the fine points of the capitulations, ordered the Ashkenazim to pay 75,000 piastres as their half of the tax burden. Ashkenazim were beaten, and one distinguished Hasidic leader was threatened that, if he did not pay 17,000 piastres within twenty-four hours, he and other leaders would be tortured by a red-hot iron and "other tortures that the ears of a listener should be spared hearing about."[65]

Luckily for the Tiberias Ashkenazim they were saved by Pasha Abdullah's decree reaffirming consul Katafago's decision that the Ashkenazim pay the Sephardim 50,000 piastres. The Tiberias governor did not rush to obey the pasha's decision. He was influenced by an Egyptian traveler who pointed out that the Ashkenazim were so poverty-stricken that they

cannot afford to eat meat or fish or anything else because they are greatly impoverished and debt-ridden now that they have to pay off the financial claim of the Sephardim . . . and they have nothing to pay with because even the houses they live in are rented. And what good comes of it that they are the majority [two-thirds] if they have nothing to pay with?

The Tiberias governor assembled the whole Jewish community, showed great courtesy to the Ashkenazim, and told the Sephardim that he tried with all his strength for the Sephardim, "but what can I do if this is the will of the Pasha who writes . . . that he pardons the Ashkenazim? In order that there be real peace between you [Ashkenazim and Sephardim], I and the consul will ask the Pasha that you, the Sephardim, be pardoned for half the sum—that you should only pay 75,000 piastres and that he not claim the other half, which the Ashkenazim cannot pay."

In March 1822 the pasha pardoned the Sephardim 50 percent of the 150,000-piastre debt, and they wanted "to establish this day each year as a day of partying and happiness." This joyous occasion had cost the

Ashkenazim 50,000 piastres for back debts plus another 35,000 piastres for interest and expenses. They lamented: "And at present we have nobody to borrow money from, not even one piastre..."

After the Sephardim of Tiberias and Safed fell victim to the capitulations by having to assume responsibility for paying all millet taxes and debts, the Perushim, in April 1823, charged the Sephardim with leaving them at the mercy of the pasha.[66] With their inimitable vehemence and rectitude, the Perushim presented a comic opera script highlighting the mutual antagonisms of Sephardim and Ashkenazim. But this was no comedy, and the intense strains reflecting the divergent opinions of the two groups caused great distress and in turn produced new stresses in the community.

Why did the Perushim continue to besmirch the Sephardim verbally after having already won tax exemptions based on the capitulations? They doubted the permanence of Pasha Abdullah's decisions wiping out their debts and obligations as members of the Jewish millet. Even while the benefits of the capitulations were being implemented, Jews in Tiberias and Safed were at the mercy of the pashas of Acre and Damascus, the town governors, and corrupt officials who continued to extract money by imprisoning and torturing Jews. Such incidents convinced the Perushim that the pashas "schemed to tear out our roots in the Holy Land."[67] Ashkenazim complained that "many want to return to their homeland if the protection of foreigners cannot be properly maintained."[68]

R. Israel accused the Tiberias Sephardim of blaming the Ashkenazim for not making partial payment on about 25,000 piastres demanded by Mustafa, pasha of Damascus.[69] Sephardim were also castigated by R. Israel for writing a letter to the pasha, declaring that the Ashkenazim were not "Franks" (i.e., Europeans) and therefore were not entitled to the financial benefits of the capitulations. This letter was signed by Raphael Picciotto, an elderly wealthy Jew from Aleppo who settled in Tiberias around 1821, and whose three sons lived in northern Syria, where they served as traders and consular agents. The Perushim censured the Sephardim for conniving to have the "aged" Raphael Picciotto sign this slanderous letter without really understanding what he was doing. R. Israel asserted that because of this letter Perushim were imprisoned for debts owed by the Sephardim and were beaten until they paid 25,000 piastres plus 7,500 piastres in "expenses" and provided the kadi with guarantees for future payments of 150,000 piastres.

In order to establish their capitulation rights once and for all, a leader of the Safed Perushim set off for Beirut to meet with an unidentified consul. When he arrived there he was told that only consul Elijah Picciotto in Aleppo could help him. The Perushim immediately wrote to peripatetic

Shlomo Pach, then in Aleppo on his way to Istanbul, and frantically asked him to intercede on their behalf, prevent Elijah Picciotto from listening to the claims of the Sephardim, and write his father in Tiberias that the Sephardi allegations are "lies and nonsense."[70]

The Perushim, not famous for reticence, were in such a desperate state that they threatened to use their connections to harm Picciotto family interests if Raphael Picciotto did not retract his labeling of Ashkenazim as non-Europeans. The missive to Pach ended with the exhortation "not to delay, because this matter is most essential." When the more tactful Shlomo Zalman Shapira read this letter he diplomatically added a note advising Pach "not to mention what was written [about Picciotto] because truthfully he did not write to the pasha, but only the wicked ones surrounding him."

This Sephardim-Perushim conflict was conducted against a background of mutual reproach, utmost distrust, and bitter condemnation. R. Israel upbraided the Sephardim of Tiberias for deceit and forging documents and claimed that the Jerusalem, Safed, and Tiberias Sephardim spread "great lies" in Istanbul about the Ashkenazim and didn't tell the Ashkenazim what they were doing, creating danger by "the information they give the Gentiles about our life-blood and for no good reason."[71] R. Israel was so agitated that he repeated the rumor that the Sephardim "want to chase the Ashkenazim out of Jerusalem." In order to resolve the messy dispute, the two sides agreed to arbitrate the matter before a Sephardi rabbinical court. In May 1823 their leaders, with elderly Raphael Picciotto in tow, set off for Damascus to present their case. The judgment of the Sephardi rabbinical court was that the Perushim should pay all their back debts to the Sephardim. Lacking the necessary cash, the Perushim leaders signed promissory notes. The court also ruled that thereafter only the Sephardim should pay the exorbitant one-time taxes levied by the pasha; this was to happen in 1825.

Despite this unanticipated income from the Ashkenazim, the financial situation of the Tiberias Sephardim was shaky. In 1823 the community was burdened by an annual interest rate of 30 percent on a debt of 200,000 piastres,[72] nearly triple their 78,000-piastre debt in 1804.

While R. Israel and his cohorts were pouring vitriolic invectives on the hapless Sephardim of Jerusalem, Tiberias, and Safed, the Perushim were slowly settling into Jerusalem, gaining the physical and financial protection granted by the capitulations, winning tax exemptions from the authorities and the Sephardi kehilla, and finding the time, energy, and ingenuity to substantially increase their share of overseas contributions from Europe and North Africa.

The Perushim boosted their overseas income by a four-pronged campaign strategy:

1. Maintaining a fundraising monopoly for the Ashkenazim in their bastion of strength, Eastern Europe, and raising the maximum amount of money in this territory.
2. Collecting funds in Western and Central Europe, which traditionally channeled contributions to the Sephardim of Eretz Israel.
3. Initiating fundraising campaigns in Italy and Ottoman dominions, which had always been exclusively Sephardi territory.
4. Altering the 1810 PEKAM arrangement that funneled to the Sephardi kollelim all monies contributed by West European Jews, and trying to get the largest possible allocation for the Perushim.

Growth in Perushim revenues was largely achieved at the expense of the Sephardim and once again led to acrimonious clashes between the two groups. Passionate arguments centered about the source and size of the income each enjoyed, how to allocate funds collected by world Jewry, and which group in Eretz Israel would control which Jewish collection territory in Europe and the Ottoman Empire. The struggle for the financial future of the Perushim, Sephardim, and Hasidim of Eretz Israel was being fought on the battlefields of the Diaspora.

In Eastern Europe some monies were contributed for Eretz Israel in the Rabbi Meir Ba'al HaNes (the Miracle Worker) collection boxes.[73] Because of difficult economic times in Poland and Lithuania, local leaders were using the R. Meir Ba'al HaNes funds for community purposes instead of forwarding them to Eretz Israel. R. Israel and others were instrumental in influencing rabbis in Eastern Europe to again declare, in 1821, that Diaspora communities were forbidden to divert monies from the collection boxes to any purpose other than supporting settlers in Eretz Israel. This was a reaffirmation of similar pronouncements made by rabbis in the eighteenth century.

Another way to increase Perushim income significantly was to raise money in Western Europe. Funds collected by Ashkenazim in Europe were distributed in accordance with the precedent established by R. Israel in Vienna in 1813, when the Winer bequest was split equally between the Ashkenazim and the Sephardim,[74] and in conformance with the 1811 Perushim fundraising mission in Germany. The Perushim also believed that the time had long since passed to alter the 1810 PEKAM allocation key formulated by the Istanbul Officials back in 1744; it was outdated and no longer reflected the demographic picture of Eretz Israel Jews at the start of the 1820s. Before the Perushim settled in Eretz Israel, the Ashkenazim were nearly all Hasidim and constituted a mere 5 percent of the Jewish town population, but by 1823 the Hasidim and the Perushim totaled a substantial 1,600 persons, more than 25 percent of the Jews in the four holy cities.

As the community increased in numbers, it was not surprising if the value of the haluka share dropped when overseas contributions did not keep pace with the population growth. A letter written in 1819 reads:

> It is better not to write about the great number of pressures we suffer at this time because they [the Sephardim] have not yet given us a share in the land. Incidentally, those who receive haluka cannot subsist without additional help and welfare, and they live on what is sent to them by their overseas relatives...[75]

A person who depended only on haluka lived "a very poor, hard life" in the Jerusalem of 1835,[76] while "many" Safed Ashkenazim in 1836 "were supported by their relatives and friends in their countries of origin."[77] Difficult as it was to survive on one haluka share, it was impossible to live without it—unless you were rich.

At the start of the 1820s the unrelenting R. Israel complained that "since we have been in Eretz Israel not even once have we been given money contributed by the Ashkenazim."[78] His conclusion was simple: "Since the Sephardim... only give donations to their Sephardi brothers, therefore all contributions of our Ashkenazi brothers should go into the treasury of the Ashkenazim in Eretz Israel."[79] The tenor of this letter was soon reflected in the words and actions of the Perushim.

Jerusalem Perushim discussed with the future Sephardi chief rabbi, Moshe Suzin, the possibility of their receiving individual haluka payments from the Sephardi kollel and sending emissaries to Western Europe and Ottoman countries to raise funds solely for the Perushim community. This proposal was emphatically rejected by the debt-ridden Sephardi community. The Sephardim categorically denied R. Israel's charge that they did not pay some of the Ashkenazi bills.[80] Did they not pay the poll tax and other community taxes and expenses for all Jews, both Ashkenazim and Sephardim? The depleted Sephardi treasury certainly couldn't be expected to make haluka payments to all Perushim, when small payments were made only to the most destitute Sephardim and select Sephardi scholars studying in yeshivot. In the past the Ashkenazim had recognized the

Sephardi right to send shlihim abroad and collect money from all Jews throughout the world. This right, the Sephardim contended, could not be arbitrarily revoked by the Perushim.

While continuing their argument with the Sephardim, in 1819 the Perushim decided to press their demands for changing the PEKAM allocation arrangement for funds raised in Western Europe. To accomplish this objective the Perushim sent to Europe two shlihim, Shlomo Zalman Zoref of Jerusalem and Benjamin of Safed. The purpose of Zoref's 1819 mission makes Shlomo Zalman Shapira's comment in 1823 appear ingenuous:[81] "to date we have written nothing to Ashkenazi [countries] because we imagined that any day the Sephardim will arrange the haluka for us."[82]

Shlomo Zalman Zoref (Hebrew for silversmith) was selected by the Perushim of Jerusalem for this overseas mission because of his dynamic drive, ebullient manner, and persuasive personality. Born in Caiden, Lithuania, in 1785, Zoref studied at a yeshiva and learned the trade of silversmith before coming to Safed in 1812. In the wake of the Galilee plagues he was one of the first Perushim to settle in Jerusalem in 1813. Tall, broad-shouldered, and solidly built, Zoref was different in many other ways from the fragile-framed, hunched-over Perushim scholars. Before coming to Eretz Israel at the age of 26, Zoref learned the trade of smelting so that he could earn his living. He arrived in Eretz Israel with his wife and three sons to start a new life at a time when many immigrants were elderly and came to be buried in the Holy Land. Wishing to communicate with the Muslims and understand them, Zoref learned to speak Arabic; he moved easily among Muslims, making him one of the few Perushim able to negotiate with the authorities. Zoref's ability to grasp the reins of power with vigor, linked with his firm yet diplomatic personality and his fundraising capabilities, enabled him to be one of the commanding Perushim leaders and prominent shlihim during the first half of the nineteenth century.

Zoref was accompanied on his mission by Benjamin, a resident of Safed (formerly of London), to ensure that Safed receive its due share of financial benefits and to prevent Zoref from encouraging Perushim immigrants to settle in Jerusalem, as Pach had been accused of doing on his 1817 mission. Despite sporadic friction between Safed and Jerusalem Perushim, the two communities worked in coordination if not always in harmony. After all, the united Perushim kollel, with branches in Jerusalem, Safed, and Tiberias, shared a common leadership, treasury, and regulations and the spiritual tradition of the Vilna gaon.

Knowing the language and customs of the Western world, Benjamin helped Zoref collect contributions from donors when they visited London, Amsterdam, and other West European cities. In some of these cities Zoref and Benjamin convinced local leaders to forward to the Perushim all monies collected for Eretz Israel. Benjamin also used his facility in the English language to write to the Baltimore Jewish community asking them to donate money for Eretz Israel: "Let it not be said that our Atlantic Brethren have not the same Blood of commiseration flowing in their veins!...."[83]

Zoref's mission was a clear incursion by the Perushim into territory that by common consent of all parties had been monopolized by the Sephardim.[84] When Zoref approached PEKAM leader Zvi Hirsch Lehren in Amsterdam in 1819 he was rebuffed for overt aggressiveness; this marred their relationship, which deteriorated continually over the next twenty years. PEKAM did not think it fair to negotiate only with the Ashkenazim. "Lacking a representative of the opposing side... we stood loyal to our covenant with the Sephardi kollelim... and we did not favor the Ashkenazim..."[85] Until the Sephardim and Ashkenazim had an opportunity to present their cases jointly about three years later, PEKAM "did not wish to do anything before investigating the matter." This may have prompted the Perushim, in February 1821, to formally appoint Lehren as their "Guardian" in Western Europe,[86] with authority to represent Perushim interests similar to Lehren's appointment by the Sephardi kollelim during the 1810s.

Bolstered by this additional authority, in 1821 Lehren forwarded to the Istanbul Officials the case of the Perushim "with complaints and protests about the Sephardim in the holy cities of Safed and Jerusalem, which allocate the money... they are acting illegally in distributing all the money to the Sephardim, and to the Ashkenazim they give nothing." The Istanbul Officials answered that "if these complaints are true, they are also in our eyes most astounding and extraordinary..."

The Istanbul Officials then wrote to the Sephardi rabbis in Eretz Israel and asked them to answer the Perushim charges promptly. Eighteen months later the angry Sephardim of Jerusalem and Safed had still not responded, preferring to send to Europe two shlihim—Mordecai Asseo and Joseph David Ayish—to counter what they regarded as false accusations being spread by the Ashkenazim.

Such feverish controversies led to a series of "compromises" about how to allocate monies contributed to Jews living in the Holy Land. During 1822–1823 separate yet similar allocation compromises were negotiated in Vilna and Amsterdam. These agreements were compromises only in the sense that the Sephardim were forced to compromise their exclusive 100-

percent share of collection funds in Western Europe and surrender a large proportion of this income to the Ashkenazim. For the Ashkenazim the compromises were a large gain of revenue.

Early in 1822 opposing Sephardi and Ashkenazi shlihim appeared before a rabbinical court in Amsterdam and presented their strong opinions on how to allocate to Jerusalem funds collected in Western Europe. The Sephardi shaliah from Jerusalem was Joseph D. Ayish,[87] son of the Jerusalem chief rabbi from 1806 to 1817, who has provided us with a dense legal brief presenting the Sephardi case.[88] Joseph Ayish believed that "because the Sephardim have received the land as an inheritance, they should be granted legal preference as old-time settlers."[89] In his argument Ayish distinguished between the new Perushim settlers with their distinctive religious customs and the old-time Jerusalem Ashkenazim who were an integral part of the Sephardi kollel "and in the course of time participated in prayers according to the Sephardi ritual." How dare Ashkenazim invade Western Europe where Sephardim traditionally had a monopoly on Jewish contributions, while at the same time they shut the Sephardim out of East European fundraising territories? "Who prevents Sephardi shlihim from entering Polish cities and other places, claiming out-and-out lies that the Sephardim give nothing to the Ashkenazim and only slander them. . . . Is it possible to imagine that the Sephardim must pay while the Ashkenazim do not pay?" Although the Ashkenazim have a right to receive some funds allocated for Jerusalem, in R. Ayish's opinion these sums should be deducted from the general community expenditures disbursed solely by the Sephardim. If the Ashkenazim refuse to pay the Jewish community taxes, "they should be prevented from living on the Holy Mountain in Jerusalem."

In sharp counterpoint the Perushim shaliah, Shlomo Zalman Zoref, claimed that since the Sephardim received all the money donated in the countries of North Africa and elsewhere in the Turkish Empire, it was only right that the Perushim should benefit from all the money collected by the European Ashkenazim. In effect, Zoref contended that "the Sephardim should visit the Sephardim, and the Ashkenazim the Ashkenazim."[90] Zoref may also have argued that money from Eastern Europe was not reaching the Ashkenazim because of the intermittent Russian-Turkish conflicts, which adversely affected collection efforts in "Poland, Lithuania, and Russia,"[91] thus harming the economic position of the Ashkenazim in Eretz Israel.

The Amsterdam rabbinical court authorized a compromise that was formulated by the PEKAM leader, Lehren, who convinced the two shlihim to approve it.[92] In order to secure Sephardi consent for this 1822 compromise,
Lehren was forced to pay off Ayish, a dubious character who later converted to Christianity and then returned to the Jewish fold. "It is a crying
shame for the Holy Land that Ayish represents Eretz Israel," Lehren wrote,
because "from this shaliah Jews will judge the quality of the whole community."[93] The 1822 compromise provided that monies collected in Western
Europe by PEKAM and shlihim would be shared equally by the Ashkenazim
and the Sephardim of Jerusalem.[94] This meant that the 2,500 Sephardim and
the 200–250 Perushim would each receive an equal share of the revenues
from Western Europe. Lehren would not formulate a compromise for Safed
"because the Hasidic kollel is also there and [Zoref] does not represent
them."[95]

In retrospect Zvi Hirsch Lehren had such grave doubts about the equity
of the agreement that he "wanted to revoke the compromise of 1822 which
I myself designed."[96] He blamed Zoref for providing him with misleading
information about the number of Hasidim living in Jerusalem in 1822.
Zoref had accurately reported that hardly any Hasidim lived there, nor was
there a Hasidic kollel in Jerusalem, but Lehren did not believe him. He
voiced apprehension that "this advantage for the Jerusalem residents
[Perushim] whose haluka allocation is large, will cause Jews to leave their
homes in Safed and go to Jerusalem,"[97] a reverse twist of the 1810 Sephardi
suspicions that Jews would gravitate to Safed as a result of the over-
generous haluka system of the Perushim.

In order to secure support for the 1822 compromise, PEKAM sent the complete text to the Istanbul Officials, the Vilna Rabbis, and the chief rabbi of
London, all of whom approved it.[98] When the Jerusalem Sephardim learned
that they would lose revenues to the Ashkenazim, they raised a ruckus,
again threatened to chase the Perushim out of Jerusalem, and rejected the
compromise signed by their emissary, Ayish.

The 1822 compromise was a smashing victory for the Ashkenazim, who
for the first time received a large new source of revenue from Western Europe. The Perushim had broken the Sephardi monopoly over funds collected in Western Europe. One leader said that this great accomplishment
was sufficient to justify Zoref's existence under God.[99] PEKAM also scored a
signal success by drafting its first allocation key for the towns of Eretz Israel. It had established its central position in the Jewish philanthropic world
only twelve years after it was founded. The 1822 PEKAM compromise also

TABLE 8 Estimated Population of Jews in Eretz Israel, 1823–1824

	SAFED	JERUSALEM	HEBRON	TIBERIAS	TOTAL	PERCENT
Perushim	600	200	—	50	850	15
Hasidim	300	50	75	300	725	12
Sephardim	800	2500	325	650	4275	73
TOTAL	1700	2750	400	1000	5850	
PERCENT	29	47	7	17		100

TABLE 9 1823 Vilna Compromise: Distribution of Funds

	PERUSHIM		HASIDIM		SEPHARDIM		
	Shares	%	Shares	%	Shares	%	TOTAL
Jerusalem	5.5	20			5.5	20	11 (40%)
Safed							
Tiberias	4.0	14	4.5	16	8.5	30	17 (60%)
Hebron							
TOTAL	9.5	34	4.5	16	14.0	50	28 (100%)

was a milestone in Jewish philanthropic history because it was the first time that a Jewish community—Western Europe—provided nonpartisan support for all the Jews in Eretz Israel based on their general need and population strength, rather than on their countries of origin (Poles supporting Poles) and ideological affinities (Hasidim supporting Hasidim).

After Zoref won a new source of income for the Jerusalem Perushim in the 1822 Amsterdam compromise, he traveled to Vilna, which had replaced Shklov as the center of Perushim fundraising. There he contested with a Hasidic shaliah on how to distribute funds collected in Western Europe. This led to the 1823 compromise formulated in March by the Vilna rabbinical court.

According to the Vilna compromise, funds were distributed equally between the 1,500–1,600 Ashkenazim and the 4,200–4,300 Sephardim living in Eretz Israel (see tables 8 and 9) with the Perushim receiving more than double (34 percent) the sum of money distributed to the Hasidim (16 percent).[100]

One provision of the 1823 Vilna compromise was that all funds collected in Western Europe by the Hasidim and Perushim would be forwarded to Eretz Israel through Vilna, not Amsterdam. The agreement sought to eliminate sending emissaries of separate groups to the same area; emissaries were instructed to collect money only for their community, and personal fundraising efforts were forbidden.

When PEKAM learned the details of the Vilna compromise, Zvi Hirsch Lehren protested to the Vilna Rabbis against this "very bad" agreement that is "not honest or just" and "not formulated correctly and is lacking in balance and reason,"[101] for it favored the Perushim at the expense of the Hasidim. Miffed at Zoref and at the Ashkenazim for deciding how to allocate funds collected in Western Europe, right after the signing of the 1822 PEKAM compromise, Lehren berated Zoref for "skinning" the Hasidic emissary "and refusing to give him any part of Jerusalem's shares,"[102] although R. Israel wrote that the Jerusalem Perushim gave the Hasidim 1 of its 5.5 shares.[103] PEKAM also resented the Vilna compromise because it routed funds collected in Western Europe through Vilna, which refused to report to PEKAM on the amount of money collected.[104] Preferring not to make a bad situation worse, PEKAM quietly revoked the Vilna compromise and continued to allocate money to Jews in Eretz Israel according to the 1822 Amsterdam compromise.

Before the ink was dry on the Vilna 1823 compromise, two Safed shlihim—Benjamin of London and Mordecai Asseo—clashed in Amsterdam on how to distribute in Safed monies collected in Western Europe. Each argued before PEKAM "that he alone was entitled to collect contributions for Eretz Israel and neither refrained from scurrilities."[105] After PEKAM heard a replay of the 1822 debate between Shlomo Zalman Zoref and Joseph Ayish it decided that the Sephardim should receive one-third and the Ashkenazim two-thirds of the monies allocated to Safed in the 1810 compromise, with the Perushim and Hasidim dividing the two-thirds on a per capita basis. Further, the Sephardim should share with the Ashkenazim one-third of the money collected in Italy and the Turkish dominions, and the Ashkenazim would reciprocate by giving the Sephardim one-third of the money collected in Western Europe.

Asseo adamantly rejected PEKAM's decision, unable to accept what he regarded as the repellent idea of Ashkenazim sharing in West European funds. So, with the complete backing of the Dutch rabbinical authorities, PEKAM decided in June 1823 that through the end of the year Benjamin should take all the contributions "on behalf of his [Perushim] kehilla."

As PEKAM was seeking to reach more equitable arrangements for Jews in Eretz Israel, the several communities there were engaged in mecilessly reviling each other about who was authorized to collect money in what overseas communities. In Algeria and Italy the Ashkenazim challenged the collection monopoly of the Sephardim; in France the Hasidim bitterly fought the Perushim and required PEKAM's intervention to restore the peace.

The Sephardim even squabbled among themselves. The Tiberias Sephardi community, reestablished in 1740, zealously ensured that donations contributed to the Fund of Meir Ba'al HaNes were channeled only to Tiberias; after all, on the outskirts of town "is his place of rest."[106] On more than one occasion, a Sephardi shaliah from Jerusalem, Safed, or Hebron attempted to collect from the Meir Ba'al HaNes Fund, despite an agreement among the Sephardim that this money was specifically earmarked for Tiberias. For example, in 1821 a Sephardi emissary from Jerusalem made an attempt to take money raised in Meknes, Morocco, for that fund, but his efforts were rebuffed by the local Jewish community. When news of this incident reached Tiberias, the Sephardim there berated the Jerusalem Sephardim. To block further attempts at "robbery," the Tiberias community appointed trustees in North Africa to guard money "rightfully" due them.[107]

Hasidim and Perushim emissaries also wrangled verbally about money collected in France just after concluding the 1823 Vilna agreement. When two emissaries of the Hasidim came to Paris in 1824 to collect funds, local Jewish leaders told them that they had just given an emissary of the Perushim all their donations on the assumption that these would be divided between the two groups. At the suggestion of one Hasidic emissary, Zvi Dov Mintz, it was decided that from then on Parisian funds would be sent to the Hasidim, until the Perushim had duly shared the disputed money.[108]

When Mintz came to Amsterdam in the summer of 1824, PEKAM discovered that he had raised funds in various parts of France and appointed representatives to collect money exclusively for the Hasidim, thereby cutting off both the Sephardim and Perushim from these sources of income. After prolonged discussions during which an agitated Mintz indignantly argued that he had "toiled, troubled, and worked" to raise the funds and therefore the money rightfully belonged to the Hasidim,[109] Lehren agreed that all the money Mintz raised in France during 1824 should remain with the

Hasidim. But at the end of the year funds collected in France "would be like all other monies collected by PEKAM for Eretz Israel—the Sephardi kollel would be given its share and the portion of the Ashkenazi money would be distributed amongst the Ashkenazim of Eretz Israel—the Perushim and the Hasidim—on a per capita basis. And all monies collected there [France] will . . . be sent to the PEKAM . . ."

Another fundraising territory under contention was North Africa.[110] In 1824 the Ashkenazim of Safed and Jerusalem (probably the Perushim) riled the Sephardim by sending emissaries to Algiers and other places in North Africa where only Sephardi Jews lived. This was a brazen act considering that the Ashkenazim had shut out the Sephardim from Eastern Europe and in 1824 refused to donate "even one small piastre" to a Sephardi shaliah traveling in Poland.[111] Sephardi rabbis in Eretz Israel retaliated by ordering North African Jewish communities not to contribute "one small penny to the Ashkenazi shaliah" and threatened to excommunicate any Sephardi doing so.[112] This rabbinical stricture placed the North African Sephardim in an unenviable position: either disobey a rabbinical order or refuse to perform the mitzva of contributing to Eretz Israel. This religious dilemma was resolved by a wise Algerian rabbinical decision that allowed individual Sephardim, on their own initiative, to donate money to the Ashkenazi shaliah on the condition that they not reduce their normal contribution to the Sephardim of Eretz Israel.

The Ashkenazim next invaded Italy, which logically sent all its contributions to the Sephardim of Eretz Israel, for the Italian kehilla was predominantly of Sephardi ancestry.[113] Despite the Sephardi monopoly over Italian funds, there were at least two instances when shlihim collected money there for the Hasidim, without arousing Sephardi wrath. In 1825, however, the Perushim demanded a share of the funds collected in Italy. PEKAM initially backed these claims, threatening to cut off support to the Sephardim, unless the Sephardim in Italy "behave properly toward the kollelim of the Ashkenazim in Eretz Israel." But then PEKAM rejected the idea because "all our goals are directed at increasing powerful relations in Eretz Israel and if we repay them [the Sephardim] in kind,"[114] they will take retaliatory action against the Ashkenazim of Eretz Israel.

The Sephardim realized that after losing 50 percent of the PEKAM collections through the 1822 and 1823 compromises they might now lose it all. Thus, in July 1825, the Sephardim and Ashkenazim came to a mutual agreement, "after many pained efforts" in the words of R. Israel,[115] that Ashkenazi shlihim could collect money in Sephardi areas such as Italy and North Africa and Sephardi shlihim could collect money in Ashkenazi territories. All funds collected under this agreement would be divided 60 percent to the Ashkenazim and 40 percent to the Sephardim. Despite this agreement Ashkenazim continued "to complain about being injured by the Sephardim," prompting Lehren to advise them "to put aside these ideas and not unjustly shout at the Sephardim."[116]

By 1824 PEKAM had become the preeminent leader in collecting and allocating money to all Jews of Eretz Israel, eclipsing the Istanbul Officials, which lost importance as the Turkish Empire and its Jewish population declined, while Western Europe and its growing Jewish community gained in influence. PEKAM's importance was boosted not only by the initiatives and leadership of Lehren but by the difficulties of raising funds in Eastern Europe and forwarding them to Eretz Israel.[117]

PEKAM monies collected in Western Europe were sent to Amsterdam, where the banking house of Hollander and Lehren owned by PEKAM leaders transferred bills of exchange to Istanbul; during the 1820s transferring funds from Europe to Eretz Israel was a complicated and expensive transaction because the Ottoman Empire had no postal system, no banking or financial transfer system, and no stable currency or fixed exchange rates. Speedy and safe money transfers were obstructed by perilous overland routes, the lack of regular shipping schedules, stormy seas, and pirates that preyed in the eastern Mediterranean.[118] The interminable Turkish wars with Russia and the perpetual squabbles between pashas ruling different parts of Palestine also contributed to the difficulties of transmitting European funds to the four holy cities.

Money transferred from Istanbul to Eretz Israel arrived late and lost a large percentage of its value.[119] The Istanbul Officials used the good offices of French consular officials stationed in Istanbul, Acre, and Sidon just as Lehren was to use the English and Dutch consuls in Beirut during the 1830s.[120] Bills of exchange were handled by agents such as Anthony Katafago, who conveniently delayed payment and cashed bills at low exchange rates.[121] Because of the delays in transferring funds, Jews were obsessed with the arrival of the mail ship. While waiting for the boat, Jews frequently signed promissory notes that they cashed at a discount, with the maturity date designated as the date of the arrival of "the ship."

By solving fundraising problems and facilitating the transfer of funds, PEKAM aspired to the role of policy-setter and peacemaker among the Jews of Eretz Israel.[122] Lehren incessantly inveighed against factionalism among Jews of Eretz Israel, which worked against an imminent Messianic Redemption:

We are ashamed about the separatism among you . . . and let it not be said that this dissension happens by itself. . . . Let not one side make light of the honor of the opposite side and let no one disparage his friend. . . . If, God forbid, this hatred continues, it would then be better for all those who have malice and hatred in their heart to live a good and peaceful life in the Diaspora . . . this is a damaging sin committed on Holy Land.[123]

Lehren admonished both the Hasidim and the Perushim:

For God's sake, take pity and spare the honor of Eretz Israel and the honor of the scholars and the honor of all the Ashkenazim and come to a friendly compromise. . . . For whom do I work and toil all day long, for trouble-makers and rumor-mongers?

Eager for detailed knowledge about all Jewish activities in Eretz Israel, Lehren encouraged the various communities to write to him frequently and at length.[124] PEKAM published some of these letters to encourage larger contributions, and Lehren asked kollel leaders, "from time to time send us one letter telling about peace in the land . . . but, heaven forbid, do not mix in the letter any strife or contention with anyone."[125] Then Lehren added that "for the benefit of the Jewish community in Eretz Israel we ask only for the truth," which was heavily laden with strife and contention.

To achieve peace and unity PEKAM planned to "bring together the two communities" of Perushim and Hasidim by setting up a common treasury—"one pocket for everyone."[126] Within such a unified financial framework an equitable economic balance could be achieved among the Ashkenazim by PEKAM distributing funds on a per capita basis, as had been agreed between R. Israel and the Hasidim back around 1813. But these plans never materialized because of the fragmented structure of the kollelim.

Realizing their increasingly crucial role in supporting the Jews in Eretz Israel, PEKAM leaders searched for additional ways to increase contributions, put an end to the fracas among the feuding factions, and stop shlihim from traveling around Western Europe. Rabbi Shlomo Hirschel recommended and PEKAM agreed to the establishment of a Society for Contributions to the Holy Land,[127] similar to the organization R. Hirschel had set up in London in 1823.[128] The purpose of this society, which PEKAM founded in 1824, was to swell fundraising for Eretz Israel by initiating systematic new organizational techniques that would obviate the need for shlihim, whose expenses were very high. No longer would shlihim of the four holy cities travel widely about Western Europe grubbing for small contributions and siphoning off funds for special projects such as the Hurva. Lehren wrote: "I promised in each and every place that by pledging contributions, the shlihim of Eretz Israel will no longer travel to and fro. This greatly pleased the ears of my listeners . . ."[129] This arrangement was never approved by the communities of Eretz Israel, who were not even consulted.

This potent new PEKAM organization had other advantages. It would help surmount financial obstacles and government regulations restricting the transfer of currencies to Eretz Israel. It would also be in a better position to combat opposition to fundraising for Eretz Israel that was now being displayed by Reform German Jewry and other Jews trying to emancipate themselves by mingling and assimilating into the Gentile society.

Lehren's ringing injunctions against shlihim proved to be more intimidating than effective in keeping them out of Western Europe. Nevertheless PEKAM's financial power provided it with a weapon enabling it to intervene in the internal affairs of the Jews in Eretz Israel; and the distance between intervention and domination was at times hardly distinguishable. In 1825 PEKAM again told the communities in Eretz Israel not to send emissaries to Western Europe: "It is not for the benefit of the kollelim that more shlihim should come and go with God's help, [PEKAM] will work for the good of everyone."[130] During that summer, when the Sephardi shaliah, Jacob David Katz,[131] visited Italy, France, London, and then Amsterdam, Lehren informed him, with all due respect, that he was prohibited from collecting money in PEKAM territory. That was sufficient to stop Katz's fundraising efforts. Lehren threatened the Sephardim that if "they do not agree to our compromises and regulations preventing shlihim from traveling . . . we will withdraw our support from them and provide benefits only to the Ashkenazi kollelim." In the heat of the argument, Lehren conveniently disregarded the fact that the Ashkenazim also opposed banning emissaries.[132]

The Sephardim were distressed not only by PEKAM's ban on shlihim but on the negative effect it was producing in Jewish communities such as Venice, which wanted to emulate the collection practices of PEKAM.[133] Although the Venice Jewish community lacked the financial strength of PEKAM, Sephardi leaders in all four holy cities wrote to it about the absolute necessity for maintaining the institution of shlihim and promised that they would henceforth dispatch shlihim on a regular schedule rather than in the prevalent haphazard, uncoordinated fashion. The Sephardim also agreed that shlihim would keep only 20 percent of the funds they collected, ostensibly because improved transportation now allowed them to traverse in one year the same travel circuit that previously took more than four years.

Sephardi leaders felt tricked by PEKAM's edict against shlihim and betrayed by the Ashkenazim of Eretz Israel. At PEKAM's order, all of Western Europe was closed off to Sephardi emissaries. How could this happen just after they had agreed with the Ashkenazim that each group could collect money in the other's territory and divide the money 60 percent to the Ashkenazim and only 40 percent to the Sephardim? Once again, Sephardim lost income, this time in an agreement that both parties had concluded in good faith. The Ashkenazim did not take PEKAM's prohibition against shlihim too seriously and would continue to defy it, but the Sephardim characteristically bowed before PEKAM's edict and resigned themselves to the new situation.

The Perushim and Hasidim, fellow Ashkenazim of PEKAM, fought the abolition of the institution of emissaries. They claimed that, without the personal message of the shlihim, Diaspora Jews would forget Eretz Israel, their love of Zion would atrophy, and the flow of money would diminish from year to year. Torah would be forgotten in many places. And what would happen to impressionable children who would lack a living link with Eretz Israel? They would neglect Eretz Israel and its poor population. Certainly, the shaliah's intimate knowledge of Eretz Israel was more convincing than local volunteer collectors appointed by PEKAM.[134]

More practical matters also motivated the Ashkenazim to fight the ban against sending shlihim to Western Europe. If the coveted position of shaliah was done away with, scholars chosen as emissaries would lose large incomes and ancillary benefits.

The emotional arguments of the Ashkenazim could not overcome the stubborn stand of Zvi Hirsch Lehren. In a long letter he summarized six major reasons for this opposition to the shlihim:[135]

1. Their expenses were much too high and they were constantly increasing. In the old days shlihim traveled by horse and wagon while today they rode in expensive carriages.
2. Expenses for food and lodging had greatly increased. No longer were shlihim content to stay in second-class inns.
3. Some shlihim damaged their cause by behaving abominably; they "stank and gave off a stench."
4. A few cunning persons masqueraded as shlihim and embezzled money destined for the poor people of Eretz Israel.

5. Off-the-beaten-path Jewish communities were not visited by shlihim, who were not interested in collecting small sums. In other towns money was inadvertently not collected.
6. The salary of the shaliah is exorbitant and usually totals 20–33 percent of the collections. Shlihim deducted up to half of their collections for salary and expenses, compared to PEKAM's fundraising costs of 6 to 8 percent of the total contributions.

Lehren complained that squabbling shlihim not only produced ill-will among Jews in Europe and Eretz Israel, but aroused the suspicions of municipalities in places such as Brussels and Hamburg, which stopped their collection efforts and sometimes imprisoned them.[136] He noted that the shaliah "is interested in the personal benefit of the individual, and PEKAM, with God's help, is interested in what's beneficial for the whole group."

Led by the dauntless Lehren, in Western Europe PEKAM was partially successful in doing away with the 300-year-old custom of shlihim that provided a vibrant connection reciprocally binding Diaspora Jewry to the spiritual center of world Jewry. The revenues of the Jewish community in Eretz Israel were indeed increased, but the personal contact between Jews in Western Europe and Eretz Israel was weakened.

During 1815–1825 Perushim activities established the tone for the escalating tensions in Ashkenazi-Sephardi relations and set the pace of development for the Jews in Eretz Israel. Before and after the arrival of the volatile Perushim in Eretz Israel, money was the juncture point of the fierce internecine strife between the groups, but basic reasons for the disagreements were more complicated.[137]

When the Perushim quietly settled "temporarily" in Jerusalem, the Sephardim assisted them in many ways despite a wariness that the authorities might demand increased taxes from the Jewish community. It was mutually understood that the Perushim would pay their own expenses; they did not wish to be economically obligated and dependent on the patronage of the debt-ridden Sephardi community. Soon after settling in permanently, the Perushim realized that they had to establish an autonomous community with an independent economic base in order to grow and develop. After treading softly for two to three years, the Jerusalem Perushim resolutely adopted tactics for increasing their revenues and reducing their expenditures. Led by the irresistibly forceful R. Israel of Shklov, the Perushim paid as little money as possible to both the Turkish authorities and the Sephardim, by applying the capitulation agreements and opting out of paying local taxes, thereby pushing a greater share of the tax burden onto the Sephardim. In addition, they were fortuitously freed from repaying the 1720 debts of Judah HeHasid. The Perushim also decreased expenses by using legalistic ploys to stop remitting inheritance payments to the Sephardim, but they were unable to escape payment of the meat tax and burial and other fees because they failed to secure the approval of the authorities to be considered a separate millet.

On the income side the Perushim succeeded spectacularly in increasing the amount of money entering their treasury from overseas Jewry. They and the Hasidim received half of PEKAM allocations, which previously had been routed exclusively to the Sephardim. Then the Perushim found new sources of revenue by invading Sephardi fundraising territories in Italy and North Africa. Despite these efforts they discovered that they could not rebuild the Hurva synagogue for lack of financial means.

Unlike the Perushim, the Hasidim did not agitate to achieve autonomy and increase their income, nor did they seek to establish a beachhead in Jerusalem or rebuild the Hurva that had belonged to their ideological forefathers in R. Judah HeHasid's group. And, unlike the unified Perushim, the Hasidim, who had split in 1797 into White Russia and Volhynia groups, again fragmented in 1818 with the establishment of Habad Hasidic groups in Hebron. After long years in the Galilee, the Hasidim had learned the art of compromise and lived in peaceful coexistence with the Sephardim—except when the Perushim upset the status quo, as they did in 1822–1823, causing the Tiberias Hasidim to resort to the capitulations. Despite their passivity, the Hasidim reaped the benefits of the Perushim-inspired changes.

During the short span of less than ten years the constant efforts of the Perushim to provide greater financial resources for their growing community completely unsettled the sedate Sephardim, who had learned the importance of passivity in their relations with the Muslims and found it hard to shake off this behavior pattern in their relations with the Perushim. R. Israel declared, with a touch of patronizing indulgence, that "we [the Perushim] have not harmed nor will we harm the Sephardi Jews, not even with a pin-point."[138] However sincere his intentions may have been, the preoccupied Perushim lacked the neutrality and perspective to admit that the economic needs of their developing community clashed with those of the Sephardi community.

The Sephardi income was plummeting, but its expenses were increasing because the arbitrary Turkish authorities continued to demand a variety of tax payments for the ever-growing number of Jews in Eretz Israel. The revenue losses of the Sephardim were serious, but more important was their loss of prestige in the world Jewish community and their disparaged status in the Turkish Empire. The standing of the Sephardi millet as the representative of all Jews in Eretz Israel was undermined. Their power to command obedience among members of the Jewish comunity was crippled. The hegemony of Sephardi Jews in Eretz Israel was coming to an end.

The confounded Sephardim were abashed at the sudden turn of events initiated by settlers they had warmly welcomed a few years before. It was difficult for them to comprehend why, after having peacefully coexisted for so long with the Hasidim, the Perushim community now challenged their authority to represent the whole Jewish community. Were not the daily contacts of individual Sephardim and Ashkenazim most amicable?

In surprise and outrage the Sepharadim reacted sporadically over specific issues, trying to keep the peace yet stem the tide that was emptying their treasury, humbling their pride, and shattering their influence. They used their influence in Istanbul to block the granting of a firman that could have established the Ashkenazim as an autonomous community. In relations with the pashas of Acre and Damascus and the local governors in Tiberias, Safed, and Jerusalem, the Sephardim harassed the Perushim by using the power of the millet and their long-standing personal contacts with local officials. Sephardi complaints before the authorities were pejoratively labeled by Perushim as "slander," "informing against," and "betraying." In one outburst of unbridled invective, R. Israel lambasted the Sephardim for "stealing" and writing "great lies" in "devilish letters."[139] The Sephardim angered the Perushim by demanding payment for services such as certifying kosher meat and burying the dead in the Jewish cemetery, but the ultimate outrage was the Sephardi threat to expel them from Jerusalem.

The temporizing Sephardim were overwhelmed by the steamrolling campaign of the singleminded Perushim. A simplistic comparison of the Sephardim and Ashkenazim contains a small measure of truth about the success of the Perushim onslaught. Ludwig August Frankl, a distinguished Jewish traveler, wrote in 1856 that the Ashkenazi "restlessness, their skill in writing, and their innate love of intrigue impel them to oppose and to overreach their Oriental brethren, who are not so active, or so quickwitted."[140] It would be more accurate to state that the Perushim, never acclaimed for their collaborative impulses, were inspired by the religious spirit of true believers and could not moderate their opinions or compromise their ideals. Their religious ideology had been unleashed in absolute form, so that they could unconditionally determine how to settle in Eretz Israel.

SEVEN

English and American Missionaries in Palestine

1820–1829

Jews living in Palestine throughout the nineteenth century, "the great century of the Christian missions," were strongly affected by the activities of the English Protestant missionaries who believed in the conversion of Jews and their physical Restoration in the Holy Land in preparation for the Second Advent of Jesus Christ. Christian faith in the Millennium—after his Second Coming, Jesus would establish the kingdom of heaven on earth and reign over it for one thousand years until the Last Judgment—inspired the missionaries and guided the lives of many Englishmen. Lord Shaftesbury spoke for them when he stated that the Second Advent was "a moving principle in my life for I see everything going on in the world subordinate to this great event."[1] Intensive reading of the Bible, absorption of the Old Testament into English culture, and mass attendance at church marked turn-of-the century England, which was intoxicated with the Millennium.

The Restoration views of the millenarians were also related to the political and social upheavals in Europe brought about by the French Revolution and tied to developments in the Near East after the French invasion of Egypt.[2] The famous chemist, philosopher, and Unitarian minister Joseph Priestley and other millenarians prayed for the eventual collapse of the

Turkish Empire. Priestley wrote to the Jews that "Palestine, the glory of all lands, which is now part of the Turkish empire, is almost without inhabitants, it is wholly uncultivated, empty and ready to receive you. But till the fall of this power, which, without deriving any advantage from it, keeps possession of the country, it is impossible that it can be yours. I, therefore, earnestly pray for its dissolution."[3] British millenarians were undeterred by the fact that from the time of William Pitt's administration in the 1790s until after 1840 British foreign policy consistently bolstered the tottering Ottoman Empire.

When Napoleon overthrew the Papal States in 1796–1798 and then invaded the Turkish territories of Egypt and Palestine, the millenarians saw a confirmation of their dream that a new era was dawning. They advocated the deliverance of Jews in Palestine as a practical matter requiring the attention of the British nation. England was petitioned around the turn of the century to "take the lead" and help bring about the "final restoration of the Jews to the Holy Land . . . with the strength of the British fleet . . ."[4] The millenarians proclaimed that England should fulfill the Redemption prophecies, thwart the ambitions of France, and promote British political and commercial interests in the Near East. Political purposes and millennium prophecies were intertwined, but the political dog was wagging the prophetic tail. Anglican mission activities in Palestine were a prelude to British diplomatic moves aimed at expanding Britain's sphere of influence in the Near East. The thought of "atheistic" French revolutionaries, then at war with England, conquering Egypt and leading the Jews back to Palestine raised the hackles of British patriots.

While the Messianic fervor of Restoration authors kept the printing presses rolling with tracts about Israel's Redemption, some Englishmen took practical action by establishing the London Society for Promoting Christianity Amongst the Jews in 1809. This London Jews Society (LJS), as it was called, was founded by distinguished, establishment Englishmen to obey Christ's injunction to "make disciples of all nations" (Matthew 28:19) and specifically to teach the Jews that Jesus Christ is the true Messiah.[5] Since Jews had been chosen by God to prepare the Coming of Christ, converting Jews represented "the highest good of the Jewish people and through them of the whole world."[6] By saving Jewish souls, the missionaries aspired to improve the Jews' everlasting fate as well as their daily lives.

As true millenarians, LJS leaders preached that the return of Jews to Zion, together with their conversion to Christianity, was an indispensable prerequisite for the Second Coming of Christ on earth. The LJS felt the need to establish itself in Jerusalem. "How else can the Divine command be literally obeyed?"[7] Anglicans appear to have been oblivious to the obvious—that Jerusalem would be the last place where they could expect to make converts, since its very stones serve to remind the Jews of the wellsprings of their religion.[8] The LJS expressed a combined religious obligation and national destiny. It confidently believed that it could change the implacable ways of the Jews because the English in the nineteenth century were absolutely convinced that they could shape the world.

Although the English established the LJS one year before the American Board of Commissioners for Foreign Missions was founded,[9] the Americans were first to dispatch missionaries to Palestine. In the opinion of the stern Prudential Committee of the American Board, whose members drew spiritual sustenance from their austere New England pilgrim forefathers, "in Palestine . . . the whole mingled population is in a state of deplorable ignorance and degradation . . ."[10] Therefore the American Board unanimously resolved (September 23, 1818) "that a mission be established forthwith in Palestine."[11] That very day Levi Parsons and Pliny Fisk were "designated for Jerusalem and such other parts of Western Asia" and each was called a "missionary to Palestine."[12] These young men were instructed to "survey . . . the various tribes and classes" in Palestine and report on "WHAT can be done for Jews."[13]

Parsons and Fisk were graduates of the Andover Theological Seminary in Massachusetts, the center of missionary activity in America. Despite their theological education and on-the-job missionary training, Fisk and Parsons did not know Arabic and Hebrew, the basic languages for preaching and praying in Palestine. What skills they lacked were to be compensated for by absolute dedication and missionary fervor.

Fisk and Parsons undoubtedly were warned, like two other American missionaries who followed them to the Near East in 1823, that "the hour is near when you expect to leave the shores of your native land with the probability that you will never see them again."[14] But such dangers were inconsequential compared to the joy of establishing "a permanent station in the vineyard of Christ."[15] To light the streets of Jerusalem, Parsons was presented with a farewell gift of an elegant pocket lantern.

Three days after preaching their departure sermons, in November 1819, Parsons and Fisk sailed from Boston. They were instructed to stop at Smyrna (present-day Izmir) and "proceed to Palestine, and there fix their station at Jerusalem, if found practical and eligible; if not, at such other place, within or without the limits of Judea, as Providence shall indicate."[16]

This mission to the afflicted heathen "now sitting in darkness, in that once favored land," was motivated by the religious zeal inspiring many

Americans to participate in "the second great awakening of Christianity,"[17] but it had little in common with English millennialism and its ideology of restoring Jews in Zion. Americans believed that Palestine and its Jews were to be converted for the sake of Jesus Christ. "They are beloved for the Father's sake."[18]

Another difference that was to influence the operations of the English and American missionary organizations was the fact that the United States, in contrast to Great Britain, had no commercial or political interests in Syria. Not until 1830 did America sign a commercial treaty with the Ottoman Empire. In December 1823 President Monroe proclaimed America's "hands off" policy in the Monroe Doctrine, which declared that the United States would not intervene in the internal affairs of European nations. In the days before Manifest Destiny, the major interest of the Americans in the Mediterranean area in the 1820s was protecting American ships from Barbary pirates infesting that international waterway.

The American missionaries' ship anchored in Malta, where they received guidance and encouragement from the leaders of the British Church Missionary Society (CMS), founded in 1799.[19] Parsons and Fisk probably heard from CMS leaders William Jowett and Charles Naudi about the brief visit to Jerusalem in 1818–1819 of Christian Burckhardt, an agent of the British Foreign Bible Society, who died of fever near Aleppo shortly after distributing Bibles in the Holy City. They may have learned that, although Roman Catholics had conducted missionary work in Syria from the end of the seventeenth century, they had no contact with the Jews.

While "brothers" Parsons and Fisk were in Smyrna, Melchior Tschoudi,[20] a Swiss pastor affiliated with the LJS, toured Jerusalem and distributed Bibles to its Jewish residents. CMS missionary James Connor also visited Jerusalem, where he conducted discussions with Christians. "Among the Jews," he admitted, "I have not been able to do anything."[21] Missionaries such as Connor, Burckhardt, and Tschoudi reconnoitered Jerusalem and experienced the blatant antagonism of the Muslim population and authorities toward Christians, leading the American Board to generalize that "the nature of the Turkish government may be considered unfavorable to Christian Missions."[22]

James Connor advised Parsons and Fisk about the impossibility of establishing a permanent mission station in Jerusalem.[23] "Jerusalem should be visited every Passover by one or another of us, but I should fear the consequences of its becoming the headquarters of a mission." It was only at Easter that strangers entered the city and any foreigner, unless he was a physician, was an object of suspicion to all inhabitants. Connor also pointed out that the Christian interdenominational strife was stronger in Jerusalem than elsewhere in Palestine.

Constantly prodded by the American Board to establish a station in Jerusalem—"The importance of the station will outweigh many difficulties"—they decided that Parsons, more oriented than Fisk to laboring among the Jews, would visit Jerusalem. So, thirteen months after arriving in Smyrna and carrying a firman from the sultan, Parsons landed in Jaffa in 1821.[24] This unhurried pace indicates that the American missionaries were seized by a less than overwhelming compulsion to visit the Holy Land.

During his eighty-day stay in Jerusalem, Parsons explored the possibilities of conducting American mission activities. He distributed Bibles in nine languages, plus 4,000–5,000 religious tracts, believing that "the distribution of Bibles and tracts is the grand method of doing good" in the Ottoman Empire.[25] Parsons painted a "dismal picture of Jerusalem" and reported on the countryside "growing into a state of rebellion" at the start of the Greek revolt against the sultan. But his spirits were buoyed up by the knowledge that "Jesus Christ holds an undisputed title to this land."

The American missionary's most helpful contact, Procopus, procurator-general of the Greek convent, reported that Levi Parsons "went every day among Jews, until he was obliged to leave Jerusalem."[26] This report is not confirmed by the journal Parsons published, which contains only two entries about his contacts with Jews: one day he visited the four Sephardi synagogues, and on another day he attended a Jewish funeral that lacked "solemnity and regularity."[27] Parsons was received respectfully but suspiciously by the Jews. When he asked how many Jews lived in Jerusalem, the wary Jews queried: "Why do you ask us this question?" Some Jews told Parsons that 3,000 of their co-religionists lived in Jerusalem, but others disagreed without noting if this population estimate was too high or too low. Lacking a common language with the Jews, Parsons could not read Scripture to them or develop a dialogue with them on religious subjects.

Parsons encountered numerous obstacles that would have to be overcome in order to establish a mission station in Jerusalem. Most formidable was the order barring tourists, diplomats, and missionaries from settling in Jerusalem, with the exception of guardians of holy sites, doctors, and select clergymen of the recognized minority groups. As Protestantism was not a recognized minority religion, its missionaries could not hope to establish a mission in Jerusalem without the unlikely intervention of the United States government. Another difficulty that hindered mission activities throughout the Ottoman Empire was the legal ban on proselytizing among the Muslims. In addition, the Roman Catholic and Eastern Orthodox churches zealously opposed conversion activities among their members, and the traditional enmity between Roman Catholics and Protestants undermined mission efforts. Also troublesome to Parsons were the Muslim persecutions of Christians in Jerusalem in the wake of the Greek uprising proclaimed on March 21, 1821. These impediments to conducting missionary activities in Palestine and setting up a permanent mission station in Jerusalem were quite insurmountable in 1821.

After less than three months of reconnaissance work, Parsons left Jerusalem because of the "Greek wars and rumours of wars" and the belief that it is "not safe to pass the hot months of the year at Jerusalem."[28] Before returning to Smyrna he was fully convinced that "Palestine is a station of high importance." The Jerusalem station is "one of the most important that can be selected, and one which cannot be relinquished . . ."

Two months after leaving Jerusalem Parsons longed for the Holy City. "The probability of being kept from Jerusalem a long time is my great trial. My heart is there. I never was sensible of greater attachment to any place. I am tried with impatience."[29] Parsons concluded that Jerusalem "is indeed the centre of the world. The station must not be relinquished. The door is already open. Difficulties must be expected, but the good resulting from a mission established here will be an infinite reward." He was not suggesting the establishment of a permanent mission, but periodic visits of missionaries to be carried out from conveniently located ports such as Smyrna or Beirut, where missionaries could benefit from a healthy climate and the protection of European consuls.

Parsons's visit to Jerusalem was hailed by the American Board "as the dawn of a brighter day to the mingled people of the eastern world."[30] No specific mention was made of the Jews. Before the American Board could act upon his suggestions, in February 1822, 30-year-old Parsons died from an undetermined fever "to which severe hardship and an unfavorable climate contributed."[31]

Mission activities in Jerusalem were stymied during 1821–1826 by the anarchy that swept Jerusalem as a result of the strife between rival pashas and feuding Muslim clans and because of the Greek insurrection against Turkey.[32] The Jews of Jerusalem mourned when they received news that the Greeks, while fighting the Turks, had slain thousands of their brethren in Morea, the southern region of continental Greece. In Jerusalem, Greek Orthodox and Roman Catholics were disarmed, ordered to dress only in black for easy identification, and compelled to repair the city's fortifications—as the Jews had done during Napoleon's invasion of Palestine in 1799. Muslim clerics instigated the Jerusalem population against the Greek Orthodox patriarchate and threatened the lives of all Christians. This reign of terror was slowly brought under control by the intervention of the Turkish authorities in Istanbul, who feared the international consequences of an indiscriminate slaughter of Christians.

An uneasy quiet descended on Jerusalem as the governor, at the behest of Mustafa Pasha in Damascus, continued to levy heavy taxes upon Christians and Jews. The annual tax on Greek Catholics was increased from 60,000 to 100,000 piastres, and a heavy tax was imposed upon the Jews. In 1821 the Sephardim were taxed 81,000 piastres and the Perushim 75,000 piastres.[33] This sum excluded "taxes levied on individuals [poll tax] and many were harshly imprisoned and were chained by irons to the pasha's tent outside the city." When Christians and Jews could not raise the tax money, they were jailed and beaten until their community paid up, a wonderfully effective collection technique. To escape persecution many Christians fled to monasteries near Jerusalem, but Jews, lacking a place of refuge, remained in the city.

Undaunted by the unsettled situation in Jerusalem, Joseph Wolff, the converted son of a Bavarian rabbi, landed in Jaffa just after Christmas 1821, with the specific intention of conducting LJS mission activities among his "lost brethren of the House of Israel."[34] Wolff had first left the Jewish fold for the Roman Catholic Church and later joined the Church of England. He was admiringly described as a man "consumed with zeal, untiring energy and romantic enthusiasm . . . a comet without any perihelion and capable of setting a whole system on fire . . . " A veritable dervish of activity, Wolff was an eternal traveler, in the best wandering-Jew tradition.

Wolff first toured northern Palestine and Mount Lebanon before proceeding to Jerusalem.[35] In Acre he met consul Anthony Katafago and Joseph Amzalag, a Jew from Gibraltar who came to Palestine about 1815. Amzalag, a wealthy merchant, introduced Wolff to several learned Jews from Safed and gave him a letter of introduction to a rabbi in Jerusalem. Wolff also met two Jews who, he claimed, "are convinced of the truth of Christianity" but cannot "profess publicly" because "their lives would be in danger among bigotted [*sic*] Jews."

Not until March 1822 did Wolff enter Jerusalem and lodge at the comfortable Armenian convent. When he realized that Jews were not visiting him, he moved into a home in the Muslim quarter, "in order that I may converse with more freedom with the Jews."[36] But eleven days later he returned to the Armenian convent, "for the house of the Turk [a synonym for Arab or Muslim, used by foreigners ignorant of the local scene] has been too unhealthy."

Wolff's missionary activities in Jerusalem, like those of other Christians, were adversely affected by fierce verbal battles and physical fights among rival Christian denominations over religious rights in the Church of the Holy Sepulchre. "Oh, what gross idolatry and imposture," he complained. A Jew admonished Wolff about this display of un-Christian behavior:

You wish to convert us to Christianity. Look to Mount Calvary, where Jesus of Nazareth was crucified, of whom you say that he came to establish peace on earth. Look to Calvary; there his followers reside— Armenians, Copts, Greeks, Abyssinians, and Latins; all bear the name of Christians, and Christians are shedding the blood of Christians on the same spot where Jesus of Nazareth died.[37]

Wolff ignored the lack of Christian unity by concentrating his boundless energies on the Jews. To make contacts with the Jewish community of 700 families or about 2,800 persons,[38] Wolff distributed dozens of Hebrew copies of the Old and New Testaments, marked with the sign of the cross. One Jew paid 15 piastres for five Bibles and thereupon was given "fifteen floggings upon his feet" on orders of the kollel. Sephardi rabbis demanded that the books be burned, and two Sephardim unsuccessfully tried to have Wolff expelled from Jerusalem by accusing him before the governor of "distributing Christian books among the Jews."

The Sephardi rabbis Meyahis, Rabem, and Koba convened a meeting with Wolff to explain their viewpoint. The meeting was conducted in Hebrew and the only extant record was written by Wolff, not a good listener and obviously an interested party. Rabbi Meyahis opened the meeting: "Some of the Jews in Jerusalem are partly from Salonichi, partly from Barbary, and others from Polonia; many of them are rough and ignorant, are not able to discern good from bad, or bad from good; many of them do not know their own laws, and we must therefore watch over them, we are not bad shepherds."[39] He proceeded to explain how Wolff's Bibles were in error and concluded, "We are therefore determined to burn every copy of them." Wolff then presented his side of the case, and Rabbi Meyahis concluded in the most conciliatory tone: "Let us not quarrel, but be friendly together; we will, with all our hearts, receive from the English nation copies of our Bible, *but without notes, without commentary, without any preface and without any Latin character.*" It is interesting that Wolff is regarded by the rabbis as a representative of the "English nation." Wolff agreed not to distribute

New Testaments and Christian tracts, if only because "I perceive that they are determined to burn every copy of them," thereby grudgingly conceding that the kollel effectively controlled the actions of its members. At this point the leader of the Perushim, R. Menaham Mendel of Shklov, joined the meeting and agreed with the decision.

Such religious debates were more appropriate to Wolff's temperament than the passive role of Bible distributor. He spent most of his time in frequent, long, and loud discussions with the learned Sephardi and Ashkenazi Jews, who treated him with "the greatest kindness, and even with respect."[40] Many Jews, such as R. Menaham Mendel and S. Z. Shapira, conversed and argued interminably with Wolff—they called him "rabbi Joseph."

No doubt Wolff's erudition and ability to protect them as the representative of the "English nation" attracted the Jewish scholars, who shunned religious discussions with Gentiles like the plague. The major reason that R. Menahem Mendel (and other Perushim) maintained a constant religious dialogue with him was that, as Wolff himself wrote, "Rabbi Mendel expressed his desire of seeing me turn again to Judaism" and actively tried "converting me to Judaism."[41] This implausible desire of the Jews to reconvert Wolff, and the impossible wish of the missionaries to convert the Jews of Jerusalem, curiously formed the basis of contact between the Christian missionary and the Jewish community. This relationship also provided Jews with an opportunity to evade kollel censorship by sending letters abroad through the LJS postal packet.

In an effort to convert the missionary, R. Menahem Mendel frequently studied with Wolff, who wrote, "He offered to read Hebrew with me every day, and to converse with me on the subject of religion."[42] R. Menahem Mendel even agreed to accept a copy of the New Testament from Wolff. Both men demonstrated cordiality, but Wolff complained about R. Menahem Mendel's "obstinacy" and noted that he "has the fault of interpreting me always, especially when persons are present." Wolff admired the rabbi's scholarship and self-effacing manner. "I [was] surprised to see before me a kind looking Jew, without the least pretension, and his countenance marked with humility; he may be fifty years of age. He excused himself for sending for me saying, I never go out and I should be therefore very glad to see you every day in my house." In the best talmudic tradition, their studies were transformed into disputes. "We argued again for some hours" was the way Wolff expressed it.

Wolff's request to study in the yeshiva was denied because he refused to believe in the Talmud—a corrupt interpretation of the Mosaic Law in the opinion of all missionaries, who accepted the first revelations of the Old

Testament as a logical stepping-stone to the higher revelations of the New Testament. Adhering to the Talmud—"the great barrier . . . between the Jew and the missionary"—broke the continuity between the Old and New Testament.[43]

The longer and harder R. Menahem Mendel strove to convert Wolff, the less he succeeded. "Every word which that sincere Rabbi spake, confirmed me in the belief that Jesus of Nazareth is the Messiah." Many Jews tried to outdo their rabbi in convincing Wolff to return to the path of Judaism. Even Mordecai, the 14-year-old son of Shlomo Zalman Zoref, boldly undertook to argue with Wolff. Debating with Wolff became such a Jewish sport that R. Menahem Mendel threatened "to pronounce an anathema against those who should dare any longer to argue [with him]." Wolff reported that the majority of Jews declared they would ignore such an anathema, but that is inconceivable, in view of the religious authority and power over the community possessed by the Jewish leadership.

After spending nearly three months in Jerusalem, Wolff felt the satisfaction of achievement. In a show of self-contentment Wolff quoted a rabbi as saying that, if LJS had sent another missionary, no Jew would have taken the trouble to converse with him. Wolff boasted, "I gained so much their confidence that they consulted with me about their own business."

In July 1822 Wolff left Jerusalem because of the "increasing war between the two Pashas of Acre and Damascus." By April 1823 the peripatetic Wolff had traveled widely, crossed the Sinai desert, and was again back in Jerusalem, this time in the company of two American missionaries, Pliny Fisk and Jonah King, successor to the deceased Levi Parsons.[44]

Wolff, in his inimitable style, reported, "Fisk and King took their lodging in the Greek convent, and I took mine among the Jews upon Mount Zion. They went to the uncircumcision, and I to the circumcision."[45] Wolff sought a place to live in the Jewish quarter but this was no simple matter. He encountered opposition from Sephardim led by R. Shlomo Moshe Suzin, who had recently succeeded to the post of chief rabbi after the death of R. Yom Tov Danon, Jerusalem's chief rabbi from 1821 to 1823. R. Suzin "observed that it never was seen at Jerusalem that a Jew should come there for the purpose of persuading them that Jesus is the Messiah." Because it was "against our constitution and custom," R. Suzin invoked the Jerusalem regulation that prohibited unmarried men 20 to 60 years of age from living in the Jewish community. R. Suzin also voiced apprehension that "the Turks may suspect that we are trying to draw Europeans to our part, and to render ourself independent," so he threatened to send a protest to the pasha

Indefatigable English pioneer missionary Joseph Wolff, who tried to convert the Jews of Jerusalem in 1822, 1823, and 1829.

American missionary Jonas King.

of Damascus. But these were only excuses for trying to keep Wolff far from the Jews.

The Sephardim, unable to avail themselves of the protection the missionaries provided to foreign nationals of European countries, took a hard line against Wolff's place of residence and his mission activities. They issued several excommunication edicts against Jews loaning books to Wolff, but these bans, Wolff claimed, were disregarded. Despite Sephardi opposition, Wolff rented a Muslim-owned house in the Jewish quarter thanks to the assistance of R. Menahem Mendel, who still believed that he could return Wolff to the Jewish fold. "Wolff is sincere; he has been led astray in his early years by reading the New Testament."[46] R. Menahem Mendel again met frequently with Wolff, discussing Jewish religious law, the Talmud, the New Testament, and Jesus Christ. They even dined together at the rabbi's house, and Wolff succeeded in angering Menahem Mendel's wife when he refused to wash his hands and recite the appropriate prayer before the meal, stating that he was unwilling to perform a talmudic ceremony.

Fisk and King remained in Jerusalem for two months, touring the religious sites. They were depressed by what they saw. "I weep when I think of Zion and look to the desolation of Jerusalem," Fisk wrote. "God has forsaken the beloved city, and all her glory is departed."[47] Fisk and King mingled mainly with Catholics and Greeks and read portions of the New Testament with the Muslims. While Wolff "labored almost incessantly" among the Jews, "Jewish unbelief and hardness of heart" repulsed the efforts of Fisk and King to discuss religion with them.

The American missionaries toured the Jewish quarter and saw poor and ragged Jews "praying for the privilege of weeping [at the Wailing Wall] where their fathers sang, and rejoiced, and triumphed."[48] Twice Fisk prevented the persecution of Jews by Muslims, leading him to comment, "Poor Jews. When will they learn the true cause of their oppression, and repent and turn to God." Fisk reported that 600 Sephardim and 25 Ashkenazi families or 2,500 Jews lived in Jerusalem; there were also 10,000 Muslims, 2,000 Greeks, 1,500 Catholics, and 500 Armenians.

Wolff introduced the two American missionaries to R. Menahem Mendel and other Jews and served as translator.[49] When the rabbi met King and Fisk, he expressed regret that he was not able to speak their language. During the religious discussion, King told R. Menahem Mendel, "Christians in America and England are continually praying for your restoration; we long to have the time come when the Holy Spirit shall be poured out upon you, and when you will feel your sinfulness, and your entire need of that great

Sacrifice to expiate your sins." R. Menahem Mendel sharply disagreed with the "great Sacrifice" of Jesus, so Fisk tactfully changed the subject to America, "the only place where the Jews had not been persecuted, and enjoy equal privileges with ourselves." The rabbi replied that it was not good for the Jews to enjoy too many privileges, "lest Jeshurun should wax fat and kick." This prompted King to note that "there are not many Jews among us who are waxed fat, but they sometimes kick." He quickly regretted his quip and told Wolff not to translate it!

In the published journals of Fisk and King there is no mention of meeting R. Menahem Mendel or using Wolff as an interpreter when talking with other Jews such as Abraham Shliffro, Isaac Ben Shlomo, and Joseph Marcowitz, with whom they discussed the time of the Messiah's arrival.[50] Pressed by the missionaries for an answer, Marcowitz responded, "Daniel said, 'The time is sealed' and what fool would presume to be wiser than Daniel?" When the missionaries continued, "But are there not Jews who do endeavor to ascertain the time when the Messiah will come?" Marcowitz said, "Yes; there are some such. But they are not upright. They are wicked Jews."

Before Fisk visited Jerusalem he doubted "the expediency, and . . . the practicality of establishing a mission there," but at the end of his visit these doubts were "entirely removed" and he concluded that "I wish now to see a missionary family there." King agreed that prospects were favorable for establishing a mission station in order that "the standard of the cross shall wave triumphantly on the walls of the holy city . . ."

Wolff remained in Jerusalem after the American missionaries departed in June 1823 and continued his missionary efforts, studying with the Jews "from morning to night, and often all night" and preaching that "you must either believe, or you must perish."[51] In turn, R. Menahem Mendel, S. Z. Shapira, and others tried to convince Wolff to believe in the Talmud and abandon his Christian beliefs. Some discourses were "very violent," "very stormy, and very unpolite indeed," and each lasted "for several hours."

In the summer of 1823 Wolff suffered an attack of fever and left Jerusalem for the healthy mountain climate of Lebanon, where he enjoyed "Christian communion" with his fellow missionaries. Wolff was now recognized as "the great pioneer missionary" by the LJS, the CMS, and the American missionaries. He believed that "there is now at Jerusalem, by God's grace, a feeling and a spirit of enquiry, excited among the Jews, even according to the confession of the Rabbis, which never existed among them before." The Jews took a more sanguine view about Wolff's success. They knew that he had been permitted to discourse with Jewish community leaders only because R. Menahem Mendel and his Perushim followers had tried to return a straying Jew to the flock. When a British traveler asked the Jerusalem merchant Joseph Amzalag, "How comes it that Mr. W. asserts in his Journal that he left you all but a Christian?" Amzalag answered: "We think it uncivil to contradict people who mean well."[52]

In the autumn of 1823 American and English missionaries conferred in Mt. Lebanon on how to conduct mission activities in Palestine. Both the American Board and the LJS were committed to establishing a permanent station in Palestine; however, Jerusalem was still out of bounds for sustained mission activities. In an effort "to collect accurate information as to the state and disposition of the Jews and to find ways of overcoming the hurdles placed in their way by the authorities," the English missionaries W. B. Lewis and William Jowett and the Americans Fisk, King, and Isaac Bird left for Jerusalem at the end of 1823.[53]

Before arriving in Jerusalem Pliny Fisk and William Jowett visited Nazareth and Acre and moved on to Tiberias, which they found in a "very ruinous and filthy condition." As honored guests in the spacious home of the rich and elderly Raphael Picciotto, the missionaries dined with the Picciotto family and were impressed that Jewish women, unlike those in the Muslim society, ate with the men and joined in the conversation. From Picciotto's scholarly son-in-law and other Jews, the missionaries learned that 950–1,150 Jews lived in Tiberias and that the Hasidim slightly outnumbered the Sephardim. The few Perushim in Tiberias went unrecorded by Fisk, who erroneously noted that the Ashkenazim were all Hasidim. Jowett was impressed to see 1,500 Hebrew books, plus another 10,000 books packed in boxes, at a yeshiva. Despite the friendly hospitality of the Jews, the two missionaries, who spoke no Hebrew, felt "greatly at a loss, in talking to these misguided people."[54]

After three days in Tiberias the missionaries next stopped in Safed. Although R. Israel of Shklov was in Jerusalem, the missionaries slept in his "very wretched and cold" house and were hosted by his son and second wife, Ita Bella, the daughter of a distinguished Hasid of Safed. Jowett and Fisk admired R. Israel's large library of 500 books. The American and English missionaries visited five synagogues and yeshivot. They found the Hasidic synagogue and yeshiva a room "filthy beyond expression." The Perushim had their own synagogue and "college" with 1,000 volumes. The "best and largest" synagogue belonged to the Sephardim. Safed was populated by 400 Jewish families, divided equally between Sephardim and Ashkenazim. Not surprisingly, Jews "manifested little good inclination" toward the Hebrew translation of the New Testament distributed by the missionaries.[55]

Fisk and Jowett arrived in Jerusalem after a brief stopover in Nablus. The missionaries called on R. Menahem Mendel of Shklov, distributed Bibles, visited the Wailing Wall, observed Christian "petty politics," and noted the oppressions suffered by both the Jews and the Greeks. Jowett reported that 5,000 Jews lived in Jerusalem and that there were 600 or 700 houses of Sephardim. Fisk, who remained in Jerusalem for five months and concentrated his attention on the Christians, reported on the Christian population but made no mention of the number of Jews.[56]

Two days before Jowett left Jerusalem he and Fisk were joined by LJS missionary W. B. Lewis, who had been ordered to Jerusalem "without delay" to beat out the Americans who had resolved to establish "a missionary family" in Jerusalem. As a result of Wolff's two visits to the Holy City, the LJS decided to establish a permanent mission station in Jerusalem. This was the greatest achievement of Wolff's missionary efforts in Palestine.[57]

W. B. Lewis, an Anglican minister of Irish origin and an LJS leader, toured "every place in Palestine inhabited by Jews." On his way from Damascus to Jerusalem he stopped in Safed for four days and was favorably impressed. "The Jews, although generally poor in appearance, seem here to breathe a certain air of independence, which I have not seen elsewhere." In Lewis's opinion the Sephardim were richer than the Ashkenazim, who "are very worldly-minded, and either tainted with infidel principles, or so ignorant and fanatical as to decline all conversation on religious subjects." Jews lived far from the Muslim quarters and were not molested, allowing Lewis to conclude that Jews live "as it were in their own country." Lewis befriended Signor D., a Jewish "apothecary and physician" who had lived in Safed since 1814. Signor D. found "a good deal of sickness" in Safed, and in his opinion Tiberias was a healthier town. He reported that 400 Jewish families or 1,600 Jews lived in Safed and that the Hasidim outnumbered the Perushim.[58]

While in Safed, Lewis had religious discussions with some Ashkenazi Jews and distributed Old and New Testaments, many of which were returned to him instead of being burned or defaced. One young man politely told Lewis that the New Testament "is not a book for the Jews." Lewis found that the poor Sephardim, especially natives of the country, were rather ignorant and "consequently fanatical to an extreme." He argued at length with a Jew whether "the Talmud is the law of God" and about the "two Messiahs—one the Son of David, and the other to be the son of

Joseph" and reported on seven synagogues in Safed, four belonging to the Sephardim and three to the Ashkenazim. From Safed, Lewis traveled to Tiberias, where he stayed at the home of the "old Jew" Raphael Picciotto, who refused to discuss religion with him.[59]

Lewis arrived in Jerusalem in December 1823 to establish a permanent mission station. He disposed of Bibles and Psalters and received 63 Spanish dollars for them. This was a small sum, leading Lewis to identify with the Jews by writing that "we are poor, very poor, in Jerusalem." He discovered that "the Prophets do not sell so well as the full Bibles amongst any of the Jews . . ." Bibles containing the sign of the cross were "committed to the flames." Missionaries continued to distribute Bibles and Jews continued to tear them up, sell them to Muslims "to wrap their pepper and salt in," or burn them in the court of the synagogue. Such public conflagrations were a cautionary move rather than an act of hostility on the part of the Jews.[60]

Early in 1824 Fisk and Bird toured Jerusalem and Hebron. A letter from R. Menahem Mendel introduced the Americans to the leaders of the Hebron Jewish community. Fisk reported 40 Sephardi and 20 Ashkenazi families, or about 250 Jews living there. This brief tour produced "no important results," meaning that Hebron lacked any potential for mission activities among the Jews and the nonexistent Christian population.[61]

In Jerusalem, Fisk and Bird "usually spent the Sabbath reading the Scriptures, and conversing . . . with such as came to us." This quiet life was suddenly disrupted when the two American missionaries were arrested and arraigned before the Jerusalem judge and governor, charged by the Roman Catholics with distributing Bibles that were "not Christian books . . . but false books." Fisk and Bird reminded the judge that they were "under English protection" and that "men under English protection are not to be trifled with." The Americans knew that Greeks, priests, and Jews, "some of whom were Europeans, and had passports and firmans," had been imprisoned and suffered corporal punishment until they paid extortion money. They were told "that a present of some valuable article" was expected by the governor, plus about twenty dollars for his officials, but they stubbornly refused to pay. "It is probably the first time that they [the Turkish officials] have done all this for nothing, for the poor Greeks and Jews always have to pay dearly for being insulted and abused," wrote Fisk.[62]

After being detained for twenty-four hours, the missionaries were freed and permitted to distribute religious tracts. They realized that "all that we have as yet suffered, however, is nothing . . . compared to what the Christian and Jewish subjects of the Sultan daily suffer at the hands of their tyrants." Two days later soldiers closed "a College of the European Jews" on the pretense that it contained mission books, but the following day the ye-shiva was reopened on orders of the pasha of Damascus "that European Jews should not be molested, nor any money exacted from them."[63]

Three weeks after Fisk and Bird had been detained the missionaries left Jerusalem for Beirut. They continued to advocate that Jerusalem "must not be relinquished," concluded that it was safe to establish a permanent mission station there, and recommended enlarging the American mission staff in the Near East.[64] They also urged that a physician join the mission to serve the staff and native notables; no mention was made about treating the general population that was in dire need of medical assistance.

Lewis was now the only Protestant missionary remaining in Jerusalem. Unable to speak Hebrew, he was never able to penetrate the Jewish community as Wolff had done so successfully. R. Menahem Mendel and the other Jewish leaders were not interested in converting the Christian-born Lewis, so the Jews were formally polite and only infrequently discussed religious issues with him, but used his benevolent help for protection against the torments of insufferable authorities. Lewis was even petitioned to help secure a firman for rebuilding the Hurva, through the good offices of the English ambassador in Istanbul.[65]

Lewis was surprised to find such a small number of Jews in Palestine—about 6,000, compared with the Jewish population in other parts of the world, which totaled about 3 million. He reported, however, that new settlers were coming to the four holy cities in 1824, entertaining "ardent expectations respecting the advent of the Messiah," indicating that Jews once again were immigrating to Eretz Israel after a temporary hiatus in 1821–1822 due to the Greek revolt against Turkey and the murder of Haim Farhi by Abdullah Pasha in 1820. Lewis was astonished to learn that hundreds of Jews, though settled in Palestine many years, did not speak the language of the country. Nor were all Jews able to talk with each other, because "hundreds, especially among the Sephardim, are equally unable to converse in Hebrew." The large figure of "hundreds" may partly be accounted for by his inability to identify Sephardi-pronounced Hebrew with the Ashkenazi-accented Hebrew that he knew.[66]

Lewis encountered much greater opposition to missionary efforts from the Sephardim, especially those who were natives of the country, than from the Ashkenazim. He found the Jerusalem Ashkenazim to be the most approachable and willing to discuss religion. This conclusion may reflect the fact that Lewis could more easily converse with the Ashkenazim and protect them as foreign nationals. Recognizing the status of the Sephardim as Ottoman citizens, Lewis concluded that "under the existing state of things in these countries of Mahomedan tyranny, we must not expect to witness an open profession of Christianity on the part of an individual native Sephardi Jew, unless he be prepared to actual martyrdom in consequence or he can fly the country, or find here a protector . . ."[67]

The more Lewis thought about the obstacles that must be overcome by the mission, the more formidable they appeared, but he was consoled by the hope that a consular agent would be stationed in Jerusalem, to protect "the foreign Jews, those who are not subjects of the Ottoman Empire . . ."[68]

During his stay in Jerusalem Lewis acted as the benefactor of the Jews by ameliorating the "daily insults" and the "tyranny of the oppressor." For such help the Jews were extremely grateful and told Lewis that "no doubt the Highest Power sent you to us." The Anglican missionary detailed Turkish "barbarities" committed against the Jews of Jerusalem and described the specific grievances of the Jews, who are "frequently forced to give up their time, and to work for the ungrateful Turk without payment." If a Jew tries to make claims against a Muslim, "he is threatened with bastinado, and I know not what." A Jew on his way to Lewis was seized "by soldiers, who were going to yoke him with another Jew to one of the heavy cannons being drawn out against Bethlehem." Another incident reported by Lewis involved Rabbi Shlomo Pach:

> Solomon P** is an engraver of seals. In the open street he was accosted by a Turk who produced a large stone, and told him to cut out a seal. Solomon replied it was not in his power, for he only knew how to engrave, not to cut and prepare the stone; the Turk thereupon laid hold of him by his beard, drew his sword, kicked him, and cut and struck him unmercifully. The poor man cried, but there was no one to assist him. Turks in the street passed by unconcerned, and the wounded Jew afterwards sought redress in vain from the officers of justice.[69]

When R. Israel of Shklov hired donkeys to take him home to Safed, they were confiscated and the muleteer returned his money only after Lewis intervened with the governor.

R. Menahem Mendel also had reason to be thankful for the help he received from Lewis. One night the rabbi's front door burst open and a large party of soldiers rushed in. The rabbi was "maltreated" and charged with the offense of leaving the door facing the street open.[70] After being imprisoned and threatened with the use of "hot irons" and "sharp nails" on his body, he was released upon payment of nearly sixty pounds sterling, or about 6,000 piastres. As a result of this incident the consuls of Aleppo and

Acre secured from the pasha of Damascus an order "comanding that the European Jews should not be molested, nor any money exacted from them."

In nearly all instances money was the sole reason Jews were taken hostage, imprisoned, and tortured. Sometimes a dozen or so Jews and Greeks were arrested in one day in order to extort money from them. A British traveler wrote that "the extortions and oppressions were so numerous that it was said of the Jews that they had to pay for the very air they breathed." In one case Rabbi Balter was "dragged about the streets among his brethren as a criminal with a chain round his neck" and then jailed. In order to secure his release, a ransom of 1,500 piastres was demanded. R. Menahem Mendel left his sickbed to appear before the governor, who "told him that he should be considered responsible for the money due from the Jew in prison..." After "the avarice of the governor was satisfied," the prisoner was released.[71]

W. B. Lewis described how Jews praying over graves on the Mount of Olives were "rudely accosted and pilfered" despite having paid protection money for access to the Jewish cemetery. If Jews resisted "they are beat[en] almost to death, and this not by common highwaymen or Bedouin Arabs, but by men they may have been in the habit of seeing and talking with every day." On the streets of Jerusalem Muslims mocked Jews, robbed them, and dunned them for imagined debts. Even European Jews "are liable to be stopped by the lowest fallaah of the country, who, if he pleases, may demand money of them as a right due to the mussulman; and this extortion may be practised on the same poor Jew over and over again in the space of ten minutes." "When a Jew walked among [the Muslims] in the market, one would throw a stone at him in order to kill him, another would pull his beard and a third his ear lock, yet another spit on his face and he became a symbol of abuse."[72]

Since Jews lacked legal recourse they were an easy prey for commercial chicanery and physical assault. A Jew buying from a Muslim dared not bargain for fear of being beaten; he paid the demanded price. A Muslim meeting a Jew in the street could order the Jew to pass on his left side. If the Jew so much as touched the Arab he was severely beaten. A Muslim unable to sell merchandise left it on his Jewish neighbor's doorstep and later returned to forcibly demand payment. The water-carriers from the nearby village of Silwan also dumped their unsold water on the Jews and clamored for compensation. As late as 1839 the newly arrived British vice-consul wrote, "What the Jew has to endure, at all hands, is not [to] be told."[73]

Jews prayed on the Mount of Olives "for the preservation of the

Sultan," but such prayers did nothing to alleviate the Muslim-instigated persecutions against them. One Jew reported in 1822 that "it is not pleasant now to live in Palestine," but hastily added that *"it is a pleasure to die in this land, and all of us here have come to die in the land of Israel."*[74]

These persecutions continued throughout the reign of the "great reformer," Mahmud II, who proclaimed: "I distinguish my Muslim subjects in the mosque, my Christian subjects in the church, and my Jewish subjects in the synagogue, but there is no other difference among them. My love and justice for all of them is very strong and they are all my true children." At the behest of Jewish leaders in Istanbul, Mahmud II issued a firman protecting the Jews of Jerusalem from paying new "taxes not instituted until then." For Jerusalem (and all Ottoman) Jews it was unfortunate that there was an unbridgeable chasm between the intent of the firman and the daily practices throughout the Turkish Empire.[75]

Jerusalem Jews were persecuted more than other minorities because they lacked the protection of patrons like Russia and France. After observing the condition of the Jews, Lewis was more than ever convinced that a "European resident protector in Jerusalem . . . would be productive of great advantage . . . [for] the suffering Jews as well as Gentiles." Lewis remembered that while in Safed, Signor D. "thanked God for his lot and that there was a consul to protect him." This was a reference to consul Katafago. Lewis declared:

> I am persuaded that an European flag hoisted in Jerusalem (as in other places of the Turkish empire, for the protection of foreigners), will ever have the effect of securing travellers and strangers from their wanton insults, exactions, and barbarities. Alluding to their sufferings and miseries, one of the Rabbis of Jerusalem exclaimed with much feeling, "Oh, when will the king of England come and deliver us."[76]

Obviously Lewis wanted to hoist over Jerusalem not a "European flag" but the Union Jack, trusting that "British influence will obtain for us [the Anglicans] the same privileges, at least, which are enjoyed by the subjects of other foreign nations."

Lewis was the most vocal advocate of appointing a British consul in Jerusalem. Such a consul, who "ought to be a missionary in spirit,"[77] would protect visitors and European settlers, both Christians and Jews, and provide official British sponsorship for mission activities in Palestine. From then on, English missionaries were the main promoters of establishing a British consulate in Jerusalem, regarding this as a precondition for setting up a permanent mission station in Jerusalem.

Lewis was unsuccessful in his campaign to open a permanent mission station in Jerusalem, although he felt "that the door of access is gradually opening...to the Ashkenazi Jews." Forbidden to distribute Bibles by order of Ottoman and papal bans issued in 1824, he became completely disheartened. Lewis must have despaired that, all alone, he could overcome the hurdles set up by both the Jews and the "Mahomedan tyranny," and in the summer of 1824 he left Jerusalem after residing there for about six months.[78]

In anticipation of the Easter season of 1825, American and English missionaries started to return to Jerusalem. They were not deterred by skirmishes conducted by the aggressive governor of Jerusalem against Bethlehem and the surrounding villages, then in a state of revolt and insurrection. In April Lewis, King, and Fisk were joined in Jerusalem by Dr. George Dalton, the newly arrived LJS medical missionary, who hoped to permanently occupy the Jerusalem station with his family.[79]

In a population lacking a certified doctor, Dr. Dalton's services as a physician were "eagerly sought and gratefully acknowledged. Every door is open at his approach, and he is admitted even into the privacy of the Harem..." An English doctor noted in 1818 that in the Orient "the character of a physician is held in such esteem that a physician is pardoned for being a Christian." In Jerusalem, patients "seize upon" a doctor "as if only he stood between them and death."[80]

The missionaries found Jerusalem in "terror and distress" and "the country about Jerusalem...in a very tumultuous state." Mustafa, pasha of Damascus, camped outside Jerusalem with 2,000–3,000 soldiers "to fleece Jews and Christians of their money," according to Dr. Dalton. The Damascus pasha had steeply increased taxes and was forcibly collecting them. The pasha terrorized the Greek Catholics—"their country is at war with the Porte"—and demanded 300,000 piastres from them. To help pay this huge tax, the Greek Orthodox Church mortgaged its jewels "at a very high rate of interest" in return for a 50,000-piastre loan from a "rich Jew," Joseph Amzalag. The Armenians were treated no better than the Greeks.[81]

The Sephardi community was taxed 120,000 piastres, forcing its members to contribute their jewelry to pay off this onerous debt. When the small Ashkenazi community did not pay 30,000 piastres of tribute, "the

Turks took Rabbi Mendel and his son, with some other Jews, bound them in chains, and took them to the camp of the Pasha. All the Jews, as might be expected, were thrown into consternation. Rabbi M. has a firman, and is entitled to protection as a Frank." Thanks to the intervention of Lewis, the imprisoned Jews were released. Partial knowledge of this incident led the Ashkenazi chief rabbi of London to malign the Perushim for trafficking with the missionaries.[82]

The American missionaries had little contact with the Jews this time. Only one entry in King's published journal tells about his meeting R. Shlomo Zalman Shapira and the young R. Isaac. "Read a little with them in Hebrew, and conversed about the pronunciation of the language." In contrast, the English missionaries had easy access to the Jewish community, where they were received "with every mark of respect and attention." Lewis and Dalton were invited "to witness the celebration of the Passover" at the home of Mr. Amzalag. When they asked some questions about the Jewish "mode of keeping the feast, Mr. A. replied jocosely, 'With plenty of good beef, mutton and wine.'" Amzalag's blessing in Hebrew over the wine lacked "a semblance of solemnity" in the opinion of overly earnest Dr. Dalton, who had not learned that wisecracking joviality was Amzalag's way of turning serious talk away from religious subjects.[83]

Dr. Dalton visited R. Menahem Mendel a number of times and "found him, as usual, reclining over a charcoal fire, buried in the Talmud" and "occupied in endeavouring to get a diminution of pecuniary demands made upon him." At R. Menahem Mendel's house, Dr. Dalton met Shlomo Zalman Shapira, who was "going to Europe for some time." In an attempt to learn Hebrew Dr. Dalton hired two teachers, one of whom was about to flee Jerusalem after his son had been imprisoned. While ministering to many sick Jews, such as R. Menahem Mendel, who refused to take medicine on the Sabbath, Dr. Dalton saw that "their filth is sufficient of itself to engender disease amongst them."[84]

The English missionaries and Jonas King attended the circumcision of an Ashkenazi boy, which is described by Dr. Dalton but not noted in King's printed journal. Jonas King asked

a blessing upon the parents and [circumcised] child, to which we all added a hearty Amen; when he remarked, "I trust they may not have Moses' words applied to them of being a stiff-necked people," Rabbi Mendel replied, "It is well we are stiff-necked, or we could not withstand the Turks." Thus they pervert the meaning of Scripture.[85]

Mustafa Pasha left Jerusalem on April 15, 1825, and his departure was followed by a complete breakdown in law and order around Jerusalem. Jerusalem and Nablus residents rebelled against the pasha, who had imposed a new series of more exorbitant taxes. The Muslims were so outraged by the heavy taxes that they closed the city gates and chased the governor and his troops out of Jerusalem. Jews empathized with Muslim grievances about crushing taxes, but lacked the will or power to take an active part in the rebellion.[86]

In the midst of such anarchy it was impossible to conduct missionary activities, let alone establish a permanent mission station in Jerusalem. All the missionaries departed strife-torn Jerusalem thanks to a safe-conduct pass from Abu-Ghosh, the toll master on the Jerusalem to Jaffa road. Dalton, Fisk, and King returned safely to Beirut by way of Nazareth, Tiberias, and Safed, after being attacked by robbers on the Sharon plain.[87]

From Safed King reported that "some estimate the Jewish population at several thousands but I think this estimate is quite too large." More accurately, Dalton reported that there were said to be an equal number of Ashkenazim and Sephardim, 400 or 500 houses in all, for a total Jewish population of 1,600–2,000. Dr. Dalton observed that Jewish homes "are very wretched and confined; they felt to us like ovens. . . . Excepting the house we were in, there did not appear a single house that could be occupied with safety to health." The Jewish quarter was "very filthy," with Dr. Dalton adding that "these circumstances may somewhat influence the healthiness of the place; although as far as I could learn, Mussulmans are said to suffer equally. Many newcomers are affected by eating too largely of fruit in the season."[88]

Easter 1825 was the last time American missionaries visited Palestine for nearly nine years. King left the region, and 33-year-old Pliny Fisk died from "a bilious Fever"—meaning a cause unknown to medicine. These events convinced the American Board that no useful purpose could be served by sending Bird or another missionary back to Palestine, which was still "convulsed with political revolutions."[89]

While assessing their progress, the Americans considered how to overcome "Paganism" and "corrupt Christianity"; they never specifically mentioned the Jews or the need to learn Hebrew in order to work among them. The Americans continued to missionize among the Greek and Roman Catholics and Armenians, seeking to "rekindle the fires of Christianity upon the mountains of Judea," and paid scant attention to the Jews.[90] In July 1828 four American missionaries submitted seven recommendations to the

American Board, urging the conduct of mission activities in Beirut, Smyrna, Istanbul, Greece, and Malta, with nary a proposal about activities in Jerusalem. The American Board and the LJS had staked out different clienteles, reflecting the English belief in the role of the Jews in bringing about the Millennium and the American inclination to labor mainly among "idolatrous worshippers of Christ."

As the Americans were reluctantly retreating from Palestine, the LJS sent Dr. Dalton back to Jerusalem. Although he was suffering from ill health, Dr. Dalton left Beirut alone on December 13, 1825, and traveled overland past Sidon, Acre, Haifa, Caesarea, Jaffa, and Ramleh, reaching Jerusalem the day before Christmas. Dalton was permitted to settle in Jerusalem because he had a "knowledge of medicine" and could treat the influential local notables.[91]

Soon after his arrival, Dr. Dalton visited Joseph Amzalag, who received him cordially, promised to find a Hebrew teacher, and consulted him about "wordly affairs." R. Menahem Mendel, still "buried in his Talmud," gave Dr. Dalton "a hearty welcome...R. M. invited me to come often to see him; asked if I came empowered by the Consul to protect them. I answered that this was impossible, but that I should feel happy in serving the Jews in any way I could."[92]

Ten days after Dalton's arrival in Jerusalem he was joined by the 23-year-old LJS missionary John Nicolayson. With his arrival, the burden of Dalton's solitary mission had been lifted and the doctor rejoiced. His joy was short-lived; twenty-one days after arriving in Jerusalem Dalton died of a "fever."[93] Dalton, the pioneer medical missionary in Palestine, was the first missionary to be buried on Mt. Zion, in the Greek cemetery.

After Dalton's death, John Nicolayson tried to keep the Jerusalem mission station in operation. He conducted "introductory religious conversation[s]" with Jews and called upon the "rather indisposed" R. Menahem Mendel, who "was quite adverse to entering into any discussion on the subject of the Messiahship of Jesus...[he] kindly invited me, however, to call upon him again." Since the young, inexperienced Nicolayson had no one to consult with after the death of Dr. Dalton, was not a medical man, and could not yet speak Hebrew, he was unable to maintain the Jerusalem mission station and returned to Beirut.[94]

Nicolayson briefly visited Tiberias and Safed during the summer of 1826 and "discovered that Safed offered a very desirable situation for a Missionary to the Jews." In the winter of 1826–1827 he lived in Safed for more than two months and learned about the Jewish community. He could still see the aftereffects of the snowstorm, strong winds, and torrential rains that avalanched the Safed mountainside during the winter of 1824–1825. "A great number of the houses in the Jewish quarter were destroyed" or damaged, including the house of R. Israel of Shklov. Miraculously, no Jews were killed or injured. This disaster was followed during the winter of 1825–1826 by a drought, locusts, and epidemics. Prices spiraled and the Safed governor extorted money from the Jews. When contributions from Europe were delayed, the Jewish community was financially hard-pressed. "I have heard told," Nicolayson reported, "that some [Jews] have actually died of hunger." This rumor was incorrect. Although there was poverty and famine, and the Jewish community debt soared to 400,000 piastres, no Jew starved to death, thanks to the haluka system administered by the kollelim. Not even the most pessimistic letter written by Jews reported death due to lack of food.[95]

From the Perushim Nicolayson heard that epidemics in Safed caused the death of many Jews. In 1826 Safed Perushim without suitable housing were sent to the nearby, plague-free village of Peki'in while other Perushim were ordered by R. Israel to stay at home. Due to R. Israel's quarantine precautions only 10–12 Perushim who did not heed his warnings died, while the Sephardim and Hasidim each lost 300 members. If R. Israel's figures of more than 600 dead Jews are correct, this means that one-third of the Safed Jewish population of 1,700–1,800 was killed by the plague, and the kehilla was reduced to slightly more than 1,000, an unlikely low figure. R. Israel casualty figures appear exaggerated and were possibly written to prove the superiority of the Perushim, the only Jewish group to undertake quarantine measures.[96]

Nicolayson also learned that in Jerusalem Mustafa Pasha of Damascus failed to suppress the revolt that had been observed by the American and English missionaries. On orders from Sultan Mahmud II, ambitious young Abdullah, pasha of Acre, besieged Jerusalem in the fall of 1826. Although he bombarded Jerusalem from the Mount of Olives for two weeks, his thousands of cannonballs were incredibly ineffective. The only recorded Jewish casualty was R. Raphael Abulafia, who was wounded in the leg by a splinter while celebrating the harvest festival in his Sukka booth. Finally the psychological effect of the bombardment, the damage to property, and the shortage of food forced the rebels to surrender. By the end of 1826 peace was restored in Jerusalem (and Nablus), and Abdullah Pasha proceeded to seize control over central Palestine and the coastal plain.[97]

The Jews of Safed kept Nicolayson at a distance, permitting him to speak in his halting Hebrew with only selected rabbis of unshakable faith. Nicolayson had difficulty in convincing Jews that "I am not come to take away earthly treasures but to impart heavenly treasures." He tried to distribute Bibles, but to his dismay he discovered that the Jews tore out the New Testament pages. To the horror of the Jews, Nicolayson suggested opening a mission school for Jewish children and they peremptorily turned this proposal down.[98]

In a melancholy mood, Nicolayson wrote on New Year's Day 1827 that he was "not welcome in the homes of the Jews" and that the rabbis were putting pressure on his major link with the Jewish community, his Hebrew teacher, to leave him. All alone, Nicolayson gave vent to the frustration of working with "heretical Christians, unbelieving Jews and fanatical Muslims." He filled his time by studying Hebrew and reading the mystical book the *Zohar*. In February 1827 Nicolayson's Hebrew teacher finally bowed to rabbinical pressure and "relinquishe[d]" him, thereby effectively cutting Nicolayson off from the Jewish community.[99]

Forced to leave Safed, Nicolayson visited Beirut and Damascus, but by the end of March he was back in Jerusalem to inquire "if practical or desirable to take up my residence here" now that the Jerusalem rebellion had been put down and Abdullah Pasha of Acre had "restored . . . tranquility." Nicolayson sadly concluded that due to the unchanged status of the Jews, Turks, and Christians, and the hostility of the Jerusalem governor, "it was better for me not to attempt a residence here alone at present."[100]

In April 1827 Nicolayson left Jerusalem, his departure hastened by "the prospect of war united with the plague." After a brief visit to Safed he was back in Beirut by June. Due to the plague that raged through the region, the impending war between Turkey and Russia, and political agitation in Palestine, the missionaries departed in early 1828 for Malta. Not until 1831 would Nicolayson return to Jerusalem.[101]

The last missionary to visit Jerusalem during the 1820s was the indefatigable Joseph Wolff, who arrived in January 1829. He made his usual dynamic effort to teach and preach, but the Jerusalem rabbis looked at him with a "fierce eye" and threatened to excommunicate Jews found talking with him. R. Menahem Mendel had died and the other Ashkenazi rabbis had abandoned hope of reconverting Wolff, so they severed contact with him. Wolff was rarely visited by Ashkenazim but a number of Sephardim spoke with him, as did Joseph Amzalag, unflatteringly described by Wolff as a vain Shylock—"money is his god."[102]

The Jews of Jerusalem found that Wolff's violent temper made "sober discussion" difficult, and they were offended by his fervid admonitions. Worse yet, Wolff encounted fanatic opposition from a Greek who nearly succeeded in poisoning him. At the end of June 1829 Wolff departed from

Jerusalem, leaving it empty of Protestant missionaries, who temporarily gave up their hold on the religious terrain of Jerusalem and Palestine.

The Jews had adamantly rejected the soul-saving efforts of the missionaries. Although the Protestants' initial reconnaissance thrusts were innocuous, and they frequently helped the Jewish community, R. Menahem Mendel expressed the feelings of the Jews when he stated that "those marks of friendship are only nets to catch poor Israel." Still, Jewish opposition, the prejudices of the native population, and the bigotry of the Turkish rulers did not stop the dogged efforts of the missionaries, who were driven by absolute belief and a deep faith. The enthusiasm that animated the religious discussions of the English missionaries was not dampened by the antagonism displayed by most Jews. Not even the successive deaths of Parsons, Fisk, and Dalton could dissuade Nicolayson, Wolff, Bird, and other resilient missionaries from continuing their work, because "Jews were still far from their promised land."[103]

EIGHT

Jewish Activities in the Four Holy Cities

1825–1830

For the Jews 1827 started sorrowfully as a time for mourning the death of R. Menahem Mendel of Shklov and ended auspiciously as a season for celebrating the first visit of Moses Montefiore to Eretz Israel.

The Jerusalem Jewish community was still recovering from the chaos resulting from the siege and bombardment of the city during the 1826 rebellion when the Perushim suffered an irreparable loss. In March 1827 R. Menahem Mendel of Shklov died after leading the growing Perushim kollel for nearly twenty years and contributing to changing the conditions of the Jewish community in Eretz Israel. Disciple and student of the Vilna gaon, R. Menahem Mendel had immersed himself in the scholarly pursuits of "researching and establishing the foundations of Torah and serving God in Eretz Israel,"[1] as was inscribed on his tombstone. He was recognized as a brilliant talmudic scholar and was acknowledged, even by the Sephardim, as the greatest prodigy of his generation.[2]

By virtue of his outstanding scholarship and his pioneering settlement efforts in Safed and Jerusalem, R. Menahem Mendel was recognized as the preeminent leader of the Perushim in Eretz Israel. His self-effacing, calming presence and generosity of spirit imparted a life-enhancing serenity to the Jewish community. More suited to study than command, R. Menahem

Mendel sanctioned the overwhelming drive of R. Israel to secure financial independence and establish an autonomous Perushim community.

Reports by missionaries attest to the cordial respect they accorded the luminescent personality of R. Menahem Mendel. They were fascinated by his humility and scholastic achievements. In turn, R. Menahem Mendel respected the missionaries' utmost devotion and never doubted their integrity, as he correctly assessed the purpose of the mission and categorically rejected its religious beliefs. The compassionate R. Menahem Mendel willingly spent long hours with Joseph Wolff in an attempt to save one Jewish soul gone astray. He also maintained contact with the missionaries because he realized that the Jewish community needed the cooperation of a great foreign power like England in order to invoke the capitulation agreements and reap the benefits of consular protection.

R. Menahem Mendel helped fulfill the yearnings of the Perushim and their dreams of Zion by bonding beliefs to actions. However, his ability to assess events and evaluate new conditions was limited by his circumscribed situation and lack of experience outside his community. R. Menahem Mendel led his flock out of Exile and into the Promised Land of Safed and Jerusalem; he died before unprecedented events imposed by the outside world would change the lives of the Perushim and transform their world in Eretz Israel.

After R. Menahem Mendel's death, R. Israel assumed the community's mantle of leadership. To prevent a breakdown of the fundraising network in Poland and Russia, two Perushim emissaries from Safed and Jerusalem were instructed by R. Israel to tell the East European Jewish communities that the Perushim communities would continue to develop their settlement in Eretz Israel.[3] These shlihim were also advised to persuade families, rather than just elderly people, to migrate to Eretz Israel.

In October 1827 the Jews of Eretz Israel were blessed with the first visit of Moses Montefiore, the most famous and admired Jew of the nineteenth century. Montefiore was born in 1784 to a well-established Sephardi family in England. A man whose reliability, honesty, loyalty, and conscientiousness earned him respect in the business world, he married Judith Barent Cohen, daughter of a wealthy family, whose sister was married to the founder of the London Rothschild banking house.

With the help of family connections, Montefiore obtained one of the twelve seats on the London stock exchange reserved for Jews and brokered for the Rothschilds. Also contributing to Montefiore's success was "a fine presence"[4]—he stood six feet three inches tall—an impressive voice, and "winning manners."

At the age of 40, Montefiore accepted his wife's advice to "thank God to be content" and retired from active participation in commercial ventures. During the remaining 61 years of his long life he led a multitude of British and Jewish philanthropies, headed the English Jewish community, numbering about 15,000–20,000, and indulged his mania for traveling. A splendid product of the pre-Victorian era, Montefiore believed that those able to lead should not shirk their obligations, for they had a dutiful responsibility to be carried out humbly. He dispensed charity as "a blessing conferred by the benevolent rich on the grateful poor,"[5] a paternalistic philosophy that guided him in his efforts to alleviate the lot of the poor Jews in Palestine.

The Montefiores boldly decided in 1827 to visit Palestine,[6] an undertaking that required extraordinary courage,[7] for England, Russia, and France were then fighting Turkey over the matter of Greek independence. Moses and Judith Montefiore left London for Palestine on May 1, 1827. In the best tradition of high English society, they carried with them letters of introduction to British consular officials and to Admiral Codrington, commander of the British fleet in the Mediterranean. After four months of travel the Montefiores arrived in Alexandria, Egypt, where Moses had a 45-minute audience with the ruler of Egypt, Mehemet Ali, whose fleet was allied with the Turkish navy and facing the hostile flotilla led by Admiral Codrington.

In October the Montefiores landed in Jaffa and marveled at the "prickly pear, pomegranate, fig, orange and lemon trees."[8] They hired donkeys and mules to carry their party to Jerusalem, an uphill ride of forty-five kilometers. The Montefiore party traveled on a rough, dirt path to Ramleh, where they stayed overnight in the Greek convent, a place of lodging barred to other Jewish travelers. Early the next morning the Montefiores journeyed for a few hours on a desolate plain and observed the peasants working their fields with primitive ploughs pulled by yoked oxen. Then their party climbed the rocky, "severe and savage,"[9] Judean hills on "a road of indescribable ruggedness."[10] After passing the village of Abu-Ghosh the Montefiores pushed their "weary animals" in order to arrive in Jerusalem before sunset, when the town gates were locked.[11] Standing before the gates of Jerusalem Montefiore performed the ancient ritual of tearing a garment as a symbol of mourning the destruction of the Temple in Jerusalem.

The Montefiores lodged in the home of "the wealthiest Jew in Jerusalem,"[12] Joseph Amzalag—trader, merchant, and "dealer in money."[13] After getting little sleep due to bedbugs and fleas "which came forth during the night,"[14] Montefiore prayed at daybreak in Amzalag's private synagogue.

Lady Judith reported that six or seven years ago Amzalag had married his "exceedingly pretty" second wife when she was 13 years old and that Amzalag's daughter was already married at 14 and her husband was only one year older.[15] It was an accepted custom among Muslims and Jews in Palestine for boys and girls to marry at these young ages,[16] and it was "not uncommon to see mothers of 11 and fathers of 13 years."[17] The Montefiores expressed a moral horror at such early marriages; in England men married at 25 to 30, after achieving economic independence.

The Montefiores observed the dress and behavior of the Amzalag family. Men dressed in traditional Sephardi long flowing robes. Women were "chastely elegant" in a silk costume,[18] profusely ornamented with bracelets and gold coins and a gold belt around the waist. Their heads were "simply covered by the turban, no hair being allowed to escape from its folds."[19]

On their ten-month overseas trip, the Montefiores spent three days and four nights in Jerusalem out of a total of seven days in Eretz Israel. During their stay in the Holy City the Montefiores visited the Wailing Wall, the Jewish quarter, the sacred sites of the Holy City, the Mount of Olives, and the Valley of Jehoshafat. At the Wailing Wall, curiously described by Judith as "a large stone,"[20] the Montefiores fended off an attempt to make them pay the fee required of the Jews who wished to pray there. Montefiore viewed Mt. Moriah and the Dome of the Rock from the nearby rooftops in the Jewish quarter because it was forbidden for Jews and Christians to enter the Temple Mount. A short time before, an Englishman had been caught on Mt. Moriah and was nearly beaten to death by the enraged Muslim mob.

Montefiore paid courtesy calls on the governor of Jerusalem, Moshe Suzin, the Sephardi chief rabbi, and Ashkenazi rabbinical leaders and visited the Sephardi Tree of Life yeshiva. In some undefined way Montefiore attempted "to promote unanimity" between the Ashkenazim and Sephardim,[21] this being the "ardent desire" of Rabbi Shlomo Hirschell, the chief rabbi of London. On Saturday the Jerusalem governor hosted a reception for the Montefiores where "coffee and pipes were handed." In Montefiore's diaries, the mention of "pipes" that desecrated the Sabbath was deleted, and "refreshments" was substituted.[22]

While Montefiore was busy touring sacred Jewish sites, Lady Judith visited Bethlehem and its Church of the Nativity, built over the site of Christ's birthplace. Bethlehem, seven kilometers south of Jerusalem, was a hilly agricultural town of about 2,000 persons. No Jew cared or dared to live in this predominantly Christian town. Lady Judith also visited the whitewashed domed tomb of Rachel on the northern outskirts of Bethlehem. Here the

Rachel's Tomb on the outskirts of Bethlehem and four
miles south of Jerusalem was repaired by Moses
Montefiore in 1841.

Moses Montefiore and his signature in Hebrew.

Patriarch Jacob buried his wife Rachel after she died giving birth to Benjamin. This sepulchre was one of the few shrines in Palestine honored by Muslims, Jews, and Christians and open to members of all three religions.

The Ashkenazi and Sephardi communities sent delegations to Montefiore complaining about the oppressive local taxes and their poor circumstances—"very few families are able to support themselves."[23] Since Montefiore's basic knowledge of Hebrew limited him to reading his prayers, he required an interpreter in order to communicate with the Jews. This may explain his error in reporting 560 as the total Jewish population—200 Sephardim ("Portuguese"), 160 Ashkenazim ("German families"), and "200 elderly widows in great distress"[24]—at a time when 3,000 Jews lived in Jerusalem. The figure of 200 widows, however, does indicate their high visibility and large numbers.

On the Sabbath the Montefiores attended the largest of the four Sephardi synagogues. The synagogue was unadorned with gold or silver ornaments for fear that decorations of value would be confiscated by the authorities. Around Montefiore were long bearded Jews wearing high black, square caps, long black gowns fastened with a sash, and prayer shawls draped over their shoulders. Montefiore was honored by being asked to chant the benedictions on deliverance from danger after a long trip. "The President of the congregation requested Mr. Montefiore not to make any offering of a large amount, otherwise the local authorities might hear of it, and would still further raise their taxes."

At the conclusion of their short visit to Jerusalem, the Montefiores distributed money to poor Jews and to community charities and took back with them "specimens of whatever curiosities the place afforded."[25] Upon arriving in Jaffa the Montefiores met British consul Damiani and learned that during their Sabbath stay in Jerusalem Admiral Codrington's fleet of British, French, and Russian ships had sunk most of the Egyptian-Turkish vessels in the battle of Navarino, just off the coat of Morea, thereby assuring Greek victory in their war of independence. And England was not even at war with Turkey!

Moses Montefiore celebrated his 43rd birthday, little realizing that this was the first of seven pilgrimages he was to make to Palestine, the last visit taking place in 1875 when he was 90 years old. On his return to London in March 1828, Montefiore delivered to the Admiralty a dispatch about the Navarino battle given to him in Malta by Admiral Codrington. He also started thinking about how to help the Jews in Eretz Israel on his next journey to the Holy Land, which was to take place in 1839.

Another clear picture of the Jewish community in Eretz Israel emerges from a review of the European mission undertaken by Shlomo Zalman Shapira from 1825 to 1828.

During the first half of 1825 the Sephardi and Perushim kollelim of Jerusalem signaled an end to their incessant disagreements. The Sephardim finally accepted the 1822 Amsterdam compromise,[26] which divided PEKAM monies for Jerusalem equally between the two groups, after having previously rejected it. In turn, the Perushim consented to pay 550 piastres as their annual share of the poll tax and to comply with Sephardi regulations in Jerusalem. Based on this agreement, the Sephardim and Perushim of Jerusalem jointly sent the elderly, respected Shlomo Zalman Shapira to Europe for the purpose of convincing PEKAM to allow shlihim to collect money in Western Europe. S. Z. Shapira brought with him a letter from the Sephardi rabbis arguing in "strong harsh words against . . . he who wishes to abolish the missions of the shlihim."[27] Shapira was also charged with convincing PEKAM to reconsider its abrogation of the 1823 Vilna compromise between the Perushim and the Hasidim,[28] to raise money for the Perushim of Jerusalem, and to secure a firman in Istanbul for rebuilding the Hurva compound.

Shapira notified PEKAM that he was about to embark on his overseas mission and registered his dissent from the PEKAM policy of apportioning money on a per capita basis to each kollel.[29] When Zvi Hirsch Lehren of PEKAM received Shapira's letter he raged that the Sephardim and Perushim had banded together in order to fight against the fundraising agency he led. Lehren vented his anger in a scornful letter to the Perushim leaders of Jerusalem and demanded to know "who gave [Shapira] permission to intervene in matters of the kollel . . . and who is he to us?"[30] Categorically, he declared that no shlihim should be sent from Eretz Israel.

Lehren accused Shapira of misrepresenting the true relations between Ashkenazim and Sephardim and in the most cutting fashion stripped bare the reasons Perushim practiced different tactics in Jerusalem and Safed. Lehren wrote that, according to Shapira, the Ashkenazim

> have come to an amicable compromise with the Sephardim of Jerusalem, as if there is peace and quiet between the two groups. And from North Africa we have heard how the Sephardim, especially those from Jerusalem, wrote accusingly about . . . the Ashkenazi shlihim of Eretz Israel. . . . How can you reconcile these two stories? . . . It appears to us [PEKAM] that there is peace between the Sephardim and the Ashkenazim of Jerusalem so that the Sephardim . . . can continue to oppress the

Hasidim... the Ashkenazim in Jerusalem have adopted all the Sephardi regulations.... Why did they accept these regulations? After all, the Ashkenazim have thrown off the yoke of the Sephardim in Safed where they established their own independent kollel. Why did they not do so in Jerusalem? Because they derived great benefit in a number of matters by having their own separate kollel in Safed.

In this and other letters, Lehren clashed with shlihim invading Western Europe. He expounded the principle that "the welfare of the many certainly takes precedence and priority over the good of an individual" and cited the case of an emissary who earned about 50,000 piastres—a huge sum that may have been a gross exaggeration. Lehren also feared the establishment of special fundraising campaigns for specific—albeit worthwhile—causes in Eretz Israel such as the 1823 mission to raise funds for the Hurva compound.[31]

As Shapira traveled toward Amsterdam,[32] Lehren wrote to the Vilna Rabbis, asking them to stop the emissary for the greater good of all Jews in Eretz Israel. But Lehren was bluntly told that the Vilna Rabbis opposed the banning of shlihim in Western Europe and believed that Lehren was biased in favor of the Hasidim. The Vilna Rabbis continued to transfer Perushim funds through Vilna, consistently ignored Lehren's arguments, and only infrequently answered his letters. Shapira's mission to Amsterdam also had the support of the preeminent talmudic sage, R. Moshe Sofer of Pressburg (today Bratislava), a town of about 15,000 Jews, which was the spiritual and cultural center of Austro-Hungarian Jewry. R. Sofer ruled against Lehren's regulation banning shlihim and in favor of the mission of the Jerusalem emissary.

When Lehren did communicate with Shapira it was often to instruct him about what was best for the Jews in Eretz Israel. In a letter that runs to five printed pages,[33] Lehren expounded to Shapira his ideas about restricting the immigration of poor Jews to Eretz Israel, to prevent community funds from being squandered. He also mentions marginal characters and drifters wanting to come to Eretz Israel because they cannot or do not wish to earn their living in the Diaspora.

...in Ashkenazi countries... there are complaints that some persons migrate from Poland to Eretz Israel because they cannot earn a living in Poland and so impose themselves on the public.... And what is the benefit of everything done for the good of settlers in Eretz Israel if there is no regulation limiting immigration so that not everybody who wants to can come and enter? The Sephardim do not permit everybody to enter, with the exception of scholars and yeshiva students. I don't know if the Ashkenazim have a similar regulation. Therefore, please do me the favor of informing me if there is such a regulation, and if there is none, how this can be corrected. Although the door cannot be locked before those wanting to come to Eretz Israel, nevertheless [immigration] should be regulated so that he who does not come for sacred reasons will not burden the public.[34]

Later Lehren again discouraged the immigration of poor settlers: "Poles who now cannot earn a living in their native country" should not come to Eretz Israel because they "are not worthy of receiving even a small penny from the charity of Eretz Israel . . . and not everybody who wants to come to Eretz Israel should do so if he is not self-sustaining . . ." Throughout the 1830s Lehren continued to write with scorn about "unstable, vacuous" characters wanting to settle in Eretz Israel.

In Lehren's opinion the current number of Ashkenazim and Sephardim in Eretz Israel was more than sufficient to fulfill the mitzva of Jews settling in the Holy Land before the advent of the Messianic Redemption. If immigrants stopped coming to Eretz Israel, Lehren contended, Jews in the four holy cities would receive larger haluka allocations and live a dignified life of prayer and study. "Plain people should not be aided to immigrate for they will reduce the living of residents [of Eretz Israel]."[35] Lehren favored settling only scholars and old, self-supporting Jews in Eretz Israel. If a person wanted to work, Lehren believed that he should remain in the Diaspora.

Despite Lehren's unceasing, resolute efforts to abort Shapira's mission, the strong-willed, serenely assertive shaliah arrived in Amsterdam in October 1826. During Shapira's five-month stay in Amsterdam, he had long, in-depth discussions with Lehren, and the two men developed feelings of mutual admiration. Tight-fisted Lehren was impressed by the frugal living habits of Shapira, an affluent man, and even conceded the validity of many of Shapira's points and the justice of parts of the 1823 Vilna compromise between the Hasidim and the Perushim. To replace the previous agreements, Shapira and PEKAM concluded a complicated new compromise that allocated 57 percent of the collections to the Ashkenazim and 43 percent to the Sephardim.[36] This Shapira-PEKAM compromise was a temporary agreement that would last about six months until the Hasidim and Perushim could negotiate their own compromise or present their cases before a Sephardi rabbinical court in Aleppo.

Early in 1827 Shapira left Amsterdam, collected funds in Frankfurt,

Prague, and Vilna, and continued on to Istanbul, where he failed to obtain a new firman for the Hurva. But he was successful in dealing with the more pressing need of securing a firman for the Perushim who were threatened with expulsion from Jerusalem as citizens of Russia, which was then preparing for war against Turkey. With the help of the Prussian ambassador at the Sublime Porte, and at the cost of about 5,000 piastres, the expulsion threat was rescinded.[37]

While Shapira was on his way back to Eretz Israel, the new feeling of amity created by the PEKAM-Shapira compromise was shattered by a letter sent from the Sephardi rabbis of Jerusalem to Lehren. In this "letter causing a heart attack," Lehren's actions were deprecated by the Sephardi rabbis, who could not forget that in the first PEKAM compromise of 1822 Lehren had broken the Sephardi monopoly over fundraising in Western Europe.[38] Now, as in the past, Jerusalem's Sephardi leaders were absolutely opposed to PEKAM's abolishing the institution of shlihim in Western Europe, believing that Lehren was acting contrary to the best Sephardi interests. The Sephardi rabbis, who initially had provided PEKAM with its sweeping mandate "to manage all matters of charity... without any person being able to appeal or protest," now decided to strip Lehren of responsibilities for "all affairs dealing with Jerusalem... and Eretz Israel."[39]

Despite the "sorrow and aggravation" caused to Lehren by this letter,[40] which he labeled "the Torah of a Jew who insults his friend," his reply to the Jerusalem Sephardi rabbis was firm. Lehren wrote that he based his opposition to shlihim on the rabbinical authority of the Ashkenazi chief rabbi of London, who was the innovator of the Holy Land Contribution Society, which abolished sending shlihim to Western Europe. Only after the Sephardim consented to PEKAM's regulations banning shlihim in Western Europe would Lehren agree to transfer donations to Jerusalem. If the Sephardim "do not want to accept our compromises and regulations preventing shlihim from traveling... then we will have nothing to do with them and we will only help the Ashkenazi kollelim..."

Lehren did receive a written agreement from the Tiberias Sephardim not to send shlihim into Western Europe. Now he demanded similar agreements from Safed, Hebron, and Jerusalem. "As long as they do not respond appropriately with the desired answer, we will send no money. And concerning the Sephardi Rabbis of Jerusalem, as long as they do not correct what they spoiled in their letter to me, I will have nothing to do with them."[41] If an apology was not forthcoming, Lehren again threatened to stop collecting money for the Sephardim.

Then Lehren received a sharply worded letter from the Istanbul Officials telling him to stop "exploiting the blood of poor people" and forward funds to the Sephardim.[42] Unable to suffer such severe accusations that he was "exploiting" the poor Jews of Eretz Israel to whom he had dedicated his life with Messianic fervor, Lehren instructed the Istanbul Officials to transfer funds to Safed, Jerusalem, and Hebron as soon as a written apology was received from the Sephardim. Later Lehren beat another retreat and instructed the Istanbul Officials to "immediately send" monies to Eretz Israel, although no apologies were received. But the Istanbul Officials had not waited for Lehren's approval and had already transferred the funds, causing Lehren to explode: "Who are you to yell at us!" By November 1828 the Hebron Sephardim accepted the PEKAM-Shapira compromise but reserved their right to send shlihim to Western Europe in times of dire distress—which, for Hebron, was most of the time.

Eventually Lehren wearied of insisting on a written apology that was not in the offing, so he transferred funds to Eretz Israel and peremptorily ended the argument by declaring that he didn't need Sephardi approval for PEKAM rules. A month later he happily wrote that the Sephardim of Jerusalem had apologized, but no mention is made about their accepting PEKAM rules banning shlihim. When explanations were finally received from the Sephardim and Perushim of Jerusalem and Safed, PEKAM printed these letters, interpreting them as a justification for its actions.[43]

Shlomo Zalman Shapira left Istanbul in July 1828.[44] He arrived in Aleppo ready to present before the Sephardi rabbinical court his arguments on how to allocate funds between the Perushim and the Hasidim. But no court session was conducted because the Hasidim did not appear in Aleppo due to an epidemic that swept Syria, the Galilee, and Jerusalem and quarantined Tiberias and Safed. Differences of opinion among the Hasidim of Tiberias and Safed may also have contributed to their reluctance to argue their case publicly. More important, most Hasidim and Perushim were reluctant to divulge to a Sephardi court details about their financial "channels showering many blessings on the Ashkenazim"—the same reason that militated against adjudicating their case before a Sephardi court in Eretz Israel. Despite the quarantine in Galilee, the ailing S. Z. Shapira (he died a few months later) traveled to Safed in an unsuccessful effort to effect a compromise between the Hasidim and the Perushim, who "light the flame of contention."

In February 1829 the squabbling Hasidim and Perushim finally agreed on a compromise regarding the division of funds raised in Europe due to pressing outside factors. Jews in Eretz Israel suffered "hunger, plague, diseases of many kinds and high prices..." Jerusalem Jews were forced to pay a special tariff of 37,000 or 50,000 piastres. The Ashkenazim of Jerusalem reported total debts of more than 40,000 piastres—"it is a bitter life, it is bitter from every side and corner." Contributions from Russia were delayed and reduced by 50–75 percent as a result of the Russo-Turkish War of 1828–1829. Russian Jewry was diverting its limited financial resources to ransoming teenage boys about to be conscripted into the Russian army for 25 years, based on the horrendous 1827 czarist decree. Thus, more financially dependent on PEKAM than ever before, the Perushim and Hasidim signed their 1829 compromise. The Sephardim lauded the Hasidim and the Perushim, who "found peace and quiet and security and much goodness." The Perushim "let it be known that in the Holy City of Jerusalem we increased the peace together with our brothers, the Sephardi scholars and rabbis."[45]

But such declarations of peace were premature. PEKAM rejected the compromise of 1829[46]—"it will not be"—because it permitted Ashkenazim to send shlihim to Western Europe and decreased the share of funds allotted to the Sephardim of Hebron. After hard negotiations, the PEKAM 1829 compromise was approved by all groups. It granted 60 percent of PEKAM monies to the Perushim and Hasidim and 40 percent to the Sephardim.

The allocation of funds received from Hungary was an unresolved part of the 1829 Perushim-Hasidim compromise. This issue had been heatedly argued by the Hasidim and Perushim of Safed, for collection rights in Hungary were just outside of PEKAM's jurisdiction. Fighting between the two Jewish groups became so furious that consul Anthony Katafago was asked to intervene, but to no avail. In the not unbiased words of R. Israel: "I exerted great efforts over Hungary. We arrived at a compromise with the Hasidim, but they did not abide by it and pumped money out of this country; and they did not allow some of the money to be sent [to the Perushim]."[47] It was only later that a compromise was reached permitting Hasidim and Perushim separate fundraising activities in Hungary if they could not agree on a shaliah who would represent both groups.

When discussing collections for Eretz Israel, a Hungarian rabbi noted that Jews in Hungary

are sitting quietly and peacefully under our ruling government and we are free from a per capita tax. Not so our brothers in the Holy Land, who sit under the yoke of the Diaspora and are indentured in body and soul to pay the heavy taxes...[48]

This was a strange reversal of roles. Jews living in Eretz Israel resided under the oppressive yoke of the Diaspora while the Diaspora Jews of Hungary lived peacefully and quietly, as it should be in the Holy Land.

Guided, and possibly inspired, by the February 1829 compromise between the Hasidim and Perushim, in April of that year the Ashkenazim and
Sephardim of Jerusalem also signed a compromise regarding collection territories in Italy, Western Europe, and various Sephardi communities in the
Turkish Empire. They also established the allocation key for bequests.[49]

While negotiations about signing the 1829 compromises were under way in
Jerusalem and in Galilee, the 300 Sephardim and the 100 Habad Hasidim in
Hebron were living in quiet harmony.[50] The two groups sent joint emissar-
ies to the Diaspora and distributed haluka out of a common treasury.

Peaceful as it seemed, the Hebron community lived in hardship and suffered a heavy financial burden. The Sephardi debt totaled more than 48,000
piastres, "with savage interest payments."[51] (We do not know how this 1828
debt of 48,000 piastres had been so precipitously reduced from 60,000 piastres in 1795, 120,000 piastres in 1798, and 200,000 piastres in 1800.) In an
1828 letter of a Hebron resident we read but find it hard to believe that during seven years no one left and no one entered because of the wars between
the pashas of Damascus and Acre. In addition, there was a five-year
drought that caused a severe rise in the price of food. Because of the economic and physical battering absorbed by Hebron's Jews,[52] Lehren found a
way in 1827 to increase the allocation to the Sephardim if only for "the
time being." In 1828–1829 the Hebron Sephardim received from PEKAM
1,500 Dutch florins sold at "the extremely bad rate" of 4.5 piastres per florin. This amounted to about 22 piastres for each of the 300 Sephardim, significantly more than the 4 to 5 piastres received from PEKAM by each of the
Sephardim of Tiberias, Jerusalem, and Safed.

The Hasidim of the Galilee tried to convince Lehren that the Habad
Hasidim in Hebron received more than their proportionate share of PEKAM
monies. Lehren answered that, if this were true, the Hasidim in Eretz Israel
should correct the inequity among themselves. On an earlier occasion a
rabbinical court found that the Hasidic charges against the Habad group in
Hebron were unfounded and awarded the Habad 1 piastre for every 8.3 piastres received by the Hasidim of the Galilee, calculating this to be the accurate numerical relationship of these Hasidic communities in 1829.[53]

The peaceful situation that prevailed between the Sephardim and Ashkenazim in Hebron and in Jerusalem did not prevent disagreements and dissension from splintering the Safed and Tiberias communities. So dissonant
were the clamorous sounds voiced by the Ashkenazim and Sephardim in
the Galilee and so frequently did they complain before Anthony Katafago,
that he suggested establishing a joint rabbinical court for adjudicating dis-

putes among Jews.[54] No such court was set up; a Hasidic leader in Safed objected to such outside intervention by the representative of the czar, who "opposes Torah decisions for Jews" in Russia.

In the Galilee, rampant disease, hunger, high prices, and large debts contributed to the state of discord in 1828–1830. There was "no peace for those leaving and entering" Safed.[55] The debts of the Safed community mounted. The 1,100 Sephardim now owed 400,000 piastres, some 360 piastres per Sephardi, compared to their debt of 125,000 piastres in 1804, which amounted to 210 piastres for each person. The Perushim's debts were also most burdensome, judging from R. Israel's unanswered request to Lehren in June 1827 to conduct a special fundraising campaign for his kollel. The 700 Perushim owed 121,000 piastres in 1833, some 170 piastres per person. The 1830 debt of the 465 Hasidim totaled 125,000 piastres, some 270 piastres for each Hasid.

In 1828 the Hasidic kollel in Safed was split by a rift in its leadership;[56] Gershon Margolit was pitted against Amram Hasida Rosenbaum. Margolit was attacked for the way he distributed haluka money to the Hasidim and, according to an English missionary, for "embezzling the money of the poor." Lehren complained that the reasons for this conflict "have been silenced and nobody told us anything about it." He also chastised the Hasidim for not showing "true brotherly love," told them to "silence all arguments and contentions" out of "love for the Holy Land and the honor of its settlers," and threatened to stop PEKAM payments if they did not stop squabbling.

In an effort to eliminate the cause of the conflict, Lehren told Margolit to resign from the Hasidic executive committee of Safed,[57] thereby enabling the Safed and Tiberias Hasidic kollelim to unite, as in previous years. But Margolit stubbornly refused to quit.

Lehren proposed establishing three major Ashkenazi kollelim in Eretz Israel—for the Hasidim, Habad, and the Perushim.[58] Through such a consolidation he hoped to eliminate certain undesirable methods of distributing haluka monies. For example, funds from one endowment were allocated among the 779 Hasidim of Tiberias and Safed, contrary to the express wishes of the donor. PEKAM "could never imagine" that instead of investing the endowment and each year distributing its annual interest of 10 percent the Hasidim would distribute the entire endowment capital at one time and planned during the coming years to deduct the annual 10 percent interest from the yearly kollel haluka allocations. This unusual "investment" policy, instead of easing the future financial burden on the Hasidim, meant that "those who come after them [would] be obligated to pay."

Lehren hoped that consolidation of the three major Ashkenazi kollelim

would ensure better record-keeping and accounting practices. He was cha-
grined to discover that no lists of Hasidic haluka recipients were sent to
him, that other lists were incomplete, and that the Hasidim mixed up PEKAM
monies with other funds sent by the Hasidim of Eastern Europe. When the
Hasidim apologized for their lack of accounting knowledge, Lehren
snapped, "What does expertise have to do with this?" He "warned" the
Hasidic leaders to distribute the haluka funds properly "without favoritism,
without discrimination, and without giving more [money] to one of their
friends."[59] Lehren instituted a system of haluka in return for receipts. Lists
containing the names of haluka recipients, the number of members in each
family, and the amount allocated were to be signed by the recipients and
certified not only by the Hasidic leaders but by three other trustworthy
men of substance.

A further measure of Lehren's "trust" toward the Ashkenazim is reflected in his recommendation that leaders of the Safed Hasidim verify
haluka payments in Tiberias and that Tiberias leaders check the Safed
haluka payments.[60] If the procedure of distributing haluka against a signed
receipt was not scrupulously followed, Lehren threatened that next time he
would forward haluka money to other Hasidic leaders of greater probity.
From its position of economic strength, PEKAM tried to foist on the Hasidic
leaders actions it could approve.

In Tiberias, during the year 1828–1829, each of the 314 Hasidim received
23 piastres from PEKAM.[61] When the Hasidic kollel of Tiberias disbursed
Eastern European haluka monies there was a falling out between Hasidic
factions from Russia and Volyzhin who split off from each other. Russian
Hasidim demanded one-third or at least one-quarter of Eastern European
contributions, but the Volyzhin Hasidim objected. R. Israel of Shklov, the
head of the Perushim kollel, was asked to arbitrate this fracas, but since friction among the Hasidim was so abrasive he referred the dispute to R.
Moshe Sofer of Pressburg, who ruled that one-third of the monies collected
in Eastern Europe for Tiberias should go to the Russian Hasidim; funds collected outside Eastern Europe should be distributed on a per capita basis
only to the needy, but not the well-to-do Hasidim.

In his rabbinical decision, R. Sofer complained bitterly about the hostility between Jews in Eretz Israel:

> Woe is me that we are so shamed and insulted. Because righteous men
> have settled in the Holy Land and disagreements are acceptable to them.
> Woe to us that this has happened in our day. . . . But what can we do?
> Our sins have made it impossible to unite them, therefore, they split off
> from each other . . .[62]

R. Sofer's admonition against schisms did not deter 10 Reisen Hasidic families from breaking away from the kollel of Tiberias in 1831 and setting up their own independent kollel.

The 600 Sephardim of Tiberias were also dissatisfied and complained to Lehren that they received less than half the funds allocated to the 350 Hasidim of Tiberias.[63] Lehren agreed with the Sephardi claim and asked the Tiberias Hasidic leaders to discuss this matter with the Sephardi rabbi, Joseph David Abulafia. "How good it would be that you discuss this matter among yourselves... peacefully and in good taste and reason, without fighting and squabbling." In August 1829 this issue still remained unresolved.

After Lehren referred to R. Israel and R. Sopher the claims of the Tiberias Sephardim, and after signing a conciliatory compromise, the Sephardim and Ashkenazim of Jerusalem jointly sent Shlomo Zalman Zoref on a European fundraising mission in 1829.[64] Lehren strongly opposed this move, for he feared that the influential leader of the Perushim would threaten PEKAM's authority, question its system of fundraising, and infringe on its collection territory. When PEKAM learned that Zoref had already left Jerusalem for Italy, where he collected funds until mid-1831, Lehren slandered Zoref as a person who "does not know how to write and his language is that of a stutterer."

Zoref answered in common coin, insulting the PEKAM leaders trying to ban emissaries from Western Europe: "He who wants to institute new regulations should be considered a destroyer of Jerusalem."[65] Perushim leaders in Vilna asked PEKAM to help finance Zoref's mission, but Lehren curtly refused. However, to stay on good terms with the powerful Vilna Rabbis PEKAM agreed to buy from Zoref soil from the Mount of Olives and the Tomb of Rachel.

As he traveled about Italy, Zoref met the Sephardi shaliah from Safed, Nathan Maraji. In Venice (June 1830) the two emissaries amicably revised points contained in the 1825 Ashkenazi-Sephardi compromise about how to distribute monies collected by shlihim in Holland, France, England, Prussia, and Italy. The Safed Perushim and Sephardi kollelim approved this Venice agreement, which was most beneficial to the Sephardim of Safed.[66]

Less pleasant than this friendly compromise was an incident that may never have taken place but is retold for the way it reflects on the nature of the institution of the shaliah. In one Italian town Zoref was preceded by a Sephardi shaliah posing as Shlomo Zalman Zoref![67] The Sephardi presented forged documents attesting to his alleged identity and was warmly received by the Jewish community. When the real Shlomo Zalman Zoref arrived in town there was a blunt confrontation at the Sabbath synagogue service and the impostor was forced to admit that he was a fraud.

In Padua and other Italian towns Zoref encouraged local Jews to increase their donations by telling about the anticipated arrival of the Messiah. Throughout history Jews have displayed a singular obsession with and a sometimes fatal attraction to Messianism. R. Israel was not satisfied to wait for Redemption: he believed that Jews must act to bring about an "awakening from below."

In each town Zoref read a letter written by R. Israel of Shklov and addressed to the Ten Lost Tribes of Israel. It depicted the spiritual state of mind of the Jews in Eretz Israel and in the Diaspora and vividly projected their hope and belief in the imminent coming of the Messianic Redemption, "quickly and in our lifetime." Discovery of the Ten Lost Tribes was crucial to Jews "in order that their people be privileged to behold the days of the Messiah and life in the next world."[68]

As 1830 approached, rumors had reached the Jews in Eretz Israel from "firsthand witnesses" who reported seeing the Ten Lost Tribes in Yemen. In the opinion of R. Israel the best way to verify these rumors, which could have a cataclysmic effect on the lives of all Jews, was to send a shaliah to Yemen. The Perushim of Safed chose Baruch of Pinsk for this mission, and in November 1830 Baruch left Safed carrying a letter to the Jews of Yemen written by R. Israel.[69]

R. Israel's long letter explained the basic principles of Redemption and made three requests of the Ten Tribes, to ensure the coming of the Messiah. First, he asked them to pray for the Jews in Eretz Israel: ". . . help us, help us with prayers" to accelerate the advent of the Messiah. Second, R. Israel asked the Ten Tribes to send to Eretz Israel ordained scholars able to ordain other rabbinical scholars, a procedure that had lapsed in Eretz Israel after the destruction of the Second Temple in A.D. 70. Ordination was crucial, because before the Messiah comes, the High Court (the Sanhedrin) composed of ordained scholars must be established in Eretz Israel. R. Israel held that renewing ordination was a prerequisite for building the Kingdom of David and rebuilding Jerusalem. "At the beginning God builds Jerusalem and then the dispersed Jews will gather there." The third request in Israel's letter was the prosaic plea for money to maintain the debt-ridden Jewish community in Eretz Israel.

Such great interest and curiosity in Redemption and the Ten Tribes was evinced by European Jewry that Shlomo Zalman Zoref read R. Israel's letter to communities he visited and Zvi Hirsch Lehren distributed copies of

R. Israel's letter to West European Jewry. Many Jews perceived apocalyptic implications in everything happening around them. Lehren himself lived with the acute feeling that the coming of the Messiah was imminent in his lifetime. Initially he was so excited about finding the Ten Lost Tribes that he financed Baruch's trip to Yemen. Eventually his ardor cooled when he learned that no Sephardim had signed the letter to the Ten Tribes and that several prominent Perushim and Hasidim opposed the mission and disparaged the character of the shaliah.

Baruch of Pinsk arrived in Sana, Yemen, in August 1833, two years and nine months after leaving Eretz Israel. While searching for the Ten Tribes, he was appointed court doctor at Sana, got involved in court politics, and, in February 1834, was shot by the imam on suspicion of being a spy of the Egyptian ruler, Mehemet Ali. When news of Baruch's fate reached the Jews of Eretz Israel and the Diaspora they were crushed; yet they continued to pray in everlasting hope for their Redemption and the coming of the Messiah.

After collecting money in Italy, Zoref moved on to the PEKAM collection territory of Paris, where he exacerbated his relations with Lehren by claiming that PEKAM was disrupting efforts to collect donations from West European Jewry. In November 1831 Zoref met in London with Asher Samson and leaders of the English Holy Contribution organization, who contended that Ashkenazim in Eretz Israel were deprived of their fair share of the haluka. Lehren had good reason to believe that Zoref was stirring up antagonisms and inciting the English against PEKAM.[70]

From London Zoref traveled to Holland and met with the PEKAM leaders in an atmosphere of great tension. Once again Zoref argued the need for emissaries to collect money for the impoverished Jews in Eretz Israel, and once again PEKAM leaders explained why they abolished the shaliah institution of fundraising. In a civil manner, both parties agreed to continue to disagree. By January 1833 Zoref had returned to Eretz Israel, which now was ruled by Egypt's sovereign, Mehemet Ali.

NINE

The Egyptian Occupation of Palestine

1831–1840

From 1831 to 1840 the Egyptian armies of Mehemet Ali conquered and ruled Palestine.[1] This nine-year period of Egyptian occupation changed the history of the Holy Land and the life of the Jews in Eretz Israel. Unlike Napoleon's short-lived 1799 foray into Palestine, Mehemet Ali jolted Palestine into a new world far different from the era of pashas Ahmad al-Jazzar (1775–1804), Suleiman (1805–1819), and Abdullah (1819–1831). Who was this pasha of Egypt and why did he covet the desolate, poor territory of Palestine?

Mehemet Ali (1805–1848), the uneducated son of an Albanian fisherman, ruled Egypt for forty-three years and his descendants sat on the Egyptian throne until 1952. He first arrived in Egypt in 1798 as an officer in the Turkish army. After battling against Napoleon and proving his military abilities, in 1805 Mehemet Ali was appointed by the Sultan as pasha of Egypt. A blunt and crude man, Mehemet Ali invited 300 Mamluke leaders to a reception (1811) where he butchered all his rivals.

Mehemet Ali was a modernizer, fanatically intent on dragging Egypt up to the level of the European powers. As pasha of Egypt, he established military, technical, and medical schools; he improved methods of land cultivation and constructed irrigation projects; he streamlined the tax collection system; and he initiated health reforms by building hospitals and introducing quarantines. Mehemet Ali mobilized most of his time and money to restructure his formidable army and navy along the lines of Western technology. He appointed his stepson, Ibrahim Pasha, a brilliant military talent, as head of the armed forces.

Anxious to demonstrate his prowess in battle, annex new territory, impress the European powers, and prove his loyalty to the Ottoman Empire, Mehemet Ali, at the behest of the sultan, sent Ibrahim Pasha to Morea to crush the Greek revolt in 1825. In return for dispatching his powerful military force and in compensation for the loss of his fleet at the naval fiasco of Navarino, Mehemet Ali expected and possibly was promised by the sultan the territorial reward of the Syrian provinces.[2] Like other Egyptian rulers before him, he coveted a buffer zone to the north, contending that Syria was essential for the safety of Egypt.

When the sultan refused to give Egypt control over Syria and offered only the rebellious island of Crete, Mehemet Ali felt deceived. He refused to help the Turkish Empire fight Russia in 1828–1829 and resolved to gain independence from the Sublime Porte.[3]

Mehemet Ali sought to extend his political influence throughout Europe and the Turkish Empire. But for a believing Muslim to rebel against the sultan, the head of the Islamic world, was no simple matter. An appropriate pretext was sought and quickly found in the person of Abdullah Pasha of Acre who had forgotten his vow in the early 1820s that he was "Mehemet Ali's creature." At the end of 1831 Abdullah was close to consolidating his control over the mountain region of Palestine and boasted about his power by signing decrees as the ruler of Sidon, Tripoli, Gaza, Jaffa, Hebron, Jerusalem, and Nablus.[4] Abdullah had angered Mehemet Ali by interfering with Egyptian trade in the Sinai and Gaza and by refusing to repay a loan. Most infuriating was Abdullah's refusal in 1829 to repatriate thousands of Egyptian fellahin who had fled to Palestine to avoid high taxation, farm indenture, and army conscription. When the rankled Egyptian pasha complained to the Sublime Porte he received a cold response, making it clear that the sultan had decided to curb Mehemet Ali's growing power in favor of Abdullah Pasha, who was faithfully carrying out Mahmud's reform program in Palestine.

Mehemet Ali found 1831 to be a propitious time to inflict revenge on his enemies. The European powers were then preoccupied with the political aftermaths of the 1830 revolutions sweeping Europe: the Paris rebellion overthrew the Bourbon monarchy of Charles X and crowned citizen Louis Philippe as king; Belgium revolted against the Dutch king and established

Mehemet Ali ruled Egypt from 1806 to 1849 and conquered Palestine in 1831 with his stepson Ibrahim Pasha leading the Egyptian army.

an independent monarchy; the Polish insurrection was crushed by Czar Nicholas I (September 1831); the Italian uprising against the papal government and Austria failed and Giuseppe Mazzini founded "Young Italy" (March 1831); Greece finally achieved independence from the Turks; revolutionary movements in Germany forced reforms. Also, in 1830 French expeditionary forces conquered Algiers and the Algerian coastal towns. European powers disdained the tottering Ottoman Empire. Reflecting the views of European leaders, Czar Nicholas I said, "I lack the power to give life to a corpse and the Turkish empire is dead."[5]

In October 1831 Ibrahim Pasha led a battle-experienced Egyptian army, intent on capturing the Syrian provinces of Palestine, Sidon, Damascus, and Aleppo and lands beyond. In quick succession he seized Jaffa and overran Palestine's coastal plain, the central Judean mountains, and the Galilee hill country. Except for overt displays of distrust shown by some Muslims in Jerusalem and Nablus,[6] the Palestine population "welcomed the Egyptian invasion with open arms."[7] Residents of Palestine hoped to be liberated from the cruel persecution, high taxes, and hated reforms of Abdullah Pasha, and believed that a distant Egyptian ruler would be a welcome improvement.

After conquering nearly all of Palestine,[8] Ibrahim Pasha besieged Acre for six months. He leveled many of the town buildings and eventually overcame the courageous defense of Abdullah's 3,500 starving soldiers. In recognition of Abdullah's brave resistance Ibrahim exiled him to Egypt with full military honors, instead of following the customary practice of publicly executing a defeated foe. In an effort to obtain the cooperation of the local inhabitants, Ibrahim punished looters and ordered the return of stolen goods.

Six months after the invasion of Palestine Sultan Mahmud declared war on Mehemet Ali and deposed him as governor of Egypt. Undeterred, Ibrahim Pasha won successive battles in Syria and overran much of Anatolia. By February 1833 he had crushed the sultan's armies and advanced to within 150 miles of Istanbul, imperiling the existence of the Ottoman Empire. The sultan's anguished pleas for British and Austrian military assistance were rebuffed, leaving him in such desperate distress that he asked for help from Turkey's archenemy, Russia, which was most happy to oblige.[9]

Realizing that the European powers would not allow him to upset the European balance of power and conquer the Turkish capital,[10] in May 1833 Mehemet Ali negotiated an agreement with the Sublime Porte that provided for his giving up territory in Asia Minor in return for the governorships in Egypt, Crete, Arabia, and Syria. As the ruler of lands from the Taurus Mountains in central Anatolia to Sudan, Mehemet Ali was now received back into the Ottoman family. He consented to pay the annual tax to the sultan, who agreed, in exchange, not to garrison Turkish troops in Syria. The sultan would also continue to appoint Syrian religious leaders and issue firmans on important matters of trade, diplomacy, and the rights of European nationals. Syria was subjected to "joint Ottoman-Egyptian rule: Ottoman in theory, Egyptian in practice," with the power to govern Syria securely clasped in Mehemet Ali's hands.

While Ibrahim Pasha was bogged down in his six-month siege of Acre and when he was far away in Anatolia, the chiefs and religious leaders of Palestine began to extend their power. They disobeyed orders issued by Egyptian occupation officials and disregarded Ibrahim's order to stop pocketing local taxes. Abu-Ghosh threatened to expel Egyptians from Jerusalem and Jaffa if they did not reestablish the poll tax and the toll paid to him by travelers on the Jerusalem to Jaffa road.

Ibrahim Pasha had temporarily overlooked these ingrained habits of disdain toward central authority. But now that he had shown his strength to the Sublime Porte and concluded a peace agreement, Ibrahim Pasha started to rule Palestine with a convincing show of force. He reorganized the administrative machinery and tax system, developed commerce and agriculture, imposed law and order, and showed tolerance toward the minorities.

Mehemet Ali appointed Ibrahim Pasha as commander of the armed forces and director of the civil administration of Syria.[11] Serving under him as governor-general of Syria was Muhammad Sharif Bey (later Pasha Bey), Mehemet Ali's able son-in-law. One of Sharif Bey's first acts was to appoint Hanna Bahri, a Greek Catholic and rival of the Farhi family, as chief financial officer. Muhammad Sharif Bey built a strong centralized administration based in Damascus, the Syrian capital. Under the new organizational setup, Palestine became one political-administrative entity for the first time since Sultan Selim I conquered the country in 1516.

To obtain local cooperation and secure justice, the Egyptians established a municipal majilis or town council in places with 2,000 or more residents.[12] The majilis advised on all affairs concerning the town and its citizens. Muslim religious courts were restricted to dealing with matters of personal status, inheritances, and property-holding. The Muslim judges were put on the Egyptian payroll and deprived of an income from court litigants. Government officials were also paid a salary out of the Egyptian treasury in an effort to limit bribery and restrict local authority.

During the first years of Egyptian rule trade flourished and industry

The military camp of Ibrahim Pasha's Egyptian army in 1834.

prospered in Syria. This thriving period marked a sharp upsurge from the stagnant economic situation that characterized Palestine during the first thirty years of the nineteenth century. There was a large increase in the sale of local goods and merchandise imported from Europe. Consumption rose because of the insatiable demands of Ibrahim Pasha's military forces. This burgeoning economic activity was distinguished by escalating prices, increased wages, rising employment, high taxes, and successive currency devaluations that all contributed to a soaring rate of inflation.[13]

Between 1831 and 1840 the Turkish piastre dropped in value by more than one-third in relation to the pound sterling. Mehemet Ali manipulated the currency to increase his income and reduce expenditures, and devalued the Turkish gold coin in 1838 by 14 percent, with the devaluation going into effect on "different days in different places."[14]

Sharif Bey overhauled the tax collection system.[15] He abolished a multitude of protection fees, arbitrary tributes, and extortion payments that were siphoned off by local chiefs and then organized a comprehensive system that included a bewildering array of taxes; the miri or land tax continued to be by far the largest income producer. The most important and most remunerative new tax was the farda, a progressive income tax. Christians and Jews paid the poll tax of 22 to 60 piastres levied by previous pashas. No changes were instituted in the custom tariff system favoring foreign nationals because it was based on capitulation agreements signed by the Sublime Porte and European powers with whom Mehemet Ali wanted to curry favor.

Ibrahim Pasha's large army foisted law and order upon the Palestine population. Soldiers maintained the peace in towns and villages by executing swift, severe punishment. Lawlessness was uprooted even in the rebellious mountain areas, and Beduin incursions were stopped in populated areas. The incessant fighting between the rival gangs of Yamanis and Kays was quelled. Travel on the roads was safe and tribute-free.[16]

A contemporary Jew trying to fulfill a need to feel secure described in an exaggerated fashion how safe people felt:

> he [Mehemet Ali] wrought fearful judgments upon all wicked men and [caused] fear and trembling to fall upon everyone, so that a little girl could walk on the road carrying gold coins in her hand, and no one would address or molest her.[17]

One way the Egyptian rulers safeguarded their subjects was by taking away their firearms.[18] Officials established how many muskets and other weapons each village must turn over to the Egyptian army. If villagers could not meet their arms quota, they purchased the required guns in other places.

While maintaining the peace, Egyptian forces continued the age-old practices of an occupying army. They cut down trees in Palestine and the Lebanon to build naval vessels. Camels and mules were confiscated, and owners of such animals fled to the less accessible mountain ranges, thereby disrupting internal transportation. Workers were requisitioned at half the going wage in order to construct government fortifications, army barracks, and impressive public works such as the health baths of Tiberias and windmills for grinding flour in Jerusalem.[19]

Soldiers were billeted in Jewish and other homes. In October 1833 the English missionary John Nicolayson wrote of a Jewish family in Jerusalem, "who like many others, have been driven out of their houses to give way to the soldiers."[20] Local garrisons in towns such as Jerusalem "frequently . . . committed serious robberies upon the Jews." Since centuries-old habits could not be changed overnight, the Jews were still "exposed to continual wrongs. The soldiers occasionally break into their houses and compel them to lend articles which are never restored."[21] In some cases, however, local Muslims and Egyptian soldiers were severely punished for physically abusing Jews. The quantum improvement in maintaining security was probably the most significant change in Palestine during the 1830s, and it had a far-reaching impact on other aspects of life in the country.

Mehemet Ali radically liberalized the legal rights and social status of Christians and Jews, "a consideration hitherto unknown to them."[22] By practicing tolerance he hoped to conciliate the European powers and gain their support for any future Egyptian ventures against the Turkish Empire, as well as obtain the cooperation of the 30,000 minority members in Palestine.

Minority members gained greatly from the peace and tranquility instituted throughout Palestine by Ibrahim Pasha. Christian and Jewish lives, property, and honor were respected by the Muslim population. Minority members continued to pay the poll tax symbolizing their inferior status, but arbitrary tributes and severe one-time taxes were abolished. Fees Christians paid to enter the Holy Sepulchre were canceled. Jews were granted free access to the Wailing Wall without paying protection money and could now worship in public and purchase homes in Jerusalem. Both Christians and Jews were allowed to repair their places of worship, but construction of new church and synagogue buildings still required a firman from the sultan.[23]

The expectations of some Jews were so great that they believed they had been elevated to a status higher than the Muslims and that Mehemet Ali was "destined to rescue them from slavery and to ensure them brighter prospects."[24] They believed that the conquest of Palestine was a divine message portending true salvation and the imminent arrival of Jewish Redemption. "The start of Redemption has arrived by the grace of God, and quickly in our time the Redeemer will come to Zion."[25]

Another boon to the Jews was the increasing influence of foreign consuls who protected them, especially the European nationals. A landmark of the period was the arrival in 1839 of the first consul in Jerusalem. Jews wrote with some exaggeration that "had it not been for the consuls' supervision, we would all have been destroyed and lost, since the Gentiles wish to consume the Jews and to accuse them falsely."[26]

Abolishing special discriminatory dress for the minorities and allowing them to ride animals in town were external trappings that signaled granting them equal rights. Seating Jews and Christians on the town councils and permitting them freedom of trade also carried the message of equality. In civil court cases minority members were granted status equal to that of Muslims. In this tolerant atmosphere European pilgrims streamed into the Holy Land, while Americans and Englishmen established mission stations in Jerusalem and openly preached the gospel. Mehemet Ali's policy of tolerance toward the minorities had to be forcibly imposed by Ibrahim Pasha's soldiers because it ran directly and deeply counter to previous Muslim practices of persecution. Muslims perceived that the very fabric of Islam was being torn before their eyes and its religious values were being undermined by the Egyptian usurper who had revolted against the legitimate authority in Islam, the sultan.

Another significant change in Palestine occurred in farming the land. Mehemet Ali initiated an agricultural policy aimed at improving land cultivation in order to feed the occupying Egyptian army and the local population and earn foreign currency by exporting produce. The Egyptians only partially succeeded in their efforts to develop Palestine's agriculture because they gave higher priority to implementing their policy of conscripting local inhabitants into Ibrahim Pasha's army. This drew off able farm and town people and depressed agriculture, commerce, and industry.

Ibrahim Pasha convinced his stepfather to delay implementing this decision of conscription, realizing that it would arouse vociferous antagonism and violence among the people. Local chiefs saw conscription as draining off their small, irregular forces and subverting their independent position of power. The life pattern of the conscript would be totally destroyed since he would be detached from all that was worth while in life—land, family, village, and tribe. However, after failing to recruit 60,000 new soldiers in Egypt,[27] Mehemet Ali ordered the conscription of Syrian recruits in the first half of 1834. Using the most brutal methods of impressment, conscripts were arbitrarily arrested and dragged off to the army.[28]

By the spring of 1834 the chiefs, notables, religious oligarchy, townfolk, and peasants had all recognized their serious error in welcoming the Egyptian invader. Within two years Mehemet Ali had launched "a new era" by changing the rhythm of life and breaking up the social, political, and economic order in Palestine.[29] Initially the Syrian populace was satisfied with economic prosperity, full employment, safety for life and security for property, reclamation of abandoned lands, and fair legal recourse for the redress of grievances. Yet these substantial benefits were outweighed by overwhelming disadvantages: escalating prices, an unstable currency, strictly enforced high taxation, and the arbitrary requisitioning of manpower and beasts of burden by an iron military fist. Far more seriously, Ibrahim Pasha had disrupted the traditional order of a Muslim society.

Tolerating the influx of foreign pilgrims and tourists was strange to a Muslim. Granting equality to Christians and Jews was humiliating, and the sight of infidel Christians setting up mission stations in Jerusalem was truly an abomination. Town notables no longer benefited from tax and tribute extortions; they were fired or subordinated to Egyptian officials or rendered superfluous when the town councils changed the local balance of power. Tribal chiefs lost income from tolls and protection money that had been abolished or channeled directly into the Egyptian treasury. Now conscription threatened to deplete feudal forces of the tribal chiefs, eclipsing their power, decreasing their influence, and jeopardizing their very existence.

The first signs of insurrection had already appeared in the mountainous areas of Palestine late in the previous year, and at the start of 1834 the Beduin in Jordan joined the revolt. Finally, after the introduction of compulsory conscription, rival chiefs and their followers banded together, received the blessings of the religious leaders, and rebelled against the Egyptians.

Now that the rainy season was over and plowing had been completed, the 1834 rebellion broke out early in May. Although called the "revolt of the fellahin," this uprising was supported by the vast majority of the urban and rural population of Palestine.

The start of the rebellion and the ferocity of the rebels came as a surprise to Ibrahim Pasha. In April 1834 Palestine notables assembled in Jerusalem told Ibrahim that they accepted his plan for army conscription, but needed to return home to implement it. Ibrahim Pasha's perceptiveness may have been dulled by the tragic Easter Holy Fire ceremony that he had just witnessed from a gallery of the Church of the Holy Sepulchre.

The miracle of the Holy Fire from heaven was celebrated on the Saturday before Easter by the Greek Catholics, Armenians, Copts, and Abyssinians and symbolized the spiritual birth and resurrection of Christ.[30] Before the start of the ceremony clusters of people began dashing excitedly around the Sepulchre, clapping and wildly howling, "This is the tomb of Jesus Christ!" Holy hysteria swept through the densely packed crowd of about 15,000 persons. An uproarious frenzy broke out as pilgrims pushed forward, "madly struggling" to be the first to light their tapers at the "holy fire" from a torch that was thrust out of a hidden porthole. Then the mob ran amok. Herds of people stampeded, trampling human limbs on the ground. Bodies quickly piled up "lying in heaps . . . like bundles of skin." Before this mass madness subsided about 300 worshippers had suffocated or been trampled to death, and another 200–300 had been badly injured. Ibrahim Pasha escaped alive thanks to the strenuous efforts of his military escort. He must have wondered what pagan excesses were practiced by the heathen Christians.

The 1834 rebellion first broke out in the mountains around Nablus, Hebron, and Jerusalem while Ibrahim Pasha was in Jaffa. The astonished Egyptian forces retreated from the countryside and were attacked in Jerusalem, Jaffa, and Gaza. The Egyptian garrisons in Hebron and Nablus were overwhelmed. Fellahin swept through the Galilee, captured Tiberias and Safed, and laid siege to Acre. From May 20 Jerusalem was besieged by 20,000 fellahin and Beduin.

Ominously, on the Sunday of May 25, Palestine was struck by an earth tremor that lasted three seconds in Jerusalem; tremors were to continue throughout the week. A few houses fell, walls cracked, minarets toppled over, and the big dome covering the Church of the Holy Sepulchre was damaged. On the following day fellahin poured into town and drove the defending Egyptian garrison of about 1,000 soldiers into the citadel.[31] Rebels sacked the town, seizing "everything of value." Jerusalemites experienced "truly awful times."

Greek and Roman Catholics, Armenians, and other Christians fled to monasteries and villages outside of Jerusalem while their churches were damaged. The Jews, with no place of refuge, stayed in their quarter, suffering, starving, and being robbed, as their synagogues were defiled. The newly arrived German Jewish settler Joseph Schwartz wrote:

What a terrible night was this for us all! The echoing of the voices of thousands of warriors,—of men, women, and children, who all raised their wild Arab war-cry in the gloom of the night, at the storming of the city; the tumult of the retreating troops; the lamentations of the defenceless, abandoned inhabitants, who heard already in their midst the shouts of the infuriated conquerors,—all presented a most mournful scene.[32]

A Welsh traveler confirmed the sad plight of the more than 3,000 Jerusalem Jews:

The Jews who had no safe place wherein to flee suffered greatly. Their houses were spoiled so completely that there was not a bed to lie down upon; many of them were slain, their wives and daughters outraged, etc. In short, things were done too barbarous to relate. In the hope of receiving good pay, or for some other end, this cruelty was spared the monasteries.

To increase the misery of Jerusalemites, the plague struck town soon after the revolt and the earthquake.

Upon receiving word from the besieged Jerusalem garrison Ibrahim Pasha marched an army of 7,500 soldiers from Jaffa to Jerusalem. The fellahin rebels fled town, pursued by Egyptian forces who routed them at the Christian villages of Beit Jalla and Bethlehem. However, Ibrahim Pasha's army was badly beaten at the Pools of Solomon just outside Bethlehem and lost 800 troops.[33]

After recapturing Jerusalem, Ibrahim Pasha met Mehemet Ali in Jaffa and with a reinforced army of 15,000 and effective cannon fire pursued the rebels in the central Palestine mountains.[34] Along the march he burned villages, executed prisoners, and cut off the right hands of old men he captured. Ibrahim pursued the rebel leader with "sword and fire" and caught and summarily executed him with his followers at the end of August. Palestinian chiefs and fellahin now realized the futility of fighting against a superb, iron-willed general equipped with artillery. This was no weak-willed sultan or bribery-prone pasha.

Toward the end of May Safed Jews told the Acre governor that fellahin around Safed were preparing to join the rebellious forces. To compound the worries of the Jews, Safed, like Jerusalem, felt two earthquake tremors. "The noise and tremors grew in intensity," a Jewish resident reported. "We were therefore compelled to leave our possessions in our homes and run outside; for there is no fear in the open, but it is death to remain indoors. The walls were smashed and fell upon those near them."[35] Luckily there was no loss of life, but the earthquake was a portent of worse troubles that were to follow.

The fellahin revolt broke out in Safed on June 15. With official approval and boundless fury, the town and rural fellahin wounded and killed Jews in the Safed kehilla of about 3,500 people. A harrowing 33-day scenario of robbery and rapine ensued. "Every kind of horror was perpetrated..." Peasants broke "into the Jewish quarter plundering and violating common standards of morality and decency..." "Even a cannibal might be ashamed of such doings." Jews reported being "repeatedly beaten until blood flowed...they stripped us of our clothes and left us naked except for our underpants..." Fellahin tortured and maimed men, molested and raped women, despoiled homes, and demolished the Jewish quarter.

Roving bands of toughs pillaged whatever was detachable. The "savages" ripped open walls, dug up floors, and detached window and door frames in search of hidden treasure hoards. "Everything was carried off which could possibly be removed, even articles of no value." The lust for loot was unquenchable. What could not be carried off was burned or destroyed. Vandals smashed the recently established printing presses of Israel Bak.

A few Arab-speaking Jews courageously infiltrated among the roaming fellahin gangs, and it is claimed that "much was saved in this manner." Isolated instances of valorous opposition by Jews trying to protect their homes and families are recorded. When two Jews hid on a roof and threw rocks on the "wild beasts" below, the house was burned down; one Jew was killed and the other seriously wounded.

"Hungry, thirsty, naked, and barefoot" Jews were "frightened and in a panic like sheep being led to slaughter." Perushim led by R. Israel of Shklov took refuge in the synagogue. Rioters surrounded the building and threatened to kill R. Israel if he did not turn over to them the monies in the kollel treasury. Bribes bought the lives of men and saved the honor of women. But the thirteen synagogues of Safed were stripped, desecrated, and damaged. Fellahin shredded prayer books and scattered torn pieces of parchment from Torah scrolls. Prayer shawls and phylacteries were used as straps and coverings for cattle.

Battered Jews fled the synagogues and their sacked houses and found a haven in the homes of friends and in the nearby cemetery and caves. The kadi of Safed, out of friendship for Gershon Margolit, still a leader of the Hasidic kollel, sheltered hundreds of Hasidim, in return for payment. The wife of the 67-year-old spiritual leader of the Hasidim, R. Abraham Dov, successfully hid money on her person, enabling the rabbi to supply starving Jews with two ounces of bread each day.

Some Jews hid on the hilltops outside of town. During the summer day they were exposed to the heat and at night they froze. Mercifully, they were hunted down and imprisoned in the citadel, where they were protected from the rampaging fellahin. More fortunate Jews escaped to the villages of Meron, Bireh, and Ein Zeitun, all on the outskirts of Safed. One refugee related:

> We ate nothing for three days and then they gave us a small cake baked on live coals to sustain us for a full day. And we sat there [Ein Zeitun] for forty days in fear of death by the robbers. Our possessions were in the hands of strangers and we did not believe that we would live through this.[36]

For weeks they lived on two small loaves of bread per day; on the Sabbath this diet was supplemented by three onions.

At long last the Druze army of Amir Bashir Shihab, allies of Ibrahim Pasha, captured Safed on July 18. Fellahin rioters fled without a fight, and the Jews returned to their demolished quarter. The treasonable governor of Safed and thirteen leaders of the fellahin were publicly executed in Acre.[37]

On the intervention of the consuls, Ibrahim Pasha promised to compensate Jews of foreign nationality for their losses and instructed the new Safed governor to return to the Jews all looted possessions not "totally ruined and destroyed." Moreover, "every Jew was believed when saying that he recognized this or that Arab among the robbers." For the first time the word of a Jew took precedence over that of a Muslim.

Looted possessions were either claimed by their owners or were auctioned off, but the proceeds netted the Jews only 1 percent of their declared loss. By the end of 1834 the Egyptians taxed the local Muslim population, possibly at the instigation of the foreign consuls, and returned to the Jews 3½ percent of their declared loss with a promise to remit the balance soon. But Ibrahim's plan forcibly to collect a sum equal to the losses of the Jews was not acted upon due to the lack of cooperation among the local officials. Long, tedious compensation negotiations ensued, with the mediating consuls enriching themselves in the process.

After representing the interests of all Safed Jews, John Farren, the British consul in Damascus, with the help of English consular agent Moshe Finzi, subsequently restricted his efforts to British nationals. He reportedly succeeded in collecting the large sum of 300,000 piastres for 7 Jews of

British nationality, an achievement reflecting the strong British influence on Mehemet Ali. When the Russian consul in Egypt protested against reparation payments being made only to British nationals the Egyptians conveniently stopped payments to all Jews.

Damages of more than 6.1 million piastres were claimed by 745 "foreign" Jewish families living in Safed. Based on these claims, each family was owed nearly 8,200 piastres, an astronomical sum compared to the annual subsistence level of a few hundred piastres. The most convincing estimate of losses sustained by the Jewish community of Safed is 1.6 million piastres or $80,000.[38] By October 1837 Jews had collected compensation totaling 864,500 piastres. Based upon these large compensation claims and payments, it is clear that Safed Jews had many valuable possessions worth stealing and were not as impoverished as they claimed in their letters to the Diaspora.

Sporadic, infrequent compensation payments to the Jews helped unleash a plethora of suspicions and a spate of complaints charging Jewish officials with withholding and even embezzling some of the compensation money they had received. Austrian nationals disputed the decisions of their representative, Gershon Margolit. Others wrote: "Is that justice and honesty? Who ordered them to distribute the money as they did?" In 1839 the few Perushim remaining in Safed claimed that they had not received even "one piastre" of compensation money long since remitted to R. Israel.

Sizable compensation payments to individuals did little to reduce the escalating debt of the Jewish community. As a result of the 1834 rebellion and fundraising disruptions in Poland and Russia, the debt of the Perushim kollel in Safed more than doubled in one year, soaring from 121,000 piastres in 1833 to 260,000 piastres in 1834. Two months after the revolt the Sephardim claimed the "huge and most terrible" debt of 550,000 piastres, as compared to their 400,000-piastre debt in the 1820s. Lacking comparable figures for the Hasidim we may safely assume that their debts also increased significantly due to the fearful destruction wrought by the fellahin.[39]

Compared to the Safed community Tiberias Jews suffered only minor inconveniences.[40] The fellahin rebels locked them in the Jewish quarter and demanded a huge ransom for their release. The 1,200 Jews—300 families—could not leave town or even visit the elegant bath-house built by Ibrahim Pasha one mile south of the town walls. After hearing about the atrocities committed against Safed's Jews, the Tiberias Jews bribed the fellahin with the large sum of 50,000 piastres. When the Perushim wrote to impress PEKAM with their poverty and the need for larger contributions, they magnified the Tiberias bribe to 100,000 piastres. The Tiberias community remained in a constant state of anxiety until the Druze army drove the fellahin out of the Galilee, restored order, and forced the rioters to return the ransom money to the Jews.

By the end of August 1834 Ibrahim Pasha had crushed the rebels and reconquered the towns of Jerusalem, Hebron, Nablus, Safed, and Tiberias. He had lifted the sieges on Acre and Jaffa and controlled the countryside in the Galilee, the central mountain area, and the coastal plain. After vanquishing most of the rebel forces in Palestine, he sought revenge against Bethlethem and Hebron, whose soldiers had defeated him at the Pools of Solomon. The Egyptians razed Bethlehem's Muslim quarter and Ibrahim bombarded, stormed, and captured Hebron. During a ferocious onslaught of three hours Ibrahim Pasha allowed his troops to slaughter Muslims, plunder the population, and defile the women. When Muslims sought safety in the Jewish quarter of Hebron, the soldiers pursued them, indiscriminately killing and looting all in their path.[41]

Despite Ibrahim's promise to protect the Jews, the Jewish ghetto was "pillaged and sacked until nothing was left...we were left naked..." Synagogues were looted, Torah scrolls were torn and scattered about, and silver ornaments were carried off. Houses of Jews "were ransacked and plundered; their gold and silver, and all things valuable, carried away; and their wives and daughters violated before their eyes by brutal soldiers." The 400 Jews of Hebron were beaten and tortured; seven men were killed and "five girls, who were minors, died under the bestial licentiousness of the Egyptian soldiers." Unlike the situations in Safed and Tiberias, no stolen property was returned to the Jews of Hebron and they received no reparations for their losses. They continued to suffer a more bitter and harsh life than that of Jews in the other holy cities.[42]

The tragedy that befell the Jews of Hebron in 1834 further united the Sephardim and the Habad Hasidim and resulted in their jointly sending a shaliah to collect money in Italy and Western Europe.[43] Hebron Jews believed that their hardships were so great that they should be given this privilege, but Lehren remained unconvinced and prohibited the Hebron shaliah from collecting money in PEKAM territory.

In response to the desperate pleas of Jews in the holy cities,[44] PEKAM distributed in Western Europe the poignant letters of Hebron and Safed Jews, with a circular urging an increase in donations. European Jews responded generously, sending large sums of money to Eretz Israel. Lehren, however, refused to establish a fundraising campaign specifically for the Safed Jews, as requested by the Perushim leaders.

Despite the terrible suffering of the Jews as a result of the 1834 rebellion, from 1830 through 1836 the lives of the Jews in the four holy towns were transformed by an unprecedented population explosion that has gone unrecorded. The constant trickle of immigration from 1800 to 1829 swelled to a rising tide over a seven-year period before precipitously dropping in 1837 (see table 10). In 1830 nearly 7,500 Jews lived in the Holy Land and their numbers jumped to about 9,700 just before the terrible earthquake on New Year's Day in 1837. During this seven-year period the number of Jews burgeoned by 2,200 (29 percent) while during the previous thirty years the number of Jews had increased by only 2,700.

The doubling of the Jewish population during the first 37 years of the nineteenth century—from 4,650–4,800 in 1800 to about 9,700 in 1837—must be viewed against the background of the enormous increase in the world and Jewish populations that began around 1800. While the European population escalated from 175 million in 1800 to 255 million in 1850—46 percent in fifty years—the world Jewish population nearly doubled, growing from 2.5 million in 1800 to 4,750,000 in 1850.

Before proceeding, a strong note of caution must be sounded. Crude population estimates with generous margins of error cannot be leaned on too heavily. Nevertheless, the figures have been checked and verified to build a logical structure based on valid population patterns that display an accurate general profile and significant statistical contours.

From 1830 to 1837 Jerusalem and Tiberias each grew by about 200 Jews while the Hebron Jewish population remained unchanged. But the Safed population of 2,200 Jews in 1830 leaped by 80 percent to 4,000 persons just before the start of 1837. Ashkenazim and Sephardim, unable to replenish their ranks either from the villages or by internal growth, maintained and increased their numbers with immigrants from the Diaspora.

At the end of 1829 it was reported from "the south of Europe . . . that great numbers [of Jews] have actually embarked."[45] R. Israel wrote from Safed in 1832 that many Jews had come from Russia "and very soon the number in their kollelim will double . . ."[46] So great was the immigration that in 1834 a Jewish leader in Jerusalem noted that "the country is like cities of refuge"; and in 1835 a new immigrant observed Jews "flowing into the four holy cities." The English mission society (LJS) recorded in 1835 as "a fact well ascertained, that the Jews are now flocking to the land of their fathers . . . a fresh influx is constantly taking place."[47]

When Lehren heard about the increased immigration at the end of 1832, he saw it as another sign of the imminent advent of Messianic Redemption. Yet his intractable opposition to Jews coming to Eretz Israel continued un-

TABLE 10 Jewish Population of Palestine in 1800, 1830, and 1837

	1800	1830	JUST BEFORE 1837 EARTHQUAKE
Acre	300	250	250
Haifa	50	100	150
Jaffa	—	100	100
Nablus	50–100	100	100
Hebron	300	400	450
Jerusalem	2250	3000	3200
Tiberias	800–900	1000	1200–1300
Safed	600	2200	4000
Galilee villages	300	300	300
TOTAL	4650–4800	7450	9750–9850

abated. So extreme was Lehren's determination to block the flow of Jews into Eretz Israel that he offered a German scholar financial and other inducements to migrate to the United States rather than settle in the Holy Land.[48] To limit the number of immigrants Lehren counseled the Vilna Rabbis not to permit the migration of Perushim to Eretz Israel without official authorization.

Lehren's advice fell on receptive ears. In 1832 the Vilna Rabbis warned Perushim not to depend on haluka as their sole source of support,[49] but to mobilize independent economic resources. They only encouraged elderly immigrants who were "free of all worldly desires." "Masses" were warned not to immigrate and risk ruining what existed in Eretz Israel.

Why was there such an upsurge of Jewish immigration between 1830 and 1836, despite staunch opposition by Zvi Hirsch Lehren and the Vilna Rabbis, and the high mortality rate due to poor health conditions and frequent plagues?[50] A plague that swept the Galilee in the spring of 1832 killed 100 Tiberias Jews. After being away from Safed for four years and four months, John Nicolayson observed that "a great many [Jews] have died during my absence, and been succeeded by others." Death was a normal occurrence and a "constant presence" in the lives of the Jews. Every ten years nearly half of the Jewish population died off. Safed was able to absorb this large inflow of 1,800 new residents in seven years despite the havoc wreaked by the 1834 fellahin rebellion and the snow and rain in the winter of 1832–1833 that collapsed 100 Jewish homes.[51] Unlike Jerusalem, Safed was not restricted by town walls or constricted into a small Jewish quarter. The nearly 1 million piastres of reparations collected for damages and losses undoubtedly helped put Safed Jews back on their economic feet. We may surmise, too, that the established economic infrastructure, empty areas, and vacant houses made it less costly to settle Jews in Safed than in Jerusalem.

Hasidim, Sephardim, and Perushim immigrants all preferred settling in Safed.[52] Most Hasidim in the 1820s chose Safed, not Tiberias, as their settlement center, but during the 1830s Hasidim were attracted to Safed by the presence of their leader, R. Abraham Dov, who reached Eretz Israel from Poland in 1832. Perushim also concentrated their new settlers in Safed, a policy encouraged and monitored by R. Israel of Shklov, who was jealously intent on establishing Safed as the capital of his group. Sephardim preferred settling in Safed in order to enjoy the healthier climate and the more tolerant Muslim attitude toward the Jews prevalent in the Galilee.

Undoubtedly, the tolerance practiced by the Egyptian occupation of Palestine also contributed to the large immigration of Jews to the Holy Land. In 1833 an astonished Jew exclaimed that "the Lord is operating wonders toward our restoration. We are in our land completely set at liberty, and are there considered as such with all the other subjects."[53] Although the glad tidings about such improved conditions were quickly communicated to Diaspora Jews, it would take decisive Jews one to two years from the time they received the good news until they could wind up their personal affairs and journey to Palestine. Since travel was a slow, difficult process, at the very earliest, Jews could arrive in Eretz Israel at the end of 1834. Yet we know that many immigrants arrived much before then.

By the middle of the 1830s steamships started sailing the Mediterranean and the ever-present danger of robbery and kidnapping on the high seas was eliminated when the sailboats of the pirates could not catch the faster steamships. Traveling to Eretz Israel was now considered safe enough that rabbis ruled that a husband could force his wife to accompany him to Eretz Israel or she could suffer the consequences of divorce. However, only the affluent could afford to pay the higher costs of steam travel, so this new means of transportation first introduced on the Mediterranean in 1833–1835 had little effect on the migration of Jews to Eretz Israel up to 1837.

It was the ubiquitous, all-pervading love of Zion that motivated Jews to uproot themselves and move to Eretz Israel. This religious aspiration emanated from varied national backgrounds, reflected diverse religious experiences, and expressed a wide variety of prosaic personal situations. Different kinds of Jews came to Eretz Israel from diverse countries under varying circumstances in order to fulfill different needs. Despite such great diversity we can identify basic types of "love of Zion" immigrants. Scholars came to Eretz Israel to receive their rightful reward for studying Torah. Sephardi Jews settled in Eretz Israel to engage in commercial pursuits or earn their living by working as artisans or religious functionaries. Large numbers of widows came to receive a small share of the haluka they were denied in the Diaspora.[54] Some immigrants left their native lands because they could not earn a living wage,[55] had failed in business, or were fleeing from creditors. Other lovers of Zion settled in Eretz Israel to expiate their sins or to fulfill a vow.

A few untrammeled immigrants had run-ins with Diaspora Jewish community leaders or were misfits searching for their proper place. There were malcontents escaping a misfortune or moral delinquents abandoning difficult circumstances at home. Some were footloose adventurers seeking new experiences in a new world. Is it sacrilegious to suggest that renegades and rebels with tainted, embarrassing histories were frequent immigrants, while God-fearing, meritorious Jews usually stayed put?

Since both love of Zion and personal motivations were long prevalent before 1830–1836, we must search elsewhere to discover why there was such a huge population growth during this period. Numerous Jews moved to Eretz Israel consumed by the belief and obsessed by the hope that during the Jewish year 5600 (September 1839–September 1840) they would be blessed by the advent of the Messiah and sanctified by the Redemption of all Israel. Traditionally Jews sought to participate in the Redemption process by going to Eretz Israel to passively "hold themselves in readiness to receive" the Messiah.[56] During the 1830s numerous Jews were transfixed by the expectation that in 1840 the Messiah would end their "suffering and degradation."[57]

Jewish sources are mute about such an awakening of fearful expectations for "great things,"[58] because it was sacrilegious to calculate the date of the Messiah's arrival and dangerous to reveal to Ottoman and Russian authorities such subversive ideas that could provoke government reprisals. However, a number of English missionaries over a period of years clearly and richly documented the Jewish belief in the imminent coming of the Messiah in 1840.[59]

No doubt some Jews settled in Eretz Israel in the belief that the Messiah would appear in the year 5600; but the number of such immigrants is far from clear. If Jews had acted upon the conviction that the advent of the Messiah was imminent they should have flooded Eretz Israel just before

1840, for "the disposition of Jews in Europe to return to this land of their fathers, seems to grow stronger as the period fixed for the appearance of their great Deliverer is approaching."[60] In fact, however, few Jews entered Palestine from 1837 to 1840, when there was "little or no increase" in the Jewish population.[61] During these days of plagues the number of Jews did not increase and may even have dwindled. Scottish ministers reported a "diminution in the number of Jews returning to their own land" in 1837 and 1838 because of the "ravages of the plague," "the rise in the price of provisions," and the "embarrassed finances" of the Jewish community and its huge debt of 800,000 piastres. English missionary A. Pieretz believed that in 1838 there actually was a decrease in the Jerusalem Jewish population "for the plague carried away more than those born during the year," while Jewish immigrants dropped to "not more than twenty." Likewise, the American explorer Edward Robinson wrote that the number of Jews in Jerusalem was "much diminished" in 1837.[62]

The major reason for the wave of Jewish immigration from 1830 to 1837 was the harsh persecutions and discriminatory practices suffered by the Jews in the Balkans, Algiers, and North Africa, Russia-Poland, and the Rumanian principalities. Upheavals in these countries triggered political, economic, and physical abuses of the Jews and provided the strongest catalyst for the love-of-Zion ideology to move some Jews from their native lands to Eretz Israel, although the vast majority of Jews immigrated to Western Europe and the United States.

During the 1828–1829 Turkish-Russian War and the Greek battle for independence from Turkey, the Balkans—Greece, Bulgaria, Macedonia, and Serbia—were in a turmoil. Yet Jews, characteristically loyal to their native country, were unable to march in battle under the cross of the Greek Catholics. So before and after the Treaty of Adrianople was signed in September 1829, marking the end of yet another war between the sultan and the czar, numerous Sephardi Jews left the Balkans for Eretz Israel.[63]

In 1830 a French expeditionary force conquered Algeria and granted Algerians many rights enjoyed by French settlers. But the invasion upset the commercial activities of the Jewish population and set off a wave of persecutions against Jews. As a result, between 1832 and 1836, hundreds of Algerian Jews moved to Safed and the coastal towns of Syria.[64]

While Sephardi Jews from North Africa and the Balkans were streaming into Eretz Israel by the hundreds, East European Jews were migrating to the Holy Land due to the repressive policies and anti-Jewish practices of Czar Nicholas I (1825–1855). Political changes newly instituted in Russia endangered the Jews' legal status and sharply restricted their ability to make a living. Starting in 1825 Jews were expelled from Russian towns along the western border, and in 1830 they were chased out of villages in areas such as Kiev.[65] Most pernicious of all Russian actions was the 1827 ukase conscripting Jewish recruits as young as 12 into the Russian army for 25 years.[66] Rather than risk the loss of a young son, numerous Jewish families moved to Eretz Israel or sent their sons there.

The fate of Polish Jews was no less difficult than that of Russian Jews. When the Poles revolted against the Russians in 1830 and 1831, Polish Jews patriotically sided with the Poles. After Russia cruelly suppressed the Polish revolts, the Jews were persecuted and lost their role as commercial intermediaries between the nobles and the farmers. Many Polish Jews in Lithuania and Volhynia, as well as Jews in southern Russia and Austria, were uprooted and fled; most went in the direction of Central Europe, and some migrated to Eretz Israel. In 1832 Russia imposed on the Rumanian principalities of Wallachia and Moldavia economic measures that discriminated against the Jews, again pushing Jews westward toward the United States, with a few coming to Eretz Israel.

Thus, although the Egyptian occupation of Palestine provided a conducive atmosphere for Jews to live in the four holy cities, and the expectation that the Messiah would appear in 1840 must have motivated some Jews to settle in Eretz Israel, the principal reason for the wave of immigration from 1830 to 1837 was the intolerable situation of Jews in Eastern Europe, the Balkans, and North Africa. Jews felt an urgent need to leave behind an unbearable financial and physical situation and then, out of love for Zion, they moved to Eretz Israel. More bluntly stated, Jews were pushed out of their native lands and came to Eretz Israel because of their love of Zion, sheer necessity, and lack of a more viable alternative.

Jewish Immigrants and Their Initiatives in the 1830s

❖

During 1830–1836 a number of strictly observant young Jews from Poland, Russia, North Africa, the Balkans, and Germany came with their wives and children to live, study, and pray in the Holy Land. These immigrants did not discard their Orthodox beliefs or relinquish their traditional life-style; by living in the Holy Land, they infused a buoyant sense of religious enthusiasm into their lives.

From these new settlers, and from children of the founding Perushim fathers, were to come attempts to introduce changes into the Jewish community. Speaking in its own voice, this youthful generation sought a constructive outlet for its energies without breaching the religious proscriptions imposed by the Jewish community in the Holy Land. They searched for ways to earn a livelihood instead of depending solely on the haluka. Among this new generation were Moshe Sachs, Israel Bak, Shmaryahu Luria, Joseph Schwartz, Menahem Mendel from Kamenets, David Yellin, and Eliezer Bergmann. These enterprising seven have been chosen for closer scrutiny because they reflect the changing spirit of their time. Youth, determination, affluence, resilience, and dynamism set them apart as exceptional members of the Jewish community.

MOSHE SACHS

Moshe Sachs (1800–1870) came to Eretz Israel from Saxony in 1830. He gained the distinction of being called the first immigrant from Germany, because at the 1815 Congress of Vienna Prussia had severed Saxony from Poland and annexed it. Like most Polish-German Jews, Sachs conversed in Yiddish, spoke a corrupt German jargon, not "the true, pure German language,"[1] and wrote in a German that was "full of grammatical and stylistic mistakes."[2] The Jewish Enlightenment (Haskala) and the religious Reform and political revolutionary movements agitating German Jewry left him untainted,[3] notwithstanding the opinion of John Nicolayson that Sachs "had something of a liberal education."[4] In fact, Moshe Sachs received the traditional Torah education in a succession of yeshivot, never staying more than a year or two in one academy.

At a time when thousands of German Jews and Christians were migrating to the United States, Sachs's love of Zion led him to settle in Jerusalem at the age of 30. The fact that he received a haluka allocation did not prevent him from claiming that he was a Jerusalem "merchant."[5] As a young eligible bachelor, Sachs solved his financial problems by marrying Rachel, the only daughter of Zadok Halevi (Kroyz), called the "Jerusalem Rothschild," who had been in North Africa since 1829 collecting money for the Perushim.

A man of restless energy, Sachs criticized the stultifying atmosphere of the haluka system, claiming that it thwarted any possibility of transforming Jerusalem into a productive society. When expounding such opinions Sachs's speedy speech enlisted his whole body to animate the line of his argument; he had a vast lexicon of gestures. No less distracting to the listener were his "very abrupt manners,"[6] "haggard" look, and conflicted countenance, topped by an overabundant and disheveled crop of hair. His "unsettled expression" underlined an anxiety and a tension that were expressed by states of exploding rage and brooding depression.

Sachs argued frequently with the English missionaries and "attempted to represent the moral precepts of the Gospel as inferior to those of the Old Testament." Although he dared not visit the missionaries at their Greek convent residence in the Christian quarter, he willingly accepted the Hebrew versions of the Old and New Testaments prepared by the London Jews Society. A leader of the Perushim community chastised Sachs and threatened to excommunicate him and deprive him of his haluka income if he did not stop seeing the missionaries. For this reason Sachs told Nicolayson "not to come to his house anymore." Yet the very next day Sachs invited

Nicolayson to his home on the first day of Passover! He also asked the missionary to forward a letter to Europe "because it would otherwise be intercepted by the rabbies [sic]."[7]

Despite all his contacts with the English missionaries, Sachs never was a candidate for conversion, as alleged by Lehren. Nicolayson complained that he could not gain his "attention to the great subject" of conversion and that Sachs "seems to look on the subject with a kind of despair." After a long "conversation (without dispute)," Nicolayson concluded (in 1840) that Sachs's "mind is still very confused—but his heart is full of unutterable desires and longings after some thing of which he feels the need but cannot yet perceive..."[8]

Anxiously searching for a purpose into which to pour his talents and looking for a mode of self-expression, Sachs started to develop an idea which he continued to promote throughout his forty years in Eretz Israel. This was a vague plan to establish agricultural settlements for those "not talented to continue their studies of the Torah."[9] These farm settlements would be financed by overseas contributors and local haluka funds. Sachs argued that his agricultural proposal would transform the haluka-oriented Jewish community into a society earning its own way. He suggested that a local person be placed at the head of the agricultural colonization project, no doubt seeing himself as the prime candidate for that position.

Sachs's agricultural plan may have been his original idea, or he may have borrowed it from the father of the Russian Haskala movement, Isaac Baer Levinsohn, who published a book in 1828 championing the dignity of manual labor and the importance of working the soil. It is also possible that Sachs thought up his plan after coming in contact with Hungarian Jews, the only group of Jewish farmers in Central Europe. Sachs does not cite Hungarian agricultural experiences, nor does he mention the Jewish farmers in Eretz Israel, then tilling the soil in the small northern villages of Peki'in, Kfar Yasif, and Shfar-Am.

Even more surprising is his comment, written thirty years later, that in 1839 "I did not find in Jerusalem even one person working as a farmer,"[10] leaving us to wonder who he intended to settle on the land. Another puzzling factor is his disregard of the security situation in Palestine, much improved by Ibrahim Pasha's armies but still far from guaranteeing peace to an isolated, exposed Jewish agricultural colony.

To further confuse matters, Sachs told Dr. Ludwig A. Frankl, an Austrian Jew visiting Jerusalem in 1856:

And why should the Jew till the ground in the sweat of his brow, when the Bedouin comes with violence, at the time of harvest, and carries off with impunity, on his camels, what he has not sowed, from the place where he has not ploughed.[11]

Sachs also disregarded the opposition of Jerusalem leaders who fought any attempt to siphon off the smallest sums from the chronically short kehilla funds, although he treaded softly in his criticism out of fear of being cut off from the haluka rolls. Realizing that he could not convince the Jerusalem leadership to support his project, he traveled in 1835 to Europe, to promote his idea with foreign governments and Jewish leaders there.

While following Sachs, a man who knew a lot and believed in very little, we might heed the advice Sachs gave Frankl: "Listen to all, but believe no one; not even me."

ISRAEL BAK

Israel Bak (1797–1874) came to Eretz Israel in 1831 after having achieved the level of a master printer dedicated to publishing religious books in Berdichev, one of the Hasidic strongholds in the Ukraine.[12] The name "Bak" in Hebrew is an acronym for the words *ben kedoshin,* meaning son of a martyred ancestor. At the age of 34, married and the father of three daughters and one son, Israel Bak settled in Safed.

I came to Safed toward the end of 1831, for it was there I had elected to dwell. Soon after, Ibrahim Pasha of Egypt swept through our land like a torrential river and conquered it. . . . My heart yearned and longed for the courtyards and villages of the Lord, to join the vineyard which is the inheritance of God, our Lord, to adorn myself in the holy soil and land. And God granted my heartfelt wish to leave my native land and my father's home and family, and he allowed me the right to ascend to the holy mountain . . . to establish a new sanctuary . . . to print the books of scholars and their holy knowledge . . . [13]

Bak may have left Russia out of fear that his only son, Nissan, born in 1815, would be forcibly recruited into the Russian army. Another reason contributing to his decision to settle in Eretz Israel may have been the intimidating atmosphere created by the cast-iron censorship imposed by Czar Nicholas I in 1826 on the printing of books.

After a six-month journey to Eretz Israel Bak and his family arrived in Safed with a good sum of cash and the mechanical parts for printing presses. Bak bought a courtyard to house his family and assembled two presses, a bindery, and other printing equipment needed to cast Hebrew letters. As a "work of devotion,"[14] he founded the first Hebrew printing press operated in Palestine since 1587. His printing press preceded by one year the first press established by the Armenian Church in Jerusalem in 1833.

Bak planned to publish prayer books, Bibles, and Psalters, and sell them in large numbers to Diaspora Jews. In 1833 his shop printed its first volume, a Sephardi prayer book, on two presses operated by about thirty workers, most of whom were scholars working as part-time apprentices.[15]

Bak was described by Nicolayson as

> an intelligent, very ingenious, and interesting man. . . . of considerable property. [He] professes to have no other object than to multiply copies of their most valuable ancient works at such prices as shall make them accessible to all pious Jews; and he added "just as your societies do with the Bible."[16]

To obtain paper and printing materials, Bak, the Hasid, signed a contract with Shlomo Zalman Zoref of the Perushim community, indicating that amicable daily contacts and business relationships prevailed between the two groups. Zoref imported the requested materials; in order to pay for them Bak was forced to take a loan backed by his promissory note. When he couldn't pay the note he was forced to sell "all his houses, property and courtyard with all the rights belonging to him."[17] Despite these difficulties Bak succeeded by mid-1834 in printing four books.

Bak's business troubles were minor compared to the tragedy visited upon him by the 1834 fellahin revolt. His printing presses were damaged and his left leg was permanently crippled. Then his wife died, leaving him with four children.

Ever resourceful, never bashful, Bak traveled to see Ibrahim Pasha and demanded full reparations for his broken printing presses. Bak wrote in 1872 through the haze of years that intensify feelings and cloud facts: "I then went to the Pasha in Acre. . . and pleaded with him. . . . He had compassion on me and gave me a small village called Jermak as my possession."[18] The Jermak village is on Mt. Meron, six miles west of Safed.

It has been suggested that the Druze villagers of Jermak asked that Bak be granted their village because they believed him to be Ibrahim's friend; as such he could secure the protection of the Egyptians against the attacks of the neighboring villagers from Peki'in. This story gains some credence from the statement of a missionary that the Jewish residents of Jermak were "men of wealth and consequence who are Europeans and who can afford some protection to the Natives whom they get to labor at very low wages."[19] It is more likely that Ibrahim Pasha, in accordance with the Egyptian policy of settling farm lands, gave Bak the Jermak village to help populate the countryside with a friendly ally who could employ European techniques to develop village agriculture and might influence European countries. There is also a possibility that Ibrahim's grant of the Jermak village merely provided post-facto legal status to lands already given Bak by the local peasants.

Whatever the true situation, Israel Bak settled his son in the village, thereby selecting him as the first European Jew to settle on the soil of the Holy Land. As the landowner, Nissan did not till the soil himself, but employed the village peasants.

Israel Bak returned to Safed, repaired his shattered print-shop, and raised capital by entering into partnership with wealthy Jews from Aleppo and Damascus. In February 1836 Bak completed printing a book written by R. Israel of Shklov. This printing job was such a labor of love that the Hasid from Berdichev printed the book by the leader of the Perushim at his own expense.

After the 1837 earthquake Israel Bak again settled in Jermak. As an old man, he wrote (in 1870) with nostalgia about his life in the village:

Then I was forced to go to the village given to me by the pasha. I built myself houses, I made myself gardens, I planted seeds in the fields and that same year I ate plentifully from fruits of the earth. The next year I had cattle and sheep, lambs, goats, horses and donkeys . . . although the land has many rocks I was prosperous and God helped me. If not for many reasons and varied troubles that afflicted me in 1840 as a result of the terrible war between the sultan and the pasha of Egypt, due to which I was forced to leave that lovely village and come to Jerusalem, I would still be happy [on the Jermak].[20]

SHMARYAHU LURIA

Shmaryahu Luria settled in Jerusalem in 1832 after amassing great wealth in White Russia as a supplier to the Russian army.[21] He undoubtedly was influenced to live in Jerusalem by his father-in-law, Hillel Rivlin, who migrated to Safed in 1809 and then was one of the first Perushim to settle in Jerusalem. Luria arrived in Eretz Israel with a family entourage of 30 to 40 persons and with large sums of money entrusted to him by the Vilna Rabbis to pay off part of the Perushim kollel's debt. In Haifa the Luria family was met by R. Israel of Shklov, who accompanied them to Jerusalem, where Luria rented houses for members of his family and contributed to charitable causes. Luria planned to use his large capital and sharp business acumen in commerce, turn a profit, and help develop the Holy Land.

Few details are known about Luria's personal and business activities in

Eretz Israel. He was friendly with Moshe Sachs and Joseph Schwartz, and together they visited the English missionary John Nicolayson at least once. After two years of business activities during a period of uncertainty and instability in Palestine, Luria lost a large sum of money and saw no prospects for improvement. He had fulfilled the Jewish maxim: "How to make a small fortune in Eretz Israel . . . Come with a large fortune." With deep regret Luria decided that he had no future in Eretz Israel and left Palestine at the end of the summer of 1834.

Luria's leaving Eretz Israel is deemed a near sacrilege in the annals of Jewish settlement in the Holy Land. His daughter explained much later that her father left Palestine to protect his property from the Russian government, which was suspicious of his contact with Ibrahim Pasha, as well as to encourage rich Russian Jews to invest in the building of Eretz Israel. According to his daughter, when the Turks replaced the Egyptian rulers in 1841, Luria, a Russian subject, was unable to return. It is also related that Luria was responsible for obtaining the firman from Ibrahim Pasha to "redeem" the Hurva synagogue. In this way not only does the Rivlin family get credit for a sterling achievement but it takes the credit away from a competing founding father, Shlomo Zalman Zoref, who rightfully achieved this success.[22]

JOSEPH SCHWARTZ

Joseph Schwartz (1804–1865) arrived in Jerusalem in April 1833.[23] Born in a small Bavarian town of a well-to-do Orthodox family, Schwartz received a traditional religious education. He also graduated from a teacher's seminary and from 1821 to 1826 studied philosophy, languages, and geography at the University in Würzburg while pursuing Torah studies at night. As a university student Schwartz must have been influenced by the tumultuous aftermath of the 1819 "hep-hep" assaults on the Jews that spread throughout Bavaria.

After graduating from the university Schwartz studied Jewish history and the geography of Palestine in preparation for a scholarly life of research in Eretz Israel. He published a map, "Boundary of Palestine according to Numbers XXXIV, 1–15," in Hebrew and German, intended as a visual history of biblical learning. The map has some value as a guide to biblical sites, but was not intended for use by travelers.

In the first half of 1831 Schwartz left Bavaria; eighteen months later he arrived at Jaffa, on the eve of Passover. Schwartz settled in Jerusalem, where he first stayed with Moshe Sachs. In his home Schwartz met Shmaryahu Luria, who arranged for the 28-year-old scholar to marry his

Scholar Joseph Schwartz settled in Jerusalem in 1833 and dedicated his life to studying the biblical geography of the Holy Land.

recently orphaned niece, Rivka. Sachs also introduced Schwartz to the English missionary John Nicolayson, with whom he met a good number of times.

After initial resistance to Joseph's settling in Eretz Israel the Schwartz family in Germany financially supported him. Without having to worry about earning a living, Schwartz embarked on research that would identify Palestinian geographical sites with Jewish history. "And from the day that I was privileged to settle in the Holy Land," Schwartz wrote, "I set my heart and eyes on all matters of Eretz Israel; on its status, its quality, substance, and quantity of life, and the position and history of its settlers."[24] Schwartz was the first Jew systematically to conduct personal observations as well as engage in fieldwork on the history and geography of Eretz Israel.

> I shall write what my eyes have seen. And I went up the mountains and down into the valleys and I searched and investigated with great effort and toil. And there are things that I investigated and checked many times from reliable travellers in order to find the facts and the essence of the truth . . . and don't say that my writings do not conform to the true reality because I promise you that more than 4,000 times I worked and toiled to observe the first sunrise as I went up on my roof and fought off sleep to investigate and learn the true reality. . . . and all aspects were checked innumerable times.[25]

In order to travel freely around Palestine and conduct field observations, Schwartz exchanged his European garb for the local costume worn by the Sephardi Jews. He traveled extensively, studying plants and animals, rocks, and natural resources of Eretz Israel, and making a special effort to identify sites mentioned in the Bible. On one occasion he studied "Scriptural geography" with Nicolayson,[26] and they had an in-depth talk about the site of Gilgal (Deut 11:30). Nicolayson's suggestion that Gilgal possibly should have been transcribed as Gilead was rejected out of hand by Schwartz, who had absolute belief in "the integrity of the text."

Schwartz displayed mystical sensitivities about the Ten Tribes of Israel lost in Yemen, Ethiopia, Tibet, or China. If this mystery could be solved, Schwartz believed—like R. Israel of Shklov and others—that it would signal the beginning of the Redemption of the Jewish people.

He distinguished himself as a Jewish artist by drawing a lithograph depicting the various holy places in Jerusalem, which shaped the image of Jerusalem in the eyes of Western observers.

Joseph Schwartz developed a close friendship with many Sephardim.

Their easygoing attitude was compatible with his own reserved, low-key personality. In the Sephardi Beth El yeshiva, Schwartz studied the secrets of the Kabbala with Sephardi scholars. One room in his spacious home was used as a study-room and synagogue, the Congregation of Joseph, where most of the congregants were Sephardim and the prayers were conducted according to the Sephardi liturgy.

Schwartz refrained from participating in public activities and refused to accept official positions in the Jewish community. In this way he conserved all his time and energy for research and avoided the interminable arguments that were an integral part of the Jerusalem kehilla. Later Schwartz would bitterly discover that his determined efforts at neutrality and noninvolvement would be interpreted as opposition to specific groups, plans, and people—not that Schwartz lacked definite opinions, which were usually on the conservative side. He was concerned, but he preferred to say little. While recognizing the negative aspects of haluka, he emphasized the importance of the haluka system. The agricultural settlement idea of his friend Moshe Sachs he regarded as a delusion and a fantasy that could only harm Jews in Eretz Israel.

MENAHEM MENDEL OF KAMENETS

Menahem Mendel (1800?–1873), born in Kamenets, Lithuania, settled in Safed in 1833. Brought up in a well-to-do scholarly household, Menahem Mendel followed the prevailing Jewish custom of studying at yeshivot and marrying at an early age. When he was felled by the cholera epidemic that spread through Europe in 1832, he vowed: "When God will save me from this death, I will go and pray on the graves of our holy ancestors and relish the pure air [of Eretz Israel] and establish myself there on Torah and work. . . ."[27] Upon recovering from his illness Menahem Mendel took his family and "packet of money" and left Kamenets.

His journey to Eretz Israel took two months—one month overland from Kamenets to Odessa, and another month from Odessa to Haifa. The stormy trip on the Black Sea was difficult: "the world is spinning like a drunkard and everybody is throwing up . . . and in the morning we hardly prayed because of our great weakness." Finally Menahem Mendel and a group of 80 Ashkenazim arrived in Haifa, in August 1833.

Menahem Mendel wanted to settle in Jerusalem, but "important and influential" Perushim in his party preferred to settle in Safed or Tiberias. He followed them because "I did not wish to leave them," emphasizing the importance of group solidarity in providing spiritual comfort and material sustenance to immigrants during the process of adjusting to a new land.

Menahem Mendel settled in Safed, where he proceeded to earn a living in a way unknown to us, possibly by lending money to Jews and Muslims. Shortly after he arrived, a cholera plague struck Safed and Jerusalem. In unadorned, unsentimental words Menahem Mendel recorded the death of his son: "I thanked God that He saved both me and my wife, but my son died at that time and was rewarded with a burial in Eretz Israel . . ." Overwhelmed by personal tragedy, Menahem Mendel was nonetheless able to find consolation in the fact that his son was privileged to be buried in the Holy Land.

Ten months after he settled in Safed Menahem Mendel's home was sacked, during the fellahin rebellion of June–July 1834. He vividly described this plunder in his book *Chronicles of the Times*, the first Jewish guidebook to Eretz Israel. In clear prose that reflected the personality of the writer, the *Chronicles* told the reader about Menahem Mendel's voyage to Eretz Israel, his trips to Jerusalem, Hebron, Tiberias, and Nablus, and everyday life in Safed. Although Menahem Mendel had only a rudimentary knowledge of Arabic he prepared a short list of Arabic words and expressions, "the first attempt by an Ashkenazi Jew to inform his brethren abroad who intended to settle in Palestine of the most necessary words in Arabic." Inclusion of an Arabic word list was most unusual, because the vast majority of Ashkenazi Jews in Eretz Israel did not understand or speak the language.

One chapter in the *Chronicles*, called "Merits of the Land," described the characteristics of the country: the variety of fruits, vegetables, meat, and fowl; kinds of eating utensils; types of drinks; the water situation; prices of food; weights, measures, and the value of coins; ways of earning a living; and holiday rituals and the celebration of religious festivities in Eretz Israel. Menahem Mendel also wrote about the customs of the Sephardi men and women, who were most hospitable and occasionally married into Ashkenazi families. The title of this chapter is "The Customs of the Sephardi Jews, called Frenken." The term "Frenk" or "Frank" (from France) was first applied by Arabs and Turks to Christian merchants from Europe. Among the Jews themselves "Frank" originally referred to Ashkenazi Jews, as in 1823, when Shlomo Zalman Shapira wrote that Ashkenazi residents of Jerusalem are called "Frenken." By the 1830s the Sephardim were called "Frenken" by Menahem Mendel and the Ashkenazim. Why this transfer of names occurred and when "Frenken" became a word of derision, expressing contempt, is not known.[28]

As a result of the 1834 fellahin revolt, Menahem Mendel "realized that it was no longer possible for me to earn my living" in Safed, so he asked permission from R. Israel of Shklov to leave Eretz Israel temporarily. During the summer of 1834, after living in Safed for one year, Menahem Mendel left Eretz Israel on the same boat with Shmaryahu Luria. In 1840–1841 he returned with his family and settled permanently in Jerusalem.

DAVID YELLIN

David Yellin (1803–1863) settled in Eretz Israel in 1834.[29] Born in Lamza, Poland, Yellin studied in yeshivot, prospered as a merchant, and became a leading member of the Jewish community. After an early marriage and the birth of a daughter, the Yellins had no more children for ten years. Since doctors and old-wives' methods were of no avail, Yellin considered settling in Eretz Israel; perhaps the privilege of living in the Holy Land would allow him to fulfill the commandment "be fruitful and multiply." Then David Yellin fell ill and, like Menahem Mendel of Kamenets, vowed that if he recovered his health he would move to Eretz Israel. When Yellin recuperated he left Lamza with his wife and daughter and traveled six weeks by horse and carriage to Odessa. From Odessa the Yellins embarked on a turbulent 42-day sea journey to Istanbul and Acre.

The Yellin family first settled in Safed, but David was unhappy when he discovered that "most" of the Safed Jews were Hasidim, whose "ways and customs were foreign to his nature." His negative feelings about the Hasidim led him to write that they outnumbered the Perushim, when, in fact, each community was of equal size, numbering around 800–950 persons. Fortunately, Yellin moved his family to Jerusalem just before the outbreak of the fellahin rebellion in Safed and after Ibrahim Pasha subdued the rebels in Jerusalem.

Joshua Yellin, David's only son, born in Eretz Israel, described what his father saw in Jerusalem:

When my late father came to Jerusalem in 1834 he found the city neglected and deserted, its streets in mourning. Most of its houses and courtyards were in ruins, and those that remained whole were small, narrow, low, and dark. Their tiny windows were covered with grills to hide the women from the gaze of passers-by. The shops were in a similar state. Only a few were occupied by vendors of the rough, black pottery made in Gaza and Hebron, or by leather-workers and cobblers. . . . There were but few shopkeepers.[30]

The affluent Yellin family brought from Poland 4,000 rubles (about 68,000 piastres). This easily enabled them to buy or rent a home in the Bab-el-Huta section of the Muslim quarter where "houses and shops could be bought for next to nothing." Despite low purchase prices, most "Jews did not interest themselves in purchasing [houses] . . . as they did not see any possibility of gaining a worthwhile living from them. They were more concerned with obtaining tenancy rights."[31] The Yellins lived in the Muslim quarter for two years. In 1836–1837 they and many Perushim moved out of the Bab-el-Huta neighborhood to the Street of the Jews near the Hurva that was in the process of being rebuilt. Here the Yellins obtained tenured rental rights in a comfortable courtyard of two apartments.

David Yellin searched for business possibilities, but, finding none, he invested his money in the Perushim kollel, receiving interest on the capital. He spent a good part of the day studying Talmud in a room he rented with two other students, while seeking out commercial ventures made possible by the rule of Ibrahim Pasha.

ELIEZER BERGMANN

Eliezer (Lazarus) Bergmann (1799–1852) arrived in Eretz Israel in January 1835.[32] Born in Bavaria, Bergmann received his education in a number of yeshivot where he was recognized as a promising scholar. On the recommendation of the head of his yeshiva, he was hired as a teacher for the children of a wealthy merchant, Mendel Rosenbaum. After several years of tutoring the talented scholar was rewarded in the traditional manner: he was married to one of his students, 17-year-old Rifka Celia Rosenbaum. The young couple lived in the large Rosenbaum household and raised a family of three boys and two girls while Eliezer continued to study Torah and tutor the Rosenbaum children.

Bergmann's love of Zion, instilled in him by his Torah studies as well as by the anti-Jewish atmosphere of Bavaria, convinced him to settle in Eretz Israel. In 1834, at the age of 35, Bergmann visited Amsterdam to secure financial support from PEKAM for his trip and for implementing plans to conduct trading and farming activities in Eretz Israel. To Lehren of PEKAM he expounded his theory that Jews should actively perform good deeds in Eretz Israel in order to accelerate the process of Messianic Redemption. However, Lehren, who consistently discouraged European Jews from settling in Eretz Israel, was not about to finance the wild ideas of the son-in-law of affluent Mendel Rosenbaum. Lehren advised Bergmann that "he who wants to work in commerce should stay in the Diaspora. The immigrant to Eretz Israel should engage in study and prayer . . . a person cannot have it both ways."[33]

Undaunted by Lehren's aggressive refusal, Bergmann drafted a circular asking Jews for loans "to be repaid when possible" so as to fulfill the "great and special commandment to move from the Diaspora to the Holy Land." This was preferable to encouraging Jewish migration "for material purposes to North America and Greece."[34] Soon after, Bergmann abandoned the idea of raising a loan. With the financial assistance of his father-in-law, he made preparations to leave for Eretz Israel with his wife, his widowed mother, and his five children, aged 8, 6, 4, 2 years, and 6 months. Although Mendel Rosenbaum opposed his son-in-law's plans for taking his daughter and grandchildren so far from home to a holy but desolate country, he gave in to Eliezer's enthusiastic pressure and became the economic sponsor of his daughter's family.

At the end of August 1834 the Bergmann family was on its way to Eretz Israel. They traveled through Germany to Venice and then sailed to Trieste, regretting not having traveled by steamship when their sailboat did not budge for 3 days and nights for lack of wind. They spent a stormy 46 days sailing from Trieste to Beirut—25 days were travel time, while the other 21 days were spent in port on "captain's business." Luckily, their boat arrived in Beirut a few days after a quarantine had been lifted; the quarantine isolation period could last as long as 40 days.

In Beirut the Bergmanns met a group of Polish Hasidim bound for Safed, 48 "men, women, children and old folk" from the Rumanian principalities of Moldavia and Wallachia,[35] and 72 Jews who had just arrived from Istanbul. A few days before their arrival, 80 Jews came to Beirut, allowing Bergmann to report happily that "religious people" were streaming into Eretz Israel "from all economic groups and from all ages, babies and old folk 80 years and more..."

Bergmann left his family in lodgings in Sidon,[36] in January 1835, while he toured Safed, Tiberias, Nablus, Jerusalem, and other towns. He was impressed with the peace prevailing in Palestine under Egyptian rule. Safed was definitely not to his liking, due to the lack of appropriate housing in the wake of the destruction wrought by the fellahin only six months before. Although Bergmann does not say so, we sense a certain incompatibility between his Bavarian temperament and the spirit of the Hasidim in Safed.

Tiberias, where "we would have preferred to live," was an expensive town and "in the summer it is hot and hard to live here because the houses and rooms are very small." Nablus was "good and inexpensive." Eliezer was impressed by its commercial possibilities, mentioning its markets for soap, cotton, and olive oil. Surprisingly, he suggested settling Jews outside Eretz Israel in Beirut, Sidon, or Tyre now that Mehemet Ali "has given permission to buy houses any place we wish," an act previously forbidden by the sultan. Ten to fifteen adult men "can settle in a number of places and regions, wherever they prefer. The land is still large and very good."

Unlike Sachs, Bergmann took into account the lack of security for Jews in isolated villages. "It is impossible for one or two or even three families to live alone where there are no Jews in the vicinity, especially when they do not know the local language." Thus he was easily convinced by Joseph Schwartz to live in Jerusalem. In March 1835 he hired a learned member of the Perushim community to bring his family from Sidon to Jerusalem. The quickest and easiest travel route from Sidon to Jaffa was a three-day boat trip instead of a dangerous six-day overland journey. After the ship anchored in Jaffa it was driven onto the rocks by a storm and the Bergmann family lost its money and possessions. "That's the way God wanted it," explained Bergmann's daughter. Ever optimists, the Bergmanns thanked the Lord that their children had been spared. Celia wrote: "I lost all that I had. I console myself (even though I now am very poor) that I live in Jerusalem and that is a great privilege. The city is very pretty."[37]

The Bergmanns adjusted quickly to life in Jerusalem. They were helped by Perushim and by Sephardi friends such as Nahum Coronel, an Amsterdam-born Sephardi Jew who, at the age of 20, came to Safed in 1830. After the 1834 fellahin rebellion he moved his family to Jerusalem, where he, like Schwartz, immersed himself in research and writing.[38]

Eliezer Bergmann borrowed small amounts of money from Schwartz and 3,000–3,500 piastres from the Perushim kollel. He paid a little more than 1,000 piastres for a three-year rental on a courtyard in the Bab-el-Huta section where many Jews had settled since rents were "very high" in the Jewish quarter. Eliezer's business sense told him not to rent but to buy houses as the Perushim kollel and rich Ashkenazim had done now that the government permitted purchase of homes and certain types of land by minority members, or at least by Europeans protected under the capitulation agreements. Buying courtyards was inexpensive and "it is a great mitzva to buy a house in the Holy Land." Before the end of their three-year lease the Bergmann family, like the Yellins and others, moved to the Jewish quarter and rented a large home near the Hurva compound from R. Jonah Moshe Navon, who was appointed the Sephardi chief rabbi of Jerusalem in 1837.

The tolerant attitude displayed toward the Jews in Eretz Israel was most idyllically described by Bergmann: "The Muslim Gentiles are defeated and greatly downtrodden. In comparison the Jews, especially the Ashkenazim, are, thank God, blessed by a higher status . . . possibly it hasn't been this way since the time of our holy rabbis." Celia wrote about Jews receiving favored treatment and the advantages of being a Jew from a European country: "We here are exempt from many bothersome matters, not only in spiritual but in material matters. Because we are foreign citizens we do not have to pay anything to the authorities. Thank God, we can do what we want."[39] After this exaggerated reference to the tax exemptions enjoyed by Europeans, Celia noted that "there are no robberies in all of Syria, like overseas. (We do not fear that they will steal our possessions because we now have no possessions.)" Bergmann sought business outlets for his practical abilities. With funds borrowed from the Perushim kollel he ordered buttons and mirrors, which he planned to sell. He sent a barrel of holy soil from Zion and rose-colored oil to Bavaria. He also considered buying "fields and vineyards," but the required capital was not forthcoming from PEKAM or his father-in-law.[40] Bergmann became active in the public affairs of the Jewish community, especially in the small, growing group of German Jews settling in Eretz Israel—". . . five German families live here, three from Amsterdam and ourselves."

Much of Bergmann's time was spent studying Torah and teaching two adult students. He made a significant observation about the level of study and scholarship in Jerusalem in 1835: ". . . not all who come here are necessarily scholars. Not only are there Sephardim settled here who cannot speak Hebrew, but there are a few Ashkenazim in the same situation." Celia corroborated Eliezer's observation when she wrote, "He who does not wish to sit and study all day can do whatever he wishes." Scottish ministers and an English missionary also observed Jews with "abundant leisure to read and discuss." Clearly, the character of the scholar-dominated Ashkenazi community had been significantly changed by the immigration wave in the 1830s, which brought to Eretz Israel idlers and others not studying Torah and not able to work.[41]

In contrast to Schwartz, Bergmann dressed in the European costume to command respect, for it is a "great honor and an especially important matter to dress in our [German] clothes and with our hat." Yet he was most friendly with the Sephardim and even was a leader of the small Jewish community from Aleppo, praying in the Sephardi synagogue according to the Sephardi liturgy. In Bergmann's opinion the Sephardim of Jerusalem lived on a higher standard than the Ashkenazim, for overseas Sephardim "fill the hands" of their shlihim with lots of money; he noted that the Sephardi community was much more burdened by debts than the Perushim kollel.[42]

Celia Bergmann described everyday life in Jerusalem. Fruit, bread, and other produce were easily available in large quantities. But food was expensive because of the 10,000 troops stationed in Palestine by Ibrahim Pasha. Celia wrote about the delicious watermelon and an exotic vegetable unknown in Bavaria:

> They are used here, as in Italy, as a salad, in soups, and as cooked vegetables. They can be prepared six different ways—and are so tasty. . . . They are very healthy and are prescribed by doctors even for sick people. They are grown here, like potatoes with us [in Bavaria], but they are more expensive."[43]

This was the tomato!

Celia ran her large household with the help of her mother-in-law. She did not employ a domestic, for they were unavailable "because they already marry at the age of 14–15."

Although Eliezer Bergmann encouraged new settlers in Eretz Israel, his self-controlled personality prevented him from rhapsodizing about the beauties and holiness of Jerusalem. In the Bergmanns' letters, the nearby Wailing Wall is mentioned but once by Celia and in two flat, simple sentences: "This is a large, strong wall. Every Friday many Jews pray there." Bergmann's way of persuading Jews to join him was by proffering realistic advice about practical matters, without neglecting to mention the problems that would be encountered in Eretz Israel. He advised prospective settlers how much money to carry on their voyage and in what coinage; at what stage of the trip to pay the travel fare; the best season to visit Eretz Israel; what type of furniture, utensils, and clothing to bring; what food was available and how much it cost. Bergmann suggested bringing an Arabic dictionary and grammar books, but noted that Jews can get along by speaking Hebrew and other languages. His letters also included a long list of occupations and an appraisal of trading opportunities for Europeans.[44]

Bergmann wrote that Jews subsisting only on the kollel haluka allocations "live in terrible distress and poverty," but he refrained from concluding that only people of means should immigrate. He believed that "the God of our Fathers will help" new settlers. "As long as the settlers in Eretz Israel multiply . . . their prosperity will increase."[45] Celia was more practical. She stated that "when there is a little money, that is the important thing," and advised that an immigrant come with two Gs: "Gesundheit and Gelt"—health and money.

> Then you can live as a good Jew should live. You can get anything you want—for money: it is good here, like overseas. . . . He who has five to

six thousand gold guldens [105,000–126,000 piastres] can live here as a Jew should live, and be happy on Shabbat and the holidays.

Celia concluded that

it is no easy thing to live here. Therefore I do not advise a person [to come] who is not strong enough to stand all this: one must suffer greatly. But of course that depends on how one stands the test. And after all has passed, the heart is lighter. It was especially hard for me because of the baby who made things most difficult. May God grant her a long life.

But that was not to be. Baby Sara, 2½ years old, died on November 13, 1836, three weeks after the death of her 6-year-old sister, Leah. And in May 1838 on consecutive days, two Bergmann sons died, leaving only one child alive. All the children were casualties of the epidemics ravaging Jerusalem at the end of the 1830s. During a trip overseas in 1844, Eliezer Bergmann received news that his wife had been murdered while walking in the alleyways near the Church of the Holy Sepulchre. In 1852, while on a fundraising mission, Bergmann died of typhus and was buried in Berlin.[46]

These seven settlers in the Holy Land were eager to give shape to their religious vision and harness their dream in a new framework of hope and salvation. With the exception of Luria, they took root in Eretz Israel by making an intense commitment that required a restructuring of their lives. The vision of Zion and the restless vitality to break loose from their old moorings propelled them into a new world of challenge and accomplishment. In Eretz Israel they mobilized "capacities to see and say, to dream and plan, to design and construct, in new ways."[47]

Our group of seven came to Eretz Israel when they were between the ages of 28 (Schwartz) and 36 (Bergmann)—except for Luria, who was about 40 years old. All of them underwent the hardships of long, formidable overland and sea journeys. They were all married men; Schwartz and Sachs married soon after arriving in the country. Schwartz and Bergmann prevailed over family opposition to their settling in Eretz Israel.

Religious dedication added to the excitement of starting adult life in a new milieu led this restless, intense group to seek new modes of expression and avenues of activity. Although ideologically united in their love of Zion, these young settlers differed from each other in personality and in areas of

activity. Schwartz concentrated his energies on scholarship. Sachs, Bergmann, Bak, Luria, and Yellin tried to lead the Jewish community into new
opportunities and challenging enterprises in agriculture, printing, and commerce. When Sachs, Menahem Mendel of Kamenets, and Bergmann were
temporarily stymied or could not find a suitable outlet, they traveled to Europe and beyond as shlihim, to champion such innovative ideas as agricultural settlements in Eretz Israel. When the talents of Shmaryahu Luria
found no productive outlet in the new environment, he left the Holy Land,
albeit with a heavy heart.

We marvel that so many settlers remained in Eretz Israel despite suffering overwhelming physical and spiritual blows meted out by a hostile population and environment. How did Bergmann and Menahem Mendel of
Kamenets overcome grief after the death of their young children? How did
Menahem Mendel and the disabled Bak survive and prosper after the terrible privations of the 1834 plunder? Only the overriding love of Zion em-
bedded in their observance of the Jewish religion could motivate courageous
youth to adjust to Eretz Israel, where a Jew could live "like a Jew should,"[48]
in the words of Celia Bergmann. Even the vows of Yellin and Menahem
Mendel to move to Eretz Israel if they recovered from their illnesses were
motivated by deep religious feelings. Significantly, the positive factors of
the peace and quiet imposed by Ibrahim Pasha and improved transportation
to Palestine are nowhere mentioned as encouraging any members of our
group of seven to settle in Eretz Israel. In fact, Sachs, Bak, Luria, and
Schwartz had set out as immigrants to Eretz Israel before Ibrahim Pasha
had conquered and pacified the land.

But the sterling qualities of youth, inspired by religious yearnings, were
not enough to return our group of seven Jews to Zion. Economic independence was essential. Every member of this small sample was financially independent and did not have to support himself in Eretz Israel. He came to
Palestine as an affluent person (Luria, Bak, Yellin, and Menahem Mendel),
married money (Bergmann and Sachs), or received financial help from his
family overseas (Schwartz and Bergmann). Without such economic means
their love of Zion could hardly have been sustained. This incontrovertible
fact in no way minimizes the significant achievements of these early settlers. It is no shame to admit that Shmaryahu Luria left Eretz Israel because
he could not find an outlet for his commercial abilities. There is no need to
present Moshe Sachs as the propounder of the first practical plan to settle
Jews on the land rather than a self-interested proposer of a nebulous farming scheme. And it is incorrect to herald Israel Bak and his son Nissan as pioneer Jewish farmers, when they were short-term landholders working the

land with hired peasant help. The legends that have been nurtured about these early settlers may be colorful—but they are unnecessary. The real achievements of this young generation stand on their own merits.

Early in 1835, five years after arriving in Eretz Israel, Moshe Sachs temporarily left the country and traveled to North Africa and Europe. His mission, undertaken on his own initiative but with approval of the Perushim kollel, had two purposes: to find his father-in-law, Zadok Halevi, who had been in Tripoli, Tunis, and Algiers on a Perushim fundraising mission since 1829, and to secure European support for his agricultural project. In Tunis Sachs met with the English missionary F. C. Ewald, who reported that Sachs told him: "I wish I could establish schools at Jerusalem for the Jewish children there, who are much neglected."[49] No mention is made of his agricultural proposals. Whether Sachs succeeded in finding Zadok Halevi we do not know, but by 1837 Halevi had returned to Jerusalem.

From North Africa Sachs journeyed to Trieste; at the beginning of 1836 he was in the Austro-Hungarian capital of Vienna. There he mixed great faith with greater gall by submitting to the Austrian Foreign Office his scheme "for improving the cultural status in Palestine, by Jewish agriculture." With sublime confidence Sachs asked for the support of Austria, but its government took no action. A German-Jewish periodical observed that "the fanaticism of the plan is greater than its clarity of thought."[50]

While in Vienna Sachs put his agricultural plan before the banker Salomon Rothschild and asked for financial support. The cautious, skeptical Rothschild warily promised to contribute an annual stipend "if the project is established."[51] Then Sachs traveled to Frankfort-am-Main, where he presented his agricultural plan to Anschel Meyer Rothschild. The founder of the Rothschild dynasty must have wondered about the viability of a plan establishing agricultural colonies in a wild land ruled by the pasha of Egypt and settled by a few thousand Jews who prayed and studied all day and knew nothing about farming. This was not the first farming project to have been placed before Rothschild. In 1832 Bernhard Behren, a Jewish merchant from Hesse, suggested that Rothschild purchase land to settle Jews in North America, where thousands of German Jews were migrating. Rothschild took no action on the proposals of Behren or Sachs because a loyal German could not finance a plan encouraging Jews to leave Germany!

About the time Sachs was presenting his agricultural plan A. M. Rothschild also received a long, florid Hebrew letter from Zvi Hirsch Kalischer, an unknown rabbi from Thorn in East Prussia. The letter, dated August 25,

1836, presented the bold, imaginative idea of establishing a Jewish state and is considered a Zionist classic.[52]

Kalischer propounded the idea that Israel's redemption would come slowly and naturally through human actions, rather than by the intervention of "God suddenly descending on earth from Heaven telling His people to go out [from the Diaspora]." Citing biblical verses and rabbinical statements, Kalischer argued that "the beginning of the Redemption will come about in a natural way, by the desire of the scattered Jews to settle on the Holy Land, and the willingness of the nations to help them." Settling Eretz Israel with Jews, according to Kalischer, was a prerequisite for the coming of the Messiah. Half of his long letter was filled with a mystical, impassioned plea for reinstituting ritual sacrifices on the altar of God in Jerusalem, so that the Messiah might come.

At the end of his letter Kalischer switched styles and in simple words asked Rothschild to buy Eretz Israel for the Jews—so that "the Holy Land [would be] under an Israelite government," which "no doubt" would return money to him "many times over." If the "pasha government" did not wish to sell Palestine, Kalischer suggested offering Mehemet Ali "another land in exchange for this country small in size but great in quality." If all of Palestine was not for sale, Kalischer asked Rothschild to buy "Jerusalem and the surrounding area" or at least the Temple Mount and its adjacent grounds in order to "offer sacrifices to God our Lord." Rothschild may well have incredulously wondered if this fixation about ritual sacrifices in the enlightened nineteenth century was the delusion of a deranged person. Choosing silence as the best answer, Rothschild did not reply to Kalischer's letter.

Oblivious of Kalischer's plan, Moshe Sachs, after presenting his agricultural proposal to A. M. Rothschild, spent the next two years (1836–1838) promoting his project in Germany, France, Holland, England, and Hungary. During his travels in German towns Sachs criticized the haluka system, charged that much of the money contributed in Europe was being squandered, and tried to muster backing for his proposal that some money allocated for haluka be invested in productive projects such as his agricultural colonization scheme. To prevent waste, Sachs recommended that a European representative periodically visit Eretz Israel and supervise the proper distribution of the haluka funds. This was a not-so-subtle criticism of Zvi Hirsch Lehren, who had never visited Eretz Israel.

Before Sachs reached Amsterdam in the summer of 1836, he wrote to Lehren and asked his help "to try and make a yeshiva in the holy city of Jerusalem." In this way Sachs hoped to increase financial support for German settlers. Sachs also propounded plans for "a new project for buying houses and fields and vineyards, to build, to sow and to reap." Lehren proceeded to savage Sachs and his yeshiva and farming plans, contending that Eretz Israel was ordained by God to be desolate; therefore no settlement efforts should be attempted until the Messianic Redemption.[53]

No less enraging to Lehren was the Sachs plan to recruit poor European Jewish tradesmen for farming work and to collect money in Western Europe for the colonization of Eretz Israel, a project that would have diverted money from PEKAM's fundraising campaigns. Sachs's dispute with PEKAM subsided at the end of 1838 when he departed for Jerusalem. Nonetheless, Lehren and Sachs showed their mutual dislike by continuing to malign each other throughout their lives.

ELEVEN

Organizing the Jewish Community and Building the Hurva Synagogue

❖

1834–1838

In Palestine one conspicuous sign of Mehemet Ali's tolerant policy toward Christians and Jews had been manifested in his granting minorities permission in 1834 to "repair" their places of worship "based on the old foundations."[1] Mehemet Ali wrote the Governor of Jerusalem that "the firman about repairing the Jewish synagogue [the Hurva] was granted on the condition that nothing be added on to an old building." This was an unprecedented "act of benevolence not performed since the Temple was destroyed" according to a member of the Safed Perushim. John Nicolayson happily called Mehemet Ali's firman a milestone for the Jews—not only "remarkable evidence of a great change in the principles of government but also in the situation and prospect of that nation in the land of their fathers."

The Roman and Greek Catholics, Armenians, and Copts were also permitted to repair their churches, monasteries, and hospices in Jerusalem after they had been damaged in 1834 by the earthquake and by fellahin rebels. The Roman Catholic monastery was "rebuilt . . . from the foundation" and "the Franks . . . raised many new buildings" showing how "repair" work could be most flexibly interpreted.

Even the Jews "dared to speak about their synagogue," wrote Neophytos, a Greek Catholic monk. The Sephardim felt an urgent need to overhaul their complex of four ravaged synagogues with "broken steps" and "fallen roofs" built more than 200 years before and now "in a ruinous condition and in danger of falling in." The British tourist R.R. Madden in 1827 described the Sephardi synagogue as "a miserable hovel more like a stable than a place of worship" and a Trappist monk in 1832 "was struck by the wretched and disgusting appearance" of the synagogues, which in places lacked a roof. "Woe to your eyes that see such things" bemoaned a Moroccan Jew.[2]

Fearing that the Egyptian firman might be revoked as a result of hostile Muslim pressure, the Sephardim hastily initiated a large reconstruction project in 1834. "Those who did not even dare to change a tile on the roof of the synagogue at one time, now received a permit and a decree to build,"[3] in the jealous words of Neophytos. Shlomo Moshe Suzin, the Sephardi chief rabbi, favored repairing the synagogues without making major renovations in order to avoid substantial construction costs that would impose an additional burden on the Sephardi community, already weighted down by a debt of 480,000 piastres. But the Sephardi leadership overruled Rabbi Suzin and the massive repair project was initiated.

Sections of the building were demolished and rebuilt. Weak parts of the foundation were reinforced. The leaking wooden ceiling covered by mats was replaced by a stone cupola whose arched lines in the vaulted dome were designed not to meet, to avoid presenting the form of a cross. Rotted walls were broken down and rebuilt. Plain fixtures and wooden furniture were installed. Some patches on the whitewashed walls were left unplastered to remind the congregants of the destruction of Jerusalem and its Temple. The repaired synagogue complex was long and spacious. Neophytos estimated that the four Sephardi synagogues together held 1,000 persons, while Nicolayson reported that it was "not so large as I had expected, but it is a solid, capacious and, for this country, fine building."[4]

To honor the sacred with religious splendor, the Sephardim asked Mordecai Schnitzer to chisel out of stone the Ark that would contain the Torah scrolls. Schnitzer, a self-taught artist who came to Eretz Israel in 1809 and was one of the first Perushim of Safed to settle in Jerusalem, prayed with the Sephardim in the Ben Zakai synagogue. He earned his living as a grave-digger and stonemason, carved objects in wood and stone, and also produced magic amulets "against sickness or for the benefit of barren women." Schnitzer carved the stone Torah Ark and drew on the wall a pair of lions holding the holy Tablets of the Covenant. The clear, energetic beauty of the

The Shephardi synagogue in Jerusalem's Jewish Quarter around 1834.

two lions supporting the Decalogue so incensed Rabbi Suzin that he ordered them whitewashed away. Lions so artfully and sharply drawn constituted a sacrilegious graven image in the eyes of the rabbi. To Rabbi Suzin and other pious Jews, religion was not expressed in art. Delight of worship was not kindled through the eye but in the heart and mind; Jews had no time or inclination for visual pleasures, only for the concepts of the mind.[5]

After less than one year of strenuous work the reconstructed Sephardi synagogues were dedicated in the presence of a crowded and noisy congregation on the Sabbath of August 29, 1835. Neophytos claimed that the Jews spent "over one million piastres" by being "rather careless in expending."[6] More accurately, the cost of this building project was around 400,000 piastres, nearly the equivalent of the total Sephardi community debt, or 100–200 percent of the annual income of the Sephardi kehilla.

Some of the building costs were defrayed by the donations of rich Jews such as Joseph Amzalag, who contributed 20,000 piastres. A Sephardi shaliah was sent to Morocco to collect special contributions. Rabbi Suzin asked Moses Montefiore to expedite the transfer of funds contributed by English Jewry for Eretz Israel, an open admission that kehilla monies for current expenses were used to defray building costs. As a result of this huge building expenditure the Jerusalem kehilla debt increased enormously and the Sephardim were burdened with high interest rates that kept their debt spiraling upward.

The Perushim viewed with envy the construction work undertaken by the Sephardim and the Christians and once again enthusiastically resolved "to glorify and elevate the power of Jerusalem" by building their temple "on the Holy Mountain of Jerusalem,"[7] thus taking another step toward Messianic Redemption. Reconstruction of the Hurva synagogue provided the backdrop against which R. Israel of the Safed Perushim fought Jerusalem leaders headed by Shlomo Zalman Zoref, a battle that led to the splintering of the Perushim kollel.[8]

Even before the Hurva issue was debated, the united Perushim kollel had been buffeted by intermittent disagreements between the Safed and Jerusalem branches dating back to 1817 when R. Israel argued the case for the centrality of Safed. Not even the Perushim's 1823 regulation sanctioning the kollel branch in Jerusalem defined clearly what autonomy would be delegated to it. In 1829 the Perushim had agreed with PEKAM on a new haluka "key"that allocated to about 450 Jerusalem Perushim more than double the sum received by the 600 Perushim of Safed. This inequitable distribution must have ruffled the Safed Perushim. Lehren later wrote that the "Jerusalem supervisors greatly exert themselves to gain the advantage in every matter . . ."[9] We may conjecture that the younger Jerusalem branch was more aggressive than the older Safed branch, which since 1827 had been unsuccessfully negotiating with Lehren to extricate itself from its dire financial predicament by selling off some kollel assets or establishing a special fundraising campaign. Then ideological arguments broke out in 1831 when R. Israel sent R. Baruch of Pinsk to seek out the Ten Lost Tribes in Yemen. The Jerusalem Perushim saw this as R. Israel's hobby-horse and a waste of money spent to chase after an elusive Messianic rainbow far from Zion.

During the early 1830s the Jerusalem Perushim spared no effort to gain control over the kollel and were not reticent about humbling R. Israel. This is evident in a revealing incident involving Alexander Ziss Blitz, a Dutch settler in Eretz Israel and a confidant of Lehren. In 1832, while R. Israel was visiting Jerusalem, the Perushim excommunicated Blitz for letters he wrote to Lehren containing derogatory information about them.[10] Lehren stormed against R. Israel and demanded that the excommunication edict be lifted; he issued a statement that nobody is prohibited from writing the truth to Amsterdam. Lehren also angrily wrote to the Vilna Rabbis and threatened to set up an independent Ashkenazi kollel if the ban was not rescinded. He asked chief rabbi Suzin of Jerusalem to revoke the excommunication; evidently R. Israel's position had deteriorated to such an extent that he could no longer control the Perushim of Jerusalem.

R. Israel's status was further damaged by sharp criticism about the interminable meddling of his wife in official Perushim affairs. Lehren had received numerous complaints that R. Israel's wife

dominates him and has a hand in matters of the kollel. . . . He allows his wife to rule over him and the kollel. They expressly say that she shares money with crooks and takes bribes. Anyone she favors receives financial benefits and is sent overseas as a shaliah.[11]

These serious charges were categorically rejected by R. Israel.

Most serious were the arguments about the rising debt of the Perushim Safed branch. Many Jerusalem Perushim led by Shlomo Zalman Zoref hotly contested the need for a united kollel with a common debt, claiming that the Jerusalem Perushim were unfairly burdened by the crushing debts of the Safed group. Debts of the Safed Perushim had precipitously escalated to 260,000 piastres after the 1834 plunder, in contrast to the Jerusalem Perushim debt of 20,000 piastres in 1833.

R. Israel blamed the high Safed debt on the Jerusalem Perushim, who did not pay off a debt of 42,000 piastres when they left Safed and settled in Jerusalem. The Jerusalemites rejected R. Israel's unconvincing arguments and laid the blame for Safed's debt on poor financial management. Zoref and other Perushim from Jerusalem demanded that the Jerusalem and Safed branches each receive a per capita share of the Perushim income, and then each branch could deduct its own debt payments and allocate funds for whatever purposes it saw fit. In fact, the Jerusalem Perushim were advocating two independent kollelim. This dispute festered for a good number of years and was frequently resolved by the Perushim executive committee, with the full backing of the Vilna Rabbis, in favor of the Safed branch.

The strongest challenge to the united Perushim kollel and its director and supervisor, R. Israel, was mounted by the majority of Jerusalem Perushim led by Shlomo Zalman Zoref, who were vitally interested in rebuilding the Hurva synagogue. The aspirations of this group were raised in 1833 by the pledge of Zvi Hirsch Lehren's younger brother Akiva to contribute the substantial sum of 20,000 piastres to build a synagogue in Eretz Israel, on the condition that it be registered as his private property, not as a religious trust. The Lehren brothers were intent on linking their family name to the historic Hurva.

The Perushim kollel was unhappy about recording the Hurva as Lehren's private property and instead asked Moses Montefiore, London's Ashkenazi R. Hirschel, Baron Rothschild, and the wealthy English Jew Asher Samson to donate 100,000 piastres for the Hurva project. When Lehren learned about this request he exploded in rage, particularly remembering that after his 1831 visit to Eretz Israel Samson had accused PEKAM of discriminating against the "starving and thirsty" Ashkenazim of Eretz Israel and had declared in the name of the Perushim that the Sephardim "are lacking in nothing" and do not need contributions from European Jewry.[12]

The financially hard-pressed Jerusalemites continued to oppose "building a synagogue for one individual when all Jews in Eretz Israel have a right to it." This firm stand may have led Lehren to increase his brother's donation from 20,000 to 44,000 piastres and then to 100,000 piastres. R. Israel suggested to Lehren, as an alternative to the Hurva, the purchase of "a good courtyard and a place suitable for a large synagogue and study hall."[13] Before Lehren could respond, R. Israel signed a commitment for the purchase of the "good courtyard," called Sukkat Shalom, the Tabernacle of Peace.

Spearheading the courtyard group in opposition to Zoref and the Hurva faction of Perushim was R. Isaiah Bardaki,[14] R. Israel's son-in-law, a distinguished scholar and one of the three Jerusalemites on the Perushim executive committee. R. Bardaki dressed in the Polish garb of a black caftan that prominently set off his pale face, which was surrounded by a long, graying beard and curled side-locks. His sparkling eyes always seemed to be only half open, hiding more than they revealed. Blunt and petulant, R. Bardaki had a voice and physical presence that served to intimidate rather than to persuade. Lacking the mature graces developed by his venerable father-in-law, R. Bardaki badgered opponents and succeeded in converting adversaries into enemies. He turned controversial issues into confrontations and, by polarizing positions, quickly pushed beyond the ken of compromise. R. Isaiah Bardaki was aptly named: his initials, "R. I. B.," form the Hebrew word "strife."

Since the great majority of Jerusalem's Perushim had set their hearts on rebuilding the Hurva, they were not deterred by R. Bardaki's opposition and the lack of Akiva Lehren's endowment. The Hurva, although not a traditional holy site consecrated in Jewish tradition, had taken on great historical significance and symbolic importance in the eyes of the Perushim. No less important were the ambitions of Shlomo Zalman Zoref to build the Hurva and to best his rivals R. Israel and R. Bardaki for leadership of the Perushim kollel.[15]

The Perushim in Jerusalem were now bitterly arrayed in two contentious groups: the Hurva faction led by Shlomo Zalman Zoref, and the courtyard group headed by R. Bardaki. Many Perushim from the Vilna area supported R. Bardaki's Sukkat Shalom group while most Perushim from Shklov favored the Hurva faction. "There is now a split between the leaders and also between the individual Perushim and the leaders," Lehren wrote to Vilna. "One person favors this leader and another person that friend."[16]

In June 1836 Zoref borrowed 1,000 piastres and traveled to Egypt to secure a firman for repairing the Hurva, basing his claim on old official documents. Joseph Schwartz helped Zoref draft his petition to Mehemet Ali asking that Jews be granted "permission to reoccupy the property of their ancestors and to rebuild the ruined ancient synagogue."[17] In Alexandria Zoref was assisted by the Austrian and Russian consuls and succeeded in obtaining the Hurva firman from Mehemet Ali in July 1836. While still in Alexandria, Zoref tried to convince Lehren to earmark his brother's bequest for the rebuilding of the Hurva now that he had obtained the coveted firman, but Lehren turned Zoref down. No doubt Lehren was strongly influenced by his long-nurtured hatred of Zoref, whom he regarded as power-hungry, greedy, and untrustworthy.

In September 1836 Zoref returned triumphantly to Jerusalem brandishing a letter from Mehemet Ali revoking old debts and a firman approving the rebuilding of the Hurva complex.[18] He was greeted by the Perushim with a great swelling of community thanksgiving. "Speedily will the Sanctuary be rebuilt. Soon the Temple will be restored," they prayed. With "zeal and industry" they quickly set to work cleaning out the rubble that littered the Hurva compound.

Dignitaries and important members of the community rolled up their sleeves. With their fingers they dug and with their hands they took out dirt and on their shoulders they carried away the rubbish and soil from that holy place. Older men carried baskets of soil and they sang songs of praise to God. Suddenly Jews gazed at the original buildings that rose out of the ground—the synagogue, the ritual bath, and other buildings on three levels. And they all were strong with good foundations. . . . And then we laid the cornerstone for the large synagogue.

Construction work commenced. Foundations were dug and repaired. When Muslims disturbed the progress of work and demanded payment of back debts on the Hurva, Zoref secured a Muslim court order invalidating the old Hurva debts, long since canceled by the sultan's firman of 1820. R. Bardaki realized that he could not stop the feverish pace of reconstruction work on the Hurva so he completed the purchase of the Sukkat Shalom courtyard, agreeing to pay 75,000 piastres for the courtyard, which had many defects.[19]

In November 1836 the Hurva group, still hoping to gain control over the Lehren bequest, appealed to the Sephardi rabbinical court for an injunction against R. Bardaki's courtyard purchase, claiming that it had not been expressly approved by Lehren. Then the Hurva group convinced Moses Picciotto of Beirut to freeze the 100,000-piastre bequest that he held in trust, until Lehren specifically designated its recipient. Picciotto was told that the purchase of the Sukkat Shalom courtyard could not be approved by the authorities because it contravened Muslim law that forbade a local person from buying property in the name of an overseas resident.

Now it was the turn of the Muslim owner of the courtyard to appeal before the Sephardi court and demand that R. Bardaki conclude the transaction by paying him the purchase price. The Sephardi court headed by chief rabbi Navon ordered R. Bardaki to complete his purchase within the following month.

On receipt of this court order R. Israel borrowed 44,000 piastres from Austrian consul Laurella in Beirut at the high interest rate of 22 percent. On December 18, 1836, R. Israel sent his wife and daughters to take the baths at Tiberias while he set off for Jerusalem, where he promptly concluded the purchase of the Tabernacle of Peace. As the new year of 1837 approached, tension among the Perushim ran so high that most Jews boycotted R. Bardaki's study sessions and refused to pray with him.

While R. Israel was in Jerusalem concluding the purchase of the Sukkat Shalom courtyard, Jerusalem and Hebron suffered slight earth shocks that cracked the walls of a number of houses. But the full brunt of the violent 1837 earthquake struck the Galilee in the most catastrophic natural disaster of nineteenth-century Palestine.[20] Hardest hit by the rupture in the earth were Safed and Tiberias.

On Sunday, January 1, 1837, at 4:20 P.M. the Lord

> poured out His wrath like fire, and the earth trembled and quaked mightily in Safed and Tiberias. The earth... heaved, like a horse tossing its mane. Domes of houses fell upon those inside, making their homes their graves. The destruction was especially severe in the houses on the hills.

From inside the earth rumbling concussions exploded, opening up fissures that swallowed homes and people in villages and towns along the path of the fault. After the undulating ground stopped moving, clouded skies darkened the face of the earth in an eerie stillness. Then a torrential rain poured down. Survivors groped blindly in the darkness, seeking an escape from the chaos.

In Safed "the calamity in its full weight fell with relentless fury upon the ill-fated Jews," while the Muslim quarter built on level ground suffered much less destruction. Since the Jewish quarter located on the steep western side of the mountain was built in tiers, with the roofs of the lower-level houses forming the streets on a higher level, the earthquake collapsed one tier on top of another, "burying each successive row of houses deeper and deeper under accumulated masses of rubbish. . . . Not a house remained standing" as buildings cascaded down the mountainside in a landslide.[21] All fourteen Safed synagogues were destroyed. Congregants chanting the late-afternoon minha prayers were buried alive under the debris. Some Jews with broken limbs were lucky to dig themselves out. Hundreds were maimed for life. Jewish survivors who were outdoors during the quake or escaped the falling masonry asked if the Day of Judgment had arrived.

Buffeted by blustering January winds and the chilling rains of the Galilee mountains, the living remnants listened in horror to the painful screams of people trapped under the ruins and begging for help. Pinned beneath buildings many injured persons died slow, agonizing deaths from starvation and asphyxiation. Safed was a ravaged town—"in every quarter the wounded, the dying, and the dead, without shelter, without attendance, without a place to lay their heads."[22] During the following weeks a series of shocks produced intermittent earth tremors of small intensity that further frightened the traumatized residents of the Galilee.

The head of the Hasidic community, R. Abraham Dov, organized the surviving Jews and built a wooden hut on top of the mountain where the injured, sick, and hungry were brought for shelter, food, and clothing. One "native doctor" ministered to all the wounded.[23] In the midst of this terrible scene of death and agony, Muslims ransacked the collapsed Jewish homes. They stole whatever was intact until soldiers sent from Acre by Ibrahim Pasha arrived to protect the helpless Jews.

It took eight days for news about the earthquake to reach Beirut. Ten days later a mercy team composed of the American missionary William M. Thomson and the English missionary Erasmus Calman arrived in Safed "to promote the glory of God by alleviating the sufferings of the poor, the sick, the wounded and orphan." Thomson reported what he saw:

> It is not in the power of language to overstate such a ruin. . . . Safed *was* but is not . . . most hideous spectacle, may I never see its like. Nothing met the eye but a vast chaos of stone and earth, timber and boards . . . mingled in horrible confusion.[24]

The missionaries erected a temporary hospital shed, collected the wounded, distributed medicine and bandages, and treated the injured. Survivors were in such a deplorable state, according to Thomson, "as rendered it impossible for us to remain with them long enough to do them any good." Lack of medical skills also handicapped the missionaries.

Thomson charged the Jews with callousness in a book written many years later. He claimed that "it is scarcely credible, and yet it is a fact that after we labored night and day to build the hospital we had to carry the wounded to it ourselves, or *pay their surviving friends* exorbitant prices to do it." Thomson exaggerated, but since it is not conceivable that he would write an outright lie, we may surmise that some Jews found it expedient to accept mission money in order to defray their heavy expenses for the rescue operation. After two days of strenuous work Thomson and Calman left to treat the casualties in Tiberias.

Immediately after the departure of the missionaries a Perushim rescue mission from Jerusalem reached Safed. R. Bardaki and Aryeh Neaman headed the rescue team of twenty persons, including "gravediggers who know how to dig graves and bury the dead."[25] The Perushim evacuated some of the injured to Haifa and Acre and sent widows and orphans to be cared for in Jerusalem. But the major task of the Jerusalem rescue team was to extricate the mangled bodies from under the rubble, identify them, and perform a proper Jewish burial.

Aryeh Neaman initially paid the large sum of 50 piastres a day to hired workmen, but since the arduous work was so repellent he was forced to increase their pay. Part of these expenses were covered by the Jerusalem kollel, which borrowed 12,000 piastres from the Jerusalem Sephardim, took a loan of 7,000 piastres in Safed, and borrowed money from consul Laurella in Beirut. Rescue operation expenses for food, clothing, and hired labor cost the Perushim about 50,000 piastres. The kollel debt also increased due to the defaulted loans of dead Perushim.

Although Safed was shaken by earth tremors in 1822, 1823, 1830, and 1834, Jews best remember the 1837 earthquake, estimated at 6.75 on the Richter scale, because "since the destruction of the Temple there never was such a disaster." The earthquake of 1759 "seems to have been not less terrific than that of 1837," but the larger population of 4,000 Safed Jews led to a far higher number of casualties in 1837. About 2,000 Jews, half of the Jewish population of Safed, were killed by the 1837 earthquake. Out of about 800 Perushim, only about 200 perished in the earthquake disaster, for they lived on the edge of the Jewish quarter and were able "to escape and run for their lives."[26] However, the Perushim despaired of reconstructing the Jewish quarter, and by 1839 only about 30 of their group remained in Safed.

Of the 850–900 Hasidim in Safed, some 300 were killed by the earthquake. Nearly all the surviving Hasidim remained in Safed, staying close to their leader, R. Abraham Dov. Among those who left Safed was Israel Bak, who gave up his shattered printing presses and moved his family to the Jermak farm where his son Nissan lived. R. Abraham Dov encouraged Hasidim to remain in Safed, telling them, "Now is not the time to cry and mourn. Let us rush aid to the needy and save what man can possibly salvage."[27]

Nearly all the 750 surviving Sephardim, headed by Moroccan and Algerian rabbis, also continued to live in Safed and mourned the 1,500 dead of their community.

As a result of the 1837 earthquake the Jewish population of Safed dropped from 4,000 to about 1,400—some 2,000 died, and 600 survivors, nearly all Perushim, moved to Jerusalem, Tyre, Haifa, and elsewhere.[28]

In Tiberias, the January 1 earthquake also took a heavy toll. "Fire came out of the Kinneret Lake and water flooded the city." The walls surrounding Tiberias cracked, and in many places they crumbled into "a pile of rocks." The Muslim quarter was demolished, and in the Jewish quarter the synagogues and all but one house collapsed. Survivors wandered about aimlessly and without hope, "as if their courage had crumbled together with the walls."[29] For weeks people lived in tents and makeshift huts outside town to escape the terrible stench of putrefied bodies buried under the wreckage. As in Safed, robbers pillaged the ruins.

A German minister, Johann Visino, arrived in Tiberias shortly after the earthquake and recounted the poignant story as told by a young married Jewish girl from Bavaria:

It was New Year's according to your calendar, and most of my people were in the synagogue with their Hasidic rabbis and Sephardi scholars. . . . I went outside of town to graze my goats. I took my baby son with me; two other sons remained at home. After half an hour I heard a terrible noise like a strong storm. The ground shook beneath me, broken rocks fell from the mountainside, and the goats crowded around me in fear. I knew nothing; full of fright I watched the town below where my most beloved husband and children remained. Great God! I will never ever see them! I gazed at the walls of the town: large gaps appeared in them. The minarets, towers, and dome of the synagogue shuddered, everything moved and swayed. Suddenly it seemed to me that all the town tilted toward the lake, and after a moment I saw nothing but a cloud of thick, gray dust that covered the whole town. Then a thunderous whirlwind-like noise was heard and the terrible screams and cries from thousands and I fainted on the ground.[30]

The young woman related that the synagogue was destroyed and all who were inside perished. "The whole town was a pile of rubble." The woman's

Tiberias before and after the catastrophic earthquake on January 1, 1837.

husband and children were buried under the ruins and she was unable to dig them out. Despite her tragedy she concluded that "we could not leave this town so beloved to us even in its destruction. Here we will live and here we will die."

The missionary team of Thomson and Calman helped treat the wounded and bury the dead. The Perushim rescue squad also came to Tiberias, where it extricated bodies from the ruins and buried them at the high cost of 1,000 piastres a grave. A temporary first-aid station was set up south of Tiberias, near the sturdy buildings of the hot baths, which withstood the earthquake. R. Israel's wife and daughters were taking the hot mineral baths at the time and were unharmed.[31]

Since the Jewish quarter was situated on level ground near the Lake of Galilee, damage and loss of life were not as extensive as in Safed. Of the 1,200 Jews of Tiberias, about 400–500 died in the earthquake.[32] Survivors totaled 700–800: 400 Hasidim, 300 Sephardim, and a handful of Perushim. For the first time in the nineteenth century, one of the four holy cities was populated by more Ashkenazim than Sephardim.

In a cataclysmic stroke of nature the number of Jews in Eretz Israel plummeted by 25 percent, dropping from 9,800 to 7,400. During one frightful moment, seven years of unprecedented population growth was abruptly erased.

Soon after the earthquake R. Israel and Aryeh Neaman wrote to PEKAM describing the catastrophe and urgently requested financial assistance for the decimated Jewish community in Eretz Israel.[33] In response to PEKAM appeals Jews generously contributed about 140,000 piastres, a sum somewhat smaller than the annual PEKAM contributions to Eretz Israel, which in 1837 totaled about 171,000 piastres.

Special prayers of mourning were written and recited in Eretz Israel and throughout the Diaspora for the 2,500 Jews who perished in the earthquake disaster.[34] In Jerusalem, memorial services conducted by the Sephardi chief rabbi Jonah Navon and R. Israel bound the Jewish community together in public mourning and repentance in the large, newly refurbished R. Ben Zakkai synagogue. In anguish, R. Israel filled his passionate sermon with rhetorical oratory, quoting biblical allusions that were as terrifyingly meaningful in 1837 as in the times of the Prophets. The content and cadence of R. Israel's jeremiad caused "a stream of tears to flow from all our brothers, the Sephardim and Ashkenazim,"[35] as he described the great tragedy and the signs of imminent Redemption. Then R. Israel was overcome and fainted.

Some Jews interpreted the destruction of Safed as God wreaking vengeance upon the Jews for neglecting the settlement of Jerusalem. R. Moshe Sofer consoled his Pressburg congregation by preaching that "the Galilee will be laid waste with the coming of the Messiah." R. Sofer believed that the "earthquake is a result of the jealousy in Jerusalem . . . and for nearly the last hundred years they settled in Safed . . . and all the settlers went only to Safed and Tiberias. Jerusalem was completely forgotten . . ." He concluded his sermon by praising R. Israel: "And R. Israel is righteous for he has gathered together the refugees of Safed and brought them to Jerusalem,"[36] where they would remain until Jerusalem was rebuilt.

Zvi Lehren and R. Israel saw the hand of God in sending R. Israel to Jerusalem on his courtyard mission, thereby saving him from possible death in the Safed earthquake. In deciphering evidence about the divine intent, some Perushim leaders of Jerusalem construed God's will to destroy Safed as punishment for R. Israel's trying to prevent the consecration of the Hurva. Other Jews saw the destruction of Safed as divine retribution signaling the imminence of Messianic Redemption.

On January 3, nine days before news about the earthquake calamity reached Jerusalem, the Perushim community was convulsed by demands of the Hurva group to dismiss R. Bardaki from the kollel's six-man executive committee. They charged him with unauthorized borrowing of money at high interest rates in the name of the kollel and with misusing kollel funds for the partisan purchase of the Sukkat Shalom courtyard. A special court was quickly convened to judge the argument that R. Israel's presence in Jerusalem negated the need for R. Bardaki to sit on the executive committee. This secular, improvised court composed of Eliezer Bergmann, Joseph Schwartz, and Mordecai Minsker heard both sides and, based on its findings, the executive committee and other distinguished Perushim voted to discharge R. Bardaki from his position as a member of the executive committee. So sudden, arbitrary, and embarrassing was Bardaki's expulsion from the executive committee that the neutral Aryeh Neaman "cried out" and wanted to "escape from his position" as a trustee of the kollel.[37]

One day after R. Bardaki was removed from his kollel post, the conflict between the Hurva and the Sukkat Shalom courtyard protagonists reached a climax. In a last, desperate attempt, rabbis Israel and Bardaki appealed to the Sephardi High Court for a Torah judgment to halt the Hurva reconstruction work that was proceeding at a frenzied pace and to issue an injunction against bringing a Torah scroll into the Hurva—for without a Torah the synagogue could not be consecrated.

In presenting his case before the Sephardi court R. Israel argued that Zoref's group could not establish a synagogue at the Hurva without his permission, since the Vilna Rabbis had appointed him to "direct and supervise all [Perushim] activities in the Holy Land of Jerusalem." R. Israel and Bardaki were now willing to concede the building of homes in the Hurva compound, but they contended that the synagogue must be located in the

View of Jerusalem from the Mount of Olives.

Sukkat Shalom courtyard. R. Israel requested a court decision on the same day "because we have heard that tomorrow they wish to enter the Hurva." The Sephardi court promptly ruled in favor of the Hurva group and refused to intervene in the disagreement among the Perushim.[38]

On January 8, 1837, at the end of eighteen weeks of concentrated, hectic work, the Hurva was consecrated for worship, "one hundred and sixteen years, two months, and three weeks" after it had been razed by Muslims. The Perushim called their Hurva synagogue Menahem Zion, meaning consoler of Zion. They exulted that the Lord had been glorified, that the gates of heaven were open to receive the prayers of all Jews throughout the world, and that the holy spirit could now shine forth from Jerusalem. Sephardim participated in the celebration fully convinced, like the Perushim, that the consecration of this new Temple of God was a further step toward hastening the imminent Messianic Redemption. Numerous Perushim now moved their homes from the Muslim quarter of Bab-el-Huta to the enlarged Jewish quarter near the Hurva, which became the center of the Jewish community of Jerusalem.[39]

Within six months the Perushim constructed in the Hurva compound study halls, ritual baths, and houses for scholars and visitors. By 1841 many destroyed stores and homes had been rebuilt despite the opposition of Muslims and the Sukkat Shalom courtyard group.[40]

Four days after the consecration of the Hurva, Jerusalemites first heard news about the horrendous earthquake in the Galilee. After sending a rescue team to Safed and Tiberias and learning of the appalling number of casualties, the Perushim were faced with the problem of deciding whether the homeless Galilee Perushim survivors should move to Jerusalem or resettle in Safed and Tiberias and rebuild the town's Jewish quarters, as the Sephardim and Hasidim were doing.

Hasidim and Sephardim in Safed must have urged R. Israel to return and help restore the town's glorious Jewish tradition. Consuls in Sidon and Beirut also "implored" R. Israel to resettle in Safed.[41] Nevertheless Z. H. Lehren convinced R. Israel to house his Safed followers in Jerusalem. Lehren feared the huge cost entailed in rebuilding the Safed Jewish quarter and was apprehensive about R. Israel's standing in the kollel.

> Why should he [R. Israel] want to return and burden himself with the problems of leadership of the kollel and deal with the public matters of housing and food after his leadership has been questioned? . . . it is better for him to stay away from all building matters that require an investment of hundreds and thousands and create great doubt.

By decision of the kollel, nearly all Perushim emulated the example of R. Israel and left Safed for Jerusalem in 1837, while other Perushim who might have wished to settle in Safed now went to Jerusalem. As a result of the 1837 earthquake the Jews said: "From the destruction of the Galilee, Jerusalem was built. From the devastation of Safed, Jerusalem was repopulated."[42] To enforce its decree, the Perushim kollel simply refused to distribute haluka to Safed Perushim. The handful of Perushim families in Safed in 1838–1839 complained that they were hungry and thirsty, naked, and barefoot and received financial help only from the Hasidic kollel of R. Abraham Dov.

R. Israel settled in Jerusalem and with R. Bardaki took possession of the Sukkat Shalom courtyard. The large, comfortable house—"one of the nicest buildings of our Jerusalem brothers"[43]—overlooked the Wailing Wall and was consecrated as both synagogue and study hall. Expansion of the Sukkat Shalom courtyard increased the absorptive capacity of the Perushim community and facilitated the resettlement of many refugees from Safed. The costs of relocating Safed refugees in Jerusalem totaled about 300,000 piastres.[44]

The physical separation of the courtyard and the Hurva completed the irrevocable division between the antagonists. Ironically, the Hurva and the Sukkat Shalom synagogue, which were to symbolize the centrality of Jerusalem and the unity of world Jewry, displayed the friction and factionalism so rampant in the Jewish community of Eretz Israel.

Hurva and courtyard antagonists excoriated each other and wrote malevolent letters to the Vilna Rabbis, who intervened in an attempt to defuse the feud. In May 1837 the Vilna Perushim issued regulations that restored the balance of power between the two rival groups, with the Hurva group gaining an advantage when R. Israel lost control over kollel financial matters. It has been suggested that the Vilna Rabbis humbled R. Israel when his PEKAM allies decided to transfer contributions from Western Europe to the Perushim through Rothschild's Paris bank rather than via Vilna. It is more likely that R. Israel was relieved of financial authority because of the way he handled the purchase of the Sukkat Shalom courtyard—Lehren was "aghast" when he learned its details—and because numerous Perushim accused him of economic irregularities.[45]

From mid-1837 on Lehren tried repeatedly to convince R. Israel to retire from the kollel leadership. "I certainly knew that I was not very satisfied with him but because of his scholarship and piety I covered up his errors. . . . I say if his wife rules and he cannot stop her from interfering in kollel matters, then it is better that the learned rabbi completely quit the leadership."[46] Nevertheless, Lehren was troubled about the prospect of Zoref assuming leadership of all the Perushim in place of R. Israel and R. Bardaki. In an agitated letter he expressed his fear that Zoref might receive the financial backing of Moses Montefiore, then planning his second trip to Eretz Israel. The large Hurva group conspicuously defied R. Israel's authority. When the Sephardim agreed to R. Israel's proposal to declare a public fast and a time of mourning during the 1838 drought, "Hurva members did not want to hear about it and they ate and drank in public just to diminish his honor . . .".[47] With such public flouting of R. Israel's religious authority, his position and prestige ebbed to its lowest level. He wrote to Lehren about his intention of returning to Safed in order to rebuild the Perushim community there.

Not only did the Hurva-courtyard controversy provide a battleground for the leadership of the Perushim, but it also hindered PEKAM fundraising attempts to help the Jews of Eretz Israel in the aftermath of the 1837 earthquake. The Hurva group, lacking internal financial resources, the largess of Akiva Lehren's endowment, and the support of PEKAM, sent at least four shlihim overseas asking benefactors to contribute money to the Hurva project.[48] The shlihim emphasized the special character of the Hurva compound, signaling the imminence of Redemption; the traditional refrain about supporting the poor Jews in Eretz Israel was played down. In an attempt to encourage new contributors, the Hurva group enjoined their European followers to learn a lesson from the fine example of the Sephardim, who had refurbished their four "luxurious" synagogues in the course of one year.

One shaliah, Aaron Zelig Mann,[49] was dispatched in 1837 to Western Europe to raise money for the Hurva without infringing on the collections of PEKAM. Mann's mission was approved by both the Hurva group and the leading Sephardi rabbis of Jerusalem, who signed a circular recommending support of the project now that Ashkenazim "are living here together with us in peace; may God help them . . ."[50]

Lehren was furious at this "invasion" of Western Europe, the exclusive collection territory of PEKAM. Not only were Zoref and the Hurva group openly defying PEKAM, R. Israel, and Bardaki, but they were willfully injuring PEKAM's collection effort. Lehren realized that, if funds collected overseas were channeled into specific projects determined by the Jews in Eretz Israel rather than according to the allocation keys decided upon by PEKAM, PEKAM's influence would decline.

PEKAM did all in its power to prevent Mann from collecting money for the Hurva in Germany, Holland, and France. But Mann must have achieved a certain measure of success, because in 1838 Lehren appealed to R. Moshe

Sofer of Pressburg and asked him to render a Torah judgment about the right of Mann and other shlihim to collect money for the Hurva project.[51]

R. Moshe Sofer's rabbinical decision praised both the Hurva group for wanting to build a glorious synagogue in Jerusalem and PEKAM's tireless fundraising efforts. He stated that it was unthinkable for Lehren to try to stop Jews from performing the mitzva of collecting money for a synagogue—unless it actually damaged collections for the poor people in Eretz Israel. Thereupon he decided in favor of PEKAM, basing his decision on the principle that the needs of the poor take precedence over building a synagogue.

R. Sofer expounded the concept that Diaspora Jewry is responsible for supplying the needs of the Jewish settlement in Eretz Israel because

> it is known that the residents of other countries settled in the Holy Land sit there under siege and in distress and lead a sorrowful life. . . . They are all engaged in the study of Torah, each according to his capability. Therefore we [in the Diaspora] have the responsibility to maintain a settlement in Eretz Israel, . . . to follow the Torah's precepts that without their settlement in Eretz Israel the Torah can disappear . . . from the face of the earth.

The rabbinical opinion emphasized that the haluka system provides greater spiritual sustenance for Diaspora Jews than economic support for the Jews in Eretz Israel.[52]

Despite the decision of R. Sofer, Mann continued to collect money, because R. Sofer refused to ban his Hurva mission, as Lehren categorically demanded. European rabbis and notables also continued to raise funds for the Hurva project, which they viewed favorably.[53] Quite isolated, Lehren met Mann in Amsterdam and expressed PEKAM's willingness to collect money for the Hurva, on condition that Mann abort his mission in Western Europe. Mann refused Lehren's offer in what must have been an acrimonious confrontation, if we may judge from his attack on Lehren in 1842 in the pages of a German-Jewish newspaper, where he hinted at the need to supervise the unpublished PEKAM accounts. (Not until 1854, one year after the death of Zvi Hirsch Lehren, did PEKAM first make public a detailed financial statement.)

In anticipation of receiving significant sums of money from overseas, the Hurva group in Eretz Israel borrowed the amount of 150,000 piastres from Joseph Amzalag in January 1839, paying him 9 percent interest and giving him a mortgage on the Hurva. Then the group loaned 100,000 piastres to the Perushim kollel so that it might pay pressing debts and "save endangered lives." The Perushim kollel promised to return the loan to the Hurva group from monies collected overseas. By 1840 this loan was repaid and, most miraculous of all, the Perushim kollel found itself absolutely debt-free, and even showed a cash surplus of 2,000 piastres.[54]

The year 1837, so inauspiciously inaugurated by the earthquake, continued to blight the lives of the Jews. A terrible drought in Palestine was followed from Easter through the summer by a cholera epidemic that killed over 150 Jews and 315 Muslims and Christians in Jerusalem. Famine followed as prices shot up. The cost of living in Jerusalem increased threefold, and Sephardim of Tiberias complained that the price of wheat jumped by more than 400 percent.[55]

Against this melancholy background of the devastations of nature, in 1837 eight Dutch- and German-Jewish families established an independent kollel called HOD (Holland and Deutschland).[56] Little is recorded about why and when the kollel was organized; the authoritative book about HOD devotes a scant half-page to its founding. Most probably, kollel HOD was set up as the result of a gradual consensus reached over a period of many months rather than an event that occurred on a specific date.

Kollel HOD was headed by Eliezer Bergmann. Moshe Sachs was overseas; Joseph Schwartz and Nahum Coronel were research types disinclined to involve themselves in public activities; Aberli Haas was 75 years old; and it is inconceivable that Alexander Blitz, Lehren's friend, and Judah Leib Goldschmidt, Lehren's relative, would have headed the newly established kollel, which was founded against the wishes of PEKAM.

Before kollel HOD was set up, the German and Dutch settlers willingly received their haluka from the Perushim, which was the only Ashkenazi kollel in Jerusalem. But Sachs and other members of HOD criticized the PEKAM haluka system. They cited the fact that all contributions from Ottoman Jews went exclusively to the Sephardim, while donations from Eastern Europe were distributed only to Perushim and Hasidim. If it was correct to allocate monies by countries of origin, the HOD people asked, why should the German and Dutch settlers not receive all funds collected by PEKAM in Germany and Holland? Moshe Sachs doubtless argued this case with force when he met Lehren in Holland in the summer of 1836.

The logic of Sachs's argument was impeccable, but its economics were absurd. If the 25 to 30 HOD settlers received all monies collected by PEKAM in Western Europe, they would be extremely wealthy in comparison to

Eretz Israel and Diaspora Jews and would deprive more than 99 percent of the Ashkenazi and Sephardi population in Eretz Israel of a major source of income. HOD members may have been encouraged to set up their kollel by the example of the Hasidim of Tiberias, who split into two kollelim in 1831 and received separate allocations from PEKAM. German and Dutch settlers looked on with interest in 1834 as the large Moroccan community in Jerusalem tried without success to organize itself as an independent community separate from the Sephardi kehilla.

The new kollel HOD was organized after PEKAM turned down Sachs's proposal and after Lehren rejected requests from R. Moshe Sofer and R. Wolff to increase the personal haluka allocations of Moshe Sachs and Joseph Schwartz.[57] Possibly kollel HOD came into being because Sachs and Bergmann clashed with Lehren about using haluka funds for buying land, courtyards, and merchandise so that the Jewish community might strive toward economic independence. In effect the establishment of kollel HOD was a veiled warning to PEKAM that HOD members who had influential, wealthy German contacts might initiate their own competing fundraising campaigns and control these funds.

The fact that Lehren was then under massive attack by Sachs, Bergmann, and the Hurva group backed by the Jerusalem Sephardim may have made it easier to establish kollel HOD. PEKAM leaders may also have felt a certain sympathy for the arguments put forward by their HOD compatriots.

Kollel HOD sent one of its members to Holland to negotiate with PEKAM;[58] "negotiation" included threats to set up a separate fundraising campaign in Western Europe. Reluctantly, PEKAM agreed to a new allocation key that provided kollel HOD with one-quarter of the 66 percent of PEKAM monies that went to all Ashkenazim in Eretz Israel or about 16 percent of all PEKAM monies distributed in Eretz Israel. Nevertheless, HOD members continued to complain about their being discriminated against, although PEKAM consented to increase this allocation when the number of their families increased.

How much money was collected by PEKAM and what sums were distributed to the HOD kollel and to individual HOD members?[59] In 1822 PEKAM collected only 21,175 piastres, but it improved its organizational techniques so that between 1826 and 1831 annual donations totaled between 102,000 and 116,000 piastres (see table 11). During the 1830s PEKAM sent up to 191,000 piastres to Eretz Israel each year, in addition to significant sums donated to victims of the earthquake and the 1834 fellahin revolt. These sums should be compared with the 130,000 piastres distributed by East European Perushim in 1838 and again in 1840 to all the Perushim in Eretz Israel.

TABLE 11 Total PEKAM allocations in 1822–1840

YEAR	PIASTRES
1822	21,175
1823	44,340
1824	37,150
1825	68,275
1826	107,540
1827	102,430
1828	105,435
1829	116,030
1830	111,700
1831	108,990
1832	97,350
1833	161,145
1834	152,445
1835	191,450 (plus 72,430 for a special donation after the 1834 sacking of Safed)
1836	149,925 (plus 19,190 for a special donation after the 1834 sacking of Safed)
1837	171,690 (plus a 135,250 donation for earthquake victims)
1838	184,930 (includes 5,750 for earthquake victims)
1839	80,280
1840	142,860

SOURCE: A. Morgenstern, *Messianism and the Settlement of Eretz Israel in the first half of the Nineteenth Century*, 180 (a Dutch dukart is calculated at 9 piastres).

During 1831–1836, before kollel HOD was established, individual HOD members received munificent benefits from PEKAM (see table 12).[60] But in 1837–1839, after HOD was founded, allocations to its members more than doubled and tripled, although total PEKAM funds for Eretz Israel did not increase, except for the earthquake victims. Compared to the thousands of piastres received annually by each HOD member, the Safed Hasidim in 1836 received 150 piastres per person plus 175 piastres for the family rent,[61] an increase of "about ninety piastres per annum" over the amount each Jew received from the kollel in 1825. These rough figures show fairly conclusively that by organizing kollel HOD, its members enjoyed spectacular financial benefits and that the large allocations to that kollel reduced the

TABLE 12 Haluka sums received by Kollel HOD members and others

	1831	1832	1833	1834	1835	1836	1837	1838	1839
Blitz	900	1180	775	815	800	850	2550	2945	2455
Sachs			130	185	270	115	1050	1335	880
Schwartz				40	425	675	1950	2560	2235
Bergmann					830	1175	5100	4470	3955
Coronel				590	575	1150	2500	1760	2130
Goldschmidt					1840	1470	4300	4020	2365
Haas	640	1425	810	1290	910	750	2600	2790	2370
R. Israel**		60		220	490	1100	1775	3505	1420
S.Z. Zoref**			245						4500**

*In addition to haluka received from the Perushim kollel.
**Montefiore Census-Microfilm at Hebrew University.

TABLE 13 PEKAM Allocations to Kollelim, 1831–1839 (%)

	1831	1832	1833	1834	1835	1836	1837	1838	1839
Sephardim in Eretz Israel	39	35	42	35	31	38	40	38	31
Perushim in Eretz Israel	31	31	25	24	38	33	18	17	40*
Habad Hasidim in Hebron	7	10	7	8	6	5	4	2	3
Hasidim in Safed	23	17	17	19	17	19	16	19	11
Hasidim in Tiberias									
Reisin		6	1	4	2	4	2	4	1
Volyzhin		2	8	10	6	2	6	11	5
HOD							14	9	9
TOTAL	100	100	100	100	100	100	100	100	100

*Including earthquake donations.

SOURCE: Z. Karagila, "Source Material on Haluka in Eretz-Israel," in *Cathedra for the History of Eretz-Israel and Its Yishur*, 57–76.

funds distributed to the Perushim in 1837 and 1838 and to the Sephardim and Safed Hasidim in 1839. (See table 13).

It is enlightening to consider how monies distributed to HOD members compared with food prices, housing rentals, wages, and the general standard of living in Eretz Israel. In Safed, where prices were lower than in Jerusalem, a nice apartment in a courtyard rented for 150 piastres a year, while the comfortable courtyard bought in 1831 by the Englishman Asher Samson—who permitted R. Israel to live there—cost 1,200 piastres. A substantial Jerusalem courtyard in the Muslim quarter, rented by Bergmann for his family of five children, wife, and mother, cost about 375 piastres annually. Bergmann reported that in the Muslim quarter Jews bought courtyards for 4,500, 3,000, and 2,000 piastres and even less. In 1836 the Perushim kollel in Jerusalem purchased a courtyard with ten modest apartments for 1,300 piastres. The affluent Hillel Rivlin estimated that a large courtyard in the Muslim quarter, with good apartments and an excellent water supply, cost 5,000 piastres, while on the Street of the Jews, the main street in the Jewish quarter, homes were hardly available, were costly, and had a poor water supply. A better-class house rented by the American missionaries in the Christian quarter in 1836 cost 1,050 piastres a year. In 1834 John Nicolayson considered renting a courtyard with numerous buildings in the Armenian quarter for 1,500 piastres. From these scattered rental figures we may tentatively estimate that a family paid annual rentals of about 150 piastres in Safed and 200 piastres in Jerusalem.[62]

Food and clothing were "very inexpensive," but prices were constantly rising because of successive devaluations, rampant inflation, droughts, and epidemics. Joseph Schwartz did not complain about high prices in 1837; however, as an orderly German he was irked by the fact that, unlike the situation in cultured countries, "here there is no official price list for food products, but the price is set according to the satisfaction of the seller." Prices listed by David Beit Hillel for 1824 were at least 100 percent lower than those noted for the 1830s, while some prices tripled and quadrupled between 1833 and 1839. A random price list of the 1830s in Damascus and Aleppo is of no help in establishing prices in Palestine. Therefore we must fall back on the generalization that in Eretz Israel fruit and vegetables were plentiful and inexpensive, while meat and wheat were expensive. If the cost of lemons, eggs, and flour are indicative of other prices, we can conclude that prices jumped by 400 percent between 1819 and 1834.[63]

How much money was needed in the 1830s to provide for the basic needs of Jews? A Palestine farmhand in 1839 could earn three piastres a day plus bread and water. In Jerusalem in 1840 the Anglican missionaries offered

Jewish boys 2–4 piastres a day for doing construction work on Christ Church; adult laborers were paid 3–4 piastres, skilled masons earned 5–14 piastres a day, and eleven years later a laborer earned 150 piastres a month.[64]

Lacking reliable numbers about prices paid and wages earned by Jews, and not having an adequate definition of subsistence living in the mid-nineteenth century, we depend on the general impressions of a British official living in Syria and Egypt. John Bowring observed that clothing and lodging were "good." He described the healthy Syrian diet: daily meals of bread, rice, yogurt, cheese, eggs, fruits, and vegetables, with "mutton . . . several times a week."[65] At that time English, French, and Russian laborers in Europe at best tasted meat once or twice a month. What Bowring knew about England and what he saw in Syria led him to the optimistic conclusion that "the condition of the labouring class in Syria is, comparatively with those in England, easy and good." This may, however, reflect a low standard of living among the British working class, enduring the industrial revolution and the inhumane 1834 Poor Law, more than a good standard of living in Syria. Is it too risky to assume that the prosperity prevalent in Syria also applied to the Jews in Eretz Israel? Is it unacceptable to suppose that rising prices in Palestine inflated at the same rate as increases in the local value of the constantly devalued foreign currency that sustained a large part of the Jewish community?

To determine the level of subsistence living in the kehilla, we rely on Jewish sources.[66] A Safed Hasid in 1835 lived with great difficulty on 150 piastres for each person above 3 months of age, plus 175 piastres for family rent money. A member of the Safed Perushim wrote in 1836 that "four gold pieces" or about 200 piastres should be enough for the needs of a whole year, but did not mention if he was referring to a person, a couple, or a family. This figure of 200 piastres is corroborated in 1839, when Montefiore donated to each Jew about "one month's income," which amounted to 21 piastres. A missionary reported in 1842 that 350 piastres (3 pounds sterling and 10 shillings) is as much an annual "annuity . . . as can be expected" by Jews from their overseas friends. Based on these figures, and remembering that it is reasonable to assume that a Safed Jew could live on 100 piastres a year at the start of the nineteenth century, we may estimate, with a tolerable margin of error, an annual subsistence living of 200–300 piastres for a couple and 300–500 piastres for a whole family, excluding rent. This contrasts sharply with the 4,000–4,500 piastres spent annually by the extremely wealthy Hillel Rivlin for his large entourage.

When comparing the subsistence living of 300–500 piastres for a whole family with the sums allocated by PEKAM in 1837 to Blitz (2,550 piastres),

Schwartz (1,950), Bergmann (5,100), Coronel (2,500), Goldschmidt (4,300), and Haas (2,600), we may conclude that HOD members, men of modest habits, could live a life of luxury on their PEKAM income. Moreover, these prodigious sums may not include other monies received by HOD members from their overseas families, from scholarships, and from the kollel.

Large incomes, expressed in piastres, were also enjoyed by the Perushim leadership:[67]

	1838	1840
R. Israel	3,700	
R. Bardaki	1,755	1,955
Shlomo Zalman Zoref	1,215	
Aryeh Neaman	1,575	
Nathan Neta, son of R. Menahem Mendel of Shklov	2,520	1,700
David Yellin	———	1,700

Such ample incomes juxtapose starkly with the meager 25 piastres of haluka distributed to 500 "acknowledged paupers" and the small amount of "relief in charity" donated to another 500 Jerusalem Jews in 1839.[68] Most of those having a marginal existence were Sephardi Jews, which allows us to hypothesize—in the face of Ashkenazi disclaimers[69]—that during the late 1830s Sephardim generally lived on a lower economic level than Ashkenazim, although many Sephardim earned their livelihood by working.

Even after considering the fragility of our figures it is apparent that the haluka allocated to HOD members, like that received by Perushim leaders, served to vastly differentiate their economic status from the great majority of the Jewish community. The great disparity of income indicates that Jews in Eretz Israel and the Diaspora had no interest in establishing an egalitarian society. Munificent sums of haluka helped forge an aristocracy, usually of scholarly abilities, which was rewarded with an economic prize. The Dutch and German settlers, like other groups of Jews with a common background and shared interests, lacked a feeling for the total Jewish community.

The separatist tendencies in Eretz Israel led to the establishment of kollel HOD in order to secure for its members a larger share of PEKAM funds and to a much lesser extent "to create new sources of livelihood and to establish constructive activities, first for themselves and later for the whole community."[70] It is difficult to accept the rationalization that HOD members "not only took care of themselves but considered the needs of the whole Jewish community and specifically the needs of Jerusalem."[71] It is true that they aspired to be the recognized agency for receiving PEKAM funds and distributing them among members and the Jews of Eretz Israel. The more financial support kollel HOD received from overseas, the stronger and more influential it would be in Eretz Israel. Power to effect changes in the Jewish community and the acquisition of ample financial blessings for its members were the dual objectives of the HOD members, who demanded what they believed was rightfully theirs.

Kollel HOD served as a model for a dozen kollelim that organized according to places of origin and burgeoned in Jerusalem during the 1840s and 1850s. The divisive event of the founding of kollel HOD contributed to the friction that developed at a progressively faster pace throughout the nineteenth century, when Jews "beat each other with sticks and stones." Incessant conflicts that accelerated community fragmentation were the most dominant, distinguishing characteristics in the social dynamics of the contentious kehilla.

TWELVE

Pilgrims, Travelers, and Explorers

❖

During the years of Egyptian rule in Syria Mehemet Ali's domestic and foreign policies produced unanticipated repercussions in Palestine that greatly affected the Jews. By maintaining law and order, the Egyptian ruler encouraged an increasing number of pilgrims, explorers, and travelers to visit the Holy Land. By bestowing near-equal rights on the Christian and Jewish minorities, the Egyptians facilitated missionary activities in Palestine and permitted the British and Americans to set up the first permanent mission stations in Jerusalem. By seeking to curry favor with the European powers, Mehemet Ali allowed consuls greater freedom in utilizing the capitulation agreements, and in 1838 he approved the British decision to establish the first consulate in Jerusalem. Let us look more closely at the development of these three landmark events in Palestine: the promotion of travel for pilgrims, tourists, and explorers; the growth of mission activities; and the establishment of the first European consul in Jerusalem.

Even before Ibrahim Pasha imposed order in the Syrian towns and countryside, travelers and explorers began venturing to Palestine as a result of the increased interest in the Levant aroused by Napoleon's 1798–1799 expedition to Egypt and Palestine. Despite the prevailing dangers in the desolate Holy Land, travelers came to satisfy their curiosity and give expression to their spirit of wanderlust, to feel "the charm and intoxication of the land,"[1] and to learn about an exotic part of the world.

François Chateaubriand (1768–1848), the celebrated French romanticist, toured Palestine in 1806–1807 and poured out descriptions of the Holy Land in his "eloquent and superficial" book *Travels from Paris to Jerusalem*.[2] More famous for his rhetoric than for his accuracy, Chateaubriand, with a great splash of flowery words and flowing phrases, rhapsodized about the Jewish "nation":

> The Persians, the Greeks, the Romans, have vanished from the face of the earth; and one small nation, whose nativity preceded the birth of those great ones, still exists unsullied in race, on the ruins of its ancestral soil. If there is anything amongst the nations of the world marked with the stamp of the miraculous, this, in our opinion, is that miracle.[3]

Chateaubriand's book became a best seller and popularized Palestine among the early-nineteenth-century European reading public.

Two pioneer explorers who made significant discoveries about the history and geography of Palestine and gave new impetus to Palestine cartography and archeology were Ulrich J. Seetzen and Johann Lewis Burckhardt.[4]

Seetzen (1767–1811), a medical doctor, was possibly the most important explorer in the Holy Land during the first third of the nineteenth century, and to him we are indebted for information about the occupations of Jerusalem Jews. From 1802 onward, "Mussa," as Seetzen was called, lived in the Near East, learned the Arabic language and Muslim customs, and converted to Islam in order to facilitate his explorations. Seetzen was the pioneer explorer of the Gulf of Eilat and the Dead Sea and first identified Massada. In 1806–1807 he toured Jerusalem, Bethlehem, Hebron, Ramleh, Jaffa, Haifa, Nablus, and Nazareth. While in Yemen in 1811, Seetzen was murdered by robbers or poisoned by the imam. J. L. Burckhardt (1784–1817) was a Swiss explorer who traveled extensively during 1810–1812 in Syria and the Sinai. In order to allay suspicions of the local Muslims, "Sheikh Ibrahim" (Burckhart's nickname) spoke Arabic, wore Muslim dress, and played the varied roles of a doctor searching for plants with medicinal properties, a merchant selling gunpowder, and a Greek Orthodox monk stationed in Damascus.[5] Buckhardt has provided us with valuable observations about Safed, Tiberias, and the Galilee, but he did not tread the beaten path and never visited the coastal areas or Jerusalem, somewhat akin to visiting

Intrepid Swiss explorer Jean Louis Burckhardt, nicknamed "Sheikh Ibrahim," spoke Arabic, traveled in disguise as a Muslim, and posed as a doctor, gunpowder merchant, and priest of the Greek Orthodox Church.

England without seeing London.[6] Burckhardt's career was cut short in Cairo by fever that killed him in 1817, at the age of 33.[7]

When Ibrahim Pasha made possible safe travel on the roads of Palestine in the 1830s, travelers began to stream into the country. At the same time there was a quantum improvement in transportation on the Mediterranean

Sea. In the decade when railroads began operating in England and the United States, steamships started to ply the Mediterranean, promoting commerce and providing greater comfort, safety, and speed for passengers. Steamships significantly shrank the size of the world and had an impact on travel no less revolutionary than that of air transportation 100 years later.[8]

Steamship lines moving people and products on the Mediterranean were opened by the French, Russians, Italians, Austrians, and British. But most passengers and cargo were dispatched by sailboat to the shallow waters of Jaffa, Haifa, and Acre. Poor port facilities and the lack of a commercial hinterland prevented Palestine harbors from docking steamships and rivaling the importance of Beirut and Alexandria.

Steamboats were the major postal links between Palestine and Europe and accelerated the frequency of mail deliveries to once or twice a month. This was a major communications advancement, considering that Turkey launched the first postal system in the Ottoman Empire only in 1834.[9]

The major obstacle to speedy transportation in the Mediterranean was the quarantine system that impeded trade and travel.[10] Overland travel was also seriously hindered. One traveler from Cairo to Jerusalem was on the road for forty-three days, of which thirty-seven were spent in quarantine because of the incidence of epidemics. But traders and travelers frequently flouted the corruptly administered regulations of the Palestine quarantine stations set up in 1835–1836 in Jaffa and Haifa.[11]

At the start of the nineteenth century pilgrim traffic to Palestine was significantly reduced by the Napoleonic Wars,[12] insecure travel conditions on the Mediterranean, and the French Revolution's spirit of rationalism, which dampened religious fervor. Only 1,000–2,000 Christian pilgrims visited Palestine in 1806–1807, while 2,700–5,000 pilgrims journeyed to Palestine each year between 1815 and 1825.

A growing number of pilgrims wishing to endow their lives with religious significance visited Palestine after the Egyptian conquest ensured free access to the Christian holy sites in Jerusalem, Bethlehem, and Nazareth.[13] Each year thousands of Greek Catholics and Armenians came from Russia, Anatolia, Istanbul, Syria, Egypt, and the Aegean islands. Hundreds of European Roman Catholics and Jews also made pilgrimages to their Holy Land, as did many Muslims from the Turkish Empire. Some 5,000–15,000 pilgrims toured the country annually from 1825 to 1834. The year 1834 marked the zenith of such expeditions, when 15,000 pilgrims attended the tragic Holy Fire ceremony in Jerusalem. Between 1836 and 1840 the outbreak of chronic cholera epidemics and the periodic imposition of quarantines in Jerusalem and elsewhere drastically decreased the number of pilgrims to a few thousand a year.[14]

During the 1830s a "rage for travel" also seized affluent Europeans, who produced a plethora of travelogues. Some, like the bored Alexis de Tocqueville, invested inexhaustible energy on trips to the new, huge world of the United States. Others added Palestine to the itineraries of their fashionable continental Grand Tours. The sense of adventure and the balmy Englishman's penchant for dashing around Levantine lands prompted some sightseers to poke about the Holy Land. Many were fascinated by sites such as the Sea of Galilee, the Dead Sea, and the foreboding Sinai desert. In the vastness of the wilderness the majestic Sinai landscape moved travelers to humility and unity with God. Coupled with the unquenchable taste for seeking romance and history was the Christian interest in visiting "the scene of our Savior's sufferings" and following in the footsteps of the patriarchs and prophets.[15]

Although most European tourists were men of means and traveled in luxury, they nonetheless suffered the oppressive heat, droughts, mosquitoes, bugs, sandstorms, and the lethal plague.[16] Travel was less than a joy in a country where distances between towns were measured in hours and days of traveling on camels, donkeys, and mules. Riding from 7 A.M. to 4 P.M. through the pitiless Sinai desert, the artist David Roberts wrote that "thirty miles a-day, sitting on a camel, rather unfits me for sketching them."[17] One Jewish writer recorded (1856) the unexpressed feelings of many tourists:

A man, to enjoy travelling in the East, must have a frame of iron. Often the most beautiful scenes and the most interesting spots produce little impression on the traveller, when his blood is boiling in his veins with feverish heat, or his frame is worn out by excessive fatigue.[18]

Despite the ordeal of traveling, writers, soldiers, politicians, clergy, missionaries, and ladies of leisure were seized by a compulsion to see the Holy Land, regale friends with tales about the land of Jesus, and put quill to paper to record their impressions for posterity. Such an odd array of persons produced a blizzard of rapturous travel books for the receptive reading public. During the eighty-year period 1800 through 1879 about 2,000 new books streamed into the literature at the rate of 25 books a year,[19] compared to 1 book a year between 333 and 1800. This wave of travel books shaped the European frame of mind about the Holy Land, created an atmosphere of biblical nostalgia and fantasy, and conjured up a Levantine mystique.

Authors transplanted from their native countries the emotional set of tourists and pilgrims: religious notions, eccentric sensibilities, romantic illusions, and biblical visions of unfulfilled prophecies. Imaginative constraints of the writers frequently led them to describe their homeland more accurately than the places they visited. Many a writer described "not what he actually saw but what his age thought it natural to see."[20] Travelers projected dreams of the millennium on an imagined Holy Land. Programmed by books, myths, and expectations and laden with the predispositions of their national backgrounds and religious values, writers admired what they had been taught to believe in. They described Palestine as a backward Turkish province graced by historical holiness and crowned by the dazzling halo of Jerusalem. The Western eye determined what the authors saw, and European mental images limited what they could describe. Writers were also influenced by what others before them had reported, occasionally plagiarizing ideas, texts, and illustrations.[21]

Extremely differing descriptions of the same site were not uncommon. Compare Pastor Clarke's 1801 description of the Jerusalem that was "grandeur" and "inconceivable splendour,"[22] with that of Chateaubriand and most others who found nothing to compensate for the dullness of Jerusalem's exterior. Only a Disraeli could see both a "gorgeous city" and a "wild and terrible and barren" one.[23]

Unable to communicate in Arabic or Hebrew, writers neglected the "human geography" of Palestine.[24] Because travelers could not establish contacts with Muslims and Jews and knew nothing about the Egyptian government of occupation, or its Ottoman predecessors, their travel books contain many errors and considerable misleading information. The authors' ignorance was mingled with a spirit of arrogance and a cocksure feeling of superiority about their national tradition, European culture, and Christian religion.

The writers' fascination with the Muslim was only matched by their inability to understand the inscrutable local residents. Fellahin were regarded as noble savages, filthy but innocent children of nature, and a vestige of the medieval days. Europeans interpreted Muslim apathy and resignation as indolence, irresponsibility, deficient intelligence, and the "inertness of Oriental character."[25] Tourists knowingly proclaimed the truism that tropical heat debilitates the character of the natives, making their organism languid. This explained to Westeners the prevalence of fatalism, lack of ambition, "indifference to the progress of decay," and "unwillingness to repair the ravages of time." More perceptive observers, however, knew that passivity, inaction, and apparent laziness had been imposed upon the people by arbitrary officials who persecuted and brutalized them, causing the Muslims to accept their fate without aspiring to improve this situation. Muslims did not complain or think about instituting changes, because questioning the will of God was blasphemous.

Christian visitors to Palestine patronizingly viewed the poverty-stricken Jewish community as a philanthropic asylum supported by monied European Jews, and as a place of refuge for elderly, indigent people who came to spend their last days in the Holy Land before being buried in the Valley of Yehoshafat, outside the walls of Jerusalem. Since travelers could not penetrate the religious urges and emotional experiences of the insular Jewish community, they disdainfully viewed the Jews as pitiable fanatics and lazy idlers unwilling to earn their living and content to dream about their vanished splendor.

Among the travelogue authors were several distinguished explorers and writers who documented their discoveries in Palestine and described the Jews in Eretz Israel.

Benjamin Disraeli (1804–1881), visited Jerusalem for one week in February 1831 during his sixteen-month Grand Tour of the Mediterranean. On approaching Jerusalem, Disraeli "was thunderstruck. I saw before me . . . a gorgeous city. Nothing can be conceived more wild, and terrible, and barren than the surrounding scenery, dark, stony and severe. . ." This "beautiful and sublime" scene was the view from the Mount of Olives rather than the more prosaic entrance to Jerusalem through the Jaffa gate. Although Disraeli proudly identified with Jews and "aggressively" boasted about the superiority of the Jewish people, his letter from Jerusalem does not mention visiting Jewish religious sites or making contact with Jews or Arabs, possibly explaining his peculiar comment that "Arabs are only Jews on horseback."[26]

The future British prime minister's visit to Palestine left an indelible impression upon him, colored his views on British imperial foreign policy, and provided him with material for his romantic-exotic novels. *Alroy* (1833), *Tancred* (1847), and *Coningsby* were filled with purple prose telling tales about a Jewish *Arabian Nights*. In *Alroy* Disraeli revealed religious fervor and projected a glorious vision of the Jewish nation by making the High Priest declare:

You ask me what I wish: my answer is a national existence, which we have not. You asked me what I wish: my answer is, the Land of Promise.

You ask me what I wish: my answer is, Jerusalem. You ask me what I wish: my answer is, The Temple, all we have forfeited, all we have yearned after, all for which we have fought, our beauteous country, our holy creed, our simple manners, and our ancient customs.[27]

One of the most famous dreamers who ever toured Palestine was Alphonse de Lamartine (1790–1869), French poet and politician. In his *Souvenirs and Impressions*,[28] Lamartine's imagination orbited at the same rarefied height as that of Disraeli's David Alroy. Both called for the establishment of a Christian state in Palestine. Now that the Turks had been pushed out of Palestine, Lamartine called on the great European powers to grant Jews the "political advantages of peace and freedom." This proposal was acidly greeted by the semiofficial organ of the British Foreign Office, which wrote in 1840:

M. de Lamartine intends to found a Christian kingdom at the sources of the Jordan and at the foot of Mount Lebanon. . . . But what is odd in the whole affair is that Lord Palmerston has chosen the same spot. Where the celebrated Deputy dreams of a Christian state, Lord Palmerston projects a Jewish Republic.[29]

The notion of establishing a state for the Jews in Palestine—not the Jews establishing their own country—was echoed by a future bishop of Glasgow[30] who visited Palestine in 1830 and by Lord A. W. Lindsay, a Holy Land tourist in 1838.

An account of Palestine after its conquest by Mehemet Ali was written by Marie Joseph de Géramb, an Austrian baron and officer in the Napoleonic Wars who later became a Trappist monk.[31] During his 1832 visit to Jerusalem de Géramb noted that the Jews believed Mehemet Ali was "destined to rescue them from slavery, and to ensure them brighter prospects." When? "Cursed be he who computes the days of the Messiah," he was answered.

De Géramb was nauseated by the filthy Jewish quarter and by the "wretched and disgusting appearance" of the Sephardi synagogue. He observed that Jews were neatly dressed, polite, industrious, and educated in contrast to the impertinent, indolent, ignorant Muslims. De Géramb understood the Jews' "anxiety to conceal their riches . . . in a country ruled by the despotic will of a pacha, who never perceives any thing illegal in extortion and oppression." On the Sabbath he reported that veiled Jewish women dressed up and displayed "a sort of luxury." As a devout Christian, de Géramb could not bring himself to believe that only on the threat of "the severest penalties" including "death itself" could Jews pass near the Church of the Holy Sepulchre. He admired the Jews' "profound respect for the Old Testament" and Jewish educational achievements but he felt pity for a people

> Obliged to submit to the most terrible punishment that ever befell a guilty people, and stubbornly resolved not to acknowledge his crime, he would cease to be of his religion, if he were to cease to expect. Hence, look at him in history, look at him at the present day: always disappointed, he still continues to hope.[32]

In 1835 a future Russian minister for the enlightenment of the nation, Abraham S. Norov, visited Palestine and wrote his book about the Holy Land. Although able to speak Hebrew, Norov met but a few Jews during the month he stayed in Jerusalem and wrote unflatteringly about them: "The strong greedy appetite of this people appears to be less prominent in Jerusalem although most of the Jews here are craftsmen or traders in the market."[33] Norov mistakenly reported that Jews pay Muslims a large sum in exchange for permission to pray at the Wailing Wall, a practice discontinued by Ibrahim Pasha three years before Norov visited Jerusalem.

John Lloyd Stephens (1805–1852), "the greatest of American travel writers,"[34] was a lawyer-writer with a spirit of adventure who visited Palestine in 1836. Stephens wrote a brash, colorful best seller that is seriously flawed by many errors resulting from his soaring imagination and his not taking notes on his travels.[35] Later Stephens was to achieve fame by discovering the Mayan civilization during his explorations in the Yucatán.

In his book *Incidents of Travel in Egypt, Arabia Petraea and the Holy Land* Stephens described the adventures of one of the first explorers of the Dead Sea, the "rash, romantic" Christopher Costigin, a courageous 25-year-old Irishman.[36] During the month of August 1835 Costigin explored the Dead Sea, the lowest point on earth, and one of the most hellishly hot places on the globe. Since many parts of the Jordan River are mere trickles of a stream during the summer, Costigin transported his boat overland past Jericho to the northern end of the Dead Sea. This did not prevent Stephens from writing that Costigin sailed down the Jordan and "narrowly escaped with his life among the rocks and rapids . . ."

For eight days Costigin sailed in his open boat on the Dead Sea taking depth soundings. Under a fiercely blazing sun and in mind-melting temperatures of 110 degrees, Costigin ran out of water and collapsed (Stephens wrote that Costigin "was thoroughly prepared [for this voyage] with all the knowledge necessary for exploring it to advantage"). An Arab messenger from Jericho summoned help from the Jerusalem-based Anglican missionary John Nicolayson, not from the Latin monks, who "showed little sympathy" toward European Catholics.

There being no available "medical man" in Jerusalem, Nicolayson promptly set out for Jericho and succeeded in returning Costigin to Jerusalem, where he was treated by the pasha's doctor "who happened to be here." Two days later the ill-fated Irishman "breathed his last."

Based on talks with Costigin's servant, Stephens drew a map of Costigin's journey on the Dead Sea. The scholar Edward Robinson wrote in a footnote that this Dead Sea map "has little resemblance to that sea, except in being longer than it is broad."

In 1837 two German tourists visited Palestine and reported about the state of the country and the situation in Tiberias and Safed immediately after the 1837 earthquake. Johann N. Visino, a German military pastor, wrote a book in the familiar format of letters and told the stories of the Tiberias and Safed Jewish survivors. During his visit to Jerusalem Visino showed pity for the poor Jews worshipping in their "dirty, decrepit synagogue." He reflected the stereotyped attitudes of many Christian pilgrims toward the Jews when he wrote: "It is a shame that stubborn rejection [of Christianity] and running after money that knows no bounds clouds the capabilities, excellent in most cases, of this wonderful nation."

The second German tourist was Herman von Pückler-Muskau (1785–1871), who had met Moshe Sachs in Tunis in 1835.[37] Von Pückler visited Tiberias just after the January 1 earthquake. He discussed Jesus with the Jews of Tiberias and bemoaned the fact that both Jews and Christians maintained the same religious prejudices they had 1,900 years before. After some talks he concluded that it was hopeless to discuss Christianity with Jews.

Despite the hardships of journeying to Palestine, two highborn, strong-spirited British women, Mrs. G. L. Dawson Damer and Lady Francis Egerton, visited the Holy Land during 1840 and recorded their impressions.[38] Lady Egerton reported that many Jews believed they were living in fateful times because 1840 was the year God had destined for the restoration of the Jewish people to their land of Zion. "The Jews . . . looked to us as the probable nation upon whom the possession of this country will devolve." Yet Lady Egerton "cannot think the Jews will be restored as a nation, until they are converted to the Christian faith." Noting that the Jews were in the same moral state as at the time of Jesus, she reported that when Jews could not "confute" the arguments of a missionary they "usually drowned his voice by clamour." She mistakenly wrote that John Nicolayson had "never made one convert" during his fifteen years in Palestine.

The Hon. Mrs. G. L. Dawson Damer wrote that the Jewish year that ended in September 1840 had been a catastrophic one for the Jews.[39] Since 1840 was declared to be the year of Redemption, Jews in Eretz Israel looked forward with complete faith, hope, and ecstasy to the coming of the Messianic Era. Jews were so confident that this apocalyptic event would take place that, according to Mrs. Dawson Damer's apocryphal story, 30,000 Jews petitioned the czar "for permission to migrate to the Holy Land." When the Messiah failed to arrive the Jews were so deflated that "a good many Jews left Jerusalem." In the opinion of Mrs. Dawson Damer, the Messiah had not come because Jews rejected the Redeemer.

Dawson Damer like Egerton noted the incongruity of the rich costumes worn by the Jews during the holidays and their shabby appearance during the weekdays. She reported that the Jews live in "misery and desolation" and the Muslims are "suspicious and uncultured."

Mrs. Dawson Damer, like Visino and Russian consul Basili,[40] wrote that the hatred between Muslims and Jews was much more intense than the antagonism between Jews and Christians. This commonly accepted but incorrect idea was refuted by the British vice-consul, W. T. Young, who knew that "the prejudice of the Christian against the Jews in Jerusalem amounted to a fanaticism . . ." Young wrote that "if a Jew were to attempt to pass the door of the Church of the Holy Sepulchre, it would in all probability cost him his life—this is not very Christian-like, considering Christ Himself was a Jew." The Scottish ministers visiting Jerusalem in 1839 observed that "the professing Christians here—Greeks, Armenians and Roman Catholics—are even more bitter enemies to Jews than Mahometans: a Jew would betake himself to the house of a Turk for refuge, in preference to that of a Christian . . ."[41] The ministers grieved over "how little have the Christians the mind of Christ!" That the relations between Jews and Muslims were better than between Jews and Christians was attested by Jews living in the Muslim quarter, while none dared reside in the Christian quarter.

In contrast to Visino, who found the Jews "running after money," and de Géramb, who wrote that the Jew is an "indefatigable" worker at "all trades, of all professions . . . I have not seen a Jew asking for charity," Mrs. Dawson Damer found that Jews were lazy and "to beg they are not ashamed." She showed contempt for rabbis imposing "general tyranny" on the Jewish population, and she decried the kehilla regulations that forbade overseas relatives from inheriting the property of the deceased in Jerusalem. For Mrs. Dawson Damer another indication of the dictatorial rabbinical rule was the interception of correspondence by Sephardi agents, which led Jews to use the mail services of the British vice-consul and the English missionaries. A "strict... police" is maintained over Jews with "European connections." The Scottish ministers also reported that "the rabbis sometimes intercept the letters of poor Jews, which they fear may be complaining of their conduct."[42]

Mrs. Dawson Damer constructively suggested that part of the mission funds should be allocated to provide Jews with medical services by bringing a doctor to Jerusalem. To alleviate the poverty of the poor Jews, she advocated distributing to them "soup, bread, and biscuits" and warm clothing, as practiced in England.[43]

Travel books also provide us with romantic, idyllic drawings of the biblical landscape and sites. This is the legacy of the most famous artist who visited Palestine in the 1830s, David Roberts. Other artists had visited Palestine, but their charming drawings were simple illustrations for travel books rather than pictures on an artistic level.

The Scottish painter David Roberts (1796–1864) was inspired by the travelogues and sketches of tourists visiting Palestine as well as by his own Mediterranean tours of Spain and Morocco. Roberts was also influenced by the great British artist William Turner (1775–1851). Although Turner never visited Palestine, he contributed twenty-six watercolors to *Landscape Illustrations of the Bible* (1836), to which Roberts added twelve of his own illustrations. Turner's watercolors were so evocative that fellow artist Sir David Wilkie wrote from his Easter pilgrimage to Jerusalem in 1841:

> I thought of him [Turner] when I passed the ancient city of Jericho. . . . I can fancy what our friend would make of this and the Vale of Jordan, of the Dead Sea, the Wilderness of the Temptation and above all, the Mount of Olives, Mount of the Ascension . . .[44]

During 1838–1839 Roberts visited Egypt and crossed the Sinai wilderness in nineteen days before arriving at the small fortress of Akaba (Eilat) on the Red Sea. A number of times Roberts referred in his journal to the journey of Moses and the Jews through the Sinai desert, but the true inspiration for his trip was Jesus. To Roberts the Jews were an important but

Jewish pilgrims outside Jaffa. The only picture of Jews painted by David Roberts.

ossified fact of history and he drew them in only one picture, showing pilgrims at Jaffa about to return to Poland.

In Palestine Roberts first visited Hebron for two days and erroneously reported that four Jewish families lived in the town, rather than the 400–450 Jews residing in the Jewish quarter. Then he traveled to the coastal towns of Gaza and Jaffa because Jerusalem was quarantined by the plague. He finally arrived in Jerusalem on Good Friday, just as the quarantine was lifted. With the Jerusalem governor, armed soldiers, and 4,000 Christian pilgrims, Roberts visited the Dead Sea and watched pilgrims dipping themselves ecstatically in the Jordan River.

> The scene in the river was most exciting. Young and old, male and female, were in the stream in one promiscuous mass—some nude, some slightly dressed. The dresses I was told were taken home, and reserved for the funeral shrouds of the wearers. One poor young Greek was drowned and many others narrowly escaped the same fate.[45]

Pictures by artists and descriptions by writers were the only ways of capturing views of the Holy Land until 1839. This situation changed with the invention of photography and its ability to preserve the miracle of the moment. The new photographic process was labeled the "Pencil of Nature" or "the Art of Photogenic Drawing, or, The process by which natural objects may be made to delineate themselves without the aid of the artist's pencil" (the title of a book and essay by Henry Talbott Fox, the inventor of the positive-negative process of photography).

During the winter of 1839 the French painter Horace Vernet and his nephew lugged bulky photographic equipment from Egypt to Jerusalem in order to capture the Holy City on film. These photographers used the daguerreotype process to record only scenery; no person could sit still for the twenty-five minutes required to snap one exposure. In his book, Vernet described his method of photographing:

> A steady rain accompanied me nearly everywhere but did not prevent me from taking a number of pictures. A picture of the walls from the Citadel area seemed to me to be especially appropriate. . . . I approached the nearest hill and aimed my "black room" at the desired angle. After investigating the site I found small stones that helped me stabilize the camera because one has to find an especially stable place like a portrait painter who sits himself opposite the subject he is immortalizing: frequently the view that actually looks perfect produces a most terrible pic-

ture. . . . On the Camera is attached a mirror intended to guide the amateur to correctly evaluate the results. The hour I aimed my camera there was a strong wind that disturbed its equilibrium and blurred the picture. Much to my chagrin, two Jews walked back and forth before the lens of the camera without my being able to explain to them the trouble they were causing me. When they approached me I motioned them to go away but to no avail. One of them starts laughing and deliberately stands in front of my lens to annoy me.[46]

The advent of the camera established new visual habits for the viewer. An accurate photograph recalling the past aroused poignant nostalgic memories. The idyllic image on canvas was now replaced by a new pictorial perspective that caught a literal representation of Palestine in its bare desolation and Jerusalem in its forlorn ruins. These dull, somber pictures are completely different from the colorful lithographs and engravings of the same period produced by Roberts and other artists.

The most significant explorer of Palestine during the first half of the nineteenth century was Edward Robinson (1794–1863).[47] Before taking up the position of professor of biblical literature at the New York Theological Seminary (today called the Union Theological Seminary of New York), Robinson toured Palestine in 1838 and earned his nickname "Old Waddy" because of the frequent references in his books to wadis or dry watercourses in the desert. He wrote:

My first motive in exploring Palestine was simply the gratification of personal feelings. . . . I had long meditated the preparation of a work on Biblical geography, and wished to satisfy myself by personal observation as to points on which I could find no information in the books of travellers.[48]

Out of such a modest motive was born *Biblical Researches in Palestine, Mt. Sinai, and Arabia Petrea in 1838*, a classic of clear, condensed writing, meticulous scholarship, and academic honesty. Although Robinson wrote the two volumes of *Biblical Researches*, his generosity of spirit moved him to grant co-author credits to his "pupil and friend," Eli Smith, an Orientalist and American missionary stationed in Beirut who accompanied Robinson on his Palestinian journey.

In March 1838 Robinson and Smith left Cairo bound for their two-and-a-half month exploration in Palestine. They crossed the Sinai desert to Akaba, journeyed through the Negev, and visited Hebron, Gaza, the Dead

American professor of biblical literature Dr. Edward Robinson was the most important explorer of Palestine from 1800 to 1850

Sea, the Jordan Valley, and Jerusalem. Energetic, indefatigable travelers, Robinson and Smith could start their journey at 2:15 in the morning and ride their camels for sixteen hours straight, arriving at their Jerusalem destination at 6 P.M. The next morning at 9 they explored the Church of the Holy Sepulchre and witnessed the Easter ceremonies.

In Jerusalem Robinson and Smith were guests of the two resident American missionaries, George Whiting and John Lanneau. Robinson explored the city in depth, discovered Robinson's Arch near the Wailing Wall, and was the first to report on the Siloam tunnel. He concluded that the Church of the Holy Sepulchre was "not the real place of the crucifixion and resurrection of our Lord,"[49] thereby inviting attacks on himself for destroying traditional religious dogma and convent legends.

Robinson charted a map of Palestine that was a model for similar maps. Robinson and Smith measured the length and width of the Dead Sea and correctly located the biblical site of Beersheba. They identified biblical ruins and confirmed the historicity of the Bible. Based on their knowledge of Palestine's history and geography, they discovered many instances where the Arabic names of locations transmitted the Hebrew names of the sites mentioned in the Bible. Contrary to the revolutionary conclusions of Charles Darwin, who had recently returned from his epic five-year voyage abroad the HMS *Beagle*, Robinson found biblical accounts to be credible and verifiable. Biblical sites tallied with his on-the-spot topographical and archaeological observations. Therefore he concluded that a literal reading of the Bible was an accurate guide for Palestinian geography and history. Note his sweeping dictum that

> all ecclesiastical tradition respecting ancient places in and around Jerusalem and throughout Palestine is of no value, except so far as it is supported by circumstances known from the Scriptures, or from other contemporary testimony.[50]

So outstanding were Robinson's achievements in the fields of physical geography, geology, natural history, and archaeology that the prestigious Royal Geographical Society of London awarded to this American its coveted gold medal for his two pioneering works. Robinson's books "serve as a beacon for all future explorers,"[51] and to this day they are avidly studied.

Explorers and travel writers have discovered significant facts about Palestine and provided us with interesting observations about the Jews. Although many travelogues are superficial and misleading, "they have contributed much that was new," enriched us with invaluable *Souvenirs and Impressions,* and enlarged our understanding of Palestine and its people in the first half of the nineteenth century.

THIRTEEN

Missionary Activities in the 1830s

❖

The peace established in Palestine under Egypt's rule, coupled with Mehemet Ali's tolerant policies toward the minorities, led to the establishment of the first missionary stations in Jerusalem. In the words of the Anglican missionary John Nicolayson, "only when the Egyptian forces headed by Ibrahim Pasha first entered Palestine could I really settle down in Jerusalem . . ."[1] Missionaries were strictly forbidden to work among the Muslims, but the authorities "viewed with indifference" conversion activities among the Jews and Christians.[2] This new situation allowed the London Jews Society (LJS) and the American Board of Commissioners for Foreign Missions to advance from survey and reconnaissance activities to the establishment of permanent Protestant mission stations in Jerusalem, where they conducted open but circumspect efforts to convert Jews and Catholic Arabs.

John Nicolayson was designated the English missionary responsible for "Syria and Palestine" after the irrepressible Joseph Wolff left the LJS in 1830, "not being able to fetter himself by regulations in any way, or to consider himself as a man under authority."[3] In the summer of 1831, before Ibrahim Pasha conquered Palestine, Nicolayson visited Safed, Tiberias, and Jerusalem, which he had last seen four years before.

Nicolayson had been preceded in Safed by S. Farman, a Christianized Jew who spent six weeks meeting with R. Israel of Shklov, Moshe Finzi (the English consular agent), Gershon Margolit (leader of the Hasidim), and other Jews. Moshe Finzi told Farman that 2,000 Jews lived in Safed: 1,200 Sephardim prayed in four synagogues, 550 Hasidim in one synagogue and two study halls, and 250 Perushim in "one large synagogue." Farman dined with a Jewish family who "exhorted [him] to become a true Jew." He discussed biblical topics with Gershon Margolit and reported perennial complaints against Margolit's manner of distributing the haluka. From such discontent Farman generalized that European funds are "sent to the rabbis, who embezzle and lie. The people, each one to get a greater proportion, lie in their turn."[4]

Three weeks after Farman arrived in Safed the rabbis forbade Jews from meeting with him. He complained that even Moshe Finzi "rarely comes to me now, and when he does come, he says, I cannot speak with you about religion..." Finzi and other Jews told Farman that "the rabbis say that the Messiah will certainly come within eight years..." Farman reported that "several" Russian families came to Safed anticipating the advent of the Messiah. At the end of August Farman was joined in Safed by Nicolayson, who also noted the "disposition of the Jews to return to Palestine, in expectation of the Messiah,"[5] and the fact that the Jews were as reluctant as ever to engage in a religious discussion.

Nicolayson and Farman visited Tiberias, bathed in the Sea of Galilee, visited the study halls of the Hasidim and Sephardim, and found the Sephardim "more open and conversant" than the Hasidim. The English missionaries "called on Mr. Levi, a rich English Jew from Gibraltar who has lately come with his family to this country to await the coming of the Messiah, or to lay his bones in holy ground." After one day in Tiberias the English missionaries spent a few days in Nazareth and Jerusalem, where the excommunication against Wolff still applied to all missionaries. Returning to Beirut, Nicolayson considered obtaining "a footing" in Safed or Sidon or joining the Americans in forming a Jerusalem station.[6]

In October 1831 Nicolayson hoped that Palestine would soon come "into our hands" and added that "the Lord will provide in due time." Within one month "due time" arrived, as Ibrahim Pasha swept through Palestine and subdued the country.[7]

With the British government's firm support and protecting prestige, the LJS was the first mission group to take full advantage of the tolerant religious policies of Mehemet Ali. LJS was not deterred by the situation in Jerusalem, where "the Turk has his mosque, and the Jew his synagogue. The pure Christianity of the Reformation alone appears as a stranger." When it became evident that Mehemet Ali was, in fact, willing to grant freedom of religious practice to the Christian and Jewish minorities, Nicolayson went back to Jerusalem in January and again in April 1833 "to make arrangements for a permanent settlement in that city."[8]

In January 1833 Nicolayson visited the Jewish synagogues and noted the "affecting contrast" between the "small, cold, wretched" study hall of the Perushim and the "magnificent temple" where the Jewish multitude once assembled in "splendid worship." It appeared to Nicolayson that "the religious light and feeling enjoyed by the ancients" was replaced by "the darkness and sadness which rest upon the present worshipers."[9]

During his two weeks in Jerusalem Nicolayson was assisted by the lay missionary Mr. Erasmus Scott Calman, "a Christian Israelite" (a euphemism for a converted Jew), who helped Nicolayson gain access to the Jewish community.[10] More proficient in Hebrew than Nicolayson, Calman took the lead in engaging Jews in conversation about religion. However, as a Polish-born Jew, he could not converse with the Sephardi Jews because of the great difference between Sephardi and Ashkenazi Hebrew pronunciations. So the missionaries concentrated their attention on the Jerusalem Ashkenazim, nearly all of them Perushim. But discussing religion with the Perushim was most difficult. While displaying cordiality toward the missionaries, Perushim evaded discussion despite persistent, "repeated attempts" by the missionaries.[11]

Nicolayson and Calman succeeded in talking with some Jews in their study hall about "a great variety of subjects."[12] When Nicolayson and one Aryeh Halevi could not clearly express themselves due to "the difference of our dialects" Moshe Sachs translated for them.

A number of times Nicolayson discussed religious topics with the rich merchant Joseph Amzalag.[13] After their talk Amzalag lent the missionaries "a rare Hebrew work." Now Nicolayson was deeply impressed by Amzalag, who until then had appeared to him as "the most callous and indifferent Jew that ever I met with."

The missionaries also spoke with R. Nathan Neta, son of R. Menahem Mendel of Shklov, but "the rabbi . . . endeavored to keep the course of conversation upon general subjects." When Calman persisted in trying to talk about religious subjects, "the rabbi rose and begged to be excused, it being time to go to the 'minha' [written in Hebrew] afternoon service." On another visit, R. Nathan Neta received the missionaries with "much civility" and invited Nicolayson to spend the Sabbath at his house.[14] When horrified Jews learned about this invitation they forced R. Nathan Neta to withdraw his offer of hospitality.

Undaunted and ever-believing—"our reception at Jerusalem had been quite beyond our expectation"—Nicolayson was "deeply convinced of the high importance of having a mission to the Jews" in Jerusalem. Amzalag urged Nicolayson "very much to take up residence here," and Nicolayson encouraged Amzalag to find him a residence in the Jewish quarter "where inquiring Jews may freely come."[15] Regretfully, Nicolayson temporarily left Jerusalem due to previous commitments and "family considerations."

Nicolayson and Calman briefly visited Tiberias, where "the rabbis had announced excommunication against whosoever should receive us." Nevertheless Jews spoke with the missionaries in a civil manner in the home of the Hasidic chief rabbi, but kept "aloof" from religious subjects. During a Torah study session the determined missionaries frequently tried to guide the discussion toward their Christian viewpoint. Each time, the chief rabbi interrupted their conversation by loudly singing Hasidic melodies. Finally "one of the rabbis got so enraged" at the missionaries' behavior "that he ordered" them "out of the room."[16]

In Safed the missionaries were "at a loss of lodging" because Moshe Finzi was out of town and every Jewish home was crowded "in consequence of the fall of more than one hundred houses from the snow and rain." Finally they were housed in an office belonging to Israel Bak, "the printer," with whom they had "much interesting conversation," and thanked him for his "friendship and affection."[17] Calman conducted discussions with "many" Jews, particularly a Jewish tourist from Poland and a German Jew bound for Cairo, neither of whom were members of the local community or subject to its discipline.

The missionaries were "very kindly" received by the Hasidic leader Gershon Margolit, who tried to bring Mr. Calman back to Judaism "not by arguments, but by promises of comfortable settlement, marriage . . ." Attending a Jewish wedding ceremony provided the missionaries with another opportunity for meeting with Jews. On another occasion they were disappointed by the "remarkable fact that on the Sabbath the Jews do not like to enter into religious discussions." However, at the end of the Sabbath the missionaries initiated a discussion with Jews that lasted from 8 P.M. until 1:30 in the morning, when it abruptly ended as the oil in the lamp was consumed "leaving us in the dark."[18] After twelve days in Safed Nicolayson returned to his family in Beirut and planned to set up a permanent mission station in Jerusalem.

One month later Nicolayson returned to Jerusalem for the Easter celebration, in the company of the recently arrived 28-year-old American missionary William Thomson, who had been instructed to establish an American mission station.[19] Nicolayson promptly called on Amzalag and was assured that once the "throng of pilgrims" left town he would find a good house for Nicolayson near his own home.

On the last day of Passover Nicolayson visited the Sephardi synagogues and the "one small" synagogue of the Perushim, whom he continued to call the "German Jews." Nicolayson compared the Ashkenazi and Sephardi Jews and found that

> there is a very considerable difference in the external manners between the two classes in their worship. Those of the Spanish have much more appearance of solemnity and those of the German more of zeal and warmth and vehemence of feeling.[20]

In Jerusalem, as in Tiberias, Nicolayson found Sephardim more "friendly and social" than Ashkenazim. Interestingly this runs counter to Dr. Dalton's conclusion in 1825 that the Jerusalem Sephardim displayed more aggressiveness and unfriendliness to the missionaries than the Perushim.

In contrast to Nicolayson's numerous Jewish contacts and his references to the Jews, Thomson's published journal entries tell about celebrating Palm Sunday and visiting the Holy Sepulchre, Jericho, the Jordan River, and the Dead Sea, with nary a mention of the Jews of Jerusalem.

Before leaving Jerusalem Nicolayson signed a rental contract for the residence of the first permanent mission. He felt greatly indebted to Amzalag, the "first to invite and encourage me to settle here, and the chief instrument in securing us this suitable lodging."[21] On his way back to Beirut for the purpose of transferring his family to Jerusalem, Nicolayson visited Tiberias and Safed with Thomson. In Tiberias they visited two synagogues and observed 80 Ashkenazim and 150 Sephardim in prayer; this would indicate that the Sephardim were double the number of Ashkenazim and that about 1,000 Jews lived in town.

By May Nicolayson had returned to Beirut and arranged to move his family to Jerusalem. Despite opposition from the American Roman Catholic churches in Jerusalem, in October 1833 Nicolayson established the first permanent Protestant mission station in Jerusalem. LJS wrote effusively of the "high privilege reserved to our church and nation to plant the Cross on the Holy Hill of Zion . . . to light such a candle in Jerusalem as by God's blessing shall never be put out."[22]

The English mission station in Jerusalem, located in the Armenian quarter where "Jews may freely come,"[23] was staffed by Nicolayson, S. Farman, and E. S. Calman, who focused their attention on converting Jews. Mission members distributed Old and New Testaments and religious tracts in Hebrew and other languages. Rather than attracting potential converts, the distribution of mission Bibles provoked most Jews, who burned and defaced them.

To make a "direct and vigorous attack upon the grand stronghold of Rabbinism, the Talmud," Nicolayson suggested writing tracts and printing them on a small press. In this way he hoped to develop a written dialogue with the "learned rabbies" who refused "descending into the arena of discussion" and retired "into the impenetrable recess of mystical contemplation secured with the hermetical seal of silence."[24] Despite Nicolayson's championing the "necessity of a Printing shop," for lack of a master printer no mission press operated in Jerusalem during the 1830s.

In 1835 Nicolayson entertained the notion of establishing a mission school for Jewish children, as he had suggested for Safed in 1826. Nicolayson tried but failed to establish for ten Aleppo families a school that would have taught the traditional Jewish curriculum, with missionaries being granted "free access to it at any time." A mission school proved impossible to implement in Jerusalem; no Jew would dare dream of sending his child to a Christian institution. In 1840 Nicolayson sadly concluded that even a school for the children of the converts is "not near."[25]

Lacking a Protestant church in Jerusalem, the first LJS place of worship was opened in Nicolayson's house in the Armenian quarter, near the citadel and bordering on the edge of the Jewish quarter. This was an ideal location—close and accessible to the Jews without settling provocatively in their midst. At prayer services Nicolayson preached to a small number of convinced Christians, with hardly a glimpse of a Jew in attendance. Only Jews visiting Jerusalem "occasionally attend the service."[26]

Jewish leaders warned their members to stay far from the missionaries and to avoid religious disputes. A ban was imposed on Jews having contact with the persistent and persevering missionaries. But this ban was only partially effective, because the intelligent, humane, and knowledgeable LJS missionaries held a strange, forbidden fascination for the Jews. It was temptingly difficult for Jews not to answer missionaries able to address them in German and Hebrew. "We cannot resist the holy language,"[27] Jews told an Englishman.

Missionaries did not preach in public for fear of arousing clamorous opposition. They discreetly engaged individual Jews in discussions about religious subjects by walking about the Jewish quarter, waiting outside a Hebrew bookshop, and visiting the schools and synagogues, especially on Jewish holidays. It was not demeaning for the dignified Nicolayson "to

Christ Church. John Nicolayson purchased the land in 1839, started to build the church in 1840, and consecrated it in 1848.

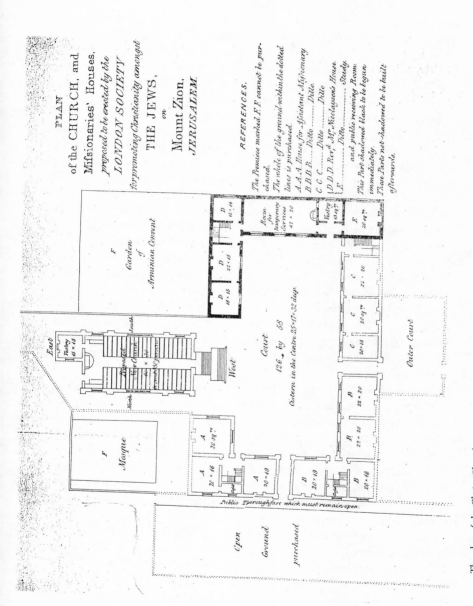

PLAN

of the CHURCH, and
Missionaries' Houses,
proposed to be erected by the
LONDON SOCIETY
for promoting Christianity amongst
THE JEWS,
on
Mount Zion,
JERUSALEM.

REFERENCES.

The Premises marked F.F. cannot be pur-
chased.
The whole of the ground within the dotted
lines is purchased.
A.A.A. House for Assistant Missionary
B.B.B.B. Ditto ___ Ditto ___ Ditto
C.C.C. Ditto ___ Ditto ___ Ditto
D.D.D. Rev.d Mr. Nicolayson's House
E. ___ Ditto ___ Ditto ___ Study.
and public receiving Room
That Part shadowed black to be begun
immediately.
Those Parts not-shadowed to be built
afterwards.

Mosque

F
Garden
of
Armenian Convent

F

East

Vestry
15 × 18

Proposed
New Church
42 × 34

South

North

West

Court
126. by 58

Cistern in the Centre 25 × 17 × 3½ deep.

A
20. sq.r.

A
22 × 16

A
20 × 19

B
22 × 20

B
20 × 19

B
22 × 20

B
20 × 16

Open
Ground
purchased

Public Thoroughfare which must remain open.

D
18 × 14

D
22 × 18

D
18 × 15

Room
for
temporary
Services
42 × 20

Vestry
16 × 9½

E
20 × 9½

C C C
22 × 20

C C C
20 × 9½

C
20 × 16

Outer Court

The plan of the Christ Church compound and homes for the missionaries proposed in 1840 by the London Society for promoting Christianity amongst the Jews, on Mt. Zion, Jerusalem.

search out the Jews" and literally chase after them. When admonished by Jews to "let us alone, we want none of your instruction," Nicolayson replied, "No, my friend, I cannot let you alone,"[28] for it grieved his heart to see Jews straying from the Christian truth.

Frequent quarantines that prevented Jews from leaving their homes and strolling in the streets disrupted mission activities. "Scarcely anybody stirs out of his house," Nicolayson complained during the 1834 plague.[29] Nevertheless, missionaries succeeded in speaking with Jews by writing letters for them in foreign languages. An additional incentive for both Ashkenazim and Sephardim to talk with missionaries was their willingness to post letters for Jews through the mail services of the mission, thereby circumventing community censorship of Jewish correspondence.

Jews whom the missionaries met were invited to Nicolayson's house, and, "notwithstanding frequent disappointments," the missionaries invited themselves to the homes of the Jews. If a Jewish acquaintance fell ill, the missionaries visited him at home and offered medical advice, as when Nicolayson visited Bergmann, who in May 1836 had "been long suffering from fever and ague." During such visits missionaries politely derided the faults in Jewish tradition and the fallacies of certain Jewish religious practices. Nicolayson attempted to convince a rabbi that at Purim time a Jew was literally "duty bound to become [so] intoxicated." He criticized the traditional Ashkenazi practice of killing a fowl as a sacrament of atonement the day before Yom Kippur, unaware that Sephardim also "strongly opposed this custom."[30]

Selected Jewish community leaders such as Amzalag, Sachs, Bergmann, Schwartz, Zoref, R. Bardaki, and Sephardi rabbis met with the missionaries. Only learned Jews considered beyond the temptations of conversion were permitted, usually in pairs, to talk with the missionaries. Normally Jews kept the conversation to general subjects "so as to avoid direct discussion." Sachs was one of the few Jews brash enough to dispute theological matters with Nicolayson. Another topic Sachs discussed with Nicolayson, after returning from his three and a half years in Europe, was the "plan for agriculture which he has in view for the Jews here." Nicolayson wrote that Sachs "burdened me to obtain the support of the new English Vice Consul in Jerusalem but I could do nothing for him that way." Details about the "plan for agriculture" remain for us as nebulous as ever.[31]

When Nicolayson visited Sachs on Passover he was received by both Sachs and Schwartz with "the warmest friendship and goodwill." Sachs told Nicolayson that Joseph Schwartz "laughs at Rabbi Nathan's authority, being independent of him" by virtue of receiving financial support from his family in Germany. After studying "Scriptural geography" with Schwartz, Nicolayson concluded that this was "an excellent substitute for Talmudic reveries" and would force Jews to use "sober reason and sound interpretation."[32]

Nicolayson's most frequent contact with the Jewish community was through his neighbor Joseph Amzalag. They conversed in both Hebrew and English on general topics, current events, and religious subjects. When discussions got out of hand, Amzalag cut them off by confessing "ignorance of Talmudic learning." After one religious discussion, Nicolayson concluded that "the stronger light of the New Testament is excluded" from Amzalag "by insurmountable prejudices." Amzalag frowned on religious discussions between Jews and missionaries, so when a Jew tried to talk with Nicolayson about "the time of the Messiah's coming," the authoritative Amzalag "put a stop to it by sending him away."[33]

These close contacts mutually benefited both Nicolayson and Amzalag. Amzalag provided Nicolayson with his chief channel to the Jewish community. Information from Amzalag about the Jewish communities in Jerusalem and other towns was essential for guiding mission activities and reporting to the LJS. At times Nicolayson was invited to Jewish celebrations by Amzalag, who promised to take Nicolayson to the consecration service of the refurbished Sephardi synagogues, but "did not send for me" because the place was "crowded full,"[34] in the naive words of Nicolayson.

Why did Amzalag so actively help Nicolayson settle in Jerusalem and then maintain frequent contacts with the mission? For Amzalag, Nicolayson was a splendid source of reliable current news about what was happening throughout Syria and beyond. On more than one occasion Nicolayson reported: "Amzalag came in . . . enquiring for news."[35] Such early, accurate news about commercial events enriched Amzalag. When devaluations occurred on different days in different Syrian towns, rapid, correct information was worth lots of money to a savvy merchant.[36]

Few Sephardi Jews maintained ties with the missionaries.[37] One exception was the Sephardi scholar Yedidya Abulafia, who conducted frequent and lengthy "discussions, conversations and investigations" with Nicolayson. These talks were conducted in Hebrew, enabling Nicolayson to overcome his "deficiency of skill in the Hebrew language." But at the end of 1834 Abulafia's "almost daily" calls ceased. Once Nicolayson and Calman visited the Sephardi scholar Mercadero Gaggi, "who received us with great civility, though entire strangers to him . . . but he kept so completely aloof from the

Christ Church with the Citadel to its right.

great question between us, that all our attempts to get into discussion were ineffectual."[38] Gaggi skillfully managed "to keep the very friendly discussion on general subjects."

Ashkenazim speaking with the missionaries also steered clear of religious discussions. When the English missionary Alexander Levi talked with R. Solomon he was told: "Mr. Levi, I begged you several times not to talk to me about religion; we are and always will be good friends, only do not talk to me on that subject." To which Levi answered:

> Don't you know what even the Talmud says: "Three that sit and eat, and the word of the law is not amongst them (i.e., they do not converse on the word of the Lord) is as if they were to eat from the sacrifices that are sacrificed unto the dead."[39]

Nicolayson complained that "Polish Jews" were unfriendly and "almost entirely inaccessible" to the missionaries. Shlomo Zalman Zoref was particularly antagonistic toward the intrusive missionaries. Expressing the official position of the Jewish community, Zoref told Nicolayson: "Let us alone and we will let you alone." Nicolayson did meet with a member of the Perushim, David Beit Hillel, who read Christian books including the New Testament, which was banned by the kehilla. But Nicolayson was disappointed when he concluded that Beit Hillel's reading was "to little purpose."[40]

R. Bardaki occasionally consulted Nicolayson on current events and community affairs, such as how minorities should deal with the authorities. When the 1840 Damascus blood libel shocked the world, and the Jerusalem kehilla was threatened by the Greek Catholics and Muslims, R. Bardaki tried to obtain from Nicolayson information about the state of the Jews in Damascus. Nicolayson obligingly dispatched the missionary Pieretz to intercede with consuls in Damascus, from where he sent news to Jerusalem and published articles defending Jews against the libel accusing them of using Christian blood in the baking of Passover unleavened bread. Nicolayson also gave Alexandria-bound Shlomo Pach a document categorically refuting the ritual blood libel.[41]

Jewish leaders in Jerusalem invited Nicolayson to a meeting convened to discuss ways of countering the effects of the blood libel. At this meeting Nicolayson sat next to the Sephardi leader, R. Raphael Navon, who just one month earlier had threatened to destroy Christ Church, which Nicolayson had just started to build. So esteemed was Nicolayson's assistance in the Damascus incident that Jerusalem's Sephardi chief rabbi, Jonah Navon, praised Nicolayson and berated Tiberias Jews for trying to chase the Jewish convert Simeon out of town. Although R. Bardaki agreed with the Sephardi letter praising Nicolayson's support of the Jewish position in the Damascus blood libel, he did not sign it for fear that it would be used against him by his Perushim antagonists in the Hurva faction. Four Hurva members flirting with the mission exacerbated the conflict between Zoref's Hurva faction and R. Bardaki's Sukkat Shalom group.

Nicolayson helped Jews by providing them with shelter, "employment and support." A mission method of proselytizing was to provide housing for a poor Jewish "stranger," and permit a potential convert to live in a missionary house in order to escape the wrath of other Jews. A usual method of attracting converts was to give "trifling" sums of money to employ "prospects," but nowhere did Nicolayson define what such trifling "pecuniary assistance" amounted to. By providing money to Jews from a "special fund for the employment and support of Proselytes," the mission tried to overcome the "fear of the Jews" that they would be struck off the haluka lists. But Nicolayson did not throw his money around, as demonstrated by his telling one of the Jewish prospects that "so long as his desire to know Christianity is not sufficient to overcome his fear of the Jews, we can do nothing further for him than lend him books . . ."[42]

Nicolayson also loaned money to the Jewish community. Some Perushim believed they were punished by plagues that beset them in 1838–1839 because they had borrowed money from the mission, so they resolved to return the tainted money and cut contact with the English missionaries.[43]

The American Board of Commissioners for Foreign Missions was less intensely involved in Palestine than the LJS, but it was just one year behind the English in setting up a permanent Jerusalem mission station. In 1832 the American Board appointed two American missionaries, William Thomson and Dr. Asa Dodge, to establish its Jerusalem station. American missionaries could act more confidently now that they were protected by the 1830 American-Turkish commercial agreement that established diplomatic relations between the young American republic and the Ottoman Empire and defined the status of U.S. consular representatives throughout that empire.[44]

Early in the spring of 1834 William and Eliza Thomson settled in Jerusalem. Shortly thereafter Thomson left Jerusalem in order to bring his belongings from Jaffa, while his wife tended their newborn baby in the

Nicolayson home. A series of earthquake tremors chased the Thomsons and Nicolaysons into the open garden, where they were forced to sleep. Amzalag and several other Jewish families also took shelter in Nicolayson's garden, leading Eliza Thomson to write sharply about the Jews:[45]

> It was truly afflicting to see these bigoted descendants of Abraham coming for protection in the hour of danger to the house of a *Christian*, really appearing to derive comfort from our composure and confidence that God would protect us.[46]

Thomson returned to Jerusalem and found his wife suffering from "violent opthalmia [*sic*]" and a "high inflammatory fever" before she "silently fell asleep in Jesus." Thomson was then excused by the American Board from the dangerous Jerusalem station. He continued to serve the mission in Beirut, the center of American missionary activities in the Near East.

In place of William Thomson the American Board appointed George Whiting to head the Jerusalem mission.[47] Whiting took up his new post in November 1834, when he arrived in Jerusalem with the medical missionary, Dr. Asa Dodge. While Dr. Dodge was "doing good to their bodies, a wide door was opened for giving instruction suited to benefit their souls." From Jerusalem Dr. Dodge and Whiting observed the "depressed and wretched state of the whole country . . . and the condition of this oppressed and degraded people."[48]

Less than three months after Dr. Dodge settled in Jerusalem he died of typhus fever, supposedly "occasioned by a hurried journey, in which he was much exposed."[49] Dr. Dodge was buried near Dr. Dalton and Mrs. Thomson in the Greek Orthodox cemetery on Mt. Zion. Due to the subsequent outcry of the Greek convent that it would never again permit a Protestant to be buried in its cemetery, the American mission purchased a nearby plot of land on Mt. Zion for its own cemetery. In life and in death the Christians of Jerusalem were divided. The Greek Orthodox, the Roman Catholics, the Armenians, and now the Americans (and soon the English Protestants) had separate cemeteries on Mt. Zion.

The mortality rate among the American missionaries was fearsome. Five out of seventeen American missionary staff in Syria died between 1822 and 1836—Parsons, Fisk, Mrs. Thomson, Dr. Dodge, and Mrs. Eli Smith. Among the children the mortality rate probably was higher. For an unknown reason the death rate among the English missionaries was much lower than that of the American mission, with Dr. Dalton the only LJS casualty.[50]

George Whiting and Nicolayson worked together in a most Christian-like manner, despite LJS's fear of American propaganda championing "Antimonarchism." Nicolayson assisted at the American Sunday service, which was not attended by Jewish converts or potential candidates for conversion. Whiting's printed journals omit reference to meeting with Jews, except for attending a Jewish wedding "by special invitation" and visiting the Jewish quarter of Hebron, where "there are about one hundred and twenty families."[51] Comments by Whiting about Jews and the boisterous Jewish festival of Purim reflected the stern attitude of the American missionaries.

Some American missionaries showed great disdain toward the Jews. Note the torrid polemic launched by William Thomson against the Jews of Safed:

> I have no heart to enter into their history, or dwell on their absurd superstitions, their intense fanaticism, or their social and domestic institutions and manners, comprising an incredible and grotesque melange of filth and finery, Pharisaic self-righteousness and Sadducean licentiousness. The following is a specimen of the puerilities enjoined and enforced by their learned rabbis . . . [52]

Lacking a living Hebrew voice to preach the Word, the message of the American missionaries could not be heard by the Jews. More important, the American missionaries showed an affinity toward Muslims. Although both the English and American missionaries displayed parental concern for the Jews as strayers from the true path of Jesus Christ, the Americans played the role of the strict, severe father harshly berating his errant son, while the English were patient, loving parents trying to convince their child of his mistakes. It also was common sense for the Americans to marshal their limited mission resources for a specific clientele only indirectly served by the English mission. The Americans and English sensibly recognized that dividing the mission terrain would allow each group to focus its efforts and improve what Nicolayson called the "little [that] has been done."[53]

Moreover, Whiting must have realized that the Americans lacked the English evangelical spirit in working with Jews so as to bring about the Second Advent. A different set of priorities was signaled by the fact that Whiting lived in the Christian quarter, where no Jew would dare enter, while Nicolayson's residence in the Armenian quarter was right on the edge of the Jewish quarter. (However, during his three years in Jerusalem,

1836–1839, the American missionary John Lanneau lived in the Muslim quarter, which was easily accessible to the Jews.) Whiting and Nicolayson amicably agreed that LJS and its Hebrew-speaking staff would give "greater attention to the Jewish subject,"[54] while the American mission would labor among Arab Christians, as they were doing in Beirut and elsewhere in the Turkish Empire.

The American missionaries in Syria pressed the American Board in Boston to obtain consular protection for the mission station in Jerusalem, similar to English consular protection. American missionaries recommended the appointment of a consul in Jerusalem because it "was often visited by American travellers, and was already the home of an American [missionary] family."[55] This recommendation was not acted upon for several reasons: few Americans lived in Syria, American commercial interests in the area were insignificant, and the American Board wielded no influence with the United States government.

American missionary activities in Jerusalem were at a low ebb at the end of the 1830s. Funds from America were in short supply, prompting Whiting to snap irritably that "if you expect your reapers to accomplish any thing in the harvest field, you do not take away their sickles, nor tie their hands."[56] Whiting temporarily returned to the United States between 1838 and 1840 due to his wife's illness. John Lanneau suffered from an eye disease and was replaced in the autumn of 1839 by Charles Sherman, who worked with Betsy Tilden and Tannoos Keren, a Roman Catholic. In 1840 an American missionary doctor, Dr. Van Dyck, ministered to the sick of Jerusalem for several months.

The prevailing American idea of the early 1830s that Jerusalem was "a most important missionary station" was slowly supplanted by Thomson's idea "that Syria was not a productive missionary field" and there was "increasing doubt here as to the expediency of continuing a station in Jerusalem." An influential member of the American Board visiting Palestine reported that "I saw nothing which should give [Jerusalem] a special claim on our attention." In 1843 the Americans suspended, but did not abandon, mission activities in Jerusalem and Palestine. One reason for such action was given from Beirut by a missionary who claimed that Jerusalemites "are notoriously more debased in moral character, and less impressible by gospel truth, than almost any other people in the land, if not in the world." Another rationalization of the Boston-based Board for suspending mission action in Palestine was the "English intruders." The Americans also blamed "the diplomacy of the Protestant powers of Europe which is seeking the establishment of a Protestant sect as the basis of political influence" in the Orient. In fact the Americans rejected the idea of restoring Jews to Palestine and concluded that "the Jew has had his day."[57]

With the small American mission team working among Greek and Roman Catholics, LJS secured a monopoly on the Jewish clientele; Nicolayson garnered enough knowledge and experience to push mission activities in the Jewish community energetically. But the kehilla enjoyed a respite from the insistent pressures of the English mission when, in August 1836, Nicolayson was recalled to London for consultations on LJS's highest priority project—building Christ Church in Jerusalem. To Nicolayson this undertaking was essential, to build a "nucleus of a living Church . . . to keep a congregation together" as well as to provide the Jews with employment and support.[58]

During Nicolayson's fifteen-month absence from Jerusalem LJS mission activities were so innocuous that they hardly troubled the Jews. When he returned to Jerusalem in October 1837 Nicolayson, with the aid of the United States vice-consul in Jaffa, made the most strenuous efforts to buy land for a Protestant church, a mission house for four missionary families, and a cemetery.[59] After nearly ten frustrating months of persevering work Nicolayson paid 80,000 piastres (800 pounds sterling) for land opposite the citadel, near Jaffa gate.[60] Although this site was in the Armenian quarter, it was significantly described as on Mt. Zion, "on the very confines of the Jewish quarter."[61] Construction of Christ Church commenced in September 1839; in 1840 the cornerstone was laid: in 1841 the British passed an Act of Parliament establishing the Protestant Bishopric in Jerusalem; and in January 1842 Bishop Alexander opened the Anglican Bishopric in Jerusalem. Only in 1845 was the requested firman for the Bishopric finally issued by the Sultan.

From 1837 through 1841 the establishment of Christ Church so preoccupied Nicolayson that it bordered on an obsession and preempted his other missionary activities. For the Jews the building of Christ Church proved to be a blessing, because Nicolayson had "little time for intercourse with the Jews, except so far as some call on me."[62]

Since LJS wanted to continue ambitiously developing the Jerusalem mission it sent additional personnel. In July 1838 Nicolayson and Simeon, a proselyte-in-training, were reinforced by the arrival of two lay missionaries who were converted Jews, G. W. Pieretz,[63] a former rabbi at Yarmouth, England, and Alexander Levi, "a mere youth."[64] In place of Nicolayson,

Pieretz went out talking to the Jews. He carried out the normal missionary activities so effectively that he was peremptorily excommunicated by the Jewish community.

Recognizing the crucial role a medical team can play in developing the activities of a mission station, the LJS worked energetically to collect money for a Fund for the Poor Sick Jews at Jerusalem.[65] As a result of these efforts, the mission station in Jerusalem received a strong forward thrust with the arrival on December 7, 1838, of the medical missionary Dr. Albert Gerstmann, accompanied by the pharmacist Melville Peter Bergheim and a prospective convert. For the third time missionaries attempted to set up a medical station in Jerusalem. We can only wonder how Dr. Gerstmann felt, knowing that his two predecessors, Drs. Dalton and Dodge, had died one and three months after starting their medical practice. Once in Jerusalem, Gerstmann wrote that he was "moved... to tears... I found more than I expected and more than I sought."

The purpose of the medical mission was "to form something that may grow into a hospital," by which Nicolayson meant "a room or two where poor sick creatures could come to have a little broth and be kept alive."[66] Gerstmann discussed with Nicolayson the possibility of "forming a hospital for poor patients" that would also employ indigent Jews who were prospects for conversion. Dr. Gerstmann suggested using one room in Nicolayson's house as a hospital and providing kosher food for the patients. Nicolayson agreed because "if we make them [the Jews] comfortable in their own houses we can never expect them to come in to our plans for a Hospital."

As the only resident doctor in Jerusalem, Dr. Gerstmann was exceedingly busy treating dozens of sick Jews who received free medical attention from him and medicines from the pharmacist Bergheim.[67] While making house calls at Jewish homes Dr. Gerstmann was shocked by the filth and misery, "the sight of destitution and wretchedness... and abject poverty." Nicolayson concluded that "one great cause of the shocking diseases and accumulated wretchedness among Jews here, is the manner in which they are compelled to crowd and herd together; three or four families in one little dark, damp, and dirty room."

Due to the great demand for Dr. Gerstmann's medical services, there was greatly increased contact between the Jews and the mission.[68] "The necessities of the poor suffering Jews broke through every restraint.... This has found the most ample employment for the whole mission, whom it has brought into daily intercouse with the Jews." Nicolayson wrote that "the spell of the 'Herem' [written in Hebrew and meaning excommunication] seems already completely broken.... The work that was anguishing has again revived; everything is now alive and stirring among us and around us."

Kehilla leaders warned Jews to stay far from Dr. Gerstmann or suffer the penalty of excommunication.[69] Shlomo Zalman Zoref wanted to impose excommunication edicts to prevent contact with the missionaries, but R. Israel demurred for fear that the bans would not be observed, according to Nicolayson. Shortly afterward, he claimed that, while the Jewish leadership was determined to issue an excommunication edict, this dread threat was "forgotten" by Jews seeking relief from illness. "Nothing was able to stand against the doctor, or rather against the necessity and eagerness of the poor Jews for medical aid," concluded Nicolayson, who was "thankful to God that the appearance of things is very promising."

Even R. Israel received Dr. Gerstmann kindly and used his medical services when his daughter fell sick. "Being Saturday he would only converse in Hebrew," wrote Levi.

> Our conversation was not directly upon religion, but chiefly concerning the sufferings of the Jews during the late revolution at Saphet. Many respectable Jews came in while I was conversing, and were quite astonished to see Rabbi Israel so friendly, and treating us, as it is the custom among the Jews on Saturday, with oranges, and said that he was very sorry that we did not come a little sooner, or we might have tasted his Sabbath cake. Thus the Jews... receive us in a friendly and kind manner, for they are convinced that we love them, and desire their welfare.[70]

Ten days later R. Israel was not reticent about asking Levi "to translate a letter into English." So grateful were the Jews for receiving devoted medical attention from the missionaries that when Dr. Gerstmann and Bergheim fell seriously ill Jews prayed for their recovery at the Wailing Wall.

Charges by Jewish leaders that the medical mission was not a humanitarian effort but a fishing expedition for Jewish souls in misery did not dissuade sick Jews from visiting the mission doctor. They argued that Jewish law sanctioned the saving of one Jewish life by all means, including resorting to mission medical services. Jews wracked by debilitating pains easily convinced themselves that their spirit was strong enough to withstand proselytizing pressures. Initially, little or "no attempt at proselytizing was made," yet while ministering to the body the doctor undoubtedly dropped "a healing word for the soul,"[71] a clear sign that mission efforts to preserve the body were inextricably tied to liberating the soul.

The great need for medical assistance was recognized by Jews such as R. Israel, who contacted Z. H. Lehren about sending a doctor to Safed in 1835. No similar request was made for Jerusalem because Bergmann reported that "here there are three doctors, experts in my opinion, one from Poland and one from Izmir."[72] No mention is made of Isaac Russee, described by Dr. Gerstmann as

an ignorant native Jew... who practices medicine but does more evil and destroys more life than the plague itself. Patients die through his ignorant treatment: he accepts bribes, but where poverty prevents gifts he certifies the sick have the plague, when they are shut up and die from starvation and lack of medical attention.... Jerusalem will never be clear of plague while these natives are allowed to practice. Many Jews assert it would be of great service to them if this Isaac could be forbidden to practice.[73]

In August 1837 the Perushim of Jerusalem set up the Bikur Holim organization for visiting sick persons and ministering to their needs throughout the night. Charter members of this organization included S. Z. Zoref, Hillel Rivlin, David Yellin, and David Hirschel, the son of London's Ashkenazi chief rabbi. Prominent by their absence from membership were R. Israel and R. Bardaki, reflecting the split between the Hurva and courtyard groups. When Jerusalem Perushim wrote PEKAM about the need to establish a hospital, Lehren brushed their request aside, but in 1840 he started to send small sums of money to the Bikur Holim society.[74]

The threat posed by the medical mission to the Jewish community could easily have been thwarted by bringing a Jewish doctor to Eretz Israel, as was recommended in 1842 by the German editor and Reformed rabbi Ludwig Philippson, who proposed establishing a Jewish hospital in Jerusalem. Philippson implored the Jewish people: "From the beginning of the year to its end we *pray* for the peace of Jerusalem; let us therefore also *do* something for her!" Then he twitted Orthodox Jewry: "Let... the strict Jew, who on no account would shorten the length of a single prayer for the welfare of Jerusalem, now show that they [sic] are in *earnest* in these their supplications."[75]

This obvious proposal of Philippson for a Jewish hospital was not implemented because it ran counter to the prevalent Jewish Orthodox belief, which maintained that Jews studying medicine or other university subjects were tainted by their secular outlook and corrupted by the heretic notions of the German Reform and European Enlightenment movements.

Orthodox Jews held that doctors were estranged from Jewish tradition and conspired to undermine the Jewish religion. In addition, Jews believed that health was a gift from God, not from physicians.

While enjoying the medical facilities in Western Europe, Lehren wrote:

> ... there is no reason to worry about the Gentile doctor brought to Palestine by the Mission; what we have to worry about is the presence there of a Jewish doctor who is a heretic and a skeptic ... and during these many years they did not miss a doctor in Eretz Israel. . . . It is better that the Jews of Eretz Israel not have Jewish doctors ... and that they be treated by learned Gentile doctors.[76]

In one outburst Lehren declared (in 1844) that "as long as I live, a doctor will never go to Jerusalem . . ." But one year later Lehren confessed that it was imperative to set up a Jewish hospital, after the mission established its hospital.

Despite the rabid opposition of Lehren, in 1843 Moses Montefiore sent to Jerusalem the first Jewish doctor, Shimon Fraenkel, who served the Jewish community for fifteen years.

Mission medical activity in Jerusalem was constantly disrupted by the plagues that struck Jerusalem in the first half of 1839, quarantined its population, and kept the Jews homebound and out of reach of the mission. The ineradicable cholera epidemic and recurring natural disasters were not new to Jerusalem. In March 1838, at the end of the rainy season, there was a drought and the hot season arrived early. "Many of the poor Jews are almost in a state of starvation," Nicolayson reported as he distributed two camel-loads of wheat to the Jews and worried about "what will this be among so many." Between May and August 1838, and in October, plague struck Jerusalem. In June Hillel Rivlin, one of the first Perushim immigrants, died of the plague, and in July 100 deaths were reported, "the majority Jews."[77] A quarantine was declared and the town gates were once again closed.

The next year was even worse—a year of "misery, a bad winter, a high price for wheat, and cholera which appeared among the Jews and Muslims in the middle of January" and killed many Jerusalemites. So lethal were the plagues of 1838 and 1839 that the Perushim of Jerusalem assembled to discuss why these epidemics were visited upon them. Some Jews believed they were punished "owing to the free intercourse which so many have had with the missionaries" and because of "the advantages which they have derived" by borrowing mission money. Lehren attributed the casualties of the epidemics to the evil spirits filling the Hurva. In the opinion of Nicolayson, the plagues and deaths were caused by "a visitation of the Divine displeasure."[78] During these days of plagues the number of Jews living in Jerusalem did not increase and may even have dwindled.[79]

After months of sporadic but intensive efforts, the activities in the medical mission were abruptly halted in May 1839 because of the plague. Unable to practice medicine in quarantined Jerusalem, and at odds with Pieretz, Dr. Gerstmann decided to accompany the sick missionary Levi to Beirut. When Gerstmann returned to plague-ridden Jerusalem in the fall he treated "at least four hundred patients during October, with half the patients being Jewish." Then Gerstmann fell sick with "severe and frequent cramps" and showed little chance of recovering in the Palestine climate.[80]

Thirteen months after his arrival Dr. Gerstmann left Jerusalem to open a medical mission in Istanbul, where he "died quite unexpectedly" in May 1841.[81] Gerstmann's departure from Jerusalem closed down the short-lived medical mission and marked the end of the most active and effective period of the LJS Jerusalem mission station during the 1830s. Nicolayson's repeated requests to send another medical missionary to Jerusalem were answered in 1842 with the arrival of Dr. Edward Macgowan, who opened the first mission hospital in Jerusalem in 1844.

What were the achievements of the mission in Palestine? How did it affect the Jewish community and influence its actions? If we judge the success of the mission by counting the number of Jewish converts to Christianity, it was a total failure. In April 1839, after three and a half years of instruction, Nicolayson administered the holy sacrament to the four members of the Simeon Rosenthal family. Although the Rosenthals were touted to be "probably the first Jewish family . . . received into the Church at Jerusalem since early Christian times," Simeon was "awakened" in Bucharest and came to Jerusalem with Nicolayson to receive religious instruction.[82] Shortly thereafter Paul Hyman Sternchuss was converted by Nicolayson and quickly sent to England to escape the wrath of the Jews. In September 1838 Rabbi Joseph, "a learned young man," was sent to Istanbul for baptism and "three rabbies have very lately become inquirers after the truth and seem determined to profess Christianity openly." However, under pressure from the Jewish community they temporarily recanted. In February 1840 Nicolayson recorded that a Jew named Jacob was baptized into the Christian faith; and in May 1843 the mission scored a tremendous triumph by converting four Jews, including two prominent Perushim. The American mission was less successful than the LJS, having converted only four persons from the eastern churches in all of Syria up to 1840.

The reason why so few Jews abandoned the ways of the Jewish community is quite evident. Despite the intensive efforts of Nicolayson's competent mission team and the conspicuous success of the short-lived medical mission, the fractious and divided Sephardi and Ashkenazi communities instinctively closed ranks in unalterable opposition to the mission. Leaders of the kehilla viewed the missionaries as a disruptive, corrupting force that must be kept as far as possible from the rank and file. When Nicolayson's mission staff established contact with individual Jews, the missionaries were repulsed by massive pressure of the total Jewish community. Yet kehilla leaders maintained correct relations with the English mission because Nicolayson and his missionaries treated the Jews with utmost courtesy, consulted and counseled with Jewish leaders, and helped the Jewish community overcome the persecutions of the authorities.

It was clearly most difficult for the LJS to break into the "impenetrable phalanx of Rabbinism at Jerusalem."[83] The Perushim, Hasidim, and Sephardim came to Eretz Israel out of profound religious motivation, absolute commitment to Messianic Redemption, and unswerving conviction that settling in the Holy Land would accelerate their personal salvation. Without a cataclysmic event that would undermine the faith of the Jews, it was preposterous to entertain the wild notion that you could convert the believing followers of R. Israel of Shklov, R. Abraham Dov, and Rabbis Suzin and Navon.

The daily routine of prayer and study in the Jewish community was conducted in the public area of the synagogue under the vigilant scrutiny of other Jews.[84] Males assembled in the synagogue each morning and late afternoon to pray and to exchange current news about who was doing what. At the synagogue, which served as the religious and social center of the community, Jews displayed a high moral concern for the conduct of their neighbors. Synagogue attendance was somewhat similar to passing muster at roll call and answering charges about personal conduct that might be pressed by any member of the congregation. Jews suspected of attachments to the missionaries were closely policed. In one case, a Jew was forced to leave a Christian home by the back door, and a hole was opened "in the garden wall, that he might escape unobserved."[85]

Social pressure and community harassment were unhesitatingly exerted on any straying Jew and his family. A potential convert was physically removed from his children and wife, and his wife quickly secured a divorce.[86] In extreme instances, intransigent Jews were banished from Eretz Israel by the kehilla and shipped back to their former homes in Europe.

If the ideological commitment to Zion, the close supervision, and daily social pressures did not keep a wavering Jew in line, unleashing the blunt economic weapon of the haluka provided a deterrent to all but wealthy Jews. The moment a Jew inquired "after Christ, he is cut off from all share in this [haluka] fund, and is thrown utterly destitute... [and] left to starve." A Jewish candidate for conversion was told that he might just as well butcher his family "as become the cause of their perishing of hunger and want" due to the cutting off of their haluka.[87] Even providing housing to a missionary passing through Tiberias could draw the threat of being struck from the life-sustaining haluka roster. Nevertheless, economic sanctions were largely empty threats. The Jewish leadership realized that denying a Jew sustenance would only drive him into the open arms of the mission, which would gladly provide for his economic needs.

When economic threats and social intimidations did not persuade a Jew to stay away from the missionaries, the rabbis brandished the ultimate weapon of excommunication,[88] particularly during the height of activity by the medical mission. Excommunication meant that a Jew was ostracized from the cohesive Jewish community and damned to everlasting condemnation. Not only was his haluka cut off, but no other Jew was allowed to have business or social contacts with the excommunicated person. Socially he was abandoned and economically he was ruined. His religious rights and privileges were canceled, and he was denied burial in a Jewish cemetery, a mortal blow to his hopes of entering the next world.

Only a disturbed, marginal character would expose himself to a denial of material rewards in this world and spiritual rewards in the next world. The convert Simeon Rosenthal, who threatened to return to the Jewish fold in 1861, was far from balanced. He was "overbearing" toward the American missionary George Whiting—he "act[ed] the great man" and "he is never in the wrong." Nicolayson was forced to rebuke Simeon for intentionally enraging Jews by ostentatious "Sabbath breaking,"[89] a practice contrary to mission policies. There is little doubt that, like Simeon Rosenthal, some prospective proselytes were strange, insufferable characters and "far from creditable acquisitions." Jews hoping to better their economic condition flirted with the mission, but when the illusory nature of their hopes was revealed they quickly backed off.

The missionaries understood the punishments for apostasy:

when a Jew becomes a proselyte to Christianity, he must literally give up every thing; he is mourned over by his brethren sitting on low stools, as if he were dead; he is thenceforward looked upon and shunned by Turk, Arab, Armenian, Greek, and Papist, as an unclean thing; he at once finds himself homeless, moneyless, friendless, utterly helpless and forsaken, without the least thing in the world to fall back upon for his body, and destitute of even hope to sustain his mind. Pretty much the same must be the case of a Jew who may be only inquiring into the truths of Christianity.[90]

Knowing the social dynamics of the kehilla, did Nicolayson and the LJS really believe that the mission was such an irresistible force that it could budge the immovable kehilla? Did Nicolayson not realize that the impregnable "Hill of Zion is not a likely place for a Jew to forsake the faith of his father"?[91] Nonetheless, as sincere, intelligent, humanitarian people, Nicolayson and the other missionaries unflinchingly faced the realities of the intransigent Jewish community with absolute, unconditional dedication to the purpose of preaching the Gospel and converting Jews to Christianity.

By using "practical benevolence" in place of "angry denunciation,"[92] Nicolayson and other English missionaries persisted in recruiting Jews for the Christian life so that their Christ Messiah could return and redeem all humankind. Salvation by grace and redemption through faith in Jesus Christ was essential, but not sufficient for Christians. Without the active participation of the Jews, Christian believers could not reach the millennium. The involvement of the "banished children of Palestine, who never advanced beyond the knowledge of God's Law and never accepted the fulfilling of that law in the words and works of the Savior of mankind" was vital for the Coming of the Second Advent.[93] "Not love for the Jewish nation but concern for the Christian soul... moved all these good and earnest" missionaries who encouraged the return of Jews to Palestine.[94]

To question missionaries about tangible results such as the number of conversions was both demeaning and irrelevant to their Christian beliefs for the salvation of souls. "The true missionary acts from a higher policy than that which sways the kingdoms of this world," in the words of Jonas King. "He reckons not the victories he is to win, by the number he can bring into the field. . . . The true missionary walks by faith . . ."[95] The burden of the heretical Jewish soul weighed heavily on the missionaries' Christian consciences. They believed they must convince the Jews about "the errors and absurdities" of their opinions and if they did not "see much success, those that come after you will. This is not the work of a day."[96]

The missionaries, no less than the Jews, were fervently inspired by the supreme faith that they were following in the path of the Lord and revealing His infinite form. Despite feelings of loneliness and futility that caused periods of deep depression, the missionaries tried not to allow themselves the luxury of doubt that occasionally afflicted believers such as Lord Shaftesbury, who in 1845, mourning the premature death of the first Anglican bishop in Jerusalem, wrote: "Have we run counter to the will of God? Have we conceived a merely human project, and then imagined it to be a decree of the Almighty? . . ."[97]

Missionaries dedicated their lives to the service of God. They all lived, and some died, cultivating the vineyards of the Lord by shedding the pains of earthly life and the attachments and desires of other people. Like other missionaries, Nicolayson performed work "dear to every truly Christian heart" because "I know not how to desist."[98] Through their religious beliefs and actions missionaries found tranquillity, fulfillment, and spiritual freedom. Missionary achievements were measured not by the number of conversions, but by feeling God's pleasure, and attaining profound inner contentment and deep serenity. With joy in their hearts, missionaries praised the Lord and persevered in the belief that "God has not called me to be successful. He has called me to be faithful."[99]

FOURTEEN

The British Consulate in Jerusalem

1839–1840

reat Britain established the first consulate in Jerusalem in 1839 and it
G significantly influenced the lives of the Jews in the Holy Land. The
British consulate was set up because of the conciliatory attitude of
Mehemet Ali toward the European powers and the initiatives of foreign
minister Palmerston. This diplomatic move neatly fit the British concept of
empire, and their objectives of maintaining overland connections with India, developing overseas commercial interests, and gaining advantages in
international politics.

The newly appointed British consul in Damascus, John Farren, had visited Jerusalem in October 1834 and toured the countryside with his guide,
John Nicolayson, who reported that at Bethlehem there were crowds of
people imploring the consul to "interfere on their behalf and provide them
with consular protection.[1]

Farren recommended settling a British vice-consul in Jerusalem,

the chief and largest city in the extreme south of Syria and the centre of
provinces which have [lately] attracted much attention and where it is
desirable to have an efficient agent for reporting intelligence of public
events . . . [2]

Colonel Patrick Campbell, the ranking British Foreign Office representative in all countries ruled by Egypt and responsible for consular agents in Syria, could not "give a positive opinion" about establishing a consular post in Jerusalem for he "never heard any complaints from English travellers who had been in Syria respecting the want of an Agent in that city." In any event, he did not suppose that "the circumstances of two or three British subjects residing in an inland town should render necessary the appointment of a British Agent there." Reporting news from Jerusalem could easily be handled by the British vice-consular agent in Jaffa since "the port of Jaffa is so near, and every event, as well as every information reported from Jerusalem must necessarily be forwarded by Jaffa." Although Campbell did not favor appointing a vice-consul in Jerusalem, he was willing to appoint a consular agent, for "it might be a considerable accommodation to British travellers to have an Agent at Jerusalem in order to forward any letters for them, or to take charge of any part of their baggage." The consular agent was to act as postman and porter!

Nonetheless, on November 6, 1836, Palmerston decided that "it w[oul]d be expedient to have an English Consular Agent at Jerusalem. State this to Col. Campbell and request him to select a person. Query what pay."[3] This decision was made as a result of Palmerston's "intense hatred and suspicions" of Russian activities in the Near East, which greatly influenced British foreign policy. Palmerston was most perturbed by Russia using the Greek Catholic Church to further its interests in Jerusalem and throughout Syria.

Niven Moore, Consul in Beirut, recommended a candidate to serve as the British consul in Jerusalem—John Nicolayson, "a most respectable man, and to great intelligence adds the further qualification of a knowledge of the Arabic language."[4] Campbell vetoed this suggestion, for "the nomination of a missionary to be Vice-Consul would . . . be most objectionable in every point of view."[5] Then, on the joint recommendation of Niven Moore, Patrick Campbell, and John Nicolayson, Palmerston appointed William Tanner Young as the vice-consul in Jerusalem.[6] Well educated but of modest economic means, the youthful W. T. Young had toured Egypt, Palestine, and Syria in 1836 and favorably impressed Moore, Campbell, and Nicolayson.

The English missionaries were "jubilant" that a British consul would soon settle in Jerusalem; undoubtedly this would help bolster missionary efforts.[7] When Nicolayson learned about Young's appointment he recorded that "this is a kind of providence."[8] The missionaries waved the English flag with stronger fervor than the diplomatic consuls engrossed in trade and urged a strong British presence in areas where they were active. The bishop of London yearned "to hoist the flag of the Church of England . . . on the hills of Judea."[9] LJS missionary Farman wrote that the Jews in Beirut and Acre asked him, "Why does not England send an army, and rid us out of the hands of our cruel oppressors?"

After a drawn-out 20-month process of selecting, appointing, and obtaining a firman for a British vice-consul, Palmerston wrote William T. Young on September 19, 1838, that he had been appointed vice-consul in Palestine, to be stationed in Jerusalem. Young's job was "to cultivate a friendly feeling towards Great Britain amongst the inhabitants of the country" and to use his best efforts "to introduce desire for British commodities and to extend the commercial relations between the two countries."[10] To fulfill the reporting responsibility of a consul, Young was instructed to transmit information about "commerce, navigation, agriculture and any other branch of statistics . . . "

As for protecting foreign subjects, Palmerston cautioned Young that

Her Majesty's Government have been informed that in some provinces of Turkey British Patents of Protection have been granted to the subjects of other powers. Such a practice is highly reprehensible . . . I have therefore to desire that in the exercise of the important privilege of issuing such patents you will be particularly careful to investigate the claims of the persons who may apply to you for them.[11]

The position of vice-consul in Jerusalem was defined no differently than that of other consuls. However, Young proved to be the first diplomat in Palestine who subordinated the promotion of British commercial interests to that of representing the political interest of a major European power.

Ten days after Palmerston appointed Young as British vice-consul in Jerusalem Lord Shaftesbury, a convinced millenarian, made an excited entry in his diary:

Took leave this morning of Young, who has just been appointed Her Majesty's Vice-Consul at *Jerusalem!* He will sail in a day or two for the Holy Land. If this is duly considered, what a wonderful event is this! The ancient city of the people of God is about to resume a place among the nations, and England is the first of Gentile Kingdoms that ceases "to tread her down" . . . ; I shall always, at any rate, remember that God put it into my heart to conceive the plan for His honour, gave me influence to prevail with Palmerston, and provided a man for the situation who can remember Jerusalem in his mirth.[12]

Shaftesbury believed that the presence of a British consul would make Palestine more secure, enabling Jews to "betake themselves to agriculture . . . [the Jews] having found in the English Consul a mediator between their people and the pasha, will . . . become once more the husbandmen of Judea and Galilee."

William Tanner Young landed in Jaffa on February 4, 1839, to take up his post.[13] He was promptly quarantined for twenty-one days due to another outbreak of the cholera epidemic in Jerusalem and Jaffa. Undeterred by the Jerusalem quarantine, Young hired a "health guardian" and seized the first opportunity of going to Jerusalem, where he arrived in late March.

While lodged at the Convent of the Cross, three kilometers west of the city walls (located near the contemporary Israel Museum and the Knesset Parliament building),[14] Young wrote to Palmerston and sounded the theme that would guide his actions:

> There are, My Lord, two parties to be noticed who will doubtless consider themselves entitled to some voice in the future disposition of affairs here: The one is the Jew unto whom God originally gave this land for a possession, and the other the Protestant Christian, his legitimate offspring. Of both Great Britain seems, I would humbly suggest, the natural guardian.[15]

Later Young and his wife moved into a house opposite the citadel and next to Christ Church. This compound consisting of the consul's residence and Christ Church became the center of British activity in Jerusalem and symbolized to both Muslims and Jews the inextricable connection between British diplomatic efforts and LJS missionary activities.

Patrick Campbell, Young's superior officer, defined the size of his consulate territory and instructed him how to protect foreign nationals. Young's jurisdiction covered the inland and coastal regions of Palestine from the port of Jaffa north to Sidon. The consular agents in Jaffa, Haifa, Acre, and Sidon were now subordinate to Young rather than to British consul Moore in Beirut.

Campbell wrote Young to strictly limit his actions for the protection of foreign nationals.

> I have to inform you that in the Levant it has always been customary for the Consuls of any power to afford his protection to the subjects of another power, not having any Consul on the spot, and you are therefore authorized to afford such protection if demanded. Great care and all

attention however must be observed by you in regard to the right of Foreigners who may claim such protection, and you will not grant it to any
persons who have not a clear right to such protection under the capitulation with the Porte.[16]

Young was warned by Campbell to pay "great attention" to protection permitted by the capitulations because

many abuses on the part of Foreign Consuls in regard to protection by
them to Native Rayahs have taken place in Syria, and indiscriminate
protection by you of persons claiming such protection as Foreign subjects might tend to involve you in disputes with the Local Authorities.

Campbell's instructions were similar to those Young had received from
Palmerston while still in London.

In mid-May 1839 the Foreign Office sent Young a short letter telling
him "to afford Protection to the Jews generally."[17] Young acknowledged
this letter without comment, but he must have wondered how to reconcile
Palmerston's "Protection" with a capital P and Campbell's limiting instructions to provide protection only in the case of a "clear right." If literally interpreted, Palmerston's instructions would provide protection for foreign
nationals as well as for Turkish citizens against their own government. This
"Protection" clause would cause Young many problems during his term of
office as vice-consul (1839–1841) and then as consul (1841–1845) and was
to become the major concern of successive British and other consuls in Palestine.

Young interpreted the "Protection" clause in a broad manner, assuming
that the more recent order of Palmerston, the secretary of state for foreign
affairs, took precedence over the previous instructions of his immediate superior. Moreover, even before receiving Palmerston's "Protection" instructions, Young had been sympathetic to acting as guardian of the Jews.[18] He
wrote to Campbell about the Jews in warm language, concluding that fanatic Christian prejudices against the Jew "quite defeat the object of gaining
them the protection they require." Later Young reported to Palmerston
that, in his opinion, Jews

are not wanting in many of the best feelings of our nature. Gratitude is
eminent among the good qualities of their hearts, and if the Protection
could everywhere be accorded to the Jews—which Your Lordship has

commanded me to afford them here, a short time would, I am persuaded, give sufficient evidence that the Jew is worthier of a higher consideration than it is now his lot generally to find.

The Jews in the Holy Land reciprocated Young's friendliness. Upon hearing that a British consul was going to be stationed in Jerusalem, they were full of joy, according to the missionary Levi.

A great many I have heard myself say, Now we shall have more liberty, and we will be able to work for our own bread, and no more have to depend on others. They being convinced that the English nation desires their welfare, they look out for protection... [19]

When Young entered the city, Sephardi and Ashkenazi rabbis came out to meet him, hoping that now Jews would be protected by a British diplomat instead of by the missionaries.

After serving in Jerusalem for less than three months Young was reprimanded several times by Campbell for exceeding his instructions about protecting the Jews. [20] Campbell first wrote Young:

you misunderstand the nature of protection to be afforded by Her Majesty's Consular officers in the Levan.... In regard to Rayah Jews it is clear that they cannot have any right of British Protection any more than any other Rayahs, and I have to request that you will strictly conform to the instructions...

The very next day Campbell chided Young that "no British Consul has a right to protect subjects of Morocco, whether Jew or Musulman," because British protection

does not apply to Rayah Jews, whom you have no more right to protect, than Austria or France would have to protect Rayah Catholics, or Russia or Greece to protect Rayahs of the Greek Religion, and indeed not even so much right, as they would be protecting people of their own Religion, while we have not even that pretext for protecting Jews.

Two days later Campbell again castigated Young: "By the indiscriminate and inconsiderate manner in which you appear to protect all Jews, you will not only compromise yourself, but also your superior Authority here..."

On the same day, in another letter, Campbell cast aspersions on Young's probity by charging him with collecting unnecessary passport fees for his own personal aggrandizement. Later in the same month Campbell condescendingly addressed Young:

> I would recommend you to read carefully the 7th Article of the general instructions to Consuls, and to recollect that you are not in any way the Protector of the Rayah Jews, and that they are not in the slightest manner under your Jurisdiction.

Then he insulted Young's intelligence: "you are stepping beyond the bounds of your duty, and taking authority upon yourself to which you are not entitled."

Young answered Campbell's serious charges in a frosty tone:

> I would respectfully state, that I was not aware that I had in any way departed from my duty . . . I do not know that I have in any case interfered between the Authorities here and the Rayah Jews—whom you observe "cannot have any right to British Protection any more than any other Rayahs" although I had concluded from the Despatch ordering me to consider it part of my duty to grant protection to the Jews generally, that it was Viscount Palmerston's wish that the Hebrew nation generally residing in Palestine should be sensible that England is kindly disposed towards them and willing to grant them a countenance which would in some measure shield them from the oppression of their neighbours, as well as of the local Authorities.[21]

While writing, Young became so incensed that he dispatched a second letter asking Campbell to point out "what the 'proper legal documents' are, which they should produce, in order to prove themselves entitled to European Protection."

So severe, unjust, and tarnishing was Campbell's condemnation in the eyes of Young that he appealed to Palmerston, contending that he had not exceeded his instruction "to afford Protection to the Jews generally." In his letter to Palmerston—which was sheer insubordination—Young touched on the British foreign minister's sore point by noting that the Russian consul-general had promised the Jews his protection.

While awaiting a vindicating answer from Palmerston, Young had still another tiff with Campbell about protecting the Jews. Young wrote that he declined the Governor's visit at the moment that I heard of his barbarous treatment of two innocent Jews: a young Jew of Salonica [who was] beaten, imprisoned and burned before he mercifully died, [and] an aged woman . . . taken under the suspicion of concealing her son—She was tied up and beaten in the most brutal way.[22]

For his conduct in this matter, Young earned the "unqualified disapprobation" of Campbell.

Another point of contention between Young and Campbell was the vice-consul's conduct when an Egyptian soldier beat Joseph Amzalag.[23] Young wrote that "I addressed myself to Ibrahim Pacha and I required satisfaction, in having the soldier beaten on the same spot where he had beaten Mr. Amzalag. . . . " In a caustic reply, Campbell concluded that "Mr. Amzalag was in the wrong, and in a great measure brought his difficulties upon himself, and I shall not therefore interfere farther in this case—"

Young and Campbell were also at loggerheads about the need for the Jerusalem vice-consul to employ a Jewish dragoman[24]—a combination Hebrew interpreter and intelligence agent able to report news about the Jewish community. Soon after his arrival in Jerusalem Young, who did not know Hebrew, asked Campbell to hire a dragoman in order

to afford protection to the Jews generally—I have thought it advisable to appoint a Jew for the especial purpose of communicating more freely and with great advantage with the Jews—without such assistance it would have been difficult for me to have met the wishes of Her Majesty's Government. A Christian Dragoman could not be found equal to the task of reading Jewish papers . . .

Not wishing to rubber-stamp the request of an insubordinate official whom he considered incompetent, Campbell refused Young's request for a Hebrew dragoman by explaining, incorrectly, that not only is

Arabic the language spoken, and in use in all documents between the . . . Jews in Palestine, but even the greatest number of Jews there are ignorant of Hebrew . . . which language is never made use of, written or verbally, in the common relations of life.

Young knew that "the languages in which the Jews chiefly communicate are Spanish and Arabic" (referring to Sephardim rather than Ashkenazim), and that "contracts among them and their writing generally are done in Hebrew." Hebrew was known by nearly all Ashkenazim, the major Jewish clients of the vice-consul, and it was the conversational language that linked the Yiddish-speaking Ashkenazim with most Arabic and Ladino-speaking Sephardim.

Again Young went over the head of his immediate superior and appealed to Palmerston, who quickly approved the appointment of a Hebrew drago-man, knowing that his services were needed in order to report on the "present state of the Jewish Population in Palestine." Palmerston set the drag-oman's salary at 3,000 piastres. It proved to be a good investment for Young, who later wrote that he learned "what is going on among the Jews" from "his intelligent old Jewish dragoman, Joseph."

In addition to numerous arguments about how to protect the Jews and the need for a Hebrew dragoman, there was yet another matter of disagreement between Young and Campbell. Young suggested establishing a consular agent in Hebron to help "the numerous travellers who now make their Tour into Palestine by the Mt. Sinai from Cairo, all of whom came through Hebron."[25] Campbell did not see "the least necessity" for such an appointment because

> if agents were named at all the places where British Travellers resort, I should have to name Agents in every Town in Syria and indeed there are so many Consular Agents now in Palestine, that I am rather inclined to diminish than Augment the number of them."

Once again Young proved to be a difficult subordinate and appealed Campbell's decision to Palmerston. And once again Palmerston decided that Young "may appoint a Vice Consul at Hebron."

This was the last conflict between Young and Campbell.[26] In September 1839 Colonel Campbell was removed from the Foreign Service because he undiplomatically extolled the virtues of Mehemet Ali and stridently complained to Palmerston about the actions of the Sublime Porte. Campbell was succeeded by another colonel, Mr. Hodges. Campbell's ouster from the Foreign Service probably saved Young's job and vindicated his protection of the Jews. In effect Young was informed that his interpretation of "Protection" with a capital P was correct when the Foreign Office wrote to him that "I am now directed by Lord Palmerston to acquaint you that His Lordship has instructed Colonel Hodges to give you all proper support in your official character of British Vice Consul at Jerusalem."

Young probably realized that Palmerston's policy of "Protection" over-stepped the bounds of conventionally accepted diplomatic practices.[27] "Palm-erston, a foreign secretary who was ready to bully Turkish ministers," was not reticent about vigorously authorizing British protection for Ottoman and Russian Jews and other non-British nationals. He acted out of humani-tarian motives and a wish to satisfy Shaftesbury, the well-connected LJS missionary organization, and the rising tide of millenarianism. Yet his pri-mary motivation was to secure for England the greatest influence in the Ot-toman Empire. It was most fortunate for the Jewish community that mis-sion activities, millenarianism, and a humanitarian attitude toward Jews were congruent interests that converged and fitted into British diplomatic and commercial plans in the Near East. Palmerston helped the Jews in Pal-estine in order to insert a British wedge into the Turkish provinces. The fostering of a friendly Jewish group that required protection permitted Brit-ain to penetrate places—such as Jerusalem—that were previously closed to it. Palmerston was not averse to using the Jews as a countervailing factor against his European rivals. By protecting the Jews, Britain established a base of operation in the Holy Land, thereby asserting its influence as well as thwarting the efforts of Russia, France, and Egypt. Palmerston had shrewdly perceived how to use the Jewish aspirations in Zion for the best interests of British policy in the Near East

When Young was instructed by Palmerston to provide protection for the Jews, he was also told to report on the "present state of the Jewish popula-tion in Palestine." Happily, Young wrote that

> the appointment of a British Vice Consul in Jerusalem has not been without its effect on the Jewish population. The remotest village in Eu-rope, that contains a Jewish resident, will hear the news that Great Brit-ain has been the first among the nations to show herself the friend of the Children of Israel, by sending to the City of David a representative.[28]

Young knew that Jews "huddle together for mutual safety" in the four holy cities where they live in "idleness and misery." He noted that it was most difficult to determine the correct number of Jews in Palestine because "the religious prejudice [is] so strong against their being numbered at all," referring to the biblical injunction against census-taking. Nevertheless Young reported that 9,310 Jews lived in Palestine:

Jerusalem	5500
Nablus	150
Hebron	750
Tiberias	600
Safed	1500
Acre	200
Haifa	150
Jaffa	60
Villages in the Galilee	400
TOTAL	9310

These figures are fairly accurate, with the glaring exception of Jerusalem, where about 4,000 rather than 5,500 Jews resided.

Young bemoaned the intolerance shown toward the Jews of Palestine.[29] "The spirit of tolerance towards the Jew is not yet known here to the same extent as it is in Europe," no doubt referring to Western Europe. "The poor Jew, even in the nineteenth century, lives from day to day in terror of his life." The Jew is forced "to purchase toleration" by paying higher prices for such items as rent. Both Muslims and Christians evinced a "fierce spirit of oppression" toward the Jew. "The Jew in Jerusalem is not estimated in value much above a dog . . ."

In two instances Young intervened to obtain justice for Jews and he surmised that this may have been detrimental to his influence with "Christians as well as Turks."[30] Young reported that the authorities forbid Jews "under pain of being severely punished" to pray in their own houses, meaning that the Jews could only pray in a synagogue that had been officially approved by a firman, such as the Hurva. To make matters worse for the Jews, according to Young (and Joseph Schwartz) Egyptian soldiers enter Jewish homes "and borrow whatever they require without asking any permission—sometimes they return the article but more frequently not."

Another "species of persecution" and extortion was related to Young by the medical missionary Dr. Gerstmann.[31]

So soon as the Plague is reported to be in the City, the Jews at once become the object of cupidity, to every employe in the quarantine service, who, with the Native practitioners in medicine, rob and oppress them to the last degree. From one individual alone, of the better class, they succeeded lately in obtaining 4,000 piastres, equal to £40 Sterling in bribes—His son was sick with the fever—they declared it to be Plague—set a guard on his house, deprived him of all means of obtaining medical assistance—the patient died, and then, on his refusing to satisfy their demands—they threatened to burn everything in his House. This My Lord is not a solitary instance.

Young sagely explained why the Jews lived in "fear and suspicion."

To seek redress he is afraid, lest it bring worse upon him; he thinks it better to endure than to live in the expectation of his complaint being revenged upon him. Brought up from infancy to look upon his civil disabilities everywhere as a mark of degradation, his heart becomes the cradle of fear and suspicion—he finds he is trusted by none—and therefore he lives himself without confidence in any.

It is difficult to reconcile Young's 1839 description about the disheartening situation of the Jews with cheery reports from Bergmann and others about "great tolerance displayed toward Jerusalem's Jews who are ostensibly blessed by a higher status" than "Muslim Gentiles."

Jews often came to Young for protection.[32] "In cases of injustice or insult they have no redress from the Mussulman authorities." Young arbitrated differences between litigating Jews and helped them by distributing PEKAM monies forwarded from Amsterdam through Beirut. This prompted Lehren to warn Jerusalem Jews not to become enmeshed in the missionary network operating out of the British consulate.

In addition to reporting regularly about the Jews, Young closely tracked the activities of the Greek Orthodox and Catholic churches and their patrons, Russia and France. He wrote about forty Russian Jewish families in Jerusalem who "consider themselves Russian Subjects or Proteges."[33] They petitioned and received protection from the Russian consul-general, "but since the departure of the late Russian Consul-General from Egypt, and the death of their late Vice-Consul at Jaffa they are no longer recognized." Young explained that these Russian Jews were stateless and without protection.

At the end of August 1839 Young was agitated by the arrival of the newly appointed Russian consul, Constantine M. Basili.[34] For the first time Russia posted to Palestine a respected member of the Russian Ministry of Foreign Affairs. After Russia transferred Basili from Jaffa to Beirut and appointed him Russian consul for all of Syria, Basili visited Jerusalem. He appointed a wakiel, a kind of consular liaison officer, for Russian Jews in Palestine; Young interpreted this to mean all European Jews, which no doubt was Basili's intent.

On October 8, 1839, Basili appointed R. Isaiah Bardaki wakiel. R. Bardaki was a man of influence, a leader of the Sukkat Shalom group of Perushim and a trustee of PEKAM. This was an opportunity for him to advance his leadership in the Jewish community after having lost the battle to stop the Hurva faction from consecrating its new synagague.

In the letter of appointment, Basili noted that R. Bardaki was recommended as consular liaison officer by Zvi Hirsch Lehren.[35] Basili promised R. Bardaki the protection of the Russian government in carrying out his tasks as wakiel for "Palestine Jews holding Russian citizenship." R. Bardaki was charged with

> granting them legal assistance, to take care of their interests, to supervise their behavior and to maintain the peace and unity among them. I have no doubt, Sir [Basili wrote Bardaki] that your sensitive character and your astute efforts will resolve all the disputes that have recently broken out among [the Jews].

The reference to Bardaki's sensitivity is most questionable, as is the expectation that the chief protagonist of the Sukkat Shalom group could resolve any disagreements with the antagonistic Hurva faction. But an astute diplomat like Basili knew what he was doing. He wanted to appoint a powerful, combative member of the European Jewish community, and he concluded that Bardaki was his man. That the abrasive R. Bardaki had not the slightest chance of resolving disputes among the Jews was of no interest to Basili.

Young reported Bardaki's appointment to Palmerston, stressing that "the political state of the country lends importance to the position of the Russian Consul...the Jews...under their new Wakiel...look to the Russian Consul as their protector." Young "directed the English Jews to take no notice" of the proceedings of the Russian consul, neglecting to mention that only two or three English Jewish families lived in Jerusalem. Upon receiving Young's dispatch, Palmerston unhesitatingly ordered him to "appoint a Vakeel for the British Jews, in the same manner in which the Russian Consul has appointed one for the Russian Jews."

Since there were so few Englishmen and English-speaking Jews in Jerusalem, Young's choice of a wakiel was quite limited. He offered the position to David Hirschel, the son of the chief rabbi of the Ashkenazim in London. An unstable character who was not interested in assuming community leadership, David Hirschel "begged to decline for the present" because he was desirous of keeping aloof as much as possible from their quarrels. Young "endeavoured to impress upon him, the duty which rested with those, who had any Authority—to endeavour to keep order and unity among their Brethren," but to no avail. Herschel may have declined the position because of his suspicions about Young's connection with the missionaries, or he may have suspected that the wakiel must serve as a British informer.

Young cushioned his failure by noting that "should the British Jews become more numerous the appointment of a Vakiel will be very desirable." He also consoled himself by reporting that "the person appointed by the Russian Consul—is anxious already to be freed from his charge—he finds the constant difficulty he is involved in, more than he can endure." This report about R. Bardaki wanting to opt out of his new appointment is highly doubtful considering his appetite for authority and leadership, especially in light of a letter written by Shlomo Zalman Zoref in 1842: "And I report that Rabbi Isaiah of Pinsk rules as he pleases and wishes . . . and every day they beat our people [Hurva members] and there is no one to stop them . . . "[36] By virtue of his new appointment, R. Bardaki strengthened his power within the Jewish community.

In April 1840 Young again reported to Palmerston on the actions of the Russian consul in Beirut and his Jerusalem wakiel, noting the growing influence and encroachment of Russia in Palestine.[37] In reality, the situation was completely different from the rumors reported by Young about the imposing presence of the meddling Russian consul.

Up to 1841 foreign minister Nesselrode did not consider stationing a Russian clergyman or diplomat in Jerusalem "in order not to arouse the 'suspicions' of the Sublime Porte and the 'jealousy' of the other Powers."[38] Nesselrode proceeded slowly and with a hesitation bordering on "excessive timidity," because he knew that Russia had the advantage of protecting 20,000 Greek Orthodox, the largest minority group in Palestine. Only in mid-1842, after the arrival of the Anglican bishop in Jerusalem, did Nesselrode send an archimandrite to Jerusalem. Not until 1847 did the Greek patriarch of Jerusalem settle in Jerusalem, and only in 1858 was a Russian consul stationed in the city.

Although Campbell had already retired from the foreign service, Young was still agitated over the lack of support from his former superior in Alexandria. Young wrote that "when I first took up my residence in this country" European Jews "consulted" him and he rendered them protection according to Palmerston's instructions. But due to Campbell's instructions

I have relinquished all official interference on behalf of Foreign Jews—
They on finding this to be the case, have ceased to apply to me, and have
readily accepted the protection which the Russian Consul has shown
himself willing to afford them.[39]

It seems not to have occurred to Young that the Jews preferred the protection of another Jew, R. Bardaki, rather than a Christian who spoke no Hebrew and was connected with the missionaries. Another reason for this apparent decline in Young's influence among the Jews may have been their
fear of being attacked because of their association with him in the event that
the consul would leave town upon the imminent cessation of Egyptian rule
in Palestine.

Young left Jerusalem at the end of the summer of 1840. When he re-
turned at the beginning of 1841 he found a Jerusalem again ruled by the
Turkish sultan in Istanbul, after Ibrahim Pasha's forces retreated back to
Egypt.[40]

FIFTEEN

Montefiore's Second Trip to Eretz Israel

1839

In 1839 Moses Montefiore visited Palestine for the second time. Since his first trip in 1827 the retired Montefiore had become actively involved in a multitude of Jewish and English community affairs. In recognition of his stellar public service, he had been elected sheriff of London and a member of the prestigious Royal Society and was knighted by the newly ascended Queen Victoria. Montefiore strove to remove the civil disabilities then imposed on British Jewry, but he was opposed by millenarians such as Lord Shaftesbury, who were more eager to return Jews to Zion than to encourage them to remain comfortably in Britain.

The purpose of Montefiore's trip to Palestine was to improve the situation of the impoverished Jews. "I sincerely pray that my journey to the Holy Land may prove beneficial to the Jews," he wrote, defining in the most general terms the reason for his voyage. He desired "to do something towards ameliorating the conditions of the Jews in Palestine,"[1] according to a similar generalization of vice-consul William T. Young. More specifically, Montefiore sought to find a way to make Jews in Eretz Israel "productive"—able to earn their own living. With the benefit of hindsight, Montefiore wrote in 1875 that his 1839 trip to Palestine was "to ascertain the practicality of the cultivation of the soil by the Jews settled in Palestine"

333

and to initiate efforts "for the development of the industrial resources of the country . . ."

Moses and Judith Montefiore left London for Palestine in November 1838, carrying letters of introduction from foreign minister Palmerston. Traveling in leisurely fashion by carriage through France, Belgium, Prussia, and Italy, Montefiore learned about the condition of the Jewish communities located along the route, as part of his constant efforts to maintain extensive contacts and help Jewish communities in Europe, Asia, and Africa. The Montefiores celebrated the Passover festival in Rome, where they again met the 29-year-old Oriental scholar Dr. Louis Loewe, who was doing research in the Vatican archives. Because of his stable, scholarly personality, his knowledge of Hebrew, Arabic, and English, and his firsthand experience with life in Eretz Israel, Loewe was invited to accompany Montefiore on his visit to Eretz Israel. Loewe readily accepted this invitation, which initiated a close, 47-year association with Montefiore.

During his first visit to Palestine in 1838 Louis Loewe had suffered through the rebellion of the Druze,[2] a small, bellicose people with their unique faith, neither Christian or Muslim. In order to ensure the safety of the Jews of Safed in the face of the Druze-Muslim threat to sack the city, the leader of the Hasidim, R. Abraham Dov, asked Loewe to intercede with the Safed governor. Loewe was promised by the governor, on his "head and eyes," that he would not desert Safed and would protect the Jews.

Shortly thereafter the governor fled the city! Most of the Jews huddled together in the courtyard of R. Abraham Dov, who bribed the Druze and local Arabs with all the money in the kollel treasury, 75,000 piastres. The marauders took the money and then avariciously demanded another 50,000 piastres. When the Jews could not pay, the saintly Hasidic rabbi was beaten. R. Abraham Dov bravely prayed and "blessed the Lord on the sentence He has judged upon me today."[3]

Realizing that they could extort no more money from the Jews, the Druze and local Muslims vandalized the Jewish quarter. During three days they enacted a replay of the 1834 plunder, looting homes and desecrating synagogues—but no deaths were reported. What could not be stolen was smashed and burned. Jews caught outdoors were robbed and beaten. Some Jews ran to the cemetery and caves outside of town. Others like Louis Loewe fled to the nearby Druze village of Ein Zeitun, which had sheltered Jews during the 1834 rebellion. Villagers threw rocks at the Jews and locked them up in a small synagogue. Loewe reported being "beaten on the most tender parts of our body and they seriously wounded us causing the flow of blood."[4] Then Jews were stripped of their clothes and possessions and tortured, before being allowed to flee back to Safed. Even Jews living in outlying villages, such as the Bak family on the Jermak, did not escape the looting and destruction of the Druze.

Hasidim asked Dr. Loewe to convince R. Abraham Dov to move the Hasidic community to a defensible site in Acre or Haifa, where foreign consuls could protect them. R. Abraham Dov said that he would abide by the wishes of the Hasidim but,

> in his opinion, they have an obligation to remain in their place regardless of what happens to them, in order to maintain this old settlement in its place and to save synagogues that would be destroyed if the Hasidim leave the city.[5]

In "holy resignation" R. Abraham Dov also quoted from the Talmud that the Galilee would be destroyed before Redemption, implying that the coming of the Messiah might be close at hand. The 600 Hasidim were convinced, remained in Safed with the 750 Sephardim, and once again started to repair their homes and synagogues and rebuild the Jewish quarter.

While traveling toward Palestine aboard an English steamer, Montefiore and Loewe discussed how they could improve the economic condition of the Jews in Eretz Israel. They realized that a basic change of direction was essential for Jews to acquire a means of livelihood. Yet they recognized the importance of haluka funds in keeping the Jews fed, clothed, and housed; thus they opposed suggestions to stop the flow of haluka so that Jews "would all be forced to seek support by their own industry."[6]

It clearly was not feasible to develop the "industrial resources" of Palestine, due to the lack of investment capital, local know-how, and trained personnel. Setting up cottage industries was not a practical alternative since there was only a small market and no chance to export competitively priced merchandise to industrial Europe. The possibility of employing Jews as artisans and craftsmen was also limited. Many Ashkenazim were physically incapable of performing manual work and lacked the skills of craftsmen. Trade and commerce could employ few Jews, for purchasing power was small; nor was there much local produce to sell, because many commodities were monopolies of the Egyptian government.[7] Montefiore also knew that it would be difficult to develop commercial opportunities in a country continually struck by pestilence and closed down by quarantine.

Since industry, trade and commerce, and crafts and artisanship were not viable employment solutions for most Jews, this left only one alternative: farming. Although Jews lacked agricultural knowledge and experience,

Montefiore believed that a large number could be transformed into productive tillers of the soil by training them in Peki'in and other farming villages that Loewe had heard about during his 1838 visit in the Galilee. Loewe probably knew that the Egyptian government encouraged peasants to settle in villages by exempting them from taxes and compulsory military conscription. In 1837 the Kadi of Jaffa acquired land outside the town walls and had it worked by peasants, in line with Mehemet Ali's policy of reclaiming waste lands and planting trees. If the Kadi could obtain land in Palestine, Montefiore was confident that with the backing of the British government he too would acquire land so that the Jews could cultivate it.

In order to determine how many Jews needed assistance, Montefiore instructed Loewe to conduct a census of "The Children of Israel living in the Holy Land in the Year 5519–1839." This was not a simple matter, because Jews objected to being counted. They remembered that when King David enumerated the people of Israel the Lord sent a plague punishing him. Montefiore and Loewe ingeniously overcame the resistance of the Jews to being counted by integrating census-taking with charity distribution. In return for answering the questionnaire prepared by Loewe, Jews were financially rewarded:[8] a child under 13 years of age received half a Spanish dollar, an adult one dollar (21 piastres), and a blind person two dollars. Jews could ill afford to pass up the opportunity of receiving the equivalent of one month's income just by filling out a questionnaire and waiting in line for a few hours.

Although it took many years to tally the results of the Jewish population census—to date there is still no comprehensive statistical analysis of the data—it provides a variety of information about certain unique characteristics of the Jewish community in Palestine.

In 1839–1840 nearly 7,500 Jews lived in Eretz Israel, a precipitous drop from the high figure of 9,800 reached just before the January 1837 earthquake. The rapid population growth of 2,200 persons experienced by the Jewish community between 1830 and 1837 was erased by one vengeful blow of nature.

A radical change in the population mix of Sephardim and Ashkenazim occurred between 1800 and 1839. In 1800 only 5 percent of the fewer than 5,000 Jews in Eretz Israel were Ashkenazim; by 1839 the percentage of Ashkenazim had passed 30 percent as a result of the influx of Perushim and Hasidim from Eastern Europe.[9] In 1839 about 1,100 Perushim and an equal number of Hasidim lived in Eretz Israel. The Sephardim numbered 5,300 and constituted almost the entire Jewish population of Haifa (150), Jaffa (125), Acre (250), Nablus (100), and the three northern agricultural villages

(250). Poor Ashkenazim with no work skills could afford to live only in the holy cities of Jerusalem, Safed, Tiberias, and Hebron, where they received haluka.

The Jewish community of Eretz Israel remained a predominantly immigrant population; two out of three Jews (68 percent) were born abroad.[10] But there was a large disparity between the numbers of native-born Ashkenazim and Sephardim. Less than one out of ten Ashkenazim counted by Montefiore were born in Eretz Israel, while four out of ten Sephardim were native-born. One quarter of the Sephardi immigrants living in Eretz Israel in 1839 came from Algiers,[11] Morocco, and Tunis, 17 percent from Greece and the Balkans, and about half from other Ottoman Empire countries. Among the Ashkenazim, seven out of ten originated in Russia and Poland, one out of ten in Rumania,[12] and one out of six (16 percent) in the Austro-Hungarian Empire.

Most of the Jews living in Eretz Israel in 1839 had arrived during the seven-year span 1830–1837. A Jew told a missionary in 1838 that most Jewish settlers were "newcomers" who had lived in the Holy Land for about four years.[13] About six out of ten settlers in 1839 came to Eretz Israel between 1830 and 1839. In comparison to the previous decade, Ashkenazi immigration soared by 270 percent, while Sephardi immigration rose by 150 percent.[14]

Contrary to many tourist reports, Montefiore's census failed to reveal an overwhelmingly elderly Jewish population. Nearly two out of ten (19 percent) were above the age of 50, a figure significantly higher than the 11.5 percent in the Jewish population of Russia in 1817.[15] And one out of ten Jews in Eretz Israel were over 60 years of age, nearly twice the number found in the 1817 Russian Jewish population (5.4 percent). Immigrant Jews were a slightly younger group than native-born Jews, possibly because the long and difficult journey to Eretz Israel was not an appealing prospect for many elderly Jews.

Seeing so many old people, the Scottish ministers logically concluded that people who came to Palestine "are generally elderly and do not leave families behind them to increase the population or supply its vacancies."[16] But this generally accepted opinion is erroneous and misleading. The meaningful key to understanding the characteristics of the Jewish population is not found in the somewhat older group of Jews, but in the cohort of Jews under age 40,[17] specifically in the small percentage of children under 10 years.

Although two out of three Jews living in Eretz Israel were under 40 years of age—significantly fewer than the 80 percent in the 1817 Russian census—in the childbearing ages of 20 to 40 there was little difference between the two populations. Most important are Montefiore's census figures showing that only 15 percent of the Jewish population was under 10 years old, much less than the 28 percent in the Russian census of 1817 and also much less than the 22 percent recorded in Montefiore's 1855 census of the Jewish population in Eretz Israel. This significant difference was the result of a low birth rate and an extremely high death rate among very young children.

Most Jewish children died before reaching age 10.[18] Montefiore's 1839 census shows that 9 percent of the population, a smaller than normal number, were 0–4 years old, indicating that newborn infants ran the highest risks of dying. The Swiss physician and researcher Titus Tobler observed in 1845 that two-thirds of the newborn babies in Palestine "die after a few days or weeks . . . about two-thirds view the light of the world for no more than a few days or weeks. One rarely finds a family with many children, whereas childless young couples were very frequent." Another physician, Dr. Robert Richardson, reported after his trip to Palestine in 1818 that "the want of children is as great a heartbreak to them now as it was in the days of Sarah."[19]

Despite the fact that the percentage of Jewish men in Eretz Israel in the child-producing ages of 20 to 40 was nearly identical to that of the 1817 Russian census, men in the Holy Land did not come close to producing and raising the slightly more than two children needed to replenish their ranks. Men in Eretz Israel barely begat one child per family.[20]

As a result of the low birth rate, the staggeringly high infant mortality, and the somewhat elderly population, there was a large population deficit.[21] The estimated annual population deficit was 40 per 1,000 Jews—the death rate was 80 per 1,000 Jews while the birth rate was 40 per 1,000.

This rough calculation of the population deficit does not take into consideration the number of Jews who left Eretz Israel. Since emigrants from the Holy Land were considered "deserters" performing a profane act,[22] as in the case of Shmaryahu Luria, it is difficult to obtain reliable information regarding their numbers. However, both Christian and Jewish sources attest to Jews returning to their native lands.[23] In 1836 Nicolayson wrote about a Jew who would gladly return to Europe but lacked the means to do so. Nicolayson was surprised to find in Beirut a number of Eretz Israel families returning to Eastern Europe, an unusual occurrence in his opinion. Jews told Nicolayson that they tried to persevere in Eretz Israel but the 1834 fellahin revolt and continuous poverty—they ate but one meal a day—drove them out of the Holy Land. At the end of the 1830s one source recorded complaints of Jews that Eretz Israel is a "land which consumes its inhabitants" and that some embittered Ashkenazim demanded to be sent back to Poland.[24] Lehren also wrote about some Jews who left Eretz Israel in the 1830s to escape their debtors.[25] Nevertheless, the factor of emigration did not contribute greatly to the population deficit, for the number of Jews leaving Eretz Israel was probably quite negligible—"very small, hardly noticeable."[26] Jews wishing to return to Europe simply lacked the necessary financial means.

What, then, caused the appallingly large annual population deficit of 40 per 1,000 Jews? Since the percentage of men aged 20 to 40 was not low; the population was not overwhelmingly elderly; nearly all the eligible men were married; and the traditional Jewish religious society prohibited the practice of birth control, we may conclude that the huge negative demographic imbalance was caused by two major factors:[27] the abominable health and economic conditions in the towns and the premature marriages of 13- to 15-year-old girls with 14- to 16-year-old boys.

Few 15-year-old girls were listed in the 1839 census as living with their parents, indicating that most were already married. Such early marriages were customarily contracted by both Jews and Muslims in the Near East. Many writers reported about baby brides and grooms, "children converted into married people."[28]

Early marriage and childbirth injured the health of both the infant and the mother and endangered their very survival. Dr. Titus Tobler wrote:

Before the persons become nubile, before their organs and ability of procreation are duly developed, those latter are utterly misused. When the boy or girl reaches the age at which the cycle of physical development is completed and nature calls only then for procreation, the best strength is already wasted; weaklings produce, with utmost effort and exertion, little weaklings . . .[29]

With the death of a baby, the young breast-feeding mother lost the contraceptive protection of lactation, so that another pregnancy ensued. This deadly cycle of early pregnancy and infant death was repeated until the exhausted mother was sapped of her ability to give birth. We can only wonder about the widespread bereavement caused by the high infant mortality and the psychological suffering of mothers no longer able to conceive.

Young mothers who did not produce a child contributed to a high divorce rate because, according to Jewish law, a husband can divorce his wife if she does not conceive after a number of years. John Nicolayson wrote that divorce occurs "frequently . . . almost daily." This is echoed by the Scottish ministers, who reported that "divorce occurs every day." Such a high divorce rate reflected a highly charged emotional situation and must have greatly disrupted the social fabric of the Jewish community.

The poor health conditions prevailing in the urban community also contributed to the high death rate. Throughout the nineteenth century (and before), in Palestine as well as in Europe, the death rate was higher in the towns where the Jews lived than in villages, which were less afflicted by epidemics. "Man-eating" towns could not maintain their population levels "without a substantial influx of immigrants from surrounding countrysides."[30] Interestingly, wars and rebellions hardly reduced the Jewish and Muslim population.

In Palestine, the disregard of filth and the neglect of proper sanitation methods were detrimental to health. With no sewage and garbage disposal, rubbish, debris, excrement, and dead animals accumulated in the town streets. Drinking polluted water spread dysentery and cholera. Jewish immigrants who had yet to adjust to the country and develop immunities were easy prey for the pernicious "ague"—chills, fever, and sweating—that was rampant, recurring, and debilitating. Contributing to poor health conditions were crowded housing quarters—damp "dens of filth" with little light, fresh air, or ventilation.[31] Inadequate clothing and lack of heating in the frigid winters also damaged the health of the Jewish population, as did malnutrition. Persons who died from a disease might have survived had they been adequately nourished. This is especially true of children under 5 years of age, whose cause of death today in many underdeveloped countries is listed as malnutrition.

In this disease-infested environment of Palestine there was not one qualified resident doctor to treat the sick, probably not such a great disadvantage in the days that mandated medical treatment by bleedings and purgings. And there was not one hospital in Palestine, no great loss in times when "hospitals were lethal death traps" spreading infections.[32]

A number of striking facts about widows, orphans, and the numerical relationship between men and women were also revealed by the 1839 census, giving Montefiore good cause to worry about the development of the Jewish community in Eretz Israel.

Widows constituted an extremely large segment of the female Jewish population, as was frequently reported by tourists.[33] Slightly more than one out of three Jewish women of marriageable age (35 percent) were widows; in Jerusalem 49 percent of Jewish women were widows. Some widows had come to Eretz Israel to live off haluka funds that were not distributed in their native lands.

A corollary of the preponderance of widows and another abnormal characteristic distinguishing the Jewish population in Palestine was the fact that women outnumbered men seven to six. Yet in the age group 0 to 14 there were five boys for every four girls.

Another strange demographic characteristic reflecting the atypical nature of the Jewish community was the large number of orphans. In Jerusalem three out of ten Jewish children (29 percent) did not have a living father.[34] The large numbers of orphans and widows provide circumstantial evidence of the high mortality rate, especially among Jewish men. If Jewish men were reported to be "more sickly and suffer[ing] from a greater variety of non-febrile diseases than other classes of the population," it was because of prolonged study hours in close, unsanitary quarters and perhaps also because of frequent fasts, self-abnegation, and mortifying the body as a means of atonement.

Montefiore's census gathered superficial information about the economic status and occupations of the Jewish population. Since there was no definition of "poor" and some Jews mistakenly believed that only poor Jews were entitled to receive Montefiore's charity; 90 percent of the Jews declared themselves "poor" and living in "distress."[35]

The occupations of the Jews listed in the census highlighted the disparity between the jobs of Ashkenazim and Sephardim. More than three out of four Ashkenazi males, but only half that number of Sephardi men, were engaged in religious occupations as rabbis, scholars, scribes, meat slaughterers, undertakers, and tombstone engravers. While only slightly more than one out of ten Ashkenazim earned their living by manual labor, nearly half (45 percent) of the responding Sephardim subsisted by "the sweat of their brow." The Ashkenazim, 25 percent of the Jewish population recorded by Montefiore, constituted only 15 percent of the working population. Slightly more than 15 percent of both Sephardi and Ashkenazi Jews listed their occupation in the undefined category of "trade." "Many [Jews] occupy themselves in Bartering and pedlery, about the Country, and in this way they eke out an existence," according to vice-consul Young. The Scottish ministers reported that "a few are shopkeepers; a few more are hawkers; and a very few are operatives."[36]

Montefiore's census shows that hardly any Jews farmed the land except in the northern villages of Peki'in (75), Shfar-Am (107), and the Jermak (18).[37] Contrary to vice-consul Young, who wrote that no Jews are "engaged in Agricultural pursuits," Nicolayson knew from David Beit Hillel that "many Jews are engaged in agriculture," referring to the three northern villages.

When Montefiore landed in Beirut on May 11, 1839, he was greeted by the governor of Beirut and the news that Mahmud II had sent Turkish armies to battle his Egyptian vassal, Mehemet Ali, in revenge for the humilating agreement of 1833, which forced Ottoman acceptance of Egyptian sovereignty over greater Syria. Sir Moses noted in his diary that "our visit is not most timely for our comfort, pleasure or safety; the political state of the country is most unsatisfactory and uncertain; a single day may bring about a complete change in the government of Syria and Palestine."[38] Montefiore also received upsetting reports about "a bad winter" in Palestine, with 40 to 50 Jerusalemites dying daily from cholera. Only one month before, the Jerusalem quarantine had prevented vice-consul Young from entering town. At this time "the roads and the country" were "generally . . . very unsafe," but having traveled so far, Montefiore was resolved to tour Palestine. The armed Montefiore party traveled overland on horseback and donkey and arrived safely in Safed on May 17.

An advance party escorted the Montefiore entourage into Safed, where it was welcomed by large crowds. Leaders of the Ashkenazi and Sephardi communities, the governor, the Kadi, and other Muslim dignitaries all paid their respects to Montefiore. The request of the Druze to visit Montefiore was declined since Montefiore and Loewe thought it "undesirable to encourage their presence in Safed" less than one year after the 1838 Druze rebellion.[39]

The indisposed R. Israel of Shklov apologized for not greeting Montefiore, who was invited to visit R. Israel taking the baths in Tiberias. R. Israel proffered his invitation despite Lehren's jealousy of Montefiore. When Lehren learned about Montefiore's impending trip to Eretz Israel, he had told R. Israel that the Jews "should provide him [Montefiore] with no control over Ashkenazi money coming from London and England and the United States of America." Lehren instructed the Jewish community to cooperate with Montefiore but "not to give him an appointment concerning the money of Eretz Israel,"[40] thereby zealously guarding PEKAM's special relationship with Eretz Israel and blocking potential competition.

While touring Safed the Montefiores saw terrible poverty in the Jewish quarter as a result of the 1834 rebellion, the 1837 earthquake, and the Druze rebellion in 1838. Although at least one synagogue and many houses in the Jewish quarter had been rebuilt, "rubbish had not been removed from the street," and Safed "was still little more than one great mass of ruins"; all around were piles of rubble. Montefiore reported:

> At the present moment the ruins of the town present an awful spectacle of destruction; the few miserable hovels they have erected are for the most part little better than caves, more fit for beasts of the field than for human beings. Many are merely four mud walls, with a mat for a roof. I think the poverty of the Jews in Safed to be great beyond anything that can be imagined.[41]

Montefiore reported incorrectly about "great numbers" of Jews dying of hunger, possibly because he was repeatedly told by Safed Jews that "it is two years that starvation stalks the country" and "prices are sky-high like they have never been."

The Montefiores visited two Sephardi synagogues and the Ashkenazi synagogue, where they prayed on the Sabbath and celebrated the spring festival of Pentecost. Montefiore contributed to paying off the loan and the high interest charges on money borrowed to refurbish one Sephardi synagogue that had collapsed in the 1837 earthquake.

Before sunset on Friday evening, the Montefiores observed

> preparations going on in every Jewish dwelling for the Sabbath. The women brought out of the oven the bread they had baked, beautifully white wheaten bread. The houses were all set in order, the table arranged, the couches spread; in every dwelling the Sabbath lamp was lighted, and a low murmur was heard, while the father of the family repeated the appointed benediction. Soon after, all hurried to the synagogue, to bring in the Sabbath there.

This Sabbath ceremony was witnessed by Scottish ministers who visited Safed two months after the Montefiore visit. One difference between the narratives of Montefiore and the Scottish ministers is that Montefiore played down the Jewish rituals, while the Scottish ministers highlighted the specific characteristics of the Jews and their religious practices.

Montefiore visited the Hasidic synagogue, whose prayer service was vividly described by the Scottish ministers:

> We . . . found it very neat and clean, beautifully lighted up with lamps of olive oil. Several very venerable men were seated all round; more than

half of the worshippers had beards verging to pure white, and grey hair flowing on their shoulders. . . . In reading their prayers, nothing could exceed their vehemency. They read with all their might; then cried aloud like Baal's prophets on Mount Carmel; and from time to time, the tremulous voice of some aged Jew rose above all the rest in earnestness. . . . One old man often stretched out his hand as he called on the Lord, and clenched his trembling fist in impassioned supplication. Some clapped their hands, others clasped both hands together, and wrung them as in an agony of distress, till they should obtain their request. A few beat upon their breasts. One man, trembling with age, seemed to fix on the word "Adonai," and repeated it with every variety of intonation, till he exhausted his voice. All of them, old and young, moved the body backward and forward, rocking to and fro, and bending toward the ground.[42]

Louis Loewe introduced Montefiore to R. Abraham Dov, the leader of the Hasidim, whom he described as "one of the most scholarly and precious persons that I have ever met. He works for the community without receiving a salary and he shares with the poor whatever he has; ten to fifteen people always eat at his table."

"From nine to six" Montefiore personally distributed charity to the Jews of Safed and collected their census questionnaires.[43] By this method he counted 1,400 Jews in Safed—750 Sephardim, 600 Hasidim, and a mere 30 Perushim.

Montefiore discussed with Sephardim their system of giving most of the haluka money to scholars, "leaving but little for the other sufferers." The Sephardim explained that their haluka system was equitable because scholars did not engage in business or income-producing occupations, so they "ought naturally to have some additional share in the offerings of their wealthier brethren abroad, offerings intended not only for the relief of distress but also for the preservation of a religious unity." Montefiore remained unconvinced.

Poor Safed Jews voiced serious complaints against the method of distributing PEKAM and other monies. Montefiore was asked to intervene so that PEKAM monies would be allocated only to the needy, who claimed that the rich were financially able to support themselves and rebuild their homes. Other Jews, afraid to sign their names to a letter, charged that out of the "huge sum" donated in the Diaspora after the 1837 earthquake, some Jews received 45 piastres of haluka while others "took" 500 piastres. And then the leaders "took back from us more than double the haluka monies they gave us." Protesting Jews were told by some kollel leaders to go back from where they came. "You have no share in our inheritance . . . it suffices for us to have only a minyan of ten males. And each of you can return to your family" in Europe. These Jews were outraged when they saw their leaders use overseas donations to "build houses that they never had, while we sit without homes, boiling during the day and freezing at night."[44]

The large sums of money donated in the Diaspora after the 1837 earthquake contributed to this "atmosphere of accusation and counteraccusation" in Safed. PEKAM's representative, Shmuel Heller, was singled out for special vilification. Heller tried to keep the Jews away from Montefiore in conformance with the wishes of Lehren, who had warned that the English philanthropist—who regularly contributed "to idolatrous causes"—wanted to set up a school where young children would learn subjects "contrary to the holy Torah."[45]

One letter writer, Nahum Halevi, was threatened that he and his family would be chased out of Eretz Israel if he dispatched his letter to Montefiore. When this threat did not dissuade Halevi, he was turned over to Muslims, beaten, and chased out of Safed, before Jewish public opinion forced his return. Then he was refused his fair share of PEKAM money: "I was left with nothing and did not even have a sliver of bread." Halevi implored Montefiore: "Father, father, save me."[46] Such stormy relations between discontented Jews depressed Montefiore, who recognized that the Jews could not silently suffer offenses and was distressed to learn that there was more than a kernel of truth in their exaggerated, disheartening diatribe.

Montefiore was relieved that at least the large Hasidic community of 600 seemed satisfied with the leadership of R. Abraham Dov and his method of distributing earthquake compensation funds "according to the amount of loss sustained by each individual." The Sephardi chief rabbi, Haim Mizrahi, and two Sephardi leaders, Samuel Aboo and Abraham Shoshana, were reproved for submitting two census lists double-counting the Sephardi leaders and then asking Montefiore for special financial benefits. Montefiore tried to placate eleven complaining Sephardi scholars by donating to each of them 50 Spanish dollars, but the scholars scrupulously insisted on distributing this 11,500 piastres among all Sephardim as prescribed in the kollel regulations.

Perushim leaders were also savagely attacked. Twelve affluent Hasidim petitioned Montefiore to get back monies loaned to the Safed Perushim when R. Israel headed the kollel in Safed. The few Perushim remaining in Safed told the Hasidim to collect their money from R. Israel, who had signed the loan agreement and now permanently resided in Jerusalem.

R. Israel maintained that he had acted in the name of the Perushim kollel of Safed, which was duty bound to honor payments on the loan, but he did not explain how this debt could be repaid by the Safed kollel, which had transferred itself to Jerusalem and stopped distributing haluka to Safed Perushim. In fact, the few Perushim who chose to stay in Safed, against the decision of the kollel, had been economically deserted by the Perushim Kollel, which invested all its resources in resettling its members in Jerusalem.[47]

Six Safed Perushim castigated the leadership in Jerusalem because they had "not received even one piastre" of haluka from PEKAM monies, contributions from Hungary, or the two large donations of Baron Rothschild. They were left "naked, bare-foot and hungry" and would have starved if not for the largess of R. Abraham Dov, who loaned them money "on the condition that he be repaid. . . . And how can we dare ask additional help from the saintly rabbi?" Montefiore was asked to negotiate with the Perushim kollel in Jerusalem on behalf of the remaining Safed Perushim.

Montefiore visited the countryside around Safed and stopped at the graves of famous rabbis buried in Meron, where scholars at the yeshiva asked for donations. He also learned that about 75 Jews lived in Peki'in and over 100 in Shfar-Am, all farmers of Sephardi origin. Montefiore then traveled to the Jermak farm that had been granted by Ibrahim Pasha to Israel Bak. He contributed money to the enterprising Bak and evidently was impressed by his achievements and by his industrious 25-year-old son Nissan, for one year later he sent Bak a press for his newly opened printing shop in Jerusalem.

While touring Safed and distributing charity, Montefiore conversed at length with the Jews. Since Montefiore did not know Hebrew, except to recite his prayers, Louis Loewe interpreted for him. Among the many requests, he was asked to intervene with the British and Austrian consuls in order to expedite government compensation payments for losses suffered by the Jews in the 1834 fellahin revolt.[48]

Safed Jews told Montefiore that they were eager to overcome their poverty by "working the land" or acting as "shepherds" or "planting vineyards or olive trees, whatever finds favor in your eyes"—a key phrase. Jews in Safed and elsewhere were willing to say whatever they thought would please Montefiore, in a nothing-to-lose effort to improve their financial position. They wrote that "if he wishes to give us land, we will work the soil." The kind of financial assistance and the type of agricultural settlements were quite vague and also irrelevant. Montefiore was greatly impressed by the declared wish of Jews "to earn their living by working," and by the successful agricultural villages of Jermak and Peki'in, which neatly fit into his plans for settling Jews in villages and then training them to be farmers. Wanting to believe what he was told, Montefiore concluded: "I have found all the men anxious to be employed in agriculture."[49]

Although the Montefiore census revealed that only two Safed Jews were agricultural workers, his enthusiasm for Jewish farming could not be contained. He was carried along by the euphoria of Lady Judith, who wrote that "energy and talent exist. Nothing is needed but encouragement and instruction."[50] It was made clear to Montefiore that agricultural work was for youths not talented for scholarly work and that farming would not distract the Jews from their traditional studies. It was also emphasized that before settlement in villages the area must be secured against robbers and marauders. For Montefiore the defense problem in the villages and in Safed could easily be solved, as in England, by requesting protection from government authorities. Indeed, Montefiore dispatched a letter to the governor of Acre asking that Safed Jews be protected against all molesters and thiefs.

Montefiore was presented with a plan to install Jewish farmers on the land by Joseph Ashkenazi, an affluent 40-year-old Hasid born in Eretz Israel. Ashkenazi's occupation in the census is listed as "negotiator," meaning moneylender and business trader. He was an absentee farm owner who "with Mussulmans" cultivated "some small farms in the vicinity of Safed." In his detailed plan Ashkenazi listed names of villages sited on government-owned (miri) land, knowledgeably described the agricultural characteristics of the land such as acreage and water supply, estimated crop yields, and attached an estimate of income and expenditures.[51] Appended to the plan was a list of 32 Jewish applicants for agricultural work, most of whom were newly arrived poor Sephardim from North Africa with experience as farmers.

In order for his plan to be implemented, Ashkenazi listed a number of crucial conditions that Mehemet Ali must agree to:

1. The pasha must send soldiers to protect the villages and the surrounding lands in order to prevent plunder;
2. Arabs should not be allowed to settle near the planted fields;
3. Villagers must not be conscripted into the army, or at least they should be granted leave during the harvest season;
4. Taxes should be remitted in cash, not in produce; all produce exported should be tax exempt;
5. Taxes should be paid directly into the Egyptian treasury, not through tax collectors in Safed or Acre.
6. These conditions should be put in writing and signed by Mehemet Ali.

Profits from Ashkenazi's farming scheme would be split five ways:
  —33 percent for taxes and government levies;
  —22 percent for scholars studying in Safed;
  —22 percent "to the Israelites who undertake the work";
  —17 percent "to the Israelitish servants employed therein";
  —5 percent to investors in the project.

A close reading of the original request in Hebrew, and Louis Loewe's English translation, leaves the reader wondering who would be working the land. An examination of this and other agricultural projects points to the conclusion that the "cultivators" of Safed and those "who undertake the work" would be the managers and supervisors of the fellahin, while the "people of the villages" and "the Israelitish servants employed" would be the farmers tilling the soil. Since most Ashkenazim lacked experience working with their hands, they could only qualify as supervisors of the Muslim fellahin, while the Sephardim would be relegated to the role of "Israelitish servants."

Safed Sephardim also requested that Montefiore secure relief from the Egyptian farda tax and the poll tax levied on Turkish but not European nationals of the minorities. Some Sephardim suggested that they receive village land on which they would only pay the miri tax, like "all Gentiles."[52] Montefiore was also asked to intervene with Mehemet Ali in order to reduce the efficiently collected poll tax that had skyrocketed to 60 piastres per person annually.

Numerous personal requests for financial assistance were submitted by individuals or small groups.[53] A number of Safed Jews wanted capital to work the land as absentee owners, by hiring fellahin and providing them with seeds, animals, and tools in return for receiving a substantial part of the harvest. Some Jews asked for capital to finance workshops. A Safed honey merchant, one of the few Jews who did not define himself as "poor," petitioned for financial assistance to cultivate beehives and to produce perfume and medicines from local olive oil.

Other financial requests of Safed Jews were to buy a courtyard within Safed to raise sheep and goats; to donate money to a number of rich Jews who became impoverished after settling in Safed; to reimburse a formerly rich widow for the 18,000 piastres extorted from her by the Druze in 1838; and to compensate a Jew for half his haluka stipend that was no longer provided by the Perushim kollel. Moroccan Jews who fled to Ein Zeitun after the 1837 earthquake asked to buy the village's land. The wealthy Sephardi leaders Abraham Shoshana and Samuel Aboo, both "land owners in a neighboring village," requested money for "work on the land" and for financing commercial activities.

How did Montefiore react to these schemes and plans? From many diary entries, which were heavily edited by Louis Loewe, Montefiore appears to have been favorably impressed by the Jews' positive attitude toward farming and by their detailed proposals. He was no less excited by the fruitful potential of the Palestine soil. Montefiore marveled at this "most fertile land" and reckoned that Palestine "is a land that would produce almost everything in abundance, with very little skill and labour." His diary entries abound in extravagant praise about the fertility of "the richest land imaginable."

The stark contrast between the beautiful land that appeared so fertile and the poverty-stricken Jews convinced Montefiore that his agricultural plan was the correct solution for their plight. He therefore proposed in a celebrated diary entry to settle Jews on

land favourable for agricultural speculation. I shall apply to Mohammad [Mehemet] Ali for a grant of land for fifty years; some one or two hundred villages; giving him an increased rent of from ten to twenty percent. The grant obtained, I shall, please Heaven on my return to England, form a company for the cultivation of the land and the encouragement of our brethren in Europe to return to Palestine. Many Jews now emigrate to New South Wales, Canada, etc., but in the Holy Land they would find a greater certainty of success; here they will find wells already dug, olives and vines already planted, and a land so rich as to require little manure. By degrees I hope to induce the return of thousands of our brethren to the Land of Israel. I am sure they would be happy in the enjoyment and the observance of our holy religion, in a manner which is impossible in Europe.[54]

After ten days of tours, discussions, and distributing charity in Safed, the Montefiores traveled to nearby Tiberias. Again they received a royal reception. Jews turned out in force, sang Hebrew songs, played on drums and fife, and shouted "Long live our Protector!" The governor, mounted on an Arabian steed, warmly addressed the Montefiore party. Recognizing Montefiore's influence with Mehemet Ali, the governor asked that Montefiore obtain from the Egyptian ruler a firman to repair the town walls damaged by the earthquake.

Montefiore toured Tiberias and saw the devastating impact of the 1837 earthquake—rubble, cracked walls, crumbled houses, and "temporary huts." "Every part" of town was "more or less destroyed."[55] Montefiore distributed charity to 750 Jews—350 Sephardim and 400 Ashkenazim, nearly all Hasidim—who were still recovering from the earthquake and the state of near starvation in the wake of the severe drought of 1838.

As on his first trip, Montefiore was appalled to see girls married at the age of 13 and horrified to learn that in many cases these girls married men of 60 or boys of 14 to 16. It was not uncommon to see a 30-year-old grandmother. Montefiore discussed with Jewish community leaders the effects of such early marriages and remained unconvinced by their view that early marriage, a normal Levantine practice, "brought great blessings and strengthened the family and peace at home." Montefiore accepted the Victorian tradition that a man should delay marriage until he could buy a house and support a family with a decent standard of living.

Most of the discussions with Montefiore centered on agricultural subjects. He was overjoyed to believe that Tiberias Jews also wanted to work for their living, rather than subsist on haluka. "They want to work and they are able to work," Lady Judith exclaimed. Montefiore received many proposals from Jews who "wanted with all their heart to learn agricultural work." In accordance with the general practice throughout the Ottoman Empire, Tiberias Jews, like those in Safed, suggested renting government land and buying seed and animals so that fellahin could cultivate the land and return to the renter a good share of the agricultural produce.

During their five-day stay in Tiberias the Montefiores paid a condolence call on the widow of R. Israel of Shklov,[56] whose husband had died while they were in Safed. R. Israel, a Talmudic scholar and writer of religious commentaries, analyzed the commandments that could be performed only in Eretz Israel and explained the importance of Jews settling in the Holy Land. According to R. Israel, Jewish immigration to Eretz Israel was so paramount that this mitzva overrode the biblical injunction of being an obedient son. "If a father and mother living in the Diaspora protest against their son's settling in Eretz Israel, the son does not have to obey his parents."

Near the end of his life R. Israel summarized his work in Eretz Israel:

I greatly love Eretz Israel so I persevered, despite my great privations, in order to earn the right of joining the land of the Lord. . . . During the last twenty-seven years I have greatly suffered . . . I have witnessed many troubles from the day I settled here. I have tasted fright, plague, and starvation. I sat in captivity; all around me enemies encircled and surrounded my soul. . . . I worked with all my strength for the Holy

Land. Motivated by the purest reasons, I led the kollel, I set a time to study Torah, and I established in Eretz Israel and overseas the strongest foundations [for the Perushim] . . .

R. Israel was a man of deeds, a talented organizer, an energetic leader of the Perushim, an excellent negotiator, and a persuasive fundraiser. Frequently at the vortex of controversy, he fought with indomitable courage and fanatical ferocity of purpose for the rights and privileges of the Perushim in Eretz Israel. Unlike the sedate R. Menachem Mendel of Shklov, R. Israel was an audacious activist able to cajole and cabal to achieve the objectives of the Perushim. His commanding, aggressive presence coupled with absolute commitment provided the Perushim with inspired, decisive leadership that only waned during his last years. R. Israel was always convinced of the rectitude of his opinions and never knew the torments of ambivalence. His enduring contribution was to reveal the heretofore unknown possibilities made possible by creative action, devoted to settling Perushim in Eretz Israel and to developing the Jewish community in Palestine during the first decades of the nineteenth century.

After five full days in Tiberias "hundreds of persons" bade farewell to the Montefiore party.[57] From June 2 to 6 the Montefiores traveled in an unhurried fashion to Jerusalem. Near Nablus they camped for two days and were visited by many of its nearly 100 Sephardi Jews, who "did not enter our tents, as we were fearful of contagion."

When Montefiore reached the outskirts of Jerusalem on June 6 he pitched tents on the Mount of Olives and "fixed a cord round the tents at a little distance, that he might keep himself in quarantine." The plague was so debilitating that it had chased three of the five steadfast LJS missionaries out of Jerusalem and shut down the medical station.

Despite the quarantine, "multitudes of the Jews went out daily to lay their petitions" before Montefiore. He also hosted Muslim and Christian notables and talked about "the temporal good of his brethren." One of the Scottish ministers suggested employing Jews in road building, for the necessary materials were easily available. Montefiore acknowledged the benefit that would attend the making of roads, but feared that they would not be permitted by the authorities. He was also undoubtedly aware that most of the Jews in Palestine were physically unable to undertake such arduous manual labor. Montefiore explained to the Scottish ministers his intention of "employing . . . young people in the cultivation of the vine, the olive and the mulberry."[58]

Vice-consul Young expressed sympathy for the very poor Jews and told

Montefiore that he approved of the plan to employ them in agriculture, but "advised beginning in a small way, so as not to excite the suspicions of Mehemet Ali."[59]

John Nicolayson was sorry that he met only once with Montefiore. "I endeavoured to direct his attention to the necessity of an internal and moral improvement of the Jews in this country, as an indispensable pre-requisite to the improvement of their civil condition, even by colonization which is what he has in view."[60] Montefiore's journal records meeting with Young but omits mentioning Nicolayson.

After much persuasion the governor of Jerusalem finally allayed Montefiore's fear of catching cholera, and the visitors entered Jerusalem. Their entrance was like a triumphal procession. Within the city the Montefiores visited the four Sephardi synagogues under one roof and the Sukkat Shalom and Hurva synagogues. They paid courtesy calls on the leading Ashkenazi and Sephardi rabbis, the governor, the British vice-consul, and Joseph Amzalag. Like all Jewish and most Christian tourists, the Montefiores visited the Wailing Wall. "How wonderful that it should have so defied the ravages of time," emoted Lady Judith. Accompanied by the governor and John Nicolayson, the Montefiore party entered the room on Mt. Zion venerated by Jews and Muslims as the site of King David's palace and considered to be the place where the Last Supper was conducted. This rare privilege was hardly ever granted to Jews or Christians.

Montefiore distributed charity to 3,007 Jews—2,508 Sephardim and 449 Ashkenazim, nearly all Perushim.[61] One Menahem Aryeh suggested that Montefiore improve the housing conditions of fifteen poor people by buying five vacant courtyards containing gardens, trees, and wells in the Bab-el-Huta section of the Muslim quarter. To make his proposal more attractive the productivity factor was added; within these large courtyards "they could make cloth screens for olive oil and sesame oil." Prices in the Bab-el-Huta section were depressed because many courtyards had been vacated by Jews when they moved to the Jewish quarter to be near the new focus of Jewish life in Jerusalem, the Hurva. Nearby a large courtyard bordering on the Armenian quarter had recently been purchased by Jews to increase the absorption capacity of the Jewish quarter. A number of Jerusalemites tried unsuccessfully to sell Montefiore homes and parcels of land. He listened politely, but contributed no money toward these personal requests, which explains Nicolayson's observation that "the Jews seem to be much disappointed in his visit."

Montefiore much preferred discussing agricultural proposals with the Jews. As in Safed, Ashkenazi and Sephardi leaders voiced their support for farming and any other activity that Montefiore cared to finance and that would provide them with an ample income. R. Bardaki, Aryeh Neaman, the Sephardi chief rabbi, Jonah Moshe Navon, and others drafted a highly rhetorical letter to Montefiore urging his help to erase the shame of impoverishment. They proposed that Jews work the land to support the scholars of the community by "choosing loyal people who are agricultural experts." Such a farming effort would strengthen the basic purpose of the Jewish community—to study Torah, to pray, and to perform the mitzva of settling in Eretz Israel. This general letter sent by the community leaders refers to a letter written by Aryeh Neaman that contained specific agricultural proposals. Neaman, a veteran settler and active leader and trustee of the Perushim kollel, had joined with Bergmann, Zadok Halevi, and two others in 1837 in an attempt to raise money in the Diaspora to buy fields, vineyards, and buildings, provide houses for rental, and establish workshops and a mill for grinding wheat.[62] Due to the lack of capital this group never became active.

In his letter to Montefiore, Neaman wrote that he had a Sephardi partner with five years of agricultural experience; if he received Egyptian government approval he planned to work the land. Before Neaman detailed his agricultural proposal, he noted two factors preventing Jews from undertaking many agricultural activities: they are forbidden to work on the Sabbath and they are "too weak" to plow and plant.

The Neaman plan, similar to that drafted by Safed's Joseph Ashkenazi, is detailed, thoughtful, and lists specific villages on government land near Jerusalem and Ramleh that could be purchased. Neaman proposed that Montefiore purchase villages, which would be supervised by Jews and worked by fellahin for the purpose of supporting the Jews of Jerusalem. However, Louis Loewe's translations of this proposal originally written in Hebrew have been doctored to leave the impression that Jews themselves were "embarking on agricultural pursuits."[63] Two unstated purposes of Neaman's farming project were to fight starvation and to lessen dependence on PEKAM and other Diaspora contributors, which also were the aims of Neaman's 1838 request that Mehemet Ali approve the purchase of land around Jerusalem by the Perushim kollel.

Perushim leaders in the Hurva camp, such as Lehren's nemesis, Shlomo Zalman Zoref, also encouraged Montefiore's agricultural pursuits if only to become as independent as possible of PEKAM. This may have been one strong motive behind the letter to Montefiore written by Zoref's son Mordecai, who had once rented a farm in partnership with a Sephardi and a Christian. This letter has been hallowed in Zionist lore as the pioneering effort in agriculture, and Zoref, like Bak, has been mythologized as the first Jewish farmer in Eretz Israel.

Mordecai Zoref started his letter by effusively praising the fertile land of Eretz Israel: "Even in desolation she is a land flowing with milk and honey." He enviously noted the example of a rich Christian who rented a farm and employed fellahin. "Why should we be worse off than Christians in this country?" asked Zoref. He then presented a logical, detailed plan suggesting that Montefiore purchase a plot of government-owned land (near present-day Rehovot) "three hours from Ramleh" and a full day's ride from Jerusalem. The village would be called "Moses Village" and include "Judith's courtyard." Zoref listed estimated expenditures and income and calculated the cost of establishing the village at 500,000 piastres, with 40 percent of this sum to be invested in oxen from plowing, indicating an emphasis on field crops.[64]

Finally Zoref proposed that ten Arabic-speaking scholars live permanently in the village and supervise the work of the fellahin. "It is known to you . . . that the work of ploughing and planting cannot for the time being be performed by Jews since that requires skills . . . " The kollel members, other than scholars who would remain in Jerusalem and study, would be divided into four shifts—each shift working for one month in the village, to take care of "all matters and needs of the village." Widows, "who are numerous," would work on the farm at such light tasks as tending sheep and milking cows. The village would provide the Perushim kollel with enough wheat, fruit, and vegetables to feed its members in Jerusalem. Sale of village produce would also provide funds to rent houses and clothe kollel members. As an alternative Zoref later suggested that Montefiore buy land for individual Perushim outside the auspices of the kollel.

After eight days of touring in and around Jerusalem the Montefiore party proceeded to Hebron, an eight-hour trip, traveling along the road on which Jews were frequently attacked and plundered by the "half famished peasantry," who stripped Jews of their clothing.[65] Just outside Bethlehem the Montefiore party visited the dilapidated, neglected Tomb of Rachel and Lady Montefiore contributed money to repair the building.

On the outskirts of Hebron, Montefiore, as usual, was met by many Jews hailing him as their benefactor, but for the first time the town governor did not make an appearance. The next day, the Sabbath, the governor paid a courtesy visit on the Montefiores. Only after he offered "profound apologies" and blamed Jewish notables for neglecting to notify him of Montefiore's arrival time was his gift accepted and was he honored with coffee and a nargila pipe.

Hebron and the Cave of the Patriarchs.

Montefiore adamantly pressed the governor for permission to visit the Tomb of the Patriarchs in the splendid building called the Cave of Machpelah, a site holy to Jews and Muslims, where the father of the Semites, Abraham, is believed to be buried. The building, which served as a mosque, was closed to Jewish and Christian visitors. When Montefiore's party tried to enter, a large Muslim mob turned the event into a riot. Jews accompanying Montefiore were beaten and forced to retreat from the building. Violence then spread to the Jewish quarter of Hebron, leading Montefiore to urgently request the Jerusalem governor to send troops to protect the Jews.[66]

Montefiore distributed charity and talked with many of Hebron's 251 Sephardim and 172 Hasidim. He visited the smaller Hasidic and the larger Sephardi synagogues described by the Scottish ministers. One Sephardi synagogue

is not more than forty feet in length, and though clean, is but poorly furnished. The seats were half-broken benches. The lamps were of ornamental brass; the reading-desk nothing more than an elevated part of the floor railed in. There was nothing attractive about the ark; and the only decorations were the usual silver ornaments on the rolls of the law, and a few verses in Hebrew written on the curtain and on the walls. Fourteen children were seated on the floor, with bright sparkling eyes, getting a lesson in Hebrew from an old Jew. The Polish synagogue was even poorer than the Spanish. It had no reading-desk at all, but only a stand for the books. However, it surpassed the other in its lamps, all of which were elegant; and one of them of silver—the gift of Asher Bensamson, a Jew in London.[67]

At the end of four not so pleasant days in Hebron the Montefiores departed for Jaffa but could not enter the town because the plague had struck again and Jaffa was quarantined,[68] as it had been at various times during 1836, 1837, and 1838. Despite the quarantines, Jaffa had grown and prospered as a commercial port during the rule of Mehemet Ali, since it served as the major communications link between Egypt and Palestine.

Camped outside of Jaffa's walls, near the seashore, the Montefiores repeated the ritual of receiving the town's Muslim notables, the British and Russian consuls, and Jewish leaders. Out of 5,000 Jaffa residents, who lived mainly from farming, the Jewish community comprised 26 families totaling 122 persons—mainly young North African Jews,[69] and 9 Ashkenazim. In 1838 Moroccan Jews had settled in Jaffa after their sailboat sank off the Haifa coast with the loss of 12 lives. These commercially oriented Jews

Jaffa at the beginning of the nineteenth century.

found Haifa too small to earn a living, attempted to settle in Nablus but did not like it, and tried to live in Jerusalem, where their commercial talents were stifled in the haluka-oriented town.

Jews were dissuaded from settling in Jaffa by old rabbinical strictures that directed them to live only in the four holy cities and by the fears of Jerusalem leaders that money contributed to Jews in Jaffa would reduce the haluka allocations to the holy cities.[70] For these reasons, not until 1820 was a Jewish community established in Jaffa.

Jaffa Jews were not scholars and received no haluka, but earned their living in commerce, in metal-work shops, and in physical labor as artisans and porters. Throughout the nineteenth century the economic self-sufficiency of the Jewish community in Jaffa (and in Acre, Haifa, Nablus, and the northern villages) shaped its development in ways quite different from those in the four holy cities.

Jews in Jaffa petitioned Montefiore to donate charity for "eighty persons, all of whom are poor . . . and do not have anything to eat because the town is quarantined." They requested help in finding a ritual slaughterer to settle in Jaffa and in repairing their one synagogue where Ashkenazim and Sephardim prayed together; they promised to name the synagogue after him. One Ashkenazi Jew asked Lady Montefiore for money, after complaining that his requests for financial assistance had not been answered by R. Abraham Dov, the Jerusalem Jewish community, or Zvi Hirsch Lehren.

The Montefiores toured the area around Jaffa and found blossoming gardens and orchards worked by Egyptian and other fellahin, but owned by rich Muslims, the Kadi of Jaffa, and the Greek Orthodox Church. The beauty of the celebrated gardens so impressed Judith Montefiore that she accorded them the ultimate accolade: these gardens "would not be embarrassed to raise their heads in comparison to English gardens."[71]

Montefiore decided that it would be faster to travel overland from Jaffa to Beirut and then board a steamer for Alexandria, rather than wait outside quarantined Jaffa for a boat bound for Egypt. So the Montefiore party traveled up the coast from Jaffa past Caesarea to Mt. Carmel where, to their "mortification,"[72] they were quarantined for one week. In quarantine Montefiore met the Scottish ministers and most reluctantly discussed with them the fulfillment of prophecies about the desolation of Palestine, "but he positively declined all reference to the New Testament." He was also visited by 34-year-old Moshe Abraham Finzi, scion of a distinguished Italian Jewish family, who had lived in Palestine for twelve years and served as British consular agent in Acre and Safed.

Reporting the latest news about Ibrahim Pasha's battles in Syria and their upsetting effect on the Galilee, Finzi told Montefiore that some Safed Jews found temporary shelter in the garrison town of Haifa after fleeing their homes "in a very distressed condition" for fear of another Druze riot.[73] Finzi and Montefiore discussed political matters and exchanged ideas about agricultural proposals. Probably at the request of Montefiore, Finzi submitted his own plan containing a list of villages located around Haifa, Safed, and Tiberias that might be available for purchase and an estimate of expenditures for working the land.

While in the Haifa quarantine station the Montefiores learned about the death of the legendary Hester Stanhope.[74] At the age of 34 the niece and private secretary of former British prime minister William Pitt had left England forever to settle in the mountains of Lebanon and play the role of queen among the Druze. So magnetic was her mystical personality that travelers considered it a high point of their trip to see the reclusive Lady Stanhope and listen to her declaim gems such as "I have not read a book since childhood, for books file away the mind." Her unconventional mode of living included borrowing money and then forgetting about the debt, as Amzalag complained to the missionary Joseph Wolff in 1829. Amzalag tried to sell Lady Stanhope's note of 150,000 piastres at a 50-percent discount but the American tourist Stephens declined such a "bargain."

On Sunday, June 30, the Montefiore party heard a loud cannonading celebration in Acre after a courier brought news that, six days earlier, Ibrahim Pasha had routed Sultan Mahmud's armies at Nezib in northern Syria. This victory once again opened the road to Istanbul for the Egyptian army and created the distinct possibility of Egypt toppling the Turkish sultan and his empire. For the second time in ten years the European powers were confronted with the diplomatic crisis of containing Mehemet Ali and preserving Turkish sovereignty and territory.

When the Montefiore party was released from seven days of quarantine, it was accompanied by Moshe Finzi to Haifa, "a neat little town . . . enclosed with walls" and a population of 2,000–2,500.[75] Montefiore visited the Jewish community synagogue and met with the poor Haifa Jews—116 Sephardim and 20 Ashkenazim—who worked for their meager livelihood since they received no haluka monies.

Then the Montefiores proceeded to Acre, still the largest town in Palestine with 12,000 residents. The largely Sephardi Jewish population of Acre, which had dwindled after the murder of Haim Farhi, totaled 233 Jews.

From Acre Montefiore traveled overland to Sidon and Beirut,[76] where he was visited by members of the Jewish community. Now that he had access to Beirut's financial facilities, he stepped up his philanthropic activities.

Acre in 1839, by David Roberts.

He contributed charity to the poor Jews of Beirut and dispatched 53,500 piastres to Jews in Safed, 11,770 piastres to Hebron, and 50,000 piastres to Joseph Amzalag for Jerusalem's Jews. He also gave money to the poor Christians in Beirut and Jerusalem.

Montefiore met with the LJS missionary, Erasmus Calman, who explained his plan to purchase part of Palestine "in the hope of inducing the Jews to cultivate the soil." Fervently waving the Union Jack, Calman declared that Jews would only settle on the land if "Sir Moses procured for them British protection..." No mention is made in Montefiore's edited diaries of Calman and his agricultural plan. More surprising is Montefiore's omitting any comment about Moshe Sachs and his agricultural project. Sachs met the Montefiores in Beirut, having just "returned from Vienna where he studied the science of medicine,"[77] according to Lady Judith.

On July 10 the Montefiores sailed from Beirut by steamship and two days later docked in Alexandria. "The first news we learned on our arrival" was that Sultan Mahmud II had died on June 30, having been spared hearing the news about the crushing defeat suffered by his armies at Nezib.

The day Montefiore landed in Alexandria he presented specific requests to the Egyptian minister of commerce and foreign affairs. The very next day he met with Mehemet Ali, whom he had last seen in 1827 on his first visit to Eretz Israel. This speedy official reception for Montefiore had been arranged despite the hostility of the British government toward Egypt. Mehemet Ali knew that Britain opposed his aspirations to rule Syria and realized that the British Mediterranean fleet had cut sea communications between Egypt and its Syrian territories.

After exchanging the normal pleasantries, Montefiore asked Mehemet Ali's permission to rent land and villages, "particularly for those at Safed and Tiberias... on lease of fifty years, free from all taxes or claims of governors, the rent to be paid at Alexandria." This was a less grandiose plan than Montefiore's Safed diary entry about renting "one or two hundred villages." Mehemet Ali told Montefiore that he had no government land to rent in Palestine. However, any private land rentals contracted by Montefiore with a Muslim would receive his approval and be sent to Istanbul "for confirmation."[78] This was a legal ploy. Mehemet Ali was playing for time, hinting to this Englishman that not he but the English ally, Turkey, might delay approving his request.

Montefiore insisted, based on accurate information provided by Finzi, Ashkenazi, and Neaman, that the Egyptian government did possess government miri land for rental. Mehemet Ali replied (according to Montefiore) that "if I could point out the parts belonging to him I could have them." This too was a polite way of stalling. As a show of his good faith, Mehemet Ali promised to ensure the security of the land and its farmers and agreed that Montefiore could "send proper persons with agricultural implements" to teach the Jews how to farm.

When Montefiore requested that Jews be allowed to give evidence against Muslims in the courts of Safed, Tiberias, and Hebron, as he claimed was the practice in Jerusalem, Mehemet Ali replied evasively that "Jews and Christians should be treated alike and there should be no difference between them." The Egyptian ruler never dreamed of granting to minority members the same status as Muslims; that would contravene Muslim law and tradition and would uselessly alienate the vast majority of the Palestine population.

Montefiore then suggested establishing "joint stock banks" in Cairo and Alexandria, Jerusalem and Jaffa, Beirut and Damascus, with a capital of £1 million sterling. Mehemet Ali's "eyes sparkled" and he "assured me the bank should have his protection, and he should be happy to see it established," realizing the importance of an inflow of foreign capital for the Egyptian economy.

These proposals were submitted, Montefiore explained, not only to help the Jews in Palestine "but to [benefit] many others who may settle in the Holy Cities, either from love for the Land of Promise, or from a desire to quit countries where persecution prevents their living in peace." Mehemet Ali did not respond, but he could only be dismayed at the prospect of a large influx of Jewish immigrants constantly appealing to European powers to invoke their capitulation rights.

As requested by the governor of Tiberias, Montefiore asked permission to repair the city wall, which had been damaged by the 1837 earthquake. Mehemet Ali said "he would order a report to be made immediately to him, and the wall repaired."

Numerous attempts by Montefiore and Loewe to obtain Mehemet Ali's approvals and answers in writing were met with courteous evasions. The Egyptian pasha tried to convince Montefiore to establish the bank as soon as possible and promised to send Montefiore the official Egyptian reply in writing. Despite repeated reminders, Montefiore never received the promised letter of approval. Little wonder—while Mehemet Ali was negotiating with Montefiore about privileges and parcels of land for the Jews, Palmerston was mounting strenuous diplomatic and military efforts to oust Egypt from Syria.

During his lifetime of 101 years Moses Montefiore showed intense dedication and fervent loyalty to the Jews of Eretz Israel. He endured seven exhausting trips to Palestine, searching for ways to alleviate the wretched poverty of the Jews and help transform Eretz Israel into a "productive" community.

No less devoted to the welfare of Jews in Eretz Israel was Zvi Hirsch Lehren,[79] who during forty years expended great energy for the same cause but never felt a need to subject himself to the hardship of travel to Palestine. Lehren thought that he knew best what was needed for the Jews in Eretz Israel, so he considered a long trip a waste of valuable time that could be better invested in raising more money for them. In contrast to Lehren, Montefiore—instilled with English patience and ability to compromise—listened to what the Jews of Eretz Israel told him even if he had his own preconceived notions about how to help them.

New ideas and dynamic action to solve the problems of the Jewish population in Eretz Israel had to come from outside of Palestine because of the insular character of the kehilla. Jews in the four holy cities were totally engrossed in preserving their body so they could dedicate their brain to study and their soul to prayer. Community leaders were immersed in a multitude of crises and catastrophes, struggling against each other, contending with overseas Jews on how to allocate the haluka, opposing the extortionist authorities, and resisting the blandishments of the missionaries. The preoccupied inbred Jewish community imprisoned in traditional, petrified patterns of living had neither time nor inclination to search for new concepts that could alleviate chronic problems.

Jews were encrusted in a past from which they could not break loose. A few leaders such as Zoref, Neaman, and Bak initiated new economic activities that appeared to be a return to the land, but actually were efforts toward economic self-sufficiency and personal benefit, not an introduction of basic changes into their inert, dormant society. New ideas could not grow and a new leadership style could not take hold in such a torpid, slumbering society. The concept of productivity generated by the European Enlightenment and the industrial revolution had to be initiated from the outside. Montefiore served as the first agent of change by presenting his agricultural proposal to Mehemet Ali and sending the first Jewish doctor to Eretz Israel in 1843. Thanks to Montefiore, a spirit of change started seeping through the Jewish community by the slow process of osmosis.

Montefiore realized that the agricultural proposals suggested by the Jews were different from his own farming program. He recognized that Jews did not want to transform the purpose of their settling in Eretz Israel from prayer and study to productivity. He understood that agriculture was a way of life with unique spiritual and human values that Jews did not possess. He was also wise enough to know that Jews agreed with his ideas when they entailed his spending money to solve problems that so sorely beset them. It also was obvious to Montefiore that an inability to understand Hebrew prevented his establishing direct contact with the Jews, contributing to the semantic similarity between widely different farming ideas. The distinction between tillers of the soil and supervisors of the fellahin probably went unnoticed by Montefiore. And the European definition of agricultural pursuits as understood by Montefiore was completely contrary to the concept of absentee landowner that the Jews were suggesting.[80]

Montefiore paid little heed to these communication problems and the possibilities for misunderstandings. His common-sense and straightforward intelligence told him that the correct solutions for the Jews of Eretz Israel would surface naturally by conducting trial-and-error experiments, rather than imposing plans from the outside. Implementing agricultural proposals in Eretz Israel would teach the Jews to work and allow daily life to determine how the plans would develop. Nearly any change would be for the better and the Jews would reap the benefits. In Montefiore's opinion, the worst scenario was to maintain the stifling status quo devoid of all prospects of progress.

A contemporary of Montefiore, R. Judah Bibas of Corfu,[81] also agreed that a change in the status of the Jews in Eretz Israel was absolutely necessary. But Bibas considered Montefiore's plan to purchase land in Palestine useless, "as long as there is no security for property there." Bibas was anxious to meet with Montefiore (an encounter that never took place) in order to explain why Jews should follow the example of the Greeks, who had recaptured their land from the Turks. In Bibas's opinion, Jews should take up arms and force the Turkish Empire to return Palestine to its rightful owners, the Jewish people. The way to achieve this objective was for Jews to train in the use of arms, learn secular sciences in addition to Torah studies, and abolish the system of haluka. During his lifetime Bibas's curiously modern ideas were never seriously considered and after his death they were relegated to the historical shelf as a dusty curiosity.

In contrast to Bibas, Montefiore was a product of nineteenth-century English society, a man of his times. His thoughts and actions accurately reflected the best motives, behavior, and social propriety of the British upper class, with which he was in business and social contact. Montefiore's philanthropic efforts illuminated the prevalent idea that charity was "a blessing conferred by the benevolent rich on the grateful poor."[82] He was able to improve the situation of the Jews in Palestine because he was a realist anchored in his world, rather than a prophetic man of vision looking far beyond his time. As a believer in the stolid virtue of performing one's duty, Montefiore probably did not realize that he was the first world Jewish figure to intercede with sovereign states on behalf of less fortunate fellow Jews. As a proud Jew and a well-connected citizen of the world's greatest power, Montefiore felt no inhibition about filling this role because he was simply doing what had to be done.

In his proposals about "agricultural pursuits" for the Jews, Montefiore recommended not a modest plan "beginning in a small way," as W. T. Young had advised, but a radical plan with revolutionary implications. This proposal to work the land in agricultural villages would have exposed Jews to the dangers of Beduin marauders and Moslem robbers. His proposal to make the Jews economically independent by earning their own living would have completely transformed the relationship between Jews in Eretz Israel and those living in the Diaspora. His plan to establish a bank with investment capital of £1 million sterling to provide credit for Jewish villages and other Jewish undertakings would have created an economic upheaval not only in the Jewish community but in all of Palestine and Syria. His suggestion to teach the secular subject of agriculture, if only to those "not talented to study Torah," would have disrupted the educational and religious system of the Jews. His proposal to provide Jews with equal status in Muslim courts would have completely revolutionized the relationship between Jews and Muslims. His suggestion to pay taxes directly into the Egyptian treasury would have severely altered the ties of the Jews to the local authorities. His proposals to introduce "happiness and plenty for thousands" of Jews in Canada, Wales, and elsewhere by encouraging them to settle in Eretz Israel would have created insurmountable absorption problems in that land.

Montefiore propounded upheavals in Jewish life in Eretz Israel and in the Jews' relationships with their Muslim neighbors, government authorities, and Diaspora Jews. It is difficult to conceive that cautious Montefiore of the "let us advance slowly but steadily" school would knowingly propose such manifold and far-reaching changes. This leads to the inevitable conclusion that Montefiore did not sufficiently comprehend the status and aspirations of the Jews of Eretz Israel and that he knew even less about the Muslim social and economic structure in Palestine and the status of the Egyptian government within the framework of the Turkish Empire. Nonetheless, even had Montefiore truly understood the cataclysmic implications of his proposals that Jews plow, plant, and reap, in all probability he would have proceeded pragmatically, relying on the realities of life to alter impractical plans.

Ignorance about the consequences of his agricultural proposals does not detract from Montefiore's contribution to the development of the Jewish community. He was the first person to strive to reshape Jews into a productive group able to earn their own livelihood. Although Montefiore's proposals never came to fruition, he started the first small ripple in the waters of Eretz Israel that over the years was to grow and influence later proposals about settling Jews on their Holy Land. For the first time European ideas of productivity had penetrated the Jewish community and started the incubating process toward change.

SIXTEEN

The End of Egypt's Occupation of Palestine

1840

During the eventful year of 1840 four great powers—Britain and the three absolute monarchies of Russia, Prussia, and Austria—ended Egypt's occupation of Syria and thereby shaped the future prospects of both the Ottoman Empire and the Jews in Eretz Israel.[1] France was alone in backing Mehemet Ali's efforts to retain Syria.

After Ibrahim Pasha resoundingly defeated the Turkish armies at Nezib, Mehemet Ali once again resolved to split Egypt off from the Turkish Empire. Since the common interests of Russia and England dictated preventing the collapse of the Sublime Porte, the two powers jointly initiated diplomatic efforts to push Mehemet Ali back to the borders of Egypt and to restore Syria to the truncated Turkish Empire.

After six months of political maneuvering the four great powers signed the London agreement of July 15, 1840, to maintain the Turkish Empire intact. When Mehemet Ali indignantly rejected the terms of the London agreement, which would have relegated him to the status of just another pasha, military action was initiated by the great powers to detach Syria from Mehemet Ali's grasp and return it to the rule of the sultan. A British flotilla reinforced by Austrian warships cruised threateningly near Beirut in September 1840, cut Ibrahim Pasha's communication in the Mediterranean, and shelled the coast. Then Turkish troops and English marines went ashore and distributed muskets to local rebels opposing Ibrahim Pasha's army. At that same time Sultan Abdul Mejid (1839–1860), successor to Mahmud II, deposed Mehemet Ali as ruler of Syria and Egypt.

A flotilla of English, Austrian, and Turkish ships set siege to Acre and bombarded the town. On November 3, after two hours of shelling, a direct hit struck the main powder magazine and demolished the arsenal, a good part of town, and its walls. About 1,700 garrison soldiers and many civilians were blown up in the fearful explosion. Completely demoralized and in shock, Egyptian forces surrendered or fled. Acre, which had so successfully thwarted Napoleon's ambitions during his two-month siege, was now conquered from the sea in a few hours. With "one whiff of grapeshot" the city of Acre was blasted to bits, its importance vanished, and its role in Palestine deteriorated throughout the nineteenth century.

The victories in Acre and Beirut excited the English public, many of whom agreed with Lord Shaftesbury's inspired opinion that God and the British sailor guided the destiny of England and protected the Jews.

It is really heart-stirring to read of our successes in Syria. . . . One midshipman does more than a hundred Turks. . . . What materials for greatness! What instruments, should it so please God, for the alliance and protection of His ancient people and for His final purposes on earth![2]

With Egyptian lines of communication and supply threatened by the capture of Beirut, Sidon, and Acre, and Egypt's demoralized army harassed by the hit-and-run tactics of Beduin and mountain tribesmen, the British fleet blockaded Alexandria. This left Mehemet Ali with no alternative but to sign an agreement with British Admiral Napier. In return for being confirmed as hereditary governor of Egypt, Mehemet Ali handed over to Turkey its fleet, which had deserted after the Nezib defeat, submitted to the sultan as his suzerain, and agreed to abandon all Syrian territory. These basic terms of the London July 15 agreement, which Mehemet Ali had so emphatically rejected in August, he was forced to accept in November.

Ibrahim Pasha evacuated Syria and started his retreat back to Egypt with his army of 60,000–80,000 soldiers.[3] He marched his hungry and thirsty troops out of Damascus and down the eastern bank of the Jordan River. By February 1841 Egypt had completely withdrawn from Palestine and the Holy Land was returned to the Turkish Empire.

In Palestine, the sheikhs and peasants had revolted against the Egyptians when it became obvious that Ibrahim Pasha's depleted forces could not control the towns and the countryside. Tribal clans received "firelocks" and took vengeance on Ibrahim Pasha's soldiers. Local government collapsed, law and order disappeared, and old tribal feuds were revived. Once more Palestine was in a state of anarchy and "the whole country was rendered anew insecure."

Hebron formally declared itself "independent" and the whole district was "in a very unsettled and disturbed state" after the Egyptian-nominated governor was slain. British vice-consul Young reported that the town of Hebron was "quite deserted by all except the aged and the Jews; the latter, many of them being Europeans, have applied to me for protection. They are in a state of great alarm, and have already been pillaged."

In Jerusalem the governor remained loyal to the Egyptians, and his force of 400 soldiers waited for orders to move against the insurgents. The governor ordered R. Bardaki, as Russian wakiel, to deliver the passports of all the foreign Jews or leave the country. Unwilling to comply, R. Bardaki traveled to Jaffa in October 1840 to arrange for the protection of the Jews by the foreign consuls. Security on the road between Jerusalem and Jaffa was so bad that Jerusalem was cut off from the coast and R. Bardaki could not return home. Then the governor and his troops were besieged in the citadel before fleeing town. A rapacious kadi seized control of Jerusalem and threatening peasants surrounded the town walls. Food and water were in short supply and "great alarm was felt, especially by Christians and Jews."

Vice-consul Young, whose country had reinstated the sultan as sovereign over Palestine, was appalled by the situation. Palestine was again divided into provinces. Governors could not "speak the language of the people" and therefore were unable to govern the country. Sheikhs assumed the role of independent sovereigns. Throughout Palestine there was "no tranquility"; "utter confusion" reigned, especially in Nablus and around Tiberias. Safed Jews suffered persecutions and complained about the seizure of their homes and the confiscation of their animals. William Young wrote about "bigotry and outrages" against Christians and Jews in Acre, Haifa, and Jerusalem. Jerusalem Jews once more walked "in expectation of being stoned or insulted."[4]

Now that the peasants had been rearmed, fighting resumed between the Kays and Yamani tribes, and the Beduin were pillaging everywhere. The Abu-Ghosh family plundered and reinstated the toll tax on travelers going to and from Jerusalem. Travel on all roads was insecure and the system of traveling in caravans was reinstituted. Adding to the confusion was the lack of rules governing domestic taxes and commercial duties.

The consul of the greatest power on earth was insulted on the Jerusalem streets, leading him to "fear [that] British subjects could expect but little assistance at my hands." Such a state of lawlessness and the inability of the consul to protect foreign nationals signaled the "return to old religious prejudices and oppressions." The English mission was temporarily suspended. John Nicolayson concluded that everything must be started anew—but "with renewed vigour," he added optimistically.

The Turkish system of "selling justice to the highest bidder" was reestablished. "Abominable abuses" were the law of the day and "everything is seized by force, and no redress [can be] obtained in either the civil or judicial courts." William Young agreed with the governor of Nablus, who told him that "he preferred the conscription and taxation of the Egyptian Government to the present state of things" and that he wished "to see Ibrahim Pasha back again in Syria."

Seeking to find a sense of order, Young advocated "the continued aid of the British Government to advise and assist in enforcing measures for the general good and tranquility of the country." Believing that many public functionaries such as the old, inefficient Jerusalem governor were totally incompetent, he wanted Great Britain to maintain its influence and power in Palestine "to enable the Turks to carry out the reforms without regard to the prejudices of the people." Young agreed with the governor of Nablus that "the Osmanlis never can govern Syria."

In order to secure the backing of the great powers, as well as relieve internal pressure for reforms and increased revenues, Sultan Abdul Mejid had issued the Hatt-I-Sherif of Gulhane on November 3, 1839.[5] This landmark Tanzimat legislation of "new rules" in the Ottoman Empire created "new institutions" for carrying out the proclaimed principles of security of life and property; equitable tax assessments and a systematic tax collection system; a fair system of conscription; and a just public trial for persons accused of crimes. The most revolutionary part of this imperial edict promised equality before the law for all Ottoman subjects.

Ironically, many of the liberal principles promulgated by the sultan to gain the goodwill of the European powers had already been implemented in Syria by Mehemet Ali. More celebrated on paper than in practice, the Tanzimat decree demonstrated the chasm between Ottoman words and deeds. For example, Jews and Christians were legally drafted into the Turkish army, but in practice minority members continued to be relieved of military service by payment of a new "exemption" tax.

While the sultan launched the Tanzimat reform era and the four great powers diplomatically and militarily pressured Mehemet Ali, Montefiore immersed himself in a multitude of public activities in England as he tried to put into practice some of his agricultural plans for the Jews of Eretz Israel. However, in February 1840 his attention shifted abruptly to Damascus, where Jews were accused of murdering Franciscan Friar Thomas and using his blood in the baking of unleavened bread (Matzot). Bitter hatred of the Jews led to the imprisonment and torture of numerous Jews charged with murdering the vanished clergyman. Several Jews died in prison, others confessed under duress, and some were killed when the Jewish quarter in Damascus was sacked. Because Friar Thomas was under French protection the French consul-general conducted a trial, found the Jews guilty of his murder, and decided that Christian blood was an essential ingredient in the matzot baked for the Jewish Passover ritual. The infamous conduct of the French consul was backed by the French government, champion of liberty and equality.[6]

World opinion was aroused in Europe and America and protest meetings were held in London, Philadelphia, and New York. In Jerusalem, where Jews were afraid of going to the market, they "were anxious to obtain authentic information" about what Nicolayson called this "calumnious fabrication."[7] In response to the requests of R. Bardaki and other apprehensive Jews, John Nicolayson obligingly sent the lay missionary, Mr. Pieretz, to Damascus to discover "the real truth." The Jewish community of Jerusalem showed a great "fervor" of interest in the blood libel and some Jews believed that such tragic news was God's final test for his Chosen People before the coming of the Messiah. For these Jews, adamantly convinced of the imminent arrival of the Messiah in the Jewish year 5600 (September 1839–September 1840), the slander about a ritual murder signaled that Redemption must be near.

Montefiore discussed the Damascus blood libel with Palmerston, who promised to use British influence "to stop such atrocities."[8] During their conversation Montefiore mentioned to Palmerston that the Jews in Palestine "were desirous of being employed in agricultural pursuits" and would appreciate whatever aid the British government could provide. But Montefiore's preoccupation with the Damascus affair and English efforts to push Mehemet Ali out of Palestine quashed any chance of securing active support for establishing Jewish agricultural villages in Palestine.

English and French Jewry displayed communal responsibility for the fate of troubled fellow Jews in a foreign country by sending a delegation to Egypt demanding that Mehemet Ali release the Jewish prisoners in Damascus. Montefiore was the English member of the delegation.

Mehemet Ali met with the Anglo-French mission on August 6,[9] immediately after receiving news about the four-power London agreement of July 15, 1840, ordering him to once again become the sultan's vassal. The delegation firmly demanded the release of Jewish prisoners from the Damascus jail and the issuance of a general acquittal from the blood libel accusation. No mention was made of the "agricultural pursuits" of the Jews in Palestine, but Montefiore did ask the Egyptian ruler to recompensate the poor Jews of Safed for losses suffered in the 1838 Druze rebellion. Despite the intimidating demands of the great powers in the July 15 agreement, and with the menacing British fleet cruising off the Syrian coast, the Jewish mission secured Mehemet Ali's approval for the release and pardon of the nine imprisoned Damascus Jews and a declaration stating that the Jews were not guilty of the blood libel.

Only after learning that Jewish prisoners in Damascus had been freed did Montefiore leave Egypt for Istanbul.[10] He spent the Sukkot festival in the Turkish capital waiting to receive a firman from the sultan absolving Jews from guilt in the blood libel. At the synagogue prayer service Montefiore met the affluent 59-year-old Moshe Rivlin and Rabbi Shmuel Salant, two distinguished Perushim on their way from Shklov to settle in Jerusalem. Moshe Rivlin, a son of Hillel Rivlin, one of the first Perushim to settle in Safed thirty years before, had been requested by the leaders of the Perushim community to settle in Jerusalem, become a leader of the kollel in place of his recently deceased father, and "plant groves of peace in the city of peace."[11] Only a neutral person from overseas could reconcile the battling factions. Rivlin was accompanied by R. Salant, a young Lithuanian Torah scholar who was ordered by his doctors to relocate to a place with a warm climate. (Not until March 1841 did Rivlin and Salant reach Jerusalem. R. Salant was appointed Torah instructor and rabbinical judge, while Moshe Rivlin preached on alternate Sabbaths at the rival synagogues of the Hurva and Sukkat Shalom.)

In November 1840 Montefiore received the imperial firman declaring the falseness of the Damascus blood libel. This historic "bill of rights for the Jews" guaranteed the security of the Jews living in the Ottoman Empire and provided that "the Jewish nation shall possess the same advantages and enjoy the same privileges as are granted to the numerous other nations who submit to our authority."[12]

At the time that the Jewish Anglo-French mission was active in the Middle East England was in the midst of a surging wave of concern for returning the Jews to Palestine. Profuse interest in Palestine and in the plight of the

Jews was nourished by the flourishing Restoration movement and stimulated by the plethora of schemes aimed at changing the international status of the Holy Land. However, the 7,500 Jews in Eretz Israel, preoccupied with the eager expectation of the impending Messianic Redemption, were untouched by this outpouring of Restoration ideas—which produced no practical results.

Plans to restore the Jews to Palestine proliferated during 1840. The semi-official organ of the British Foreign Office, the *Globe*, championed the establishment of an independent state in Palestine where large numbers of Jews could settle.[13] It was proposed that the great European powers provide guarantees for the new Jewish state after the purchase of Palestine with money contributed by wealthy European Jews.

On March 9, 1840, the influential *Times* published an appeal to the Protestant monarchs of Europe contending that now in the midst of the Levant crisis "and other striking signs of the times" it was the "duty" of Protestant Christianity to restore the Jews to Palestine.[14] This appeal, like many English Restoration proposals, showed how the British propensity for staking a proprietary interest in Palestine mingled with sincere sympathy for the restoration of Jews to their ancient homeland and was tinged by traditional hostility toward Catholic France.

English Restorationists were joined by Jews in Germany proposing projects for the Restoration of Jews. One Berlin proposal published in early 1840 rejected as futile and dangerous the idea of setting up a Jewish state in backward Palestine.[15] More constructively, the anonymous Jewish advocate suggested settling Jews in the American states of Arkansas or Oregon. In return for 10 million dollars, it was suggested that the American government provide Jews with land the size of France.

A few months later another anonymous German-Jewish writer was absolutely convinced that Palestine was *the* solution for the Jews.[16] He issued a clarion call under the bombastic headline "Now or Never":

> The Turkish government is falling to ruin. . . . Greece has severed itself. . . . *Will Israel alone hide his hand in his bosom?* The events of the East are the finger of the Lord. . . . The power of our enemies is gone . . . yet ye do not bestir yourself. . . . What hinders? Nothing but your own supineness! . . . take possession of the land of your fathers; build a third time the temple of Zion, greater and more magnificent than ever.

For this polemicist the passivity of the Jews was the main obstacle to their early return to Palestine. In retort, Reform Jews wrote that "the emigration of individuals to Palestine is of no consequence" and counseled leaving Syria "to those who contend for it." Another German Jew ventured the opinion that "for us Germans the Orient is simply too remote; perhaps our British co-religionists are cleverer than we are."

English Restorationists were intrepidly led by Lord Shaftesbury. Inspired by the great-powers agreement of July 15, 1840, Shaftesbury recorded in his diary on July 24: "Everything seems ripe for their return to Palestine. Could the Five Powers of the West be induced to guarantee the security of life and possessions to the Hebrew race, they would flow back in rapidly augmenting numbers."[17] A week later Shaftesbury dined with foreign secretary Palmerston and propounded his scheme for Jewish settlement in Palestine, which struck Palmerston's fancy.

August 1840 was the high point of Restoration pronouncements.[18] On August 14 the Foreign Office mouthpiece, the *Globe*, stressed the British historical mission of leading the Jews back to their homeland, as Cyrus, king of Persia, had done in the sixth century before Christ. Shaftesbury also mentioned King Cyrus, displaying the more than coincidental relationship between the views of the Foreign Office and the opinions of the Restorationists' guiding spirit.

The *Times* of August 17, 1840, published an article proposing "to plant the Jewish people in the land of their fathers," under the protection of the five powers, "for it is no longer a mere matter of speculation, but of serious political consideration." The article raised questions about the Jews' reactions to returning to the Holy Land. How soon would Jews be ready to leave for Palestine? Would Jews "of station and property" be willing to invest capital there? Would Jews settle in Palestine if their rights and privileges were secured to them under the protection of a "European power" that was not identified but whose name was obvious to all English readers? The English Jewish community met these questions in stalwart silence.

One week later the *Times* printed an earlier Restoration memorandum addressed to the great powers, with encouraging replies from most of the sovereigns. In the same issue a letter from "an English Clergyman" described the persecutions suffered by the Jews and demanded that "Britain should acquire Palestine for the Jews." Another letter writer stated: "I believe . . . that all individuals and nations that assist this world-renounced people to recover the empire of their ancestors will be rewarded by Heaven's blessing."

The furious frequency of articles about the Restoration of the Jews created a public commotion, much to the satisfaction of Shaftesbury, who on August 29 gleefully wrote in his diary: "The newspapers teem with documents about the Jews. What a chaos of schemes and disputes is on the horizon. . . . What a stir of every passion and every feeling in men's hearts!"

Obsessed by the return of "God's ancient people . . . to the Land of their Fathers,"[19] Shaftesbury submitted to Palmerston a practical plan for "the adjustment of the Syrian Question." Shaftesbury was convinced that "ultimately" Jews "contemplate a restoration to the soil of Palestine," especially now that the coming of the Messiah "is near at hand." In order to allay Jewish "suspicions" and "call forth . . . the hidden wealth and industry of the Jewish People," Shaftesbury suggested that the four great European powers guarantee "equal laws and equal Protection to Jew and Gentile" that would be maintained by the sultan or the "Governing Power of the Syrian Provinces."

He recorded reasons "why more is to be anticipated from the Jews than other settlers in Palestine." Jews "subsist, and cheerfully, on the smallest pittance," are "accustomed to arbitrary Rule," are "indifferent to Political Objectives," and "have no preconceived theories to gratify." Shaftesbury assured Palmerston that Jews "trained in implicit obedience . . . will acknowledge the present appropriation of the soil, in the hands of its actual Possessors" and remain "content to obtain an Interest in its Produce by the legitimate methods of rent or purchase." With the "Capital" of "their wealthy brethren"—Montefiore is mentioned—and the "hidden wealth and industry of the Jewish people," Jews will show "large Results" with "the application of small means" in agriculture and "mercantile enterprise."

This letter highlights many of the concepts of the Restorationists, who viewed the Jews as submissive subjects—backed by unlimited capital—willing to subordinate their hopes and selves so that they could live in Palestine under any conditions. With the most benevolent intentions, Shaftesbury and his fellow Restorationists "regarded the Jews as somehow passive agents of the Christian millennium. . . . Shaftesbury envisaged an Anglican Israel restored by Protestant England, at one stroke confounding popery, fulfilling prophecy, redeeming mankind."[20]

As Shaftesbury was writing to Palmerston about settling Jews in Palestine, the end of the Jewish year 5600 in September 1840 loomed close by. Palmerston and Shaftesbury were both aware "that the Time is approaching when their Nation is to return to Palestine."[21] Looking for a savior to redeem them from physical and spiritual distress, many Jews in Eretz Israel, Europe, and the Ottoman Empire during the previous fifteen years had been agitated about the imminent arrival of the Messiah in 1840.[22]

In Eretz Israel a feeling of anxiety and trepidation seized numerous members of the somber kehilla living a "life in deferment" and yearning for the cataclysmic coming of the Kingdom of Heaven.[23] Once again acute Messianic longing completely possessed many Jews, directed their thoughts, and riveted their attention. Poised on the brink of the end of the world, these Jews lived in tense expectation and suspended animation, awaiting Messianic Deliverance from Exile and the Redemption of the Jewish people in Zion.

Ever since R. Israel sent his emissary to Yemen in 1830 in search of the Ten Lost Tribes, a series of convulsive events in Eretz Israel had signaled for some Jews the approaching Redemption. They believed that "when suffering is severest, the redeemer is nearest."[24] During the 1830s these Jews were conscious of living through perilous, tragic times that were pregnant with Messianic portents and apocalyptic signs of disasters, suffering, and bloodshed. In 1831 the fearsome wars of Gog and Magog recounted in Jewish sources were reenacted by the Egyptian conquest of Palestine and the threatened collapse of the Turkish Empire. Jews designated Mehemet Ali as their Edomite king who would bring them to their kingdom. Building of the Hurva and rebuilding Jerusalem had Messianic implications. Days of wrath were visited on the Jews in 1834 when they suffered through the fellahin revolt. These terrible days were surpassed by the 1837 earthquake that buried 2,500 Jews in Safed and Tiberias and reminded Jews that according to the Mishna the destruction of the Galilee was to herald the coming of the Messiah. Such catastrophes were followed in quick succession by epidemics, the Druze sacking of Safed, the ritual murder charges in the Damascus blood libel, and the destructive wars of Mehemet Ali against the sultan, with the involvement of the great European powers.

To gauge the role Messianism played in the life of the Jews in Eretz Israel, we must observe actions more than listen to words. What impact did Messianism have on the behavior and lives of the Jews? How actively and deeply involved were they in their Messianic yearnings and how did they demonstrate this involvement? One researcher wrote: "It appears that a group of the Perushim in Jerusalem as well as a number of immigrants who had arrived from Germany [such as Joseph Schwartz and Eliezer Bergmann] changed the text of the prayers..." and stopped reciting part of two prayer rituals.[25] When a prayer ritual and "an accepted religious practice is abolished in a religious society, this is a matter of significance."[26] However, doubts have been raised about whether this change in the prayer ritual actually took place.[27]

When the year 5600 came to an end and the Messiah failed to appear, a wave of despair descended on many Jews of Eretz Israel. They had placed absolute faith in messianism and had been direly disappointed by their Lord of Redemption. The result was a spiritual upheaval of immense force. Basic religious concepts that nourished believing Jews were rendered suspect. Trusted tenets and professed creeds came crashing down as disillusioned Jews cynically concluded that "the Messiah will come only when he is no longer needed."[28] Bewildered Jews sought new answers in a desperate effort to find meaning for their lives.

Still in shock and suffering from the periodic plagues of 1836–1839, many baffled Jews tried to explain that the Messiah did not come because God had revealed a failure in His people. Having been found wanting and not worthy of living in the days of the millennium, they were being punished.[29] One Jew professed "that the accumulated sins of the Israelites made them, as yet, unworthy of their promised restoration and that many years of expiation were still before them."[30] The Perushim and Z. H. Lehren claimed that the contentions and clashes among the Jews delayed the advent of the Messiah, and they appealed to the Jews to repent these sins. An English missionary agreed that "the Messiah would have come last year [1840] if the people of Israel had not been so sinful."

Some Jews left Eretz Israel after losing their faith. Had not their Messianic belief, so inextricably bound to the Jews returning to Zion, been proven empty? A few Jews no longer believed and were tempted by the forbidden fruits so attractively presented by the English missionaries. Now that the coming of the Jewish Messiah had proven illusory, Nicolayson preached even more fervently that Jews should believe in the true Messiah, Jesus Christ. And in May 1843 LJS scored a colossal coup by converting four Jews, including two prominent Perushim.[31] The conversion of a few Jews and the possible change in the Jewish prayer ritual are two acts indicating that the yearning and disappointment about the coming of the Messiah in 1840 were experienced intensely by an undetermined number of Jews. The Messianic belief had lacked the dynamic power to move many Jews to leave the Diaspora for Eretz Israel or to inspire widespread changes in the Jewish religious mode of living. However, the unrealized Messianic expectations influenced the subsequent actions of the Jews in Eretz Israel and the Diaspora:

> As a result of the failure of the Messiah to appear . . . the belief that one could no longer believe in activities meant to hasten the coming of the Messiah was strengthened. It was felt that one had to rely only on the study of the Torah and on performing the commandments . . . not on any trades, crafts, commerce, or agriculture[32]

After Jews bitterly learned that the "apocalyptic is full of promises, but it has never kept one of them,"[33] Jewish leaders adopted an old idea of R. Israel of Shklov and others that fixed 1840 as the *starting point* for the step-by-step continuous process of Redemption, which required Jews to settle in Eretz Israel and sanctify the Holy Land before the advent of Messianic Redemption. "From the year 5600, the next world begins . . . this is the propitious year of God . . ."[34] It took a long time for this message of a divine will working toward an ordained end to reanimate hope and reinstill faith in the Jewish community. Although nearly all Jews believed that Redemption is a hope never to be despaired of, some Jews concluded that "the essence of being a Jew meant to live forever in a state of expectation for that which would not come."[35]

While Restoration plans were being bandied about and the Jewish confidence in the Messianic epoch was betrayed, Egypt was being forced out of Syria. To fill this territorial vacuum, France, Austria, Russia, and Prussia put forth separate proposals about the future of Palestine, each seeking to secure for itself political advantages and commercial privileges, in addition to religious rights in Jerusalem, Bethlehem, and Nazareth. Under the pretext of protecting Christian rights in Palestine, the European powers were trying to gain influence and acquire strategic territory in the Levant. Religion provided diplomacy with a convenient handmaiden. "The protestations of brotherly love from the other European Powers have ulterior motives . . . ," explained Russian foreign minister Nesselrode.[36]

French foreign minister François Guizot, in keeping with France's historical role as protector of Roman Catholics living in Palestine, suggested that Jerusalem be made a Christian city separate from the Pashalik, and guaranteed by all the European powers. Instead of restoring the Jews to Palestine, as proclaimed by Napoleon in 1799, Guizot proposed a vague plan for a Christian Jerusalem that was couched in sentimental terms.

The British considered the French plan to internationalize and establish "a Christian Free City" in Jerusalem, or set up an independent Christian state in Palestine guaranteed by the great-powers, "wild," "impractical," and a scheme "like one of Lamartine's poetical reveries."[37] Palmerston labeled

> Guizot's proposal for Jerusalem as a subtle plan tending to the same end which the French have steadily had in view—to weaken the Sultan as much as possible, to detach from his Empire as much territory as pos-

sible, and to obtain for France every possible opening for the exercise of domineering influence in the Levant.

He concluded that "we want to set up the Turkish Empire and not to pull it down." Guizot must have recognized the futility of implementing his plan—it was even opposed by King Louis Philippe, who considered the notion of "establishing a little independent Christian community in Jerusalem chimerical and absurd."

Opposition from King Louis Philippe and the English prompted Guizot to send a personal letter enlisting the support of foreign minister Metternich of Austria, the other Roman Catholic European power. With vital interests to protect in the Balkans, Metternich withheld his backing. Like Palmerston, he believed that peace in Europe depended on preserving the integrity of an independent Turkish Empire. Since Metternich knew full well that the sultan, as head of the Muslim world, could never agree to declare Jerusalem a "free and Christian city,"[38] he suggested broadening the rights of Christian minorities by securing great-power protection for Christians living in Palestine. On-the-spot enforcement of Christian rights and access to Christian holy places would be entrusted to a "Turkish commissioner in the Holy Land" directly subordinate to a high office in Istanbul and advised by a council appointed by the great powers.[39]

The modest Austrian proposal "does not seem to me to be required or necessary," opined Nesselrode, who voiced Russia's strong opposition to Guizot's more sweeping plan. Nesselrode believed that Palestine should be organized as a separate Pashalik, but Jerusalem should be independent and directly subordinate to Istanbul. Consuls in Palestine should be empowered to protect the rights of merchants, tourists, and pilgrims and "a special Church and Monastery should be founded for the use of Russian clergy and pilgrims." Nesselrode preferred to go it alone rather than establish partnerships with other European powers because "we want to avoid general European interference in the Christian East."[40]

Contrary to strong British suspicions, Russia had but limited objectives in Palestine:

To obtain as independent pasha of Jerusalem a reliable man to protect the pilgrims; to put an end to the squabbles over the Holy Places; to prevent the *mufti* and *qadi* of Jerusalem from extorting rewards from Greek monks who appealed to them in cases of persecution; and if such persecutions were once stopped by the Ottoman authorities, to persuade the Patriarch of Jerusalem to live in his see.[41]

A concrete proposal about Palestine was presented by D. P. Tatitschew, the Russian representative at the London conference that adopted the July 15, 1840, agreement.[42] Tatitschew suggested placing the Church of the Holy Sepulchre under the protection of the Carmelite sect, but this impractical proposal was rejected. In October 1840 Tatitschew recommended putting Christian holy places in Jerusalem under the protection of a permanent military guard composed of European soldiers and allowing each sect to participate in the refurbishing of the Holy Sepulchre. These inconsequential notions were never seriously considered.

The Prussians, inspired by the religious romanticism of the newly ascended King Friedrich Wilhelm IV, who proposed establishing the Anglo-Prussian Bishopric in Jerusalem, put forth their own detailed, thoughtful plan for Palestine. Prussia proposed signing a treaty between Turkey and the great European powers that would place the three Christian holy cities—Jerusalem, Nazareth, and Bethlehem—under the direct protection and control of the Christian European powers. Christians in Palestine would remain minority members paying a fixed annual tax into the Turkish treasury, but their security would be guaranteed by residents appointed by the five great powers. Russia would appoint the Greek Catholic resident; Austria and France would appoint the Roman Catholic resident; and Prussia and Great Britain would appoint the Protestant resident. Each resident would be provided with a guard of 60 soldiers.

> The Protestant Church, under the joint protection of Great Britain and Prussia, was to be recognized as on an equal footing with the other Churches, and to establish its headquarters and other institutions— including schools for Jews—on Mount Zion, which was to be fortified.[43]

Later (in July 1841) the Prussians suggested extending religious protection to the Jews as well. This was the first mention of the Jews in all the great-power plans.

Early in 1841 the Prussian military attaché in Istanbul, Lt. Helmuth Von Moltke, who at Nezib had watched the defeat of the Turkish troops he had trained (after warning against the disastrous results of a frontal assault), proposed establishing Palestine as a buffer state and placing it under the protection of Prussia.[44] The Prussian proposals were not accepted because of their widespread implications, the almost certain opposition of Turkey, and the staunch opposition voiced by Austria, Russia, and England.

The French proposal to internationalize a Christian Jerusalem, the Austrian proposal to protect Christians and their holy places in Palestine, the

Russian proposals for establishing a separate Pashalik with consuls protecting the rights of minority members, and the far-reaching Prussian proposal to set up a Christian protectorate over Jerusalem, Nazareth, and Bethlehem were discussed by the leaders of the great powers in 1839, 1840, and 1841. The future of Palestine, however, was just a marginal subject that diverted the attention of the great powers from more pressing matters. Lacking common interests, it was inevitable that the great powers would reject each other's plans and separately try to promote their influence in the Middle East. These international plans "for the future of Palestine as a separate, semi-independent entity whether wholly, mainly or partly Jewish or Christian" had no effect on the Jews of Eretz Israel, who were probably ignorant of the existence of such proposals.[45]

Although Palmerston was the major diplomatic manipulator of plans about the future of Palestine, England conspicuously did not put forth a proposal of its own. Palmerston had already taken the initiative by setting up the first European Consulate in Jerusalem to promote English interests in Palestine. Rather than protect Christians, Palmerston pushed British commercial and political interests in the Near East by affording Protection with a capital P to the Jews.

After listening to Shaftesbury "argue politically, financially, commercially" about Jews settling in Palestine,[46] Palmerston in August 1840 wrote to Lord Ponsonby, the British ambassador in Istanbul, about the imminent return of the Jews to Palestine and the great contribution the Turkish government could make by holding out "every encouragement to the Jews of Europe to return to Palestine." Palmerston started his dispatch to Ponsonby by informing him that during 1840 the Jews anticipate the coming of the Messiah "and consequently their wish to go thither [Palestine] has become more keen, and their thoughts have been bent more intently than before upon the means of realizing that wish." Always the consummate politician, Palmerston did not appeal to religious or humanitarian motives, but described how the sultan could profit from Jewish money, and check Egypt's expansionary ambitions, while earning the support of rich, influential Jews in European countries.

In order that the sultan benefit from Jews settling in the Ottoman Empire he must guarantee "full and complete security for Person and Property [by establishing] some impartial Courts of Justice . . . before which Jew and Mahometan might be equally sure of obtaining a just Sentence." Palmerston allowed himself the luxury of such sweeping claims because England was the major protector of Turkey against Egypt and its staunchest military ally. While writing his dispatch to Ponsonby, Palmerston knew that the

British fleet had cut Egypt's sea lanes with Syria and was sailing close to Beirut, intimidating Mehemet Ali and preparing to shell the Lebanese coast.

Three months later Palmerston found another opportunity to enlarge on his previous request to Ponsonby that the sultan encourage the settlement of European Jews in Palestine. This was occasioned by Palmerston's receiving a memorandum from the Commission of the General Assembly of the Church of Scotland that requested special protection for Protestant missionaries working among the Jews. At the same time the assembly asked for "ample protection of Jews . . . [in order] to prevent the occurrence of the Cruelties to which they have been recently subjected at Damascus . . . and might greatly tend to disarm that People of their Prejudices against Christianity itself."[47]

Palmerston sent this memorandum to Ponsonby. Without explicitly agreeing with its objectives, he wrote that such "matters . . . excite a very deep interest in the minds of a large number of Persons in the United Kingdom" and again encouraged the sultan to issue some formal edict or declaration granting protection to the Jews in his dominions. Palmerston imperiously suggested that Ponsonby secure the permission of the Sublime Porte so that all Jews, including Ottoman citizens, "be at liberty" to submit "complaints to the Turkish Government through the British Consular Officers, and through the British Embassy at Constantinople." This was another transparent effort to infiltrate English influence throughout the Turkish Empire.

What reason did Palmerston proffer for such brazen requests?

> There can be no doubt that very great benefit would accrue to the Turkish Government, if any considerable number of opulent Jews could be persuaded to come and settle in the Ottoman Dominions; because their wealth would afford employment to the People, and their Intelligence would give a useful direction to Industry; and the Resources of the State would thereby be considerably augmented.

Palmerston felt no compunction about making such an extravagant request after British naval forces bombarded Acre and were actively helping the sultan push Mehemet Ali out of Syria and Palestine. British influence at the Sublime Porte was at its peak.

Impatient, arrogant, and self-confident, Palmerston kept pressing Ponsonby to convince the Sublime Porte to provide protection for the Jews.

He was not put off by Ponsonby's warning that "the Porte is likely to object" to his proposal of safeguarding the Jews. So in February 1841, with Mehemet Ali out of Syria, Ponsonby was again instructed by Palmerston:

> ... use every exertion to obtain this permission. You will endeavour to impress upon the minds of the Turkish Ministers that it would be highly advantageous to the Sultan that the Jews who are scattered through other countries in Europe and Africa, should be induced to go and settle in Palestine.[48]

Again we hear the familiar refrain about Jewish "wealth" and "industry . . . to promote the progress of civilization" in Palestine. The sultan should provide "real and tangible security" for the Jews of Europe for the purpose of inducing "wealthy Jews to come and settle permanently in Palestine, and to lay out their money in buying houses and land and in making improvements in the agriculture and commerce of the Country." Once more Ponsonby politely demurred and wrote Palmerston that it "might be in fact inconvenient to the Porte and not useful to the Jews to give them *special immunities.*"

Still not dissuaded, Palmerston mailed Ponsonby a copy of the dispatch sent to "British Consuls and Consular Agents in the Turkish Dominions" telling them that the Porte had guaranteed the Jews "complete freedom in the exercise of the religion" and had given assurance that "it will attend to any representation which may be made to it by Her Majesty's Embassy, of any Instance of Oppression practiced against the Jews." Consular agents were instructed to "make a diligent enquiry" into all complaints of Jews and "report fully" to Ponsonby in Istanbul. Palmerston then confused the consular agents by warning them against interfering with the local authorities.

> But nevertheless you will, upon any suitable occasion, make known to the Local Authorities that the British Government feels an interest in the welfare of the Jews in general and is anxious that they should be protected from oppression.

These befuddling instructions came to an abrupt halt when the Whig government was defeated in September 1841 on an issue concerning Spain and Palmerston was swept out of office. Out with Palmerston went his protection policy for the Jews in the Turkish dominions, and the concept that the British "duty" was "to lead the way and to direct the march of other nations."[49] The new foreign secretary, Lord Aberdeen, despised the Turks, "for I consider their government the most evil and the most oppressive in the world."[50] He added that "it is quite enough to govern England, and if we are to regulate the affairs of Turkey also I fear the task will be too heavy." Lord Aberdeen coupled his repugnance for the Turkish Empire with a "frigid distaste" for the Jews.[51]

Back in Jerusalem William T. Young was instructed by Aberdeen, as he had been by Campbell, to interpret protection of the Jews narrowly, so that

> the number of persons who receive British Protection shall be strictly limited to those who by birth are entitled to it, and also to those whom the capitulations to Turkey, construed in the strictest sense, permit to be withdrawn from the immediate control of the Turkish Law.[52]

The wheel had once again turned.

Despite these political changes, Restoration plans continued to be championed by Christians who thought that the return of the Jews to their ancient homeland was politically and commercially advantageous to England, essential for the Second Advent of Jesus, and, incidentally, also good for the Jews. A mixture of these motives prompted Col. Charles H. Churchill, British consul in Damascus, to write enthusiastically to Moses Montefiore in June 1841 about his "anxious desire to see your countrymen endeavour once more to resume their existence as a people...burning to return to that land which you seek to remould and regenerate."[53]

Colonel Churchill considered it "perfectly attainable" to secure "a refuge and resting place" for Jews "scattered throughout the world." To achieve this objective two conditions were indispensably necessary. "Firstly, that the Jews will themselves take up the matter universally and unanimously. Secondly, that the European Powers will aid them in their views."

Churchill counseled Montefiore on how to organize a "movement" for concerted

> agitation...throughout Europe...that...would conjure up a new element in Eastern diplomacy—an element which under such auspices as those of the wealthy and influential members of the Jewish community could not fail not only of attracting great attention and of exciting extraordinary interest, but also of producing great events...and that would end by obtaining the sovereignty of at least Palestine.

Jewish opulence and influence were invoked once more.

A turn of events was necessary according to Churchill, who sounded a typical Victorian theme:

> . . . the march of civilization *must* progress, and its various elements of commercial prosperity *must* be developed. It is needless to observe that such will never be the case under the . . . Turks or the Egyptians. Syria and Palestine must be taken under European protection and governed in the sense and according to the spirit of European administration.

In soaring prose Churchill invited Jews to summon the "Powers on whose counsels the fate of the East depends to enter upon the glorious task of rescuing our beloved country from the withering influence of centuries of desolation . . . "

Churchill advised that Jews petition foreign secretary Aberdeen

> to accredit and send out a fit and proper person to reside in Syria for the sole and express purpose of superintending and watching over the interests of the Jews residing in that country. The duties and powers of such a public officer to be a matter of arrangement between the Secretary of State of Foreign Affairs and the Committee of Jews conducting the negotiations.

No mention is made about securing the approval of the "ignorant and fanatical . . . blundering and decrepit . . . Turks."

Churchill concluded his letter with a clarion call reminiscent of ardent Zionist proclamations:

> . . . a *beginning* must be made—a resolution must be taken, *an agitation must be commenced,* and where the stake is "Country and Home" where is the heart that will not leap and bound to the appeal? . . . National Regeneration . . . makes every Jewish heart vibrate. The only question is—*when* and how.

Montefiore, acting as president of the Board of Deputies of British Jews, submitted Churchill's proposal to the board, which resolved:

> . . . [it] is fully convinced that much good would arise from the realisation of Colonel Churchill's intentions, but is of opinion that any measures in reference to this subject should emanate from the general body

of the Jews throughout Europe, and that this Board doubts not that if the Jews of other countries entertain the proposition those of Great Britain would be ready and desirous to contribute towards it their most zealous support.[54]

English Jewry was willing to donate money for the settlement of European Jews in Palestine, provided that this was the wish of their nonexistent "general body." Such a cold reception by British Jewry for a passionately presented manifesto by a Christian calling for Jewish "National Regeneration"!

Although Restoration projects planned for the Jews peaked around 1840–1841, they continued to be persuasively proposed well past the mid-nineteenth century. However, practical conditions for settling Jews in Palestine did not exist. The feeble, propped-up Turkish government was unwilling to provide special status for the Jewish minority. Nor would the Sublime Porte countenance a potential multitude of Jews flooding into Palestine now that the Hatt-I-Sherif of 1839 guaranteed minority rights. Also nonexistent were the rich Jews who would consider investing the large sums required to settle Jews in Palestine and develop a prosperous community.

World Jewry was unable to exploit the abundance of proposed Restoration projects and settlement schemes. The Jews of Western Europe were preoccupied with the Damascus blood libel or were placing their hopes on Emancipation, Enlightenment, and Reform, or opting for assimilation and conversion, or finding their way to America. East European Jewry had to invest all its efforts in eking out a subsistence living in czarist Russia that permitted little freedom for political action. And the religious yearning of orthodox Jews to return to Zion was squelched by the failure of the Messiah to appear in 1840. So immersed was world Jewry in its own problems and interests that it could not even produce a paper scheme for settling Jews in Eretz Israel until the plan of an orthodox German rabbi was printed in 1842.[55]

Diaspora Jewry lacked a united world organization to promote activities on an international scale. Also crucially missing was a visionary leader, able to understand the international political scene, grasp the proffered opportunities, and turn them to the advantage of the Jews in Paletine. More was required than the stolid dedication of Montefiore.

A Jewish national movement had not yet developed independently or in tandem with the religious belief of returning to Zion. And the concept of pioneering in a homeland located in a backward country arbitrarily ruled by

Muslim Pashas was an outlandish idea considered by few Jews. Although European powers, notably Great Britain, might aid Jewish colonization in Palestine, no substantial number of prospective immigrants wishing to return to their homeland was in sight. "Not a voice was raised among the Jews for the restoration of the land to them." Since, according to Churchill, it was "for the Jews to make a commencement," for lack of Jewish settlers, there was no beginning.

EPILOGUE

Reconstructing the nineteenth-century world of the Jews in Eretz Israel required overcoming the intractable problem of how modern minds can gain insight into the Jewish soul, which, in past generations, was guided by divine instruction and experienced life in terms of Messianic visions. Telling the story of the Jews in their Land also necessitated removing the foliage of myths and legends that obscured the true picture. With an awesome historical memory, Jews frequently conceptualized their past as they wanted to remember it. Ideology triumphed over reality, and preconceived ideas distorted facts. Families of founding fathers dispensed an idyllic history of piety and patriotism that romanticized the past and justified the heroic efforts of their ancestors. For historically conscious Jews questing after their past, Jewish history existed to reshape images and change the Jewish consciousness in order to lead the Jews into their Promised Land, where they could build a glorious Third Commonwealth, a veritable third Temple.

Jewish interest in historiography was minimal to nonexistent. History for the Jews was a "chronicle justifying the ways of God to man," a "memoir of suffering," "Jewish martyrology," or "a chronicle of genealogy."[1] As a result, the history of the Jews in Eretz Israel from 1799 to 1840 is a mixed-up catalogue of events recorded by Jews disregarding dates and ignoring numbers. While trying to establish order, coherence, and meaning in linking the start of the story to its end, I hope that the danger of picturing an overly tidy, purposeful, and sequential history of the period, which in fact was chaotic and quite messy, has been avoided.

In the life of a people the past has a connection with its future. Although the past illuminates the present and provides insights into contemporary issues, the dangers of reading present meanings into the past are constantly with us. Trying to identify this "diabolical and inseparable couple" of the past and the present is never easy.[2] And explaining how past acts shape future behavior is frequently speculative.

Friction and factionalism were the most dominant distinguishing characteristics in the social dynamics of the contentious Jewish community divided into separate kollelim. Virulent fights produced a shower of invective. A rain of righteous morality, stormy verbal clashes, and ferocious fights enveloped and decisively influenced the Jews in Eretz Israel.

As a new, dynamic force the committed Perushim demanded what they regarded as their rightful place in Eretz Israel and were ready to do what was required to achieve their destined goal. If this promoted debate, forced confrontations, badgered compliance, and provoked contentions, so be it. If this propelled Ashkenazim and Sephardim into battle over Jewish funds and spawned irreconcilable differences that ruptured the community, no matter. Each group's angle of vision frequently proved to be its angle of attack. Sacred fires stoked by inflamed religious enthusiasts proved hard to dampen.

Perushim and Hasidim transplanted to Eretz Israel the ideological adversities, social antipathies, and personal antagonisms brought from Eastern Europe. Adjustment anxieties of a predominantly immigrant population sharpened inveterate suspicions. The intimacy of living in close quarters apparently made Jews overly conscious of their neighbors' deficiencies. Diversity of objectives and conflicts of interest, particularly in distributing limited financial resources in a needy community, inevitably escalated into implacable hostility that polarized the Sephardim, Perushim, and Hasidim and pitted one group against the other.

Christian observers frequently commented on the mud-slinging and "the hateful spirit of sect" manifest among the Jews.[3] Joseph Wolff wrote that the Perushim and Hasidim tried to keep each other from settling in Jerusalem "and accuse...each other to the Turkish Governor." John Nicolayson noted "divisions" among the Jews. The perceptive and sympathetic British vice-consul W. T. Young observed the Jews in 1839: "I fear the want of union among themselves, and their internal caballing—the natural fruits of their poverty—tend to increase their wretchedness."

Scottish ministers touring Palestine in 1839 remarked that "no Jew trusts his brother. They are constantly quarrelling, and frequently apply to the Consul to settle their disputes."

The problem of the Jewish community was not how to stop the splintering of the kehilla into competing factions or how to achieve a consensus and harmonize divergent interests. Its problem was how to continue to disagree under an array of pressures, yet live together in tolerably amicable conditions and act in concert for the benefit of the total Jewish community. Why did this remain an unsolved problem? Is it really true, as the historian Barbara Tuchman has argued, that the Jews "are the most contentious people alive.... Their quarrels are legion, they abuse each other incessantly and without compunction, and settle differences of opinion within any group by splintering instead of submitting to majority rule."[4]

Psychologists may explain why the Ashkenazim found relief in lambasting each other and how a constant state of confrontation triggered impulsive, aggressive responses. Sociologists may analyze how too much leisure time produced verbal battles, and how living under different influences— the Ashkenazim in Christian countries, and the Sephardim mainly in Muslim lands—led to the great distinctions between these communities.[5] Economists can demonstrate how "sharp divergences of an economic character aggravated the separation between Ashkenazim and Sephardim in Palestine and produced conflicts."[6] Political scientists can interpret Jewish factionalism as the natural consequence of long centuries lacking political power or responsibility and contend that without a power ruling them Jews "would swallow each other alive."[7] And historians can tell about the twelve separate tribes in the divided kingdom of Judah and Israel and describe how centuries of subjection generated among the Jews "petty ambitions which lead people to destroy each other..."[8]

Setting aside such encompassing theories about the results of protracted persecutions and precarious living conditions, we can explain why many Jews saw "conflict as inevitable, accommodation as impossible and communication as nothing more than an exchange of threats."[9] An underlying factor feeding this factionalism was the system of financial assistance extended to the Jewish community in Eretz Israel by European philanthropic organizations. This framework and approach emphasized group differentiations and accented a disparity of interests. Although most clashes in the Jewish community centered around money matters rooted in the religious and social issues, bitter antagonisms were exacerbated by personality fights.

Consecration of the Holy Land through study and prayer did not fully occupy all Ashkenazi settlers. With abundant free time, they applied the combative keenness of mind learned in Talmudic disputations. In a verbal tradition where the tongue was the Jewish sword, Ashkenazim boisterously debated by bullying and abusing each other with scorn, mockery, and personal animus. Honoring an opponent and respecting differing views were alien concepts; that reasonable people can amicably disagree was an unknown idea. Creeds outweighed courtesy and principle prevailed over manners. Vituperation displaced civility and shouted expletives substituted for reasoned thought. While working for Redemption in the next world, Jews made life miserable for their opponents in this world.

The rough rhetoric and unbending attitudes of individuals and groups expressed the absolute values and unwavering principles that governed Jewish life in Eretz Israel. Conflicts were imprinted with compelling religious fervor. Each Jewish group was convinced that it was a sacred instrument chosen to fulfill the divine intent and thus became arrogantly contemptuous of the inadequacies and errors of fellow Jews. In a society based on divine authority, compromising sacred truths was unconscionable and therefore inconceivable. Tolerance was heresy and shifting opinions was an abomination. In times of disagreement the Jews of Eretz Israel lacked a culture of conciliation. They stood fast and unequivocally asserted their rights; the only compromises they made were forced upon them by the outside world. Such unyielding behavior had long preserved Jewish life in the hostile Diaspora environment; now it contributed to the divisiveness of the Jewish society of Eretz Israel.

World Jewry's spiritual center in Eretz Israel lacked a sense of communal unity based on shared values, a feeling of mutual responsibility, and a quest for community. Identity of faith and a shared fate could not fuse the disparate ways of life of the Sephardim, Perushim, and Hasidim, which remained particularistic groups. Partisan loyalty to a specific ideology or place of birth overpowered a sense of belonging to a total Jewish community.

The seeds of discord planted in the fertile soil of the Holy Land flourished in constantly growing disharmony, controversy, and hatred, encouraging separatist religious groups to multiply in amoeba-like divisions. Kollel HOD set the style for the many kollelim that later burgeoned in Jerusalem. Friction and factionalism determined the character, temper, and direction of the Jewish community throughout the nineteenth century and begat a similar situation throughout the twentieth, which witnessed political parties and religious organizations loathing each other and frequently splitting apart.

Both the Hasidim and the Perushim transferred their East European way of life to the Holy Land. Different Jewish customs, forms of worship, and religious observances existed side by side. No effort was made to fuse the various groups in one common melting pot. The Sephardim, Hasidim, and Perushim lived within the socially cohesive framework of their own kollelim, where Jews were free but not equal. Each group was governed by men of learning or wealth. Leaders of the Sephardi kollel were chosen by the local oligarchy, while heads of the Perushim and Hasidim were appointed to kollel positions by their supporting fundraising organizations in Poland. Even the Sephardi chief rabbi, a most influential member of his kollel who served as chief justice of the rabbinical court and as head of the Jewish millet, had no monopoly on community power and did not rule a theocracy. In a people living under God there was no government by a priesthood that interpreted the revealed laws of the Deity. By command of their cultures rather than by order of a ruling religious hegemony, Ashkenazi and Sephardi values gained the compelling force of law.

Kollel leaders legislated regulations and governed their members by the rule of law and a stern system of penalties that included public flogging, putting straying members in a stockade built in the Hurva courtyard, and excommunicating them. Such extreme measures were only infrequently needed to keep Jews in line. Social and ideological unity created pervasive conformity to community values that quelled divergent opinions and squelched actions by recalcitrant members. Nevertheless, solidarity within each group started to disintegrate as the kollelim grew in size with the significant increase of new immigrants.

During 1830–1837 the most significant, dramatic, and overlooked phenomenon in the Jewish community was its population explosion. Within seven years the number of Jews swelled from 7,500 to 9,600 before the lethal 1837 earthquake reduced the Jewish population again to 7,500. This unprecedented 30-percent population growth was the direct result of persecutions that impelled Jews to leave Algiers, the Balkans, Poland, Russia, and the Rumanian principalities. Throughout Jewish history this pattern has been repeated; Jews do not leave their native lands in significant numbers until they are pushed out or worse consequences befall them.

The tremendous population growth between 1830 and 1837 was in stark contrast to the slow growth of the kehilla from 1800 to 1830. During these thirty years the number of immigrants had been kept to a minimum because the practical realities of feeding the flock took precedence over the rhetoric about the religious-Messianic ideologies of settling in Eretz Israel. Unrestricted, nonselective immigration was never a cardinal plank in the Return to Zion ideology of the Hasidim, Perushim, Sephardim, and their overseas financial benefactors, who did not want to redeem the Jewish people by establishing a mass movement that would send a multitude of Jews swarming into the Holy Land. Opening the doors of Eretz Israel for people unable to support themselves was a luxury that nineteenth-century Jews believed they could not afford. In bold polarity stands the Law of Return legislated by the newly created state of Israel affirming the right of all Jews to enter Israel despite the threatening economic and security conditions prevailing since 1948.

Around 1800 the Jewish community in Palestine was composed of about 95 percent Sephardim; however, by the end of the nineteenth century the Ashkenazim would outnumber the Sephardim due to large waves of immigration from Eastern Europe. The growing city of Jerusalem would be populated by a Jewish majority, while the number of Jews in the other three holy cities would increase quite slowly. After the establishment of the Jewish state, masses of Sephardi immigrants from North Africa and Asia transformed Israel once again into a predominantly Sephardi community.

As the power of Diaspora fundraising organizations increased, they assumed a more dictatorial attitude toward the Jews of Eretz Israel. In a most unequivocal manner, Zvi Hirsch Lehren, the leader of PEKAM, told the Sephardim that "distributing charity depends on the opinion of the donor, not the ideas of the recipients."[10] He threatened that if the Sephardim "do not distribute [money] as we see fit, we have the power to institute changes and give all to the Ashkenazim..." But the intemperate outbursts of the petulant PEKAM leader were bluff and bluster. Much as the Jews of Eretz Israel needed the funds collected in the Diaspora, overseas Jews needed Eretz Israel to focus their religious dedication on a consecrated purpose.

Zvi Hirsch Lehren tried to impose his views against what he regarded as the insidious encroachments of change. Like some present-day Jews, he believed that Jews throughout the world should have a decisive say in conducting the affairs of the community in Eretz Israel. To an extent Lehren unified that community by deciding on equitable allocations and compromises. PEKAM provided the discursive forum where rival groups argued their case and secured a certain level of satisfaction and a large measure of justice. However, by financially supporting specific ideological and geographical associations, PEKAM emphasized the separatist tendencies of the communities in Eretz Israel and encouraged different groups to split apart at a rapidly increasing tempo.

Despite the fact that the Egyptians decisively defeated the Turks in 1833 and again in 1839, and introduced Western-style reforms, the four great European powers pushed Mehemet Ali out of Palestine, returned the Holy Land to the sultan, and propped up the Ottoman Empire for another eighty years until its demise in 1922. Although nine years of Egyptian rule were too short a period to make an indelible impression, certain irreversible changes provided the base for further progress and an impetus toward the development of European concepts and practices. Traces of Westernization planted in Palestine at the end of the eighteenth century by Napoleon and by French traders were intensively developed by Mehemet Ali, and the results were reaped in the course of the nineteenth century.

Moses Montefiore tried to reshape Jews into a productive group. Although his proposals never came to fruition, the incremental changes he initiated gathered momentum and set off other innovations, which had a deep impact on the kehilla. Yet only when nonreligious, enlightened Jews were willing not just to contribute money but to settle in Eretz Israel were these changes carried out. This was not to happen until the 1882 czarist pogroms pushed young Russian Jews out of their native land in the direction of their secular Zion called Zionism.

A Jewish national movement had not yet developed independently or in tandem with the religious belief of returning to Zion. And the concept of pioneering in a homeland located in a backward country ruled arbitrarily by pashas was an outlandish idea considered by hardly any Jews. Although European powers, notably Great Britain, might aid Jewish colonization in Palestine, no substantial number of prospective immigrants wishing to return to their homeland was in sight. "Not a voice was raised among the Jews for the restoration of the land to them." Since, according to Churchill, "it is for the Jews to make a commencement," for lack of Jewish settlers, there was no beginning.

Montefiore was recognized for half a century as the foreign minister of the world Jewish community. His activities touched the lives of world Jewry and wherever he traveled he raised the morale of his brethren. Montefiore's greatest contribution to the Jewish cause was lending it his name and reputation. This was still the day of the shtadlan, when distinguished, rich Jews intervened to improve the lot of oppressed Jews. Like other well-meaning shtadlanim, Montefiore felt no need for concerted group action undertaken by a representative organization, as is the present accepted mode of operation.

Diaspora Jewry lacked a united world organization to promote activities on an international scale. Also crucially missing was a visionary leader able to understand the international political scene, grasp the proffered opportunities, and turn them to the advantage of the Jews in Palestine. More was required than the stolid dedication of Montefiore.

Establishing the English consulate and the Anglican mission station in

Jerusalem helped the Jews. James Finn, the second British consul in Jerusalem, did not doubt that the Jews were extricated from "a condition of oppression . . . mainly through the protection" extended by the British consul at the direction of Lord Palmerston. Setting up the British consulate in 1839 triggered a chain reaction of diplomatic appointments in the Holy City. Within the coming years Prussia (1842), France and Sardinia (1843), the United States (1844), Austria (1849), and Russia (1858) established consulates in Jerusalem. Truly, "after God the Consuls were the highest persons in Palestine."[11]

The existence of the LJS mission spurred the Sephardim to set up a hospital in Jerusalem in 1844, encouraged the Rothschilds to found a Jewish hospital in 1854, helped convince Montefiore to send an orthodox Jewish doctor to minister to the health needs of Jerusalem's Jews, and forced the reluctant kehilla to accept his medical philanthropy. The mission greatly improved the city of Jerusalem not only in the field of health. The simple Gothic Christ Church, consecrated in 1849, improved the architecture of the city, provided work for Jews and Muslims, and permitted natives to learn the trade of stonecutter. A mission school of industry, Miss Cooper's school for girls, and Bishop Gobat's school for boys, all set up in the 1840s and 1850s, led Montefiore, Rothschild, and other overseas Jews to found Jewish schools in defiance of the vocal opposition of the Jewish establishment. Despite the mission's promoting progress and instituting modern improvements that changed the Holy City, Jews rabidly fought the missionaries and to this very day instinctively oppose any activity remotely resembling proselytizing.

In the land of Israel we discern a cord of continuity between the era 1799–1840 and later historical periods. The remote, neglected area of Palestine, which lacked recognition as a separate administrative entity in the Ottoman Empire, still has no agreed-upon national boundary. Geography also shaped the development of the cities of Jaffa and Haifa in ways quite different from those in the four holy cities. Knowing they would receive no haluka subsidies, Jews in Haifa and Jaffa worked for a living rather than depending on the largess of Diaspora Jews. Today these port cities have expanded to meet the commercial needs of the country and its residents display a modish, unfettered life-style. Tribal enmities and blood feuds among the Muslims and Beduin still continue to cause frequent fights. Many Jews today, like the Ashkenazim at the turn of the nineteenth century, still show a dismissive disdain toward Muslims and an outward defiance of the Gentile world. Rigorous Talmudic studies are still conducted in religious study halls, while the Jewish tradition of learning, in a somewhat diluted fashion, is carried on in Israeli schools with special emphasis on the Bible serving as the geographic guide of the country. Girls as well as boys today study at public educational facilities, marry at their convenience, and act as equal family partners, in sharp contrast to 150 years ago, when girls learned to recite their Hebrew prayers by rote and were confined to their homes and domestic chores until they were married off at an early age. To a large extent a Jew is still measured by his ability to expand the dimensions of the mind in a country needing to develop high technological products. The common language of the Sephardim and Ashkenazim in 1800 and today was and is Hebrew, the holy language of ritual, responsa, and legal contracts. Although different pronunciations initially made it difficult for Sephardim and Ashkenazim to understand each other, there was no need to revive a language that was spoken alongside the Yiddish of the Ashkenazim and the Ladino of the Sephardim. Eventually the lilting, soft-singing Sephardi pronunciation won out in Israel over the harsh, quavering, Yiddish-accented inflection. Repugnance of Israelis toward those leaving the country, like Shmaryahu Luria, has changed little in 150 years. Those "going down" from Eretz Israel are still reviled as deserters performing a profane act and most present-day departers leave with a heavy heart and a guilty conscience.

From the vantage point of modern Israel we view nineteenth-century Jews in Eretz Israel not as exotic creatures of a patriarchal past but as forerunners of a living legacy in a dynamic country that has revolutionized the total condition of the Jewish people. In retrospect we see religiously motivated Jews building a national monument that links their concepts and activities in Eretz Israel during 1799–1840 with the secular, socialist-inspired society launched at the end of the nineteenth century for the purpose of regenerating the Jewish people in its own country. Jews of different decades exercised their inalienable right to pursue their Promised Land, mold it as they saw fit, and transform it into the Jewish state. At the start of the nineteenth century the trajectory of modern journeys to Eretz Israel was charted. Jews continue to travel in its path toward a Redemption that each defines for himself.

NOTES

1 NAPOLEON'S INVASION OF PALESTINE, 1799

1. F. Bourrienne, *Memoirs of Napoleon Bonaparte*, 3, 86.
2. N. Barber, *The Lords of the Golden Horn*, 124.
3. A. L. Tibawi, *British Interests in Palestine 1800–1901*, 230. Translated as "really to conquer England" by J. A. R. Harriott, *The Eastern Question* (Oxford, 1918), 8.
4. Albert Sorel, *L'Europe et la révolution française*, vol. 5, "Bonaparte and the Directory" (1903), as cited in Jacques Bainville's *Napoleon*, English translation (New York, 1970), 97.
5. Tallyrand quoted by D. G. Chandler, *The Campaigns of Napoleon*, 211.
6. Bourrienne, 68.
7. Bainville, vol. 3, p. 135, quoting the academician Arnault in "Souvenirs d'un sexagénaire," recorded by H. A. B. Rivlin, *The Agricultural Policy of Muhammad Ali in Egypt*, 8.
8. A. Cohen (ed.), *The History of Eretz-Israel under Mamluke and Ottoman Rule (1260–1804)*, 140.
9. R. Mahler, *A History of Modern Jewry, 1780–1815*, 618, 688: P. Guedella, *Napoleon and Palestine*, 21; I. Ben-Zvi, *Eretz-Israel under Ottoman Rule: Four Centuries of History*, 329; M. Gichon, "History of the Gaza Strip," 158; Y. Zahavi, *From the Hatam Sofer to Herzl*, 38.
10. Y. Ben-Arieh, "The Development of the Twelve Major Settlements in Nineteenth-Century Palestine," 127–128.
11. J. Schwartz, *Descriptive Geography and Brief Historical Sketch of Palestine*, 142.

12. R. Kark, "The Jewish Community of Jaffa in the Late Ottoman Period," 13.

13. S. C. Herold, *Bonaparte in Egypt*, 273.

14. C. F. C. Volney, *Travels through Syria and Egypt in the Years 1783, 1784 and 1785*, vol. 2, 227.

15. D. Kinross, *The Ottoman Centuries*, 222.

16. M. Eliav, *Eretz-Israel and Its Yishuv in the Nineteenth Century (1777–1917)*, 38–39; N. Sokolow, *History of Zionism*, vol. 1, 63; Ben-Zvi, *Ottoman Rule*, 322.

17. F. Kobler, "Napoleon and the Restoration of the Jews to Palestine." In 1936, the only copy of the proclamation, in a German translation, was found in London. Neither the French nor Hebrew original version has been found.

18. J. D. Popkin, "Zionism and the Enlightenment," 113–120.

19. A. L. Tibawi, *A Modern History of Syria including Lebanon and Palestine*, 39.

20. C. Watson, "Bonaparte's Expedition to Palestine in 1799," 29.

21. J. L. Burckhardt, *Travels in Syria and the Holy Land*, 339.

22. Mahler, 650: A. Yaari, *Eretz-Israel Emissaries*, 688.

23. Mahler, 650.

24. Y. Ben-Arieh, *Jerusalem in the Nineteenth Century*, vol. 1, 228, 318.

25. I. Rivkind, "Separate Pages," 143–144. All quotes are from this source unless otherwise noted.

26. Yaari, *Emissaries*, 566.

27. Schwartz, *Geography*, 449.

28. Ibid., 373.

29. Watson, 30.

30. Herold, 303.

31. Bourrienne, 86.

32. C. de la Jonquière, *L'Expédition en Egypte 1798–1801*, vol. 4, 632–633.

33. D. G. Chandler, *The Campaigns of Napoleon*, 248.

34. An important explorer-soldier, Captain Jacotin, commanded a group of French engineers and geographers who accompanied Napoleon's army and hurriedly charted the geography and topography of Palestine and Egypt. Despite its many inaccuracies, Jacotin's "Carte Topographique de la Egypte," published in 1810, was the greatest cartographic work of its day and marked the beginning of modern mapping in Palestine. Jacotin best mapped the areas of Palestine where Napoleon moved his army—along the coastline from Gaza to Acre, the Valley of Jezreel, and the Galilee. Maps of Jerusalem and Nablus are worthless, "being apparently mere fancy sketches" (Y. Ben-Arieh, *The Rediscovery of the Holy Land in the Nineteenth Century*, 21).

35. "By the easy victory which they won the French shattered the illusion of the unchallengeable superiority of the Islamic world to the infidel West, thus posing a profound problem of readjustment to a new relationship. The psychological disorders thus engendered have not yet been resolved" (B. Lewis, *The Arabs in History*, 166–167).

36. Schwartz, *Geography*, 375.

2 NINETEENTH-CENTURY PALESTINE; THE LAND AND ITS PEOPLE

1. The term "Middle East" was coined in 1902 by the American naval historian Alfred Thayer Mahan, to define the area between Arabia and India; it superseded the term "Near East" (B. Lewis, *The Middle East and the West*, 9–10).

2. Cook and Kurat in V. J. Parry et al., *A History of the Ottoman Empire to 1730*, 8, 185.

3. Kurat in Parry et al., *158*.

4. C. Issawi (ed.), *The Economic History of the Middle East, 1800–1914*, 18.

5. Cicero.

6. The sultan was humiliated by a consecutive series of unfavorable treaties and the loss of territories in the treaties of Passarowitz (1718), Kutchuk Kainardji (1774), Sistoria (1791), and Jassy (1792).

7. B. Lewis, *The Emergence of Modern Turkey*, 36.

8. C. Berenger, *Chateaubriand* (Paris, 1931), 136.

9. H. Temperley, *England and the Near East: The Crimea*, 69.

10. R. Bachi, "The Population of Israel," 24.

11. R. Mahler, *A History of Modern Jewry, 1780–1815*, 611.

12. M. Ma'oz, *Ottoman Reform in Syria and Palestine*, 4.

13. A. Cohen, *The History of Eretz-Israel under Mamluke and Ottoman Rule (1260–1804)*, 106.

14. A. Cohen (ed.), *Palestine in the Eighteenth Century*, 327.

15. C. F. C. Volney, *Travels through Syria and Egypt in the Years 1783, 1784 and 1785*, vol. 2, 280.

16. Ibid., 384.

17. W. Wittman, *Travels in Turkey, Asia Minor and across the Desert into Egypt...*, 209–210; also in other tourist accounts.

18. T. Philipp, "The Farhi Family and the Changing Position of the Jews in Syria and Palestine, 1750–1860," 102; M. Ish-Shalom, *Christian Travels in the Holy Land*, 410, 415, 428, 433.

19. J. L. Burckhardt, *Travels in Syria and the Holy Land*, 180.

20. M. Ma'oz, *Studies on Palestine during the Ottoman Period*, 144.

21. Burckhardt, 180.

22. Burckhardt, 327.

23. A. M. Lunz, "The Jews in Palestine," in *Jerusalem Yearbook*, vol. 1, 210.

24. J. H. Plumb, *England in the Eighteenth Century* (New York, 1983), 33.

25. Volney, vol. 2, 409.

26. A character in a Sardinian novel quoted by F. Braudel in *The Mediterranean World in the Age of Philip II*, vol. 1, 39.

27. B. Abu Manneh in I. Bartal (ed.), *The History of Eretz-Israel*, 175.

28. N. Katzburg, "From the First Letters of the English Vice Consul in Jerusalem," xxiii.

29. G. A. Smith, *The Historical Geography of the Holy Land*, 181.

30. Volney, vol. 2, 326.

31. S. J. and E. K. Shaw, *History of the Ottoman Empire and Modern Turkey*, vol. 1, 166.

32. H. R. Gibb and H. Bowen, *Islamic Society and the West*, vol. 1, part 2, 69.

33. Volney, vol. 2, 143.

34. *Hebrew Encyclopedia*, vol. 6, 500.

35. Cohen, *Eighteenth Century*, 324.

36. Burckhardt, 169, 188, 194.

37. Cohen, *Eighteenth Century*, 203, 326.

38. Bachi, 34.

39. Gibb and Bowen, vol. 1, part 1, 280–281.

40. S. Avitsur, *Daily Life in Eretz-Israel in the Nineteenth Century*, 103.

41. Dr. Chapin, a missionary doctor living in Jerusalem in 1862; in M. O. Schmelz, "Some Demographic Peculiarities of the Jews of Jerusalem in the Nineteenth Century," 124.

42. J. Bowring, *Report on Commercial Statistics of Syria*, 98.

43. R. R. Madden, *Travels in Turkey, Egypt, Nubia and Palestine in 1824, 1825, 1826 and 1827*, vol. 2, 315, 320.

44. L. A. Frankl, *The Jews in the East*, vol. 2, 241.

45. Volney, vol. 2, 480.

46. Lewis, *Modern Turkey*, 109.

47. M. Eliav, "The Austrian Consulate in Jerusalem and the Jewish Community," 76–77.

48. A. Carmel, "Russian Activity in Palestine during the Late Ottoman Period," 86.

49. S. N. Spyridon, "Annals of Palestine 1821–1841," 18.

50. Braude and Lewis, vol. 2, 1, quoting J. S. Furnival, *Colonial Policy and Practice* (New York, 1956), 304.

51. Ma'oz, *Ottoman Reform*, 195.

52. Braude and Lewis, vol. 1, 6.

53. E. Robinson, *Biblical Researches in Palestine, Mount Sinai and Arabia Petrea in 1838*, vol. 3, 452–464.

54. Ibid., vol. 2, 90; W. Jowett, *Christian Researches in the Holy Land in 1823 and 1824*, 214.

55. Carmel, "Russian Activity," 86.

56. Jowett, *Holy Land*, 230.

57. N. Lestchinsky, *Jewish Migration for the Past Hundred Years*, 8.

58. Mahler, 7.

59. I. Ben-Zvi, "Musta'rabs in Eretz-Israel," 379–386.

3 HASIDIC IMMIGRATION TO ERETZ ISRAEL, 1777–1807

1. I. Ben-Zvi, *Eretz-Israel under Ottoman Rule: Four Centuries of History*, 282, A. Shohat, "Three Eighteenth-Century Letters on Eretz-Israel," 236–237.

2. Y. Barnai, *The Jews in Eretz-Israel in the Eighteenth Century*, 49–54; Y. Barnai (ed.), *Hasidic Letters from Eretz-Israel*, 23–24; A. L. Frumkin, *The History of the Scholars of Jerusalem*, 58–60.

3. A. Yaari, "The Travels of David Beit Hillel in Eretz-Israel," 383, 391; Frum-

kin, 71–72; Barnai, *Eighteenth Century*, 55–57; Barnai, *Hasidic Letters*, 26, 52–54; I. Heilprin, *The First Aliyot of the Hasidim*, 16–19; B. Weinryb, *The Jews of Poland*, 330; Y. Hisdai, "Early Settlement of '*Hasidim*' and of '*Mithnaggedim*' in Palestine," 236–237.

4. For good descriptions of the Hasidic movement, see R. Mahler, *A History of Modern Jewry, 1780–1815*, 430–535; Weinryb, *Jews of Poland*, 262–303.

5. S. Sontag, *New York Review of Books* 26, no. 14, Sept. 25, 1980, in a review of a book by Elias Canetti.

6. G. Scholem, *Major Trends in Jewish Mysticism*, 330.

7. Mahler, 489; Scholem, 342–343.

8. Mahler, 445; H. J. Zimmels, *Ashkenazim and Sephardim*, 120–121.

9. A. Cohen, *Palestine in the Eighteenth Century*, 18.

10. A. Yaari, *Eretz-Israel Emissaries*, 518–519; I. Rivkind, "Separate Pages," 138–139.

11. B. Halprin, *The Idea of the Jewish State*, 185.

12. *Missionary Herald*, Jan. 1818, 10; "The Jews are indeed possessed with an irresistible desire, or rather frenzy, for dying in this place, relinquishing everything for this," according to J. Conder, *The Modern Traveller*, 340.

13. The following quotes are from Hasidic letters written in 1788 and 1789 (Barnai, *Hasidic Letters*, 181–194).

14. M. Eliav, *Eretz-Israel and Its Yishuv in the Nineteenth Century (1777–1917)*, 10–11.

15. Barnai, *Hasidic Letters*, 68.

16. Mahler, 676.

17. A. Yaari, *Letters from the Land of Israel*, 313; Barnai, *Hasidic Letters*, 72.

18. Yaari, *Emissaries*, 518–519; Rifkind, "Separate Pages," 138–139.

19. Barnai, *Hasidic Letters*, 77.

20. Ibid., 75.

21. Ibid., 57–59, 72, 76; Yaari, *Letters*, 317.

22. Barnai, *Hasidic Letters*, 58.

23. Ibid., 72.

24. Ibid.

25. Ibid., 74.

26. Ibid., 71, 75.

27. Ibid., 76.

28. Y. Barnai, *The Jews in Eretz-Israel in the Eighteenth Century*, 257; Barnai, *Hasidic Letters*, 67; Yaari, "Travels," 323–368.

29. A. M. Lunz, *Jerusalem Yearbook*, vol. 2, 156; Yaari, "Travels," 448.

30. Y. Barnai, "The Leadership of the Jewish Community in Jerusalem in the Mid-Eighteenth Century," 285–290; Cohen, *Eighteenth Century*, 18; Yaari, *Emissaries*, 540; A. Shohat, "The Jews in Jerusalem in the Eighteenth Century," 44; A. Cohen, "Arabic Documents on the Settlement of Debts of the Jewish Communities of Jerusalem and Hebron in the Eighteenth Century," 321–322.

31. Barnai, *Hasidic Letters*, 67; Shohat, "Three Letters," 255.

32. Barnai, *Hasidic Letters*, 72.

33. Rivkind, "Separate Pages," 137–138.
34. Barnai, *Hasidic Letters*, 66–67.
35. Ibid., 75; Yaari, "Travels," 399.
36. Barnai, *Hasidic Letters*, 74; Yaari, "Travels," 399.
37. Rivkind, "Separate Pages," 124; M. Ish-Shalom, *Christian Travels in the Holy Land*, 137; Yaari, "Travels," 399, *Letters*, 289, 293, *Emissaries*, 450, "The Earthquake in Safed in 1759," 349–363; Barnai, *Hasidic Letters*, 51–52; A. R. Malachi, *Chapters in the History of the Old Yishuv*, Eliav, *Eretz-Israel*, 93.
38. Barnai, *Hasidic Letters*, 52; Barnai, *Eighteenth Century*, 8–9, 215.
39. Barnai, *Hasidic Letters*, 74.
40. Ch. Katz-Steiman, "The Immigration of the Hassidim from Its Start until the First Quarter of the Nineteenth Century," 30–32.
41. Barnai, *Hasidic Letters*, 151.
42. Ibid., 25.
43. H. J. Zimmels, *Ashkenazim and Sephardim*, 119.
44. Solomon Maimon in his 1772 "Epistle of Zeal," quoted by Mahler, 475.
45. A. Curzon, *Visits to the Monasteries of the Levant*, 209.
46. Zimmels, 329.
47. J. Wilson, *The Lands of the Bible Visited and Described . . .*, vol. 2, 615.
48. J. L. Burckhardt, *Travels in Syria and the Holy Land*, 326–327: The medical missionary D. Dalton witnessed a Hasidic prayer service in Tiberias and reported "screeching, roaring, and crying, with wringing their hands, striking their heads against the wall, and jumping" (LJS, 18th Report, 261).
49. Barnai, *Hasidic Letters*, 75.
50. Weinryb, *Jews of Poland*, 329; Heilprin, 29–30.
51. Barnai, *Hasidic Letters*, 75.
52. Yaari, "Travels," 406–407.
53. Barnai, *Hasidic Letters*, 67.
54. Ibid., 74.
55. Ibid., 255.
56. Barnai, *Eighteenth Century*, 128
57. Y. Barnai, "The Ashkenazi Community in Eretz-Israel, 1720–1777," 204.
58. Barnai, *Hasidic Letters*, 67–68; Mahler, 658.
59. Heilprin, 24.
60. Barnai, *Hasidic Letters*, 75, 77.
61. Ibid., 67, 75.
62. Ibid., 73, 77.
63. Ibid., 79, 81, 94.
64. Ibid., 84–87.
65. Mahler, 661.
66. Barnai, *Hasidic Letters*, 25, 64–65.
67. Heilprin, 34.
68. Barnai, *Hasidic Letters*, 84–85.
69. Ibid., 87, Katz-Steiman, 3.
70. Frumkin, 75, Lunz, *Jerusalem Yearbook*, vol. 9, 189–190.

71. Barnai, *Hasidic Letters*, 67, 87.

72. Ibid., 100.

73. Ibid., 97–103.

74. Wilson, vol. 2, 133.

75. Barnai, *Hasidic Letters*, 87.

76. Rivkind, "Separate Pages," 146; Yaari, *Emissaries*, 532–633; M. Kosover, *Arabic Elements in Palestinian Yiddish*, 85–86.

77. Rivkind, "Separate Pages," 180–181, Yaari, *Emissaries*, 640–647.

78. Yaari, *Emissaries*, 596, 669.

79. Rivkind, "Separate Pages," 182–183.

80. O. Avisar (ed.), *Book of Tiberias*, 110, 159–160.

81. M. O. Schmelz, "Some Demographic Peculiarities of the Jews of Jerusalem in the Nineteenth Century," 119–142.

82. Barnai, *Hasidic Letters*, 113–115, 126–132, 142–143, 149, 152–153, 172–176; Avisar, *Tiberias*, 110–111, 390–391; Yaari, *Emissaries*, 639; Lunz, *Jerusalem Yearbook*, vol. 5, 196.

83. Barnai, *Hasidic Letters*, 90.

84. Scholem, 330; Weinryb, *Jews of Poland*, 327.

85. Barnai, *Hasidic Letters*, 75, 77.

86. Yaari, "Travels," 368; Kosover, 30.

87. Barnai, *Hasidic Letters*, 51–52.

88. Yaari, *Letters*, 306.

89. Barnai, "Leadership of the Jewish Community," 284–285.

90. N. Sokolow, *History of Zionism*, vol. 1, 79.

91. Barnai, *Hasidic Letters*, 234–235.

92. Ibid., 84.

4 PERUSHIM SETTLE IN SAFED, 1808–1812

1. R. Mahler, *A History of Modern Jewry, 1780–1815*, 624–625.

2. A. Morgenstern, "The Pekidim and Amarcalim of Amsterdam and the Jewish Community in Palestine," 90–91.

3. M. M. Rothschild, *The Haluka*, 86–87.

4. Moses Hagiz, in Mahler, 625.

5. T. H. Rivlin, *The Vision of Zion, Shklov to Jerusalem*, 15.

6. Mahler, 399–409.

7. Ibid.

8. Ibid., 365.

9. A. Yaari, *Letters from the Land of Israel*, 330.

10. Y. Ben-Arieh, "The Development of Twelve Major Settlements in Nineteenth-Century Palestine," 113.

11. A. Yaari, *Memoirs of Eretz-Israel*, 111.

12. Morgenstern, "Pekidim," 92–93.

13. PEKAM, *Letters of the Pekidim and Amarcalim of Amsterdam*, vol. 1, 219.

14. I. Rivkind, "Separate Pages," 137–138.

15. Yaari, *Letters*, 339.
16. Rivkind, "Separate Pages," 145.
17. Yaari, *Letters*, 339.
18. Based on Burckhardt's 600 houses in 1810: J. L. Burckhardt, *Travels in Syria and the Holy Land*, 317.
19. A. M. Lunz, *Jerusalem Yearbook*, vol. 5, 217; M. Ish-Shalom, *Christian Travels in the Holy Land*, 201–205.
20. A. L. Frumkin, *The History of the Scholars of Jerusalem*, 139.
21. Y. Y. Rivlin, "The 'GRA' and His Students in the Settlement of Eretz-Israel," 122.
22. Yaari, *Letters*, 329–331.
23. Frumkin, 140; Yaari, *Memoirs*, 111.
24. Yaari, *Letters*, 338.
25. Frumkin, 138–139.
26. I. Ben-Zvi, *Eretz-Israel under Ottoman Rule: Four Centuries of History*, 389; A. Yaari, *Eretz-Israel Emissaries*, 756.
27. Frumkin, 140.
28. Yaari, *Letters*, 335.
29. Yaari, *Memoirs*, 112.
30. Yaari, *Letters*, 329–330, 332.
31. Yaari, *Emissaries*, 760.
32. Rivlin, "The 'GRA' and His Students," 141; Frumkin, 141; Yaari, *Letters*, 113.
33. Frumkin, 146–147, Rivlin, "The 'GRA' and His Students," 145.
34. Mahler, 636; N. N. Gelber, "Immigration of Jews from Bohemia and Galicia to Eretz-Israel 1811–1869," 243–244.
35. Frumkin, 142.
36. Frumkin, 90, 139; Y. Barnai, *The Jews in Eretz-Israel in the Eighteenth Century*, 180.
37. A. Yaari, "Letter from Safed in 1835," 345; *Monthly Intelligence*, July 1832, 101.
38. Burckhardt, 327; I. Heilprin, *The First Aliyot of the Hasidim*, 29.
39. Rivkind, "Separate Pages," 145.
40. Ibid.; A. I. Katsh, "Three Emissaries from Safed in Italy," 237; A. M. Haberman, "A Compromise between Two Emissaries from Safed in Amsterdam," 357; N. Michman, "The Emergence of Pekidim and Amarcalim of Amsterdam," 78.
41. M. Sharon and Y. Baeck, *From Ancient Archives of P. Grayevsky*, 17–18; A. Shohat, "Three Eighteenth-Century Letters on Eretz-Israel," 235–236; A. Cohen, "Arabic Documents on the Settlement of Debts of the Jewish Communities of Jerusalem and Hebron in the Eighteenth Century," 317–330.
42. PEKAM, *Letters*, vol. 1, 264, 267; Morgenstern, "Pekidim," 66–67.
43. M. Toledano, *Archives of R. Toledano*, 87.
44. PEKAM, *Letters*, vol. 1, 267.
45. Yaari, *Emissaries*, 508; Barnai, *Eighteenth Century*, 122.

46. Lunz, *Jerusalem Yearbook*, vol. 9, 51–52, vol. 13, 217.

47. PEKAM, *Letters*, vol. 1, xi–xii; M. Eliav, *Eretz-Israel and Its Yishuv in the Nineteenth Century (1777–1917)*, 119.

48. I. Bartal, introduction to PEKAM, *Letters*, vol. 3, xiii.

49. M. Montefiore, *Diary and Letters from Voyages*, vol. 1, 165.

50. Yaari, *Letters*, 339.

51. B. Gat, *The Jewish Community in Eretz-Israel (1840–1881)*, 105.

52. Frumkin, 150.

53. Yaari, *Letters*, 341.

54. Rivkind, "Separate Pages," 145.

55. Yaari, *Letters*, 330.

56. Rivkind, "Separate Pages," 142.

57. Frumkin, 142–143.

58. Toledano, 120–121.

59. O. Avisar (ed.), *Book of Tiberias*, 112; Yaari, *Emissaries*, 638, 640, 643; Rivkind, "Separate Pages," 146; Toledano, 119–120; Rivkind, "Separate Pages," *Zion* 5 (1933), 180–181.

60. Frumkin, 143; PEKAM, *Letters*, vol. 1, 93; I. Bartal (ed.), *The History of Eretz-Israel*, 199; A. Morgenstern, "Messianic Concepts," *Cathedra* 24, 58.

61. Yaari, *Letters*, 341.

62. Ibid., 339.

63. Ibid., 336; P. Friedman, "Letters from Eretz-Israel from the Years 1814–1822," 270.

64. Journal of English missionary W. B. Lewis, Dec. 2, 1823, in LJS, 17th Report, 113.

65. Y. Barnai, "The Regulations (Taqanot) of Jerusalem in the Eighteenth Century," 307; Barnai, *Eighteenth Century*, 296; Yaari, *Memoirs*, 168.

66. A. M. Lunz, *Jerusalem Yearbook (1881)*, 58.

67. Yaari, *Letters*, 336, 341.

68. Rivlin, *Vision of Zion*, 177.

69. Katzburg, "Documents about the History of the Ottoman Law Regarding Purchasing Property by Foreign Nationals," in Rivlin, *Vision of Zion*, 155.

70. Yaari, *Letters*, 336; Bartal, *The History of Eretz-Israel*, 226.

71. In 1746 it was claimed that one person in Jerusalem needed 150 piastres a year for subsistence and in 1760 the Istanbul Officials set annual minimum requirements for Jerusalemites at 140–150 piastres for a couple, 80–100 piastres for a bachelor, and 75 piastres for a single widow or orphan. A Tiberias Hasid wrote in 1789 that during a regular year a couple needed an income of 150 piastres. A year earlier (1788) R. Menahem Mendel bequeathed to his wife 1,000 piastres, which earned an annual income of 150 piastres, a most generous sum for a single person. In 1812 Burckhardt erroneously reported that no Jew could live on less than 50 pounds sterling a year or 5,000 piastres (Y. Barnai, "The Leadership of the Jewish Community in Jerusalem in the Mid-Eighteenth Century," 209, 310; Barnai, *Eighteenth Century*, 294; Y. Barnai, *Hasidic Letters from Eretz-Israel*, 210; Mahler, 658).

72. Yaari, *Letters*, 338, 339; Barnai established 75–100 piastres as the minimum annual subsistence at the end of the eighteenth century (Barnai, *Eighteenth Century*, 293).

73. Yaari, *Letters*, 339; Friedman, 270.

74. Yaari, *Letters*, 339.

75. J. Huizinga, *The Waning of the Middle Ages*, 9.

76. Frumkin, 150.

77. S. Dubnow, *History of the Jews in Poland and Russia*, vol. 1, 127.

78. Mahler, 148.

79. G. Scholem, *Major Trends in Jewish Mysticism*, 252.

80. Henry Wadsworth Longfellow.

81. Frumkin, 150.

82. Yaari, *Letters*, 341.

83. T. B. Shabbath, 119b.

84. L. A. Frankl, *The Jews in the East*, vol. 1, 312: The famous admonition in Proverbs 13:24 is "He who spares the rod hates his son, but he who loves him is diligent to discipline him."

85. E. Robinson, *Biblical Researches in Palestine, Mount Sinai and Arabia Petrea in 1838*, vol. 1, 422.

86. *Missionary Herald*, 1823, 386.

87. H. J. Zimmels, *Ashkenazim and Sephardim*, 274.

88. M. Kosover, *Arabic Elements in Palestinian Yiddish*, 100–101.

89. Yaari, *Letters*, 331, 339.

90. E. Rivlin, *The Enactments concerning Legacies in Jerusalem and Palestine*, 607; Kosover, 103.

91. Letter of English missionary W. B. Lewis on Feb. 23, 1824, in LJS, 17th Report, 119.

92. A. Yaari, *Travels in Eretz-Israel*, 505.

93. Zimmels, 309–310.

94. Y. Kaniel, "Social Relations between Sephardim and Ashkenazim in the . . . Nineteenth Century," 50–51; Zimmels, 66.

95. Kosover, 214; Zimmels, 280.

96. Yaari, *Letters*, 341; Yaari, *Memoirs*, 111.

97. Y. Ro'i, "Jewish Arab Relations in the First Aliya Settlements," in *The Book on "The First Aliya,"* ed. M. Eliav and I. Rosenthal (Jerusalem, 1981), vol. 1, xviii.

98. Unless otherwise noted, all regulations are from A. Rivlin, "Perushim Regulations, about the Haluka from 1823," 149–170. The Perushim accepted the regulations invoked by the Sephardim; however, it is impossible to identify these Sephardic regulations of Safed because no records have survived. We must therefore warily resort to the hazardous practice of transposing the regulations of the Jerusalem Sephardi community to Safed while remaining alert to the fact that these Jerusalem regulations were stricter and more detailed because Jerusalem Jews lived in closer proximity to a more hostile Muslim population. Similarities between Perushim and Hasidic regulations remain unknown for lack of documentation about the Hasidic regulations, so we can only surmise in the most general fashion that Perushim

learned from the experience of the Hasidim (Barnai, "Regulations," 271–316).

99. A. E. Bonar and R. M. M'Cheyne, *Narrative of a Mission of Inquiry to the Jews from the Church of Scotland in 1839*, 278.

100. M. D. Gaon, *Oriental Jews in Eretz-Israel*, vol. 1, 113–115.

101. Menachem Mendel of Kamenets, *Chronicles of the Times*, 61.

102. Yaari, *Letters*, 341.

103. Frumkin, 151.

104. PEKAM, *Letters*, vol. 1, 48, vol. 3, 28, 30.

105. Rivlin, *Vision of Zion*, 59.

106. B. Weinryb, "Problems of Researching the History of the Jews in Eretz-Israel," 73.

107. Heinz Kohut in C. E. Schorske, *Fin-de-Siècle Vienna* (New York, 1981), xviii.

5 THE PLAGUE YEARS AND THE JEWISH COMMUNITY OF JERUSALEM, 1812–1815.

1. J. Schwartz, *Descriptive Geography and Brief Historical Sketch of Palestine*, 281.

2. A. Yaari, *Memoirs of Eretz-Israel*, 113.

3. Y. Barnai, *Hasidic Letters from Eretz-Israel*, 152.

4. Another Jew related that hardly one out of five persons escaped alive; and an English tourist traveling in Palestine in 1815 wrote that no less than 3,000 Jews died in Eretz Israel or more than half of the total Jewish population (Schwartz, *Geography*, 479; M. Ish-Shalom, *Christian Travels in the Holy Land*, 412).

5. Yaari, *Memoirs*, 118–119.

6. Yaari, *Memoirs*, 119.

7. P. Grayevsky, *From Ancient Archives*, vol. 3, 35.

8. Schwartz, *Geography*, 471.

9. M. Ma'oz, "Jerusalem in the Last 100 Years of Turkish Ottoman Rule," 261–263; W. G. Browne, *Travels in Africa, Egypt and Syria*, 416–417; A. Cohen, *Palestine in the Eighteenth Century*, 171.

10. N. Schur, *Jerusalem in Pilgrims' Accounts*, 95; J. Conder, *The Modern Traveller*, 70–72; W. H. Bartlett, *Jerusalem Revisited*, 192; W. H. Bartlett, *Walks about the City and Environs of Jerusalem*, 14.

11. J. Wilson, *The Lands of the Bible Visited and Described*, 49.

12. A. W. Kinglake, *"Eothen" or Traces of Travel*, 129.

13. R. Blake, *Disraeli's Grand Tour*, 71.

14. Y. Ben-Arieh, *Jerusalem in the Nineteenth Century*, vol. 1, 228; E. Robinson, *Biblical Researches in Palestine, Mount Sinai and Arabia Petrea in 1838*, vol. 1, 452–464.

15. A. M. Lunz, *Jerusalem Yearbook (1881)*, 118; *Monthly Intelligence*, Dec. 1833, 187; *Jewish Intelligence*, Nov. 1839, 266, and Aug. 1842, 268; Robinson, *Biblical Researches*, vol. 1, 328, vol. 2, 393.

16. A. E. Bonar and R. M. M'Cheyne, *Narrative of a Mission of Inquiry to the*

Jews from the Church of Scotland in 1839, 199.

17. U. J. Seetzen, *Reisen durch Syrien, Palästina, Phönicien*, vol. 2, 36–37, 199, 204–205, in Ben-Arieh, *Jerusalem*, vol. 1, 233.

18. B. Braude and B. Lewis (eds.), *Christians and Jews in the Ottoman Empire*, vol. 1, 8.

19. A. M. Hyamson, *The British Consulate in Jerusalem in Relation to the Jews of Palestine, 1838–1914*, vol. 1, 7–8. As late as 1839 Scottish ministers reported what happened to a Christian mistaken for a Jew: "the monks mistaking him for a Jew, rushed out upon him, and pursued him through the streets, into a house where he took refuge, threatening to kill him, unless he kissed a picture of the Virgin, in a New Testament which they held out to him. This he did, and saved his life."

20. J. Nicolayson *Journals, 1826–1842*, Jan. 29, 1833; *Monthly Intelligence*, Dec. 1833, 188.

21. Kinglake, 123.

22. C. F. C. Volney, *Travels through Syria and Egypt in the Years 1783, 1784 and 1785*, vol. 2, 306.

23. Robinson, *Biblical Researches*, vol. 1, 371, vol. 2, 91, 92.

24. Ben-Arieh, *Jerusalem*, vol. 1, 228, 318.

25. Bartlett, *Jerusalem Revisited*, 44.

26. *Missionary Herald*, Apr. 1827, 105.

27. Wilson, 12.

28. Ish-Shalom, 156–157, 479.

29. J. E. Hanauer, *Walks in and around Jerusalem*, 153; J. L. Porter, *Jerusalem, Bethany and Bethlehem*, 40.

30. When information is lacking for the beginning of the nineteenth century, I have projected the Jerusalem and kehilla situation at the end of the eighteenth onto the 1812–1815 period, a tradition-bound, slow-changing society; this risky practice appears acceptable, unless concrete evidence points in another direction.

31. I. Rivkind, "Separate Pages," *Zion* 5, 182; R. Mahler, *A History of Modern Jewry, 1780–1815*, 651.

32. A. Yaari, *Eretz-Israel Emissaries*, 540, 560–561, 566, 704; Rivkind, "Separate Pages," 153; Y. Barnai, *The Jews in Eretz-Israel in the Eighteenth Century*, 286; Rivkind, "Separate Pages," *Zion* 5, 182–183.

33. A. Elimelech, *Chief Rabbis*, 102, 155; Barnai, *Eighteenth Century*, 186; N. Sokolow, *History of Zionism*, vol. 1, 77–79; Bartal, *The History of Eretz-Israel*, 242.

34. M. Eliav, *Eretz-Israel and Its Yishuv in the Nineteenth Century (1777–1917)*, 144; Y. Kaniel, "Social Relations between Sephardim and Ashkenazim in the . . . Nineteenth Century," 52.

35. Y. Barnai, "The Status of the 'General Rabbinate' in Jerusalem in the Ottoman Period," 47–69; Y. Barnai, "The Leadership of the Jewish Community in Jerusalem in the Mid-Eighteenth Century," 271–315; Barnai, *Eighteenth Century*, 184–189.

36. For details about serious disagreements within the kehilla, see Y. Barnai, "The Regulations (Taqanot) of Jerusalem in the Eighteenth Century as a Source on the Society, Economy, and Daily Activities of the Jewish Community," 278–279;

Barnai, "Jewish Community in Jerusalem," 201–205; Elimelech, 104–105; Barnai, *Eighteenth Century*, 170; Ch. Katz-Steiman, "The Immigration of the Hasidim from Its Start until the First Quarter of the Nineteenth Century," 98–109.

37. Lunz, *Jerusalem Yearbook*, vol. 2, 153.

38. M. Kosover, *Arabic Elements in Palestinian Yiddish*, 83.

39. Yaari, *Emissaries*, 258–260, 459–460.

40. R. Mahler, *A History of Modern Jewry, 1780–1815*, 642, 659–660, 665, 670.

41. Barnai, *Eighteenth Century*, 230–250.

42. E. Finn, *Reminiscences*, 53.

43. PEKAM, *Letters of the Pekidim and Amarcalim of Amsterdam*, vol. 2, 191, vol. 3, 9.

44. Mahler, 659; Bonar and M'Cheyne, 168.

45. Mahler, 665. In 1758 an average grant was 50, 55, 65, 70, 125, 140, or 150 piastres, depending on the wealth of the yeshiva. In the middle of the eighteenth century the richest Jerusalem yeshivot paid scholars an annual stipend of 120 piastres, and the poorest yeshivot paid 50 piastres. In fact there was no "average" grant because the amount of a yeshiva fellowship was determined by "scrupulous scaling of salaries," based on the academic rank of the scholar. As yeshiva "heads" Rabbi Shmuel Meyuhas received 450 piastres in 1762 and Rabbi Isaac HaCohen Rappaport was granted 504 piastres each year during 1749–1754. Abraham Ben Asher received 465 piastres and another rabbi was offered 300 piastres annually. The income of the yeshiva head was usually double the amount awarded to the sage, which partly explains the occasional jousting over the position of yeshiva head.

46. Barnai, *Eighteenth Century*, 289.

47. Bonar and M'Cheyne, 168.

48. Bartlett, *Jerusalem Revisited*, 42.

49. Seetzen, vol. 2, p. 23, quoted by Mahler, 642.

50. M. J. Géramb, *A Pilgrimage to Palestine, Egypt and Syria*, vol. 1, 313.

51. Mahler, 642.

52. T. Zeldin, *France 1848–1945*, 32.

53. Sokolow, vol. 1, 78. The only available professional medical service was provided by European physicians touring Palestine or military doctors visiting troops in the citadel garrison. The health situation may not have been improved by Jewish and Muslim doctors who practiced medicine according to old wives' tales and prevalent witchcraft practices. There were barber-surgeons in Syria who performed on a creditable level. Their operating techniques "would do honour to any hospital surgeon in England" according to the reputable English physician Dr. Richard Madden, who toured the Middle East in the 1820s and 1830s and described how the barber-surgeons set dislocations, bled patients, cured work diseases, made incisions, and performed eye operations. Possibly Dr. Madden's opinion, which sharply differed from the "capricious and immethodical" treatment observed by Dr. Wittman in 1800, reflected more on the sad state of European medicine in the 1820s than on good medical practices in Palestine.

54. Mahler, 643, 655; Barnai, *Eighteenth Century*, 174, 231, 284, 293.

55. Mahler, 641, 643, B. Weinryb, "Problems of Researching the History of the

Jews in Eretz-Israel," 80; M. Ish-Shalom, *Christian Travels in the Holy Land*, 158–159.

56. L. Forbin, *Travels in Greece, Turkey and the Holy Land* (London, n.d.).

57. Conder, 138.

58. A. M. Lunz, *Pathways of Zion and Jerusalem*, 164.

59. Mahler, 655.

60. Barnai, *Eighteenth Century*, 151–154.

61. Yaari, *Emissaries*, 20–21, 718; Ish-Shalom, 414.

62. M. Wallenstein, "An Insight into the Sephardi Community of Jerusalem in 1855," 75–96; L. A. Frankl, *The Jews in the East*, vol. 2, 23–26. Even had we extrapolated the 1855 figures at 25 percent, or 30 percent or 40 percent for 1812–1815, instead of 50 percent, income and expenditures would have remained in approximately the same relationship to each other.

63. Wallenstein, 95; Barnai, "Regulations," 292–298; E. Rivlin, "The Enactments concerning Legacies in Jerusalem and Palestine," 559–619; Lunz, *Jerusalem Yearbook*, vol. 5, 190; Y. Kaniel, "Organizational and Economic Contentions between Communities in Jerusalem in the Nineteenth Century," 111–116; Mahler, 655.

64. Mahler, 655.

65. Rivlin, "Legacies," 586–587.

66. Eliav, *Eretz-Israel*, 151.

67. Mahler, 654; Barnai, *Eighteenth Century*, 267–268; Barnai, "Regulations," 298–299.

68. M. D. Gaon, *Oriental Jews in Eretz-Israel, Past and Present*, vol. 1, 115.

69. Mahler, 654.

70. Barnai, "Regulations," 301–302; Frankl, vol. 2, 23; Wallenstein, 95; Barnai, *Eighteenth Century*, 269–270.

71. Barnai, *Eighteenth Century*, 270–274; A. Cohen, *Palestine in the Eighteenth Century*, 257.

72. Kosover, 204–206; Barnai, *Eighteenth Century*, 268–269; A. M. Hyamson, vol. 1, 297, 343; Frankl, vol. 2, 24.

73. Yaari, *Emissaries*, 719–720; *The British Consulate in Jerusalem in Relation to the Jews of Palestine, 1838–1914*, Toledano, 67–68; Barnai, "Regulations," 302.

74. Gaon, vol. 1, 116.

75. Frankl, vol. 2, 144.

76. Barnai, *Eighteenth Century*, 157, 174, 292.

77. Ibid., 282.

78. Wallenstein, 84; Ish-Shalom, 160.

79. *Missionary Herald*, 1825, 38.

80. Frumkin, vol. 3, 162; Yaari, *Emissaries*, 714.

81. Frankl, vol. 2, 24; Mahler, 605.

82. Mahler, 654.

83. S. Halevy, *The First Hebrew Books Printed in Jerusalem*, 7.

84. Mahler, 654.

85. For details about 1843 funds, see Yaari, *Emissaries*, 717–718.

86. Wallenstein, 92–93; Rivkind, "Separate Pages," *Zion* 5, 164; Lunz, *Pathways of Zion,* 164.

87. Lunz, *Pathways of Zion,* 164. Abraham Moshe Lunz calculates kollel expenditures as "one-third for expenses of the town, one-third for supporting widows, orphans, and the poor who are unemployed, and one-third for the scholars . . ." Lunz does not mention interest payments, which according to our figures constitute nearly half of the community's expenditures and greatly overshadow the 50,000 piastres or 30 percent of the kollel's expenses for the upkeep of scholars and poor people. By omitting monies paid for interest, Lunz's estimates are approximately correct. Payments for protection and the poll tax total 35,000 piastres or 37 percent of the total kollel expenditures of 95,000 piastres and nearly two-thirds (63 percent) or 60,000 piastres were spent on kehilla operating expenses and for maintaining the poor and the scholars.

88. A. Cohen, "Arabic Documents on the Settlement of Debts of the Jewish Communities of Jerusalem and Hebron in the Eighteenth Century," 321.

89. Yaari, *Emissaries,* 704; Rivkind, "Separate Pages," *Zion* 5, 182.

90. Yaari, *Emissaries,* 719; Wallenstein, 94.

91. Barnai, *Eighteenth Century,* 264–265.

92. Mahler, 655.

6 FRICTION AND FACTIONALISM, 1815–1825

1. A. Morgenstern, "The Pekidim and Amarcalim of Amsterdam and the Jewish Community in Palestine—1810–1840," 95–96.

2. I. Werfel, "The History of the Ashkenazi Community in Eretz-Israel," 79; P. Grayevsky, *From Ancient Archives,* 17, 9–10; Morgenstern, "Pekidim," 79.

3. A. R. Malachi, *Chapters in the History of the Old Yishuv,* 16; letter of R. Menahem Mendel, in A. M. Lunz, *Jerusalem Yearbook,* vol. 4, 114.

4. *Hazfirah Newspaper,* 1889, no. 94.

5. This narrative is mainly based on A. L. Frumkin, *The History of the Scholars of Jerusalem,* 128–149; M. Eliav, *Eretz-Israel and Its Yishuv in the Nineteenth Century (1777–1917),* 168; Y. Yellin, *Memoirs of a Native of Jerusalem, 1830–1918,* 6.

6. *Jerusalem* 4, 113; Grayevsky, *Archives,* no. 10, 7.

7. Goldman, "HA-ASIF" (1886–1887), 72, quoted by B. Gat, *The Jewish Community in Eretz-Israel (1840–1881),* 195.

8. Frumkin, 154, 194–195.

9. Grayevsky, *Archives,* no. 16, 1.

10. Frumkin, 162.

11. Werfel, 78–80.

12. Grayevsky, *Archives,* no. 17, 9–10.

13. M. Benayahu, "Document about Distributing Money in Eretz-Israel from Germany," 114.

14. Y. Barnai, "The Regulations (Taqanot) of Jerusalem in the Eighteenth Century," 292–298; Y. Kaniel, "Organizational and Economic Contentions between

Communities in Jerusalem," 111–116.

15. Frumkin, 149; E. Rivlin, "The Enactments concerning Legacies in Jerusalem and Palestine," 607; Kaniel, "Organizational and Economic Contentions," 114–115.

16. Rivlin, "Legacies," 607–609; M. Kosover, *Arabic Elements in Palestinian Yiddish,* 87.

17. A. Rivlin, "Perushim Regulations about the Haluka from 1823," 155, 162, 166–167; P. Friedman, "Letters from Eretz-Israel from the years 1814–1822," 272.

18. Werfel, 93; Eliav, *Eretz-Israel,* 157.

19. Friedman, 272; Kaniel, "Organizational and Economic Contentions," 116–119.

20. Kaniel, "Organizational and Economic Contentions," 119–124. In the mid-nineteenth century Ashkenazi Jerusalem Jews unsuccessfully attempted to buy kosher meat directly from the Arab meat dealers in order to cut out the middleman brokerage fee of the Jewish butcher. But the Sephardi rabbis thwarted these attempts both to ensure the kashrut of the meat and to maintain the income of the Sephardi Kollel.

21. Grayevsky, *Archives,* no. 17, 7; LJS, 17th Report, 120.

22. Benayahu, 113.

23. Grayevsky, *Archives,* no. 17, 9.

24. M. Solomon, *Three Generations in the Yishuv, 1812–1913,* 25; Werfel, 77.

25. Frumkin, 154.

26. Solomon, 37; Morgenstern, "Pekidim," 168; *Jewish Expositor* 1822, 15–16; A. Yaari, *Eretz-Israel Emissaries,* 781; Werfel, 82–83; M. M. Rothschild, *The Haluka,* 61.

27. A. Morgenstern, "The Organizational Unity of the Perushim Kollel in Eretz-Israel," 298.

28. Morgenstern, "Pekidim," 116; Grayevsky, *Archives,* no. 17, 20–21; Werfel, 84.

29. For details of this 1823 mission, see Werfel, 85–90.

30. Grayevsky, *Archives,* no. 17, 6.

31. Quotations from Werfel, 94, 102, 95, 93, 89, 88.

32. Grayevsky, *Archives,* no. 17, 21, 23; Werfel, 103; A. Braver, "The First Use of the Capitulation Rights by the Jews in Eretz-Israel," 165.

33. Frumkin, 154–155; Werfel, 106; Yaari, *Emissaries,* 781; Solomon, 38; M. Sharon and Y. Baeck (eds.), *From Ancient Archives of P. B. Grayevsky,* 68.

34. Frumkin, 154, 158–159; Werfel, 106.

35. Yaari, *Emissaries,* 763.

36. Rothschild, 83.

37. Yaari, *Emissaries,* 624, 679; O. Avisar (ed.), *Book of Hebron,* 45; Y. Barnai, *Hasidic Letters from Eretz-Israel,* 252–259, 262–267; M. Shapira, "The Habad Hasidic Community in Hebron," 67–117. Basic theological controversies and acrimonious, odious personal quarrels escalated so quickly that by 1801 R. Abraham refused to receive contributions that R. Shneur Zalman collected for the Hasidim in Eretz Israel—"and he need not send us even one piastre and not lend us even one piastre." Not wanting to submit to the Habad, Rabbi Abraham disassociated his Hasidic flock in Eretz Israel from R. Shneur Zalman and his collection system and set

up his own independent European collection system among Hasidim in Eastern Europe (1803). This conflict diverted Habad settlers to Safed, curtailed contributions, and created financial hardships for the Hasidim. R. Abraham reported: "the little money that arrived was so small that we could not fulfill our obligation to pay each of the Hasidim some small amount of the haluka...the interest charged on the loan eats us up and continues to grow...there are many large debts placed on us...our life is not livable because of the debt collectors."

38. Y. Ben-Arieh, "The Development of Twelve Major Settlements in Nineteenth-Century Palestine," 88, 90; J. L. Stephens, *Incidents of Travel in Egypt, Arabia Petraea and the Holy Land*, 309, 313.

39. C. Ritter, *The Comparative Geography of Palestine and the Sinaitic Peninsula*, 317; I. Rifkind, "Separate Pages," *Zion* 5, 168.

40. Rivkind, "Separate Pages," 126–143; Rivkind, "Separate Pages," *Zion* 5, 154–155, 167–169; Yaari, *Emissaries*, 593–594, 596; A. Cohen, "Arabic Documents on the Settlement of Debts of the Jewish Communities of Jerusalem and Hebron in the Eighteenth Century," 324–325; Grayevsky, *Archives*, no. 16, 10.

41. A. M. Lunz, *Jerusalem Yearbook*, vol. 5, 317; Avisar, *Hebron*, 45, 432.

42. Yaari, *Emissaries*, 679, 681.

43. Kaniel, "Organizational and Economic Contentions," 116.

44. Journal of missionary W. B. Lewis, Nov. 11, 1823, in LJS, 17th Report for 1824–1825, 106; W. Jowett, *Christian Researches in the Holy Land in 1823 and 1824*, 151; K. M. Basili, *Memoirs from Lebanon 1839–1847*, 57.

45. T. Philipp, "The Farhi Family and the Changing Position of the Jews in Syria and Palestine, 1750–1860," 106; N. Schur, "The Death of Haim Farhi as Reflected in Travelers' Reports," 179–181; H. Temperley, *England and the Near East: The Crimea*, 8–9; LJS, 17th Report, 106; N. Sokolow, *History of Zionism*, vol. 1, 74; Basili, 57. Putting a wealthy man to death and seizing all his property was an everyday occurrence. Abdullah "had killed several of his creditors for demanding repayment." Jewish sources and the English missionary believed that Haim Farhi "remonstrated with the pasha on account of the sufferings of the people—the pasha was enraged and ordered the minister to be drowned." Other explanations are that Farhi was killed because of his personal popularity and opposition to Abdullah's order to construct fortifications or the fact that his relatives worked for the pasha of Damascus, whom Abdullah hated.

46. A. J. Rustrum, *The Royal Archives of Egypt and the Origins of the Egyptian Expedition to Syria 1831–1841*, 17, 23.

47. J. Schwartz, *Descriptive Geography and Brief Historical Sketch of Palestine*, 394–395; A. L. Tibawi, *A Modern History of Syria including Lebanon and Palestine*, 45; Basili, 59.

48. Rustrum, *Egyptian Expedition*, 18, 19, 20, 21, 22; S. N. Spyridon, "Annals of Palestine 1821–1841," 30; Basili, 60; Tibawi, *Syria*, 45.

49. Frumkin, 145; Rivlin, "Legacies," 608.

50. Z. Karagila, "The Community of Perushim in Eretz-Israel during the 1830s," 328; PEKAM, *Letters of the Pekidim and Amarcalim of Amsterdam*, vol. 1, 45.

51. Journal of Wolff, Jan. 25, 1822, in LJS, 15th Report, 170; Spyridon, 26; A.

Lamartine, *A Visit to the Holy Land or Recollections of the East*, 242; Tibawi, *Syria*, 7.

52. Frumkin, 145; Braver, 161–169; Morgenstern, "Pekidim," 40.

53. Frumkin, 145; Yaari, *Memoirs*, 115.

54. Friedman, 272; Kosover, 183.

55. Frumkin, 143, 145.

56. Frumkin, 145–146; Werfel, 95.

57. Grayevsky, *Archives*, no. 17, 12.

58. Friedman, 272; I. Ben-Zvi, "Events in Safed from the Lootings of 1834 to the Druze Attacks in 1838," 294, 296.

59. Werfel, 92.

60. Friedman, 272.

61. Braver, 165.

62. Friedman, 272.

63. Ibid., 273.

64. E. Robinson, *Biblical Researches in Palestine, Mount Sinai and Arabia Petrea in 1838*, vol. 3, 256; Jowett, *Holy Land*, 171, 172.

65. Friedman, 273–274, for the following quotations.

66. Grayevsky, *Archives*, no. 16, 4; Werfel, 91.

67. Werfel, 95.

68. Grayevsky, *Archives*, no. 16, 6.

69. For details about this incident, see Werfel, 95–97, 101; Grayevsky, *Archives*, no. 16, 4; Avisar, *Tiberias*, 113; Eliav, *Eretz-Israel*, 94; Jowett, *Holy Land*, 171, 180; Ish-Shalom, 434; J. Bowring, *Report on Commercial Statistics of Syria*, 92; Vereté, "Why Was a British Consulate Established in Jerusalem?" 332, Toledano, 129; *Jewish Expositor*, 1823, 339.

70. Werfel, 91, 92, 94, 101.

71. Werfel, 99, 103; Grayevsky, *Archives*, no. 17, 21; Avisar, *Tiberias*, 115; PEKAM, *Letters*, vol. 1, 174.

72. Yaari, *Emissaries*, 640, 647.

73. Werfel, 84; A. M. Lunz, *Pathways of Zion and Jerusalem*, 170, and *Jerusalem Yearbook*, vol. 9, 3–9.

74. PEKAM, *Letters*, vol. 1, 264; Yaari, *Emissaries*, 760.

75. Friedman, 269.

76. E. Bergmann and C. Bergmann, *Yis'u Harim Shalom*, 727.

77. A. Yaari, "Letter from Safed in 1835," 351.

78. Rivlin, "Legacies," 607.

79. Frumkin, 147.

80. Benayahu, 103–155, presents the Sephardi case.

81. Solomon, 29–30.

82. Grayevsky, *Archives*, no. 17, 23; Solomon, 27.

83. Yaari, *Emissaries*, 763.

84. Ibid., 761–762.

85. PEKAM, *Letters*, vol. 1, xiii.

86. A. M. Haberman, "A Compromise between Two Emissaries from Safed in

Amsterdam," 260–261, contains the following quotations.

87. Yaari, *Emissaries*, 683–685; N. Michman, "The Emergence of Pekidim and Amarcalim of Amsterdam," 72.

88. Benayahu, 105–155. All quotations are from this source unless otherwise noted.

89. PEKAM, *Letters*, vol. 1, 111.

90. H. J. Zimmels, *Ashkenazim and Sephardim*, 61.

91. Haberman, 285. An English missionary, Joseph Wolff, wrote in 1822 that the Russian-Turkish conflicts were seriously reducing funds contributed to the Ashkenazim of Eretz Israel: "no money for the Polish Jews arrives from Russia, the Polish Jews are in great distress" (LJS, 15th Report, 198).

92. PEKAM, *Letters*, vol. 1, 96, 187, 196, 215, 235, 265, 288.

93. Ibid., vol. 3, 184.

94. Ibid., vol. 1, 16, 215, vol. 2, 69.

95. Ibid., vol. 1, 195.

96. Ibid., vol. 1, 187.

97. Ibid., vol. 1, 266.

98. Ibid., vol. 1, 15, vol. 2, 36; Haberman, 260.

99. Morgenstern, "Pekidim," 58.

100. PEKAM, *Letters*, vol. 1, 220, 232, 285; Banayahu, 114.

101. PEKAM, *Letters*, vol. 1, 21, 55, 173, 195, 217.

102. Morgenstern, "Pekidim," 59, based on PEKAM, *Letters*, in the 1830s.

103. Frumkin, 152–153.

104. PEKAM, *Letters*, vol. 1, 232.

105. Haberman, 257–259, 262, 264; Morgenstern, "Pekidim," 60–61.

106. Toledano, 187.

107. Avisar, *Tiberias*, 113, 170–171; Yaari, *Emissaries*, 712; Toledano, 184–187.

108. PEKAM, *Letters*, vol. 1, 78, 85.

109. Ibid., vol. 1, 89.

110. Ibid., vol. 1, 23–24, 39; Yaari, *Emissaries*, 764–765; Benayahu, 109.

111. PEKAM, *Letters*, vol. 2, 94.

112. Yaari, *Emissaries*, 765.

113. PEKAM, *Letters*, vol. 1, 39, vol. 2, 95; Yaari, *Emissaries*, 682, 763.

114. PEKAM, *Letters*, vol. 1, 39.

115. Frumkin, 148.

116. PEKAM, *Letters*, vol. 2, 95, 102.

117. Haberman, 262; LJS, 15th Report, 198; Yaari, *Emissaries*, 763; PEKAM, *Letters*, vol. 3, 258.

118. Journal of Dr. Dalton, Aug. 13, 1825, in LJS, 19th Report, 149.

119. PEKAM, *Letters*, vol. 3, 248.

120. Morgenstern, "Pekidim," 14.

121. PEKAM, *Letters*, vol. 3, 24, 191, 248.

122. Ibid., vol. 3, 4.

123. For this and the following quotations, see ibid., vol. 2, 83, 86, 87, 106, vol. 3, 5.

124. Ibid., vol. 1, 48, vol. 2, 39, vol. 3, 245, 257.
125. Ibid., vol. 2, 91, vol. 3, 257.
126. Ibid., vol. 1, 89, 93, 95, 111, 266, vol. 2, 184.
127. Ibid., vol. 1, 65, vol. 2, 156.
128. Yaari, *Emissaries*, 184, 767–768; Morgenstern, "Pekidim," 63.
129. PEKAM, *Letters*, vol. 1, 13.
130. Ibid., vol. 1, 15, 43.
131. Ibid., vol. 1, 16, 82, vol. 2, 82, 96.
132. Ibid., vol. 3, 37.
133. I. Ben-Zvi, "Opposition of the Venetian Kehilla to the Institution of the Shlihim," 266–280. Sephardi leaders in Jerusalem explained to the Venice kehilla that PEKAM's new collection system of appointing local representatives, securing annual pledges, and forwarding donations every three months was inimicable to PEKAM and could only be implemented by energetic, resolute personalities like Lehren who "dedicated their bodies to heavenly purposes, put aside all private business . . . and travelled about incessantly."
134. Yaari, *Emissaries*, 689.
135. PEKAM, *Letters*, vol. 1, 186, vol. 3, 208–209.
136. Ibid., vol. 1, 65, 82, 92, 186, 196; Rivkind, "Separate Pages," 168.
137. Werfel, 100.
138. Ibid., 99.
139. Ibid., 93, 99.
140. Frankl, vol. 2, 36.

7 ENGLISH AND AMERICAN MISSIONARIES IN PALESTINE, 1820–1829

1. B. Tuchman, *Bible and Sword*, 115.
2. M. Vereté, "The Restoration of the Jews in English Protestant Thought 1790–1840," 316–345; M. Kedem, "Mid-Nineteenth-Century Anglican Eschatology on the Redemption of Israel," 55–72.
3. F. Kobler, *The Vision Was There*, 45.
4. Kobler, *Vision*, 43; R. Mahler, *A History of Modern Jewry, 1780–1815*, 690.
5. W. T. Gidney, *The History of the London Society for the Propagation of Christianity through the Jews from 1809 to 1908*, 34.
6. Tuchman, *Bible and Sword*, 119.
7. Gidney, 117.
8. W. H. Bartlett, *Walks about the City and Environs of Jerusalem*, 190.
9. L. Grabill, *Protestant Diplomacy and the Near East Missionary Influence on American Policy 1816–1927*, 5–8.
10. R. Anderson, *History of the Missions of the American Board of Commissioners for Foreign Missions to the Oriental Churches*, ix–x.
11. P. Fisk, *A Memoir*, vii.
12. A. L. Tibawi, *American Interests in Syria 1800–1901*, 12.
13. Anderson, *History*, 10.
14. Tibawi, *American Interests*, 73.

15. D. O. Morton, *Memoir of Rev. Levi Parsons, Late Missionary to Palestine,* 155.

16. *Missionary Herald,* 1819, 266.

17. A. L. Tibawi, *British Interests in Palestine 1800–1901,* 8.

18. *Missionary Herald,* 1819, 266.

19. Morton, 232; *Missionary Herald,* 1820, 111; Fisk, 34; Tibawi, *American Interests,* 20.

20. A. E. Bonar and R. M. M'Cheyne, *Narrative of a Mission of Inquiry to the Jews from the Church of Scotland,* 168–169.

21. W. Jowett, *Christian Researches in the Mediterranean from 1815 to 1820,* 430, 433.

22. *Missionary Herald,* 1820, 122.

23. Tibawi, *American Interests,* 15, 16. Parsons preached that "the Jews have a special claim upon our charity." His departure sermon was nearly exclusively devoted to improving the conditions of the Jews in Palestine, while Fisk only incidentally mentioned the Jews in his departure sermon.

24. *Missionary Herald,* 1822, 17; I. Bird, *Bible Work in Bible Lands,* 37.

25. Morton, 295, 296, 304.

26. LJS, 15th Report, 190.

27. Morton, 324, 327.

28. Bird, 43, 53; Fisk, 257; Anderson, *History,* 13; Morton, 337, 342.

29. Morton, 347; *Missionary Herald,* 1822, 19.

30. Morton, 381.

31. Fisk, vii.

32. For a vivid firsthand description, see S. N. Spyridon, "Annals of Palestine 1821–1841," 18–29, 31, 32, 35.

33. A. L. Frumkin, *The History of the Scholars of Jerusalem,* 162.

34. LJS, 19th Report, 40; Gidney, 111, 105.

35. Journal of Wolff in LJS, 15th Report, 169, 170, 186.

36. Journal of Wolff in LJS, 15th Report, 188–189, 199, 205, 217.

37. Bartlett, *Walks,* 190–191.

38. Journal of Wolff, LJS, 15th Report, 192, 196, 197, 201.

39. Journal of Wolff, LJS, 15th Report, 202–203.

40. LJS, 15th Report, 63, 66, 266, 275, 295.

41. Journal of Wolff, LJS, 15th Report, 199, 200; *Jewish Expositor,* 1822, 417.

42. Journal of Wolff, LJS, 15th Report, 200, 207, 217, 218; *Jewish Expositor,* 1822, 503.

43. Journal of Wolff, LJS, 15th Report, 65, 79, 204, 209, 218, 221.

44. Fisk, 258; *Missionary Herald,* 1824, 34; LJS, 16th Report, 102.

45. Gidney, 104; Fisk, 270, 279; Journal of Wolff, LJS, 16th Report, 112; Journal of Wolff, LJS, 17th Report, 71, 112, 113.

46. Journal of Wolff, LJS, 16th Report, 110, 111, 121.

47. Fisk, 264, 265, 271, 278–279; Anderson, *History,* 17.

48. Fisk, 285.

49. Journal of Wolff, LJS, 16th Report, 111, 112.

50. *Missionary Herald*, 1824, 67–68, 99; Bird, 57; Fisk, 265; LJS, 17th Report, 55. But this meeting was recorded in the unpublished "Journal of J. King and P. Fisk," dated 1823, in Houghton Library, Harvard University.

51. Fisk, 288; Anderson, *History*, 117; Journal of Wolff, LJS, 16th Report, 53, 117, 120, 121.

52. W. Jowett, *Christian Researches in the Holy Land in 1823 and 1824*, 66–67; LJS, 18th Report, 54, 82; Gidney, 101, 105; LJS, 17th Report, 54; LJS, 16th Report, 53; R. R. Madden, *Travels in Turkey, Egypt, Nubia and Palestine*, vol. 2, 335. King called Wolff one of the "ablest missionaries." LJS extolled his "characteristic simplicity and humility." Both W. B. Lewis and Dr. Naudi claimed that in spite of the "pride, bigotry and pretended wisdom" of the Jews Wolff "has cleared the way" so that now "the door is fully open for proclaiming the Gospel in Jerusalem amongst the Jews."

53. LJS, 15th Report, 62.

54. Jowett, *Holy Land*, 171, 172, 177, 178–179, 185; Fisk, 315, 316; *Missionary Herald*, 1835, 451.

55. Jowett, *Holy Land*, 181, 182, 184–185; Frumkin, 142; A. Yaari, *Travels in Eretz-Israel*, 516.

56. Fisk, 323; Jowett, *Holy Land*, 231, 232, 234–235, 236, 238, 243; LJS, 16th Report, 102–103.

57. Jowett, *Holy Land*, 265, 268; *Jewish Expositor*, 1825, 341; LJS, 16th Report, 55.

58. Gidney, 119; *Jewish Expositor*, 1825, 294, 336–339; Journal of Lewis, LJS, 17th Report, 112, 113, 114.

59. Journal of Lewis, LJS, 17th Report, 112; *Jewish Expositor*, 1825, 295, 297, 299, 337, 339, 340.

60. Journal of Lewis, LJS, 17th Report, 53, 123; M. Ish-Shalom, *Christian Travels in the Holy Land*, 167; Spyridon, 25.

61. *Missionary Herald*, 1825, 65; Anderson, *History*, 22.

62. *Missionary Herald*, 1825, 33–38; Fisk, 328–337; Anderson, *History*, 20–21; Bird, 107—117.

63. *Missionary Herald*, 1825, 36; LJS, 17th Report, 126.

64. Tibawi, *American Interests*, 24, 32.

65. *Jewish Expositor*, 1824, 108.

66. LJS, 17th Report, 112, 119, 121.

67. Ibid., 124–125.

68. Ibid., 124.

69. Ibid., 116, 117, 118; PEKAM, *Letters*, vol. 1, 203; A. Yaari, *Memoirs of Eretz-Israel*, 116–120.

70. Jowett, *Holy Land*, 233; *Missionary Herald*, 1825, 36; Frumkin, 162.

71. LJS, 17th Report, 116, 117; *Missionary Herald*, 1825, 38; Jowett, *Holy Land*, 233.

72. LJS, 17th Report, 117; Yaari, *Memoirs*, 180.

73. Yaari, *Memoirs*, 127–128; A. M. Hyamson, *The British Consulate in Jerusalem in Relation to the Jews of Palestine, 1838–1914*, vol. 1, 7.

74. LJS, 17th Report, 70, 207.

75. M. Sharon and Y. Baeck (eds.), *From Ancient Archives of P. B. Grayevsky*, 29; S. J. Shaw and E. K. Shaw, *History of the Ottoman Empire and Modern Turkey*, vol. 2, 59.

76. LJS, 17th Report, 112, 118, 120, 127; Yaari, *Memoirs*, 124.

77. LJS, 18th Report, 80.

78. Ibid., 77; LJS, 17th Report, 55; Tibawi, *British Interests*, 10.

79. *Missionary Herald*. 1825, 38–39; LJS, 18th Report, 79, 153–154.

80. N. Schwake, *Studien zur Geschichte des Krankenhauswesens*, 112; J. Conder, *The Modern Traveller*, 119.

81. *Missionary Herald*, 1827, 35, 37; LJS, 18th Report, 146; Spyridon, 35; J. L. Stephens, *Incidents of Travel in Egypt, Arabia Petraea and the Holy Land*, 371; Fisk, 360; LJS, 16th Report, 103; LJS, 19th Report, 169. Fisk and King gladly welcomed their English brethren, and Dalton and Lewis displayed a similar spirit of collegiality, showing no signs of jealousy toward potential competitors. Fisk exlaimed: "You do not know what happiness we enjoy when we are allowed to welcome new fellow labourers to the field." When Dalton arrived in Jerusalem, King wrote that "our hearts are gladdened by the unexpected arrival of Dr. A. Dalton from Beyroot." This spirit of collegiality was also shared by the English, whose leader, L. Way, wrote that he "could act [myself] with an American brother in most perfect harmony." Later in Beirut Mrs. Dalton and her children lived with the American missionary family the Goodells while Dr. Dalton was in Jerusalem and Nicolayson boarded at the home of Isaac Bird.

82. Yaari, *Emissaries*, 714; PEKAM, *Letters*, vol. 1, 174, 203, 250; Bird, 173; *Missionary Herald*, 1827, 36; Frumkin, 162; LJS, 18th Report, 149.

83. *Missionary Herald*, 1827, 36; LJS, 19th Report, 88; LJS, 18th Report, 146, 147, 152.

84. LJS, 18th Report, 152, 156.

85. Ibid., 155.

86. Ibid., 80; *Missionary Herald*, 1827, 37; Spyridon, 32–42; LJS, 19th Report, 148; I. Ben-Zvi, *Eretz-Israel under Ottoman Rule: Four Centuries of History*, 351.

87. LJS, 18th Report, 158–160; Fisk, 365; Anderson, *History*, 25.

88. *Missionary Herald*, 1827, 68; LJS, 18th Report, 161.

89. *Missionary Herald*, 1827, 103; Anderson, *History*, 30; Fisk, 379, 386; *Missionary Herald*, 1826, 214.

90. *Missionary Herald*, 1826, 214, 1828, 351.

91. LJS, 19th Report, 144–145, 148, 149, 156, 158; J. Nicolayson, *Journals, 1826–1842*, 162.

92. LJS, 19th Report, 160–161.

93. Ibid., 89, 161–169; Gidney, 120–121.

94. LJS, 19th Report, 91, 164, 168.

95. Gidney, 121; LJS, 19th Report, 92–93; Yaari, *Memoirs*, 120; *Jewish Expositor*, 1829, 149, 1828, 237; Nicolayson, *Journals*, Nov. 1826, 101; PEKAM, *Letters*, vol. 1, 125; A. I. Katsh, "Three Emissaries from Safed in Italy," 247.

96. PEKAM, *Letters*, vol. 2, 79, 85, vol. 3, 19, 246. If the number of deaths had

420 / Notes to Pages 181–187

been so disastrously high, as claimed by R. Israel, Lehren would hardly have written with such equanimity about "a number of beloved souls taken from us" in Safed, although nine months later he reported on the death of 250 Jews in Eretz Israel. Also, it appears highly improbable that 300 Hasidim died in the 1826 plague, which would have reduced their numbers to nearly zero, while in 1829 there were 465 Hasidim in Safed, based on detailed haluka lists Lehren received from the Hasidim. See S. Lieber, "The Development of the Jewish Population of Safed," 13–44.

97. Morgenstern, "Pekidim," 35; Basili, 57; Spyridon, 32–42; Yaari, *Memoirs*, 108–109; Yaari, *Emissaries*, 714–715.

98. Nicolayson, *Journals*, Nov. 18, 1826, 97, 109; LJS, 20th Report, 62; Gidney, 121.

99. Nicolayson, *Journals*, 135, 156.

100. *Jewish Expositor*, 1829, 151, 152; Gidney, 121; Nicolayson, *Journals*, 161.

101. Nicolayson, *Journals*, 163, 255; *Jewish Expositor*, 1829, 33, 152, 153, 155; Gidney, 121; LJS, 21st Report, 63, 64.

102. H. P. Palmer, *Joseph Wolff*, 151; *Jewish Expositor*, 1829, 358–359; *Monthly Intelligence*, 1834, 149.

103. Gidney, 122; Madden, vol. 2, 231–232.

8 JEWISH ACTIVITIES IN THE FOUR HOLY CITIES, 1825–1830

1. A. L. Frumkin, *The History of the Scholars of Jerusalem*, 158–161, 163.
2. LJS, 15th Report, 64.
3. A. Yaari, *Eretz-Israel Emissaries*, 770.
4. L. Wolff, "The Queen's Journey 1837–1897," 31.
5. M. Samuel, *Harvest in the Desert*, 44.
6. (Sir) M. Montefiore and Lady J. Montefiore, *Diaries*, vol. 1, 36.
7. R. R. Madden, *Travels in Turkey, Egypt, Nubia and Palestine*, vol. 2, 395.
8. Montefiore *Diaries*, vol. 1, 40.
9. Disraeli in R. Blake, *Disraeli's Grand Tour*, 64.
10. W. H. Bartlett, *Jerusalem Revisited*, 14.
11. Lady Judith Montefiore, *Private Journal of a Visit to Egypt and Palestine (1827)*, 192.
12. W. H. Bartlett, *Walks about the City and Environs of Jerusalem*, 191; *Jewish Intelligence*, 1842, 166.
13. J. L. Stephens, *Incidents of Travel in Egypt, Arabia Petraea and the Holy Land*, 369, 372.
14. Judith Montefiore, *Journal*, 203.
15. Ibid.
16. J. Nicolayson, *Journals*, 1826–1842, 604.
17. J. L. Burckhardt, *Travels in Syria and the Holy Land*, 307.
18. Bartlett, *Walks*, 192.
19. Judith Montefiore, *Journal*, 203.
20. Ibid., 204.
21. Ibid., 214–215.

22. Montefiore *Diaries*, vol. 1, 41–42.

23. Judith Montefiore, *Journal*, 210.

24. Montefiore *Diaries*, vol. 1, 40, 41.

25. Judith Montefiore, *Journal*, 215.

26. PEKAM, *Letters of the Pekidim and Amarcalim of Amsterdam*, vol. 1, 23, 57, vol. 2, 37.

27. B. Rivlin, "The Mission of Shlomo Zalman Shapira from Jerusalem to Amsterdam during 1825–1829," 134.

28. PEKAM, *Letters*, vol. 1, 56, 72; *Jewish Expositor*, 1825, 108–109.

29. Rivlin, "The Mission," 112–113.

30. PEKAM, *Letters*, vol. 1, 56–57, 93.

31. Yaari, *Emissaries*, 715–716.

32. PEKAM, *Letters*, vol. 1, 56, 86, 172; A. Morgenstern, "The Pekidim and Amarcalim of Amsterdam and the Jewish Community in Palestine—1810–1840," 66, 82.

33. Rivlin, "The Mission," 119–124.

34. PEKAM, *Letters*, vol. 1, 95; Morgenstern, "Pekidim," 166.

35. PEKAM letter quoted by Morgenstern, "Pekidim," 166.

36. PEKAM, *Letters*, vol. 1, 116, 171, 173, 221; vol. 2, 73, 79, 80, 105, 190, 201. Shapira and PEKAM concluded the following complicated compromise, which set different keys for funds contributed according to the "old" system and monies pledged by individuals based on the "new" collection system.

PEKAM-Shapira 1826 Compromise

	"OLD" COLLECTIONS		"NEW" COLLECTIONS	
	No. of Shares	%	No. of Shares	%
Perushim in Eretz Israel	5.5	20	3.9	14
Hasidim in Eretz Israel	8.6	31	9.9	35
Habad of Hebron	1.7	6	2.0	7
Sephardim	12.1	43	12.1	43
Jerusalem	5.5	20	5.5	20
Hebron	3.0	11	3.0	11
Safed	2.33	8	2.33	8
Tiberias	1.33	4	1.33	4
TOTAL	28.0	100	28.0	100

37. Morgenstern, "Pekidim," 118; PEKAM, *Letters*, vol. 2, 175, 177.

38. Morgenstern, "Pekidim," 71, 77; PEKAM, *Letters*, vol. 2, 37, 82, vol. 3, 179, 207.

39. PEKAM, *Letters*, vol. 1, 188–189.

40. Rivlin, "The Mission," 134; PEKAM, *Letters*, vol. 1, 186, vol. 2, 37, 67, 189.

41. PEKAM, *Letters*, vol. 2, 37, 69, 82, 190.

42. PEKAM, *Letters*, vol. 2, 220, 236, vol. 3, 8.

43. PEKAM, *Letters*, vol. 3, 180, 207; I. Rivkind, "Separate Pages," 147–153.

44. PEKAM, *Letters*, vol. 2, 72, 73, vol. 3, 3, 25–26, 27, 34, 185.

45. Morgenstern, "Pekidim," 68; Yaari, *Emissaries*, 771; Rivkind, "Separate Pages," 148–151; PEKAM, *Letters*, vol. 3, 14, 57, 197, 212, 241; R. Mahler, *A History of Modern Jewry, 1780–1815*, 583; W. B. Lincoln, *Nicholas I*, 290; document 107 in City of Jerusalem Archives. According to this compromise in Jerusalem the Perushim received 4.5 shares and the Hasidim 1 share. The remaining 11⅓ shares for the Ashkenazim were distributed as follows: 7⅔ shares to the Hasidim of Tiberias and Safed; 2 to the Safed Perushim; and 1⅔ share to the Habad of Hebron.

46. PEKAM, *Letters*, vol. 3, 241, 244; Morgenstern, "Pekidim," 69.

1829 Compromise

	SEPHARDIM		PERUSHIM		HASIDIM	
	Shares	*%*	*Shares*	*%*	*Shares*	*%*
Tiberias	8	5			18	11
Safed	14	8	39	23	35	21
Jerusalem	33	20				
Hebron	12	7			9	5
TOTAL	67	40	39	23	62	37

This PEKAM 1829 compromise enacted some minor changes in the Shapira-PEKAM compromise by dropping the total Sephardi share from 43 percent to 40 percent and increasing the Perushim allocation from 20 percent to 23 percent, while the Hasidim gained 1 percentage point at the expense of the Habad.

47. Morgenstern, "Pekidim," based on unpublished letters of PEKAM in the 1830s; PEKAM, *Letters* vol. 2, 185, vol. 3, 242; Yaari, *Emissaries*, 777; Frumkin, 148–149. Paragraph nine in the aborted 1829 compromise between the Perushim and Hasidim infuriated Lehren. This paragraph specifically granted the Ashkenazi Kollelim a license to send shlihim into Western Europe. Lehren wrote that "we absolutely do not agree with this and we do not want to hear anything about it striking the fancy of any kollel to send shlihim . . ." Lehren ranted against dispatching shlihim to Western Europe and threatened to quit his PEKAM post if the Ashkenazi and Sephardi Kollelim continued to disregard the PEKAM ban against shlihim in Western Europe.

48. Yaari, *Emissaries*, 778.

49. Rivkind, "Separate Pages," 153–156; Yaari, *Emissaries*, 765–767, 774–775; Frumkin, 146–148. One provision of this compromise stipulated that if an overseas bequestor was a Sephardi two-thirds of his inheritance would to go the Sephardim. But if the bequestor was Ashkenazi the inheritance would be split fifty-fifty between the Ashkenazim and Sephardim. This was similar to the agreement signed by R. Israel in 1813 in Vienna whereby the bequest of an Ashkenazi was divided evenly between the Sephardim and the Ashkenazim. Another provision of this Jerusalem compromise allocated to the Sephardim two-thirds of all donations collected in Italy. This was a considerable financial improvement for the Sephardim, who in 1825 had been forced to accept only 40 percent of monies collected in Italy. In the totally Sephardi communities of Spain, North Africa, and Morocco, Ashkenazim were permitted to collect "new" donations without "touching traditional contributions," a good copy of the 1824–1825 Sephardi-Ashkenazi agreement. The Jerusalem compromise also provided that contributions collected in Germany by Sephardim and Ashkenazi shlihim would be divided fifty-fifty between them. This is one more instance of the Ashkenazim and the Sephardim blatantly defying PEKAM's prohibition against sending shlihim to Western Europe.

50. PEKAM, *Letters*, vol. 2, 81–82. No evidence backs up the Ashkenazi warning that the aggressive Sephardi leader of Hebron could chase the Hebron Ashkenazim out of Eretz Israel by virtue of his control over the common treasury.

51. Rivkind, "Separate Pages," 146; A. Cohen, "Arabic Documents on the Settlement of Debts of the Jewish Communities of Jerusalem and Hebron in the Eighteenth Century," 325; Rivkind, "Separate Pages," *Zion* 5, 167–169; Yaari, *Emissaries*, 596, 683–684, PEKAM, *Letters*, vol. 2, 82. A most expressive letter written in English to raise money in the United States of America described in the rhetoric of the day the pathetic state of the Jews in Hebron in 1828: "The terrible glaive weighs always upon their heads—they have to support daily false accusations! What enormous taxes! How many vexations! How many punishments and inventions to sustain their injustice and cruelty! What silver or gold, and what precious treasure, could satisfy the voracity of their enemies! If you want resources to appease their ferocity, slavery presents itself immediately before you, with all its horrors! If one complains of such ill treatment, the cruelty increases, the evil becomes always heavier and more awfull [sic].—Every body is struck with fear. Here the war displays itself with all its dreadful preparations—there piracy exerts its enormous crimes. If you dare to cross the seas, death will follow you.—But who can yet believe it?—in such a calamitous position, without any means, and without resource, we are forced to pay an imposition of Thirty Thousand Dollars.—"

52. PEKAM, *Letters*, vol. 2, 82, 114, vol. 3, 181, 197, 248.

53. PEKAM, *Letters*, vol. 2, 23, 34, 84, 111, 114, 185, 254, 262. Lehren granted the 100 Habad Hasidim 16 percent of the monies allocated to all the Hasidim in Eretz Israel, although they constituted only 10 percent of the Hasidic population. In the compromise of 1829 the Habad Hasidim of Hebron received 14.5 percent of the money allocated to all Hasidim (9 shares out of 62).

54. PEKAM, *Letters*, vol. 2, 200; Morgenstern, "Pekidim," 39.

55. Rivkind, "Separate Pages," 166; A. I. Katsh, "Three Emissaries from Safed

in Italy," 247; Yaari, *Emissaries*, 669; Frumkin, 149.

56. PEKAM, *Letters*, vol. 3, 25, 26, 31, 32, 248, 256; *Jewish Intelligence*, 1832, 100.

57. PEKAM, *Letters*, vol. 3, 33, 248.

58. PEKAM, *Letters*, vol. 3, 245, 246, 249. The Hasidim in Safed would distribute funds to all Hasidim in Eretz Israel; the Perushim in Jerusalem would distribute funds to all Perushim in Eretz Israel and the Hebron Habad would also distribute monies to the few Habadnikim outside Hebron.

59. PEKAM, *Letters*, vol. 3, 29, 246, 251.

60. PEKAM, *Letters*, vol. 3, 31–32, 247, 252; Yaari, *Emissaries*, 778. The Hasidim of Safed further ruffled the feathers of PEKAM in 1830 by sending a shaliah to collect money in Germany, Sweden, and Denmark, countries within the jurisdiction of PEKAM where emissaries had been banned. Although the Hasidim pleaded about their large debt, PEKAM aborted this mission and publicized the fact.

61. PEKAM, *Letters*, vol. 3, 248.

62. Y. Zahavi, *From the Hatam Sofer to Herzl*, 83–84; Z. Karagila, "Source Material on Haluka in Eretz-Israel," 70.

63. PEKAM, *Letters*, vol. 3, 27, 181, 242.

64. Yaari, *Emissaries*, 774–777; Z. Karagila, "The Community of Perushim in Eretz-Israel during the 1830s," 309–312. Karagila discerned a strong current of friction and strife and Byzantine power struggles among the Perushim leaders of Eretz Israel.

65. Karagila, "Community of Perushim," 311.

66. Katsh, 247; Yaari, *Emissaries*, 775, 776; PEKAM, *Letters*, vol. 2, 190. They concluded that two-thirds of the monies collected in Western Europe would go to the Sephardim and one-third to the Ashkenazim, which significantly revised the 1825 compromise whereby 60 percent of the monies went to the Ashkenazim and 40 percent to the Sephardim. To reduce expenses the Sephardim and Ashkenazim agreed to send one joint shaliah to Western Europe in haughty disregard of PEKAM's ban on all shlihim in its collection territory but in keeping with PEKAM's injunction to send one rather than many shlihim from the same town. It was reaffirmed that Ashkenazi shlihim in North Africa would collect only "new" donations and not take monies from the traditional collection system. Sephardim would receive 40 percent of these "new" contributions. In addition, Sephardi shlihim could collect money in "Poland and Russia," with the Sephardi receiving 60 percent and the Ashkenazim 40 percent of the donations from Eastern Europe.

67. Yaari, *Emissaries*, 776; M. Solomon, *Three Generations in the Yishuv, 1812–1913*, 47–49.

68. Yaari, *Letters*, 342–357; Morgenstern, "Pekidim," 96–105.

69. Yaari, *Emissaries*, 147–148.

70. Karagila, "Community of Perushim," 312.

9 THE EGYPTIAN OCCUPATION OF PALESTINE, 1831–1840

1. H. Dodwell; *The Founder of Modern Egypt, Muhammad Ali*; S. Shamir, "The Beginning of Modern Times in the History of Palestine," 138–158; S. J. Shaw

and E. K. Shaw, *History of the Ottoman Empire and Modern Turkey*, vol. 2, 9–10; Spyridon, "Annals of Palestine 1821–1841," 13; E. Robinson, *Travels* in Palestine and Syria, vol. 1, 43; Rustrum, *The Royal Archives of Egypt and the Origins of the Egyptian Expedition*, 7; K. M. Basili, *Memoirs from Lebanon 1839–1847*, 94.

2. M. S. Anderson, *The Eastern Question (1774–1923)*, 77; D. Kinross, *The Ottoman Centuries*, 467.

3. Rustrum, *Origins*, 42, 59, 78; A. L. Tibawi, *A Modern History of Syria including Lebanon and Palestine*, 67.

4. M. Abir, "Local Leadership and Early Reforms in Palestine 1800–1834," 299–301; Tibawi, *Syria*, 64–65; Rustrum, *Origins*, 25–26, 78.

5. H. Temperley, *England and the Near East: The Crimea*, 67.

6. Rustrum, *Origins*, 45.

7. Y. Hofman, "The Administration of Syria and Palestine under Egyptian Rule (1834–1840)," 312; Abir, "Local Leadership," 302; Basili, 64; Spyridon, 64.

8. Basili, 64; Tibawi, *Syria*, 66; Hofman, 311–312.

9. W. B. Lincoln, *Nicholas I*, 201–203; J. Ridley, *Lord Palmerston*, 221.

10. Lincoln, 203–207; Basili, 83; Hofman, 318.

11. Hofman, 311–333.

12. M. Ma'oz, *Ottoman Reform in Syria and Palestine*, 88; Basili, 91; J. Bowring, *Report on Commercial Statistics of Syria*, 103.

13. Bowring, 29–30, 37–45, 61, 92, 131; Abir, "Local Leadership," 306; Ma'oz, *Reform*, 12–13; H. A. B. Rivlin, *The Agricultural Policy of Muhammad Ali in Egypt*, 209; Basili, 110; Rustrum, *Origins*, 69.

14. Temperley, 405; B. Lewis, *The Emergence of Modern Turkey*, 109; Bowring, 94, 99; E. Robinson, *Biblical Researches in Palestine, Mount Sinai and Arabia Petrea in 1838*, vol. 2, 94; Rivlin, *Agricultural Policy*, 121.

15. Basili, 91, 336–339; Bowring, 118, 131. In the opinion of the British consul in Egypt, "although taxes . . . have been progressively raised" such an increase was less "by a considerable difference" than the depreciation of the piastre "or any other Turkish coin." Native merchants continued to pay as much as a 12-percent tariff rate while European merchants and natives in alliances with foreign merchants paid a maximum of 3.5 percent. Foreign merchants were also exempt from tax payments on merchandise moving from one district to another.

16. *Missionary Herald*, 1835, 370. When the formidable Abu-Ghosh clan continued to ignore Egyptian orders to stop collecting tolls on the Jerusalem–Jaffa road, some of its members were hauled off to chain gangs in Acre prison.

17. A. Yaari, *Memoirs of Eretz-Israel*, 109.

18. Basili, 97; Robinson, *Researches*, vol. 2, 162; *Missionary Herald*, 1835, 374. Lacking means to buy arms, villagers would be tortured, "thrown into prison, and sometimes marched off as conscripts."

19. *Hebrew Encyclopedia*, vol. 5, 501; Ma'oz, *Reform*, 17; Bowring, 47, 62, 91, 131; Spyridon, 131, 134.

20. J. Nicolayson, *Journals; 1826–1842*, 426, 442, 732, 768.

21. A. E. Bonar and R. M. M'Cheyne, *Narrative of a Mission of Inquiry to the Jews from the Church of Scotland in 1839*, 149.

22. A. L. Tibawi, *American Interests in Syria 1800–1901*, 61.

23. Robinson, *Researches*, vol. 2, 94; Tibawi, *Syria*, 85; A. Morgenstern, "The Pekidim and Amarcalim of Amsterdam and the Jewish Community in Palestine—1810–1840," 155: E. Bergmann and G. Bergmann, *Yis'u Harim Shalom*, 76, 93.

24. M. J. Géramb, *A Pilgrimage to Palestine, Egypt and Syria*, 314; M. Ish-Shalom, *Christian Travels in the Holy Land*, 444.

25. Bergmann and Bergmann, 76, 98.

26. Ibid., 76; Bowring, 137; Tibawi, *American Interests*, 87–88.

27. Rivlin, *Agricultural Policy*, 201–202; Abir, "Local Leadership," 309; Tibawi, *Syria*, 73.

28. Basili, 100; Bowring, 26; *Missionary Herald*, 1835, 374; A. Yaari, *Letters from the Land of Israel*, 73; R. R. Madden, *Travels in Turkey, Egypt, Nubia and Palestine*, 11, 298; Ish-Shalom, 178, 485.

29. Ma'oz, *Reform*, 12.

30. D. O. Morton, *Memoir of Rev. Levi Parsons, Late Missionary to Palestine*, 330; LJS, 18th Report, 151; Spyridon, 71, 72; A. W. Kinglake, *"Eothen" or Traces of Travel*, 124; A. Curzon, *Visits to the Monasteries of the Levant*, 230–243; P. Fisk, *A. Memoir*, 270; J. Conder, *The Modern Traveller*, 133–136.

31. For descriptions of the rebellion in Jerusalem, see Spyridon, 73–105; I. Bird, *Bible Work in Bible Lands*, 302–309; *Jewish Intelligence*, 1835, 188–191, 200–208.

32. J. Schwartz, *Descriptive Geography and Brief Historical Sketch of Palestine*, 380; Spyridon, 88.

33. M. Gichon, *Carta's Atlas of Palestine from Beitar to Tel Chai*, 93.

34. A. J. Rustrum, *The Royal Archives of Egypt and the Disturbance in Palestine 1834*, 69–70; Tibawi, *Syria*, 74.

35. For descriptions of the revolt, see M. Abir, "The Claims of Safed Jewry after the Lootings of 1834," 267–274; Menachem Mendel of Kamenets, *Chronicles of the Times*, 35–36, 93–95; Yaari, *Memoirs*, 129; Bowring, 129; Rustrum, *1834*, 63; L. A. Frankl, *The Jews in the East*, vol. 1, 256; I. Ben-Zvi, "Events in Safed from the Lootings of 1834 to the Druze Attacks in 1838," 285–286; Schwartz, *Geography*, 403–407; Z. Karagila, "S. Shmuel Ben R. Israel Peretz Heller Describes the Sack of Safed," 109–116; I. Rivkind, "Separate Pages," 170–176.

36. Malachi, 68.

37. A. M. Lunz, *Jerusalem Yearbook*, vol. 5, 292.

38. Schwartz, *Geography*, 407. The British consul in Egypt, Colonel Campbell, reported a Jewish property loss of 7 million piastres but later he itemized losses of 6,135,416.5 piastres. This list is nearly identical with claims presented to the Russian consul in Acre, which totaled 6,135,250.8 piastres. We can understand how huge these claims were in comparison to the 44 million piastres Egypt collected in taxes from all of Syria in 1835. Therefore, like John Farren, we conclude that these Jewish claims were grossly exaggerated, for like all compensation claims they were submitted to collect the greatest amount of money. In 1839 Campbell wrote that "payments have been made on account and I understand the whole affair is in a train of final settlement." The knowledgeable Z. H. Lehren confirmed that the Jews were paid 1,729 purses or 864,600 piastres. John Farren claimed that one-third of about 4 million piastres was paid to the Jews. Jewish sources reported: by 1839 Jews

had collected 8 percent of the claims; "Jews were repaid scarcely one-fourth of what they had lost"; the Ashkenazim received 75 percent of their claimed compensation; in the summer of 1837 the Perushim received 302,000 piastres of compensation. One English tourist, A. W. Kinglake, incorrectly reported that the Jews received no compensation and no stolen property was returned to them (Bowring, 104–105, 129; Morgenstern, "Pekidim," 51; Abir, "Safed Jewry," 270, 272–274; Lunz, *Jerusalem Yearbook*, vol. 5, 293; Rustrum, *1834*, 63–64; Ben-Zvi, "Events in Safed," 279; Kinglake, 462).

39. Ben-Zvi, "Events in Safed," 23, 290–291; Z. Karagila, "The Community of Perushim in Eretz-Israel in the 1830s," 90–291, 313, 328; A. L. Frumkin, *The History of the Scholars of Jerusalem*, 149; A. I. Katsh, "Three Emissaries from Safed in Italy," 247.

40. Spyridon, 89; Robinson, *Researches*, vol. 2, 256; C. Ritter, *The Comparative Geography of Palestine and the Sinaitic Peninsula*, 11, 247; Menahem Mendel of Kamenets, 74, 98; Malachi, 72–73; Rivkind, "Separate Pages," 171; Schwartz, *Geography*, 409–410.

41. *Missionary Herald*, 1836, 253; *Jewish Intelligence*, 1835, 283–284.

42. Schwartz, *Geography*, 398–399; Lunz, *Jerusalem Yearbook*, vol. 2, 82; Yaari, *Emissaries*, 687; *Jewish Intelligence*, 1835, 283–284; J. L. Stephens, *Incidents of Travel in Egypt, Arabia Petraea and the Holy Land*, 321; Robinson, *Researches*, vol. 2, 453; Nicolayson, *Journals*, 444, 557; *Missionary Herald*, 1836, 253; Spyridon, 100.

43. Yaari, *Emissaries*, 650, 686–688, 780–781: I. Ben-Zvi, *Eretz-Israel under Ottoman Rule*, 370; M. Toledano, *Archives of R. Toledano*, 60–62.

44. Rivkind, "Separate Pages," 170–178; Menahem Mendel of Kamenets, 96–101.

45. *Monthly Intelligence*, 1830, 14.

46. Morgenstern, "Pekidim," 28, 29, based on PEKAM, *Letters*.

47. Bergmann and Bergmann, 70.

48. Morgenstern, "Pekidim," 166.

49. B. Kluger (ed.), *From the Source—The Old Yishuv on Bulletin Boards*, 45; Morgenstern, "Pekidim," 29.

50. *Jewish Intelligence*, 1839, 18, 266, 267; Morgenstern, "Pekidim," 32A; *Monthly Intelligence*, 1832, 124; L. Stone, *The Family, Sex and Marriage in England*, 54; M. O. Schmelz, "Some Demographic Peculiarities of the Jews of Jerusalem in the Nineteenth Century," 132, 134. This high mortality rate was calculated for the ten-year period of 1856–1866 in Jerusalem. Lacking a comparable figure for Safed, we have adopted the 50-percent mortality rate because it was well known that during 1800–1840 "entire generations" of the Jewish population were "cut down by pestilence, earthquake, or the sword, in the space of very few years" (LJS, 31st Report, 71). Housing, health, and sanitary conditions in Safed were abominable, as in Jerusalem. In 1823 missionaries commented on R. Israel of Shklov's "very wretched and cold" house and found the streets and houses dirty (W. Jowett, *Christian Researches in the Holy Land in 1823 and 1824*, 181, 183). In 1824 a Jew told missionaries that there was "a good deal of sickness" in Safed and that Tiberias was a

healthier town (Journal of Lewis in LJS, 17th Report, 112). In 1825 the medical missionary Dr. Dalton observed that Safed Jewish homes are "very filthy" and "are very wretched and confined; they felt to us like ovens. . . . Excepting the house we were in, there did not appear a single house that could be occupied with safety to health" (Journal of Dr. Dalton in LJS, 18th Report, 16). In the 1820s, as previously noted, Safed suffered from snow and rainstorms, a drought, locusts, and epidemics that obviously had a detrimental affect on the population level. In 1833 Jewish homes were overcrowded "in consequence of the fall of more than 100 houses from the snow and rain" (Journal of Nicolayson, Feb. 17, 1833, in *Monthly Intelligence*, 1834, 19). In 1831, when Nicolayson returned to Safed after a four-year absence, he noted that "a great many" of his Jewish friends had "died during my absence" (Journal of Nicolayson, Aug. 21, 1831, in *Monthly Intelligence*, 1832, 126), indicating a high mortality rate. A similar comment was made by a missionary on October 20, 1838, about Jerusalem (*Jewish Intelligence*, 1839, 8).

51. *Monthly Intelligence*, 1834, 19.

52. PEKAM, *Letters*, vol. 3, 246; M. Eliav, *Eretz-Israel and Its Yishuv in the Nineteenth Century (1777–1917)*, 83–84, 104.

53. *Monthly Intelligence*, 1834, 180.

54. J. S. Buckingham, *Travels in Palestine*, 399, quoted by Schmelz, 132.

55. PEKAM, *Letters*, vol. 1, 97; Morgenstern, "Pekidim," 165.

56. *Jewish Expositor*, 1821, 74.

57. G. Scholem, *Major Trends in Jewish Mysticism*, 287.

58. *Missionary Intelligence*, 1834, 180.

59. Morgenstern, "Pekidim," 151–153. As early as 1823 an English missionary reported "only seventeen years more" for the restoration of Israel. In October 1827 a Hebron shaliah in Alexandria told John Nicolayson "that within twelve years the period of the Messiah's coming would arrive"; Jews also told this to the missionary Mr. Farman. Joseph Wolff reported in 1829 that "a great number of Jews" were going to Jerusalem "in expectation of the near coming of the Messiah" and Farman recorded in his Journal in August 1831 that "all the rabbies [sic] in Safed say that the Messiah will come after eight years which opinion they affirm to be supported by the Cabala." John Nicolayson repeated this report after meeting Farman in Safed. In December 1832 Nicolayson told about 180 Jews from Oran traveling to Eretz Israel for two reasons: "for their inducement lies in their persuasion of the sacredness of the soil and the nearness of Messiah's coming." Two months later Nicolayson wrote that "three Spanish rabbies from Jerusalem . . . are quite persuaded that the Messiah they look for will come within eight years" (*Jewish Expositor*, 1821, 74, 1823, 426, 1829, 157; *Missionary Intelligence*, 1830, 14, 91, 1832, 103, 124, 1833, 180, 1834, 22, 133).

60. *Monthly Intelligence*, 1832, 124.

61. Bonar and M'Cheyne, 164.

62. Ibid., 164–165, 246; Robinson, *Researches*, vol. 2, 87.

63. Ben-Zvi, *Eretz-Israel*, 362; J. Meisel, "The Jewish Settlement in Eretz-Israel in 1839," 445.

64. Ish-Shalom, 527; *Jewish Expositor* 1829, 111; Bonar and M'Cheyne, 164, 171; *Monthly Intelligence*, 1833, 180, 1834, 27, 63, 180; S. Schwarzfuchs, "The Jews

of Algeria in Northern Eretz-Israel and the French Protection," 333; A. M. Hyamson, *The British Consulate in Jerusalem*, 11; Lunz, *Jerusalem Yearbook*, vol. 5, 293. Even before the French invasion Joseph Wolff reported in 1828 about "fifty Jews besides their wives and children... coming from Tunis and Tripoli for the purpose of residing at Jerusalem, expecting there the arrival of the Messiah" and less than a year later Wolff wrote about "one hundred [North African] Jews at Jaffa, on their way to Jerusalem to die there." At the end of 1832 John Nicolayson learned that about 180 Jews came "direct from Oran (not from Algiers)... for two purposes: the sacredness of the soil and the nearness of the Messiah's coming..." In the middle of 1833 LJS missionary Ewald wrote about five Tunisian Jews going to Jerusalem and then reported that 100 Tunisian Jews sailed "for Jerusalem, in order to die at the Holy City." An LJS correspondent in Malta wrote in the middle of 1834 about 38 Jews immigrating "from some interior parts of Morocco" and "many other such families" were "from day to day" expected at Gibraltar on their way to Eretz Israel. In addition, he corroborated Ewald's report that in the summer of 1833 "a more considerable number... went to reside... in Palestine." Research has revealed that "about 200 families from Algiers and Oran left North Africa for Eretz-Israel during the initial stages of the French conquest of Africa" and that about 130 of these families settled in Safed and 70 families in Tiberias. "Jews of Algiers and its dependencies, are numerous in Palestine" reported the British vice-consul in 1839. Many of these Algerian Jews were listed among the 126 "French" families—about 500 people—requesting restitution payments for loss of property after the 1834 fellahin plunder in Safed.

65. I. Bartal, "On the Beginnings of Jewish Settlement in Jaffa," 359.

66. Mahler, 583; Lincoln, 290; Morgenstern, "Pekidim," 165; Nicolayson, *Journals*, July 1836, 780. Lehren as well as John Nicolayson noted that Russian Jews came to Palestine "to avoid being enlisted in the Russian army."

10 JEWISH IMMIGRANTS AND THEIR INITIATIVES IN THE 1830S

1. N. N. Gelber, "Moshe Sachs," 576.

2. S. Baron, "History of German Jews in Eretz-Israel," 116.

3. On the Enlightenment (Haskala), see W. Laquer, *A History of Zionism*, 6–27.

4. J. Nicolayson, *Journals, 1826–1842*, Mar. 12, 1834, 483; *Missionary Intelligence*, 1834, 12; A. Yaari, *Eretz-Israel Emissaries*, 809; M. Eliav, *Israel and Its Yishuv in the Nineteenth Century (1777–1917)*, 215; Eliav, *Love of Zion and Men of HOD*, 215; Gelber, "Moshe Sachs," 569.

5. Gelber, "Moshe Sachs," 570.

6. L. A. Frankl, *The Jews in the East*, vol. 2, 9.

7. *Missionary Intelligence*, 1834, 12–13; Nicolayson, *Journals*, Dec. 1833, 453, Mar. 12 and 14, 1834, 483, 486, 487, Apr. 13, 1834, 503.

8. A. Morgenstern, "The Pekidim and Amarcalim in Amsterdam and the Jewish Community in Palestine—1810–1840," 177; Nicolayson, *Journals*, June 16, 1840, 1028.

9. Gelber, "Moshe Sachs," 570, 576.

10. B. Gat, *The Jewish Community in Eretz-Israel (1840–1881)*, 307. To confuse matters Sachs claimed in 1861 that his updated 1853 plan for agricultural settlements was intended for the vicinity of Jaffa for security reasons. Yet in 1870 Sachs wrote about community leaders who threatened that "every person who wants to devote himself to agricultural work will receive no financial support."

11. Frankl, vol. 2, 10, 11.

12. S. Halevy, *The First Hebrew Books Printed in Jerusalem in the Second Half of the Nineteenth Century (1841–1890)*, 1–31.

13. A. Yaari, *Memoirs of Eretz-Israel*, 144.

14. F. Braudel, *The Mediterranean World in the Age of Philip II*, vol. 1, 437.

15. M. Ish-Shalom, *Christian Travels in the Holy Land*, 494.

16. *Monthly Intelligence*, 1834, 18.

17. Halevy, 19.

18. Yaari, *Memoirs*, 144.

19. A. M. Hyamson, *The British Consulate in Jerusalem in Relation to the Jews of Palestine, 1838–1914*, vol. 2, lxix.

20. Yaari, *Memoirs*, 144–145.

21. A. L. Frumkin, *The History of the Scholars of Jerusalem*, 175–176; A. Morgenstern, "The Organizational Unity of the Kollel Perushim in Eretz-Israel," 304–305; E. Rivlin, "Letter from Hillel Rivlin to His Father-in-Law, Shmaryahu Luria," 141–147; A. M. Lunz, *Jerusalem Yearbook*, vol 5, 230–231, vol. 13, 238–239; Nicolayson, *Journals*, May 6 and 7, 1834, 507; *Jewish Intelligence*, 1835, 185.

22. T. H. Rivlin, *The Vision of Zion, Shklov to Jerusalem*, 87, 91–95.

23. Eliav, *HOD*, 225–228; E. Bergmann, and G. Bergmann, *Yis'u Harim Shalom*, 112; Gat, 247–248; Frumkin, 233–236; Y. Fisher, "Art in Nineteenth-Century Palestine," 110–116. Thousands of Jews accepted the antagonistic advice of the Bavarian Diet that "the Jews must clear out and go to America."

24. Nicolayson, *Journals*, Mar. 14 and 24, 1834, Apr. 27 and 28, 1834, May 7, 1834, 486, 491, 507; *Jewish Intelligence*, 1835, 183.

25. J. Schwartz, introduction to his *Descriptive Geography and Brief Historical Sketch of Palestine*.

26. Nicolayson, *Journals*, June 30, 1834, 839; *Jewish Intelligence*, 1835, 213.

27. Menahem Mendel of Kamenets, *Chronicles of the Times*, 53, 55, 57, 59, 62, 71–78, 82, 83; M. Kosover, *Arabic Elements in Palestinian Yiddish*, 110.

28. Kosover, 214–217.

29. Y. Yellin, *Memoirs of a Native of Jerusalem, 1830–1918*, 3–15.

30. Yaari, *Memoirs*, 153–154.

31. Rivlin, "Hillel Rivlin," 146; Yaari, *Memoirs*, 154; Yellin, 6–7.

32. Eliav, *HOD*, 228–232; Morgenstern, "Pekidim," 168, 170, 173, 174, 188.

33. A. Morgenstern, "The Correspondence of Pekidim and Amarcalim as a Source for the History of Eretz-Israel," 105.

34. Bergmann and Bergmann, 23–26.

35. Ibid., 60, 62, 70.

36. Ibid., 68, 77, 82, 84, 93, 97.

37. Ibid., 58, 78, 85, 98.

38. Ibid., 90, 93, 98, 103, 114, 116, 120; Frumkin, 274–275.

39. Bergmann and Bergmann, 76, 82, 101, 105, 106.

40. Ibid., 79, 125.

41. Ibid., 92, 101, 102; A. E. Bonar and R. M. M'Cheyne, *Narrative of a Mission of Inquiry to the Jews from the Church of Scotland in 1839*, 284; Frankl, vol. 2, 66. In 1856 Ludwig August Frankl caustically commented: "The idleness of the parents produces its natural effect on the children, the feeling of honour, even when excited, is soon blunted by the universal receipt of alms. In Jerusalem alone, where every word of the Bible is regarded as sacred, the command of the Bible, 'In the sweat of thy face shalt thou eat bread,' is practically ignored."

42. Bergmann and Bergmann, 72, 92, 107.

43. Ibid., 58, 105–106.

44. Ibid., 43, 47, 58, 61, 62–63, 65, 66–70, 79, 81, 91–92, 107. In an effort at occupational counseling he wrote that bookbinders, cobblers, locksmiths, metal workers, copiers of scripture, weavers, jewelers, carpenters, and an "expert doctor" have good chances for employment.

45. Bergmann and Bergmann, 72, 79, 99, 101, 105.

46. Nicolayson, *Journals*, 851.

47. E. Erikson, *Young Martin Luther*, 12.

48. Bergmann, 105.

49. Yaari, *Emissaries*, 773; *Jewish Intelligence*, 1836, 100.

50. Gelber, "Moshe Sachs," 570, D. Stock, "Moses Sachs," 332; Eliav, *HOD*, 215. Sachs flatteringly called Austria a great country with the highest cultural and moral standards. "Only the moral participation of the Austrian government," he claimed, "will allow this program to be carried out." Despite the vagueness of his plan and the anonymity of its author, the Austrian government asked Baron Stirmer, its consul in Istanbul, to request a report from consul Picciotto in Syria and to evaluate the plan. Lacking a record of Stirmer's answer we must assume that either he recommended against the plan or the Austrian government concluded that the proposal and its proposer were unworthy of a serious answer. In any case, the Austrian government took no action.

51. Stock, 332.

52. I. Klausner (ed.), *Drishat Zion* by Z. H. Kalischer, 209–222; Rothschild may have been reminded of an unsavory article published in 1830 in the American weekly advising the Rothschilds to purchase Jerusalem (*News Weekly Register*, 1829–1830, cited by R. Glanz, "The Rothschild Legend in America," *Jewish Social Studies* 19 [1957], 20).

53. Morgenstern, "Pekidim," 176, 177, 186. If Sachs did not tell Lehren about these plans, Lehren learned about them by unashamedly opening and reading the letter from Sachs dispatched to Joseph Schwartz. Nevertheless, in 1828 Lehren chastised the Perushim for reading a letter intended for the Hasidim (PEKAM, *Letters*, vol. 2, 30–31). Sachs is described by Lehren as an idler wandering aimlessly between yeshivot before immigrating to Eretz Israel for the express purpose of finding a wife. In Lehren's slandering opinion Sachs was so close to joining the English mis-

sionaries that he should be restrained from returning to Eretz Israel and a divorce should be obtained for his wife.

11 ORGANIZING THE JEWISH COMMUNITY AND BUILDING THE HURVA SYNAGOGUE, 1834–1838

1. Z. Karagila, "The Community of Perushim in Eretz-Israel during the 1830s," 318; A. Yaari, "Letter from Safed in 1835," 355; J. Nicolayson, *Journals, 1826–1842*, July 2, 1834, 663.

2. H. Temperley, *England and the Near East: The Crimea*, 281; S. N. Spyridon, "Annals of Palestine 1821–1841," 109–110, 120–122; R. R. Madden, *Travels in Turkey, Egypt, Nubia and Palestine*, vol. 2, 338; M. J. Géramb, *A Pilgrimage to Palestine, Egypt and Syria*, vol. 1, 308; Yaari, *Eretz-Israel Emissaries*, 724.

3. Spyridon, 122; Yaari, *Emissaries*, 719; R. Mahler, *A History of Modern Jewry, 1780–1815*, 651.

4. Nicolayson, *Journals*, July 2, 1834, 663.

5. H. Baer, in the newspaper, *HaAretz*, May 18, 1979, 25–26; L. A. Frankl, *The Jews in the East*, vol. 2, 79, 229. Schnitzer's lions were still considered idolatrous more than thirty years later (in 1867) when the Sephardi chief rabbi attributed them to a "Gentile builder."

6. Spyridon, 123; Nicolayson, *Journals*, Aug. 29, 1835, 675; Yaari, *Emissaries*, 719, 724–725, 782; M. Solomon, *Three Generations in the Yishuv, 1812–1913*, 66; Nicolayson, *Journals*, Mar. 27, 1835, 624; *Jewish Intelligence*, 1836, 123; A. Morgenstern, "The Pekidim and Amarcalim of Amsterdam and the Jewish Community in Palestine—1810–1840," 124; M. Wallenstein, "An Insight into the Sephardi Community of Jerusalem in 1855," 78.

7. P. Grayevsky, *From the Hidden Treasures of Jerusalem*, no. 2, 1; Morgenstern, "Pekidim," 155–156.

8. Details of this conflict are liberally documented in Karagila's "Community of Perushim," 306–330, and Morgenstern, "Pekidim," 120–132, from which I have liberally borrowed.

9. A. Rivlin, "Perushim Regulations about the Haluka from 1823," 160–168; PEKAM, *Letters*, vol. 2, 107–108; Morgenstern, "Pekidim," 120. Perushim 1823 regulations legally sanctioned the kollel branch in Jerusalem and granted each kollel branch veto rights over expenditures and the initiation of new activities by its sister community. Only in cases of life and death could the kollel branch act independently. Each Perushee branch was authorized to send shlihim overseas without the approval of the other Perushee kollel. It was unclear, however, how much autonomy was delegated to the Jerusalem branch. One possible reason for this lack of clarity was that the Perushim regulations were drafted as a compromise rather than as a legal basis for cooperation. The Jerusalem branch received 4½ shares and the Safed branch 2 shares out of a total of 28 shares distributed to the Jews in the four holy towns.

10. Morgenstern, "Perushim Kollel," 306.

11. PEKAM letter in Karagila, "Community of Perushim," 318.

12. Z. Karagila, "The Struggle over the Distribution of Monies from England in Palestine from 1831 to 1835," 462; Morgenstern, "Perushim Kollel," 305.

13. Karagila, "Community of Perushim," 320.

14. M. Eliav, *Eretz-Israel and Its Yishuv in the Nineteenth Century (1777–1917)*, 90.

15. G. Kressel, *Planters of Hope*, 74, views the Hurva-Sukkat Shalom issue as basically a battle for the leadership of the Jerusalem Perushim between Zoref and Bardaki.

16. Karagila, "Community of Perushim," 323.

17. Karagila, "Community of Perushim," 321–323; A. Yaari, *Memoirs of Eretz-Israel*, 154; J. Schwartz, *Descriptive Geography and Brief Historical Sketch of Palestine*, 281; Morgenstern, "Pekidim," 39, 128, 131. Lehren wrote: "we cannot believe him [Zoref] because he is not honest and never performed a mission without being paid . . ." As the Hurva-courtyard battle heated up Lehren threatened to cut Zoref and his son Mordecai from the haluka rolls if they did not obey the authorized Perushim leadership of R. Israel. Lehren even recommended banishing Zoref from Eretz Israel.

18. Kressel, *Planters*, 122–127; Schwartz, *Geography*, 282; B. Gat, *The Jewish Community in Eretz-Israel (1840–1881)*, 196; M. Sharon and Y. Baeck, *From Ancient Archives of P. B. Grayevsky*, 91: ". . . even dignitaries and important personalities rolled up their sleeves and participated in the labor, digging with their own hands and carrying away the rubbish and soil on their own shoulders. The elderly too helped to cart away the soil, all the while singing songs of praise to God . . ."

19. Morgenstern, "Pekidim," 40, 130–131; weak foundations, cracked walls, and too little room for all the Jerusalem Perushim, and the legal status of the courtyard as private property was questioned.

20. A. R. Malachi, *Chapters in the History of the Old Yishuv*, 27; W. Thomson, *The Land and the Book*, 277–280; A. Yaari, *Letters from the Land of Israel*, 360; E. Robinson, *Biblical Researches in Palestine, Mount Sinai and Arabia Petrea in 1838*, vol. 3, 186, 324, 471–475; *Missionary Herald*, 1837, 433, 436–437, 439; Menahem Mendel of Kamenets, *Chronicles of the Times*, 95.

21. Robinson, *Researches*, vol. 3, 321; Thomson, *The Land*, 278; Yaari, *Letters*, 364; M. Ish-Shalom, *Christian Travels in the Holy Land*, 673.

22. Robinson, *Researches*, vol. 3, 321–322.

23. Thomson, *The Land*, 277–280.

24. *Missionary Herald*, 1837, 434; Thomson, *The Land*, 278, 280; Robinson, *Researches*, vol. 3, 473.

25. Solomon, 54–55; Yaari, *Letters*, 364–366; Y. Zahavi, *From the Hatam Sofer to Herzl*, 86; A. M. Lunz, *Jerusalem Yearbook*, vol. 9, 157; Morgenstern, "Pekidim," 40.

26. M. Vered and H. L. Striem, *The Safed Earthquake of 1.1.1837*; Zahavi, 86; Lunz, *Jerusalem Yearbook*, vol. 9, 155, 159; Robinson, *Researches*, vol. 3, 255, 322, 475; I. Bird, *Bible Work in Bible Lands*, 327; Ish-Shalom, 189, 673; I. Ben-Zvi, *Eretz-Israel under Ottoman Rule*, 387; Yaari, *Letters*, 361, 365; Menahem Mendel of Kamenets, 51, 95; I. Ben-Zvi, "Events in Safed from the Lootings of 1834 to the

Druze Attacks in 1838," 298, 308; Schwartz, *Geography*, 407; J. Wilson, *The Lands of the Bible Visited and Described*, vol. 2, 154.

27. Yaari, *Letters*, 381.

28. 1,338 in Montefiore's 1839 Census, J. Meisel, "The Jewish Settlement in Eretz-Israel in 1839," 429; A. E. Bonar and R. M. M'Cheyne, *Narrative of a Mission of Inquiry to the Jews from the Church of Scotland in 1839*, 164, 263; Jewish Intelligence, 1839, 282. It is methodologically permissible to use 1839 population figures because during the years 1837–1840 there was "little or no increase" in the Jewish population.

29. Yaari, *Letters*, 361; Lunz, *Jerusalem Yearbook*, vol. 9, 152, 182; Ish-Shalom, 477, 481, Ben-Zvi, *Eretz-Israel*, 396–397.

30. Ish-Shalom, 477, 478.

31. Bird, 332; Yaari, *Letters*, 362; Lunz, *Jerusalem Yearbook*, vol. 9, 154. Despite Jewish burial efforts an American missionary, Isaac Bird, a close friend of Thomson, maliciously reported that "not a Jew, Christian or Turk lifted a hand to assist us except for high wages . . . I never saw a Jew helping another Jew except for money."

32. Lunz, *Jerusalem Yearbook*, vol. 9, 156, 157; Ish-Shalom, 486, 673; Zahavi, 86–87; M. Eliav, *Eretz-Israel and Its Yishuv in the Nineteenth Century (1777–1917)*, 102; Robinson, *Researches*, vol. 3, 475; Bird, 331; O. Avisar (ed.), *Book of Tiberias*, 117; Meisel, 430.

33. Yaari, *Letters*, 363–366; M. Eliav, *Love of Zion and Men of HOD*, 21–22; Morgenstern, "Pekidim," 227.

34. Malachi, 31–32; Lunz, *Jerusalem Yearbook*, vol. 9, 166–168.

35. Yaari, *Letters*, 362.

36. Morgenstern, "Pekidim," 156, 133; Zahavi, 86; Lunz, *Jerusalem Yearbook*, vol. 9, 156.

37. Karagila, "Community of Perushim," 324–325; Morgenstern, "Pekidim," 131.

38. Morgenstern, "Pekidim," 131–132; Lunz, *Jerusalem Yearbook*, vol. 5, 233; Y. Alfasi, "Documents about the History of the Old Settlement," 216–224.

39. Schwartz, *Geography*, 282; Morgenstern, "Pekidim," 132, 142; Solomon, 64; Y. Yellin, *Memoirs of a Native of Jerusalem, 1830–1918*, 6; Yaari, *Memoirs*, 154–155; Sharon and Baeck, 90; E. Bergmann and G. Bergmann, *Yis'u Harim Shalom*, 93, 120: In remembrance of both R. Menachem Mendel, who championed the rebuilding of Jerusalem, and the prayer "Blessed art Thou Consoler of Zion and Builder of Jerusalem" recited while mourning the destruction of the second Temple.

40. Lunz, *Jerusalem Yearbook*, vol. 9, 381–384; Yaari, *Emissaries*, 782–783; Nicolayson, *Journals*, Nov. 20, 1840, 1075–1076; Morgenstern, "Pekidim," 142.

41. Karagila, "Community of Perushim," 326.

42. Ben-Zvi, "Events in Safed," 306.

43. S. Halevy, "R. Israel of Shklov," 371.

44. Frumkin, 140, 149 (350,000 piastres plus 50,000 for burial expenses).

45. Karagila, "Community of Perushim," 323–324, 325, 330, 332; Z. Karagila, "Source Material on Haluka in Eretz-Israel," 58–60; Zahavi, 87–88.

46. Karagila, "Community of Perushim," 327, 329.

47. Morgenstern, "Perushim Kollel," 308; Morgenstern, "Pekidim," 180.
48. A. L. Frumkin, *The History of the Scholars of Jerusalem*, 252; Yaari, *Emissaries*, 782.
49. Yaari, *Emissaries*, 783–784. He was instructed "not to touch the edge of the holy funds of Eretz Israel that were established to save endangered lives" but to collect funds so that "a new light [will] illuminate Zion by building a small Temple... and this mitzva will protect them and take them from darkness to light, from slavery to redemption..."
50. Grayevsky, no. 1, 31.
51. Kressel, *Planters*, 75. In his appeal to R. Moshe Sopher, Lehren claimed that "if we burden these countries with shlihim and their upkeep and various donations for a synagogue that is not needed, we will weaken donors' contribution money to the poor people..." By phrasing the problem Lehren tried to dictate the answer. Nowhere in Lehren's appeal is there mention of redeeming an old synagogue from Muslim hands or building the synagogue for Jerusalem, Eretz Israel, and world Jewry. But R. Moshe Sopher understood that "they want to glorify and raise on high the house of God in place of the ruins."
52. Zahavi, 89–90; Kressel, *Planters*, 134; Yaari, *Emissaries*, 784. This decision of R. Sopher startled the Hurva leaders for it ran counter to a 300-year-old rabbinical decision that stated: "There is no greater mitzva than building a synagogue in the Holy City of Jerusalem where prayers can be lifted up to heaven... especially when we consider that this [building of a synagogue] is a mark of excellence for the poor of Jerusalem so that members of other peoples will act toward them with love and friendship." In this old "Responsa" first priority was given to building a synagogue in Eretz Israel because without such a Temple the Jews of Eretz Israel could not come close to God and could not establish contact with the Shehina, the holy spirit.
53. Morgenstern, "Pekidim," 157–158; Yaari, *Emissaries*, 784.
54. Solomon, 72–73; Yaari, *Emissaries*, 786; Frumkin, 149.
55. Spyridon, 126–127; Robinson, *Researches*, vol. 1, 95; M. Toledano, *Archives of R. Toledano*, 141.
56. Eliav, *HOD*, 241, 250, 258, 379.
57. Morgenstern, "Pekidim," 70, 173, 174, 188.
58. Lunz, *Jerusalem Yearbook*, vol. 9, 17, 56; Eliav, *Eretz-Israel*, 130.
59. Morgenstern, "Pekidim," 227. Five non-Jewish sources reported that each year PEKAM distributed 125,000, 250,000, 280,000, and 350,000 piastres. The picture is further filled out by knowing that at the time the Sephardim received one-third of PEKAM funds they were allocated by PEKAM, about 24,000 piastres in 1827 and about 47,700 piastres in 1829. In comparison the Vilna Rabbis sent 120,150 piastres to 419 Perushim in 1838 and 127,150 piastres to 470 Perushim in 1840. Bergmann and Bergmann reported the amount of overseas funds distributed in Eretz Israel in 1836: the Perushim were "any day" expecting to receive 90,000 piastres, the Hasidim had already received four times that amount, 360,00 piastres, while PEKAM had forwarded 90,000 piastres to Eretz Israel: Ish-Shalom, 465, 504, 526, 542, 560; Bergmann and Bergmann, 72; Eliav, *HOD*, 35; G. L. Dawson Damer, *Diary of a Tour in*

Greece, Turkey, Egypt and the Holy Land, vol. 1, 310; K. M. Basili, *Memoirs from Lebanon 1839–1847*, 330; Malachi, 98–104.

60. A. M. Hyamson, *the British Consulate in Jerusalem in Relation to the Jews of Palestine, 1838–1914*, vol. 1, 5. Could the few HOD members taking funds from the Perushim, Sephardim, and the Hasidim have caused the newly arrived British vice-consul in Jerusalem to write in 1839 that the "pecuniary means have diminished" for "those who are dependent on" haluka?

61. A. Yaari, "Letter from Safed in 1835," 349; LJS, 18th Report, 154; Hyamson, vol. 1, 5.

62. Menahem Mendel of Kamenets, 77; Yaari "Letter," 349–350; Z. Karagila, "S. Shmuel Ben R. Israel Peretz Heller Describes the Sack of Safed," 112; Bergmann and Bergmann, 64, 75, 77, 85, 90, 98; E. Rivlin, "Letter from Hillel Rivlin to His Father-in-Law, Shmaryahu Luria," 146; Robinson, *Researches*, vol. 1, 327; *Monthly Intelligence*, 1834, 137; J. Bowring, *Report on Commercial Statistics of Syria*, 50; LJS, 15th Report, 182. Nicolayson was willing to take a ten-year lease and pay 2,000 piastres annually if the owner would "erect certain additional buildings." At the other end of the price scale a convent room in 1825 rented for 4 piastres a day. In the 1830s "lodging generally in Syria for all classes is cheap comparatively with most other countries" in the opinion of the knowledgeable Englishman John Bowring.

63. Yellin, 18; *Jewish Intelligence*, 1842, 271; S. Olin, *Travels in Egypt . . . and the Holy-Land*, vol. 2, 325; A. Yaari, "The Travels of David Beit Hillel in Eretz-Israel," 504; Bowring, 49, 51, 83, 96, 123; Bergmann and Bergmann, 62, 93; Menahem Mendel of Kamenets, 77, 78. "The price of food is now double what it once was, and some things are four times as high as when Mr. Nicolayson first came. This arises from there being more money in the country. If boarding could be obtained in Jerusalem, then an individual might easily live on less than 100£ a year."

64. Bowring, 51, 82, 84; J. W. Johns, *The Anglican Cathedral Church of St. James, Mount Zion*, 8; Hyamson, vol. 1, 28.

65. Bowring, 49, 50. "Tolerable wages ranged from 5 to 10 piastres per day."

66. Yaari, "Letter," 349, 350; Ben-Zvi, "Events in Safed," 296; (Lady) Judith Montefiore, *Notes from a Private Journal of a Visit to Egypt and Palestine (1839)*, 124; Robinson, *Researches*, vol. 1, xvi; Bowring, 57; Rivlin, "Hillel Rivlin," 145.

67. Malachi, 98–104.

68. Hyamson, vol. 1, 5.

69. Bergmann and Bergmann, 116.

70. Eliav, *HOD*, 242; Eliav, *Eretz-Israel*, 131.

71. M. Eliav, "Notes on the Development of the Old Yishuv in the Nineteenth Century," 51.

12 PILGRIMS, TRAVELERS, AND EXPLORERS

1. G. A. Smith, *The Historical Geography of the Holy Land*, 84.

2. E. Robinson, *Biblical Researches in Palestine, Mount Sinai and Arabia*

Petrea in 1838, vol. 3, 23; F. R. Chateaubriand, *Itineraire de Paris à Jérusalem et de Jérusalem à Paris* (Paris, 1812).

3. R. Mahler, *A History of Modern Jewry, 1780–1815*, 622; M. Ish-Shalom, *Christian Travels in the Holy Land*, 409.

4. U. J. Seetzen, *Reisen durch Syrien, Palästina, Phönicien.* J. L. Burckhardt, *Travels in Syria and the Holy Land.*

5. P. J. Bliss, *The Development of Palestine Exploration*, 179, 180; Y. Ben-Arieh, *The Rediscovery of the Holy Land in the Nineteenth Century*, 38–39.

6. *Journal of David Roberts in The Holy Land*, Jan. 21, 1839, vol. 1, 17.

7. N. A. Silberman, *Digging for God and Country*, 27.

8. In 1835 the French opened a direct line from Marseilles to Beirut, Alexandria, and Istanbul; the subsidized Russian Steam Navigation Company and an Italian steamboat sailed intermittently from Odessa to Istanbul and Mediterranean ports; and the Austrian Lloyd Steamship Co. provided the best service in its scheduled sailings from Trieste to Beirut and Alexandria, "calling at Jaffa twice in each month." Starting in 1835 each month the British sailed a steamer from Liverpool to Malta, Alexandria, and Beirut. The price of a London to Beirut ticket, for instance, was a costly 29 pounds sterling or 2,900 piastres, double the price of a trip by sailboat (N. Katzburg, "From the First Letters of the English Vice Consul in Jerusalem," xiv; D. Chevallier, "Western Development and Eastern Crisis in the Mid-Nineteenth Century," 206; Z. Karagila, "The Community of Perushim in Eretz-Israel during the 1830s," 329; A. Yaari, *Letters from the Land of Israel*, 370; Robinson, *Researches*, vol. 2, 334; J. Nicolayson, *Journals, 1826–1842*, Apr. 1836, 732.

9. D. Kinross, *The Ottoman Centuries*, 465; J. Bowring, *Report on Commercial Statistics of Syria*, 86. Once a month the English steamer transported mail to the Mediterranean and this postal service was probably utilized for Dutch diplomatic mail, which carried the eagerly awaited PEKAM correspondence between Holland and Palestine. About every six weeks postal messengers carried the mails between Istanbul and the capitals of the provinces. Internal communications had improved to the extent that gold and silver were transported by "horse post" from Istanbul. On the Via Maris Egypt ran a postal system from Cairo to Gaza, Jaffa, and then to Damascus; however, this service may not have been too efficient judging from Lehren's suggestion that R. Israel petition Mehemet Ali to improve the postal service in Palestine. Since Jerusalem was bypassed on this postal route, Jerusalemites used the infrequent government express going directly from Jerusalem to Alexandria or resorted to the private "pony express" services that shuttled mail each week between Jerusalem, Jaffa, and Beirut.

10. S. J. Shaw and E. K. Shaw, *History of the Ottoman Empire and Modern Turkey*, vol. 1, 264; Katzburg, x, xiv; Robinson, *Researches*, vol. 1, 369; W. E. Polk and R. L. Chambers, *Beginnings of Modernization in the Middle East*, 10; Bowring, 86, 96. Quarantine regulations were "habitually evaded and scorned by the adventurous and dishonest. No irregularity, no violation of the sanitary code, but was purchasable by a bribe." From Jerusalem British vice consul Young complained about "the maladministration of the Quarantine" and contended that "the Quarantines . . . absorb half the benefit which would arise from this improved

method of communication." He deplored the fact that "quarantines offer a serious obstacle" to the flow of free trade the consuls were developing. Although a great cholera epidemic killed tens of thousands of Europeans in 1831–1833, 50,000–80,000 Cairenes died in the plague of 1835, and the deadly plague frequently swept large parts of Palestine during the 1830s, European consuls and traders loudly complained that a "quarantine jail" was a relic of a superstitious age, absurdly managed, ineffective, and most vexatious. Sultan Selim III and Mehemet Ali adopted sixteenth-century European quarantine regulations that isolated ships and passengers in plague-ridden areas for periods up to forty days.

11. Katzburg, x; S. N. Spyridon, "Annals of Palestine 1821–1841," 117–118; Bowring, 100. In Haifa Ibrahim Pasha established a quarantine station specifically for his soldiers, not for pilgrims and travelers. Christian minorities unsuccessfully tried convincing Ibrahim Pasha to establish the quarantine station inside Jaffa for the convenience of the pilgrims by arguing that Haifa was the wrong site and "too far distant from Jerusalem." Ibrahim Pasha answered, "I must think of my soldiers who I prefer to die in war than in a dreadful plague." Despite the complaints of the consuls and the mismanagement of the quarantine stations, Mehemet Ali recognized that the quarantine "played a major role in preventing the spread of plague in Syria."

12. Seven hundred Christian pilgrims arrived in the autumn of 1806 (Mahler, 610). Seetzen reported on 1,000 Greek Catholic and 1,000 American pilgrims in 1807. By 1815 the number of pilgrims had increased to 2,000 to 3,000—1,000 Greek Catholics, 1,000 Armenians plus Roman Catholics (Y. Ben-Arieh, *A City Reflected in Its Times*, vol. 1, 198, 233; W. Turner, *Journal of a Tour in the Levant*, vol. 2, 175–176; H. Temperley, *England and the Near East: The Crimea*, 462). Turner reported on the detailed census of 4,705 pilgrims in Jerusalem in May 1815. In 1820, based on estimates of Abu-Ghosh's income from his toll tax, 4,000 Christians and 600 Jewish pilgrims visited Jerusalem, while the English missionary James Connors reported on 3,130 pilgrims. For the year 1824 the American missionary Isaac Bird estimated that 5,000 pilgrims and others attended the Holy Fire ceremony and Levi Parsons recorded exactly 2,706 pilgrims in Jerusalem. From 1825 to 1834 the Greek Catholic monk Neophytos reported that "more than 4,000" Armenian pilgrims came each year, many financially encouraged by their churches in Anatolia, and "never more than 3,000" Greek Catholics. "For the Easter of 1828 the Armenians had over 4,000 pilgrims," while only 253 Greek Catholics came from Egypt and Anatolia because of the Greek battles against the Turks for their independence and the Russian-Turkish war. Trappist monk M. J. Géramb visited Jerusalem at Christmas 1831 and reported a town "thronged with pilgrims." He found only 4 Roman Catholics out of 4,000 pilgrims and was "told that at Easter there might be twenty out of ten thousand." In 1833 pilgrims came "in unusual numbers . . . particularly Armenians," according to John Nicolayson. During 1833 and 1834 10,000 Armenians and Greek Catholics journeyed to Jerusalem each year according to the soon to be appointed Russian consul, K. M. Basili. So great was the number of pilgrims that the superior of a Jerusalem convent was forced to cede his room to some pilgrims (Turner, vol. 2, 175–176; Temperley, 283, 462; W. Jowett,

Christian Researches in the Mediterranean from 1815 to 1820, 438; J. Conder, *The Modern Traveller*, 136; I. Bird, *Bible Work in Bible Lands*, 140; D. O. Morton, *Memoir of Rev. Levi Parsons, Late Missionary to Palestine*, 330, 334; Spyridon, 48, 50, 70; K. M. Basili, *Memoirs from Lebanon 1839–1847*, 67; M. J. Géramb, *A Pilgrimage to Palestine, Egypt and Syria*, vol. 1, 318; Nicolayson, *Journals*, Nov. 12, 1833, 429; *Monthly Intellignce*, 1834, 134.

13. In the late fall months Christian pilgrims started to arrive in Jerusalem for the Christmas season. At Easter the great influx of pilgrims peaked. Pilgrims doubled Jerusalem's population of 11,000–12,000 and settled at the monasteries, which provided hotel-like services for a small fee. Other young, healthy, and poor pilgrims camped outdoors with their sleeping gear, pots, and pans. Russian pilgrims, dressed in long black peasant garb covered by sheepskins to protect against the cold, filled the air with their kapusta (cabbage) cooking. Poor pilgrims brought from their native lands merchandise such as cloth, which they set out for sale on the pavement in front of the Church of the Holy Sepulchre. Although many pilgrims defrayed expenses by this barter method, they brought economic prosperity to Jaffa, Bethlehem, Jerusalem, and Nazareth and were a lucrative source of income for the church, the government authorities, town merchants, and storekeepers. Trade with pilgrims flourished because even the poorest had to buy food and felt a need to purchase a crucifix and other religious mementos. During the 1830s an estimated 10,000 pilgrims annually must each have spent at least 400 piastres, leaving 4 million piastres in Jerusalem.

14. Bowring, 97, 99; Spyridon, 132. In 1838 2,000 Christian pilgrims were quarantined for twenty-one days before Easter. By Easter 1840 Neophytos reported on only 1,000 Greeks and 1,300 Armenian pilgrims, and a British tourist wrote about "3 to 4,000 Russian pilgrims."

15. Journal of Roberts, in *The Holy Land*, vol. 1, 21.

16. LJS, 19th Report, 145–163.

17. Journal of Roberts, in *The Holy Land*, Feb. 12, 1839, vol. 1, 51. Missing the comforts of home, fatigued, and in pain from saddle-soreness, only in retrospect did many tourists entertain pleasurable memories about Palestine.

18. L. A. Frankl, *The Jews in the East*, vol. 2, 364.

19. R. Röhricht, *Bibliotheca Geographica Palestinae*.

20. M. Bloch, *The Historian's Craft*, 107.

21. C. Ritter, *The Comparative Geography of Palestine and the Sinaitic Peninsula*, vol. 2, 65; Bliss, 181. Gibbons unflatteringly labeled Palestine "a territory scarcely superior to Wales, either in fertility or extent." Many Englishmen described sites in Palestine that reminded them of English locations. The Judean hills recalled the Scottish highland glens; the village fellahin "were something like the old Highland clans"; "a beautiful valley" near Nablus "might almost pass for a scene in England"; and the walls of Jerusalem "nearly resemble those of York and other ancient cities in England." The Englishman, inbred in the spirit of the Bible, compared the Sea of Galilee to the "gentle Windemere—she had still the winning ways of an English lake," while the dyspeptic Mark Twain (in 1867) wrote about "the dim waters of this puddle" (Journal of Roberts, in *The Holy Land*, vol. 2, 69,

and vol. 4, 11; A. E. Bonar and R. M. M'Cheyne, *Narrative of a Mission of Inquiry to the Jews from the Church of Scotland in 1839*, 119; Finn, 58; W. H. Bartlett, *Walks around the City and Environs of Jerusalem*, 15; A. W. Kinglake, *"Eothen" or Traces of Travel*, 93–94; Twain, *Innocents Abroad*, 225).

22. Conder, 69.

23. R. Blake, *Disraeli's Grand Tour*, 65.

24. C. G. Smith, "The Geography and Resources of Palestine as Seen by British Writers in the Nineteenth and Early Twentieth Century," 90.

25. A. Lamartine, *Visit to the Holy Land or Recollections of the East*, 242; Bowring, 28.

26. Blake, 66, 106, 126, 128.

27. I. Cohen, *The Zionist Movement*, 49.

28. A. Lamartine, *Souvenirs, impressions, et paysages pendant un voyage en Orient* (Paris, 1835). Lady Hester Stanhope, the strange English recluse in the Mountains of Lebanon, claimed that half of what Lamartine wrote about their meeting was fiction and the other half was full of errors. When "inaccuracy possessed a truly pathological fascination," French historian Marc Bloch suggested calling "this psychosis Lamartine's disease" (Bloch, 101).

29. F. Kobler, *The Vision Was There*, 62.

30. Ibid., 59; Y. Ben-Arieh, *Rediscovery*, 56, 82, 223.

31. Géramb; M. Ish-Shalom, *Christian Travels in the Holy Land*, 35, 441–445; Ben-Arieh, *Rediscovery*, 61.

32. Géramb, vol. 1, 307, 308, 309, 311, 312, 313, 314, 315, 317; Ish-Shalom, 456. Curzon was perceptive enough to realize, like Géramb, that rich Jews hid their valuables from the avaricious Muslims but he was incorrect in reporting that there were "many rich Jews" in Jerusalem (A. Curzon, *Visits to the Monasteries of the Levant*, 94).

33. Ish-Shalom, 464.

34. Van Wyck Brooks in H. Finnie, *Pioneers East*, 6. Edgar Allan Poe praised Stephens's prose as "highly agreeable, interesting and instructive" with "claims to public attention possessed by no other book of its kind." Other reviewers objected to its "spice of the irreligious" and the "levities... which occasionally give a queer air of irreverence... about sacred things" (J. L. Stephens, *Incidents of Travel in Egypt, Arabia Petraea and the Holy Land*, viii, xxxv.

35. Von Hagen's introduction to Stephens, *Incidents*, viii.

36. Nicolayson, *Journals*, 529, 591, 676–677; Robinson, *Researches*, vol. 2, 339–340; Stephens, *Incidents*, 386–387, 394–399, is marred by many errors; E. O. Eriksen, "Christopher Costigin (1810–1835), Irish Explorer of the Dead Sea," *Holy Land* (Spring 1985), 41–49; E. O. Eriksen, "Dead Sea Explorer," *Jerusalem Post*, Sept. 4, 1985, 5; E. O. Eriksen, "Exemplary First Aid," *News Centre Journal* 5/1, 9; E. O. Eriksen, "The Illness of Christopher Costigin—A Case of Heat Stroke," *Dublin Historical Record* 39/3 (June 1986), 82–85; E. O. Eriksen, "Heroic Maltese Sailor," *Maltese Herald*, May 21, 1985, 2; Ritter, vol. 3, 125. Others followed in the footsteps of Costigin and explored the lowest point on the globe, 1,290 feet below sea level. During 1836–1838 determining how far the Dead Sea was below sea level

became a scientific obsession with numerous explorer-scientists such as W. G. Beke and G. H. Moore (1837), G. H. Schubert (1837), C. Cailler (1837), and C. J. de Bertou and J. Russeger (1838).

37. Ish-Shalom, 37, 480–484. A prince from Silesia, von Pückler was a renaissance man—he studied education and law, reached a high military rank in the Saxony army, and was a famous landscape gardener as well as a widely traveled, prolific, and well-known writer. While visiting Jerusalem Pückler-Muskau succeeded in entering Mt. Moriah, drawing his sword and threatening to cut down anyone who obstructed his passage (G. L. Dawson Damer, *Diary of a Tour in Greece, Turkey, Egypt and the Holy Land*, vol. 2, 11).

38. F. Egerton, *Journal of a Tour in the Holy Land in 1840*, 17, 19, 22; Ish-Shalom, 534.

39. Ish-Shalom, 39, 525–531; Dawson Damer, vol. 1, 310–311, 317, 319.

40. Ish-Shalom, 479; Basili, 330.

41. A. M. Hyamson, *The British Consulate in Jerusalem in Relation to the Jews of Palestine, 1838–1914*, vol. 1, 8, 5–6; Bonar and M'Cheyne, 149.

42. Ish-Shalom, 443, 479, 531; Géramb, 313; Dawson Damer, vol. 1, 312, 313, vol. 2, 40; Bonar and M'Cheyne, 166.

43. Dawson Damer, vol. 25, 29, 30.

44. M. Omer, *Turner and the Bible*, 14.

45. Journal of Roberts, in *The Holy Land*, vol. 3, 13, 27, 45.

46. E. Schiller, *The First Photographs of Jerusalem*, 11; Y. Nir, *The Bible and the Image, The History of Photography in the Holy Land 1839–1899*, 164.

47. Ben-Arieh, *Rediscovery*, 68–70, 74–77; Bliss, 193; Finnie, 181.

48. Robinson, *Researches*, vol. 1, 1–2, 46.

49. Ibid., vol. 2, 80; Ritter, vol. 2, 82; Ben-Arieh, *Rediscovery*, 76.

50. Robinson, *Researches*, vol. 3, 263.

51. Ritter, vol. 2, 71.

13 MISSIONARY ACTIVITIES IN THE 1830S

1. J. Nicolayson, "Mittheilungen für eine Skizze der Geschichte der englishen Mission und des evangelischen Bithums zu Jerusalem," *Zions-Bote* 1 (1852), 7–9, quoted by A. Carmel, "Russian Activity in Palestine during the Late Ottoman Period," 83.

2. A. L. Tibawi, *American Interests in Syria 1800–1901*, 61.

3. LJS, 25th Report, 88; W. T. Gidney, *The History of the London Society for the Propagation of Christianity through the Jews from 1809 to 1908*, 155–156. Wolff had refused LJS's request "to return to England" and explain the contents of a letter he sent to the Jews and published without authorization in the *London Morning Herald*.

4. *Monthly Intelligence*, 1830, 15, 1832, 73, 100, 101.

5. *Monthly Intelligence*, 1832, 103, 104.

6. *Monthly Intelligence*, 1832, 124, 130, 134, 146.

7. *Monthly Intelligence*, 1832, 147.

8. *Jewish Intelligence*, 1835, 1; Gidney, 178, 179.

9. *Monthly Intelligence*, 1833, 185; J. Nicolayson, *Journals, 1826–1842*, 372.

10. A. E. Bonar and R. M. M'Cheyne, *Narrative of a Mission of Inquiry to the Jews from the Church of Scotland in 1839*, 249.

11. *Monthly Intelligence*, 1833, 185; Nicolayson, *Journals*, 372.

12. *Monthly Intelligence*, 1834, 11.

13. *Monthly Intelligence*, 1833, 186–187. On at least one occasion they had a three-hour discussion that "embraced every point of importance between us and Jews, from the office and character of the Messiah to the mystery of the Trinity . . ."

14. *Monthly Intelligence*, 1833, 187; Nicolayson, *Journals*, 384.

15. Nicolayson, *Journals*, 372–373, 384; *Monthly Intelligence*, 1834, 13, 15, 18. Nicolayson naively noted in his unpublished journal that this invitation was canceled as a result of R. Nathan discovering that Nicolayson was "a believer in Christianity," a most unlikely explanation considering that Nicolayson had contact with R. Nathan's father and was known to the Jewish leadership from his previous visits to Jerusalem.

16. *Monthly Intelligence*, 1834, 18–19.

17. Nicolayson, *Journals*, Feb. 26, 1833, 389; *Monthly Intelligence*, 1834, 11, 20.

18. *Monthly Intelligence*, 1834, 20–22.

19. *Missionary Herald*, 1833, 41, 1834, 134.

20. *Monthly Intelligence*, 1834, 135; Nicolayson, *Journals*, 606; *Jewish Expositor*, 1825, 15.

21. *Monthly Intelligence*, 1834, 143; Nicolayson, *Journals*, 408; *Missionary Herald*, 1834, 322.

22. *Missionary Herald*, 1833, 441; *Monthly Intelligence*, 1834, 148; Nicolayson, *Journals*, 425; Gidney, 153. Nicolayson was disturbed but not discouraged by letters from Jerusalem reporting "intrigues to prevent a Protestant mission at Jerusalem." To shut out the missions, the Armenian Convent outbid the missionaries on renting a courtyard and the Roman Catholics used their influence against the Protestants. An undesignated consul and the rabbis warned against the arrival of the missionaries.

23. *Monthly Intelligence*, 1834, 13, 15; *Jewish Intelligence*, 1835, 177, 179; Bonar and M'Cheyne, 172.

24. *Jewish Intelligence*, 1835, 177, 178; A. L. Tibawi, *British Interests in Palestine 1800–1901*, 14; Nicolayson, *Journals*, 796.

25. Nicolayson, *Journals*, Apr. 4, 1835, 628, Mar. 28, 1840, 998; LJS, 31st Report, 73.

26. *Jewish Intelligence*, 1835, 202, 1839, 143, 1840, 11; LJS, 31st Report, 75. Nicolayson conducted early morning daily prayer services in Hebrew using the newly translated (1836) liturgy of the Church of England into Hebrew. On Sunday mornings and Christian holidays, prayers were chanted in English, Hebrew, and occasionally also in German and Arabic. On Sunday Nicolayson preached three sermons in three languages to prove that Jesus was also the Messiah for the Jews. The congregation at the daily Hebrew services was "small"; by 1839 it had not yet at-

tracted "any attention among the Jews." Sunday services attracted eight persons in January, "12 communicants" on March 3, 1839, and ten in July. Participants were mission people and their families, one tourist, and "one . . . native." On October 14, 1838, "for the first time two Jews" attended Sunday services; in 1840 one British tourist reported a few Jewish converts in attendance and another wrote about "only nine or ten persons" at the service. At another 1840 service Nicolayson preached in Hebrew to "about eighteen, amongst whom were three or four converted Jews."

27. *Jewish Intelligence*, 1835, 179, 1840, 11, 1842, 109.

28. *Jewish Intelligence*, 1835, 295; *Monthly Intelligence*, 1833, 181.

29. *Jewish Intelligence*, 1835, 182, 208; Nicolayson, *Journals*, June 18, 1835, 647. In 1835 Perushim sent letters via the Russian consul in Jaffa. In the 1830s some Ashkenazi and Sephardi Jews bypassed kollel censorship by sending letters to Europe using the postal services of English missionaries, the British vice-consul in Jerusalem, and Dutch diplomatic mail.

30. Nicolayson, *Journals*, Sept. 28, 1835, 686, May 30, 1836, 612, 688, 745; H. J. Zimmels, *Ashkenazim and Sephardim*, 108; *Jewish Intelligence*, 1835, 183.

31. Gidney, 179; Nicolayson, *Journals*, Apr. 1834, 500, June 16, 1840, 1025. They argued at length about whether the moral precepts of the Old Testament were superior to the Gospel and spoke about the Messianic interpretation of Isaiah (49:1–7).

32. *Jewish Intelligence*, 1835, 181, 183, 214.

33. Nicolayson, *Journals*, 182, 183, 200, 212, 283, 284, 503, 504, 510, 537, 557, 665, 683, 686.

34. Ibid., 675.

35. Ibid., July 3, 1835, 664.

36. E. Robinson, vol. 2, 94. No specific date was set for devaluations to go into effect in Palestine. They were "proclaimed on different days in different places, and in each [place] went immediately into operation." Jaffa, being the first Palestinian town to receive news from overseas, devalued money a few days before inland Jerusalem. This enabled nimble merchants knowing the latest news to reap large profits. These merchants also grew rich by buying and selling coins that had different values in different towns. For example, "in Jerusalem gold currency was cheaper than in Beirut, and silver more expensive."

37. *Jewish Intelligence*, 1835, 214–221, 282–283, 293.

38. *Jewish Intelligence*, 1835, 295; Nicolayson, *Journals*, 572.

39. *Jewish Intelligence*, 1839, 177.

40. Nicolayson, *Journals*, 740, 748, 822; A. Yaari, *Travels in Eretz-Israel*, 500.

41. Nicolayson, *Journals*, 1063; *Jewish Intelligence*, 1839, 174, 1840, 167, 195, 260, 294, 295.

42. LJS, 31st Report, 74; *Jewish Intelligence*, 1840, 190; Nicolayson, *Journals*, Mar. 1835, 602, 893, Dec. 20, 1838, 893, Nov. 13, 1840, 1071; *Jewish Intelligence*, 1839, 9, 143, 179.

43. *Jewish Intelligence*, 1840, 96.

44. Tibawi, *American Interests*, 61; *Missionary Herald*, 1833, 441.

45. *Jewish Intelligence*, 1835, 183.

46. *Missionary Herald*, 1835, 47, 51; R. Anderson, *History of the Missions of the American Board of Commissioners for Foreign Missions to the Oriental Churches*, 35; Tibawi, *American Interests*, 73.

47. Tibawi, *American Interests*, 59; Nicolayson, *Journals*, Nov. 1, 1834, 569; *Jewish Intelligence*, 1835, 292–293.

48. *Jewish Intelligence*, 1835, 177, 195, 293; *Missionary Herald*, 1832, 287–288, 1834, 374, 375, 1838, 420.

49. *Missionary Herald*, 1835, 281, 374; Tibawi, *American Interests*, 73; Bonar and M'Cheyne, 172.

50. Tibawi, *American Interests*, 73; H. Finnie. *Pioneers East*, 119; Anderson, *History*, 234; Nicolayson, *Journals*, 418; *Missionary Herald*, 1832, 130. American missionary Eli Smith was convinced "that enfeebled health and shortened life are among the sacrifices necessary to the work of the missions."

51. Nicolayson, *Journals*, 677, 694, 745; *Missionary Herald*, 1835, 421, 1836, 251, 252, 253, 1837, 302; *Jewish Intelligence*, 1836, 116. Nicolayson sincerely wished "to strengthen Brother Wh-s' hands . . ." They had cooperated in providing spiritual sustenance to Costigin, the Irish adventurer, during his last two days on earth. At the Sunday services conducted in English in Whiting's home, Nicolayson assisted Whiting after he had completed the LJS early Sunday service in Hebrew. Since Whiting spoke no Hebrew and was acquainted with few Jews, the Talmudic injunction about Purim must have been told to Whiting by Nicolayson, who quoted the Hebrew version and its translation in his *Journals*.

52. W. Thomson, *The Land and the Book*, vol. 1, 275.

53. Tibawi, *American Interests*, 96; *Missionary Herald*, 1835, 368; Nicolayson, *Journals*, June 6, 1836, 763.

54. Nicolayson, *Journals*, 734; Tibawi, *American Interests*, 74.

55. Tibawi, *American Interests*, 76. There is no mention of the consular issue in the *Missionary Herald*. In 1835 the American Board's annual report noted that the Turks continued to deny Protestants the status of Jewish and Catholic minorities, and in 1836 Whiting and others urged "the necessity of consular protection for Americans residing in Syria and Egypt."

56. *Missionary Herald*, 1840, 203, 465; Anderson, *History*, 37; Robinson, *Researches*, vol. 1, 333; Nicolayson, *Journals*, 866; LJS, 33rd Report, 53.

57. *Missionary Herald*, 55; Tibawi, *American Interests*, 92, 100, 105; Anderson, *History*, 38; I. Bird, *Bible Work in Bible Lands*, 340; William Miller quoted by E. R. Sandeen, *The Roots of Fundamentalism*, 52.

58. Nicolayson, *Journals*, Dec. 1, 1836, 794.

59. *Jewish Intelligence*, 1839, 155.

60. S. Lieber, "The Purchase of Land for 'Christ Church' by John Nicolayson," 201–203.

61. *Jewish Intelligence*, 1839, 155, 1841, 36; H. Temperley, *England and the Near East: The Crimea*, 443.

62. Nicolayson, *Journals*, Aug. 11, 1838, 867.

63. Bonar and M'Cheyne, 170, 240. Pieretz, a Prussian Jew and former rabbi at Yarmouth, England, was a man of "mature mind, established character and ad-

vanced experience" (Nicolayson, *Journals*, July 4, 1838, 849).

64. Nicolayson, *Journals*, 849, 850; *Jewish Intelligence*, 1835, 155.

65. Gidney, 180; Nicolayson, *Journals*, 891; Bonar and M'Cheyne, 170; *Jewish Intelligence*, 1839, 62.

66. Gidney, 180; *Jewish Intelligence*, 1839, 98; Nicolayson, *Journals*, Dec. 18, 1838, 892, Oct. 1839, 957; E. Finn, *Reminiscences*, 32.

67. Nicolayson, *Journals*, Jan. 23, 1839, 899; LJS, 31st Report, 76; *Jewish Intelligence*, 1839, 62, 97, 98, 144, 1840, 34–35.

68. Nicolayson, *Journals*, Dec. 12, 1838, 892; *Jewish Intelligence*, 1839, 97.

69. Nicolayson, *Journals*, Feb. 1838, 902, 903, Jan. 1839, 894, Jan. 21, 1939, 897; Gidney, 180–181.

70. A. Yaari, *Letters from the Land of Israel*, 404; *Jewish Intelligence*, 1839, 178–179, 1840, 36.

71. Finn, *Reminiscences*, 32; *Jewish Intelligence*, 1840, 302.

72. E. Bergmann, and G. Bergmann, *Yis'u Harim Shalom*, 92.

73. A. M. Hyamson, *The British Consulate in Jerusalem in Relation to the Jews of Palestine*, vol. 1, 9.

74. I. Freiden, "Bikur Holim Perushim in Jerusalem," 120, 122; A. Morgenstern, "The Correspondence of the Pekidim and Amarcalim as a Source for the History of Eretz-Israel," 105.

75. J. Kellner, *For Zion's Sake*, 12–14; Freiden, "Bikur Holim Perushim," 122; *Jewish Intelligence*, 1842, 366–367.

76. This viewpoint expressed in 1847 by Zvi Hirsch Lehren was no less true in 1839. Lehren wrote: "We know the character of most of the doctors in our time concerning their belief in our sacred faith. They are sons lacking all faith. And if any of them come to our holy city they will, God forbid, plant seeds of apostasy in the Holy Land. Even if they cure the bodies they will contaminate the souls—and there is no greater evil than this . . ." B. Z. Dinur, "From the Archives of the Chief Rabbi Haim Abraham Gaugin," 114; G. Kressel, *Planters of Hope*, 88; A. Morgenstern, "The Pekidim and Amarcalim of Amsterdam and the Jewish Community in Palestine—1810–1840," 212; B. Gat, *The Jewish Community in Eretz-Israel (1840–1881)*, 126–127.

77. N. Katzburg "From the First Letters of the English Vice Consul in Jerusalem," x–xii; A. Yaari, *Memoirs of Eretz-Israel*, 156; Nicolayson, *Journals*, Mar. 1838, 828, Apr. 28, 1839, 908; *Missionary Intelligence*, 1832, 130; Robinson, *Researches*, vol. 2, 321, vol. 3, 72–73; S. N. Spyridon, "Annals of Palestine 1821–1841," 127, 129, 130; Nicolayson, *Journals*, 849, 850, 881, 887, 888, 890; A. L. Frumkin, *The History of the Scholars of Jerusalem*, 175.

78. Spyridon, 130; *Jewish Intelligence*, 1839, 199, 1840, 96; LJS, 32nd Report, 45; Morgenstern, "Pekidim," 111; Nicolayson, *Journals*, Nov. 27, 1838, 887.

79. Bonar and M'Cheyne, 164, 165, 246; Robinson, *Researches*, vol. 2, 87. During these days of plagues the number of Jews living in Jerusalem did not increase and may even have dwindled. Scottish ministers reported a "diminution in the number of Jews returning to their own land" in 1837 and 1838 because of the "ravages of the plague," the rise in the price of provisions," and the "embarrassed fi-

446 / *Notes to Pages 313–316*
nances" of the Jewish community and its huge debt of nearly £8,000 or 800,000 piastres. LJS missionary Pieretz believed that in 1838 there actually was a decrease in the Jerusalem Jewish population, "for the plague carried away more than those born during the year" while Jewish immigrants dropped to "not more than twenty." Likewise, the American explorer Edward Robinson wrote that "the number of Jews in Jerusalem has been much diminished" in 1837.

80. Nicolayson, *Journals*, May 20, 1839, 920, May 24, 1839, 921, May 27, 1839, 922, June 17, 1839, 927, July 8, 1839, 929, Sept. 26, 1839, 949, Oct. 1, 1839, 950; *Jewish Intelligence*, 1840, 343–345. Friction developed between Nicolayson and Gerstmann and fractured the Jerusalem mission station. Nicolayson frequently complained about Gerstmann's character, hot temperament, lack of cooperation, "vanity and folly," and refusal to participate in the service baptizing Simeon Rosenthal and his family. Gerstmann was vaguely accused by Nicolayson of disclosing his feelings, "which appear utterly inconsistent with his connection with the Mission," but no specific charges were recorded. Nicolayson and Gerstmann also disagreed about the prospective convert Libas, so in April 1839 Libas was sent to the missionary Ewald serving in Tunis, possibly without the concurrence of Gerstmann. When Gerstmann decided to accompany the sick missionary Levi to Beirut, "without waiting to consult," Nicolayson sharply responded that this was further proof of Gerstmann's deficiency of moral qualification. Before Gerstmann returned to Jerusalem (with Levi) Nicolayson concluded that he would have "to recommend Gerstmann's removal" because of "some other evidence." This undisclosed evidence may be the "want of kinship . . . on the part of Dr. G." toward Levi or Pieretz's undefined charges against Gerstmann for conduct unbecoming a missionary.

81. Nicolayson, *Journals*, Jan. 17, 1840, 980, May 25, 1841, 1095; Gidney, 174; Nicolayson, *Journals*, Mar. 28, 1840, 998, May 26, 1840, 1017; Freiden, "Bikur Holim Perushim," 122.

82. Nicolayson, *Journals*, 882, 911, 913, 975; Gidney, 181; Bonar and M'Cheyne, 171; *Jewish Intelligence*, 1839, 97, 142, 155, 175–177, 199, 241; 1842, 270–271.

83. *Jewish Intelligence*, 1843, 281.

84. Nicolayson, *Journals*, Feb. 1839, 903; G. L. Dawson Damer, *Diary of a Tour in Greece, Turkey, Egypt and the Holy Land*, vol. 1, 312; *Jewish Intelligence*, 1839, 172–174.

85. Nicolayson, *Journals*, July 1, 1839, 928; *Jewish Intelligence*, 1839, 243.

86. Nicolayson, *Journals*, May 31, 1836, 748, October 17, 1838, 882.

87. Bonar and M'Cheyne, 131; *Jewish Intelligence*, 1839, 8, 9, 180.

88. Nicolayson, *Journals*, 1839, 902, 903.

89. Ben-Arieh, *A City Reflected in Its Times*, vol. 2, 520; Nicolayson, *Journals*, Sept. 1841, 1154, 1186; W. H. Bartlett, *Jerusalem Revisited*, 78; Nicolayson, *Journals*, 1839, 898, 901; A. Blumberg, *A View from Jerusalem 1849–1858*, 151, 241–242, 306, 307.

90. *Jewish Intelligence*, 1840, 188.

91. E. Warburton, *The Crescent and the Cross*, quoted by B. Tuchman, *Bible and Sword*, 133.

92. W. H. Bartlett, *Walks about the City and Environs of Jerusalem*, 191.

93. C. Ritter, *The Comparative Geography of Palestine and the Sinaitic Peninsula*, vol. 2, 2.

94. Tuchman, *Bible and Sword*, 121.

95. *Missionary Herald*, 1827, 70.

96. *Missionary Herald*, 1838, 334.

97. Tibawi, *British Interests*, 81; Tuchman, *Bible and Sword*, 133. "But what is our condition! Have we run counter to the will of God! Have we conceived a merely human project, and then imagined it to be a decree of the Almighty, when we erected a bishopric in Jerusalem, and appointed a Hebrew to exercise the functions? Have we vainly and presumptuously attempted to define the times and seasons which the Father hath put in His own power? God, who knoweth our hearts, alone can tell. It seemed to us that we acted in faith for the honor of His name, and in the love of His ancient people; but now it would appear that the thing was amiss, and not according to God's wisdom and pleasure."

98. Nicolayson, *Journals*, Aug. 1834, 561.

99. 1979 Nobel Peace Prize winner Mother Teresa, the "saint of the gutters" of Calcutta.

14 THE BRITISH CONSULATE IN JERUSALEM, 1839–1840

1. *Jewish Intelligence*, 1835, 290–292; J. Nicolayson, *Journals, 1826–1842*, Oct. 18, 1834, 567; E. Robinson, *Biblical Researches in Palestine, Mount Sinai and Arabia Petrea in 1838*, vol. 2, 162.

2. M. Vereté, "Why Was a British Consulate Established in Jerusalem?" 320, 323.

3. Ibid., 325, 328.

4. J. Bowring, *Report on Commercial Statistics of Syria*, 121.

5. Vereté, "British Consulate," 324.

6. As soon as Palmerston agreed to Young's appointment, Campbell asked Mehemet Ali to approve stationing a British consul in Jerusalem. Knowing of Palmerston's foreign policies, Mehemet Ali could not have been happy about approving another English consular agent in the Syrian territory he conquered against the express wishes of the British government. But the Egyptian ruler could not risk a rift in his relations with the British government. So he reverted to the same tactic he used when consenting to the erection of the Christ Church in Jerusalem. He endorsed the opening of a British consulate in Jerusalem on the condition that the legal sovereign of the Syrian territory, the sultan, approved the British request. Palmerston promptly instructed the British ambassador in Istanbul to secure a firman for the British consulate in Jerusalem. Seven months later, in July 1838, Palmerston learned that the sultan had granted the firman for a Jerusalem-based British consul. Why should the sultan object to a British consul in Jerusalem that he did not control? He was happy to provide his Egyptian foe with a new headache, wishing all possible trouble that the British Empire could bring down on the head of Mehemet Ali.

7. A. L. Tibawi, *British Interests in Palestine 1800–1901*, 33.

8. Nicolayson, *Journals*, Nov. 8, 1838, 889.

9. *Monthly Intelligence*, 1832, 69, 99; A. M. Hyamson, *The British Consulate in Jerusalem in Relation to the Jews of Palestine, 1838–1914*, vol. 2, lxviii, lxix, lxvii; The missionary Calman also suggested (in 1840) that Moses Montefiore should secure British protection for the Jews. Calman even went to the extreme of claiming that not only the Jews but also the Muslims asked pleadingly: "When will you English come and take possession of this our country?" The Church of Scotland missionary organization was understandably "most anxious that, in any future settlement of that country," Palestine be placed "under the auspices of Britain."

10. Tibawi, *British Interests*, 32.

11. Hyamson, vol. 1, xxxiv.

12. Vereté, "British Consulate," 316–317.

13. Nicolayson, *Journals*, Jan. 6, 1839, 900; Hyamson, vol. 1, 2, 3; N. Katzburg, "From the First Letters of the English Vice Consul in Jerusalem," x; *Jewish Intelligence*, 1839, 174.

14. Nicolayson, *Journals*, 1839, 900, 920; *Jewish Intelligence*, 1839, 174.

15. Hyamson, vol. 1, 4; Tibawi, *British Interests*, 137.

16. Hyamson, vol. 1, 2–3.

17. Ibid., vol. 1, xxxv, 4.

18. Ibid., vol. 1, 4, 7, 8.

19. *Jewish Intelligence*, 1839, 180; Hyamson, vol. 1, 8; E. Bergmann and G. Bergmann, *Yis'u Harim Shalom*, 65.

20. Hyamson, vol. 1, 11–12, 22–24.

21. Ibid., vol. 1, 12–13.

22. Ibid., vol. 1, 8–9, 14, 15.

23. Ibid., vol. 1, 17, 20–21, 22.

24. D. Kinross, *The Ottoman Centuries*, 384; Hyamson, vol. 1, 2, 4, 7–8, 16, 28; G. L. Dawson Damer, *Diary of a Tour in Greece, Turkey, Egypt and the Holy Land*, vol. 2, 10.

25. Hyamson, vol. 1, 16–17, 18, 19.

26. H. Temperley, *England and the Near East: The Crimea*, 107, 109; J. Ridley, *Lord Palmerston*, 303; Tibawi, *British Interests*, 41, completely misread the evidence when he wrote about "Campbell's steadying influence" on Young; Hyamson, vol. 1, 27.

27. A. Cunningham, "Stratford Canning and the Tanzimat," 249; Kenneth Bourne, *The Foreign Policy of Victorian England 1830–1902*, 239. Throughout the decade of 1830–1840, with the exception of a five-month period, Palmerston vigorously and decisively dominated British foreign policy. He aimed at curtailing French and Russian commercial and religious interests that had penetrated into the Turkish Empire. For Palmerston, the disrupting influence of that "ignorant barbarian" Mehemet Ali must be held in check in order to prevent upsetting the equilibrium in the Near East and ensure the stability of the Ottoman Empire. He declared that "the integrity and independence of the Ottoman Empire are necessary to the maintenance of the tranquility, the liberty, and the balance of power in the rest of Europe." These objectives could best be achieved by pushing Ibrahim Pasha's forces out of Syria and Palestine and returning Egypt to a strengthened Turkish Empire. When necessary, British military and political assistance must be provided to the sultan to

prevent the predatory Mehemet Ali and the carnivorous European great powers from biting pieces out of the Turkish provinces. While thwarting the ambitions of Czar Nicolas I, Louis Philippe, and Mehemet Ali, Palmerston advanced the English economic and political position in the Turkish dominions by promoting British trade, signing commercial agreements, and appointing as many consular agents as possible to show the Union Jack.

28. Hyamson, vol. 1, 1, 4, 5, 8. Since Young still had no Jewish dragoman and his contacts with the Jewish and Muslim communities were extremely limited—he spoke no Hebrew or Arabic—we assume that much of Young's valuable information about the Jews was garnered from helpful, Hebrew-speaking John Nicolayson. Young admitted that his "means of communication" with the Jews "are very limited," but attributed this restriction to the "Quarantines" that prevented him from moving freely around Palestine.

29. Hyamson, vol. 1, 9.

30. Ibid., vol. 1, 8.

31. Ibid., vol. 1, 6–7; Bergmann and Bergmann, 76, 82, 101, 106.

32. F. Egerton, *Journal of a Tour in the Holy Land in 1840*, 21; Dawson Damer, vol. 1, 312; A. Morgenstern, "The Pekidim and Amarcalim of Amsterdam and the Jewish Community in Palestine—1810–1840," 17.

33. Hyamson, vol. 1, xxxv.

34. Spyridon, 131; Hyamson, vol. 1, 25.

35. G. Kressel, *Planters of Hope*, 132–133; Hyamson, vol. 1, 25–26, 28.

36. M. Eliav, *Love of Zion and Men of HOD*, 36; A. M. Lunz, *Jerusalem Yearbook*, vol. 5, 234.

37. Hyamson, vol. 1, 29; Katzburg, xx, xxi, xxvii. Russian consul Basili visited Jerusalem for the Easter Festival; according to Young, "his presence gave a character to the Greek and Armenian ceremonies—he appeared in his uniform, and was attended by the Russian pilgrims, many of them old soldiers in their regimentals." That the vast majority of Russian pilgrims were poor village peasants rather than soldiers was not reported. Recognizing Palmerston's sensitivity about Russia's influence in the area, Young reported rumors: "The pilgrims from Russia have been heard to speak openly, of the period being at hand when this country will be under the Russian Government." Young's troubled frame of mind is reflected by his complaining that the Greek and Latin priests teach that "England is 'Protestant and not Christian'" in an effort "to extend the influence of the Governments who support and protect their churches"—a clear reference to French and Russian support for the Roman Catholics and Greek Orthodox.

38. D. Hopwood, *The Russian Presence in Syria and Palestine, 1843–1914*, 2, 33–35; W. B. Lincoln, *Nicholas I*, 199; Temperley, 73.

39. Hyamson, vol. 1, 29.

40. Nicolayson, *Journals*, Sept. 8, 1840, 1047.

15 MONTEFIORE'S SECOND TRIP TO ERETZ ISRAEL, 1839

1. (Sir) M. Montefiore and Lady J. Montefiore, *Diaries of Sir Moses and Lady Montefiore*, vol. 1, 197; A. M. Hyamson, *The British Consul in Jerusalem in Rela-*

tion to the Jews of Palestine, 1838–1914, vol. 1, 14; G. Yardeni-Agmon, "John Gawler and His Trips to Palestine," 16.

2. M. Eliav, *Eretz-Israel and Its Yishuv in the Nineteenth Century (1777–1917)*, 11–12.

3. A. Yaari, *Letters from the Land of Israel*, 385, 388, 391.

4. A. M. Lunz, *Jerusalem Yearbook*, vol. 5, 305–307; Yaari, *Letters*, 390.

5. Yaari, *Letters*, 392; Montefiore *Diaries*, 1, 162.

6. A. E. Bonar and R. M. M'Cheyne, *Narrative of a Mission of Inquiry to the Jews from the Church of Scotland in 1839*, 246.

7. A. L. Tibawi, *A Modern History of Syria including Lebanon and Palestine*, 70, 86, 87.

8. Montefiore *Diaries*, vol. 1, 165; (Lady) Judith Montefiore, *Notes from a Private Journal of a Visit to Egypt and Palestine (1839)*, 164; I. Ben-Zvi, "Events in Safed from the Lootings of 1834 to the Druze Attacks in 1838," 296.

9. 26 percent in J. Meisel, "The Jewish Settlement in Eretz-Israel in 1839," 429.

10. Meisel, 434–437.

11. S. Schwarzfuchs, "The Jews of Algeria in Northern Eretz-Israel and the French Protection," 333.

12. 9.24 not 0.24 in Meisel, 446.

13. *Jewish Intelligence*, 1839, 9.

14. M. O. Schmelz, "Some Demographic Peculiarities of the Jews of Jerusalem in the Nineteenth Century," 132. Ashkenazim came to Eretz Israel in equal numbers during 1810–1819 and 1820–1829 (104 in 1810–1819 and 114 in 1820–1829) but show a slight drop in immigration during 1820–1829 after a statistical adjustment for the 50-percent death rate every ten years (260 in 1810–1819 and 228 in 1820–1829). During 1810–1829 the immigration picture of the Sephardim is significantly different from that of the Ashkenazim. From 1820 to 1829 Sephardi immigration increased by 2½ times compared to 1810–1819 (103 in 1810–1819 and 257 in 1820–1829); after adjusting for the 50-percent mortality rate over a ten-year period, the Sephardi immigration doubled (258 in 1810–1819 and 514 in 1820–1829). This significant increase reflects Sephardi immigration at the end of the 1820s, probably as a result of the Greek revolt and the Balkan wars.

15. Z. Kovac, "The Immigration to Eretz-Israel in the Mid-Nineteenth Century," 201.

16. Bonar and M'Cheyne, 148.

17. This prevalence of young families is corroborated by three reliable travel writers in 1815, 1845, and 1856. In 1815 British tourist William Turner reported that young Jewish families had recently started to settle in Eretz Israel. The knowledgeable Titus Tobler, based on his visit of 1845–1846, wrote that "younger couples constitute the majority" of the population." Frankl, after his 1856 trip, wrote that "the Jews arrive mostly with wife and children or sufficiently young to have expectation of this blessing" (M. Ish-Shalom, *Christian Travels in the Holy Land*, 158, 413; Schmelz, 135; L. A. Frankl, *The Jews in the East*, vol. 2, 170).

18. Schmelz, 128, 131; Meisel, 438. Indirect proof of a huge death rate among

the young is provided by the results of a survey of Ashkenazi-Perushim buried between 1840 and 1908 in the Mount of Olives cemetery, which shows that 35 percent of the tombstones were those of children up to age 12. It should be noted that a high infant mortality rate is one indicator of a backward economic country such as Palestine where a rich variety of diseases and disasters of nature mercilessly weeded out the weakest members of society—babies and young children.

19. *Missionary Herald*, 1823, 386.

20. Meisel, 440–441.

21. Schmelz, 132–134. Sephardi fathers born overseas produced one child (0.99) and foreign-born Ashkenazi men produced an average of three-quarters (0.72) of a child. Among the Sephardi fathers born in Palestine the situation was slightly better. They produced one and one-third (1.34) children, but native-born Ashkenazi fathers produced only half (0.54) a child. One out of three Ashkenazi families were childless and the average Ashkenazi family had less than one child. In Jerusalem seven out of ten families headed by men 15 to 24 years old had no living children "and the average of children alive per family was 0.37."

22. *Jewish Intelligence*, 1836, 282–283; A. Morgenstern, "The Pekidim and Amarcalim of Amsterdam and the Jewish Community in Palestine—1810–1840," 36; T. H. Rivlin, *The Vision of Zion, Shklov to Jerusalem*, 87, 91–95.

23. *Jewish Expositor*, 1829, 154; J. Nicolayson, *Journals, 1826–1842*, 828, 833; Bonar and M'Cheyne, 165; F. Egerton, *Journal of a Tour in the Holy Land in 1840*, 21; G. L. Dawson Damer, *Diary of a Tour in Greece, Turkey, Egypt and the Holy Land*, vol. 1, 317–318; Ish-Shalom 528.

24. Rivlin, *Vision of Zion*, 56.

25. Morgenstern, "Pekidim," 36.

26. Frankl, vol. 2, 175, for 1856.

27. Following the evidence and reasons presented by Schmelz.

28. Frankl, vol. 1, 341; vol. 2, 18, 67, 125; LJS, 15th Report, 207; Nicolayson, *Journals*, 604; Burckhardt, 307. Burckhardt (812) noted that in Tiberias Jews married at a very early age—"it is not uncommon to see mothers of eleven and fathers of 13 years." Missionary Joseph Wolff wrote about 12-year-old boys being married off and John Nicolayson told about a 14-year-old bridegroom. Much later (872) the Jewish historian Heinrich Graetz, after a visit to Eretz Israel, called such early marriages "a deeply rooted evil . . . nothing less than infanticide."

29. Schmelz, 128.

30. M. Eliav, "The Jewish Community in Jerusalem in the Late Ottoman Period (1815–1914)," 152; Schmelz, 130; Nicolayson, *Journals*, April 1836, 733, June 1836, 753; Bonar and M'Cheyne, 246.

31. A. M. Lunz, *Jerusalem Yearbook (1881)*, 118.

32. L. Stone, review of M. Foucault's book on *Madness* in *NY Review of Books*, Dec. 16, 1982, 28.

33. N. Schur, *Jerusalem in Pilgrims' Accounts*, vol. 1, 11.

34. Schmelz, 132.

35. N. Katzburg, "From the First Letters of the English Vice Consul in Jerusalem," xii–xiii.

36. A. M. Hyamson, *The British Consulate in Jerusalem in Relation to the Jews of Palestine, 1838–1914,* vol. 1, 5; Bonar and M'Cheyne, 148.

37. Meisel, 429; Hyamson, vol. 1, 7; Nicolayson, *Journals,* Apr. 1838, 833.

38. Montefiore *Diaries,* vol. 1, 157, 159; S. N. Spyridon, "Annals of Palestine 1821–1841," 130; *Jewish Intelligence,* 1839, 240.

39. Montefiore *Diaries,* vol. 1, 163.

40. Morgenstern, "Pekidim," 76; I. Bartal, "Settlement Proposals during Montefiore's Second Visit to Eretz-Israel, 1839," 258. Lehren accused Montefiore of coming to Eretz Israel "to boost his reputation" and of "regularly giving money to idolatrous causes," a reference to Montefiore's Christian philanthropies (Eliav, *Eretz-Israel,* 124).

41. Montefiore *Diaries,* vol. 1, 168; Ben-Zvi, "Events in Safed," 301, 302–303, 307, 320–322; Bonar and M'Cheyne, 278; Ish-Shalom, 516–517, 519; *Jewish Intelligence,* 1839, 284.

42. Yaari, *Letters,* 385.

43. Montefiore *Diaries,* vol. 1, 164, 165, 166.

44. Ben-Zvi, "Events in Safed," 306, 307, 309.

45. Morgenstern, "Pekidim," 178.

46. Ben-Zvi, "Events in Safed," 288–289, 303–304, 310–311; Montefiore *Diaries,* vol. 1, 164.

47. Ben-Zvi, "Events in Safed," 304–306.

48. M. Abir, "The Claims of Safed Jewry after the Lootings of 1834," 267–274.

49. Montefiore *Diaries* vol. 1, 166, 168.

50. Meisel, 454, 456; (Lady) Judith Montefiore, *Notes from a Private Journal of a Visit to Egypt and Palestine (1839),* 162.

51. Meisel, 461; Montefiore *Diaries,* vol. 1, 166; Bartal, "Settlement Proposals," 261–262, 263, 271; M. Montefiore, *Diary and Letters from Voyages,* 241.

52. Ben-Zvi, "Incidents in Safed," 293–295, 297. The Egyptians effectively collected the poll tax based on actual kollel population records rather than negotiating a total fixed sum for all Jews of Safed regardless of their number, as practiced by the previous pashas. Annual tax payments would have amounted to 21,000 piastres (based on 350 heads of families or 1,400 Jews) in comparison to 5,000 piastres paid each year to Pasha Abdullah from 1818 to 1830 and 2,000 piastres paid annually up to 1818.

53. Bartal, "Settlement Proposals," 251; Meisel, 460; Ben-Zvi, "Events in Safed," 309–310, 313–315, 317–319; Montefiore *Diaries,* vol. 1, 167.

54. Montefiore *Diaries,* vol. 1, 166–169, 175; Judith Montefiore, *Notes,* 166, 168.

55. Journal of Roberts, in *The Holy Land,* Apr. 22, 1839, vol. 4, 23; A. Lamartine, *Visit to the Holy Land,* 240; E. Robinson, *Biblical Researches in Palestine, Mount Sinai and Arabia Petrea in 1838,* vol. 3, 254; Bonar and M'Cheyne, 290; *Jewish Intelligence,* 1839, 284–285.

56. Montefiore, *Diaries,* 166; Judith Montefiore, *Notes,* 171; introduction to Israel's book *The Corner of the Table.*

57. Montefiore, *Diaries,* vol. 1, 175, 176; Bonar and M'Cheyne, 143;

Nicolayson, *Journals*, May 29, 1839, 919; *Jewish Intelligence*, 1839, 241.

58. Bonar and M'Cheyne, 142–143.

59. Hyamson, vol. 1, 5; Montefiore *Diaries*, vol. 1, 178.

60. *Jewish Intelligence*, 1839, 241.

61. Bartal, "Settlement Proposals," 251, 255, 287–288; *Jewish Intelligence*, 1839, 241; R. Kark, "Montefiore's Second Visit to Eretz-Israel, 1839," 89. Montefiore probably learned that in 1837 an "agent of the Ashkenazi community" in Jerusalem requested permission to purchase plots of land to plow, plant, and harvest, raise sheep and cattle, and process agricultural products. R. Israel of Shklov was finally convinced that the Perushim should buy property in Eretz Israel, much to the chagrin of Lehren, who wrote R. Israel that "buying fields and vineyards appears to all of us [PEKAM] a mad matter... how can you imagine putting all living residents of Eretz Israel into farming!" In 1837 rich European Jews were asked to support the scholars of Jerusalem on income derived from fields and vineyards, from cloth or other kinds of workshops, or from the rent of stores, or even by bringing over craftsmen from Europe. Such a proposal resembled the practice of the Greek Orthodox Church, which supported its monks by selling the produce of fields surrounding the Church in the Valley of the Cross. The plan also was similar to the common practice in Muslim villages of contributing some of the income received from "miri" lands to mosques and other religious institutions.

62. Morgenstern, "Pekidim," 178–179; Montefiore, *Diary and Letters*, 271–275.

63. Bartal, "Settlement Proposals," 254, 272; Kark, "Montefiore's Second Visit," 71; Montefiore, *Diary and Letters*, 247–263.

64. M. Solomon, *Three Generations in the Yishuv, 1812–1913*, 93; S. Avitsur, *Daily Life in Eretz-Israel in the Nineteenth Century*, 28; Bartal, "Settlement Proposals," 272.

65. Nicolayson, *Journals*, 833; Montefiore, *Diaries*, vol. 1, 182.

66. Montefiore, *Diaries*, vol. 1, 184.

67. Bonar and M'Cheyne, 183.

68. Nicolayson, *Journals*, Apr. 1838, 836, May 7, 1838, 842; J. Bowring, *Report on Commercial Statistics of Syria*, 97, 99.

69. A. Yaari, *Memoirs of Eretz-Israel*, 148–149.

70. Lunz, *Jerusalem Yearbook*, vol. 5, 323; Eliav, *Eretz-Israel, 1777–1917*, 95; I. Bartal, "On the Beginnings of Jewish Settlement in Jaffa," 355–357; Tibawi, *Syria*, 87. A rich, distinguished Jew from Istanbul bought a courtyard with a three-story building near the Jaffa port to serve as an inn for Jewish settlers and pilgrims on their way to and from Jerusalem. This Jewish community facility was registered in the name of the Sephardi community and was run by a few Jews who lived in Jaffa on a permanent or temporary basis. Settlers and pilgrims stayed at the inn a number of days until a convoy was assembled to accompany them to Jerusalem. To facilitate the 24–36 hour trip from Jaffa to Jerusalem the Sephardi kollel of Jerusalem purchased a house in Ramleh, a three-hour donkey ride from Jaffa. For lodging and transportation to Jerusalem Jewish travelers paid 50 piastres.

71. Judith Montefiore, *Notes*, 197.

72. Montefiore *Diaries*, vol. 1, 188; *Jewish Intelligence*, 1839, 199; Bonar and M'Cheyne, 229–230, 232; Katzburg, xii. The normal quarantine period of fourteen days was reduced to seven since the Montefiores agreed to wash all their clothes and tents in the sea and fumigate nonwashable possessions.

73. Montefiore *Diaries*, vol. 1, 189.

74. Montefiore *Diaries*, vol. 1, 63–65; A. Lamartine, *Visit to the Holy Land or Recollections of the East*, 142–163; A. Yaari, *Travels in Eretz-Israel*, 525; J. L. Stephens, *Incidents of Travel in Egypt, Arabia Petraea and the Holy Land*, 371–372.

75. Bonar and M'Cheyne, 237; Y. Ben-Arieh, "The Development of Twelve Major Settlements in Nineteenth-Century Palestine," 141; Meisel, 429.

76. Montefiore *Diaries*, vol. 1, 189, 196.

77. Hyamson, vol. 2, lxviii, lxix; Judith Montefiore, *Notes*, 214.

78. Montefiore *Diaries*, vol. 1, 196, 197, 199; Dawson Damer, vol. 1, 321; Ishshalom, 529.

79. Morgenstern, "Pekidim," 5.

80. Bartal, "Settlement Proposals," 285–286.

81. Bonar and M'Cheyne, 395, 393; I. Klausner, "R. Yehuda B'ibas." Possibly R. Bibas was influenced by the nationalistic spirit of the newly founded (831) "Young Italy" movement planning to establish an independent Italian nation.

82. M. Samuel, *Harvest in the Desert*, 44.

16 THE END OF EGYPT'S OCCUPATION OF PALESTINE, 1840

1. W. B. Lincoln, *Nicholas I*, 202, 218; M. S. Anderson, *The Eastern Question (1774–1923)*, 88–109; S. J. Shaw and E. K. Shaw, *History of the Ottoman Empire and Modern Turkey*, 11, 56; J. Ridley, *Lord Palmerston*, 319–320; H. Temperley, *England and the Near East: The Crimea*, 114–16, 120, 124–125; 127–130; K. M. Basili, *Memoirs from Lebanon*, 136, 150, 167, 171.

2. B. Tuchman, *Bible and Sword*, 128.

3. A. L. Tibawi, *A Modern History of Syria including Lebanon and Palestine*, 93; Anderson, *Eastern Question*, 88–109.

4. N. Katzburg, "From the First Letters of the English Vice Consul in Jerusalem," ix–xxx; J. Nicolayson, *Journals, 1826–1842*, Oct. 1840, 1057, Oct. 19, 1840, 1059, Oct. 26, 1840, 1070, Dec. 1840, 1080, 1082; J. Schwartz, *Descriptive Geography and Brief Sketch of Palestine* 384; A. M. Hyamson, *The British Consulate in Jerusalem in Relation to the Jews of Palestine, 1838–1914*, vol. 1, 41.

5. English translation in J. C. Hurewitz, *Diplomacy and the Middle East* (Princeton, 1956), vol. 1, 113–116; B. Lewis, *The Emergence of Modern Turkey*, 105–108; M. Ma'oz, *Ottoman Reform in Syria and Palestine*, 21–25; Anderson, *Eastern Question*, 108; Shaw and Shaw, vol. 2, 60–61.

6. *Encyclopedia Judaica*, vol. 5, 1250; *Jewish Intelligence*, 1840, 167, 165–185, 196–206, 209–259, 283–291, 311–312, 325–329, 352–359.

7. Nicolayson, *Journals*, Mar. 16, 1840, 991, 993–994.

8. (Sir) M. and Lady Judith Montefiore, *Diaries of Sir Moses and Lady Montefiore*, vol. 1, 214; Abraham Geiger wrote: "For me it is more important that

Jews be able to work in Prussia as pharmacists or lawyers than that the entire Jewish population of Asia and Africa be saved although as a human being I sympathize with them." At the opposite end of the spectrum was the violent reaction about the destiny and passivity of all Jews expressed by the 16-year-old vengeful firebrand Ferdinand Lasalle: "The Jews in Damascus suffer cruel actions that only contemptible people—sons of wild tribes could suffer without taking a terrible blood vengeance on their enemies. Therefore even the Christians are amazed at our restraint, at our failure to rebel. . . . Cowardly people, you deserve no better lot! The trodden worm turns, but you only bow deeper! You do not know how to die, to destroy, you do not know what is a just vengeance . . . You were born to be slaves!" (B. Halprin, *The Idea of the Jewish State*, 67–68).

9. Tuchman, *Bible and Sword*, 126; *Jewish Intelligence*, 1840, 328, 353; Temperley, 115, 119: Anderson, *Eastern Question*, 103.

10. T. H. Rivlin, *The Vision of Zion, Shklov to Jerusalem*, 14; M. Eliav, *Eretz-Israel and Its Yishuv in the Nineteenth Century (1777–1917)*, 92; Y. Yellin, *Memoirs of a Native of Jerusalem, 1830–1918*, 78; A. Yaari, *Memoirs of Eretz-Israel*, 159.

11. H. Z. Hirschberg, "The Oriental Jewish Communities," 212.

12. Montefiore *Diaries*, vol. 1, 279.

13. W. Laqueur, *A History of Zionism*, 43.

14. Tuchman, *Sword and Bible*, 126; F. Kobler, *The Vision Was There*, 161.

15. Laqueur, 44–45. Pretty expensive considering that the Louisiana Territory between the Mississippi and the Rocky Mountains was bought in 1803 for $16 million and Seward's Folly—the purchase of Alaska in 1867—cost $7,200,000 or about 2 cents an acre.

16. *Jewish Intelligence*, 1840, 345–347, 351; Laqueur, 45–46.

17. E. Hodder, *The Life and Work of the Seventh Earl of Shaftesbury*, vol. 1, 310.

18. Kobler, *Vision*, 61–62; Tuchman, *Bible and Sword*, 113–114.

19. Tuchman, *Bible and Sword*, 127–128; Hyamson, vol. 2, lxxi–lxxiii; N. Sokolow, *History of Zionism*, vol. 2, 229–231; Hodder, vol. 3, 314–315.

20. Tuchman, *Bible and Sword*, 114, 128.

21. Hyamson, vol. 1, 33.

22. *Jewish Intelligence*, 1840, 131, 141, 266; A. Morgenstern, "The Pekidim and Amarcalim of Amsterdam and the Jewish Community in Palestine—1810–1840," 192–195.

23. G. Scholem, *Major Trends in Jewish Mysticism*, 287.

24. I. Klausner, *The Messianic Idea in Israel*, 441.

25. Morgenstern, "Pekidim," 7.

26. Y. Katz, "1840 as a 'Year of Redemption' and the Perushim," 73.

27. I. Bartal, "Mission Regulations and Their Place in the Reality of History" and Morgenstern's answer, "Historical Reality or Heartfelt Feelings in the Research of the 'Old Settlement,'" *Cathedra* 31 (Apr. 1984), 159–181.

28. Franz Kafka.

29. *Jewish Intelligence*, 1842, 166, 167.

30. G. L. Dawson Damer, *Diary of a Tour in Greece, Turkey, Egypt and the Holy-Land*, vol. 1, 318; M. Ish-Shalom, *Christian Travels in the Holy Land*, 528; Morgenstern, "Pekidim," 150, 205, 209–210.

31. *Jewish Intelligence*, 1843, 280; J. Wilson, *The Lands of the Bible Visited and Described*, vol. 2, 270.

32. Morgenstern, "Pekidim," 8.

33. R. T. Herford, *The Pharisees*, 191.

34. G. Kressel, *Rabbi Yohanan Alkali—R. Zvi Kalischer—Selected Writings*, 45; Morgenstern, "Pekidim," 206.

35. I. Howe, *World of Our Fathers*, 461.

36. D. Hopwood, *The Russian Presence in Syria and Palestine, 1843–1914*, 13.

37. Unless otherwise noted all quotations are from M. Vereté, "The Plan to Internationalize Jerusalem in the Years 1840–1841," 9–25.

38. N. N. Gelber, "The Palestine Question 1840–1842," 46.

39. L. Wolf, *Notes on the Diplomatic History of the Jewish Question*, 113, 105.

40. Hopwood, 13.

41. Hopwood, 33; A. Carmel, "Russian Activity in Palestine during the Late Ottoman Period," 94.

42. Gelber, "Palestine Question," 47–48.

43. Wolf, *Notes*, 105.

44. Eliav, *Eretz-Israel*, 48.

45. Wolf, *Notes*, 116, 117.

46. Hyamson, vol. 1, 33–34.

47. Ibid., vol. 1, 34–35, vol. 2, lxxiv.

48. Ibid., vol. 1, 37, 40.

49. Canning in A. Cunningham, "Stratford Canning and the Tanzimat," 26.

50. Lincoln, 335.

51. Tuchman, *Bible and Sword*, 129.

52. Hyamson, vol. 1, 46–47; Temperley, 444.

53. For the text of Churchill's Letter to Montefiore, see Wolf, *Notes*, 119–121.

54. Wolf, *Notes*, 123; M. Kedem, "Mid-Nineteenth-Century Anglican Eschatology on the Redemption of Israel," 55–72.

55. R. Horowitz, "The Idea of Independence of Jews in Eretz-Israel of Rabbi Zeharia Frankel in 1842," 5–26.

EPILOGUE

1. E. Voegelin, *Order and History, Israel and Revelation*, vol. 1, 132; I. Berlin, "Benjamin Disraeli, Karl Marx and the Search for Identity," in *Against the Current*, 253; D. H. Freundlich, *Peretz Smolenskin*, 57.

2. F. Braudel, *The Identity of France* (New York: 1989), vol. 1, 27.

3. C. Ritter, *The Comparative Geography of Palestine and the Sinaitic Peninsula*, vol. 3, 323; *Jewish Expositor*, 1822, 507; L. A. Frankl, *The Jews in the East*, vol. 2, 27; J. Nicolayson, *Journals, 1826–1842*, Nov. 14, 1840, 1072; A. M. Hyamson, *The British Consulate in Jerusalem in Relation to the Jews of Palestine*,

1838–1914, vol. 1, 6, 28; A. E. Bonar and R. M. M'Cheyne, *Narrative of a Mission of Inquiry to the Jews from the Church of Scotland in 1839*, 131, 148, 168.

4. B. Tuchman, *Practicing History*, 133.

5. M. Kosover, *Arabic Elements in Palestinian Yiddish*, 76.

6. H. J. Zimmels, *Ashkenazim and Sephardim*, 76.

7. Tuchman, *Practicing History*, 133; R. Hanina lived in the first century, Avot 3:2.

8. S. Laskov, "Zamenhof's Letter to the Biluim," *Zionism* 2 (Autumn 1980), 154.

9. John F. Kennedy speech.

10. B. Z. Dinur, "From the Archives of the Chief Rabbi Haim Abraham Gaugin," 91–92.

11. F. Rosen, *Oriental Memories* (London, 1930), 9.

BIBLIOGRAPHY

ABBREVIATIONS OF PUBLICATIONS

Cathedra	*Cathedra for the History of Eretz-Israel and Its Yishuv.* Jerusalem: Yad Izhak Ben-Zvi, 1976.
Chapters	*Chapters in the History of the Jewish Community in Jerusalem, Jerusalem in the Early Ottoman Period, Jerusalem in the Modern Period.* 4 vols. Jerusalem: Yad Izhak Ben-Zvi, 1973, 1976, 1979, 1981.
Missionary Herald	*Missionary Herald,* 1819–1840 (periodical of American Board of Commissioners for Foreign Missions).
Safed Volume	*Safed Volume, Studies and Texts of the History of the Jewish Community in Safed from the Fourteenth through the Nineteenth Centuries.* 2 vols. Vol. 2. Ed. I. Ben-Zvi and M. Benayahu. Jerusalem, 1963.
Shalem	*Shalem: Studies in the History of the Jews in Eretz-Israel.* 4 vols. Jerusalem: Yad Izhak Ben-Zvi, 1974, 1976, 1981, 1984.
Sinai	*Sinai, A Monthly for Torah and Judaic Studies.* Jerusalem: Mosad ha-Rav Kook.
Tarbiz	*Tarbiz, A Quarterly for Jewish Studies.* Jerusalem: Institute of Jewish Studies of the Hebrew University.
Vatiqin	*Vatiqin, Studies in the History of the Yishuv.* Ramat Gan: Bar-Ilan University, 1975.
Yad Rivlin	*Joseph J. Rivlin Memorial Volume.* Ed. H. Z. Hirschberg. Ramat Gan: n.p., 1964.
Zion	*Zion, A Quarterly for Research in Jewish History.* Jerusalem: Historical Society of Israel.

Abir, M. "The Claims of Safed Jewry after the Lootings of 1834." In *Safed Volume*, 267–274 (Hebrew).

———. "Local Leadership and Early Reforms in Palestine 1800–1834." In *Studies on Palestine during the Ottoman Period*, ed. M. Ma'oz, 284–310. Jerusalem, 1975.

Alfasi, Y. "Documents about the History of the Old Settlement." *Bar-Ilan Yearbook* 3 (1965), 216–224 (Hebrew).

Anderson, M. S. *The Eastern Question (1774–1923)*. London, 1966.

Anderson, R. *History of the Missions of the American Board of Commissioners for Foreign Missions to the Oriental Churches*. Vol. 1. Boston, 1873.

Avigdori, S. "The Abu Family in Safed." *Echo from the East* 2/2 (1944), issue of Dec. 24, 1943 (Hebrew).

Avisar, O. (ed.). *Book of Hebron*. Jerusalem, 1970 (Hebrew).

———. *Book of Tiberias*. Jerusalem, 1973 (Hebrew).

Avitsur, S. *Daily Life in Eretz-Israel in the Nineteenth Century*. Tel Aviv, 1972 (Hebrew).

———. "The Occupations of Safed Jewry: 1837–1948." In *Safed Volume*, 323–350 (Hebrew).

———. "The Population of Safed." *Nature and the Land* 7/2 (1964), 88–93 (Hebrew).

Avneri, A. L. *The Jewish Land Settlement and the Arab Claim of Dispossession (1878–1948)*. Tel Aviv, 1980 (Hebrew).

Bachi, R. *The Population of Israel*. Institute of Contemporary Jewry, Hebrew University Demographic Center, Jerusalem, 1977 (Hebrew).

Baeck, Y., and M. Sharon (eds.). *From Ancient Archives of P. B. Grayevsky: Documents and Sources*. Jerusalem, 1977.

Barber, N. *The Lords of the Golden Horn*. London, 1973.

Barnai, Y. "The Ashkenazi Community in Eretz-Israel, 1720–1777." In *Shalem*, vol. 2 (1976), 193–230 (Hebrew).

———. "Changes in Nineteenth-Century Jerusalem." *Sinai* 81 (1977), 151–155 (Hebrew).

———. *The Jews in Eretz-Israel in the Eighteenth Century*. Jerusalem, 1982 (Hebrew).

———. "The Leadership of the Jewish Community in Jerusalem in the Mid-Eighteenth Century." In *Shalem*, vol. 1 (1974), 271–316 (Hebrew).

———. "The 'Mughrabi' Community in Jerusalem in the Nineteenth Century." In *Chapters*, vol. 1 (1973), 129–140 (Hebrew).

———. "R. Eliezer Bergmann's Assistance to the Mughrabis in Jerusalem." In *Vatiqin*, 117–126 (Hebrew).

———. "The Regulations (Taqanot) of Jerusalem in the Eighteenth Century as a Source on the Society, Economy, and Daily Activities of the Jewish Community." In *Chapters*, vol. 3 (1979), 271–316 (Hebrew).

———. "The Status of the 'General Rabbinate' in Jerusalem in the Ottoman Period." *Cathedra* 13 (Oct. 1979), 47–70 (Hebrew).

———(ed.). *Hasidic Letters from Eretz-Israel, from the Second Part of the Eigh-*

teenth Century and the First Part of the Nineteenth Century. Jerusalem, 1980 (Hebrew).

Baron, S. "History of German Jews in Eretz-Israel." In *In Memory of David (Volume in the Name of David Yellin),* 116–128. Jerusalem, 1935 (Hebrew).

Bartal, I. "Eastern European Jewry and Eretz-Israel 1777–1881." *Cathedra* 16 (July 1980), 3–12 (Hebrew).

———. "The Immigration and Structure of the Ashkenazi Yishuv, 1777–1881." *Cathedra* 16 (July 1980), 3–12 (Hebrew).

———. "Messianic Expectations in the Context of Historical Reality." *Cathedra* 16 (Apr. 1984), 159–171 (Hebrew).

———. "Mission Regulations and Their Place in the Reality of History." *Cathedra* 31 (Apr. 1984), 159–171.

———. "Montefiore and Eretz-lsrael." *Cathedra* 33 (Oct. 1984), 149–160 (Hebrew).

———. "On the Beginnings of Jewish Settlement in Jaffa." In *Shalem,* vol. 3 (1981), 351–363 (Hebrew).

———. "Settlement Proposals during Montefiore's Second Visit to Eretz-Israel, 1839." In *Shalem,* vol. 2 (1976), 231–296 (Hebrew).

———. "Some Marginal Notes on the Memorandum of the Sefardi Kollel of Jerusalem, to Sir Moses Montefiore, 1885." *Zion,* 42/1–2 (1978), 97–118 (Hebrew).

———(ed.). *The History of Eretz-Israel, The Last Phase, Ottoman Rule 1799–1917.* Jerusalem, 1983 (Hebrew).

Bartlett, W. H. *Jerusalem Revisited.* London, 1855.

———. *Walks about the City and Environs of Jerusalem.* London, 1844.

Bashan, E. *Captivity and Ransom in Mediterranean Jewish Society (1391–1830).* Ramat Gan, 1980 (Hebrew).

Basili, K. M. *Memoirs from Lebanon 1839–1847.* Jerusalem, 1983 (Hebrew).

Ben-Arieh, Y. *A City Reflected in its Times, Jerusalem in the Nineteenth Century.* Vol. 1, *The Old City.* Vol. 2, *Emergence of the New City.* Jerusalem, 1977, 1979 (Hebrew).

———. "The Development of Twelve Major Settlements in Nineteenth-Century Palestine." *Cathedra* 19 (April 1981), 83–144 (Hebrew).

———. "The Growth of the Jewish Community of Jerusalem in the Nineteenth Century." In *Chapters,* vol. 1 (1973), 80–122 (Hebrew).

———. *Jerusalem in the Nineteenth Century.* Tel Aviv, 1980 (Hebrew).

———. "The Jewish Quarter in the Old City: Site, Growth and Expansion in the Nineteenth Century." In *Chapters,* vol. 1 (1973), 9–51 (Hebrew).

———. "The Jewish Settlement in Jerusalem and Eretz-Israel in the Nineteenth Century." In *Arts and Crafts in Nineteenth-Century Palestine,* ed. Y. Fisher, 9–12. Jerusalem, 1979 (Hebrew).

———. "Nineteenth-Century Western Travel Literature to Eretz-lsrael: A Historical Source and a Cultural Phenomenon." *Cathedra* 40 (July 1986), 159–188 (Hebrew).

———. "The Population of the Large Towns in Palestine during the First Eighty

Years of the Nineteenth Century according to Western Sources." In *Studies on Palestine during the Ottoman Period*, ed. M. Ma'oz, 49–69. Jerusalem, 1975.

————. *The Rediscovery of the Holy Land in the Nineteenth Century*. Jerusalem, 1970 (Hebrew).

Benayahu, M. "Document about Distributing Money in Eretz-Israel from Germany." In R. David Ayish (ed.), *Sura*, vol. 1, 103–155. Jerusalem, 1954 (Hebrew).

Ben-Gurion, D., and I. Ben-Zvi. *Eretz-Israel in the Past and in the Present*. New York, 1918 (Yiddish); Jerusalem, 1979 (Hebrew).

Ben-Zvi, I. *Eretz-Israel under Ottoman Rule: Four Centuries of History*. Jerusalem, 1962 (Hebrew).

————. "Events in Safed from the Lootings of 1834 to the Druze Attacks in 1838." In *Safed Volume*, 275–322 (Hebrew).

————. "Musta'rabs in Eretz-Israel." *Sinai* 30–31 (1939–1940), 379–386 (Hebrew).

————. "Opposition of the Venetian Kehilla to the Institution of the Shlihim." In *Studies and Sources*, ed. I. Ben-Zvi, 266–280. Jerusalem, 1969 (Hebrew).

————(ed.). *Studies and Sources*. Jerusalem, 1969 (Hebrew).

Bergmann, E., and G. Bergmann. *Yis'u Harim Shalom: Aliya and Travel Letters, Jerusalem 1834–1836*. Ed. A. Bartura. Jerusalem, 1969 (Hebrew).

Berlin, I. *Against the Current*. London, 1982.

Bird, I. *Bible Work in Bible Lands*. Philadelphia, 1872.

Blake, R. *Disraeli's Grand Tour—Benjamin Disraeli and the Holy Land, 1830–1831*. London, 1982.

Bliss, P. J. *The Development of Palestine Exploration*. London, 1906.

Bloch, M. *The Historian's Craft*. New York, 1953.

Blumberg, A. *A View from Jerusalem 1849–1858*. Cranbury, N.J., 1980.

Bonar, A. E., and R. M. M'Cheyne. *Narrative of a Mission of Inquiry to the Jews from the Church of Scotland in 1839*. Edinburgh, 1846.

Bond, A. *Memoir of the Rev. Pliny Fisk*. New York, 1973.

Bourne, Kenneth. *The Foreign Policy of Victorian England 1830–1902*. Oxford, 1970.

Bourrienne, F. *Memoirs of Napoleon Bonaparte*. London, 1904.

Bowring, J. *Report on Commercial Statistics of Syria*. New York, 1973.

Braude, B., and B. Lewis (eds.). *Christians and Jews in the Ottoman Empire—The Functioning of a Plural Society*. 2 vols. New York, 1982.

Braudel, Fernand. *The Mediterranean World in the Age of Philip II*. 2 vols. Translated by Siân Reynolds. New York, 1972–73.

Braver, A. "The First Use of the Capitulation Rights by the Jews in Eretz-Israel." *Zion* 5 (1940), 161–169 (Hebrew).

Browne, W. G. *Travels in Africa, Egypt and Syria*. London, 1806.

Buckingham, J. S. *Travels in Palestine*. London, 1821.

Burckhardt, J. L. *Travels in Syria and the Holy Land*. London, 1822.

Carmel, A. *The History of Haifa under Turkish Rule*. Jerusalem, 1977 (Hebrew).

————. "Russian Activity in Palestine during the Late Ottoman Period." In

Chapters, vol. 4 (1981), 81–116 (Hebrew).

Carne, J. *Syria, the Holy Land, Asia Minor, etc.* 3 vols. London, 1835.

Cassuto, D. "An Eighteenth-Century Italian-Jewish Traveler on the Structure of the Sephardic Synagogues in Old Jerusalem." *Cathedra* 24 (July 1982), 41–50 (Hebrew).

Chandler, D. G. *The Campaigns of Napoleon.* New York, 1966.

Chateaubriand, F. R. *Travels in Greece, Palestine, Egypt and Barbary during the Years 1806 and 1807.* London, 1811.

Chevallier, D. "Western Development and Eastern Crisis in the Mid-Nineteenth Century." In *Beginnings of Modernization in the Middle East*, ed. W. E. Polk and R. L. Chambers, 205–218. Chicago, 1968.

Cohen, A. "Arabic Documents on the Settlement of Debts of the Jewish Communities of Jerusalem and Hebron in the Eighteenth Century." In *Shalem*, vol. 1 (1974), 317–330 (Hebrew).

———. "Ottoman Rule and the Re-emergence of the Coast of Palestine." *Cathedra* 34 (Jan. 1985), 55–74 (Hebrew).

———. *Palestine in the Eighteenth Century.* Jerusalem, 1973.

———(ed.). *The History of Eretz-Israel under Mamluke and Ottoman Rule (1260–1804).* Jerusalem, 1981 (Hebrew).

Cohen, I. *The Zionist Movement.* New York, 1946.

Cohen, S. Y. "The Gaon of Vilna and His Disciples as Founders of the New Yishuv in Eretz Israel." In *Chapters*, vol. 1 (1973), 237–249 (Hebrew).

Cohen, T. *From Dream to Reality, Eretz-Israel in the Enlightenment Literature.* Ramat Gan, 1982 (Hebrew).

Conder, J. *The Modern Traveller.* London, 1849.

Cunningham, A. "Stratford Canning and the Tanzimat." In *Beginnings of Modernization in the Middle East*, ed. W. E. Polk and R. L. Chambers, 245–264. Chicago, 1968.

Curzon, A. *Visits to the Monasteries of the Levant.* London, 1849.

Dawson Damer, G. L. *Diary of a Tour in Greece, Turkey, Egypt and the Holy-Land.* 2 vols. London, 1841.

Dinur, B. Z. "From the Archives of the Chief Rabbi Haim Abraham Gaugin." *Zion* 1 (1926), 85–121 (Hebrew).

Dodwell, H. *The Founder of Modern Egypt, Muhammad Ali.* Cambridge, 1931.

Dubnow, S. *History of the Jews in Russia and Poland.* 3 vols. Philadelphia, 1916–1920.

Ducker, H. G. "The Tarniks." In *The Joshua Starr Memorial Volume*, 191–201. N.p., 1953.

Egerton, F. *Journal of a Tour in the Holy Land in 1840.* London, 1841.

Eliashar, E. "The Rabbi Yohanan Ben Zakkai Synagogues." *Chapters*, vol. 1 (1973), 61–79 (Hebrew).

Eliav, M. "The Austrian Consulate in Jerusalem and the Jewish Community." *Cathedra* 18 (Jan. 1981), 73–110 (Hebrew).

———. *Eretz-Israel and Its Yishuv in the Nineteenth Century (1777–1917).* Jerusalem, 1978 (Hebrew).

———. "Intercommunity Relations in the Jewish Community of Eretz-Israel in the Nineteenth Century." *Pe'amim* 11 (1982), 118–133 (Hebrew).

———. "The Jewish Community in Jerusalem in the Late Ottoman Period (1815–1914)." In *Chapters*, vol. 4 (1981), 132–173 (Hebrew).

———. *Love of Zion and Men of HOD: German Jewry and the Settlement of Eretz-Israel in the Nineteenth Century.* Tel Aviv, 1970 (Hebrew).

———. "Notes on the Development of the Old Yishuv in the Nineteenth Century." In *Chapters*, vol. 1 (1973), 44–60 (Hebrew).

Elimelech, A. *Chief Rabbis.* Jerusalem, 1970 (Hebrew).

Elliot, C. B. *Travels in the Three Great Empires of Austria, Russia, and Turkey.* London, 1938.

Erickson, E. *Young Martin Luther.* London, 1958.

Eriksen, E. O. *Holy Land Explorers.* Jerusalem, 1989.

———. "The Illness of Christopher Costigin—A Case of Heat Stroke." *Dublin Historical Record* 39/3 (June 1986), 82–85.

Field, J. *America and the Mediterranean World 1776–1882.* Princeton, 1969.

Finn, E. *Palestine Peasantry, Notes on Their Clans, Warfare, Religion and Laws.* London, 1923.

———. *Reminiscences.* London, 1929.

Finnie, H. *Pioneers East, The Early American Experience in the Middle East.* Cambridge, 1967.

Fisher, Y. "Art in Nineteenth-Century Palestine." In *Arts and Crafts in Nineteenth-Century Palestine*, ed. Y. Fisher, 88–109. Jerusalem, 1979 (Hebrew).

Fisk, G. *A Pastor's Memorial of Egypt . . . Jerusalem and Other Principal Localities of the Holy Land Visited in 1842.* London, 1843.

Fisk, P. *A Memoir of . . . Pliny Fisk, Late Missionary, to Palestine.* Edinburgh, 1828.

Forbin, L. N. P. A. *Travels in Greece, Turkey and the Holy Land, in 1817–1818.* London, n.d.

Frankl, L. A. *The Jews in the East.* 2 vols. London, 1859.

Freiden, I. "Bikur Holim Perushim in Jerusalem—From Society to Hospital." *Cathedra* 27 (Mar. 1983), 117–140 (Hebrew).

———. "The Hasidic-Sephardic Hospital in Jerusalem, 1844." *Cathedra* 37 (Sept. 1985), 177–183 (Hebrew).

Freundlich, D. H. *Peretz Smolenskin.* New York, 1965.

Friedman, P. "Letters from Eretz-Israel from the Years 1814–1822." *Zion* 3 (1934), 267–274 (Hebrew).

Frumkin, A. L. *The History of the Scholars of Jerusalem.* 3 vols. Vol. 3. Jerusalem, 1929 (Hebrew).

Gaon, M. D. *Oriental Jews in Eretz-Israel, Past and Present.* 2 vols. Vol. 1. Jerusalem, 1928 (Hebrew).

Garrett, C. *Respectable Folly: Millenarians and the French Revolution in France and England.* Baltimore, 1976.

Gat, B. *The Jewish Community in Eretz-Israel (1840–1881).* Jerusalem, 1963 (Hebrew).

Gelber, N. N. "Immigration of Jews from Bohemia and Galicia to Eretz-Israel 1811–1869." *Jerusalem* (1953), 143–151 (Hebrew).

———. "Moshe Sachs." *Sinai* 1 (1937), 568–583 (Hebrew).

———. "The Palestine Question, 1840–1842." *Zion* 4 (1930), 44–46, and appendices, 1–41 (Hebrew).

Géramb, M. J. *A Pilgrimage to Palestine, Egypt and Syria.* 2 vols. Vol. 1. London, 1840.

Gibb, H. R., and H. Bowen. *Islamic Society and the West.* 2 vols. Oxford, 1950.

Gichon, M. *Carta's Atlas of Palestine from Beitar to Tel Chai.* Jerusalem, 1974 (Hebrew).

———. "History of the Gaza Strip." *Cathedra* 6 (Dec. 1977), 133–165 (Hebrew).

Gidney, W. T. *The History of the London Society for the Propagation of Christianity through the Jews from 1809 to 1908.* London, 1908.

Goodman, P. *Moses Montefiore.* Philadelphia, 1925.

Grabill, L. *Protestant Diplomacy and the Near East Missionary Influence on American Policy 1816–1927.* Minneapolis, 1971.

Grayevsky, P. *From Ancient Archives, Documents and Sources,* ed. M. Sharon and Y. Baeck. Jerusalem, 1977 (Hebrew).

———. *From the Hidden Treasures of Jerusalem.* 24 vols. Jerusalem, 1927–1935 (Hebrew).

Guedella, P. *Napoleon and Palestine.* London, 1925.

Haberman, A. M. "A Compromise between two Emissaries from Safed in Amsterdam." In *Safed Volume,* 255–266 (Hebrew).

Halevy, S. *The First Hebrew Books Printed in Jerusalem in the Second Half of the Nineteenth Century (1841–1890).* Jerusalem, 1975 (Hebrew).

———. "R. Israel of Shklov." *Sinai* 5 (1939), 30–37 (Hebrew).

Halprin, B. *The Idea of the Jewish State.* Cambridge, Mass., 1961.

Hanauer, J. E. *Walks in and around Jerusalem.* London, 1926.

Hebrew Encyclopedia. Jerusalem, 1949–1985.

Heilprin, I. *The First Aliyot of the Hasidim.* Jerusalem, 1947 (Hebrew).

Herford, R. T. *The Pharisees.* Boston, 1962.

Herold, S. C. *Bonaparte in Egypt.* London, 1962.

Hirschberg, H. Z. "The Oriental Jewish Communities." In *Religion in the Middle East,* ed. A. J. Arberry, 196–212. Cambridge, Eng., 1969.

———. "The Turning-Point in the History of Jerusalem in the Nineteenth Century." In *Yad Rivlin,* 78–107 (Hebrew).

Hisdai, Y. "Early Settlement of 'Hasidim' and of 'Mithnaggedim' in Palestine— Immigration of 'Mitzva' and of 'Mission.'" In *Shalem,* vol. 4 (1984), 231–269 (Hebrew).

Hodder, E. *The Life and Work of the Seventh Earl of Shaftesbury.* 2 vols. London, 1887.

Hoexter, M. "The Role of the Qays and Yaman Faction in Local Political Divisions: Jabal Nablus Compared with the Judean Hills in the First Half of the Nineteenth Century." *Asian and African Studies* 9 (1973), 251.

Hofman, Y. "The Administration of Syria and Palestine under Egyptian Rule

(1831–1840)." In *Studies on Palestine during the Ottoman Period*, ed. M. Ma'oz, 311–333. Jerusalem, 1975.

Hopwood, D. *The Russian Presence in Syria and Palestine, 1843–1914: Church and Politics in the Near East.* Oxford, 1969.

Horewitz, R. "The Idea of Independence of Jews in Eretz Israel of Rabbi Zeharia Frankel in 1842." *Directions* (Feb. 1980), 5–26 (Hebrew).

Horn, S. E. "The Jerusalem Bishopric." Doctoral thesis, University of Minnesota, 1978.

Howe, I. *World of Our Fathers.* New York, 1976.

Huizinga, J. *The Waning of the Middle Ages: A Study of the Forms of Life, Thought and Art in France and the Netherlands in the Fourteenth and Fifteenth Centuries.* London, 1976.

Hyamson, A. M. *The British Consulate in Jerusalem in Relation to the Jews of Palestine, 1838–1914.* 2 vols. London, 1939, 1941.

Ilan, T. "The First Hebrew Translation of Lady Judith Montefiore's Notes from a Private Journal of a Visit to Egypt and Palestine." In *Shalem*, vol. 3 (1981), 363–366 (Hebrew).

———. "Lady Stanhope and the First Archaeological Excavation." In *Book of Vilnai: Essays on the History, Archaeology, and Lore of the Holy Land*, ed. E. Schiller, vol. 1, 401–407. 2 vols. Jerusalem, 1984 (Hebrew).

Irby, C. L., and L. Mangles. *Travels through Nubia, Palestine and Syria in 1817 and 1818.* London, 1823.

Ish-Shalom, M. *Christian Travels in the Holy Land, Descriptions and Sources on the History of the Jews in Palestine.* Tel Aviv, 1965 (Hebrew).

Israel of Shaklov. *The Corners of the Field.* Jerusalem, 1968 (Hebrew).

Issawi, C. (ed.). *The Economic History of the Middle East, 1800–1914: A Book of Readings.* Chicago, 1966.

Johns, J. W. *The Anglican Cathedral Church of St. James, Mount Zion.* Jerusalem, London, 1844.

de la Jonquière, C. *L'Expédition en Egypte 1798–1801.* 5 vols. Paris, 1899–1907.

Jowett, W. *Christian Researches in the Holy Land in 1823 and 1824.* London, 1826.

———. *Christian Researches in the Mediterranean from 1815 to 1820.* London, 1824.

Kalisher, Z. H. *Drishat Zion.* Introduction by I. Klausner, 209–222. Jerusalem, 1974 (Hebrew).

Kaniel, Y. "Cultural and Religious Cooperation between the Ashkenazim and the Sephardim in the Nineteenth Century in Jerusalem." In *Chapters*, vol. 1 (1973), 289–300 (Hebrew).

———. "Organizational and Economic Contentions between Communities in Jerusalem in the Nineteenth Century." In *Chapters*, vol. 2 (1976), 97–126 (Hebrew).

———. "The Relationship of the Sephardim and Ashkenazim in the Old Yishuv in Jerusalem." Master's thesis, Bar-Ilan University, 1970 (Hebrew).

———. "Social Relations between Sephardim and Ashkenazim in the . . . Nineteenth Century." *Vatiqin* (1975), 47–65 (Hebrew).

Karagila, Z. "The Community of Perushim in Eretz-Israel during the 1830s." *Zion* 4 (1981), 306–330 (Hebrew).

——. *The Jewish Community in Palestine during the Egyptian Rule (1831–1840), Social and Economic Patterns.* Tel Aviv, 1990.

——. "The Leadership of Kollel Perushim in Jerusalem, 1839–1843." *Cathedra* 37 (Sept. 1985), 33–48 (Hebrew).

——. "S. Shmuel Ben R. Israel Peretz Heller Describes the Sack of Safed, 1834." *Cathedra* 27 (Mar. 1983), 109–116 (Hebrew).

——. "Source Material on Haluka in Eretz-Israel." *Cathedra* 20 (July 1981), 56–76 (Hebrew).

——. "The Struggle over the Distribution of Monies from England in Palestine from 1831 to 1835." In *Shalem*, vol. 4 (1984), 459–470 (Hebrew).

Kark, R. "Agricultural Land and Plans for Its Cultivation by Jews during Montefiore's Second Visit to Eretz Israel, 1839." *Cathedra* 33 (Oct. 1984), 57–92 (Hebrew).

——. "Jaffa—The Social and Cultural Center of the New Jewish Settlement in Palestine." *Jerusalem Cathedra* 3 (1983), 212–235.

——. *Jaffa 1799–1917.* Jerusalem, 1985 (Hebrew).

——. "The Jewish Community of Jaffa in the Late Ottoman Period." *Cathedra* 16 (July 1980), 13–24 (Hebrew).

Karmon, I. "Changes in the Urban Geography of Hebron during the Nineteenth Century." In *Studies on Palestine during the Ottoman Period*, ed. M. Ma'oz, 70–86. Jerusalem, 1975.

Katsh, A. I. "Three Emissaries from Safed in Italy." In *Safed Volume*, 229–254 (Hebrew).

Katz, Y. "1840 as a 'Year of Redemption' and the Perushim." *Cathedra* 24 (July 1982), 73–74 (Hebrew).

Katzburg, N. "From the First Letters of the English Vice Consul in Jerusalem." In *Vatiqin*, ix–xxx.

Katz-Steiman, Ch. "The Immigration of the Hasidim from Its Start until the First Quarter of the Nineteenth Century." Ph.D. thesis, Bar-Ilan University, 1981 (Hebrew).

Kedem, M. "Mid-Nineteenth-Century Anglican Eschatology on the Redemption of Israel." *Cathedra* 19 (Apr. 1981), 55–72 (Hebrew).

Kellner, J. *For Zion's Sake.* Jerusalem, 1976 (Hebrew).

Khalaf, S. "Communal Conflict in Nineteenth Century Lebanon." In *Christians and Jews in the Ottoman Empire*, ed. B. Braude and B. Lewis, 107–134. New York, 1982.

Kinglake, A. W. *"Eothen" or Traces of Travel.* New York, 1845.

Kinross, D. *The Ottoman Centuries—The Rise and Fall of the Turkish Empire.* New York, 1977.

Klausner, I. *The Messianic Idea in Israel.* London, 1956.

——. "R. Yehuda Bibas." In *The Ways of Zion*, 110–114. Jerusalem, 1978 (Hebrew).

——(ed.). *Drishat Zion* by Z. H. Kalischer. Jerusalem, 1974 (Hebrew).

Kluger, B. (ed.). *From the Source—The Old Yishuv on Bulletin Boards*. Jerusalem, 1978 (Hebrew).

Kobler, F. "Napoleon and the Restoration of the Jews to Palestine, Discovery of An Historic Document." *New Judea* (London) 16 (Sept. 1940).

——. *The Vision Was There*. London, 1956.

Kosover, M. *Arabic Elements in Palestinian Yiddish—The Old Ashkenazic Jewish Community in Palestine, Its History and Its Language*. Jerusalem, 1966.

Kovac, Z. "The Immigration from Eastern Europe to Eretz-Israel in the Mid-Nineteenth Century." *Cathedra* 9 (Oct. 1978), 193–204 (Hebrew).

Kressel, G. *Planters of Hope, From Jerusalem to Petah-Tiqva*. Jerusalem, 1976 (Hebrew).

——(ed.). *Rabbi Yohanan Alkali—R. Zvi Kalischer—Selected Writings*. Tel Aviv, 1945 (Hebrew).

Lamartine, A. *Visit to the Holy Land or Recollections of the East*. 3 vols. Vol. 1. London, n.d.

Laqueur, W. *A History of Zionism*. London, 1972.

Lestchinsky, N. *Jewish Migration for the Past Hundred Years*. New York, 1944.

Lewis, B. *The Arabs in History*. New York, 1967.

——. *The Emergence of Modern Turkey*. London, 1961.

——. *The Middle East and the West*. London, 1964.

Lewis, B., and B. Braude. *Christians and Jews in the Ottoman Empire: The Functioning of a Plural Society*. 2 vols. New York, 1982.

Lieber, S. "The Development of the Jewish Population of Safed, 1800–1839." *Cathedra* 46 (Dec. 1987), 13–44 (Hebrew).

——. "The Purchase of Land for 'Christ Church' by John Nicolayson." *Cathedra* 38 (Dec. 1985), 201–203 (Hebrew).

Lincoln, W. B. *Nicholas I, Emperor and Autocrat of All the Russias*. Bloomington, Ind., 1978.

Lipman, V. D. *Sir Moses Montefiore—A Symposium*. Oxford, 1982.

London Society for Promoting Christianity amongst the Jews. *Annual Reports*, 1825–1901.

——. *Jewish Expositor*, 1816–1830.

——. *Jewish Intelligence*, 1835–1866.

——. *Monthly Intelligence*, 1830–1835.

Lunz, A. M. *Jerusalem Yearbook for the Diffusion of an Accurate Knowledge of Ancient and Modern Palestine*. 13 vols. 1 (1882); 2 (1887); 3 (1889); 4 (1892); 5 (1898–1901); 6 (1902–1904); 7 (1907); 8 (1909); 9 (1911); 10 (1914); 11–12 (1917); 13 (1919) (Hebrew).

——. *Jerusalem Yearbook for the Diffusion of an Accurate Knowledge of Ancient and Modern Palestine* (1881). Jerusalem, 1882.

——. *Pathways of Zion and Jerusalem*. Selected and ed. G. Kressel. Jerusalem, 1970 (Hebrew).

Macalister, R. A. S. "Browne's Travels in Palestine 1797." *Palestine Exploration Fund Quarterly* (1906), 133–142.

McNeill, W. H. *Plagues and Peoples*. New York, 1976.

Madden, R. R. *Travels in Turkey, Egypt, Nubia and Palestine in 1824, 1825, 1826 and 1827.* 2 vols. Vol. 2. London, 1829.

Mahler, R. *A History of Modern Jewry, 1780–1815.* New York, 1971.

Malachi, A. R. *Chapters in the History of the Old Yishuv.* Tel Aviv, 1971 (Hebrew).

Manuel, F. E. *The Realities of American-Palestine Relations.* Washington, D.C., 1949.

Ma'oz, M. "Jerusalem in the Last Hundred Years of Turkish Ottoman Rule." In *Chapters,* vol. 1 (1973), 260–272 (Hebrew).

———. "Nineteenth-Century Jerusalem: Political and Social Developments." In *Chapters,* vol. 4 (1981), 66–80 (Hebrew).

———. *Ottoman Reform in Syria and Palestine: The Impact of the Tanzimat on Politics and Society.* Oxford, 1968.

———(ed.). *Studies on Palestine during the Ottoman Period.* Jerusalem, 1975.

Margalit, M. "Some Aspects of the Cultural Landscape of Palestine during the First Half of the Nineteenth Century." *Israel Exploration Journal* 13 (1963), 208–223.

Meisel, J. "The Jewish Settlement in Eretz-Israel in 1839." In *Safed Volume,* 425–479 (Hebrew).

Menahem Mendel of Kamenets. *Chronicles of the Times.* Ed. G. Kressel. Jerusalem, 1956 (Hebrew).

Michman, N. "The Emergence of Pekidim and Amarcalim of Amsterdam." *Cathedra* 27 (Mar. 1983), 69–84 (Hebrew).

Montefiore, (Lady) Judith. *Notes from a Private Journal of a Visit to Egypt and Palestine (1839).* London, 1844.

———. *Private Journal of a Visit to Egypt and Palestine (1827).* Jerusalem, 1975 (first published in London, 1836; only 128–234 reproduced).

Montefiore, M. *Diary, and Letters from Voyages: Palestine in the 1830's.* Jerusalem, 1974.

Montefiore, (Sir) M. and Lady J. Montefiore. *Diaries of Sir Moses and Lady Montefiore.* Ed. L. Loewe. Chicago, 1890.

Morgenstern, A. "The Construction of the Courtyard of 'The Hurva of R. Yehuda the Hasid' in Jerusalem." In *Shalem,* vol. 4 (1984), 271–305 (Hebrew).

———. "The Correspondence of Pekidim and Amarcalim as a Source for the History of Eretz-Israel." *Cathedra* 27 (Mar. 1983), 85–108 (Hebrew).

———. "The Correspondence of Pekidim and Amarcalim of Amsterdam as a Source for the History of Eretz Israel." In *Dutch Jewish History,* ed. J. Michman and T. Levie, 433–463. Jerusalem, 1984.

———. "The First Jewish Hospital in Jerusalem." *Cathedra* 33 (Oct. 1984), 107–124 (Hebrew).

———. "Historical Reality or Wishful Thinking in Research of the Old Yishuv." *Cathedra* 31 (Apr. 1984), 172–181 (Hebrew).

———. "Messianic Concepts and Settlement in the Land of Israel." In *Vision and Conflict in the Holy Land,* ed. J. Cohen, 141–162, 182–189. Jerusalem, 1985.

———. "Messianic Expectations with the Approach of the Year 1840." In *Messianism and Eschatology,* ed. Z. Barras, 343–369. Jerusalem, 1983 (Hebrew).

———. *Messianism and the Settlement of Eretz-Israel in the First Half of the*

Nineteenth Century. Jerusalem, 1985 (Hebrew).

——. "The Organizational Unity of the Perushim Kollel in Eretz-Israel." *Zion* 47/3 (1982), 293–310 (Hebrew).

——. "The Pekidim and Amarcalim of Amsterdam and the Jewish Community in Palestine—1810–1840." Ph.D. thesis, Hebrew University, 1981 (Hebrew).

Morton, D. O. *Memoir of Rev. Levi Parsons, Late Missionary to Palestine.* Poultney, Vt., 1824.

Nicolayson, J. *Journals, 1826–1842* (photostatic copy in Jerusalem City Archives, pagination as in Jerusalem City Archives).

Nir, Y. "The Beginnings of Photography in the Holy Land." *Cathedra* 38 (Dec. 1985), 67–80 (Hebrew).

——. *The Bible and the Image: The History of Photography in the Holy Land, 1839–1899.* Philadelphia, 1985.

Olin, S. *Travels in Egypt . . . and the Holy-Land.* 2 vols. New York, 1843.

Omer, M. *Turner and the Bible.* Jerusalem, 1979.

Pach, S. Collection of Letters in the Manuscript Department of the National Library in Jerusalem, 4/468 (Hebrew).

Palmer, H. P. *Joseph Wolff—His Romantic Life and Travels.* London, 1935.

Parfitt, T. *The Jews in Palestine 1800–1882.* Woodbridge, 1987.

Parry, V. J., et al. *A History of the Ottoman Empire to 1730* (chapters from the Cambridge History of Islam and the New Cambridge Modern History). Cambridge, 1976.

Paxton, J. D. *Letters from Palestine . . .* London, 1839.

PEKAM. *Letters of the Pekidim and Amarcalim of Amsterdam.* Vol. 1, 1826–1827, ed. J. J. and B. Rivlin. Jerusalem, 1965 (Hebrew). Vol. 2, 1828, ed. J. J. and B. Rivlin. Jerusalem, 1970 (Hebrew). Vol. 3, 1828–1829, ed. B. Rivlin; introduction by I. Bartal. Jerusalem, 1978 (Hebrew).

Philipp, T. "The Farhi Family and the Changing Position of the Jews in Syria and Palestine, 1750–1860." *Cathedra* 34 (Jan. 1985), 97–114 (Hebrew).

Polk, W. E., and R. L. Chambers (eds.). *Beginnings of Modernization in the Middle East.* Chicago, 1968.

Popkin, J. D. "Zionism and the Enlightenment: The Letter of a Jew to His Brethren." *Jewish Social Sciences* (Spring 1981), 113–120.

Porter, J. L. *Jerusalem, Bethany and Bethlehem.* London, 1886.

Ridley, J. *Lord Palmerston.* London, 1972.

Ritter, C. *The Comparative Geography of Palestine and the Sinaitic Peninsula.* Trans. and adapted by W. L. Gage. Edinburgh, 1866.

Rivkind, I. "The Perished of Safed in the Earthquake of 5597 (1837)." *Palestine Annual* 2–3 (1926), 100–109 (Hebrew).

——. "Separate Pages (Documents on the History of the Jewish Settlement in Palestine in the Eighteenth and Nineteenth Centuries." In *Yerushalayim (Collection of Papers in Memory of Abraham Moses Lunz),* 111–178. Jerusalem, 1929. Also in *Zion* 5 (1933), 148–163 (Hebrew).

Rivlin, A. "Perushim Regulations about the Haluka from 1823." *Zion* 2 (1927), 150–170 (Hebrew).

Rivlin, B. "The Mission of Shlomo Zalman Shapira from Jerusalem to Amsterdam during 1825–1829. In *Yad Rivlin*, 108–150 (Hebrew).

Rivlin, E. "The Enactments concerning Legacies in Jerusalem and Palestine." In *Memorial, Part V: Palestine*, ed. Y. L. Ha Cohen Fishman (Maimon), 558–619. Jerusalem, 1937 (Hebrew).

———. "Letter from Hillel Rivlin to His Father-in-Law, Shmaryahu Luria." *Zion* 5, 141–147 (Hebrew).

Rivlin, H. A. B. *The Agricultural Policy of Muhammad Ali in Egypt*. Cambridge, Mass., 1961.

Rivlin, T. H. *The Vision of Zion, Shklov to Jerusalem*. Tel Aviv, 1947 (Hebrew).

Rivlin, Y. Y. "The 'GRA' and His Students in the Settlement of Eretz-Israel." In *The Book of the GRA*, ed. Y. L. Ha Cohen Maimon, vol. 2, part 4, 111–162. Jerusalem, 1954 (Hebrew).

Roberts, D. *The Holy Land*. 5 vols. Tel Aviv, 1982 (reproduction).

Robinson, E. *Biblical Researches in Palestine, Mount Sinai and Arabia Petrea in 1838*. 3 vols. London, 1841.

Robinson, G. *Travels in Palestine and Syria*. 2 vols. London, 1837.

Röhricht, R. *Bibliotheca Geographica Palestinae, von 333 bis 1878*. Berlin, 1890.

Rothschild, M. M. *The Haluka*. Jerusalem, 1969 (Hebrew).

Rustrum, A. J. *The Royal Archives of Egypt and the Disturbance in Palestine 1834*. Beirut, 1938.

———. *The Royal Archives of Egypt and the Origins of the Egyptian Expedition to Syria 1831–1841*. Beirut, 1936.

Samuel, M. *Harvest in the Desert*. Philadelphia, 1944.

Sandeen, E. R. *The Roots of Fundamentalism*. Chicago, 1970.

Schiller, E. *The First Photographs of Jerusalem: The Old City*. Jerusalem, 1978.

Schmelz, M. O. "Some Demographic Peculiarities of the Jews of Jerusalem in the Nineteenth Century." In *Studies on Palestine during the Ottoman Period*, ed. M. Ma'oz, 119–142. Jerusalem, 1975.

Scholem, G. *Major Trends in Jewish Mysticism*. New York, 1946.

Schur, N. "The Death of Haim Farhi as Reflected in Travelers' Reports." *Cathedra* 39 (Apr. 1986), 179–190 (Hebrew).

———. *The History of Safed*. Tel Aviv, 1983 (Hebrew).

———. *Jerusalem in Pilgrims' Accounts—Thematic Bibliography*. Jerusalem, 1980.

———. *Napoleon's Expedition to Eretz-Israel*. Tel Aviv, 1984 (Hebrew).

———. "The Numerical Relationship between the Number of Households and the Total Population in the Cities of Eretz-Israel during the Ottoman Period." *Cathedra* 17 (Oct. 1980), 102–106 (Hebrew).

Schwake, N. *Studien zur Geschichte des Krankenhauswessen . . . Des 19 bis zum Beginn des 20. Jahrhunderts*. Herzogenrath, 1983.

Schwartz, J. *The Produce of the Land*. Jerusalem, 1845; 3rd ed., Jerusalem, 1900 (Hebrew). English translation by Isaac Leeser: *Descriptive Geography and Brief Historical Sketch of Palestine*. Philadelphia, 1850.

Schwarzfuchs, S. "The Jews of Algeria in Northern Eretz-Israel and the French Protection." In *Shalem*, vol. 3 (1981), 333–350 (Hebrew).

Seetzen, U. J. *Reisen durch Syrien, Palästina, Phönicien . . .* 4 vols. Berlin, 1854–1859.

Shamir, S. "The Beginning of Modern Times in the History of Palestine." *Cathedra* 40 (July 1986), 138–158 (Hebrew).

Shapira, M. "The Habad Hasidic Community in Hebron, Its History and Image, in the Years 1820–1929." In *Vatiqin*, 67–116 (Hebrew).

Sharon, M., and Y. Baeck (eds.). *From Ancient Archives of P. B. Grayevsky: Documents and Sources.* Jerusalem, 1977.

Shaw, S. J., and E. K. Shaw. *History of the Ottoman Empire and Modern Turkey,* 2 vols. London, 1976.

Shohat, A. "The Jews in Jerusalem in the Eighteenth Century." *Cathedra* 13 (Oct. 1979), 3–46 (Hebrew).

———. "Three Eighteenth-Century Letters on Eretz-Israel." In *Shalem* 1 (1974), 235–256 (Hebrew).

Silberman, N. A. *Digging for God and Country: Exploration, Archeology, and the Secret Struggle for the Holy Land, 1799–1917.* New York, 1982.

Sim, K. *Desert Traveller—The Life of Jean Louis Burckhardt.* London, 1969.

Simon, R. "The Struggle over the Christian Holy Places during the Ottoman Period." In *Vision and Conflict in the Holy Land,* ed. Richard I. Cohen. Jerusalem, 1985. Also in *Cathedra* 17 (Oct. 1980), 107–126 (Hebrew).

Sir Moses Montefiore: A Life in the Service of Jewry. Jerusalem, 1965.

Smith, C. G. "The Geography and Natural Resources of Palestine as Seen by British Writers in the Nineteenth and Early Twentieth Century." In *Studies on Palestine during the Ottoman Period,* ed. M. Ma'oz, 87–102. Jerusalem, 1975.

Smith, G. A. *The Historical Geography of the Holy Land.* Jerusalem, 1983.

Sokolow, N. *History of Zionism.* 2 vols. London, 1919.

Solomon, M. *Three Generations in the Yishuv, 1812–1913.* Jerusalem, 1951 (Hebrew).

Spyridon, S. N. "Annals of Palestine 1821–1841." *Journal of Palestine Oriental Society* 18/1–2 (Jerusalem, 1938), 63–152.

Stampfer, S. "The Collection Box—The Social Role of Eretz-Israel Charity Funds." *Cathedra* 21 (Oct. 1981), 89–102 (Hebrew).

Stanislawski, M. F. *The Transformation of Jewish Society in Russia 1825–1855.* Cambridge, Mass., 1979.

Stempler, S. (ed.). *The History of the Yishuv, Landmarks before Statehood.* Tel Aviv, 1983 (Hebrew).

Stephens, J. L. *Incidents of Travel in Egypt, Arabia Petraea and the Holy Land.* New York, 1837.

Stern, S. "The First Jewish Hospital in Jerusalem—An Addendum." *Cathedra* 37 (Sept. 1985), 184–188 (Hebrew).

Stock, D. "Moses Sachs." *Sinai* 2 (1938), 331–333.

Stoler, J. "The Semiotics of Food in the Bible." In *Food and Drink, Selections from the Annales: Economies, Sociétés, Civilisations,* vol 5, ed. Robert Forster and Orest Ranum, trans. Elborg Forster and Patricia M. Ranum, 126–138. 5 vols. Baltimore, 1978.

Stone, L. *The Family, Sex and Marriage in England.* New York, 1979.

Temperley, H. *England and the Near East: The Crimea.* London, 1936.

Tennenbaum, M. "The British Consulate in Jerusalem, 1838–1890." *Cathedra* 5 (Oct. 1977), 83–108 (Hebrew).

Thomson, W. "Journal of a Visit to Safed and Tiberias." In E. Robinson, *Biblical Researches in Palestine, Mount Sinai and Arabia Petrea in 1838,* vol. 3, 471–475. London, 1841.

———. *The Land and the Book: Southern Palestine and Jerusalem, Central Palestine and Phoenicia.* 2 vols. New York, 1876.

Tibawi, A. L. *American Interests in Syria 1800–1901.* Oxford, 1967.

———. *British Interests in Palestine 1800–1901.* Oxford, 1961.

———. *A Modern History of Syria including Lebanon and Palestine.* Edinburgh, 1969.

Toledano, M. *Archives of R. Toledano.* Jerusalem, 1960 (Hebrew).

Tuchman, B. *Bible and Sword: England and Palestine from the Bronze Age to Balfour.* New York, 1956.

———. *Practicing History, Selected Essays.* New York, 1981.

Turner, W. *Journal of a Tour in the Levant.* 3 vols. London, 1820.

Vered, M., and H. L. Striem. *The Safed Earthquake of 1.1.1837.* Israel Atomic Energy Commission, 1976.

Vereté, M. "The Restoration of the Jews in English Protestant Thought 1790–1840." *Middle Eastern Studies* 8 (1972), 3–50.

———. "Why Was a British Consulate Established in Jerusalem?" *English Historical Review* 85 (1970) 316–345.

Voegelin, E. *Order and History, Israel and Revelation.* Baton Rouge, 1958.

Volney, C. F. C. *Travels through Syria and Egypt in the Years 1783, 1784 and 1785,* 2 vols. London, 1787.

Wallenstein, M. "An Insight into the Sefardi Community of Jerusalem in 1855" (Gaster MS 975). *Zion* 42 (1978), 75–96 (Hebrew).

Watson, C. "Bonaparte's Expedition to Palestine in 1799." *Palestine Exploration Fund Quarterly* (1917), 17–55.

Weinryb, B. *The Jews of Poland—A Social and Economic History of the Jewish Community in Poland from 1100 to 1800.* Philadelphia, 1972.

———. "Problems of Researching the History of the Jews in Eretz-Israel." *Zion* 2 (1937), 189–215; *Zion* 3 (1938), 58–83 (Hebrew).

Weinstein, M. "The Religious and Social Life of Jerusalem in the Eighteenth Century." In *Chapters,* vol. 1 (1973), 178–188 (Hebrew).

Werfel, I. "The History of the Ashkenazi Community in Eretz-Israel." *Sinai* 5 (1939), 69–117 (Hebrew).

Wilson, J. *The Lands of the Bible Visited and Described . . .* 2 vols. London, 1847.

Wittman, W. *Travels in Turkey, Asia Minor and across the Desert into Egypt, during the Years 1799, 1800 and 1801 . . .* London, 1803.

Wolf, L. *Notes on the Diplomatic History of the Jewish Question.* London, 1919, esp. 114–119.

———. "The Queen's Journey 1837–1897." In *Essays in Jewish History,* ed. Cecil Roth.

———. *Sir Moses Montefiore, A Centennial Biography.* London, 1884.

Wolff, J. *Missionary Journal and Memoirs of the Rev. Joseph Wolff, Missionary to the Jews, written by himself*, rev. and ed. John Bayford. London, 1921.

Yaari, A. "The Earthquake in Safed in 1759." *Sinai* 28 (1951), 349–363 (Hebrew).

———. *Eretz-Israel Emissaries*. Jerusalem, 1951 (Hebrew).

———. "Letter from Safed in 1835." *Sinai* 28/11–12 (1951), 345–358 (Hebrew).

———. *Letters from the Land of Israel*. Ramat Gan, 1971 (Hebrew).

———. *Memoirs of Eretz-Israel*. 2nd ed., Ramat Gan, 1974 (Hebrew). English translation: *The Godly Heritage*. Jerusalem, 1958.

———. "The Mission of R. Israel of Shklov." *Sinai* 5 (1939), 52–65 (Hebrew).

———. "The Suffering of Ashkenazi Jews in Jerusalem at the Beginning of the Nineteenth Century." *Sinai* 5 (1939–1940), 270–278 (Hebrew).

———. *Travels in Eretz-Israel*. Tel Aviv, 1946 (Hebrew).

———. "The Travels of David Beit Hillel in Eretz-Israel." *Sinai* 4 (1939), 24–31.

Yardeni-Agmon, G. "John Gawler and His 1874 Settlement Plan in Eretz Israel." *Zionism* 1 (1970), 84–120.

Yellin, Y. *Memoirs of a Native of Jerusalem, 1830–1918*. Jerusalem, 1928 (Hebrew).

Zahavi, Y. *From the Hatam Sofer to Herzl*. Jerusalem, 1972 (Hebrew).

Zeldin. T. *France 1848–1945—Love and Ambition*. Oxford, 1979.

Zimmels, H. J. *Ashkenazim and Sephardim*. London, 1958.

Index

Abdullah Pasha, 133–39, 181, 203, 205
Abdul Mejid, Sultan, 368, 370–71
Aberdeen, Lord (George Hamilton-
  Gordon), 384
Aboo, Samuel, 345, 348–49
Abraham, R. (Kolisk), 37, 46, 50, 54,
  131
Abu-Ghosh family, 25, 179, 369,
  425n.16
Abulafia, R. Isaac, 80
Abulafia, Yedidya, 301
Acre, 8, 10, 11, 13, 359, 368
Age, distribution of population, 337–38,
  450n.17
Agriculture, in Palestine
  Egyptian occupation, 210
  Hasidic immigration, 40
  Montefiore census of 1839–1840,
    341–42
  Montefiore's plan, 335–36, 346–49,
    350, 352–54, 359, 363–64, 365–66

Perushim settlement in Safed,
    72–73, 453n.61
  Sachs's plan, 226, 243, 430n.10
  village life in nineteenth century,
    25–26
Alexander I, Czar, 57
Algazi, R. Yom Tov, 12, 100
Algeria, 148, 149, 222
Ali, Mehemet
  aid to Pasha Abdullah, 134
  British foreign policy in Ottoman
    Empire, 448–49n.27
  conflict with Mahmud II over
    agreement of 1833, 342
  deposed as ruler of Syria and Egypt,
    368
  Egyptian occupation of Palestine,
    202–3, 205–6, 209, 210–11, 367,
    372
  meeting with Montefiore, 361–62
  missionaries and tolerant religious

policies, 293–94
policies and travelers to Holy Land, 275
Alroy (Disraeli), 281
American Board of Commissioners for Foreign Missions, 159, 161, 162, 179–80, 292, 304
Amzalag, Joseph
    British consulate and, 325
    Christian missionaries and, 163, 170, 178, 180, 182, 294, 295–96, 301
    moneylending and, 177
    Judith Montefiore on marriage of, 187
Andover Theological Seminary, 159
Apostasy, 315–16
Arabic language, 79, 234
Armenians, 34, 95, 98
Art and artists, 247, 249, 286, 288
Artisans, 105–6
Aryeh, Menahem, 352
Ashkenazi, Joseph, 347–48
Ashkenazim. *See also* Hasidim; Perushim
    changes in population between 1800 and 1839, 336–37, 393
    closure of Jerusalem to, 42
    friction and factionalism in Jewish community, 102, 196–99, 390–92, 424n.66
    immigration from 1810 to 1829, 450n.14
    Jewish community in 1800, 35
    occupations compared to Sephardim, 341
    PEKAM and Sephardi-Ashkenazi agreement of 1824–1825, 423n.49
    scholars and haluka, 69
    Zoref's fundraising efforts in Europe, 199–201
Asseo, Mordecai, 143, 147–48
Austria, 378, 379, 431n.50
Ayish, R. Jacob Moshe, 100
Ayish, Joseph David, 143, 144, 145

Ba'al Shem-Tov, Israel, 36–37
Bak, Israel, 227–29, 256, 295, 346
Balter, R., 175
Banks, 362, 365
Bardaki, R. Isaiah
    appointment as liaison to Russian consulate, 330, 332
    end of Egyptian rule in Jerusalem, 369
    Hurva synagogue controversy, 252, 253–54, 260, 262
    Montefiore's agricultural plan, 353
    Safed earthquake of 1837, 256
Baruch of Pinsk, 200, 201
Bar Yohai, R. Simeon, 43
Basili, Constantine, 329–30
Bavaria, 230
Beduin, 24, 211
Behavior, regulation of, 81–83
Behren, Bernhard, 243
Beirut, 359, 361
Beit midrash, 74
Benjamin of Safed, 142–43, 147
Bergheim, Melville Peter, 309
Bergmann, Celia, 236, 238–41, 242
Bergmann, Eliezer, 236–41, 271
Beth El synagogue, 98
Bethlehem, 187, 189, 217
Bibas, R. Judah, 364
Biblical Researches in Palestine, Mt. Sinai, and Arabia Petrea in 1838 (Robinson), 289
Bikur Holim society, 311
Birth rate, 338, 451n.21
Blitz, Alexander, 266
Blood libel, 303, 371–72
Bohemia, 63–64
Bowring, John, 272
British Church Missionary Society (CMS), 160
Bubonic plague, 29, 87–89, 181, 312–13, 420n.96, 438n.10–11
Burckhardt, Christian, 160
Burckhardt, Johann Lewis, 276–77

Burial fees, 111–12, 126
Burial Society, 112, 126

Calman, Erasmus, 255, 294–95, 361
Campbell, Colonel Patrick, 319, 321–26, 331–32
Capitulation agreements, 31, 134–39
Cartography, 15, 284, 291, 398n.34. *See also* Geography
Cemeteries, 93, 305. *See also* Burial fees; Burial Society
Censorship, 84, 226, 227, 300, 443n.29
Census, 336–42, 344
Charity, 115, 117
Chateaubriand, François, 18, 276, 280
Chief rabbi, 100–101
Children, 338. *See also* Infant mortality; Orphans
Cholera epidemics, 234, 266, 278, 312, 438n.10
Christ Church, 308, 321, 395
Christians and Christianity. *See also* Churches; Greek Orthodox Church; Missionaries; Christian; Monasteries; Pilgrims; Roman Catholic Church
    Egyptian occupation of Palestine, 209–10
    Jewish converts to, 313–14
    as minority group in early nineteenth-century Palestine, 33–34
    persecution of Jews in Jerusalem, 408n.19
    quarter in Jerusalem, 93, 95
    repair of churches and monasteries in Jerusalem, 246
    travelogues on relations between Jews and, 285
Chronicle of the Times (Menaham Mendel), 234
Churches, 93, 95, 98, 297
Church of the Holy Sepulchre, 93, 95
Churchill, Col. Charles H., 384–86, 387

Church of St. James, 98
Church of Scotland, 382
Circumcision, 178
Clarke, Pastor, 280
Climate, 43
Commerce, 17, 27–31. *See also* Merchants
Community, Jewish. *See also* Ashkenazim; Hasidim; Perushim; Sephardim
    friction and factionalism as characteristic of, 389–92
    response to Christian missionaries, 314–15
    Sephardi and Perushi organization of, 64–66
Coningsby (Disraeli), 281
Connor, James, 160–61
Conscription, 210–11, 212, 223, 227
Consulates, 31, 210, 318–32, 395, 447n.6
Cooper, Anthony Ashley. *See* Shaftesbury, Lord
Coronel, Nahum, 238
Costigin, Christopher, 283–84
Courts, rabbinical, 101
Craftsmen, 105–6
Currency, 30–31, 208, 443n.36
Cyrus, king of Persia, 374

Dalton, Dr. George, 177, 178, 179, 180
Damascus, 19, 303, 371–72
Damer, Mrs. G. L. Dawson, 284, 285–86
Darwin, Charles, 291
Darwish, pasha of Damascus, 133
Dead Sea, 284
Death, 89. *See also* Mortality rates
Debts, Jewish community, 118, 127, 197, 216, 249, 250–51
Deficit spending, 118
Demographics. *See* Population, Jewish,
Dhimmis, 32–33
Directory of Five, 6
Disraeli, Benjamin, 280, 281–82

Divorce, 3, 339–40
Doctors, 106, 177, 309–10, 311–12, 340, 409n.53, 445n.76
Dodge, Dr. Asa, 305
Dome of the Rock, 93
Dov, R. Abraham, 220, 255, 256–57, 334, 335, 344, 345
Dov Baer, R. (Mezhirech), 37, 38
Dress, 33, 82, 187, 210, 239
Droughts, 266, 312
Druze, 228, 334–35, 342

Earthquakes, 43, 212, 213–16, 254–60, 350
Eastern Orthodox Church, 161–62. See also Greek Orthodox Church
Economics. See also Debts, Jewish community; Fundraising; Income; Poverty; Taxation
    Christian missionaries and Jewish community, 315
    Hasidic immigration to Eretz Israel, 47–48, 49–50, 51
    Jerusalem Sephardi kollel in 1812–1815, 109–15, 117–19
    Montefiore and development of Eretz Israel, 335, 365
    Perushim settlement in Safed, 61–62, 66–70
    status of Jewish communities in Palestine in 1800, 35
    Tiberias Sephardim in 1823, 139
Education, 77–78. See also Scholars; Schools
Egerton, Lady Francis, 284–85
Egypt
    administration of Palestine, 3, 202–3, 205–6, 208–23
    end of occupation of Palestine, 367–87, 393–94
    Napoleon's invasion of Palestine, 6–7, 14–15
Elderly, 337
Emigration, from Eretz Israel, 338–39
England
    consulate in Jerusalem, 318–32, 394–95, 447n.6
    diplomatic presence in early nineteenth-century Palestine, 32
    end of Egyptian occupation of Palestine, 367–68
    French proposal for future of Jerusalem, 378–79
    Greek war of independence, 189
    Jews and future of Palestine, 372–75, 381–87
    Mehemet Ali and foreign policy in Ottoman Empire, 448–49n.27
    missionaries in Palestine, 157–59, 170–83, 306
    Napoleon's invasion of Palestine, 5–6, 15
    travelogues and descriptions of Palestine, 439n.21
Epidemics. See Bubonic plague; Cholera epidemics; Health, in Palestine
Ewald, F. C., 243
Excommunication, 38, 315
Explorers, 276–77
Extortion, 174–75, 328–29

Family, Jewish community, 28–29, 108. See also Marriage
Famines, 266, 312
Farhi, Haim
    administration of Palestine and protection of Jewish community, 23, 134
    murder of, 133, 413n.45
    Napoleon's invasion of Palestine, 10
    Perushim settlement in Jerusalem, 121
    welcome to Perushim immigrants, 61
Farhi, Shlomo, 134
Farman, S., 293, 320
Farren, John, 215–16, 318
Fellowships, scholarly, 104
Finn, James, 395
Finzi, Moshe, 215, 293, 358–59

Firmans, 127, 128–29, 130
Fisk, Pliny, 159–63, 166, 168–69, 170–71, 172–73, 179
Folk medicine, 106, 409n.53
Food, prices of, 73–74, 239–40, 271, 272. *See also* Famines; Kosher practices; Malnutrition
Foreign trade, 31
Fox, Henry Talbott, 288
Fraenkel, Shimon, 312
France, 148, 367, 371, 378–79. *See also* Napoleon and Napoleonic Wars
Frank, Jacob, 38
Frankl, Ludwig August, 156
Frenken, 234
Friedrich Wilhelm IV, King, 380
Fundraising. *See also* Istanbul Officials; PEKAM
    friction and factionalism in Jewish community, 102–3, 132–33, 139–47, 190–96, 199–201
    Hasidic immigration to Eretz Israel, 48–49
    HOD kollel and, 267–68, 271–74
    Hurva synagogue controversy, 264–65
    Muslim revolt of 1834, 217

Gabella tax, 112, 113, 126
Gaggi, Mercadero, 301, 303
Galicia, 63
Gambling, 83
Gaza, 7–8
Geography, 232, 291. *See also* Cartography
Géramb, Marie Joseph de, 282–83
Germany, 225
Gerstmann, Dr. Albert, 309–10, 311, 313, 328–29
Gilgal, 232
Goldschmidt, Judah Leib, 266
Governors, Jerusalem, 115
Grand vizier, 17
Great Britain. *See* England
Greek Orthodox Church

    agriculture in Jerusalem, 453n.61
    influence as minority group in Palestine, 34
    Muslims and Greek war of independence, 162–63, 177
    Russian diplomatic and religious ties to, 31–32, 319, 329, 331
Greek war of independence, 162, 189, 222
Guizot, François, 378

Habad Hasidim, 131–33, 196, 412–13n.37, 423n.53
Haifa, 359, 395
Halevi, Nahum, 345
Halevi, Zadok, 243
Haluka, 68–69, 108, 315, 344, 432n.9
Hamilton-Gordon, George. *See* Aberdeen, Lord
Hasidim. *See also* Ashkenazim; Habad Hasidim
    conflicts with PEKAM, 424n.60
    description of prayer service, 343–44
    distribution of haluka, 68–69
    distribution of PEKAM funds in Hebron, 196
    division of Winer inheritance, 63
    friction and factionalism in Jewish community, 131–33
    immigration to Eretz Israel, 2, 36–56, 220
    peaceful coexistence with Sephardim, 155
    Perushim and distribution of PEKAM funds, 345–46
    Perushim settlement of Safed, 61, 79–80
    Safed and Druze-Muslim rebellion, 335
    Safed earthquake of 1837, 256–57
    Yellin's negative attitude toward, 235
Hatt-I-Sherif of Gulhane, 370
Hazaka, 72
Hazzan, R. Joseph, 124

Health, in Palestine. *See also* Bubonic
plague; Cholera epidemics;
Doctors; Infant mortality;
Mortality rates; Sanitation
of Christian missionaries, 179,
444n.50
life in early nineteenth century, 29
medical services in 1820s and 1830s,
409n.53
missionaries and medical services,
309–10, 395
travelers and quarantine regulations,
278
urban community compared to
villages, 340
Hebrew language, 44, 80, 294, 325–26,
396
Hebron
appointment of British consular
agent in, 326
distribution of funds from Istanbul
Officials, 67
economic hardships in 1820s, 196
end of Egyptian occupation of
Palestine, 369
friction and factionalism in Jewish
community, 131–33
Hasidic immigration to Eretz Israel,
42–43
Montefiore's visit to, 354, 356
Muslim revolt of 1834, 217
Perushim settlement of Safed, 59
Heller, Shmuel, 345
Hillel, David Beit, 271, 303, 342
Hirschel, David, 330–31
Hirschel, R. Shlomo, 151
Historiography, 388
History, Jewish, 388–89
HOD (Holland and Deutschland) kollel,
266–68, 271–74, 391
Hospitals, 309, 311–12, 395
Housing
cost of living in Jerusalem in 1830s,
271
descriptions of Jews by Christian

missionaries, 179
Palestinian towns in early
nineteenth century, 28–29
Perushim settlement in Safed,
71–72, 73
provision of by missionaries, 304
Hurva synagogue
building of synagogue as mitzva,
435n.52
organization of Jewish community
and building of, 246–47, 249–60,
262–68, 271–74
Perushim and firman to repair and
rebuild, 127–28, 130–31

Ibrahim Pasha
end of Egyptian occupation of
Palestine, 203, 205, 206, 210–11,
367–68, 368–69
granting of Jermak village to Israel
Bak, 228–29
insurrection of 1834, 212, 213, 215,
217
Immigration. *See also* Emigration, from
Eretz Israel
Ashkenazim from 1810 to 1829,
450n.14
encouraged by R. Menahem Mendel,
129–30
Hasidic to Eretz Israel, 36–56
Jewish community in 1830s, 218–23,
224–30, 232–45, 337
Lehren on poor settlers, 191–92
*Incidents of Travel in Egypt, Arabia
Petraea and the Holy Land*
(Stephens), 283–84
Income. *See also* Wages
Perushim standard of living in Safed,
73–74, 272–73
scholars and yeshiva heads in
Jerusalem, 105, 409n.45
Sephardi kollel in Jerusalem, 118
strategies for increase by Jerusalem
Perushim, 155
subsistence in Jerusalem of

eighteenth century, 405n.71,
406n.72
Income tax, 111
Infant mortality, 3, 338, 339, 451n.18
Inflation, 110
Inheritance tax, 110–11, 124–26
Isaac, R., 48–49
Islam, 11, 17, 18, 132. *See also* Muslims
Israel, R. (Polotsk)
   Hasidic immigration to Eretz Israel,
      41, 45, 46, 47, 48, 53
Israel, R. (Shklov)
   allocation of PEKAM funds in Tiberias,
      198
   Christian missionaries and, 170, 174,
      310, 311
   disagreements between Safed and
      Jerusalem branches of Perushim
      kollel, 250, 251, 346
   earthquake of 1837, 259, 260
   friction and factionalism in Jewish
      community, 124–25, 129, 130,
      138, 139, 141, 149, 155, 156
   fundraising in Diaspora
      communities, 140
   Hurva synagogue controversy, 254,
      260, 262
   leadership of Jewish community, 185
   Lehren and kollel leadership, 263–64
   Messianism and fundraising,
      200–201
   Montefiore's second visit to Eretz
      Israel, 342
   Muslim revolt of 1834, 214
   opposition to Perushim settlement in
      Jerusalem, 120, 123, 127
   Perushim community and bubonic
      plague, 87–88
   Perushim settlement in Safed, 61,
      62–63, 64, 65, 66, 79, 80, 220
   summary of work in Eretz Israel,
      350–51
   taxation and government of
      Palestine, 135
Israel, state of, 393, 395–96

Istanbul Officials for Palestinian Jewry
   chief rabbi of Jerusalem, 101
   conflict between Sephardim and
      Perushim, 130, 143
   currency exchange and transfers of
      funds, 150
   Hasidic immigration to Eretz Israel,
      41, 42, 46, 53
   immigrants and tax collection, 113
   influence on eighteenth- and early
      nineteenth-century Jerusalem
      community, 101
   PEKAM and, 193–94
   Perushim settlement of Safed, 60,
      66–68
   Torah Judgments and taxation in
      Jerusalem, 114
Italy, 148, 149

Jacotin maps, 15
Jaffa, 8, 356, 358, 395, 453n.70
al-Jazzar, Ahmad
   description of Palestine under rule
      of, 21, 23–25
   Napoleon's invasion of Palestine, 7,
      8, 10, 13, 15
   tolerant attitude toward Jews in
      Safed, 43
Jermak village, 228–29, 346
Jerusalem
   closure to Ashkenazi settlers, 42,
      58–59
   conflict between Perushim and
      Sephardim, 139–47
   cost of living in 1830s, 271
   Disraeli's description of, 281
   disagreements between branches of
      Perushim kollel, 249–51
   distribution of Istanbul Officials'
      funds, 67
   end of Egyptian occupation of
      Palestine, 369
   establishment of Perushim
      community in, 2, 262–63
   Jewish community from 1812 to

1815, 87–89, 91, 93, 95, 98,
100–115, 117–19
Jewish population in 1830s,
445–46n.79
missionaries in 1820s, 160–62, 171,
173, 177, 179, 182
missionaries in 1830s, 296–97, 304,
307
Montefiore's visit to, 351–54
Napoleon's invasion of Palestine,
12–13
Jews. See Ashkenazim; Hasidim;
Perushim; Sephardim; specific
topic headings
Jowett, William, 160, 170–71
Judges, rabbinical, 101

Kabbalism, 76
Kalischer, Zvi Hirsch, 243–44
Katafago, Anthony, 134–39, 150,
196–97
Katz, Haim, 71, 73, 77
Katz, Jacob David, 152
King, Jonas, 166, 168, 178, 179, 316
Kollels, 64–66, 69, 117–19, 122–23,
197–98, 249–51. See also
Hasidim; Perushim; Sephardim
Kosher practices, 47, 112–13, 126,
412n.20

Lamartine, Alphonse de, 282
Land tenure, 26
Lanneau, John, 291, 307
Law, Perushim, 82–83
Law of Return, 393
Lehren, Akiva, 251
Lehren, Zvi Hirsch
British consulate in Jerusalem and,
329
compromise on PEKAM funds
allocation, 145
dictatorial attitude toward Jews of
Eretz Israel, 393
earthquake of 1837 and divine
intent, 260

emigration in 1830s, 339
friction and factionalism in Jewish
community, 143, 148–49,
150–51, 152, 190–94
HOD kollel and, 267
hospitals and medical services, 311,
312
Hurva synagogue controversy,
252–53, 264–65
R. Israel and kollel leadership,
263–64
Messianism and, 201, 377
Montefiore and, 342, 345, 363
Muslim revolt of 1834 and
fundraising, 217
opposition to immigration, 218–19,
236
opposition to shlihim, 153–54
PEKAM collection system and,
416n.133
proposed consolidation of major
Ashkenazi kollelim, 197–98
Sachs's agricultural plan, 245
on Vilna compromise, 147
Zoref's fundraising efforts and, 199
Letter-writing, 84–85. See also
Censorship
Levi, Alexander, 303, 308
Levinsohn, Isaac Baer, 226
Lewis, W. B., 171–72, 173, 178
Literacy rates, 78
Loewe, Dr. Louis, 334, 335, 344
London agreement (July 15, 1840), 367,
368
London Jews Society (LJS), 158–59, 180,
292, 308, 395. See also
Missionaries
Louis Philippe, King, 379
Luria, Issac, 44
Luria, Shmaryahu, 229–30

Macgowan, Dr. Edward, 313
Madden, R. R., 247
Mahmud II, Sultan, 18, 133, 134, 176,
205, 342, 361

Malnutrition, 340
Mann, Aaron Zelig, 264–65
Maraji, Nathan, 199
Marcowitz, Joseph, 169
Margolit, Gershon, 197, 293, 295
Marriage. *See also* Divorce
  early age of among Muslims and
    Jews in Palestine, 187, 339–40,
    350, 451n.28
  intermarriage between Hasidim and
    Sephardim, 47
  Perushim community life and, 78
  Perushim and Sephardi regulations
    on immigration, 83
Medievalism, 18
Meir Ba'al HaNes Fund, 140, 148
Menahem Mendel (Kamenets), 233–35
Menahem Mendel, R. (Shklov)
  accomplishments of and death,
    184–85
  Christian missionaries and, 165–66,
    168, 169, 174–75, 178, 180, 183
  friction and factionalism in Jewish
    community, 120, 121, 122,
    129–30, 130–31
  Perushim settlement in Safed, 58,
    59–60, 61, 66, 70, 71, 72
Menahem Mendel, R. (Vitebsk), 41–42,
  44, 47, 48, 49, 50–51, 52–53
Merchants, 30–31, 107, 425n.15. *See
  also* Commerce
Meron, 346
Messianism
  and fundraising, 200–201
  Hasidic immigration to Eretz Israel,
    39–40
  imminent arrival of Messiah in 1840,
    375–78
  increased immigration in 1830s,
    221–22, 428n.59
  Perushim settlement in Safed, 57, 58
Metternich, Klemens von, 379
Meyahis, R., 164
Meyuhas, R. Mordecai Joseph, 12–13,
  54, 100, 106

Millenarianism, 157–58
Millets, 32
Minority groups, early nineteenth-
  century Palestine, 32–33. *See also*
  Ashkenazim; Christians and
  Christianity; Hasidim; Perushim;
  Sephardim
Mintz, Zvi Dov, 148–49
Missionaries, Christian
  activities in 1820s, 157–66, 168–83
  activities in 1830s, 225–26, 292–97,
    300–301, 303–17
  activities after 1840, 395
  British consulate in Jerusalem,
    319–20
  establishment of mission in
    Jerusalem, 442n.22
  friction among in Jerusalem, 446n.80
  Jewish Messianism and, 377
  prayer services, 442–43n.26
  relations between English and
    American, 419n.81
  respect for R. Menahem Mendel, 185
  Safed earthquake of 1837, 255
Mitnaggedim, 38, 49
Mizrahi, Haim, 345
Monasteries, 30, 95, 98
Moneylenders, 107
Monroe Doctrine, 160
Montefiore, Judith
  first visit to Eretz Israel, 186–87, 189
  second trip to Eretz Israel, 334, 347,
    350, 352, 354, 358, 361
Montefiore, Moses
  Damascus blood libel, 371–72
  doctors and Jewish community, 312
  first visit to Eretz Israel, 185–87, 189
  influence on Eretz Israel, 394
  protection of Jews during Egyptian
    occupation of Palestine, 3–4
  second trip to Eretz Israel, 333–54,
    356, 358–59, 361–66
Moore, Niven, 319
Mortality rates. *See also* Infant
  mortality

of American missionaries, 305
high levels in Jewish community, 3,
   340, 427–28n.50
Montefiore census of 1839–1840,
   338
poor health conditions and plagues in
   1830s, 219, 241
Tiberias Jewish community in early
   nineteenth century, 52
Mount of Olives, 91, 93
Muslims. *See also* Islam
   European travelogues on, 280–81,
      285
   kosher practices in Jerusalem,
      112–13
   legal ban on Christian proselytizing
      among, 161
   payments to for protection and
      services by Jewish community in
      Jerusalem, 114–15
   Perushim attitude toward, 81
   quarter of Jerusalem, 95
   rebellion of 1834, 216–17, 234
   tolerance of minority groups, 32–33
Mustafa, Pasha of Damascus, 177, 179,
   181
Mustafa IV, Sultan, 18

Napoleon and Napoleonic Wars, 1, 5–8,
   10–15, 16, 58, 70
Naudi, Charles, 160
Navon, Jonah, 303–4, 353
Nazareth, 10
Neaman, Aryeh, 256, 259, 260, 353
Nelson, Lord Horatio, 6
Nesselrode, Karl Robert von Graf, 331,
   378, 379
Neta, R. Nathan, 294
Newspapers, British, 373
Nicholas I, Czar, 133, 205, 222, 227
Nicolayson, John
   agriculture and Jews, 342
   and American missionaries, 306–7
   arrival in Jerusalem, 180–82
   on blood libel, 371

character of converts to Christianity,
   315
cost of housing in Jerusalem in
   1830s, 271
description of Bak, 228
on divorce rate among Jews, 339–40
end of Egyptian occupation of
   Palestine, 370
on firman for Hurva synagogue, 246
friction and factionalism in Jewish
   community, 389
Jewish emigration in 1830s, 338
Jewish messianism and, 377
meeting with Montefiore, 352
missionary activities in 1830s,
   292–97, 300–301, 303–4, 308,
   316, 317
plagues as divine retribution, 313
protection of Jews of Jerusalem, 3
recommended as British consul, 319
Sachs and, 225–26, 232
Norov, Abraham S., 283
North Africa, 149, 429n.64

Occupations, 30–31, 69, 105–6, 341
Officials and Wardens of Amsterdam.
   See PEKAM
Olim. *See* Immigration
Orphans, 341
Orphans Fund, 117
Osman I, Sultan, 17
Ottoman Empire
   British foreign policy and, 157–58
   description of Palestine in early
      nineteenth century, 1, 16–21
   end of Egyptian occupation of
      Palestine, 367–87
   European support until demise in
      1922, 393–94
   Jewish community and British
      influence in, 327
   Napoleon's invasion of Palestine,
      7–8, 10–15
   persecution of Jews, 174–76

Pach, R. Shlomo, 127, 128, 139, 174
Palmerston, Lord (Henry John Temple)
   British consulate in Jerusalem, 319,
      320, 322, 326, 327, 330
   end of Egyptian occupation of
      Palestine, 362
   on French proposal for future of
      Palestine, 378–79
   protection policy for Jews in
      Ottoman Empire, 381–84
   Shaftesbury and settlement of Jews
      in Palestine, 374, 375
Parsons, Levi, 159–61
Pashas, Ottoman Empire, 19–21, 115
PEKAM
   allocation formula of Istanbul
      Officials, 67–68
   conflicts between Ashkenazim and
      Sephardim over allocation of
      funds, 142–56, 190–96, 424n.66
   conflicts with Hasidim over
      fundraising, 424n.60
   earthquake of 1837, 259
   HOD kollel and distribution of funds,
      266–68, 271–74
   Hurva synagogue controversy, 131,
      264–65
   Lehren and collection system,
      416n.133
   Montefiore and distribution of
      funds, 344–45
   Muslim revolt of 1834 and
      fundraising, 217
   PEKAM-Shapira compromises of 1826
      and 1829, 421n.36, 422n.46
   Sephardi-Ashkenazi agreement of
      1824–1825, 423n.49
   volume of funds distributed, 435n.59
   Zoref's fundraising efforts for Jeru-
      salem Perushim, 199, 201
Peki'in, 346–47
Perushim. *See also* Ashkenazim
   allocation of PEKAM funds, 190–96,
      345–46
   Christian missionaries and, 294

disagreements between Safed and
   Jerusalem branches of kollel,
   249–51
friction and factionalism in Jewish
   community, 120–56
haluka regulations, 432n.9
Hurva synagogue controversy, 252
immigration and Jewish community
   in early nineteenth century, 2–3
Jewish community of Jerusalem,
   87–89, 91, 95, 98, 100, 262–63
Messianism and, 377
Safed earthquake of 1837, 256, 263
settlement in Safed, 56–86, 220
de Phelipeaux, Louis-Edmond, 10
Philippson, R. Ludwig, 311–12
Photography, 288–89
Piastre, Turkish, 31
Picciotto family, 31, 135, 138, 139, 170
Pieretz, A., 222
Pieretz, G. W., 308–9
Pilgrims, 278–79, 438n.12, 439n.13,
   449n.37
Plonski, Shlomo, 131
Poland, 37–38, 85, 223
Poll tax, 114, 134, 348, 452n.52
Ponsonby, John William, 383
Population, Jewish, in Palestine. *See
   also* Age, distribution of
   population; Birth rate; Infant
   mortality; Mortality rate;
   Occupations; Sex, distribution
   of population
   British consulate report on, 327–28
   and Christian in 1800, 33–34
   earthquake of 1837 and decline, 259
   explosion of from 1830 through
      1836, 218–23, 392–93
   Jerusalem community in 1812–1815,
      108–9
   Jerusalem community in 1830s,
      445–46n.79
   Montefiore census of 1839–1840,
      336–42
   Palestinian towns in 1800, 27

Perushim in Jerusalem from 1815 to 1821, 123
Postal service, 278, 437n.9
Poverty, 53–54, 70, 107–8, 117, 137
Prayer services
  Christian missionaries and, 442–43n.26
  description of Hasidic, 44–45, 343–44
  Messianism and Ashkenazi, 376
  Perushim and quorums, 121–22
  Perushim regulations and, 75–76
  relations between Sephardim and Hasidim, 51
Priestley, Joseph, 157–58
Printing, 227–28, 229
Professionals, 106–7
Protestantism, 157, 161
Provinces, Ottoman Empire, 17
Prussia, 378, 380

Rabbis, Sephardi, 100–101
Rachel's tomb, 187, 189, 354
Ransom payments, 65
Redemption. *See* Messianism
Reform Judaism, 373–74
Religion. *See also* Ashkenazim; Christians and Christianity; Hasidim; Islam; Perushim; Sephardim
  Christian missionaries and conversion of Jews, 314
  Perushim community in Safed, 74–75
  reasons for increase in immigration in 1830s, 220–21
  role of Messianism in life of Jews in Eretz Israel, 376–77
Restoration (historical period), 157–58
Restoration movement, 373–75, 384, 394
Revolutions
  Druze-Muslim of 1838, 334–35
  European of 1830s, 203, 205

Greek war of independence, 162, 189, 222
Muslim of 1834 and Egyptian occupation of Palestine, 211–17
Richardson, Dr. Robert, 338
Rivlin, Hillel, 85, 229, 271
Rivlin, Moshe, 372
Road building, 351
Roberts, David, 279, 286, 288
Robinson, Edward, 222, 284, 289–91
Roman Catholic Church, 34, 160, 161–62, 246, 329
Rosenbaum, Amram Hasida, 197
Rosenbaum, Mendel, 237
Rosenthal, Simeon, 313, 315
Rothschild, Anschel Meyer, 243, 244
Rothschild, Salomon, 243
Russee, Isaac, 311
Russia
  Bak's decision to emigrate, 227
  consulate and Jewish community, 329–30
  diplomatic position and presence in early nineteenth-century Palestine, 31–32
  end of Egyptian occupation of Palestine, 367
  Greek Catholic Church and diplomatic interests, 31–32, 319, 329, 331
  PEKAM and fundraising, 195
  Perushim settlement in Safed, 57–58
  pilgrims from, 449n.37
  political changes and status of Jews in 1830s, 222–23
  proposals about future of Palestine, 378, 379–80
Russo-Turkish War (1828–1829), 38–39, 195, 222, 415n.91

Saadia, R., 76
Sabbath ceremony, 343
Sachs, Moshe, 225–27, 243, 244–45, 266, 300–301, 361

Safed
    allocation of PEKAM funds, 147
    Christian missionaries in, 180–81
    conflicts between Sephardim and
      Ashkenazim, 196–99
    cost of living in 1830s, 271
    disagreements between branches of
      Perushim kollel, 249–51
    Druze-Muslim rebellion and
      persecution of Jews, 334–35
    earthquake of 1834, 213–16
    earthquake of 1837, 254–60
    Hasidic immigration to Eretz Israel,
      43
    immigration and population in
      1830s, 219–20
    Montefiore's visit to, 342–49
    Napoleon's invasion of Palestine and
      Jewish community, 11–12
    Perushim settlement in, 56–86
    plague epidemics, 180
Salant, R. Shmuel, 372
Samson, Asher, 271
Sanitation, 29, 309, 340, 427–28n.50.
    See also Health, in Palestine;
    Housing
Schnitzer, Mordecai, 247, 249
Scholars
    income of yeshiva heads in
      Jerusalem, 409n.45
    level of study and scholarship in
      Jerusalem, 239
    Perushim community and, 69, 77–78
    Sephardi haluka system, 344
    Sephardi society in Jerusalem,
      103–5, 117
Schools, 77–78, 297, 395. *See also*
    Yeshiva
Schwartz, Joseph, 212–13, 230, 232–33,
    238, 252, 271, 300–301
Seetzen, Ulrich, 105, 276
Selim III, Sultan, 7, 18
Sephardim
    allocation of haluka, 68, 69
    allocation of PEKAM funds, 190–96,
      424n.66
    Ashkenazim and population mix
      between 1800 and 1839, 336–37,
      393
    Christian missionaries and, 168
    community regulation of behavior,
      81–83
    decline of community in early
      nineteenth century, 3
    financial situation of Safed
      community, 70
    friction and factionalism in Jewish
      community, 120–56, 196–99, 390
    Hasidic immigration to Eretz Israel,
      45–48, 49–50, 51
    immigration from 1810 to 1829,
      450n.14
    immigration in 1830s, 220
    Jewish community in Jerusalem
      from 1812 to 1815, 89, 100–15,
      117–19
    kollel and community organization,
      64–65
    as minority group in Palestine in
      1800, 34–35
    occupations compared to
      Ashkenazim, 341
    PEKAM and Sephardi-Ashkenazi
      agreement of 1824–1825, 423n.49
    Perushim settlement in Safed, 61,
      64–66, 80–81
    regulations in Jerusalem and Safed,
      406n.98
    repair of synagogues in 1834, 247,
      249
    Zoref's fundraising efforts in
      Europe, 199–201
Servants, domestic, 69
Sex, distribution of population, 341
Shaftesbury, Lord (Anthony Ashley
    Cooper)
    British consulate in Jerusalem,
      320–21

Christian faith in Millennium, 157
on English victories at Acre and
Beirut, 368
missionaries and faith, 317
Montefiore and British Jewry, 333
Restoration movement, 374, 375,
381
Shapira, Shlomo Zalman, 70, 129, 130,
139, 190–94
Sharif Bey, Muhammad, 206, 208
Sherman, Charles, 307
Shfar-Am, 346
Shlihim, 104, 132–33, 152, 153–54,
190–94
Shoshana, Abraham, 345, 348–49
Sick Fund, 117
Sidon, 19
Smith, Eli, 289–91
Smith, Sir Sidney, 10, 15
Sofer, R. Moshe, 191, 198–99, 259–60,
265
Souvenirs and Impressions (de
Lamartine), 282
Standard of living, 272. See also Food,
prices of; Housing; Sanitation
Stanhope, Hester, 359
Steamships, 220, 278, 437n.8
Stephens, John Lloyd, 283
Sternchuss, Paul Hyman, 313
Storekeepers, 106
Subsistence. See Income
Sukkat Shalom synagogue, 263
Suleiman, pasha of Sidon, 25, 59
Sultans, Ottoman Empire, 17
Suzin, R. Shlomo Moshe, 122, 141, 166,
168, 247, 249
Synagogues, 46, 51, 74, 98, 314. See
also Hurva synagogue

Talleyrand, Charles, 6
Talmud, 76, 165–66
Tancred (Disraeli), 281
Tanzimat decree, 370
Tatitschew, D. P., 380

Taxation. See also Income tax;
Inheritance tax; Poll tax
Christian and Jews in Jerusalem and
Muslim persecution, 163
Egyptian occupation of Palestine,
208
Hasidic immigration to Eretz Israel,
48
Jerusalem kollel in 1812–1815,
109–14
merchants and tariffs, 425n.15
Montefiore and Safed Sephardim,
348
Ottoman Empire and administration
of Palestine, 20–21
Pasha Abdullah and Jewish
community, 134–39
strategies for reduction by Jerusalem
Perushim, 154–55
village life in nineteenth-century
Palestine, 26–27
Temple, Henry John. See Palmerston,
Lord
Ten Lost Tribes, 200, 201, 232, 250
Thomson, William M. and Eliza,
255–56, 295, 296, 304–5, 306
Tiberias
conflict between Sephardim and
Ashkenazim, 196–99
debt burden of Jewish community,
70
distribution of funds from Istanbul
Officials, 67
earthquake of 1837, 257–59
Hasidic immigration to Eretz Israel,
42, 50–52
Jewish community in 1808, 58
Montefiore's visit to, 349–51, 362
Muslim revolt of 1834, 216–17
Tobler, Dr. Titus, 338, 339
Tocqueville, Alexis de, 279
Tomb of the Patriarchs, 356
Towns, early nineteenth-century
Palestine, 27–31

Tradesmen, 106, 107
Transportation, 29–30, 220, 278, 351, 437n.8
Travel
    end of Egyptian occupation of Palestine, 369
    European travelers to Holy Land, 275–86, 288–91, 439n.21
    Perushim regulation of, 84
    steamships and, 220, 278, 437n.8
    transportation in early nineteenth century, 29–30
Travelogues, 279–86, 288
Travels from Paris to Jerusalem (Chateaubriand), 276
Tschoudi, Melchior, 160
Turkey. *See* Ottoman Empire
Turkish language, 80

United States, 159–62, 170–83, 304

Valley of Jehoshafat, 93
Van Dyck, Dr., 307
Vernet, Horace, 288–89
Villages, early nineteenth-century Palestine, 25–27, 28
Vilna compromise, 146–47
Vilna gaon, 38, 57. *See also* Perushim
Violence, life in nineteenth-century Palestine, 23–25
Visino, Johann, 257
Von Moltke, Lt. Helmuth, 380
von Pückler-Muskau, Herman, 284

Wages, 271–72. *See also* Income
Wailing Wall, 98, 100, 352
Wakiel, 330–31
Whiting, George, 291, 305, 306–7
Widows, 111, 340–41
Winer, Simon, 63
Wolff, Joseph, 163–66, 168–70, 182–83,

292, 389
Women. *See also* Bergmann, Celia; Montefiore, Judith
    divorce and, 3, 339–40
    early age at marriage, 187, 339–40, 350, 451n.28
    haluka regulations and domestic servants, 69
    life in Perushim community, 78–79
    Perushim regulation of behavior, 82–83
    rights in state of Israel, 396
    as widows, 111, 340–41

Yakir, 53
Yamani camp, 25
Yellin, David, 235–36
Yellin, Joshua, 235
Yemen, 200, 201
Yeshiva, 103–5, 409n.45. *See also* Schools
Yiddish language, 79
Yohanan Ben Zakai, 98
Young, William Tanner, 285, 319–32, 341–42, 351–52, 369–70, 384, 389

Zaddik, 37, 52
Zoref, Mordecai, 353–54
Zoref, Shlomo Zalman
    Bak and printing supplies, 228
    Christian missionaries and, 303, 310
    conflicts between Perushim and Sephardim over allocation of PEKAM funds, 142–43, 144, 145, 146, 147
    Hurva synagogue controversy, 251, 252–53, 331
    Montefiore's agricultural plan, 353
    PEKAM and fundraising mission to Europe, 199–201